The Russian Enigma

Ante Ciliga was born in Shegotichi (now Yugoslavia) in 1898. He joined the pro-Communist fraction of the Croation Social Democrat Party and was, in 1922, elected secretary of the Croatian Communist Party. The representative of the Yugoslav Party at the Vienna headquarters of the Balkan Bureau of the Comintern, he was sent, in 1926, to Moscow to study at the Party school. In 1929 he joined the Trotskyist Opposition and took part in the 'revolt' of the Yugoslav section of the school which condemned the Comintern's policy in Yugoslavia. Arrested in 1930, he spent three years in prison and two and a half years in exile in Siberia. Apart from the present volume (see publishing details on copyright page) he has published *La crise de l'Etat dans la Yougoslavie* (Paris, 1974), and edits the Croatian-language political magazine, *On the Threshold of a New Day*, from Rome, where he lives.

The Russian Enigma

by

Ante Ciliga

Part one translated by
Fernand G. Fernier and Anne Cliff

Part two translated by
Margaret and Hugo Dewar

INK LINKS

The first section of the present complete volume was first published in France as *Au pays du grand mensonge*, 1938, and in England by Routledge as *The Russian Enigma*, London 1940, with a book club edition in the Labour Book Service. Translation and typesetting used in this edition © Routledge.

The second section was first published by Editions des Iles d'Or as *Sibérie, terre de l'exil et de l'industrialisation*, 1950. Translation by Margaret and Hugo Dewar © Ink Links, 1979.

The chapter in the first section *'Lenin, also . . .'* was omitted from the 1940 English edition as well as the 1938 Gallimard French edition. It was first published by Editions des Iles d'Or in a 1950 edition of the first section, retitled *Au pays du mensonge déconcertant*. The World copyright for the complete work now resides with Editions Champs Libre who were the first to publish the full book in one volume.
© Editions Champs Libre, 1977

World English Language rights © Ink Links, 1979

Ink Links Ltd.,
271 Kentish Town Rd.,
London NW5 2JS.

ISBN 0906133 22X cloth; 0906133 238 paper

Section Two and Chapter 'Lenin, also . . .' typeset by Tek-Art, Croydon.
Printed and bound by Whitstable Litho Ltd., Millstrood Rd., Whitstable, Kent.

CONTENTS

PART TWO
SIBERIA: LAND OF EXILE, LAND OF INDUSTRIALIZATION

EDITOR'S NOTE

This is the first complete edition in English, of a book the history of which merits recounting. The book's history in its French version, the multiple editions, the law suits etc., must be omitted for lack of space.

Our decision to publish the full work in English involved some nail-biting suspense: first of all, the Routledge edition was not to be found either in the Routledge files, the British Museum or any of the principal libraries specializing in Soviet affairs. Two copies were eventually traced to and purchased from Anthony Hall's antiquarian bookshop in Twickenham. It then transpired that an American reprint company, Hyperion, had reprinted a short run from the Routledge edition without the permission of Routledge. We take this opportunity of warning our American readers that the Ink Links version is nearly double the length of the Hyperion edition, contains the full version of a crucial chapter 'Lenin, Also . . .. (expunged in the Routledge and, hence, Hyperion edition) and carries the world copyright in the English language, by permission of the French publishers, Champs Libre.

The second part of the book had never appeared in English and we feared the daunting cost of its translation both to ourselves and to the readership. However, we happened to be phoning Hugo Dewar about other matters and chanced to ask him if he had ever heard of Ante Ciliga. "Now wait a minute; Margaret," he said, calling his wife, "didn't we once translate a book of Ciliga's?" And indeed they had! But where was it now? "Perhaps we gave the manuscript to a bookshop in Twickenham . . ." And indeed Anthony Hall still had the manuscript which the Dewars have allowed us to use, generously waiving their translation fees. Our sincere thanks go to them for this warmhearted act which has speeded up, and indeed made possible the long delayed publication in English of Ciliga's work in full—a book which is a moving testimony of our times, the product of the intelligence, sensitivity, solidarity, combativity and wit of the international working class.

Ink Links, July 1979.

FOREWORD

Everyone knows that the world, this old world of ours, is riddled with lies, violence and injustice. Even those capitalists who enjoy privileged positions have ceased to believe in its future. If the ancient order still persists, it is not because of its creative resources ; it is merely a protracted decomposition. At this moment in History, the Soviet Union is manifest in the eyes of the workers and of the whole of humanity as the focal point of a new world. There, at the price of desperate effort, and in spite of all obstacles, a new society is being built up, a society, imperfect in many ways, but—we are told—in which is achieved the emancipation of labour together with others of humanity's ageless dreams. Unfortunately the truth is very different. Real life in the U.S.S.R., and the conditions prevailing throughout that country, prove that an inverted evolution has triumphed, an evolution which tends to consolidate society on the basis of a new form of oppression and a renewed exploitation. Modern Russia shows its originality in the fact that this new edition of the past is bedecked with the brightest colours, the most advanced theories, the most modern slogans and the most daring dream-visions.

Nowhere else in the world, therefore, exist such flagrant contradictions between official theory and real life, between hopes and their fulfilment, between word and deed. The official ideology is the only one permitted in Russia, which means that there social and political life is permeated with lies to an incredible extent. At every step one encounters them, one realizes them in the life of every citizen, whatever his condition ; the first words uttered by public orators contain them. This terrible contradiction pursued me throughout the ten long years I spent in the U.S.S.R.

The situation is still further complicated by the fact that in present-day Russia capitalist exploitation, political oppression and even slavery go hand in hand with a certain undeniable progress. Other examples of such strange wedlock could be found in history. The rise of entire social strata, genuine exploits in the conquest of a material world, the raising of the level of civilization—all are there. This rapid and breath-taking progress, added to exploitation and oppression, to the lies disguised as slogans, such as ' liquidation of classes ' and ' abolition of man's exploitation by man ', causes the U.S.S.R. to appear in the eyes of a tired and despairing Europe as a distant saviour, vaguely crowned with a halo. The myth of Soviet Russia is one of the most tragic misunderstandings of our time.

The Soviet experiment once more presents the problems of progress, socialism and of the very foundations of human life, but this time in a larger way.

The pages you will read are by no means intended to analyse or solve these problems. My aim is to describe what I heard and saw in the most widely distant provinces of this immense country, at various stages of its development, among all classes of society inside and outside prison. The picture of Soviet life as I portray it appears to me, though in sombre hue, to contain bright patches. In spite of the sufferings of a revolution, in spite of the final degeneration of that revolution, the country possesses many advantages over the West, where people are stifled in social stagnation. But it would show lack of depth and an incomplete understanding of the Western crisis to suggest to the West that it should follow the example of Russia, a suggestion that is put forward by those who imagine that the U.S.S.R. is building up a form of socialism. The emancipation of the proletariat and of humanity would demand much bolder and more profound programmes than the one that Russia is able to provide— Russia, a reactionary power, which every day is drifting farther away from socialism and is becoming more and more reconciled to the old Western outlook.

The forces that demand a renascence of the West, that wish for an effective emancipation and transformation of occidental society, should join, not with the ruling class of the U.S.S.R., but with the immense stratum of the exploited and oppressed people. The bureaucratic State still holds over them its iron rod, its fearful apparatus of coercion, preventing every free manifestation of the workers' will. In the everyday life of the U.S.S.R., one meets at every turn with ill-disguised hatred, cherished by labourers and *kolkhosians* for the triumphant bureaucratic order. Everywhere within the masses, one feels the budding wish for a different and better rule. The two currents—the bureaucrats' official lies and the secret hatred of the masses—feed Soviet life and fill the following pages.

*　　*　　*

The recent Moscow trials make it easier for the reader to understand this book. Those who have lived in Russia during the terrible years between 1928 and 1936 will see, in these bloodstained trials, the striking confirmation of the truths that could not be known before except by those outside the pale of official life, that is, in prison or in exile. The internal decomposition of the régime has now become apparent to the whole world.

I have attempted faithfully to render my impressions, which altered considerably in the course of ten years. I began by seeing Russia with the eyes of a conscientious and somewhat overwhelmed foreign tourist. It was but gradually that I felt mistrust rise within me. During the last eight years of my stay in Russia, I became more and more permeated with a spirit, critical of the system and of Trotsky, and finally even of Lenin.

I by no means pretend to throw a glaring light on Russia. My only aim is the truth, a valuable thing in these days when so many conscious and obvious lies are told about that country. I am fully convinced of the necessity of writing about the U.S.S.R. and the Russian revolution in a spirit of absolute sincerity, putting aside the Bolshevist principle of deforming facts ' in the interests of the revolution '. Experience has proved, I am sure, that all means are *not* permissible in the service of revolution. Shameful means end by compromising the best of causes.

I wish to avail myself of this opportunity to express all my grateful thanks to my numerous friends both in Russia and abroad who have helped me in the preparation of this book.

A. CILIGA.

PARIS,
July, 1937.

PART ONE

IN THE LAND OF THE DISCONCERTING LIE

Popular revolutions have no more implacable
enemies than the men they raised to power.
                                    H. DE BALZAC.

Book I

RUSSIA AND HER ENIGMAS

I

FIRST SHOCKS

For years I had wanted to go to Soviet Russia. The Bolshevist revolution which, in the face of a Europe torn by war and crushed by capitalist exploitation, boldly tried to build a society founded on a brotherhood of nations and on the enfranchisement of the workers had, from its very inception, gained my whole-hearted sympathy. A young student, I joined the ranks of the Socialist Party of Croatia in 1918. I soon evolved towards Bolshevism. Between 1919 and 1921, I was already taking an active part in the Communist movements of Yugo-Slavia, Soviet Hungary, Czecho-slovakia and Italy.

I postponed my journey to Russia until later, judging that, in order to benefit from Bolshevist experience in the land of the Soviets, I should complete my preliminary preparation by actively participating in the Communist movements of Eastern Europe. From 1922 to 1926, I worked in Prague, Vienna and Zagreb. I divided my time between Party work and academic studies. When in 1925 I joined the Political Bureau of the Yugo-Slav Communist Party, the police, deciding that I had transgressed beyond the limits of their tolerance, had me expelled from Yugo-Slavia.

The next year I spent in Vienna as foreign representative of the Central Yugo-Slav Committee and member of the Balkan Bureau of the Comintern (Communist International). I was to go to Moscow in 1926. That summer, the Comintern suddenly changed its policy with regard to the Yugo-Slav Party. The Left section to which I belonged was replaced by the section of the Right, which took over the direction of affairs. Under those conditions, in going to Moscow I seemed likely to lose my liberty of action. But the wish to study the experiment of the great Russian revolution in situ prevailed. The repeated defeats suffered by the Communist movements in Europe proved the necessity of studying and improving tactics. Would not a journey to Moscow be the most fruitful source of experience ? Again, that year and the next, Moscow was expecting the visit of a large section of the active members of the Yugo-Slav Party. Therefore the interests of the Left section of the Party also demanded a journey to Soviet Russia. I left Vienna on October 1st, 1926.

My first impressions of Russia—from the border to Moscow —offered nothing remarkable ; the country appeared to be a succession of vast spaces where the trace of man was only sporadically visible in occasional and wretched villages.

At last came Moscow—Alexandra Station. The usual hubbub of the railway platform. I left the station, intending to call a taxi, but there were none ; nothing but horse-drawn cabs—*izvostchiki* which I beheld with astonishment. Both cabs and cabbies looked dejected. Here I was confronted by old Russia, backward and poor, in spite of all revolutions. I climbed into a cab.

My clothes and my bad Russian labelled me a foreigner, and the cabby began to talk to me. " Have you come from America ? A good life, over there. You can have all the things you want ; and good quality—at a low price. Not like it is here. We can get only worthless clothes, and the prices are sky-high. We have only rags left."

This surprised me. What ! A worker of the New Russia who felt no pride, no joy in his new life ? I became entangled in a complicated answer about not believing that everyone abroad was well dressed.

The streets drew my attention. To arrive at my destination, we were crossing the heart of Moscow. The town appeared very different from what I had expected. Nothing impressive about the houses ; they all seemed old and ill-adapted to modern needs. It was the East, ' Holy Russia '. The streets were paved with enormous stones, as Europe knew them in the Middle Ages. Most of the passers-by wore old clothes, even rags. The grey of autumn twilight deepened the sadness of this belated drabness, mixture of the oriental and the medieval.

2

During those first days, this drabness, this time-lag between Russia and the rest of Europe became an obsession. Moscow could not be an obsession. It was the heart, the centre of the country. Its aspect was no doubt a reflection of the level of social and cultural life over the whole of Russia. I spent hours wandering through the streets of the town, gazing at faces, going to meetings, eating in public refectories, visiting the theatre. Itinerant tradesmen indicated the extremely low economic level of the population ; at every step I met pedlars who spent all day in the street, their entire merchandise consisting of a few apples. As to Moscow's public refectories, they were the filthiest places I had seen in my life.

Life in Russia—I told myself in those early days—is far from being so contented and beautiful as the Communist press abroad makes out and as I myself believed it to be. But this conclusion left me ill at ease. I admonished myself for having perhaps been lacking in critical spirit before coming to Russia ; I almost accused myself of judging from a ' bourgeois ' point of view.

I had known long since, as everyone had, that Russia had been Europe's most backward country, but, like all foreigners, I had no concrete and living notions of the extent of this lag. Henceforward, I told myself, I must take this historical lag into consideration ; it will be necessary to state, once and for all, that the level of the life of the masses is still lower than it appears when seen from Europe. But all this is not essential, what matters in the end is the direction of the evolution. In Russia, the level of the life of the masses is low, but it is rising, albeit slowly ; in Europe, the high pre-War level is tending to drop.

I had, moreover, one favourable impression at least. Although dressed worse than the Viennese, the people showed fresher, rounder faces. One felt that, notwithstanding their tattered appearance, people ate their fill, and above all, that they had faith in a better future. In spite of poverty, their glances and their movements were full of youth and life. When I had become more familiar with all these people, that youthfulness, that faith in the future, that conviction that life was only just beginning, that unshakable determination to secure a ' place in the sun ' appeared to me to be the outstanding characteristic of Soviet Russia. In the streets, in the offices, in the schools and in the factories, I met men who before the revolution were ' nobodies ' and now were ' somebodies ' or preparing to become such.

Coming from the despairing stagnation of post-War Vienna, in Moscow one was struck by the rise of entire social groups, the quickened rhythm of life, the desire for education felt by all, but especially by the young. The contents of Soviet books, newspapers, all recalled the vastness of the country, the magnitude of its problems, all underlined the importance of this world-capital.

In the midst of all this impetuous torrent of Soviet life, the Comintern appeared to me an institution devoid of great importance. Without yet understanding Soviet Russia and the real part played by the Comintern, I saw clearly from the very beginning that there was an abyss between the great speeches about ' the general staff of the World Revolution ' and the reality. The importance of the Comintern was considerably less in Moscow than that of any of the People's Commissariats. It was nothing but a foreign section attached to the Propaganda Service of the Central Committee. The people I met there—the permanent collaborators of the Comintern—seemed to personify the narrowness of the institution and the drabness of the building in which it was housed. They had neither scope nor breadth of view, and showed no independence of thought. I expected to meet giants, I found dwarfs. I hoped to gather wisdom from venerable masters and I met with none but lackeys.

The autumn and winter of 1926 were marked by a bitter struggle within the Communist Party, a struggle to which the present Moscow trials are the bloody epilogue. From the day of my arrival, I was admitted into the Communist Party of Russia and was thus enabled to follow the march of events from the inside. During the first half of October, the Opposition was being ' worked ' to answer for its factory demonstrations, especially those of the aircraft factory *Aviopribor*. In October took place the XVth conference of the Communist Party of Russia, during the course of which the pressure against the Opposition increased. Finally, at the beginning of December, at the VIth plenum of the Executive Committee of the Comintern, a third attack was launched against the Opposition.

At the time of my arrival in Russia, I was an adherent of the policy advocated by the majority of the Central Committee.

My first contact with the Russia of the Soviets did not inspire me with any doubts as regards the justness of that policy, at least as to its basic justness. And I was all the more astonished at the methods used against the minority.

It was sufficient to be present at a few Party meetings to be convinced that discussions of ideology played but a very secondary part in the struggle. The deciding factor consisted of threats, intimidatory actions and terrorism. One felt that any militant member who distinguished himself by a particularly cynical and brutal outburst against the Opposition in general, or against some of its members, was assured of either immediate advancement or a brilliant future.

Woe betide the speaker who put forward doubts, who declared that such or such a point of difference between the Opposition and the majority did not seem clear to him. By way of answer, he would be reproached for lack of revolutionary flair, he would be accused of being in both camps, of being a traitor in disguise. The official speaker would harangue him, raising his voice. " That does not seem clear to you ? Comrades, X—— declares that it doesn't seem clear to him ; you perceive that the basic principles of Party politics, and the petit-bourgeois characteristics of the Opposition do not seem clear to him. . . . Whom does he seek to lead into error ? We know very well what he hides behind this hypocrisy. The Party will tolerate no hesitation, no lack of clarity. . . ." In those conditions, all leaning towards doubt soon disappeared. Those who, at the outset, had dared express their doubts, in the end mounted the platform to excuse themselves for having misunderstood.

The attitude of the Opposition strengthened the feeling of uneasiness. The rare opponents who had developed their opinions in the Cells took to speech in those same Cells a few weeks later to declare that they renounced their opposition. Often they would go so far as to condemn the ideas of the Opposition. That was merely a form of tactics in accordance with the instructions of the majority of the Opposition leaders. But this Byzantine diplomacy disturbed the other side and soon they themselves no longer knew whether their retractions were sincere or not.

At the beginning of December, as I have already stated, the plenum of the Comintern's Executive Committee took place. For the last time, the doors of the Kremlin were opened to a congress of the Third International. The essential task of this congress was to condemn the Russian Opposition ; to remove Zinoviev from his post of President of the Comintern and to deliver the Opposition over to the mercy of Stalin and Bukharin. " The circle is once more closed," wrote *Pravda*, " all the world, from the Cells of the masses to the Comintern's Executive Committee, has condemned the Opposition. If the latter continues its struggle, henceforward it risks infringing Soviet legality."

That sentence, harmless as it may sound to the average European, contained to the Russian a direct threat of annihilation by the G.P.U. (the political secret police). And the destruction of what remained of the Opposition of the Left within the Russian Party, the triumph of the Russian nationalist and bureaucratic reaction which aspired only to come to terms with the ruling classes of the Old World, coincided symbolically with the expulsion of the Comintern from within the walls of the Kremlin. No further congresses of the Third International were to take place there.

Seven years earlier, in 1919, Trotsky, upon opening the first congress of the Third International, wrote in his manifesto to the Red Army : " Is it not symbolic to see today in the palace of the age-long oppressors of the workers of Russia and of the propagators of European reaction, the meeting of the Convention of World Revolution ? "

Undoubtedly, I was not yet sufficiently mature to understand the deep significance of this annihilation of the Russian Opposition. Like Clara Zetkin, I saw only " an episode, not a catastrophe ".

Nor did I sufficiently connect the events that developed within my own Yugo-Slav Party, namely, the transference of power to the Right accomplished the summer before under pretext of a reconciliation between the various sections, with what took place in the Russian Party and in the Comintern.

In the splendid hall of St. Andrew at the Kremlin, two hundred delegates and numerous visitors heard the eloquent struggle between the leaders of the Russian Party. At the exits, silent and of statuesque immobility, young soldiers of the G.P.U. division mounted guard.

Stalin, Bukharin, Zinoviev, Trotsky and Kamenev made long speeches, one after the other, in opposing groups. It was the last time in the history of the Russian revolution that the

6

leaders of that revolution—still equals in right—appeared on the same platform, face to face with the world.

The forced speeches of Bukharin and Zinoviev failed to impress me in the least ; Bukharin appeared to me pretentious, Zinoviev verbose. Stalin's unshakable determination to push matters to the extreme, the clarity with which he stated the dilemma, impressed me deeply, in spite of the heaviness of his speech. Trotsky spoke in an exceptionally intelligent and subtle way. From the point of view of oratory, his speech marked the culminating peak of the session. This triumph was all the more remarkable, as public recognition was denied him on account of political calculations.

Trotsky walked up to the platform ; a deep silence fell over the meeting. He asked leave to speak for two hours. The Chairman, a Bulgarian named Kolarov, refused to grant him more than the half-hour accorded to all the speakers whose names were down. Trotsky seemed about to descend from the platform when, after a few moments' hesitation, the Chairman offered him one hour. Trotsky remained and began his speech—his swan-song.

The hall listened breathlessly. Those among the audience who had no clear-cut mandate could not resist showing their enthusiasm at the wittier passages of the speech. Trotsky stigmatized the agents of the Comintern : Manuilsky, Pepper and Schmeral. From the Committee's bench, dear old Clara Zetkin leaned over the balustrade in order not to lose one word. Bukharin, moved and tense, was taking notes for his reply to Trotsky. Pepper, feeling himself beaten, sought help from Zetkin, but she stopped him with a sharp word ; he hastened over to Bukharin ; the latter, without saying anything, pointed to his ear to indicate that he wished to listen and pushed him aside.

However, notwithstanding the polemic brilliance of his oratory, Trotsky wrapped his exposition of the debate in too great a prudence and diplomacy. The audience was unable to appreciate its depth, the tragedy of the divergences separating the Opposition from the majority.

Kamenev's speech was sober and clear. In contrast with Zinoviev and Trotsky, he did not begin by refuting the accusations brought against the Opposition. He began his speech by affirming that there existed in Russia and in the Third International a danger from the Right, represented by the official majority of the Russian Party. This phenomenon, he declared, was not the result of chance, but was due to the petit-bourgeois character of the country and to the weakening of the revolutionary spirit of the Western proletariats. This reasoning impressed the audience. But Kamenev did not draw the bold conclusions that such premises seemed to imply.

The Opposition—I· was struck by this at the time—was not aware of its weakness ; it was also going to underestimate the magnitude of its defeat and to neglect to draw a lesson from it. Whereas the majority, led by Stalin and Bukharin, manœuvred to obtain the total exclusion of the Opposition, the latter constantly sought for compromise and amicable arrangements. This timid policy of the Opposition was instrumental, if not in bringing about its defeat, certainly in weakening its resistance.

When a little later, Viniovitch (who had, in the days of Zinoviev, been secretary to the Communist Youth International) told me by the way that the Opposition was bound to win all the same in the course of the next few months, it appeared to me that all the members of the Opposition were henceforth condemned.

II

IS ALL LOST?

I WOULD have liked to believe that the situation in Soviet Russia was, if not excellent, at least good in so far as essentials were concerned ; but new facts and new ideas came day after day to deepen my doubts and fears.

During the congress of the Comintern, a small personal incident came unexpectedly to illustrate the situation and the future in store for me. I was staying with one of the members of the Executive Committee of the Comintern who had very friendly feelings towards me. Wishing to draw my attention to the too great liberty with which I was speaking of matters concerning the Party, he gave me some friendly advice,

" Don't forget, my dear friend, that you are not in Yugo-Slavia where you can go for the Central Committee as much as you please ; don't forget that you are in Russia and that here, unless you belong to the Central Committee of the Communist Party, you are a mere nobody."

Another member of the same Committee who was present at the time added with a knowing glance,

" And don't let this go any further."

A third colleague, younger but more precocious, contented himself with preserving an eloquent silence.

I replied with vigour that such a state of affairs would be flagrantly opposed to the Marxist principle of the relations between the leaders and the masses of the Party ; that, given the fact that Russia was ruled by Bolshevism in its highest form, such relations as they implied could not possibly exist.

Alas, it was precisely these relations between the masses and the leaders that led me straight to a Soviet gaol.

As to my three friends, they are today still among the leaders of the Comintern and their influence in that body is in inverse proportion with the loquacity which they displayed on the occasion of our conversation.

I soon came across a case in which not only militant workers, but also the masses of the workers themselves had been deprived of their most elementary rights. I met a former Hungarian manual worker whom I had known very closely in 1919 in Soviet Hungary ; he was now the director of a factory in Moscow. He told me that in his factory, they had just arrested a group of anarchist-syndicalists suspected of disseminating an illegal pamphlet demanding the improvement of working conditions in their factory.

" What ! " I exclaimed. " Are there still anarchist-syndicalists in Moscow ? Yet in the demonstration of November 7th, I saw no trace of them in the procession, nor have I seen a single banner of theirs."

" Come, come," my old friend replied, " didn't you know that they represent a ' petit-bourgeois deviation ' condemned as long ago as at the Xth Party congress ? "

" I know, but they are not opposed to Soviet power, they are not counter-revolutionaries. In every country, there is a united front with them against reaction and capitalism. Would it not suffice to fight their deviation by ideological means ? All the more as the bourgeois class has been liquidated in Russia and the majority of the working class is in favour of Communism."

My friend launched into an explanation dealing with the backward character of the working class, with its waverings and its uncertainty. But all his arguments left me cold. When he told me that on the eve of the feasts of the 1st of May and the 7th of November, it was customary to arrest a number of anarchists and socialists of all shades to ensure the smooth running of the demonstrations ; that at the feast of the Internationale and at that of the October revolution, those people were not allowed to demonstrate under their own banner, albeit anti-capitalist, then I felt the ground slipping away from under my feet.

Thus workers were denied the right to demonstrate under a workers' banner, in a workers' State. This went beyond my understanding.

As to the attitude adopted by the syndicate organization faced with these workers' grievances and these arrests, it appeared to me a scandalous outrage to the working class. The ' triangle ' of the factory (i.e. the director, the secretary of the Party Cell, the chairman of the factory committee) called a meeting on behalf of the syndicate. At this meeting, the syndicate proposed to the workers that they condemn the authors of the pamphlets in question and approve of their arrest. With a hypocrisy worthy of the Inquisition, they all wanted to condemn ' those who had placed themselves beyond the bounds of lawfulness ', as if it were possible lawfully to publish a sheet of complaints, and it was decided to approve of ' the measures taken in defence of Soviet power '.

The meeting naturally took place in the absence of the accused and whosoever would have dared take up their defence would have spent the night at the headquarters of the G.P.U.

I refused to believe this incident typical of the general run ; I consoled myself by supposing that here was an isolated case of ' deformation '.

* * *

There were at that time thirty to forty militant members of the Yugo-Slav Communist Party in Moscow. To keep in touch with the working masses and to study the practice of Bolshevist experience, they had to spend one day a week in a factory. They worked like the manual workers, were present at syndicate and Party meetings and organized the work of the MOPR (International Association for Assistance to Revolutionaries in other countries). The close kinship between the Yugo-Slav and the Russian languages rapidly enabled them to mix with the workers. Most of these Yugo-Slav comrades were themselves manual workers who had received a political education and were the backbone of the Yugo-Slav Party. They had come to Russia, there to learn the revolutionary art of Bolshevism, then to return home, their apprenticeship served.

These comrades, some openly, others secretly, began to tell the most terrifying tales of the state of the manual workers in the factories.

One of them, Risto Samardjitch-Noskov, an old militant syndicalist from Bosnia, later to be executed by the Yugo-Slav reactionaries, described in detail to me the outrages and the withholding of their rights, to which the manual workers in his factory were subjected. The Soviet factory workers, he said, were prisoners of their foremen and directors, as in capitalist countries. Their lot was indeed worse, for, in the latter countries, the workers can protest in the Press and at meetings. Here there was no one to whom to turn. It was not socialism, he concluded, it was slavery.

Another comrade, Mustafa Deditch, also a militant syndicalist, former secretary of the Federation of Herzegovina, who now can look back on seven years of prison and exile in Soviet Russia, told me analogous facts. In despair at finding that the workers were as badly exploited in Soviet Russia as they were abroad, he fell ill and even intended to leave the Party.

A third, a young and not yet hardened worker of the Voyevodina, gifted and sensitive, had the same experience and left the Party to become an ordinary workman once more.

There were, I must admit, comrades who, from the same material, extracted very different conclusions. Yes, they said, the 'knout' reigns supreme in the Soviet factory, but the Russian manual worker is so backward, and lacking in conscience to such an extent, that he does not know how to look after his tools and has no pride in raising his output. One is therefore forced to use coercion so that the factory can function and in order to educate the worker himself.

They gave examples, mentioning various incidents they had witnessed. Here is one.

Two workmen had to take a barrel of oil down a flight of stairs. Instead of handling it carefully and lowering it step by step, they hurled the barrel from the top of the stairs to the bottom, at the risk of breaking it. What must one do? Surely one is obliged to be brutal.

Witnesses for and against were piling up. I began to realize the spirit that reigned in Soviet society. The contradictions I found there seemed to me inadmissible, yet in actual practice they were tolerated. The brisk rhythm of Soviet life had underlying it a lack of social principle. Entire groups of peasants and workers rose in social status and took on all sorts of directing, economic, political and administrative functions. A very large number of young peasants and manual workers, owing to their secondary or higher education, took in hand the reins of the new society. But this happy evolution entailed not only certain regrettable isolated characteristics, it had also a considerable and deeply perverted aspect. The strata that rose would at the same time be permeated with a certain bourgeois spirit, a spirit of desiccated egoism, of low calcula-tion. One felt their firmly established desire to hew themselves out a good place, regardless of others, and one recognized this as a case of cynical and spontaneous atavism. In his efforts to succeed, each man gave evidence of a totally unscrupulous capacity for adaptation and a shameless aptitude for flattery of those in power. It was written in every gesture, on every face, in every eye. It was expressed in every act, in every speech, in the coarse revolutionary phraseology. This spirit prevailed not only among non-Party members, but also and above all among the Communists themselves, who instead of being the best were often the worst of all.

" Is this our vanguard ? " I asked myself.

What seemed yet worse to me was that this tendency to assume bourgeois characteristics, far from being on the decrease, was on the contrary increasing and growing stronger, flooding all before it. The destructive torrent met with no obstacle, no attempts were made to stem its rise. It was accepted by both the masses and by the leaders as if it were inevitable.

I groped my way about this labyrinth of unforeseen sensations ; these imponderables seemed to me as precise as physical realities.

Foreseeing the triumph of the ruling tendencies, I drew the logical conclusion that the evolution towards socialism had been finally arrested, that the revolution had died and hence that ' all was lost '. For it is not machines nor factories, but human inter-relationships that make the essence of socialism.

But then, what is taking place in Russia ? The bourgeois order has been abolished, the bourgeois class has been liquidated in so far as it was a ruling class. As the domination of the bourgeois has not been re-established, capitalism has not come back to power. Then, how is it possible to say that socialism is irretrievably lost ?

Unable to answer these questions, I must remain satisfied to postpone the final conclusion until later.

* * *

During the winter from 1926 to 1927, the revolution and the civil war in China held world opinion in suspense as much as did events in Spain during 1936–37.

My Yugo-Slav comrade, Mustafa Deditch, was present at the Presentation Ceremony of the Eastern Communist

Workers' University. Rykov delivered an oration in which he declared that had the Opposition been listened to, the Soviet State would have supported the Chinese revolution. But fortunately ' we ' had not allowed ourselves to be dragged into it and thus had avoided war with Great Britain.

Which clearly meant : let the Chinese revolution drown in her own blood, provided we remain safe.

A horrible doubt assailed our minds. Were we, the foreign Communists, by any chance considered as the pawns on a chess-board ?

III

PEASANTS AND MANUAL WORKERS: WHAT THEY THINK

THE peasant question seemed to me to be of decisive importance, not only for the outcome of the internal struggles of the Party, but also for the fate of the entire revolution. Thus my adherence to the policy of the majority was based mainly, if not entirely, on the line of conduct taken on the peasant question, which seemed to me correct. What the peasants did and thought was known to me only through books and newspapers. Hence I decided to spend the summer in the country to see for myself what was happening there.

The severe Russian winter made me wish for the first time in my life to see a southern sea and sun. I decided to go to a village in the Crimea—Koktebel—between Theodosia and Sudak.

During the journey, I was struck by the amount of tea the Russians drink in an attempt to cope with the heat. But I will first relate two of the more interesting experiences of the journey.

I was travelling in the company of an old workman who was returning to Baku. He was lamenting the misery of the factory workers in great detail. What distressed him most was to see the same work done in the same workshops paid at different rates according to whether the workman was a non-Party member or, as he himself was, a Communist.

From the Marxist point of view, a difference in salary according to profession, a higher remuneration for skilled workers and employees, seemed to me justifiable. But that the same work should have better or worse remuneration, that to be a Communist should carry with it not the duty to set an example but material advantages—that seemed revolting and inadmissible. Later, when my comrades were taken on, we learned that this was engineered by a simple increase of rates in favour of the Communists.

In the Ukraine, part of the journey was passed in the company of a group of peasants. They were alert men, strongly built and intelligent, and they were talking freely about everything. They complained bitterly of being oppressed by the Soviet power. All, they said, was for the factory workers : holidays, social insurance, culture, freedom from taxation, eight-hour day. Nothing for the peasants. Today as before, the peasants were counted second-class citizens. They went on to grumble about the oppressive taxes, and above all about the difference between the prices of agricultural and industrial products.

Upon my arrival at Koktebel, I settled in at a *seredniak's* (middle peasant). He was the young head of a family and had been married only two years. He had several brothers who lived apart from each other in the same village. One of them, a member of the Communist Party, was the chairman of the local Soviet. A young sister, a non-Party member, was preparing to become a schoolmistress. Belonging to such a milieu, my host could be called ' Soviet-spirited ' as the Russians put it. On the occasion of the mobilization exercises which took place a month after my arrival at Koktebel, he showed no hostility towards the system at all, yet did not hide the fear he had of war. He had just received an annual loan from the Rural Credit Society of 100 or 150 roubles to buy a second cow and improve his equipment. The aid he was thus given by a Government institution served to strengthen his feelings of loyalty towards the State. One might even say that the revolution, by reason of its having split up the estates of the big local landowners, had materially improved his condition, as it had that of the entire village. In short, my host seemed to me the perfect type of the Soviet peasant, the incarnation of the policy of union between workers and peasants.

Yet there were dark sides to the picture and it was difficult not to notice them. My host had a child ; he had it baptized and invited a kulak (well-to-do peasant) from a distant village to be godfather. The man was rather more in the nature of a rich steppe-landowner than a kulak. In his district, somewhere in the north-eastern part of the Crimea, he possessed a flock of some two or three thousand sheep. He was therefore a capitalist. Were there still such people in Soviet Russia ? How had he succeeded in amassing this wealth ? Then I learned the best part of the story : he had grown rich by speculation during the great famine of 1921.

My host spoke of this immense flock with great admiration, revealing thereby his own wish to grow rich. The strange thing was that at the same time he remained politically on an integral Soviet plane. He had no idea of the contradiction represented by his wishes and his political views.

My frequent conversations with other peasants left me with the same impression. More so, even. The majority of the villagers expressed an even greater reluctance in the matter of the Anglo-Soviet tension and the eventuality of war. Yes, they admitted, it looks as if England wants to fight the Communists. The Communists, but not Russia. What have we farmers got to do with it ? They thus proclaimed a sort of neutrality. Sometimes one heard in their tones a shade that seemed to indicate the hope of future improvement, but often there was a certain anxiety. Things might go badly for the peasants. My spokesmen, ill at ease, would cast a glance over their village, over the grounds of the old landed proprietor, his deserted country house. . . .

The secretary of the Party Cell, employed in the local Soviet administration, expressed the opinion that the mobilization had been a roaring success : the villagers had answered the call instead of hiding in the woods. The apprehension expressed in that phrase spoke volumes about the famous ' morale ' of the peasants. I saw the gradual disappearance of the idyllic picture of the relations with the peasantry as the official Press still portrayed it.

* * *

In the village, there were both co-operative and private shops. On the beach, these two types were represented by two small shops, built side by side. The private shopkeeper did an excellent trade, her wares being good and fresh ; the co-operative store seemed apathetic, it opened late, closed early and sold shoddy stuff. One day, the shop-woman complained to me of the taxes that were crushing her business out of existence.

" Why don't you seek employment in the co-operative shop ? You have experience, you know the work ; you could make yourself very useful and you wouldn't have any more cares."

" They refuse to have me there," she answered. " I tried once, but they sent me away."

Another small mystery of great Russia.

A few summer visitors, of whom I was one, had their meals with a country-woman. One day at meal-time our hostess told us that she had just sold her vineyard.

" Sold ? Does that mean that you can sell ground ? "

" Certainly, you can sell anything," she replied, and began to enumerate various cases of sale of fields, gardens and immovable property in general. My objections as to the abolition of private ownership of land did not seem to affect her in the slightest. Later, in Moscow, I learned that those sales were made solely in the form of cessions of investments, ' investments of labour ', of course.

Along the coast, there was a row of some ten houses, some of which belonged to the Theodosian Holiday Trust and others to leading representatives of the Soviet intelligentsia. Five or six half-ruined buildings remained unoccupied.

At the end of the beach, on a picturesque hill, could be seen the villa of N——, the former landowner. At the side of it, in an old coach-house, lived the last two representatives of the family, the former owner's wife and daughter. The wife's present occupation was that of village prostitute, and her daughter, aged sixteen, had already joined the same profession. I blamed, not the lady, but the revolution.

One day we made a trip to the ancient site of Krym, the one-time capital of the Crimean Khans. A Tartar ' mulla ' showed us over the ruins of Tartar grandeur with great pride and explained the old inscriptions to us. On looking at him, on listening to his voice, I said to myself : the revolution gives to some more than to others, but it gives something to practically everybody. That constitutes the power of the system which is rising from the revolution. This ' mulla ', strange and even hostile to the general policy of Bolshevism, is ready to put up with a good many drawbacks for the sole reason that the renaissance of Tartar nationality has been allowed to take place.

18

On the way home, one of our comrades told us the history of her family during the revolution. She had belonged to a rich family of Volga farmers. Her father owned more than a hundred hectares of land which were taken from him by the revolutionaries. She had been to a secondary school and was in sympathy with them. Her father had hated Czarism. In 1917, during the Civil War, she quarrelled with him on political grounds, embraced the cause of the Bolsheviks and married a Communist. The old farmer could not forgive Bolshevism for having taken his land from him, and when, during the NEP (New Economic Policy), his youngest son joined the Communist Youth, it was a hard blow to him. But years went by, all the children had been able, under Soviet rule, to study and make their way in the world. Then the old man admitted himself won over, became reconciled with his children and to the system. " If I did cling to my land, it was not to take it into my tomb with me, it was to enable my children to study and become men. As the Soviets do all that for you anyhow, it's all the same to me."

I prepared to return to Moscow. On leaving the South, I was tempted to take some of the local fruit back with me and went to the market to buy some. I felt as if I had returned to Europe. At first sight, on reading the notices, one sensed the land of socialism ; but one had to throw only one glance behind the scenes to see the old conditions still fully active. I had come to Soviet Russia with the certainty of beholding a continuous development, untrammelled and with boundless horizons. Now, unrest seized me. What I had believed to be the very groundwork of Soviet life seemed to crumble before me.

I observed, without doubt, that the majority of the peasants were well disposed towards the Soviet power, at any rate that they felt no hostility towards it. But it was no less certain that the peasant did not conceive of any road to progress other than along lines of private economy, of agrarian capitalism. The rural masses did not yet suspect that there was antagonism between Soviet-socialist progress and capitalist progress. But that antagonism existed in reality and was increasing every day. How would the contradiction be solved ?

*　　*　　*

Shortly after my return to Moscow, I went to spend a fortnight in the country round Vladimir, in the company of a distinguished woman from Montenegro, Stoia Markovitch. The aim of our journey was to collaborate in the activities of MOPR (International Association for Assistance to Revolutionaries in other countries), which was collecting funds in that region for the benefit of political prisoners in Yugo-Slavia.

Vladimir, the ancient capital of the Russian monarchs, has retained all the characteristics of the most backward Russian provinces. The finest building in the town, the one-time governor's mansion, was occupied by the Party Committee. As to the Executive Committee of the Soviets, that was housed in a building of secondary importance. That showed even to the least well-informed where the real power lay.

After a few conversations about matters connected with the affairs of MOPR at Vladimir, we went on to the Guss-Khrustalny district, an old and important industrial centre surrounded by limitless countryside.

The secretary of the District Committee acquainted us with regional economics, with details of the local industry and the fluctuation of labour. We spoke at several large meetings in textile, glass and other factories.

The textile factory prided itself on counting among its workers one old woman who had saved the establishment during the famine years by taking all the work of the upkeep upon herself. She was now a member of the Central Executive Committee of the U.S.S.R. This high dignity with its attending honours bewildered her, for she lived for her work and was devoted to her factory.

At the glass factory we were introduced to several skilled workmen and foremen, old social-democrats. Later on I had several talks with them. They did not go in for any illegal activities, published no subversive pamphlets and were officially counted as non-Party. But they had never ceased dealing by word of mouth with concrete and current matters in a social-democrat fashion. At the workers' meetings, people were forced indirectly to take their arguments into account. They had not been sent away from the factory for the reason that there was a shortage of skilled labour.

The impression that these meetings and private conversations left on me was favourable, on the whole ; but I was struck by the passive attitude of many of the workers. One felt that they had neither interest nor enthusiasm, but on the contrary a frigidity of manner, an exaggerated reticence. It was depressing. The workers seemed to say by their silence : it is all very well but what does it mean to us ? One had to pester each person to get a word out of him. I had already observed the same attitude among the workers in Moscow, a year before, on the occasion of the collections for the English miners on strike.

Leaving Guss-Khrustalny, we penetrated into a distant forest to visit another glass factory. We were received with joy ; guests from the centre and strangers on top of that were no daily occurrence. The administration received us with ceremony and the workers listened to our speeches with, obvious interest.

Before the meeting, I communicated the principal points of my speech to the secretary of the Party Committee. One of them was the following : the level of the life of the Soviet workers still leaves much to be desired, the poverty of the land and its economic lag still make themselves felt even after the revolution ; but in Soviet Russia—and this was the real point—the level tends to rise gradually, whereas in capitalist Europe the position of the workman, which was very high before the War, is daily becoming more precarious. The secretary asked me not to talk about the proletarian level of life and to limit myself to a discussion of the difficult situation of the working class in Europe.

The following day the director of the factory invited me to dine with him. There were about twenty-five guests : the Party and syndicate leaders and some fifteen factory workers. They were old workmen with typical faces. They inspired respect and behaved with great dignity as men who are conscious of being the creators of the new wealth of Soviet society.

I enquired into their situation. They were all specialized workers or foremen who were receiving relatively high wages. There was not one unqualified manual worker, except for a packer, the widow of a foreman who had died in a factory accident. These men spoke with pride of their status in society and of all that concerned the revolution in Russia.

Yet they did not appear one with the director and seemed to be saying : we are on good terms with the administration, but please do not confuse us with it.

* * *

The autumn of 1927 was marked by an occurrence new to me : the shortage of butter, cheese and milk. Then the bread distribution too became irregular. But the public queued patiently for hours on end. No indignation, no trace of protest meeting. The newspapers did not touch upon the subject. Days, weeks, months went by. What a country, what strange people ! In Europe, a shortage one hundred times smaller would have caused a storm in the Press, the Communists would have been seen in the streets, demonstrating. Here, months of privation passed without leaving a trace in the community. Was it the spirit of sacrifice peculiar to the Russian worker ? Were they overwhelmed by a post-revolutionary fatigue ? Was it the fatalism of slaves, as the reactionary denigrators of the Russian people would have it ?

It was not before three months had passed that the Press began to murmur and that a few explanations were given. Kalinin declared at a meeting that the revolution had considerably improved the nutrition of the people which entailed as a necessary consequence a certain scarcity of butter and other alimentary produce. . . .

* * *

That same winter, I spent a couple of weeks in a rest-house near Moscow. The place, if I remember rightly, was called Peski. The rest-house had originally been the large villa of a former landowner. It now sheltered workmen with their families, clerks and young people. The relations between the visitors were marked by a pleasant simplicity. The food was excellent. Sports, among which were ski-ing and skating, were very much enjoyed. In the evenings, entertainments were improvised.

I shared my table with a group of manual workers from Kolomna and I grew very friendly with them. They were good friends, open and kindly as the people in Russia generally are. But they took very little interest in political problems. They were mechanics from the locomotive factory at

Kolomna ; each had his little house, his cow and his kitchen garden. They took pleasure in their work and earned enough to live in a small but decent way. They left to others the care of solving problems of world importance. Their simplicity and good humour delighted me and made a welcome contrast with the manners of the Moscow clerks ; but alas, what political apathy. . . .

A week later, about to take leave of one another, we were seized with the desire to seal our friendship by spending a last few pleasant hours together. But we soon found out that a Russian worker can buy no drink other than vodka in the local co-operatives.

There was also a group of students from the Institute of Higher Education, all young and full of energy. Talking politics with them, I noticed that they knew the external aspects of the history of the workers' movement excellently well, as given in the elementary Marxist textbooks ; but their attitude as regards the more actual problems was one of indifference and formalism.

Among those who spent their holidays at Peski were also a few women workers from licensed factories. They all proclaimed that both wages and working conditions were better in these private enterprises than in those run by the State. Many workers would have liked to have been taken on in them, but the syndicates obstinately opposed this. Thus, in a socialist State, conditions of work were better in private enterprises than in nationalized factories. What was to be thought of the workers' wish to be taken on in the former ? How to describe the syndicates that struggled for things other than the improvement of working conditions in the socialized factories ?

One of the women told us that she had gone to the factory in order to be able to study.

" Did you lack the means to study ? Could you not have applied for a scholarship instead of going to work ? "

" No, it was for my apprenticeship."

" What apprenticeship ? "

" The worker's apprenticeship."

At that point I learned that it was necessary to work for two or three years in a factory in order to reach the social position of worker ; after that it became easy to be admitted to a higher school.

One of the women attracted my attention by her instinctive dislike of bureaucracy. It was more than hatred, it was a passionate ardour that urged her to unmask at every turn the misdeeds of bureaucrats. Nothing escaped her notice. Every detail of administrative routine became to her an event of paramount importance. She unveiled the bureaucrats' hypocrisy, their false ' devotion ', their Communist phraseology, so often belied by their actions. These accusations helped me to probe behind the scenes of Soviet life and gave me the sort of synthesis which I was still lacking. Each one of her gestures seemed to imply : I know you are scoundrels, you bureaucrats of Communism, both big and little ; I can see right through you ; I know, from A to Z, the reasons I have for despising and hating you.

Her unbounded hostility towards the official Soviet society was instinctive and unreasoned. Her attitude was totally devoid of all theoretical backing and had no political colouring. But it was the first time that I had come across a person of working-class origin, a daughter of the October revolution, who no longer restricted herself to condemning such or such a point of the system, but who condemned the whole, lock, stock and barrel. I had come across such an attitude in the camp of the adversaries of the October revolution, among former landowners, capitalists and reformists. Now I had before me a specimen of the rising generation of workers whose very spiritual progress had brought about a horror of bureaucracy. At the time, it struck me only in a vague and general way.

The favourable impression this young worker produced on me was not modified when, one day, she began to ply me with the following questions.

" Actually, why have you come here to eat the bread of the Russian worker ? You know how welcome you are. You strangers live here like lords, whereas our workers have to put up with dry bread. Why don't you make a revolution at home instead of rushing in here where the table is already laid ? "

I still had some illusions on the subject of the Comintern, without, however, ignoring the fact that an incredible number of nonentities and parasites had worked their way into that institution and now inhabited the ' Lux ', the seat of the Third International at Moscow. The contempt shown to them by the Russian proletariat was justified. I therefore did not feel it in me to take offence at certain exaggerations that were contained in the statements of this working woman. I replied to her that there were many exceptions to the rule and I did not greatly regret only half convincing her.

I met this woman again at Moscow a few months later. How great was my astonishment when I learned that she had been a member of the Communist Youth and had only recently left it. Looking at her membership card, I was seized by a curious apprehension : was it her time in the Comsomol (League of Youth) that had contributed to the formation of such opinions in this young woman ?

I was soon to learn the influence that syndicate life had had on her development. I heard one day that she was out of work.

" What has happened to you ? " I asked.

" The syndicate, to punish me for having taken part in a strike, has left me without work."

This is what had happened. She was vice-chairman of the factory committee in the important sewing workshop where she was employed (that was how I learned that she was a militant syndicalist). The workshop had just received a considerable order from the Red Army. The new contract entailed a notable drop in the already low wages. The women workers demanded a revision. The young vice-chairman, instead of arguing with her comrades, supported their demands. These were turned down, whereupon all the workers handed in their collective resignation.

" But I do not see that there was any strike," I said with astonishment.

" A collective resignation is considered tantamount to a strike by the syndicate."

Nearly all the workers who had thus left their work found employment elsewhere. But the syndicate bureaucrats wished to punish the vice-chairman for the solidarity she had shown with her worker-comrades. As a result, she was refused all employment.

At that time I had already come into contact with the Trotskyist Opposition. Carefully I began to direct the conversation towards this subject, but I was soon convinced that the struggle between the Party leaders left the woman cold. Maybe she did not understand it, maybe she believed that from the workers' point of view there was not much to choose between the rival leaders.

But I had no time to go deeply into her feelings. On the eve of the Five Year Plan, I became too absorbed in the multiplicity of problems and mysteries which Russia was putting before my mind.

Book II

THE TURMOIL OF THE FIVE YEAR PLAN

I

A WORLD RUNS OFF THE RAILS

I HAD already been in Russia well over a year. Facts and impressions had finally melted into a complete picture of Soviet life. But the picture had more the properties of a snapshot than of a profound evolutionary view of society. I perceived novelties, quaint occurrences and contradictions visible to any foreign observer. These impressions were so different from those received in static Europe, they compelled attention so powerfully, that the stranger often limited himself to underlining the contrast between the West and Russia, neglecting to study the intrinsic laws of Soviet Russian life. He perceived an entirely new society, he was struck by the boldness of its tendencies and by the severe struggle it waged to establish itself, and that sufficed him. Yet all this was not essential ; the indispensable point was to discover the general trend, the final end of all these dynamic forces. This direction, this aim that constituted the underlying sense of events, was much more difficult to discern. One needed criteria different from those needed to study European life. European notions only just permitted perception of the contrast between the West and the land of the Soviets. As for the concepts that might help to discover the real meaning of events in Russia, they must be acquired on the spot ; they could not be taken ready-made out of one's European travelling trunk.

The winter of 1927–28 marked the end of a stage in Soviet development ; the life itself, as it were, drew some conclusions from the preceding evolution. It became easier, even for a foreign observer, to realize them.

These conclusions had nothing cheerful about them. Five years of NEP (New Economic Policy) were ending in a general economic and political crisis. No degree of State or Party censorship was able any longer to hide the facts. The Government had arrived at the point not only of admitting it but of making it the starting-point of a new line of action on which its very existence depended.

The butter, milk and bread shortage which had occurred during the autumn had revealed to the town-dwellers the existence of a deep-rooted rural crisis, the consequences of which shook the country as a whole. The complaints of Kalinin and Rykov at the Moscow meetings, their famous argument about ' the nation that ate too much ', illustrated the confusion of the leading spirits. At the XVth Party Congress in December, the failure of the deliveries of wheat and the queues outside the food-shops could no longer be passed over in silence. But the words used in speaking of them were discreet and tinged with invigorating optimism. During the first months of 1928, optimism suddenly gave place to anxiety, then to panic. In Party circles, people began openly to speak of a crisis in the deliveries of wheat, of a peasant strike. . . .

Pravda adopted a new type of phraseology where the kulaks (well-to-do peasants) were concerned, also as regards the ' more important figure in the village ', the *seredniak* (middle peasant). " The village has soared to wealth ; the kulak has enriched himself more than the others. Three successive good harvests have not been in vain," *Pravda* wrote in its famous leading article of February 16th, 1928, attributed to the pen of Stalin. The peasants have hoarded the wheat and now keep it in their villages to force the price up. In this matter, Stalin wrote, the kulak has succeeded in carrying the *seredniak* along with him.

That was word for word what the Opposition had been saying before. The Opposition had defined the situation in the countryside, it had foretold the food-problems that were to follow.

There could be no doubt about the matter. It appeared very clear to me—and to many of my acquaintances—that in this essential point of the debate, events put the Opposition in the right and the majority of the Party in the wrong. It so happened that this question was evidently decisive for Russian life after the October revolution.

Appreciating the kulak danger within the Party, Stalin proceeded, repeating word for word what Trotsky and Zinoviev had said : " Foreign elements have recently filtered into our organizations, into those belonging to the Party as well as into the others. These elements do not realize that in villages there are classes, they do not understand our class-policy, they make great efforts not to harm one single member of the village community, to live in peace with the kulak and to retain their popularity among all ' strata ' of the rural population."

At the same time as this onslaught was being made on the kulak, an attack was made on the private merchant, the *nepman*. The latter received less attention at the hands of the Press than the kulak, but the G.P.U. and the tax-collector put their claws into him. They began to tax him to such an extent that there was nothing left for him but to liquidate. The taxes became in actual fact a disguised confiscation. A large number of *nepmen*, above all those who had shown themselves too clever, were exiled to distant parts by the G.P.U.

Finally, the Press and the official orators began to stigmatize a third enemy of the proletariat : the bureaucrat.

The three Opposition-slogans which had marked the demonstration of the 7th of November, 1927, " Against the kulak, the *nepman* and the bureaucrat ", now received the consecration of the Party, resounding at all meetings and being printed in all newspapers.

The plenum of the Central Committee in April proclaimed, on Stalin's initiative, the necessity of self-criticism and democracy inside the Party. " Self-criticism is as necessary to us as air and water," Stalin said. He added, " Even if the workers' criticism contains only five per cent of the truth, its value is none the less positive."

It seemed as if the hour of renovation had struck for the Party. The unbearable atmosphere of 1926–27 seemed to clear. The bureaucratic pressure that had stifled all the thought of the masses seemed to relax. Communists began to brace themselves, muscles grew tauter ; the approach of storm and struggle could be felt.

The movement was towards civil war. The communiqués received from the ' wheat-front ' spoke of arrests, of confiscations, of acts of terrorism. All this created an atmosphere of bitter pugnacity. But the difficulties were not limited to those of a rural nature. The entire economic system of Soviet Russia was tottering.

There was corn in the villages, but the peasants were not interested in giving it up to the State at ridiculously low prices, for this same State sold them its mediocre industrial products in insufficient quantities. Peasant life was returning to natural economy. The town no longer received corn, the countryside no longer received manufactured goods. The goods shortage, calculated for the whole of the country, amounted to one thousand million roubles. The State had neither the means of buying cereals at a higher price, nor of developing its industry on a large scale.

In the towns, great unemployment had preceded the shortage of food. The Opposition, going by official figures, estimated the number of unemployed as 2,200,000. Tomsky, in refuting the statements of the Opposition, admitted to the number of 1,700,000 syndicated workers out of work and omitted to refer to the number of non-syndicated workers affected. At the same time, the rural districts were feeling the effects of over-population. The return to natural economy could, in a rough-and-ready way, assure subsistence to the middle and higher classes of the peasantry, but it created a desperate situation for the rural proletariat and the day-labourers who could no longer find employment either in village or town. In Moscow there were even street-demonstrations (at the Riazan Station), occasioned by rural elements who had come up in vain to look for work in town and whom the G.P.U. drove back to the villages in order to diminish the pressure of urban unemployment.

Russia of the NEP was agonized. Production was decomposing and no longer succeeded in fulfilling the needs of the various social groups ; exchanges were paralysed, the country's economy had reached a dead end. The Soviet world had left the rails and heroic measures were needed to rescue it from destruction.

It then appeared that the way to salvation lay along the road advocated by the Opposition and which the Party was at last following : to struggle against the private capitalist elements in town and village, to concentrate the State's resources with a view to the speeding up of industrialization,

to create large agricultural units aiming at total collectivization, to mobilize to this end the working class, the workers
as a whole, and, first of all, the revolutionary elements of
Communism.

There came a moment when I was prepared to forget all
the misery I had seen in the course of the last eighteen months,
to forget the privileges of the leaders, the oppression and the
suffering of the masses, the spirit of domination, of flattery,
of submission that permeated the entire Soviet society. I was
ready to believe, I did believe for one moment, in the possibility of a reconciliation between the masses and the administration, of a union between the workers and their leaders in
the conquest of a new world.

It was known that within the Party a group on the Right
was opposed to this new policy. In this field, too, the forecast
of the Opposition came true. It had even foretold the names
of the leaders of the section of the Right : Rykov, Bukharin,
Tomsky. Rightly, one should have believed that as Stalin
was adopting the Opposition-policy, he would have formed
a coalition with the Trotsky-Zinoviev group versus the Right.

This hope reached its zenith when the Central Committee
of the Party issued its manifesto of the 3rd of June to the
working class, containing a declaration for self-criticism, for
the workers' democracy, and for a struggle against bureaucracy. It seemed to me that here was the striking and
decisive slogan which was to rouse the workers and eliminate
the blemish of bureaucracy. The course of events dashed
my hopes and soon taught me how unfounded they had been,
and to what extent I had underestimated the ability of Communist bureaucracy to perform the very opposite of what it
proclaimed, and to disguise its worst crimes under the guise
of the most progressive slogans and most eloquent phrases.

II

FAREWELL, HOPES AND ILLUSIONS !

In many Cells, simple militants were trying to apply the new slogans of self-criticism and workers' democracy. They hoped in this way to rid themselves of the curse of bureaucracy within their own organizations and their own factories.

I was able to notice that these efforts succeeded only in those cases where they were co-ordinated with the action of higher authorities. In order to succeed it was necessary to obtain the approval of these higher authorities in each individual action against specified persons or things. If ordinary men from the rank and file, simple militant Party-members, permitted themselves to speak out on their own initiative, such daring was sufficient—apart from any other consideration —to ensure their failure and to cause them to be accused of ' disorganizing activities '.

I was present at one truly paradoxical case. Two Party-members, not belonging to the Opposition, drew upon their heads a severe reprimand from the Control Committee for having come to some agreement at their private domicile as to the attitude they were going to adopt at the next meeting in an attack on local bureaucracy. The Control Committee of the Party held the opinion that outside the meeting members had no right to speak of what they knew. To seek one another's advice, to prepare a speech before uttering it, was to give proof of sectarianism ; such behaviour was to be condemned, even if the so-called sect were in no way part of the Opposition. The right to prepare speeches, to examine subjects beforehand, belonged exclusively to the various stages of the administration. Thus, the separation of the rights of the militant masses and the administrative apparatus was not only preserved but also systematized.

Meanwhile, the struggle against the Right, against the advocates of a reconciliation with the kulaks, followed its own course. But one felt that an invisible conductor was toning down the music. It seemed as if someone were leading the masses of the Party as a child is led by the hand : forward, one more step, no, no farther now, stop. But why was one allowed to take such or such a step and not another, where did they wish to arrive, what was their destination ? The answers to these questions remained the secret of the ' apparatus '. The masses did not even dare ask the questions. Notwithstanding the most solemn assurances in the newspapers on the subject of self-criticism and democracy, there was no real change in the life of the Party nor in that of the masses. What was happening ? Was it a vast hoax ? Or was it that Stalin's new policy against the Right could not yet— for tactical reasons inside the Party—take on its full stature ?

In the spring of 1928, the Fourth Congress of the Profintern (International Council of Red Trade Unions) took place in Moscow. Among the members of the Yugo-Slav delegation at this conference I met an old friend, a railwayman and militant revolutionary of tried reliability, who had been my comrade in the days of my illegal activities in 1919. He had already stayed in Russia, from 1917 to 1918, as an Austrian prisoner of war. He had been able to observe the beginnings of the Revolution and had taken an active part in it. After having been the guest of the Moscow railwaymen and after having been able to observe their public and private lives, he condensed his new impressions of Russia in the following terms : " The situation today is very different from what it was in my time ; the manual worker is once more caught in the trap, the bureaucrats live as the bourgeois used to live and their wives play a corresponding part. What is needed is a new revolution."

Has it gone as far as that ? I wondered.

* * *

Convinced that the views of the Trotskyist Opposition were well-founded, and perturbed by the hesitation displayed by the majority, i.e. the Stalin group, in applying the new policy, several Yugo-Slav comrades, of whom I was one, decided to seek contact with the Opposition. The latter had been reduced to illegal activity. Its leaders and most important men had been sent into exile. The anti-Trotsky terror did not weaken.

In such conditions, to seek contact with the Opposition meant risking prison and exile. To be arrested and imprisoned in the land of the Soviets, what a strange prospect for a revolutionary ! It had been drummed into us that the Soviet prisons contained only counter-revolutionaries ; to be arrested in this country seemed to all of us a mark of infamy. It had needed one or two years of observation and reflection in Russia to become familiar with the idea that prison in that country was no dishonour for a revolutionary, and that risking prison might even become a duty. But what sufferings had to be undergone, what illusions lost before realizing this ! The dream had been splendid, disillusionment all the more bitter. We had clung to the flimsiest excuses for hope before surrendering to the evidence.

In spite of the most energetic repression, one could feel that, as a result of the crisis prevailing in the country and in the Party, there was a certain recrudescence of Opposition activity in Moscow. The influence of Trotskyism on Party officials was daily growing. In certain Party circles, Opposition literature was spreading with lightning rapidity. It is only from such writings that one can draw authentic data concerning the course of hostilities between the Stalin and Rykov groups. At the same time, the Opposition documents, particularly letters from Trotsky, dealt with current economic and political problems with a boldness and a clarity that compelled admiration.

The mental tension attained its maximum in Moscow during the summer of 1928, after the July plenum of the Central Committee of the Communist Party, in which the Right had acquired a majority. It considered taking the Party secretaryship away from Stalin. Rykov, in reviewing the results of this plenum before the militant Moscow Party members, pointed out that the difficulties in the matter of wheat delivery had occasioned, in certain Party circles, ideological falterings of a Trotskyist nature. The threat was scarcely veiled. The plenum had promised the peasants that no more extraordinary measures would be applied. Communist bureaucracy held on to its comfortable existence and still hoped, by means of expedients, to avoid the inevitable trial of its power and privilege.

Stalin himself did not wait for events ; he prepared them. At the most critical moment, when his fate, so it seemed, hung only by a thread, he gave proof of extraordinary energy and boldness. He acted behind the scenes, but the results of his actions were not long in manifesting themselves in the open. He was concentrating the forces of the Party apparatus immediately subordinate to him. With the aid of the heads of the Comsomol belonging to the group called ' Left-Centre ' —Kostrov, Lominadze, Chatskin—he organized a genuine group. He sent his emissaries to the provinces to ' work ' the local leaders and the provincial members of the Central Committee. In his immediate surroundings he spoke of the possibility of a provisional coalition with the Trotskyist Opposition, a coalition directed against the Right. Lenin, too, he explained, had accepted a provisional coalition with the Mensheviks loyal to the Party against the liquidating Mensheviks.

But Stalin was not satisfied with the simple combinations inside the Party apparatus. He made an appeal to the masses. He prepared popular manifestations, especially one workers' demonstration in Moscow. Everyone knew that the Right—Rykov, Tomsky, Bukharin—so long as they had the support of Kalinin and Voroshilov, had a majority in the Politbureau and in the Central Committee of the Party. It was against this majority that Stalin directed his workers' demonstration. The Right, though it had a majority, hesitated to remove Stalin from his post of general secretary. Stalin, in the minority, had no fear of workers' intervention. In spite of the importance of the individual factors which undoubtedly influenced the tactics of the opposing parties, these were, on the whole, decided by social reasons. The hesitation of the Right as regards Stalin could be explained by its fear that his departure might let loose the danger of the kulaks and so sweep bureaucracy away. The Right feared the consequences of its own intentions. As to Stalin, he linked his fortunes to the final triumph of bureaucracy in the economic and political life of the country. The thought of creating a powerful agriculture and a powerful industry lent him strength.

In these internal Party struggles, the part played by the masses limited itself to that of spectator or at the most of instrument. The fate of the Party and country was decided in the shadows ; the masses had to wait for the moment when they could carry the victor in triumph, whosoever he might be.

My friends and I could not believe such a situation possible, yet we felt that most certainly it existed. We felt that the masses would remain in the background, that their part in social affairs was bound to decrease, whatever the outcome.

III

IN THE CAUCASUS

During the summer, I joined my comrade Draguitch who was in Ingushetia, a wild and mountainous region in the Caucasus. My journey was entirely devoid of incident. I was neither the victim of a railway accident nor of the exploits of Rostov's famous bandits who were everywhere openly operating on a grand scale.

I put up at Vladicaucasus and found that it closely resembled a colonial town—a teeming crowd of miserable natives, innumerable hovels and squalid streets surrounding the prosperous little island where dwelt the civilized conquerors.

In the market I hired a coachman to take me into the mountains to my friend. In the course of the journey I conversed with the peasant and we went by a roundabout route in order to call at his home. He belonged to a family of sectarian Russians, dwelling on the outskirts of the town. They were living in modest plenty, in the usual peasant way. Religion played a great part in their lives. Within the family there were three sects : baptists, molokans and a third I cannot remember.

As we drove along, my coachman complained of the oppression of the peasants. Under cover of the fight against the kulaks, the entire peasant class was being persecuted. I agreed with him and declared that the peasant masses and the kulaks should not be confused. Immediately he gave me his confidence and began to speak openly on all questions of Soviet life.

He was firmly attached to the Soviet form of government and wanted no return either to Czar or great landowners. But he was in favour of reforms inside the system. His ideas were remarkably clear.

" These mountains," he said, pointing at the ranges that

surrounded us on all sides, " these mountains are full of mineral wealth, as everywhere in Russia. The State lacks the means to bring them into exploitation. One should allow foreign capital to come in. The State would benefit by the concessions and the people would have work."

In the field of politics, he believed in the necessity of freedom of Press and suffrage. " Let the people elect to the Soviets whom they choose and let them write in the papers what they like."

Twenty miles from Vladicaucasus, we took the military road of Georgia to cross the Terek and climb the slopes of Ingushetia. Ancient and powerful watch-towers, now derelict, bore witness to the military importance that this region had had in the days when Cossacks and mountain tribes fought each other. We had another six or seven miles to go before we reached the village for which I was bound, in the heart of Ingushetia.

Before the War, it would have been dangerous for a Russian to show himself in that region. The *aoul*, or native village, had retained its ancient aspect. The peasant dwellings were of the traditional type, crowned with ancient towers. During the revolution, the Ingushi had, to a man, sided with the Bolsheviks, as the latter were the adversaries of the Cossacks, hereditary enemies of the Ingushi. The enemies of our enemies are our friends, they argued. And indeed, those miserable mountain dwellers, despoiled by the Cossacks, who, a century before had robbed them of their fertile lowland fields, could not but gain by the revolution.

Now the Bolsheviks were bringing civilization to the Ingushi. A road had been built to Terek and cars from Vladicaucasus appeared in the mountain *aouls*. A group of geologists was prospecting the region, in search of copper and other minerals. Near the village, in a clearing in the wild forest, a rest-house had been built where officials of the autonomous region of Ingushetia could come and stay. In the village itself, there were many holiday-makers, almost exclusively office workers, from Vladicaucasus and even from Moscow.

Our valley of Arm-Khi had been rebaptized ' Valley of the Sun '. It deserved the name. The mountain-tops were bathed in the sunlight, the dense and fragrant forest had made room for terraced fields and flower-carpeted meadows. The new road wound gaily among the mountains where waterfalls hurtled down narrow gorges. Far from Moscow and its noise, far from Russian and Yugo-Slav politics, my friend Draguitch and I revelled in the freedom and the charm of Nature, as if we had foreseen the Northern ice that lay in store for us. " Siberia awaits us, let's enjoy the Caucasus," we said to one another in jest.

We were not far from Kazbek, from the gorge of Darial and the castle of Tamara. We decided to visit these remarkable places. We set out on foot shortly after midnight. At dawn we were on the Terek. From there we walked towards Kazbek in the direction of Tiflis. The road followed the valley of the Terek which, enclosed by high mountains, marked the boundary between the two autonomous regions of Ingushetia and Ossetia. In a series of sharp ranges, the mountains sloped towards us as we stood in the valley, each ridge with its own shape and colour, varied tints of green. We admired the versatility of the landscape, comparing it with the Alps, which to me had seemed cold, almost tedious in their impressive grandeur. Here, in the Caucasus, all seemed new, alive with a clamorous smiling life.

Towards the right the valley was broader. A few hills appeared between the road and the mountains. On the nearest one we perceived the ruins of an old castle, and we climbed towards it in the glory of the rising sun. Shrubs had invaded the relics of feudal grandeur ; there, where armed men used to drill, a flock of sheep was grazing. An old Georgian shepherd told us the legends of the land. He had been a shepherd before the revolution and had remained one since. In his eyes the world had never changed. He told the ancient legends with the same ceremoniousness as ever, perhaps with more, for he was grown old.

Perched on the hill we admired the freshened landscape with its play of light and shade, its verdure and forms. After having wandered through the ruins of the castle, we hastened on, assailed in the midst of enchanted Nature by the realization of the frailty of all things.

We passed through a large village without stopping. We met peasant-carts going to town. The road had but a slight incline and it was easy to walk quickly and at the same time to look about us. Nature, here, seemed to accumulate all her creative power ; at every turn of the road we were confronted by a new marvel. It became impossible not to pause and gaze upon the harmonies of this scene where Nature had surpassed herself. We were in the famous gorge of Darial.

We crossed a deep abyss between towering walls of rock and after a few more steps we beheld the castle of Tamara and behind it a vast horizon of high mountain ranges, a scene so often depicted by Russian poets and painters. Here we halted.

We were on the borders of Georgia. In a miserable inn we talked to a man employed at the Georgian custom-house. He spoke to us, as was usual, of the natural beauty and the romantic customs of the Caucasus. This official had been— at least he said he had been—a rich man before the revolution ; now he was but a poor official. He sighed as he spoke of Paris, of Nice and Geneva. The innkeeper served us with greenish tea and the custom-official offered us spirits of maize. When we spoke of visiting the castle of Tamara, he warned us that the crossing of the Terek was dangerous at that point ; the cables of the ferry were weak and two tourists had but recently been drowned.

We decided that the castle and the heroes sung by Pushkin and Lermontov were worth the risk. We crossed the Terek at a point where the stream was particularly swift, not without casting anxious glances at the abyss beneath our feet. Then we climbed the rock that dominated the opposite bank. It was there that at one time had risen the castle of Tamara. Of it there now remained only the foundations and the vaults.

Farther along, the road rose sharply above the Terek to vertiginous heights. Below, the river flowed with savage speed and called to memory the famous legends of the poets. At the end of the day we reached the foot of the Kazbek, the landscape round us taking on the character of its high altitude.

We visited the military road to Georgia, famous for its beauty, linking Tiflis to Vladicaucasus. Late in the evening we caught the Vladicaucasus bus which deposited us once more at the spot where we had crossed the Terek.

It was past midnight and we were anxious to return home, but an incident delayed us. On the other bank we found a peasant family whose cart had broken down ; there was a sick woman with her child, both in rags ; the husband was trying to make the cart cross to the other bank by sheer strength.

We could not but help these poor people. It cost us an hour and a half of united effort. In the end we had a bathe in the Terek before returning to our mountains.

It was our first day in the Caucasus. Henceforth we were ready to face the snows of exile in Siberia.

* * *

The villages of Ingushetia are miserable and backward. At first sight, no social differentiation can be perceived. On looking more closely, however, one sees poor and rich. Here one learns the relativity of our concepts of wealth and poverty. The curious fact about it was that this social differentiation had developed only after the revolution, during the NEP. The more prosperous elements of the village were very much at one with the Soviet system ; they had acquired their prosperity through the posts they occupied in that system. The chairman of the rural Soviet, the manager of the co-op (the ex-leader of an insurgent band), the contractor for public works, the lorry owner, the peasant who hired out premises to the Soviet administration—these were the well-to-do of the countryside. For that reason they were ' Soviet patriots ', but a touch of uncertainty showed through their patriotism. Vague rumours about the new rural policy had reached them. They were in favour of a free commerce in wheat, of a consolidation of markets, of an unrestricted development of small private economy. As to the poor, they were of a contrary opinion and upheld the new Government policy in the hope of a better future.

I was present at a discussion in which several Ingushi of the neighbourhood took part. The debates were coloured with the courtesy that characterized the patriarchal customs of this little people, but the divergence of opinions did not appear the less clear. A peasant from the neighbouring village, an old chieftain whose brother had been killed in the course of the Civil War, defended the point of view of the well-to-do peasantry. He was at the head of a flourishing agricultural concern and complained about the new turn of politics, by which not only was he prevented from taking new land into cultivation, but his right to what he already held was being questioned, which was threatening his enterprise with ruin. A grower, younger and less well-to-do, a *bedniak* (poor peasant) of the village where I was staying, was expressing the hopes of the poorer peasants in terms measured but full of conviction.

The Soviet Government, he thought, wanted comfort for all, but the more necessitous were the first that should be helped.

The old peasant with whom we were staying had retained some of his old comfort. Therefore he found it difficult to hide his liking for the pre-revolutionary order. One day, returning from Vladicaucasus and pointing at the loaf he had brought back with him, he said in a knowing tone, " The Bolsheviks are no doubt for the people, but in order to get a piece of bread, one must queue all day and quarrel with everybody."

We heard similar remarks made about boots, clothes and like objects. The wife of our host listened to her husband and made timid protests. One day when he was out, she opened her heart to us. " The Bolsheviks want to build up a new life ; that can't be done in a day. But look, in the past women had no rights at all, they were proper slaves ; the Bolsheviks have given us liberty, have made us the equals of men. That is what annoys my old man."

But the old man himself had gained by the revolution in securing Ivan, a little Cossack, orphan of the Civil War. My hosts, who had no children, had adopted the little Christian and no one had stopped them from turning him into a complete Ingushi Moslem.

I soon had a fresh opportunity of noticing the adherence of the women of the mountains to the new Government. In the course of a conversation with the Communist leaders of Ingushetia, I mentioned the social differentiation that had arisen among the Ingushi during the NEP. " It must be taken into account when applying the new policy," I added. I was at once asked to give a lecture on the subject at the Soviet-Communist Political School of the Mountain Peoples. I accepted.

It was an important occasion, devoted to the Party's agrarian policy. I described the result of my observations of rural life in Ingushetia. A woman student of the school, chairman of a Soviet in an *aoul* of Kabardia, spoke in the course of the discussion. This fifty-year-old woman expressed, with serious enthusiasm, the hopes that the mountain peoples were building on the Soviet rule ; with indignation she recalled the age-long oppression by the Czarist colonizers ; at last, her eyes ablaze, she spoke of the emancipation of the Caucasian women, at one time uneducated and enslaved—an emancipation, all credit for which belonged to the October revolution.

* * *

At Vladicaucasus, a small detail recalled me to the realities of Soviet life ; at the municipal park, an entrance fee had to be paid in order to enter the well-kept gardens. " A budgetary matter," a local Communist told me, by way of justification. In fact, the municipal policy of Czarist days had remained unchanged ; today, as yesterday, the people, the poor, were not allowed to walk in the best part of the park.

IV

RETURN TO MOSCOW

My stay in the Caucasus was drawing to a close. I had to return to Moscow at the beginning of August to follow the activities of the Sixth Congress of the Comintern, the session of which had already commenced.

I travelled in the company of an employee of the Party Committee in Moscow. She had made a journey to the Caucasus to further the affairs of the Stalin section. We had long conversations about the state the country was in, and in particular about the struggle that was taking place inside the Party against the Opposition of the Right. My companion was firmly convinced of Stalin's victory. " We shall win, for the administrative apparatus is in our hands." Later on I had many an occasion to test the value of that magic formula in Russian life.

The meetings of the Sixth Congress of the Third International were fairly tedious. The participants considered the public meetings as so much waste of breath. Everything was decided behind the scenes. Worse still, behind those scenes, decisions were postponed till later. Stalin did not speak at this congress. He limited himself to addressing the conference of the presidents of national delegations behind closed doors. At that conference he declared that no doubt there existed differences of opinion between the prominent members of the Politbureau of the Russian Party, but that these differences, bearing as they did on isolated questions, did not amount to two different policies. After having made this declaration, he left Moscow.

The Sixth Congress adopted the Comintern's programme. No serious discussion of this programme had taken place either before or during the congress. The document, it would seem, was of some importance ; yet it was adopted automatically, as if it had been just any resolution. Bukharin had drawn it up and the Stalinist group had introduced a few modifications into it by way of the German and Russian delegations. Many delegates had acquainted themselves with the criticism of the programme from the pen of Trotsky, who was then in exile at Alma-Ata. Thus in his speech Manuilsky could not help mentioning the " philosophy of Alma-Ata ". Trotsky's criticism, sharp and convincing on many points, had produced a visible impression on several of the delegates, even among those who leaned towards Stalin and did not agree with Trotsky's general view.

The first five Congresses of the Comintern had been held at the Kremlin ; the sixth was held at the ' Syndicate House '. The Politbureau of the Russian Communist Party had first thought of the Colossus Cinema, but it had been felt that the contrast between the Kremlin and the Colossus Cinema was too eloquent, and finally the Syndicate House had been chosen.

The delegates at the congress were uneasy about the possible developments of the struggle within the Russian Party. They feared a victory of the ' peasant policy '. They regarded Stalin with disquietude and were wondering whether he was going to launch a vigorous attack against that policy and whether he would emerge victorious. If not, they were inclined to collaborate with the Opposition. Russia's signing of the Kellogg Pact, which had recently taken place, strengthened this feeling of anxiety. Rykov's explanatory speech breathed the wish to make peace with the bourgeois world. Among the delegates rumours were circulating about mysterious transactions between the Soviet Petrol Syndicate and the Standard Oil Company.

At this period I met a group of foreign workers in Moscow. They were specialized German workmen who worked in Moscow's larger factories. Most of them were political refugees. I questioned them about their working conditions, and they answered that, even under a capitalist system, they had never known such bad conditions. One of them, who had worked not only in Germany but also in France, Switzerland and Austria, told me that piece-work had been driven up to an output unknown in Western Europe. I asked him how the factory workers reacted to this. It was true, he said, that the workers were dissatisfied, but the Russian workman was so backward, so docile, so incapable of action that this discontent-

45

ment remained sterile. Furthermore, those of the Western workers who could not succeed in explaining to themselves the historic reasons for the passive attitude of the Russian proletariat, its inability openly to fight bureaucratic oppression, ended by being imbued with a feeling of detachment and European superiority towards Russia. Their reasoning tended to reach the following conclusion : after all, there is not much to be hoped from the Russians ; their Asiatic socialism is enough for them.

I must add that that was the conclusion to which most foreigners settled in Russia came. Those strangers, be they workmen, revolutionaries or political refugees, were all in a somewhat paradoxical position. They were entrusted with interesting work, they were decently paid, well lodged, could go on holidays and enjoyed the best of comforts. They were well looked after, workers' meetings were organized at which they spoke, social consideration and various honours were accorded them. On the other hand, in the factories, in the Party, in the administration, these strangers discovered a mode of living that went against their notions of socialism. They began to feel indignation and became bitter. The representatives of the Russian Communist Party, accustomed to consider this as an ' infantile disease ' that attacked foreigners, would answer them with a brand of patience tinged with contempt.

" Yes, we know all that, all the foreigners who come to Russia begin by propounding the views of the extreme Left. Their notions of socialism are too romantic ; they do not understand Bolshevist discipline ; they are unaware of the difficulties met with when building up socialism, when directing the masses in a backward, petit-bourgeois country."

The administration treated the foreigners in a relatively liberal way, but at the same time created some sort of vacuum around them. If the foreigner grew restive and sought support from Russian workers, it soon ' talked Russian ' to him and made him lose his desire to quarrel with the system.

Moreover, the Russian workers had had time to learn what to say and what not to say at meetings. Thus, whilst being fairly communicative in private interviews with foreigners, they maintained an icy silence at public meetings and left the rostrum to professional enthusiasts.

The foreigner was generally ignorant of the fact that the Russian worker had been feeling this bureaucratic pressure for the last sixteen years. He was ignorant of the fact that the authorities had had to repress numerous strikes. He was not aware of the significance of the Kronstadt cannonades, the sound of which had deeply shaken the masses of Russian workers. He could not understand why the Russian worker of his day was reduced to silence, why this working class which had been through three revolutions was now powerless and could not, even in its own factories, react against the shameless arbitrariness of the bureaucracy. The stranger was not aware that the bureaucracy had had relentlessly to crush the workers to reduce them to this state of silence ; instead of growing angry with the administration, he began to disparage the Russian workers.

The Russian worker, on the other hand, began to envy the foreign worker or revolutionary and became hostile to him, for he could not fail to notice the material and moral privileges the latter enjoyed. Thus Communist bureaucracy applied the old principle of *divide et impera* ; the forces of the working class were smashed for the benefit of the administration.

The omnipotence of the administrative apparatus was based on the actual possession of the nationalized means of production and of the governmental machinery of coercion. The latter used the G.P.U. as its last resort. In the end, the administration ruled by relying directly on the G.P.U., which was ' the armed force of the Party ', i.e. of the administrative apparatus. Thus, logically, the leaders of the Central Control Committee of the Party were members of the Direction of the G.P.U. and presided at its Special Council, its organ of repression.

I had reached the conclusion that the political orientation of Russia depended on the administrative apparatus. Thus it was important to know the type of men running the G.P.U. How would they behave in the case of a victory of the sections of the Right in the Communist Party, in the case of a ' Thermidor ' ? The anti-Thermidorian, Gracchus Babeuf, had, for his conspiracy of the Equals, obtained the help of Robespierre's police. Would anything of an analogous nature happen in Russia ?

My, albeit incomplete, observations proved to me that no revolutionary spirit actuated the G.P.U. Its members were entirely absorbed in careerist activities. Everything was subsidiary to the sacrosanct principle of hierarchy. To be able to say, " I spoke to Yagoda today ", or " Trilisser called out to me ", was an event in the life of an official two or three rungs lower down the hierarchic ladder.

Their habits were remarkably bourgeois. One met important officials, powdered and perfumed like *demi-mondaines*. The men of the G.P.U. kissed the hands of their womenfolk. But what struck me most was their feeling of caste. They all considered one another as members of the same family, as the saviours of the revolution. They accepted their immense privileges with serene complacency as feeble rewards for their activities. It is true that they devoted the best of their years and energy to the service ; they carried out a stupendous task which to them had become one with their careers and privileges. In the struggles inside the Party, the collaborators of the G.P.U. were almost without exception fanatic adversaries of the Right and adherents of Stalin. The various services of the G.P.U. were at that time the bulwarks of the Stalinist section. When Rykov's secretary, an official of the G.P.U., went over to the Right, it was referred to in those circles as a real calamity. " Just imagine, Ferdinand has had himself influenced by Rykov," they exclaimed in despair. It was considered a dishonour to the institution as a whole.

I also came across a number of Trotsky's sympathizers in the G.P.U. The possibility of a Stalin-Trotsky coalition was considered with great enthusiasm by some. There were even a few real Trotskyists. I remember a discussion between two brothers, the one employed by the Central Committee, an adherent of Stalin, the other an important official of the G.P.U. and a Trotskyist. I rarely encountered so much hatred and loathing of Stalin as I did when meeting this last.

Later, when I found myself in the bad books of the G.P.U. and knew its prisons and exile, I was able to observe that institution from the bottom instead of observing it from the top. But let us not anticipate.

In the autumn of 1928, the struggle inside the Party was entering its decisive stage. The problem of the deliveries of wheat once more came to the fore. Members of the Central Committee were feverishly canvassed with a view to the plenum. Stalin had met with a set-back in attempting to win the Leningrad people over to his cause—Komarov and

the others—the successors of Zinoviev. But on the whole
Stalin's position had grown stronger, above all in Moscow.
The dismissal of Uglanov, the secretary of the organization,
was already being planned. *Pravda* published an article
under the title : All the levers must be pulled. What a
difference, compared with the resolution adopted by the July
plenum of the Central Committee, at which it was solemnly
declared that " extraordinary measures " were for ever to be
abolished !

At that time Trotsky once more intervened in the struggle
by publishing Kamenev's notes of his meetings with Bukharin :
the latter had made an offer to Kamenev and Zinoviev to
form a coalition of the Right against Stalin. One of
Kamenev's close collaborators, who was in favour of Trotsky,
had procured him the notes. The publication of this confidential political document roused the greatest emotions in
the organization at Moscow. Stalin was able to utilize the
document to his best advantage. His subordinates took upon
themselves the task of copying Trotsky's letter which contained
the revelations about Kamenev. At the October plenum
of the Central Committee, Stalin gained a final victory ; he
succeeded in building up a majority. First of all, Stalin
thought of dealing with the Right once and for all, but the
combinations of the administration led to a certain ' compromise ' : Stalin himself proclaimed that there was no
divergence of opinion at the Politbureau and that the supposed
deviation of the Right within the Politbureau was no more
than a counter-revolutionary and Trotskyist calumny. For
the time being, he contented himself with reducing to non-
existence the subaltern elements of the Right. The turn of
the three members of the Politbureau belonging to the Right
Opposition came in April, 1929, at the next plenum of the
Central Committee ; whilst ejecting them, Stalin made once
more all the declarations he had made the previous October
about " rumours of a counter-revolutionary nature ".

After his victory in the October plenum, Stalin hastened to
finish off Trotsky. The latter might quite well have become
dangerous to his victor, either directly or by forming a coalition
with the rest of the malcontents. Stalin had not let the
warning constituted by the parleys between Bukharin and
Kamenev go by unheeded. On November 20th, 1928, the
Direction of the G.P.U. intimated to Trotsky that he was to

leave Soviet territory. On February 12th, 1929, Trotsky set foot ashore in Constantinople. In the absence of Trotsky, the game became considerably simpler for the bureaucratic oligarchy. The Right Opposition knew it. At the meeting of the Politbureau that was to decide Trotsky's fate, therefore, the men of the Right voted against his expulsion from Russia, under pretext that " he would be still more harmful abroad ". Let us note in passing that the Moscow trials of 1936–37 were in part no more than a form of vengeance against Zinoviev, Kamenev, Bukharin and Rykov, for having attempted to form the 1928 coalition. As to Trotsky's banishment, it showed clearly that Stalin, whilst fighting the Right, was pursuing his own political ends, distinct from those of the Left.

* * *

It was at this moment that events occurred in Yugo-Slavia and in the Yugo-Slav Communist Party that were to weigh heavily in my ultimate fate in Russia. This Yugo-Slav ' affair ' may serve as an excellent illustration of the methods of the Comintern.

V

THE COMINTERN IN YUGO-SLAVIA

O<small>N</small> January 6th, 1929, there was a *coup d'état* in Yugo-Slavia. Parliament was dissolved and all Parties were forbidden. General Jivkovitch—leader of a secret Serbian military league known as ' The White Hand '—was called to power. The *coup d'état* was tinged with Fascism, but it lacked the essential element of Fascism, the character of mass-movement. The new rule was, on the whole, nothing but a military dictatorship, the justification for it being the necessity of putting an end to the struggle between the nationalities in Yugo-Slavia. The dominating nation, the Serbs, constituted a minority of five million and this explains the national conflict which has torn Yugo-Slavia from the day of its birth. The Croatians, the strongest of the non-Serbian nations, counting more than three million inhabitants, found themselves at the head of the struggle against Serbian hegemony. As, under a parliamentary constitution, the opposition of non-Serb nations could not be avoided, ruling circles in Belgrade had decided to eliminate such a constitution in favour of a military dictatorship. Given the relative national forces, this struggle demanded a disproportionate effort on the part of the Serb masses, which yet drew no noticeable benefit from Belgrade's policy of hegemony ; hence they greeted the dictatorship with coldness and reserve. From the beginning, therefore, it was doomed to be suspended in a vacuum ; in order to ensure its existence, it had to have recourse to a terror as cruel as it was senseless.

These events had the most tragic results for the Yugo-Slav Communist Party and also for the 120 Yugo-Slav Communists who were in Moscow.

In 1926, as I have mentioned before, Moscow had entrusted the direction of the Yugo-Slav Party to the elements of the Right. During the course of 1926 and 1927, these elements had so compromised themselves in the eyes of the Party that at the plenum of the Yugo-Slav Central Committee, the old Politbureau had been dismissed with indignation and a new one had been elected, consisting of elements more to the Left. But the Central Committee had forgotten who were the real masters. These—that is, Bukharin, Gorkitch and Manuilsky—annulled the decisions of the Central Committee and dissolved the new Left Politbureau. The old leaders could not very well be reinstated ; worse was done. The Bukharin-Gorkitch-Manuilsky triumvirate collected a group of bandits who had never had any connections with the Yugo-Slav movement and sent them to Yugo-Slavia as ' mandataries '. They were unprincipled adventurers, apparently haled at random from all over the world. To crown the joke, this band was called the ' Workers' Direction '. There were, it must be admitted, two or three honest workmen among them, such as Djouro Djakovitch-Bosnitch who was later killed by the Yugo-Slav reactionaries, but they were only scapegoats put there to screen the scoundrels.

The mandataries were busy preparing the Party conference and already saw themselves as victors ; a few more months and these men without background would have served the ' apprenticeship of illegal activities ' needed. Soon a world career in the Comintern would have been open to them.

All would have gone well if Belgrade had not gained the ascendancy in Yugo-Slavia. There had been the Fascist-military *coup d'état*, followed by bloody reprisals, in the Balkan manner, against the Opposition. That was the time when ' illegal activities ' became necessary. Then there should have been men who knew how to die. But the mandataries were of another stamp ; they were seized with severe panic, for this was no longer a matter of a career but of their very skins. The result was a catastrophe as incredible as it was dishonourable. The ' best ' of the mandataries left the Party to its fate, the Party, the Communist League of Youth and the workers' movement, to flee at top speed out of Yugo-Slavia, straight to Moscow. At the head of this little band was Gorkitch, the ideologist.

They were the ' best '. The worst remained in Yugo-Slavia and entered the police service. We then learned that a number of them had been *agents provocateurs*, who had from the beginning been receiving pledges from both sides.

One of them was the 'chief mandatary', Bresovitch, ex-Austrian prisoner of war in Russia, who had never belonged to the Yugo-Slav movement at all.

Gorkitch, Manuilsky and a few others saved their skins; their careers were not broken, they avoided catastrophe. But, on the other hand, the Yugo-Slav workers' movement was delivered into the hands of the most cruel reaction. Gorkitch and the other leaders of the Comintern coldly sent dozens and hundreds of men to their deaths to cover up their own desertion and to prove that they were acting and fighting against reaction. It was, in 1929–30 in Yugo-Slavia, the repetition of what had happened on a larger scale in China. It was neither the first time nor the last; one had already seen examples, one was to see more in other countries.

The cowardice and the treachery shown by the leaders of the Comintern on the day following that of the 6th of January, 1929, caused a storm of indignation to arise among the Yugo-Slav militants in Moscow, especially in a group of the Left that counted well over fifty members. It is worth while writing a few words about that group, for its example makes it possible to illustrate the mechanism of the evolution of the Comintern, as well as certain traits that characterized the Communist Parties.

The Yugo-Slav Left had been formed in 1921 after the dissolution of the Communist Party, in order to pursue illegal activities. In 1924 and 1925, the Left strengthened its position by advocating a revolutionary policy in the national and peasant questions. This group of the Left distinguished itself and still does by limiting its interests to Yugo-Slav affairs. It neither wished nor knew how to co-ordinate its action with that of groups of the Left in the other sections of the Comintern. The members of the Yugo-Slav Left did not imagine that such a line of conduct condemned their efforts to sterility; they imagined, on the contrary, that they were not giving any tricks to their competitors of the Right and thus were working their way to power with the help and by means of the Comintern.

Such tactics are characteristic of the Parties that belong to the Communist International. The method by which the representatives of the Russian Communist Party hold the reins of the Comintern is that of entirely isolating the various Parties.

Each of them knows only his own Party and the Russian one. Groups in the Comintern struggle only to retain their positions inside each Party. When they showed interest in the doings of other national sections, it was only to uphold the propositions of the Russian Party. These groups succeeded in establishing themselves by complying with every wish of the representatives of the Russian Communist Party, and by adopting an attitude of permanent servility where they were concerned. There existed no international spirit, no deep and considered interest in foreign Communist movements. Such a spirit would not be tolerated. To resolve general problems, to judge and condemn, there exists the Russian Communist Party ; the others are there merely to carry out its decisions. It seems incredible that such a system of servility could have been born and developed within an international workers' movement ; yet it exists and it triumphs.

In February, 1929, the Comintern called a general meeting to pacify the Yugo-Slavs in Moscow. The assembly, following upon tumultuous discussions, declared that the report of the Comintern was unsatisfactory and rejected the resolution proposed by it. A counter-resolution was adopted with 90 votes against 5, condemning the conduct of the directors of the Yugo-Slav Party. It was an indirect condemnation of the policy of the Comintern.

That could not be allowed to pass. " Your case is clear ; the Comintern will reduce you to non-existence," an old political refugee who had attended the debates told me with kindliness.

The Trotskyist group, then fully formed, had taken the lead among the malcontents. The critical attitude towards the system, becoming more and more general among the Yugo-Slavs as among all foreigners arriving in Soviet Russia, had given rise within our small group to a complete Opposition ideology. The peasant question, as it had presented itself during the winter of 1928, had been the determining factor of that Opposition. It had become very clear that the views of the Trotskyist Opposition on that question had been correct. The slogan of workers' democracy and self-criticism launched by Stalin had revealed itself as a simple bureaucratic manœuvre, just like his toleration of the Right accompanied by a persecution of the Left. All this drove

54

us to define our position and to seek contact with the illegal organization of the Trotskyists in Moscow.

Soviet problems constituted the core of our opposition, whereas the international policy of the Comintern (in China, in England and elsewhere) formed in some way a general framework. It was within this framework that the problems of the Yugo-Slav Communist Party fitted.

Inside our Party we not only criticized the administrative activities of the Comintern and the adventurers it had called to power ; we also became increasingly hostile to the political Line of the Comintern. Starting from the national question, we found ourselves faced with the following dilemma : socialist revolution or bourgeois revolution in Yugo-Slavia. The section of the Left had at one time favoured exploiting the nationalist problem in the interest of the revolution. But this ' exploitation ' had in the end taken on such a form that the Communist and the workers' movements had been reduced to serving the bourgeois nationalism of the oppressed peoples of Yugo-Slavia. Long before the French had reconciled the red flag and the national *tricolore*, the Internationale and the Marseillaise, Dalmatia had brought about an alliance between the Croatian three-coloured flag and the red flag of the revolution, of the Internationale and the national anthem ' Our Splendid Fatherland '. The revolutionary and international workers' movements threatened to split up into as many simple ' radical ' movements as there were nationalities in Yugo-Slavia.

Our small group declared war on these tactics and succeeded, on that point, in winning over the whole of the Yugo-Slav Left, i.e. practically all the active Yugo-Slav Communists in Moscow. The Left, which in 1924 and 1925, had been the first to advocate the exploitation of the national question, now struggled against this policy as applied by the Comintern. As for me, personally, I had battled in this field against the ideologist of the Right, Sima Markovitch ; now, in the same field, and to gain the same end, I was reduced to battling against the Comintern and its Executive Committee.

Now that we had formed a Trotskyist group, it was left for us to learn of what consisted illegal political activity in Russia. We formed a central body of six members : four Yugo-Slav Communists, Deditch, Draguitch, Heberling and myself, and two Russians, former members of the Communist Youth League, Victor Zankov and Oreste Glybovsky. This ' centre ' was assisted by a group of five militant members of the Opposition, and was in personal contact with five other ' sympathizers '. Moreover, our centre was in contact with the Trotskyist organization in Moscow through the intermediation of a trusted person. It was he who regularly handed us letters from Trotsky and from other members of the Opposition, as well as theses and like Opposition documents. As to our activities, they were developed in two distinct milieux : Russian factory workers and Yugo-Slav Communists of the Left.

The Yugo-Slav Communists were members of factory Cells and had contacts with workers in favour of the Opposition, both Communists and non-Party members. As to our countrymen, we did our utmost to interest them in Yugo-Slav questions which naturally lay closer to their hearts than did the Russian questions. We endeavoured to link these Yugo-Slav problems with the general policy of the Comintern and of the Russian Communist Party, showing that our disaster was but the particular aspect of a general disaster, which could not be remedied without a general change of policy within the Russian Communist Party. Our people were not easily convinced ; they imagined that the Yugo-Slav calamities were an exception and that all was well inside other Communist Parties, above all in the Russian Party. That was only an illusion, but one they relinquished only with regret.

To give an example I shall first quote the statement made by an old militant syndicalist from Yugo-Slavia, Risto Samardjitch-Noskov. " Trotsky is not in the wrong ; but all these bureaucrats no longer want world revolution. If Stalin wanted it they would drop him as they dropped Trotsky. Then what ? If revolution broke out in Yugo-Slavia, Gorkitch and Manuilsky would be the first, I am sure, to send me into exile. But go and tell that to our Yugo-Slav workers. They would not even listen to you."

He refused to join our group, but, all the same, he never denounced us. When one of his friends, approached by us, was about to do so, Noskov succeeded in dissuading him.

Another comrade, a humble workman who had undergone a great deal of persecution in Yugo-Slavia on account of his revolutionary activity, spoke to us as follows : " Certainly you are right. The bureaucrats prosper at the expense of the people, just like any aristocrat. But I cannot return to Yugo-Slavia ; I don't speak foreign languages ; my professional knowledge is mediocre. Here, at least, I am allowed to live and work."

We tried to draw into our ranks those Yugo-Slavs who, on their arrival in Moscow, had left the Party and had been taken on in factories. They received us well, as real comrades, but refused to take any part in politics whatsoever.

Vukachin Markovitch, the famous revolutionary from Montenegro, met with a tragic fate in Russia. Bursting with activity, he felt at ease only among the people. He was a sort of Chapaiev, yet he never succeeded in becoming acclimatized in the U.S.S.R. He had gone on tours through Russia, had worked everywhere he went, for the authorities were always willing to give him work, but nowhere had he felt at ease ; he lost his way in the maze of bureaucracy and in order to avoid being caught, he continually changed his residence. He ended by seeking a refuge in Daghistan, which reminded him of his native Montenegro, but even there bureaucracy had preceded him. When he came to Moscow, he could not be brought to stay at the Circle of Political Refugees. He could not stand the moral vacuum that prevailed there. He would spend one night with one comrade, the next with another. Often, in order to disturb nobody, to drain his cup of misery to the dregs, he slept at the tramps' shelter.

People have not yet got out of the habit of accusing the Soviet Government of fanning revolutionary activity abroad and of preparing the personnel of the future revolution. In my opinion, nothing is less true. No one has done so much towards the decay of international Communism as the Soviet Government has. Even when their agents transmit revolutionary slogans to Communist Parties, they take precautions so that these slogans may remain matters of pure phraseology and never be put into practice. As for the hundreds and thousands of foreigners who go to visit Soviet Russia, they come back from it disappointed, demoralized and incapable of action. The Russian revolution, in itself degenerating, drags the international revolutionary movement, to which at one time it had given so lively an impetus, down with it.

* * *

The militant Yugo-Slav Communists did not escape the reprisals that their attitude of opposition to the criminal policy of the Comintern in the matter of Yugo-Slavia had brought upon them. But instead of dealing with us in one fell swoop, action was taken in a progressive, slow way, by gradually tightening the meshes of the net. First a Commission was formed to investigate the affair, in actual fact to attempt to break up our group. When these tactics had been found ineffectual, a mixed Commission was formed (Central Committee of the Party and Comintern) under the chairmanship of N. N. Popov, the former Menshevik. Not before six months had elapsed did the Commission terminate its labours and call a meeting to expound its conclusions. As Russian Communist practice demanded, an attempt was first made to demoralize us by putting to the vote a resolution purely and simply to approve the findings of the Commission. As soon as the meeting was opened, one of the ' partisans of the Comintern ' threatened us with Siberia ; it was stressed that the findings of the Commission had already been approved by the Central Committee of the Party. Almost half the members of the assembly (17 votes against 21, the other Yugo-Slavs being on their holidays) voted against the resolution, however, and an appeal was made to the Central Committee to obtain a revision of the matter.

A few days later a Commission of the Comintern, presided over by Soltz, met to organize the repression. It acted with exceptional haste. Soltz allowed only a few minutes to each of the interested parties. One detail of the debates is worth mentioning. When Soltz was summing up the theses of the partisans of the Comintern and of our group, he turned to us with a look of reproach.

" Why are you so passionate ? " he asked. " To hear you speak, one would believe that we are faced with the representatives of two enemy classes. But we are the children of one single class, of one Party."

We replied by pointing at the partisans of the Comintern. " No, we do not belong to the same class as they do."

The representative of the Politbureau of the Yugo-Slav Party wanted to prove that lackeys are always more zealous than their masters. He demanded nothing more nor less than our expulsion. The decision made by Soltz's Commission was more lenient : three (of whom I was one) were to be suspended from the Party for a period of one year ; twenty comrades were ordered to leave Moscow for any other place of residence of their choice, in order to ' permit the struggle within the Yugo-Slav Party to calm down ' ; a few dozen comrades came off with a mere reprimand.

These reprisals revealed to us certain new aspects of Party tactics in Russia. What was most noticeable was the slowness of action. It was due to the fact that the Party was passing through a period of transition and also to the particular methods used in dealing with newcomers to the Opposition.

At the time an open conflict was being waged in both Party and Comintern against the section of the Right. The notes of Trotsky about the Kamenev-Bukharin parleys, published in February, had had the effect of turning the majority of the Politbureau and of the Presidium of the Comintern against the ' triumvirate ' of the Right. Bukharin, Rykov and Tomsky heard themselves openly accused of being the leaders of the Right. This accusation was sanctioned at the XVIth Party Congress in April, 1929. Bukharin was removed from his post of chief editor of *Pravda*, and Tomsky from the leadership of the syndicates. At the same time, in the field of the Comintern, Bukharin partisans were removed from the various sections.

As to the Opposition of the Left, Stalin was making a great effort to win over the Trotskyists without Trotsky. The latter's exile was his pretext. I first thought that the attempt would fail, that once Trotsky was banished, his adherents would tighten their ranks. I made a mistake there. The entire ' old Trotskyist generation ' was ready to sacrifice the person of their leader, to discard the principle of workers' democracy, to shut their eyes to the conditions of the workers, so long as the struggle against the kulaks and the industrialization of the country were kept up. Preobajensky, the most disinterested of the ' capitulaters ', and one of the foremost ideologists of the Communist bureaucracy, made this programme the *sine qua non* of all agreement with Stalin. When he reminded Stalin of the waverings of the Central Committee, the latter firmly replied, " If necessary, I shall have the entire Central Committee arrested, but I shall carry out the Five Year Plan." That brought the parleys to a close.

When we had gone to the Comintern in answer to the convocation sent us by the Soltz Commission, we had found the Preobajensky-Radek group there, gaining its footing in the Party. In these circumstances, the Stalinist administration had good reasons to cause our affair to drag ; there were hopes that we would follow the Russian Opposition on its road to capitulation, and that, abandoning our ' romantic ' conception of socialism, we would finish by returning to the good road of bureaucratic truth.

It was not merely a matter of giving us time to think. They still wanted to conquer us, convince us. I was to undergo the enquiries of a Special Commission on the eve of my exclusion from the Party ; yet it was then that I saw open before me the possibilities of political work at the Comintern which had before been refused me when I was still an irreproachable Party-member and an official delegate of the Yugo-Slav Central Committee. The task was given me of writing the history of the Yugo-Slav Party, and I was allowed to penetrate into the ' Holy of Holies ', the archives of the Comintern. It was not just chance. I was able to see later that a regular system was being applied.

Bureaucratic tactics consisted in terrorizing the opponent from outside, whilst demoralizing him from the inside by a labour of corruption. The process was known by the beautiful name of ' Communist re-education '. One began by warning the culprit and gently pushing him aside ; he was given to understand that his attitude did not correspond with the exigencies of the moment, that he ought to ' amend ', to ' Bolshevize ' himself. If this warning had no effect, he was threatened with severe administrative measures ; if he remained obdurate, he would be courted and before he could regain his composure he would be entrusted with an interesting, well-remunerated task, and he was practically told, " You see, the dictatorship of the proletariat is severe but not resentful ; the Party has its principles but it is not petty. It would be easy for us to crush you : you are an isolated individual, everyone condemns you ; yet we are offering you the widest possibilities, you may have interesting well-paid work ; all you need do is to come back from your errors and correct yourself as you work. Now go ahead, for we are short of men."

This argument is far from senseless ; it is based on realities. But it corrupts souls and deepens oppression and untruth.

At that time I was given an opportunity to study the functioning of the Comintern at close quarters. I was able to observe its highest officials : Bukharin, Manuilsky, Kuusinen, Remmele, Piatnitsky, Bela Kun, Dimitrov, Schmeral, as well as their lieutenants. Some were men of limited intelligence, as Remmele or Piatnitsky, who were not aware of what was going on around them, nor of what they themselves were doing. But the majority consisted of men at one time remarkable, but now demoralized or exhausted.

Maybe it is worth while to pause over Dimitrov who was later to shine with ephemeral brilliancy in the sky of the Comintern. Towards 1920 Dimitrov played a part of only secondary importance in the Bulgarian Party and, in the Comintern, was nobody. But after the 1923 and 1924 events in Bulgaria, he drew attention to himself and pushed Kolarov, Kabaktchiev and others into the background. In exile he learned foreign languages and in 1929 was entrusted with the secretaryship of the Comintern for Central Europe. Dimitrov's first quality was his Levantine artfulness ; next one was struck by the coarse and calculating realism of the Bulgarian peasant who still remembered the Turkish rod and who had fought for his national independence. One day, when in a speech he allowed himself a slighting remark about Zinoviev (who was then already a dead man, politically speaking), a member of the Executive Committee whispered into my ear, " What a man ! When Zinoviev was in power, Dimitrov was one of his most servile flatterers."

VI

I LEAVE MOSCOW

THE sanctions applied by the Control Commission could neither discourage nor convince my comrades, the Trotskyists no more than the other members of the Yugo-Slav Left. A short time after the Comintern had pronounced its verdict, we gathered some ten militants and decided to carry on the struggle inside the Yugo-Slav Party—illegally, if necessary. We began to draw up pamphlets in which we criticized the policy and the theories of the Yugo-Slav Central Committee.

I spent the summer in Moscow, foreseeing a possible departure in autumn. Several of my comrades had been sent to the *kolkhosi* (collective farms) in the northern Caucasus to take part in the harvesting campaign. They were present at the peasant riots. The peasants of several villages had revolted to a man and had massacred their local Communists. As to the foreigners, they had been contented to lock them up in a barn, saying, " You are not from here ; leave us alone and we shall leave you alone." The rioting was crushed in a matter of days and our comrades were liberated. Upon their return to Moscow, they did not know whom to blame : the rioting peasants or the Government. Other comrades who had spent the summer in South Western Ukraine told horrible tales of the misery of the Jews in those regions. Small trades and crafts by which they had formerly made a living had been abolished as being aspects of private capitalism. The Jews could find no form of employment ; the then undeveloped industry of the NEP could offer them none ; there were enough unemployed as it was without bringing in the Jews. Nothing was left them but to die by inches, without work, in their ancient ' Jewish zone '.

These comrades had met in the Ukraine the celebrated Marusya, who, during the Civil War, had been the leader of a very much feared band of supporters. Her days of triumph were over. Dressed in a military cloak, she wandered aimlessly through the streets. She could be seen entering a co-operative shop where she would say in a toneless voice, " Hand me a bottle." The employee would hand her a bottle of vodka ; she would take it without paying for it and go out without saying another word.

In 1929 there were several ' affairs ' with foreign Communists. A group of Bulgarians were arrested when attempting to return to their own country without permission. They belonged to a group of Left nationalists within the Bulgarian Party. Dissatisfied with the official policy of Kolarov and Dimitrov, they had tried secretly to leave Odessa in a small craft. They were arrested as they were setting foot on board. One of their comrades had betrayed them to the Kolarov-Dimitrov group ; they were arrested by the G.P.U. and sent to the mines of the Ural.

Then there was the ' affair ' of the Hungarian and Rumanian Communists. One of them was a former high syndicate official from Transylvania, called Keblesz. He had at one time been a member of the Politbureau of the Rumanian Party and had been in command of a detachment of the Red Army in Soviet Hungary. When arrested in Czechoslovakia while attempting to cross into Russia, he was very nearly handed over to the Rumanian police. On that occasion the international Communist Press waged a campaign in his favour. He was set free and arrived in Moscow. He belonged to the section of the Right of the Rumanian Party that had been removed from power. High offices were offered him in the Soviet administration ; he refused them and was taken on in a factory ; he was an excellent carpenter. When his group was arrested, it was first stated that he had been in contact with Trotskyists ; then he was accused of having linked up with the democratic centre (the decists) ; then with Chliapnikov's ' workers' opposition '. In the end official circles declared that Keblesz was in no way a member of the Opposition, but an *agent provocateur*. After my departure from Moscow, I never heard Keblesz mentioned again and was unable to discover anything further about him. Anything may happen in life, but it is incredible to see the facility and the unscrupulousness with which the G.P.U. accuses people of being spies and *agents provocateurs*.

Brandler's group, which also had difficulties, succeeded in

getting out of them and returning freely to Germany in the spring of 1929. Some of the members even obtained paid holidays before their departure. About to leave, another member of the group, R. Kreuzburg, gave before an important Cell in Moscow an exposition of his differences of opinion with the Comintern. Above all he criticized the bureaucratic rule which prevented Party-members from openly expressing their views and from debating the problems of the day. The Russian Communists listened with mixed feelings of envy and respect to this foreigner who, on the eve of his departure, permitted himself boldly to criticize the system.

After the disillusion Kreuzburg had suffered in Russia, he was to go through more in his own country. Soon came the inglorious *débâcle* of Communism and social democracy in Germany and Hitler's victory. Kreuzburg was unable to bear it. He gave up all political activity in 1931 and took his own life in 1936.

After a three years' stay in Russia, I had been able to form an opinion on Soviet public life. I then began to study private life more closely.

I had often heard it said that the private lives of the Communist leaders were far from irreproachable. I had thought those tales to be counter-revolutionary calumnies or else mere scandal-mongering. I used to say : as the policy is on the whole correct, why strain at details about people's morals. Now that I had found the policy to be incorrect, these details, such of them as I had been able to observe, began to stand out more clearly.

The members of the Government and of the Central Committee and the high officials of various administrations had themselves divorced one after the other. The women they left had, in years gone by, shared their exile ; they had lived by their sides through the difficult years of persecution and civil war. Now they were coldly left because they had grown old. Other Communists, of humble origin, divorced their wives because they found them incapable of understanding them : we 'had' to leave her, they said. Certainly each of these cases, taken in isolation, had nothing very stirring about it, but cumulatively they made me wonder whether it was necessary for a revolution to cause so much pain to those who had suffered so much in its name. I could not

64

share the Olympian serenity of the Russian Communists who thought that everything was above-board so long as they had assured their divorced wives a livelihood.

This feeling of disapproval was strengthened when one made the acquaintance of the new wives of these Communists. But for rare exceptions, they were by no means serious-minded women. They were usually drawn from the petit-bourgeois, the ' intelligentsia ', and civil servants' families. Often they belonged to the old ruling classes. Even in the case of those who had been working women, students and Communists, one felt no spiritual union between them and their husbands. It was all too clear that marriage to them had been only a means of advancement in the world, of having nice living-quarters, dresses and a car. Those who had belonged to ' good families ' before the revolution had moreover an assurance of security for themselves and their relatives.

One cannot compel one's feelings. But is it not curious to see that Russian Communists have feelings only for that sort of woman ? It is very reminiscent of what takes place in bourgeois society, where pretty girls marry rich old men. Socialists have always denounced this form of prostitution called marriage. And the analogy goes further. One day I had occasion to read a letter of the young wife of a very prominent People's Commissar to her lover, a student. It reminded me of the old cabinet ministers of Europe and the cheerful lovers kept by their wives. Nature, even in Soviet Russia, has her own back.

These men did not always seek a divorce. They often just took mistresses. A new class of Soviet-spirited courtesans had arisen. But the difference between these Soviet morals and those of the higher classes of capitalist society was difficult to appreciate.

These morals roused the indignation of the young people. On the occasion of a commemorative banquet organized by a Soviet institution—a banquet which as a matter of fact degenerated into a Homeric drinking-bout—the members of the Comsomol (Communist Youth League) of that institution noticed that one of the guests, the famous Budienny, was too tenderly kissing the hands of a young and frail girl-student of the Conservatory. They were told that she was his new wife. Later on they learnt that the former wife of Budienny, who had been in the Red Army and had fought through the Civil

War at his side, was now safely in a lunatic asylum. The Party Cell had to use a very heavy hand to stifle the scandal that these young people were about to expose.

Another example : a group of young members of the Comsomol lodged a complaint against a colleague who had been allocated to them, when they learned that he lived with his housekeeper whilst refusing to marry her. In that case, too, the administration hushed up the whole affair by remonstrating with them and dropping more than a few hints about reprisals.

I wanted to have direct knowledge of the opinion of the interested parties and formed friendships with young Communists. They were decent young people, of working class origin, themselves workers. They had already acquired a certain instruction and had reached a certain status, but they were preparing themselves for further advancement, several of them by means of University examinations. They worked with great ardour and modesty. I noticed not one trace of the depravity which, according to the foreign press, prevailed in the Comsomol. Later, when in prison, I learned from Opposition-Communists that, indeed, at one time, there had been a certain moral corruption in the Comsomol, but only in the days of the NEP and at certain stages of the hierarchy.

Yet these admirable youths drew their lessons from the private and public examples of morality shown them by the senior Communists. They refused to neglect the vast possibilities for study and work that Communist society offered them ; they would sooner have given up their moral ideals. I discreetly tested the possibilities of drawing them into the Opposition, but I soon found that they would have been incapable of engaging in a systematic and fierce struggle against the bureaucratic régime. One might have won them over in a moment of indignation, but they would have drawn back as soon as they had understood the serious consequences that Opposition activity might entail. For that reason I did not persist.

When corrupt morals prevail in the upper layer of society, one can expect to find the same in the street among the poor. In the centre of the town, in Neglinna Street, a few steps away from the State Bank, groups of prostitutes could be seen walking up and down the pavement. A little farther, in Petrovka Street and Tverskaya Street, more elegant prostitutes had their beat. In Moscow were to be found the worst vices of the big towns of Europe and the East. In the heart of the capital, in a café specializing in such things, ladies in quest of adventure could find men whose bodies were for sale. Near Nikitskaya Gate was the secret market of the homosexuals. Houses of assignation, the ' apartments of Zoika ', were tolerated and flourishing. There were places where bohemians mixed with the relics of the old society and the new Communist aristocracy. Circles of Lesbians had a certain success in Moscow as well as in the provinces. Often eroticism was tinged with mysticism.

To these ' normal ' phenomena of the capitalist world was added a phenomenon peculiar to Moscow. There was a whole group of women married to Communist dignitaries who gave themselves up to prostitution to round off their budgets and to obtain extra dresses. At the time of which I write, notwithstanding all the privileges in kind they enjoyed, such as apartments, paid holidays and so on, officials drew but relatively modest salaries ; there was a legal maximum for Party-members. This salary was insufficient to allow for luxurious clothes, and on the whole there was still a feeling that Communists should dress modestly. People had not yet reached the stage where arguments were provided advocating the ' civilized life '. Soon the G.P.U., always vigilant, learned, to its profound horror, that the wives of honourable Communist officials were prostituting themselves in secret. After it had recovered from its first astonishment, the G.P.U. decided to exploit this knowledge to the greater glory of the revolution. It shut its eyes to the private lives of these ladies, but forced them to co-operate with it. They had to watch and denounce their husbands and their friends. The G.P.U. was accustomed to avail itself on a variety of pretexts of the services of the wives of prominent Communists or of non-Party technicians.

These moral sores were not merely a heritage of the past. On the contrary, they seemed to rise and flourish on new fields of Soviet society. That was what worried me most. When the theatre unveiled these vices, it seemed to me that the criticism of past corruption was too attractive to the new *élite*, that it found a much greater satisfaction in the rendering of these vices on the stage than in their condemnation. Thus only can I explain to myself the insistence with which a number of episodes were produced on the stage, as the one of Azeff at the cabaret in the play called *Blood* at the Vakhtangov Theatre. Later, in the film *The Storm* a complacent and truly exaggerated version was given of the debauch in the Nizhni-Novgorod market. What had happened to the sacred fire of the revolution, that was to devour all the iniquities of the old world ?

*　　*　　*

Autumn was drawing near. The political season was about to commence. From now onwards my days in Moscow were numbered and for that reason I spent a great deal of time walking in the streets. After three years in Moscow I found it hard not to believe myself in a capital of Tartar Khans instead of in that of the Czars of Russia. Every stone crookedly laid, every ill-applied inscription, all the strange outlines of the buildings, the roofs, the windows and the hoardings called up thoughts about an ancient and hoary East. The new buildings were still lost in the masses of this living museum. Yet everywhere one saw the indications that a new world was being born. A large number of old churches, steeples and ancient buildings were being demolished ; streets were being widened. A new style was making its appearance. " The passion for destruction is a creative passion " were the words of a 1918 inscription on the Nikolskaya Gate. That inscription was soon to vanish along with the gate it adorned and the wall of Kitai-Gorod.

The town was overflowing with vitality. The Five Year Plan was drawing near. One may criticize Moscow as much as one likes, one may lament the discrepancy that exists between the reality and the ideal, between promises and their realization, but one cannot deny the energy that inspires it and which makes itself everywhere felt. The will to live is Moscow's supreme law.

*　　*　　*

At last the day came on which I had to present myself at the offices of the Party to receive my papers. At the Central Control Commission, Soltz handed me a personal letter to Kirov, for I had decided to go to Leningrad. When I left he wished " that all might be straightened out ". Next I went to the Central Committee to fetch some other papers. In one of the halls I saw on a high pedestal a bust of Lenin. Opposite, on a pedestal of the same height and make, there was another bust. That must be Marx, I said to myself. But it had no beard. I let my mind run over the apostles of socialism and could think of no one to resemble it. My curiosity roused, I went nearer, and to my indescribable amazement I recognized Stalin. Today a bust of Stalin at the Central Committee would astonish no one. But at that time, a few months before Stalin's fiftieth anniversary, the public had not yet grasped that Stalin was to be equal to Lenin. A short whle previously, at a Party meeting, someone had interrupted Soltz, " Why don't you carry out Lenin's Political Testament ? "

" The Party is putting Stalin to the test," Soltz answered. " If he works well, he will remain general secretary ; if not, he will be removed."

Now Stalin, during his lifetime, has been declared the equal of Lenin, or to be more accurate, since Lenin died, the greater of the two. " A live dog is worth more than a dead lion."

It was not some over-zealous provincial bureaucrat, it was Stalin himself who was propagating his own cult within the precincts of the Committee. This fact alone is more significant than all the arguments on the true situation of Party and country.

VII

IN LENINGRAD

LENINGRAD is a piece of Europe inside the Russian immensity. Its vast network of precisely planned streets, its grandiose buildings and its palaces leave an unforgettable impression. By going through Russia, in the end one forgets Europe. In Leningrad one finds the synthesis of all isolated elements present in every European town. Its numerous palaces create a harmonious entity and give the town incomparable majesty. The size of its squares, of its quays and main roads calls up the grandeur of past events. The huge blocks of Finnish granite that in its " Champ de Mars " surround the common grave of the victims of the revolution are more effective than Lenin's Mausoleum, dwarfed as it is by the Kremlin. The inscriptions hewn on the granite blocks breathe the stern enthusiasm of the first years after the October revolution. Even street-names in Leningrad tell more of the greatness of 1917 than those in Moscow. The people, too, are different from those of the capital. There is more elegance in gesture and dress, more outward manner, more culture.

The proletariat imprints its stamp on the town. At five o'clock in the afternoon, at the end of the day's toil, the workers, in their tens of thousands, leave their factories and fill the streets in all quarters of the town like an overflowing stream. They wear sombre, oil-stained work-clothes, their features are accentuated by the iron-dust of the workshops. But above all, their faces express a pride and a resolution such as I have never met with in European workmen. Their whole attitude seems to embody the feeling that they are the vanguard of the world's proletariat, that they have been the first to occupy workshops and factories and to make the greatest workers' revolution the world has yet known.

Even today when they are reduced to servitude, now that their factories have passed into the hands of a bureaucracy, a

70

'red bourgeoisie' as it is called in Russia, one still feels the pulse of the great effort of the years from 1917 to 1921. It is felt above all individual differences ; it really seems that the revolution has not been in vain for the Leningrad proletariat.

Six years later, amidst the horrors of distant Siberia, I once more was able to meet thousands of workers from Leningrad. They had been sent there after the murder of Kirov, with their wives and children, some thirty or forty thousand of them. They had been scattered right across northern Siberia and along the coast of the Arctic Ocean. But in their cold and taciturn submission one sensed their underlying contempt for the bureaucratic Government and the presence of their workers' pride along with their secret hope of revenge. They did not call themselves 'Zinovievists' ; that to them would have seemed mere talk and cowardice ; they called themselves 'those from Leningrad', and made it sound as if it meant : we are a band of the working class, not a group of bureaucratic backbiters. The Leningrad workers have defended themselves and will no doubt do so again in the future.

* * *

To return to Leningrad itself, as I saw it in the autumn of 1929. The rhythm of life seemed slow after Moscow. The mad dance of the capital had not yet whirled the rest of Russia along with it. Leningrad was, in this respect, somewhat provincial. The buildings and pavements, which were not very well kept, strengthened this feeling. In 1929 Tchernichevsky would have certainly been unable to speak of the 'smooth pavement' of the Neva Prospect.

One of my old Russian friends was staying at the nursing home of Detskoye Selo (the old Tsarskoye Selo). Draguitch and myself paid him a visit and availed ourselves of the opportunity to see the famous ancient residence of the Czars. We walked, all three, in the magnificent parks now open to the people. The autumn weather was splendid, clear and mild. The trees were already assuming coppery hues. The rays of the sun were still warm and a very light breeze played over the landscape. For the first time in my life I enjoyed the beauty of autumn. As we walked, we discussed the fate of the Russian revolution. Near the bottom of the park, at a cross-road, we discovered a tomb of victims of the revolution. We were struck by the inscription : " Never, never again shall workers be slaves."

But they are slaves today, or at any rate some of them have reduced others, the mass of the workers, to slavery. October was not the last chord in the hymn of liberation, but rather a link in a long chain of struggle that stretches from yesterday's barbarism to tomorrow's emancipated society.

The palaces of the Czars at Detskoye Selo seemed depressing to me. Their halls were majestic but glacial. I had felt the same in the Winter Palace and at the Hermitage. One felt rather the oppression of centuries than the grandeur. This beauty, created by a small *élite* for its own enjoyment, exacerbated a feeling of hostility against a world of misery, slavery and degradation.

At some distance from the Palace, in a small shady square stood the monument to Pushkin. The poet seemed to regard the world with a scowl. The Five Year Plan had no room for Pushkin. I was soon to meet the director of Pushkin House in prison. The inscriptions on the monument were not very legible. They were lines by the poet consecrated to the Tsarskoye Selo School—lines to the friends of his youth. In their simplicity they were magnificent and I re-read them. We were, here, on the most sacred place in Russian history. Here, next the Czars, lived the Decembrists. To the one side, this monument represented a reconciliation of ' society ' with the Empire ; to the other it was a challenge to the Czars. These two tendencies were wedded in Pushkin's soul. The revolution has broken all these dreams of reconciliation. But after the Five Year Plan there was a revival in Russia of the desire to link up with the national tradition, albeit on the basis of a Soviet-bureaucratic society. Pushkin became once more an obligatory symbol and his cult became a State-cult. Like Nicholas I, the Czar of the landed nobility, Stalin, the Czar of the bureaucrats, wanted to bask in the sun of Pushkin. The director of Pushkin House, I read in the papers, had been re-instated in his post and had gone back to work. The monument of the poet at Detskoye Selo had presumably been renovated and was now resplendent in its beauty.

Near the palace were some farms and schools of agriculture. One of our friends had just done some practical work there ; he was a student in the new Faculty of Tractor Construction in Leningrad and his ideological sympathies had gone out to the Lenin-Trotsky-Zinoviev trinity. But his practical life was devoted to Stalin's tractors. He advised us to abandon all Opposition activity. " You are right," he told us, " but in God's name drop it all, no good will come of it. Keep your own opinions, but keep them to yourselves." He has been an engineer now for a good many years. How many like him are there in Russia ?

A comrade of ours who was convalescing at Detskoye Selo introduced us to the wife of an influential local Communist. Before the revolution she had been the wife of a Tsarskoye Selo palace official. Nothing in her indicated the new mentality. Like so many others, she had simply resigned herself to her transition from the old to the new aristocracy.

Draguitch and I had already visited Leningrad and seen all our friends. It was time to think of work and to go to see Kirov, especially now that Deditch, the third member of our little group, had arrived. He had spent the summer in the Ukraine with his wife, an inspector of Jewish schools. Deditch was a Moslem from Bosnia, his wife a Jewess from the Ukraine. Such a marriage would have seemed curious in Europe. In Russia no one was astonished by it.

I went to see Kirov at Smolny, the Smolny for ever famous for its associations with the ten days in October, 1917. Their echo had at one time reached me in the obscure Austrian military hospital where I was. There is a large garden in front of the Smolny where twelve years earlier young aristo-cratic women of the Smolny institute used to walk. One enters the building by a beautiful colonnade which bears the following inscription : " Here met the first Soviet of the Workers' Revolution." In front of the garden and the colonnade is Dictatorship Square, from which one has a splendid view of the district. It is via Twenty-fifth-of-October Avenue, the ' Champ de Mars ' and Dictatorship Square that one reaches Smolny, where met the first Soviet. It is a living résumé of the revolution.

I went up to the third floor, to Kirov's ante-chamber. Here Nikolayev was to murder him, five years later. I passed through into Kirov's study, a large and well-appointed room, and handed him Soltz's letter. Already acquainted with my arrival, he obviously knew more about it than he was willing to admit. He asked some polite questions about the struggle inside the Yugo-Slav Party, the official pretext of my disgrace.

I belonged to the Politbureau of a feeble and uninfluential Party and yet Kirov treated me in accordance with my rank in the ' hierarchy '. To him I was part and parcel of the new class of bureaucrats possessed of rights up to the point of being allowed a certain amount of Opposition leanings.

We first agreed about my scientific work in Leningrad. I am a trained historian and had during my three years' stay in Moscow never interrupted my historical research into matters concerning Western Europe. In my presence, Kirov telephoned to the chief of the propaganda section, and two days later I was appointed reader at the Leningrad University. One telephone call from Kirov and I and my friends were provided with rooms at the Party House in Leningrad. Thus the Soviet bureaucracy gained souls ; it terrorized and corrupted at the same time and proceeded by a mixture of coercion and persuasion.

Kirov's office in no way recalled the atmosphere of enthusiasm of the October revolution. Kirov himself, by his manners and methods, reminded me of the cultured high officials of the Austrian administration I had known at Brunn, where, during the War, I had had dealings with matters concerning Istrian refugees. In the office of Kirov, governor of Leningrad in 1929, one felt that the revolution had already been tamed and canalized. I was to interpret Nikolayev's revolver-shot as an act arising from the despair of the 1917–24 generation, disappointed by the results of the revolution and of the Five Year Plan without the strength to begin all over again. Beginning all over again would be possible in Russia only to men physically and spiritually wholly new.

My comrades refused all Party appointments and went to factories as plain workmen, Deditch to the telephone factory ' The Red Dawn ', Draguitch to the factory for electrical appliances ' Electrosila ' (former Siemens-Schuckert factory).

I lived in Leningrad from October, 1929, until I was arrested in May, 1930. Apart from the Communist University, I also taught at the Regional School of the Party and gave courses for militant factory Communists. Moreover, I worked on the History Department of the Leningrad Communist Academy. With this I filled my days.

I took a great interest in my students. Those at the University constituted, in a way, the *élite* of the Leningrad proletariat ; young people from twenty-five to thirty years old, healthy and vigorous. They were nearly all working men and had long careers of public activity behind them. They were cultured and intelligent, real 'gentlemen' of the proletariat. It seemed to me that this was the ground from which were to spring the future champions of the working class against the bureaucracy. Their social origins, the links that united them to the working class, their intellectual level, their youthful energy, the opportunity that was offered them of acquainting themselves both in theory and in practice with the various aspects of the workers' movement, these indicated them for that role.

Yet I was soon to find that my forecast had no foundation. They were interested only in a very superficial way in questions of history and sociology and in theoretical debates on the working class movement. They certainly learned very well all they were taught ; they learned it too well ; for them what was not written in the manual did not exist. They asked no questions outside the official programme. Their spiritual life was entirely mechanized. When I endeavoured to guide them beyond the narrow bounds of their syllabus, to awaken their interest and their critical sense, they hung back, giving the impression that their social sense was blunted.

This attitude struck me particularly during my course of lectures on post-war Europe, in which I had to give a lecture on Fascism to an audience of two hundred students.

I carefully prepared my lecture and made a considerable effort to bring out certain analogies between a number of characteristic phenomena of the Fascist and the contemporary Soviet régimes, particularly where the relations between the administration and the mass of the workers were concerned. I tried to sketch out an idea of what was lacking in Russia, namely, the free activity of the masses. My intention did not reach the audience. Certainly up to a point they saw the analogy, but it did not astonish them, they found it entirely normal : it was the part of the leaders to take decisions ; the whole question depended on knowing what was the end in view. The final end of the Soviet leaders was good, that of the Fascists bad. My listeners thought it entirely natural that in both cases the masses should be only an instrument.

I began to observe the everyday behaviour of my students towards the working class, the class from which they had sprung and with which they remained in closest contact. I was able to note that they accepted their privileges with complacency, however great they might be from the workers' point of view. The 1929–30 session had already begun, the crisis of the food-supply was rapidly worsening, the workers were growing more and more anxious and their wives and children were going short of bread, milk and butter. As to the students, they were provided with everything and were in no way moved by the food-crisis. They considered this state of affairs natural. When one talked to them of the privations of the workers, they answered in commonplace phrases such as " the building up of socialism is not without its difficulties ". By their social position and their ideology, they were identified with the bureaucracy. In the end I was forced to accept the belief that they represented not a workers' *élite*, but a ' young guard ' of the bureaucracy ; a vitalized workers' movement would find no leaders among them. These would have to be drawn from the depths of the untutored masses. The parvenus who defend their privileges are the worst enemies of any real working class movement, for such a movement must of necessity seek the annihilation of any bureaucratic system.

Teaching at the Communist University was no light task. Every year the syllabus was altered, and historical facts and appreciations were biased with increasing insolence. Not only the recent history of the revolutionary movement in Russia was dealt with thus, but also distant events such as the Paris Commune, the 1848 revolution, the first French revolution. It had been customary at one time to criticize Jacobins in favour of the ' Extremists ' ; at the time that I was teaching at the University, one had on the contrary to make a decided stand in favour of the Jacobins and against the ' Extremists '. What was to be said about the history of the Comintern ? Every new edition of the *History of the Formation and Development of the Comintern* gave a new version, in many ways entirely opposed to the previous one. Political economy and philosophy underwent the same treatment.

The professors, obviously, were well acquainted with these falsifications, as they had to carry them out ; they were sufficiently knowledgeable to recognize the difference between their teaching of today and that of yesterday. As for the students, as far as I was able to observe them in their history classes, they did not normally notice these changes, or attached no great importance to them. They did not accept the lie in so fully conscious a way as did the professors, but unconsciously assimilated it along with the rest of the syllabus matter and the general spirit of the teaching.

As these falsifications were introduced into all branches of teaching at the same time, I came to the conclusion that they were not due to isolated accidents, but to a preconceived plan that was to transform history, political economy and the other sciences in accordance with the interests and conceptions of the bureaucracy and to adapt the traditional Bolshevist interpretation of Marxism accordingly. Indeed, a new school, a bureaucratic school of Marxism, was being formed in Russia. If one took into account the vastness of the interests it represented and the enormous influence it exercised on the international workers' movement through the intermediary Russian Communist Party and Comintern, one could not deny the importance—a negative importance—of this new school. To the historic schools of Marxism—those of Kautsky, Luxemburg and Guesde, Austro-Marxism, and the Communism of the revolutionary period—one had henceforth to add this school of Soviet-bureaucratic Marxism.

The professors fell into three groups. Those who were former members of the Opposition (the ' capitulaters ') had the greater influence owing to their better theoretic grounding and their more supple intelligences. They were spurred on by their fierce competitors, the young professors, blameless Communists of limited intelligence. Finally, the ' old guard ', who formed a third group. These men had never sinned against Communist orthodoxy, but they no longer had sufficient intellectual litheness to play leading parts. The main struggle lay between the two younger groups. The Rector of the University, who was allied to both, conscientiously tried to reconcile them.

The Regional Party school comprised young provincial Communists, mainly of peasant origin. They were real children of the people, naïve and as yet unspoiled by bureaucracy. They shared the peasants' uneasiness, and yet, in curious contradiction, clung to the official Party Line. One felt that they would turn into faithful lieutenants of the system, able to ensure the domination of the people from which they themselves had sprung. The school occupied the premises of an old religious seminary near the Finland Station. Accommodation and food were mediocre. In contrast, the University students seemed to live like Oxford undergraduates. The bureaucracy respected the principles of hierarchy in its own midst ; humbler people had to be content with little and to live in hopes of betterment.

The courses for militant Communist factory workers were given at the Detskoye Selo, in the old mansion of Countess Paley, a spacious but uncomfortable place. They were three- or six-months' courses designed for official secretaries, propagandists and agitators of Party Cells and of Youth Branches connected with the Leningrad industries. The students were nearly all working men and women. About a third of them were already minor officials, the others, whilst earning their living with the work of their hands, filled several unpaid social functions and were candidates for official posts. The selection, by the administration, of the more active and gifted workers bled the working class and explained to a large extent the unlimited power of the bureaucracy over the proletariat.

With these students, contact with the factory was much more real than was the case with the students of the Communist University. The anxiety of the working masses touched them and they did not use commonplaces as did the others. " The worker's life is unbearable, his patience is at an end ; our propaganda meets with great obstacles among the workers," they often said.

Their interest in the workers' movement abroad was of a very different nature from that shown by the University students. The latter considered the Western workers with great aloofness. " What are they compared to us ? " they asked. The course-students, on the other hand, hoped for a foreign proletariat to come to their help or even to save them. They often anxiously interrogated me about the future of the revolutionary movement in America and Germany. My position as ' Communist suspended from the Party ' increased, so it seemed, the degree of confidence shown in me by certain students.

The standard of life of the course-students was exceptionally high. I have never seen such excellent food in any other educational establishment. And that was in the spring of 1930. One must believe that the bureaucratic leaders deemed it necessary to ensure at all costs a friendly attitude in the liaison organizations that exerted an immediate influence on the working masses in the Leningrad factories.

I was enabled to make an interesting observation of a group of students from the Comsomol (Communist Youth). In the front row on the left was a young woman who was studying with both zeal and success, and looked at the universe through the eyes of the Party newspaper, the resolutions of meetings and the official manuals. In the back row on the right a very different type of student was seated, one who saw everything in black. She belonged to a family of textile workers and worked in a textile factory herself. At every opportunity she spoke of the worker's hard life. With the greatest simplicity she mentioned the most heart-breaking incidents she could daily observe at the factory and at home. She spoke of them with a subdued indignation and she was clearly moved by the contradictions between the workers' realities and the writings in books and papers. One felt in her words the unspoken question : whence those contradictions, when will they be solved, can they be solved ?

With the same instinctive ease her antagonist of the front row used to find reassuring answers. Her optimism was systematic. All the ' shortcomings ' and ' accidents ' were ironed out by this official enthusiasm. For her, life resided in factories in course of construction, in machinery, in heroic leaders ; as to the workmen, the workers in the *kolkhosi* (collective farms), the masses—they were to her but shadow without substance. Her attitude and general behaviour made me believe that she was the daughter of a petit-bourgeois family or of State officials. I consulted the card-index ; no, she, too, was of working class origin. Thus these two young women belonging to the same social class, to the same group of the Comsomol, seated in the same room, managed to represent two modes of thought, two entirely different worlds. No doubt they had had an instinctive feeling of this in choosing their desks as far apart from one another as possible. The rest of the class disposed themselves between them, according to their affinities, drawing them either towards the one girl or the other.

This case reminded me of that of a young Communist, the wife of a rather influential official of KIM (Communist International of Youth), in Moscow. She was a woman of nineteen, beautiful, intelligent and energetic. She worked in a factory and attended technical classes in the evenings. Recently she had been abroad with her husband—who was not a Russian—having been given an illegal task to perform abroad. Was this not a couple from the vanguard ? But by looking more closely one discovered the deepest corruption hidden beneath a veil of virtue. To that young woman nothing counted but her career and that of her husband. She had the gift of considering everything from the point of view of advancement in the administration. At all costs they were to rise higher in the hierarchy. Convictions, ideas, conscience—they were notions fit for imbeciles. Intelligent people knew how to use them to serve their own ends but were not duped by them.

This young militant, wife of an active member of the KIM, where had she gathered her egocentric conception of the world ? Could it be explained by the influence of the leading circles of the Comsomol and the Communist International of Youth, where the worst bureaucratic corruption prevailed ?

In the Leningrad section of the Communist Academy, work was less brisk than it was at Moscow. Yet hard work was being done. The Five Year Plan demanded all sorts of ideological justifications. The peculiar social system that was being developed in Soviet Russia had a tendency to create its own ideology in all branches of science. To be more exact, it tended to fuse its own conception of the world with that of the old science as well as with the traditional ideology of Marxism and the new scientific data. I was working in the historical section, on the History Commission of the Comintern, which was my task in the composite picture. Moreover, on my own initiative, I was doing research work on the history of the feudalism of the Southern Slavs.

The general framework of the researches of the Communist Academy was supplied by the highest authority, the Central Committee of the Party. All the same, work at the Academy had many advantages, less from a material standpoint than from that of social position and the possibilities of the scientific career offered to members of the Academy. Once they had ' rendered unto Caesar the things that are Caesar's ', that is, once they had performed the task demanded by the bureaucratic Plan, the ' scientists ' had an excellent social and material status assured them. Like all other ruling classes the bureaucracy paid the priests of its cult very well and gave them a place of honour in the social hierarchy. After they had fulfilled their official task, the scientists could retire to the recesses of their special subjects, to their disinterested researches conducted in accordance with their own judgement. Finally, one was able to study anything one wished with the greatest freedom of mind, provided that this intellectual exercise remained a strictly personal matter. It was imperative, however, publicly to profess the opinions demanded by the bureaucratic powers. In private one was allowed to think what one liked.

Even when the authorities were acquainted with these personal opinions, they put no obstacles in their way, provided that they were not expressed in public. " Restrict yourself to educating the people," they seemed to say, " in time you will succeed in re-educating yourself." This was the mechanism by which untruth was spread in maximum doses, and the conscience and will-power of those who saw the system too clearly put to sleep. This was what Soviet Russia called ' Communist education and re-education ', or sometimes ' living Leninist-Marxism '. Under these conditions did science develop in modern Russia.

Soviet science demanded that each of its acolytes should submit to the new ' emperor ' and to the high aristocracy of the Party, and that these should be adored. But at the same time it defended the interests and the privileges of the ' intelligentsia ' and of the bureaucracy as a whole, be it Communist or non-Party. Not only did this brand of science lend its support against the old ruling classes but also against the mass of the workers. For from the intelligentsia it drew its strength and its enthusiasm. As I had numerous connections with intellectual circles, I could gauge to the fullest extent the immensity of the privileges enjoyed by the intelligentsia in the U.S.S.R. ; first of all, by those belonging to the Party, then the others, in particular the technicians. The differences in social conditions were all the more striking in Russia because of the general low level of living throughout the country. It was enough to compare the lodgings, food, clothes, sanitary conditions and culture enjoyed by the intellectuals and the bureaucrats on the one hand and those by the ordinary workers on the other to perceive the gulf that separated those two strata of the population.

That was why it was so easy to understand the admiration

felt so facilely by intellectuals in capitalist countries for Soviet Russia ; that country was indeed the kingdom of the intellectuals !

Yet could one assert that the essence of the ' new world ' be that the intellectual class should replace the bourgeoisie in exploiting the workers, that the bureaucrats of all types of workers' organizations, the officials and engineers of factories and trusts, doctors, professors and academicians should simply replace property-owners, capitalists and their hangers-on ? Should education and technical knowledge be the foundation of new privileges, of a new division of society into exploiters and exploited, into masters and slaves ?

By reason of my financial and social position, I found that I belonged to the ' upper ten thousand '. I was well placed for recognizing the multiplicity of reasons that urged people to adapt themselves to the bureaucratic régime, reasons very adequate from the point of view of personal well-being. I felt, as it were, at home in the rich and spacious halls of the Academy, lodged in one of the great palaces of the " Champ de Mars ". I had at my disposal books in all languages and of all periods, not excepting current foreign publications of all tendencies, a fruit forbidden to the ordinary run of mortals and to plain Communists. I was still better placed at the Communist University, where I could walk in the magnificent and well-kept halls of the ancient palace, or sit in my private study among my chosen books obtained *ad lib.* at Government expense.

I lived in truly splendid, well-furnished apartments at the Party House, which was one of the largest palaces of the most aristocratic quarter of the town. My functions left me enough spare time to devote myself to literature, languages and those social problems that interested me. Also Russia's finest watering-places, travel and entertainments were within my reach. I had been suspended from the Party for a period of one year, but it would have been sufficient for me to show myself disposed to join the throng of right-thinkers to receive once more a membership card finally assuring my present and future privileges.

It would have been all the more easy for me to take this last step, as I was by this time convinced of the fate of the Russian revolution. The defeat of the Opposition of the Left now seemed final to me ; the only possible evolution in

Russia, for some time at least, was an evolution towards the Right. As for Europe, and Germany in particular, I expected to see a recrudescence of reaction. In short, I expected a new 1804, a new 1849, or a new 1907. One had to resign oneself to sink still deeper, not to rise till later. That situation, that moment of impotence, that passivity of the working masses, contributed just as much as terrorism and individual and collective privileges to cause many in Russia to celebrate the bureaucratic Bonapartism. Stalin, as had Napoleon in the past, seemed to be saving what could still be saved of the revolution. He was the " smallest evil " in the general current of reaction.

I knew what I was losing and what awaited me when I chose the camp of the adversaries of triumphant Bonapartism, the camp of the popular masses which, for the moment, was the camp of the vanquished. But my choice was attended by no heroic effort, it was dictated to me by an internal evolution. I should have liked combat. All these Soviet Barres, Fouchés, and Bonapartes, great or small, disgusted me. I was hostile to them by instinct as well as by conviction. Before my eyes rose the picture of my old compatriots and neighbours, the Istrian peasants. Could I betray them? Could I forget them and think merely of my own petty interests? All these workers of Croatia, Slovenia, Bosnia and Herzegovina, to whose organization I had belonged after the World War, and whom I had spurred on to fight for a better society, the peasants of the Krijevatz region, whose hopes and expectancy I had shared from 1918 to 1919—had I incited them to " fight the palaces " merely to go and live there myself, leaving my comrades-in-arms outside?

Neither the fact that the new order had ousted the bourgeoisie and the landowners in favour of bureaucrat and intellectual, nor the fact that it had supplanted the cults of Christ, Czar, and private property by those of Marx and Lenin, Soviet rule and State property-ownership, was really enough to make it palatable. There was undoubtedly an element of the incredible in this question : how was it possible that the great effort of 1917 towards emancipation should have ended in a new slavery, whilst preserving the 1917 slogans? The facts were there. It was necessary to look for an explanation, a new theory, and not to deny the facts in order to preserve the vanished theory.

I thought I began to see a conceivable explanation. I remembered a statement by Hegel to the effect that a phenomenon can preserve its form whilst its contents are completely transformed. Had not Lenin written that often the fate of great men is to serve as ikons after their death, when their ideas of liberation are adulterated to justify a new oppression and a new slavery ? It was pleasant to see a few tens, say a few hundreds, of thousands of men rise from among the people and lift themselves to the peaks of society and civilization. But tens of millions paid for this ascent, 160 millions of workers and peasants, whose condition had in no way improved. May one forget 160,000,000 for the sake of 200,000 ?

I felt that my place was not among the minority of the satisfied, but among the oppressed and unhappy majority. The work begun in Russia had come to naught.

Was it therefore necessary to leave this country of forlorn hopes and return to Europe ? No, the time had not yet come. I could not yet see with sufficient clearness for my own satisfaction how it had all happened : how it was that everything in Russia was perfect in words, in appearance, but that in reality there existed an appalling state of affairs. I was not clear in my mind as to what measures would be necessary to prevent a recurrence of this development in Europe. I had to stay in Russia in order to clear this point up entirely. I had come to study the experiment of the great revolution. I began to suspect that my studies would take me beyond Russia—to Siberia, into the unknown.

A few of my friends, Trotskyist capitulaters, made every effort to keep me from this road. When, during the spring of 1929, the Opposition began rapidly to melt away, it seemed at first as if there had been a misunderstanding. In far Siberia, people read the Party resolutions and ordinances concerning the industrialization, collectivization, self-criticism and the political uplifting of the masses ; they took these words to be realities. But when in the future they return from Siberia, they will see the workers exploited more than ever, industrialization carried out at the expense of the working class, a total disappearance of workers' democracy, even of democracy inside the Party—these people, I said to myself, will drift back into the Opposition. But I soon saw that I was wrong. All these Opposition intellectuals cared very little about the fate of the working class. That was not the factor that decided their political attitude, it was the speeded-up industrialization and the offensive against the kulaks. Their attitude towards the horrible oppression and exploitation under which the workers suffered was exactly the same as that of Stalinists and Bukharinists. To them, workers were the necessary victims on the altar of socialism, that is, of the State capitalism they mistook for socialism.

" Russia is such a miserable country," one of them told me, " that it suffices to provide a civilized man with a life that is just bearable, in order to turn him into an aristocrat and put an abyss between him and the masses."

As for the general policy, he added, " Stalin carries out the essentials of the Opposition policy. No doubt Trotsky would have done it with more go and with less brutality, and we, who are more cultured than Stalin's men, would have been at the top. But one should be able to rise above these ambitions of class and individual."

A very prominent Soviet diplomat, in talking to one of my friends, concluded as follows : " Let's not forget that Russia is an Asiatic country ; the way of Genghis Khan and Stalin suits it better than the European civilization of Leon Davidovitch."

Bukharin had given Stalin the title of " Genghis Khan of the Russian revolution " and this appellation had gone the rounds all over the land.

Another penitent Oppositionist answered my remarks about the absence of a workers' democracy : " A workers' democracy is out of the question in Russia. Here the working class is so feeble and demoralized that to give it liberty would be to ruin the revolution once and for all. What may save it is an educated minority dictatorship ; this minority must of course find its strength in the working class and slowly raise it to its level."

These people, as one sees, had been right to capitulate. After all, they represented only a special brand of Stalinist bureaucracy. I told them so, in a jocular way. They answered that I was looking at Russia with Western illusions.

Among them there were people who thought Trotsky had been wrong not to risk all in 1923. " As a victorious general of the Civil War " (this expression surprised me) " Trotsky was then more popular than Stalin. If he had wanted the victory, he could have won it easily."

" Do you really believe," I answered, " that Trotsky ought to have made a military *putsch* ? "

" No, it would have been enough for him to have shown himself at the factories. The Opposition obtained a majority in Moscow when it had only the worst orators and Trotsky had shown himself nowhere. His success would have been more complete still if he had personally addressed the workers in the principal factories. After that he should have gone to Kharkov where his victory was certain, and to Leningrad, where his mere presence would have broken down the barrier built by Zinoviev. Direct action by Trotsky in the three capitals would have ensured his victory throughout the land. The glory of a general who had successfully brought the revolution to an end, and who had the Red Army behind him, would have added weight to these oratorical manifestations in the factory Cells and would have facilitated victory."

" But if the situation was as you describe it, why didn't Trotsky act, then ? "

" Trotsky knew very well that the victory was going to be easy. But he wanted to avoid an open break. At that time the entire old guard of Bolshevism was against him ; he argued that his victory would have had the ineluctable consequence of a split inside the Central Committee. He would not hear of such a thing. He hoped to win this ' old guard ' over by loyal means and to carry off a less painful victory later. But he let his chance escape him. In 1926 and 1927, his appeal to the factories could lead only to failure. Stalin, unafraid of the scission, naturally triumphed."

My informant added, " Here is another example of the inopportune scruples that stood in Trotsky's way. During Lenin's illness, Trotsky went to see him as little as possible, although Lenin kept asking for him. Trotsky explained to him that he did not think it right to see him so often, when Lenin's most intimate disciples were received only on rare occasions. There was some truth in what Dzerzhinsky said to Rakovsky, namely, that Leon Davidoditch was too chivalrous a man, and that at the difficult moments through which the country was passing, a different sort of leader had to be found."

Many old Bolsheviks, even those who did not belong to the

Stalinist group, saw that Stalin was the man the Party needed. An influential member of the Central Committee who, at first, did not belong to the Stalinist group, said about him, " He is our Ivan Kalita " (i.e. a fifteenth-century prince who achieved Muscovite unity) ; " in spite of all his failings he has known how to bring about unity between the leaders of Bolshevism."

Whilst refusing to remain in the Opposition and pitying those who " uselessly rotted " in Siberia, those people retained a certain sympathy for Trotsky. It was manifest every time *Pravda* attacked Trotsky. On these occasions they came to see me and eased their consciences by a few lamentations : " What a low, shameful thing to do ! " The next day, grown strong again, they would tell me : " Did you know that Stalin has declared that he is going to throw out the group of Slepsky, Astrov and the other young Bukharinists ? "

At that time I also met several of the leaders of the Zinoviev Opposition. At present these men are in prison, a few have been shot. When I knew them, they still cherished certain illusions. " Stalin's men are not prepared for a fight against the Right-wing. In the course of the struggle, we shall take charge and deal with the various organizations. In Leningrad the Stalinists have to call on our men to draw up a simple resolution against the Right-wing."

In their opinion the Opposition had held the correct view and Stalin had now adopted its policy.

" But if the Opposition held the correct view," I asked, " why did it not win ? "

" We have wondered about that many a time ; we think our offensive must have been premature."

" Would it not be true to say the opposite ? If you had appealed to the workers before Stalin's administrative apparatus had triumphed, you might have won."

" Not at all. The decision does not rest with the workers in Russia. It rests with the apparatus. The Russian worker is too uncultured. In Lenin's time already, the apparatus was the decisive factor."

The affirmation of the preponderance of the ' apparatus ' over the working class in the days of Lenin reduced me to silence. I refused to believe it, but on the other hand could not shake off the belief that those who had directly taken part in those events should know more about it than I did, and that in any case they had no wish to cast aspersions on Lenin.

87

Another comment that I heard about that time and which startled me still more was, " Perhaps it is better that the Opposition should not have triumphed ; we were forming a coalition with Trotsky, and in the case of victory he would have been the leading light. But Trotsky might have dragged the revolution into the worst type of adventurism."

This was the first time that I had come across an Opposition afraid of its own victory. What remained of the Russian revolution ? The men in exile and in gaol.

VIII

THE YEAR OF THE GREAT CRISIS

THE autumn of 1929 was marked by an increasingly rapid extension of the *kolkhosi* (collective farms) and by an intensive pressure on the peasants. This policy had now come to be traditional : in spring, i.e. during sowing-time, promises and concessions were made to the peasants, in order to exert all the more pressure on them in autumn, at the time of harvesting.

The struggle for corn was the centre of interest for both peasants and bureaucrats. It was the conflict between two classes and two economic systems that at the time of the NEP had made some sort of an alliance. Peasant economy was now stifled within the framework of the NEP. The small private farms still dominated Russian economy, in spite of their fragmentary and backward nature. During the years of the NEP, these small farms had risen too much in importance to put up with the hampering rules of the bureaucratic organization and the domination of a still undeveloped State industry. The two economic systems and the two corresponding classes had become mutually exclusive. One of the two adversaries was to carry the day and reconstruct the country's economy in accordance with its own particular leanings. For bureaucracy to win this severe struggle, it had to solve two fundamental and extremely difficult problems. It had, on the one hand, to create an agriculture founded on State capitalism and, on the other hand, to call into being an industry of sufficient importance to meet the industrial needs of the country. The victory of either party was not only to determine the character of Russian economy for the coming period, but even the attitude of Russia towards the outer world and the part she would play in the world's economy. Russia was either to remain an agricultural country and be to some extent colonized by industrial capitalism, or she was to become a national independent empire, both agricultural and industrial, after the American model.

The kulaks took the initiative, in the conflict, with the famous " corn strike ". After a short hesitation, the bureaucracy answered by the most brutal counter-attack. From 1928 to 1933 bureaucrats and peasants waged one of the most grandiose class-conflicts human history has known. It was complicated by struggles between bureaucracy and proletariat, between Communist bureaucrats and non-Party technicians, and lastly by an internal struggle between the various sections of the Communist bureaucracy. One can say that the Five Year Plan, as it was carried out, represented to a certain extent the expression of a terrifying conflict between all classes and all social groups of modern Russia, Stalin's victory was a solution by means of the average, as it were, the resultant of all the social forces at work. Stalin was the product of the events more than he was their cause.

The period of the Five Year Plan is certainly the epic of Soviet bureaucracy. If the latter has come out of the struggle bespattered with mud and blood, it helps to prove that this ' epic ' has nothing in common with the heroic struggle hoped for by the masses of liberated workers, nor with the age of socialism. But it also proves that the time of the Five Year Plan is closely related to the ' heroic epochs ' of the initial stages of capitalism, from the conquest of the Americas and the Indies onwards.

Stalin may justly claim the merit of having preserved and firmly established bureaucratic domination in Russia. He did not usurp the place of leader and emperor of bureaucracy. Thus it is a fact that on the day of the emancipation of the working masses of factories and *kolkhosi*, on the day of the abolition of privileges, Stalin with his system of capitalist and State exploitation will go to join the ' great men ' of reaction in the graveyard of history.

It was during my stay in Leningrad that the bureaucratic offensive against the countryside began to develop in all its magnitude and that one could clearly see the directing part played in it by Stalin. Events went beyond the scope of familiar opinions ; entirely new problems made their appearance, new answers had to be found. It was no longer socialism, it was not liberation of labour, it was pure slavery.

Yet something new was being born. What exactly was it? That question was on all lips, mine among them.

That year was really that of the 'great crisis' in the policy of bureaucracy, for the latter had declared a ruthless war against the *status quo* of the NEP, and the traditional technical and economic backwardness of Russia. In spite of its spirit of routine and a layer of fat acquired during the NEP, the bureaucracy was up to its task. History imposed a choice upon it : either lose its dominant position, or radically transform Russia by developing its productive forces at great speed. Bureaucracy found itself master of sufficient energy and suppleness to choose the road of action.

It would be wrong to believe that the labouring masses remained entirely dumb and passive and that they had no influence. On the contrary, they expressed themselves by acting in their own way, and exerted a certain pressure on private capital and on bureaucracy. But that pressure was not strong enough to determine the course of events. That was the main point. The bureaucracy certainly had to take the state of mind of the masses into account in drawing up its general 'Line'. The masses had just enough strength and activity to impose the correction of details, 'zigzags' of the general Line—but the Line itself was a definite expression of bureaucratic interests.

One obvious concession, however, was made to the masses, a concession to the revolutionary enthusiasm of 1917–20 ; a tribute of cynical lies and unconscious illusions was paid to the past. Bureaucracy adorned its anti-worker and anti-socialist Plan with the gaudiest of socialist, proletarian and revolutionary banners. The totalitarian, Bonapartist régime made it possible to transform and falsify without difficulty the slogan of 1917–20, to meet the needs of the new hour. In this way, under pretext of workers' intransigence and class purism, the privileges of bureaucracy were affirmed and a bureaucratic struggle was waged against the workers as much as against the old property-owning classes. This explains why at the next stage—after the first Five Year Plan—it was possible to abandon with surprising speed and ease the proletarian exclusivism in favour of the 'Soviet people', the ultra-proletarian fanaticism in favour of a total confusion between the 'people' and the 'proletariat'. Well before this stage was reached, the struggle against 'excessive egalitarianism ' had made it possible for the bureaucracy to affirm with particular clarity its own economic privileges to the detriment of the proletariat.

The huge economic revolution of the Five Year Plan was made for the benefit of those who directed its operations. The Soviet bureaucracy became one of the minorities that rule the world. This revolution cost those who were ' directed ' unbelievable suffering, those, that is, who were but an instrument. The working masses saw themselves more and more riveted to the condition of the slaves and mercenaries of a capitalism that was no longer private, but belonged to State and caste.

I did not realize all this at once, nor was it with a light heart that I came thus to judge the Russian situation. On the one hand, the Stalinist interpretation was in contradiction with the facts, but on the other that of the Trotskyist Opposition did not fully cover them either.

Thought advanced along a zigzag course and often merely stored up facts without appreciating values. The great Line was hard to follow, to take in at a glance. The example of previous revolutions would throw light on events, often it would obscure them. The ancient theories, the old programmes that unconsciously guided the first steps of the investigation became a dead weight at the following stages. The authority of Marx and Lenin permitted the economizing of strength and prevented the necessity of battering down open doors ; but too often it caused entirely new phenomena to be overlooked. " All theory is hoary, but the tree of life is eternally green."

The reader will perhaps be disagreeably surprised at the slowness with which my mind worked. But I am consoled by an observation I have been able to make in Russia, and since—in Europe : the experience of the Russian revolution is so rich, so complex and so young that most of the people who earnestly reflect on ' the Russian problem ' arrive but slowly at their conclusions and must constantly revise their estimate in the light of new facts.

The events of the years 1929–30 are the principal factors in this revision of values.

After my two sojourns in the country in 1927 and 1928, and above all after the wheat strike of 1928, I understood that war was inevitable between the peasantry, whose spontaneous development was directed towards private capitalism and State economy. But this war followed a very different course from the one I visualized and took on an entirely different social significance.

Like all Communists, I had begun by unconsciously identifying bureaucratic State economy with socialism. I thought, therefore, that in this war the socialist elements of the working class as well as the poorer peasantry would oppose the capitalist elements of town and village. The Communist Opposition of Trotsky and Zinoviev seemed to me the vanguard of socialism in that struggle. When, in 1928, Stalin's group, and with it the entire Party, proclaimed war against the private capitalism of the kulaks, I first imagined that this signified a proletarian and revolutionary rebirth of the Communist Party. I began to reproach myself for my doubts about the future of the revolution in Russia. I was all the more inclined to allow the Party and its leaders new credit, as the fate of Soviet society seemed entirely to depend on these leaders, and a return to socialism to be possible only on their initiative or at least with their participation.

In the autumn of 1929 this hope in Stalin and his group had long since vanished. Self-criticism and workers' democracy as applied by Stalin and the Party were nothing but a process of bureaucratic reshuffling. The workers had as few rights as ever, the Communist Opposition continued to be subject to persecution and society had in no way evolved towards socialism. One had therefore to conclude that the trend was towards the restoration of private capital. This conclusion could quite naturally be drawn from the objection raised by the Trotskyist Opposition, an objection that appeared well-founded. From it followed that the ' Left ' attitude of Stalin reflected only the ' Centre ' waverings between socialism and capitalism and that Stalin, notwithstanding all his zigzagging to the Left, was to lean more and more towards the kulaks and private capitalism.

That is how theory would have it. Reality was very different. Stalin went on putting increasing pressure on the kulaks and the *nepmen*, whilst stifling the workers' Cells and the working class. With all his might, Stalin encouraged the war that developed in the villages around the questions of wheat and *kolkhosi* (collective farms). On November 7th, the twelfth anniversary of the October revolution, Stalin published his famous article entitled *The Year of the Great Crisis*. In this article, in bold and provocative terms, he declared war on the small peasant economy, justifying this war by the needs of industrialization. The bureaucratic slogan of the U.S.S.R. became : " Put the U.S.S.R. in a car and the peasant on a tractor." In this way the October socialist aspirations were proclaimed to the proletariat and the world at large.

A little later, on the 27th of December, Stalin spoke the final words, " To hell with the NEP ! " The country and the whole world were to know that Russia was entering into a new phase of her development.

How far one had moved from what Stalin himself had written in February, 1928 : " The NEP is the foundation of our economic policy and will so remain for a long time to come." In April, 1928, Stalin and the plenum of the Central Committee of the Party had passed a resolution to the effect that " only liars and counter-revolutionaries could spread rumours about the abolition of the NEP ". But the decision of this same plenum also contained items such as : " Maintenance of the NEP and offensive against the kulaks," which, in the later course of events, forced Stalin to make a choice. I remember very well New Year's Day of 1930 in Leningrad, which we celebrated among intimates. The entire talk ran on the brutal abolition of the NEP by Stalin, and the meaning and consequences of such an action.

A short time before this abolition, the necessity of speeding up industrialization had already been proclaimed. " Carry out the Five Year Plan in four years ! " was the cry. With the help of the syndicates, 25,000 manual workers had been sent to the country " to strengthen the organization of collective farms ". These workers were to be bureaucratic gaolers, sent to mount guard over the peasants in their collective farms.

The enormous machine, destined to transform the whole of Russia, worked at full speed. Events proved Preobrajensky to be right when he said, " Once the struggle against the kulaks has begun, there will be no retreat possible, even should we wish it." To Stalin, no retreat towards private capitalism was possible. On the other hand, how could one " send the NEP to hell " whilst stifling the proletariat ? The two

94

actions were irreconcilable, according to the old theory put forward by Trotsky. Yet the proletariat remained under the heel of bureaucracy. I saw no signs of its future emancipation. Could one conclude that Stalin would end by breaking his neck and be replaced by men from the Right? In the absence of Rykov and Bukharin—the Dantons of the Russian revolution, who had already been morally executed on the guillotine—their more fortunate heirs would succeed to Stalin. That was the direction events seemed to be following.

Then came the first months of 1930. Collectivization to the fullest extent was proclaiming its triumph. But at the same time more and more echoes were heard of peasant resistance and peasant risings.

Collectivizations and risings had all Russia in their grip. Trotskyists, Zinovievists, Right-wing Communists and Stalinists were all talking with equal anxiety of the storm that was brewing and of which no one could foretell the issue. I gathered from a conversation I had with a trusty Stalinist, a collaborator of the Central Committee, that the Moscow leaders had been particularly impressed by the peasant bands that had formed in the province of Ryazan, within reach of the capital.

From several quarters came tales of Voroshilov's resistance to Stalinist collectivization : " You reduce the country to despair and it is left to me to cope with the situation. I am not doing it." And Voroshilov refused the support of the Red Army to crush the peasant revolts. From that day special divisions of the G.P.U. conducted the punitive expeditions.

The hurricane was sweeping Russia, smashing the time-old patriarchal system of the country to atoms. Bureaucracy was imposing its own civilization. The bloody progress fought its way through towns and villages, sword in hand and starvation at its heels.

Suddenly, on the second day of March the trumpets of retreat were sounded. Stalin published his article, *The Vertigo of Success*. The forced enrolment of the peasants into *kolkhosi* (collective farms), the basis of Stalin's agarian policy, was proclaimed to be but a deformation of the general Line by the local authorities. The general Line, it was said, demanded that collectivization should be entirely voluntary.

The effect produced by this declaration was immense. The number of collective farms fell with lightning rapidity ; it dwindled from day to day, from province to province. What a speculation on the Stock Exchange of History !

The peasants marched in procession through the villages, carrying Stalin's portrait as if it were an ikon. They were to pay dearly for this confidence. Copies of the paper with Stalin's article, priced at five kopeks, were sold at ten roubles in the country. Everyone wished to possess this historic document. Markets in town and village were opened again. On the lower rungs of the administration there was a momentary confusion and bewilderment. " I am off to reinstate the kulaks in the villages," an instructor of the regional Committee of Leningrad told me, half-jokingly. He had been given the task of righting the ' local deformations ' ; two weeks previously he had been ' dekulaking ' the countryside.

Thermidor has come, I thought, we are drawing near to the dénouement. At this moment, the retreat was being carried out in good order, but at any moment a general rout could be expected. Every morning, on waking up, I wondered whether there had been a *coup d'état* at the Kremlin.

Soon ' administrative lessons ' were drawn from the events. The secretary of the Moscow Party Committee, Baumann, who had, eighteen months before, replaced Uglanov, a Right-wing man, in that capacity, was now declared guilty of ' deviation to the Left ' and appointed to the secretaryship of the Central Party Committee in Central Asia, which corresponded to a sort of exile. Baumann was expiating the Ryazan rising and the closing of the markets at Moscow.

The fate of local ' deviators ' was far worse, especially in the distant provinces, where violence had been particularly odious and the risings all the more forceful. The district leaders of the Party Soviets or G.P.U. were now being executed, and, though the number of these executions was not very considerable, they caused terrible panic. What struck me most on hearing eye-witness accounts of these events was that the people condemned should have accepted their expiatory sacrifice with such relative calm. They thought that, if these executions saved the bureaucratic dictatorship as a whole, if they calmed the rebellious peasantry (or rather if they misled them into error), the sacrifice of their lives would not have been in vain. This attitude was particularly prevalent among members of the Cheka. What an astonishing manifestation of caste-feeling ! Among the victims thrown by Stalin to the fury of the people, a few were saved by the last-minute intervention of their friends ; the rest were executed.

This original method of calming the anger of the people reminded me of Marco Polo's report of the Mongol Emperor who reigned in Pekin at that time. It was customary once every ten or fifteen years to deliver over to the crowd the minister most abhorred by it, which allowed the Emperor quietly to oppress his people for the next ten or fifteen years. What I saw in Russia was to bring this Mongol Emperor repeatedly to my mind.

The retreat of the bureaucracy lasted throughout the month of March, 1930 ; it was an organized retreat, not a rout. The flood of the peasant revolt did not succeed in swamping the system, but on the contrary returned slowly to its accustomed channels. In April all doubts were removed : the retreat of March had been a tactical move, not a capitulation. The collapse of the *kolkhosi* was stemmed, and in a few places their development even resumed an upward trend. After a few fluctuations, the percentage of collectivized land came to rest round about the figure 25, instead of the 50 per cent of February. At the same time, the rhythm of collectivization had slowed down, its methods having become ' democratized ' and the despoiling of the peasants in the *kolkhosi* having diminished. The programme originally set out for one or two years was now spread over three or four. Whereas originally everything was to be collectivized down to the last fowl, it was now decided that the peasant was to hand over " only " essential produce to the collective : his land, his ploughing cattle, agricultural implements and barns. He was to keep his house and what he needed for his own domestic purposes.

Yet the kulaks were deprived of literally everything, which meant to say that 5 to 10 per cent of all peasants suffered. Their confiscated property was given to the common fund of the *kolkhosi* : the kulaks and their entire families were packed off to Siberia, to concentration camps and to exile. The same fate was reserved for anyone who made the slightest gesture or spoke the least word against the Government policy. This latter type of victim soon outnumbered the real kulaks.

Before March 2nd, people had been forced to go into the collective farms. This was done as follows : a representative from town would come and say, " Those who want to go into the collective farms stand on the left and those who want to go to Siberia stand on the right." This method was now denounced as abuse of power on the part of the administration. Henceforward, a ' strictly voluntary ' collectivization was demanded. " Don't touch the peasants (except the kulaks), do not threaten them, but drive them into a position in which they cannot go on living as they are and they will come to the collective farms on their own initiative." That was called ' encouraging the collective movement ', ' helping the peasants to build up a new life '. Paraffin, sugar, industrial produce, agricultural implements were sold only to members of collective farms.

The private farmers could obtain nothing. On the other hand, they had to pay crushing taxes and hand over exorbitant quantities of wheat. If they could not meet these demands, all their property was confiscated and they were sent into exile. If they owned good land, the village Soviet would take it away from them and give them in return mediocre fields, far distant from their homes. Their children were not admitted to the various courses and schools of the village, only the children of members of collective farms being admitted. If they complained of this policy to their friends or at meetings, or if they as much as spoke up in their own houses, they were arrested as kulak sympathizers and sent to concentration camps or into exile, and all their possessions were confiscated.

Part of this confiscated property was transferred to the *kolkhosi* ; but often, too often, this property was merely taken by local Communists. If the dissatisfied peasants began to make mass protests, even if their dissatisfaction was but obliquely expressed, a few were immediately executed by a firing-squad, " to soothe spirits ", and the others were scattered far and wide. The district ' triumvirates ' of the G.P.U. had, at that time, the right to execute anyone on the spot, not only without any form of trial whatsoever—the G.P.U. had always had and still has the right to execute without trial—but even to do so without referring to the higher authorities of the G.P.U., as was usually demanded.

Usually the 'dekulakization' and the sending of peasants into exile took place at the same time. A band of conscripts and G.P.U. soldiers would surround houses according to a preconceived plan, or even a whole village, and would leave after a few hours, taking with them from fifty to two hundred people to be sent into exile. The representatives of the *kolkhosi* or of the rural Soviet would then immediately take charge of the property of the 'dekulaked' peasants. The victims were allowed to take with them no more than a crust of bread. A number of them would be shot in situ to encourage the militant collectivists and to terrorize their adversaries.

I must add that part of the kulak population succeeded in maintaining itself by all sorts of stratagems, and even managed to become members of collective farms. In a country where there exists no workers' democracy, where the masses have no control over the authorities, where the workers can do nothing on their own initiative, where all rights and all power belong to the administration, in such a country the relations between a kulak and the local administration are factors that weigh heavier than the fact of his being a kulak.

Similar reasons made it possible for the bureaucratic powers to persecute and exterminate people who did not bask in their favour, even if they belonged to the middle or to the indigent strata of the peasantry. It was sufficient if such were declared kulaks or kulak sympathizers. There was no one to whom appeals could be made, the administration being both prosecutor and judge, as well as dictator to the Press. As to the mass meetings, at them only opinions demanded in high quarters were allowed to be voiced.

The news from the countryside during April and May of 1930 made one see that the Party was continuing its policy of collectivization and that the March retreat had been a stratagem of Stalin's, and a successful stratagem at that. Collectivization was becoming more and more consolidated, and the new agricultural system was beginning to function. I had conversations with some ten rural Communists, or urban ' representatives ' sent to villages. They all proclaimed the greatest optimism and a feeling of victory, " The peasants have been curbed into collectivization." I also spoke to peasants and workers with relatives in the country. The impression I received concerning their attitude was, " Why worry, you can't do anything against force."

How was it possible ? A short while since, the peasant revolt was overspreading the whole land. A slight attenuation of the form of pillage and exploitation had sufficed for the villages to be ready to submit to the experiment. Had it been a revolt of despair, a revolt to preserve the last sack of corn, a last chicken ? Were 130,000,000 peasants going to submit, provided their last chicken was not to be taken from them ?

The situation could not be explained solely by the effects of the Terror. I heard incredible stories of the hopes raised among peasants by collectivization. With collectivization, technical civilization penetrated into the backward rural districts of Russia. Wireless and cinema came to villages that were without a school the day before ; where the plough was still unknown and the earth was broken with the aid of the ancestral hoe, tractors made their appearance. The people were dazzled. Countless factories were rising, armies of tractors, cars, unheard-of agricultural machines were to make their appearance in the village, along with piles of artificial manure. Postal and telephone service, medical service, agrarian experts, machinery and tractor stations, all sorts of courses and schools were introduced. All this could not fail deeply to impress the creative instinct of the masses, to fan the ancient hope of a better life in those villages that had suffered so much during the NEP.

From now onwards, a new road, though strewn with terrible sacrifices, lay open before the peasants. The storm of collectivization was clearing new horizons. Horror and hope were born at the same instant. How was it possible not to be swept along by expectation, all the more as all resistance threatened to carry the rebel off to death by starvation in the virgin forest of the great Soviet North ? Forced to make a choice, most farmers wavered, then submitted.

During April and May, 1930, I understood that no power could prevent the transformation of the petty, backward peasant economy into a mighty agrarian State economy, founded on the *kolkhosi*.

Apart from terror and technical progress, bureaucratic

collectivization found an ally in the social situation of the ancient Russian village with its class antagonisms. The traditions of the rural Russian communities and the primitive collectivism of the peasants contributed mightily to the success of collectivization. The Russian villages had never liked the capitalist peasant, the kulak, growing rich at the expense of the *mir* (village community). Bureaucracy had succeeded in exploiting this hatred for its own profit and had availed itself of this rural community instinct, at one time expressed in Tchernychevsky's programme. It often happens that the revolutionary hopes of a people are realized in a reactionary form.

The hatred felt for the kulak was the factor in the rural community not only linking the middle layers of the village, but also the poorest layers and the day-labourers, the immediate victims of the kulak. The latter farmed the land of the poorest and took the day-labourers into his service. The anti-kulak feelings of the latter element weighed heavily in the issue of the struggle between kulaks and bureaucracy, especially in those regions where community life was little developed and where kulak capitalism had made great strides and as a result the resistance to the bureaucratic collectivization was particularly bitter (the Ukraine, the Northern Caucasus and Siberia).

Agrarian collectivization was being brought about by a series of complex and often contradictory measures. To the *kolkhosi* were given the lands and cattle of the kulaks. They could have them for the taking. The rest would be worked out later. Machines made their entry into the village, rural economy was approaching that of industry, country life that of towns. The new economy upset all routine, elevated the lowest levels of the population and absorbed part of them into the administrative staff. For a middle peasant it was an undeniable rise in the world to become the president of a *kolkhos*, or even a brigade- or field-leader. Vast possibilities of action rose before him and his organizing faculties were developed. A poor young peasant, by becoming a tractor-driver, rose in the social scale. Yet he only changed his master, for instead of being a labourer in the service of the kulak, he became a salaried worker of the bureaucracy. The vast majority of the people remained as obscure as they had always been. The day-labourers of the collective farms were as cruelly exploited as ever and their condition recalled that of the former serfs.

The fruits of the labour of the collective farms, exactly as were those of industry, were snatched away by the bureaucracy, from the lowest employees of the *kolkhos* (or of the factory) to the crested bureaucrats of the Kremlin. The degree of exploitation to which the various groups of workers were subjected varied as much as did the privileges enjoyed by the various strata of the bureaucracy itself. But that made no difference to the fundamental division of the country into two camps : on the one hand, the hard-working and exploited masses, on the other the exploiting leaders.

I will cite two concrete examples to illustrate the very peculiar and in a way favourable attitude adopted by the lower levels in the country towards the new bureaucratic policy.

A short while before my arrest in May, 1930, I received several letters from a friend in the country ; he was not a Communist but a non-Party member, of democratic leanings, who had been given the task of organizing the health services in a village of the Valdai region in the province of Leningrad. My correspondent was very touched by the gratitude shown him by the members of the *kolkhosi* ; the latter were absolutely taken aback at finding that the town had thought of them, that the Leningrad hospital had provided them, free of charge, with medical aid and children's cots for the village crèche. He described the crowd of peasants, standing round the medical centre he had just organized, greybeards from distant villages. " It is the first time in my life " he wrote, " that I find myself useful to the people." What a contrast to the horrors that had been reported to me from other sources. Yet these contradictory reports were both equally true, both assistance and destruction were being doled out to the villages, civilization and exploitation marching hand in hand.

The general feeling among the peasants of the *kolkhosi* of the Valdai district could be put as follows : " We are poor ; we have nothing to lose ; the Government promises us a better life. Who knows ? Maybe it will come ; we will put ourselves in its hands and we will attempt the experiment." The peasants did not consider collectivization something of their own, their own creation as it were, but an enterprise demanded by the Government, to which they were prepared to submit. The peasant masses of the *kolkhosi* knew themselves to be clay in the hands of the administration and they resigned themselves to that part. That was the new and very unambiguous impression that arose from the simple and direct tales of my correspondent. The Valdai district was exceedingly poor. In the richer regions, in particular in the Ukraine, in the Northern Caucasus and in Siberia, this tendency was much less pronounced ; more hopes had been built on private capitalist development and more resistance was offered to the establishment of a rural State economy. But the tendencies I have just described were also in existence there ; they contributed to the final victory of collectivization.

The *kolkhosi* of Valdai, my correspondent wrote me, waited with impatience for the arrival of tractors and other agricultural machinery. They had not yet come, but rumours of their imminent arrival, strengthened by news from other districts, produced continual excitements. The feelings of the peasants towards machinery had something in common with those of the old Red Indians towards the ships and the guns of Christopher Columbus. Did not the captains of the Five Year Plan bear a resemblance to the ships' captains of Cortés ? Was there not the same thirst for pillage and conquest under a guise that was sometimes ingenuous and sometimes had the cynicism of Christian—or Communist— missionary activity ? Both ancient and modern conquistadors brought not only guns and blood but also a new order, more oppressive but on a higher level than the old. The conquerors did not bring happiness to the people, they brought them civilization.

These reflections, this interpretation of the Five Year Plan, were in direct contradiction to the official theories of Stalinism, as well as to those of the Trotskyist Opposition. Trotskyism as well as Stalinism saw in these events only a struggle between two social orders : proletariat versus bourgeoisie, the latter embracing the kulaks and the relics of the former ruling classes. As for me, I had come to the conclusion that three social systems were partaking in the struggle : State capitalism, private capitalism and socialism, and that these three systems represented three classes : the bureaucracy, the bourgeoisie (including the kulaks) and the proletariat. The difference lay in that Stalinists and Trotskyists saw State capitalism as socialism and bureaucracy as proletariat. Trotsky as well as Stalin wished to pass off the State as being the proletariat, the bureaucratic dictatorship over the proletariat as the proletarian dictatorship, the victory of State capitalism over both private capitalism and socialism as a victory of the latter. The difference between Trotsky and Stalin lay in the fact that in this victory Stalin saw the triumph of pure socialism, pure dictatorship of the proletariat, whereas Trotsky perceived and stressed the gaps and bureaucratic deformations of the system.

It is true that I still underestimated the extent of my differences with Trotskyism ; it seemed to me that I had merely gone beyond it and that our differences were but of a temporary nature.

I hoped the Opposition would overtake me. The experience of subsequent years showed me the strength of the organic bonds that united the Trotskyist Opposition with the bureaucratic régime of the Soviets ; these bonds were too tight to allow the Trotskyist to cover the distance separating a bureaucratic clique of the Left and a revolutionary struggle of the masses.

I ascribed still less importance to my disagreement with the leaders of the Trotskyist Opposition concerning the practical value of Stalinist collectivization. At that time, Trotsky was accusing Stalin of ' ultra-Left-wing ' opinions and of ' adventurism ' for having given the word for collectivization and integral dekulakization. I had no such objections to Stalin's agrarian policy which, in my opinion, was anyhow by no means socialist. But on the other hand, his policy seemed one of entire realism to me, taking into account the conflict that had arisen between the bureaucracy and the kulaks. From the point of view of the interests of the bureaucrats in office, it was even the only possible course of action. As for the prophecies of Rakovsky, who in the spring of 1930 declared that there would be nothing left of all this collectivization by the autumn of the same year, they appeared to me destitute of all grounds.

IX

THE WORKERS AND THE FIVE YEAR PLAN

THE life of the workers in Leningrad was far from providing so many new data as did peasant life and the experiment of collectivization.

That was natural. In rural economy, new social relations were being created. The technical revolution was accompanied by an economic and social revolution. The village was undergoing a crisis greater than that of the October revolution. Russia and the entire world were present at the formation—or rather at the downward construction—of a new and original rural economy, which was in many respects different from anything the world had ever seen before. Little islands of social life were emerging from a sea of blood, causing the rise of many new theoretical problems. A new sociological and philosophical significance had to be draped round these novelties.

During the course of the October revolution, the peasants had liquidated 30,000 estates of the big landowners, who between them had held half the Russian soil ; then they had shared out the private lands, the secular as well as the ecclesiastical estates. Now the task was to liquidate from ten to twenty million peasant holdings out of the 25,000,000 that existed in Russia. It was necessary to share them out between a few hundred thousand *kolkhosi*, controlled by a few thousand machinery and tractor stations belonging to the State. Whatever the importance of the ' spontaneous sharing out ' of October may have been, it had been infinitely simpler to carry out than the present collectivization. It is indeed easier to divide 30,000 large estates than to fuse ten to twenty million peasant holdings. It is easier to expropriate the possessions of a few hundred thousand noblemen than those of a hundred million peasants. The agrarian October revolution had been relatively simple, for it had made no alterations in the agricultural technique and had even allowed a retrogression in that technique. Now there was an agrarian revolution that demanded the application of the most modern technical methods, methods that, in the majority of cases, were still unknown at the time of collectivization.

Yet another difference consisted in the fact that during the October revolution, the expropriation of the aristocracy went hand in hand with its exclusion from rural economy. Collectivization demanded on the other hand the re-adaptation of the ancient type of peasant to a new life as worker in the *kolkhos*, an essential part in the rural productive scheme. To get him there, terror and technique were insufficient ; there was also needed a certain minimum of willingness on the part of the peasants.

This revolution was far more difficult to carry out than the one that took place in England in the days of " enclosures ", when the peasants were robbed of their land to transform it into manorial pastures and the peasants simply driven from their homes in an attempt to eliminate them.

The world had already seen agrarian revolutions analogous to the October one ; its theoretical significance had been studied beforehand. The agrarian revolution of collectivization was a new factor in the world and put an entirely new social and economic problem to this same world.

During the winter of 1929–30, this problem had become extremely acute. Collectivization was far from having been achieved, but a struggle for life was already opposing the ancient to the new economic system. It was not difficult to foresee that a compromise was henceforth impossible and that one of the two systems must triumph completely over the other. It became a matter of the greatest urgency to solve the following theoretical problem : what form was the new economic and social system to take if it was no longer to be based on the private economy of bourgeois capitalism but entirely on exploitation and on a division into a hierarchy of classes, thereby becoming unable to show a classless socialism ? The enormous surface of land involved, and the preponderance of agriculture in the country, made the question one of world-importance, not only in its theoretical but also in its practical aspects.

The industrial development of Russia, on the very contrary, put forward no problems of this sort, no entirely new theoretical social problems. I do not mean to imply on that score that industrialization contained no elements of greatness nor of novelty. Within the Russian framework, it was equivalent to a truly technical and economic revolution. It also modified to a certain extent the economic world-picture. The industrialization of the Ural, of Central Asia and, above all, of Siberia created economic centres of world importance. A new America, as greedy and as dynamic as the old, was born on the immensity of Eastern Europe and Northern Asia, six to seven thousand miles long and two to three thousand miles wide. The industrialization of European and Asiatic Russia is of fundamental importance to the historic progress of the Asiatic continent ; for the economic, social and political revolution that is ripening throughout Asia.

At the same time as the already existing metallurgic industry was growing and new metallurgic bases were being built (Magnitogorsk and Kuznetsk), new branches of industry were being created : the construction of machines, tractors, industrial cars ; aeronautics and chemistry, creation or remodelling of metal works. Industrialization was at the basis of the agrarian revolution, of mechanization and of the collectivization of rural economy. Simultaneously, this rural economy was drawing nearer to industry, and equally the countryside was drawn nearer to the towns ; industry as such was gaining in importance in the general picture of national economy.

But however great the national and international significance of this industrialization was, it introduced no new principles into the social structure of industry itself and produced no new theoretic problem. The immense and rapid growth of industry, the development of old factories and the creation of entire new branches of industry only reproduced on a larger scale the relations that existed in industry before the Five Year Plan. Hence, observing the life of the workers in Leningrad, I was unable to add to what I saw in the course of my three years' stay in Russia.

But—and here is one of Russia's so frequent contradictions —the fact itself that the social relations in industry had not been transformed was an enigma worth solving. The most various capitalist and bureaucratic phenomena that presented themselves in Soviet industry had always been attributed to the influence of capitalist and petit-bourgeois elements, or had been explained as inevitable but temporary concessions to these elements, the influence of which was great during the days of the NEP, and the legal existence of which had been officially recognized. Now that the NEP was being liquidated, private capitalism extirpated, the petit-bourgeoisie mercilessly destroyed, these capitalist and bureaucratic phenomena should, if logic were right, have automatically disappeared and made way for a socialist organization of industrial production.

In actual fact, nothing of the sort was happening. Capitalist and bureaucratic methods were stiffening : piecework, separation of labour and administration, concentration of all directing functions in the hands of the administration, the reduction of the functions of the workers to that of simple execution of orders, consolidation of the salary system, growing inequality of wages in favour of the bureaucrats.

All this showed that the bureaucratic and capitalist characteristics of the Soviet State industry were not solely due to the influence of the relics of the old private capitalism, but constituted the organic basis of this State industry.

Thus it was to industry as well as to agriculture, that is, to the sum total of Soviet economy, that the question applied as to which was the new social and economic system that, no longer being private capitalism, was not socialism either.

The more I studied the feelings of the workers, the more urgent it appeared to find the answer to the above question.

An old skilled workman from one of the principal Leningrad factories told me, " We live worse now than at the time of the capitalists. If we had had to face such starvation, if our salaries had been so low in the days of our old masters, we would have gone on strike a thousand times. But what can we do now ? It was we who wanted Soviet rule, how can we now fight it ? If we went on strike at present, our own wives would laugh at us and say, ' There you are, with your Soviet rule ! ' "

When the 25,000 manual workers were enrolled for work in the country, this old workman signed up as a volunteer. He came back disgusted after a few months. " There are too many injustices ; it is not collectivism, it is pillage." As a skilled workman, he demanded no privileges from the Government, he felt safeguarded by his qualifications and in a way independent. He was a non-Party member, but he had spent several years at the front during the Civil War. The fear and the bewilderment that now held him in their grip seemed to reflect the sentiments of the deepest strata of the proletariat. " We have taken the wrong turning," was the conclusion they drew from the revolution. Towards the end of the Five Year Plan, at the time of the ' better life ' proclaimed by the bureaucracy, these strata of the population were fully aware of the real nature of the present system of the U.S.S.R.

I heard similar reflections from the mouth of a foreign Communist worker employed in the textile industry. Of Southern origin, he expressed his feelings with greater passion. " Never in my life have I known such slavery as there is in my factory. If such a thing existed in a bourgeois country, I would have thrown a bomb at it a long time ago ! " But in Russia he did nothing of the sort, for he saw no way out : the mass of the workers was passive, and authority, was it not ' our authority ' ? In despair he was trying to get back to his own country ; there at least he would know against whom and how to fight. He obtained his permit to leave only with the greatest difficulty, for his ' lack of enthusiasm for the Soviet system ' was well known. Nowadays, although he has lost his faith, he continues to work in the official Communist Party. At any rate, no one could think out a better system, he told me after my return to Europe.

I also remember a conversation with a manual worker who had done some repairs to my room. Having gone to his home to pay him, I found him absorbed in reading a newspaper. I scarcely knew him and asked him, " What do the papers say ? " He pointed to the tidings concerning the limitation of social legislation in Germany which the Soviet Press had transformed into an abolition of social insurances. " Just like it is in this country," the workman said without further comment. That simplicity and that sincerity told more than a long discourse on the feelings that Soviet bureaucracy inspired in the workers. My humble workman seemed to imply the discouraged view that it was not he alone who thought so, but everyone.

At that time it was officially announced that unemployment was ' liquidated ' in Soviet Russia. The result of that announcement was that all unemployment benefits were equally ' liquidated '. Moreover, a number of regulations protecting the workers had been curtailed. Newspapers, on the other hand, violently attacked those workers who, in some way or other, put up a resistance to bureaucratic exploitation, declaring them to be ' undisciplined, lazy and drunken '. Under the guise of ' socialist emulation ' a sweating system was introduced, combined with the corruption of a small workers' minority by means of all sorts of ' advancements '.

A worker with whom I discussed the possibilities of fomenting a factory-strike spoke to me in a way which threw a very clear light on such a policy. He was a man of well-considered opinions, a non-Party worker and a genuine proletarian. Knowing his inclinations, the bureaucrats had already attempted to buy him over and force him to accept the post of syndicate representative of the corporation to which he belonged. He found it very difficult to shake off this attempt to enlist him into the administrative apparatus ; it was not easy to refuse such a post when the general meeting of the workers, called on the initiative of a straw man of the administration, decided that " you, the best worker among us," had to become the representative of the syndicate, or an *udarnik* (a shock-brigader), or a member of the Party. Plebiscite lies and violence penetrated the entire social life of Soviet Russia.

The above-mentioned worker considered that the main obstacle in the way of so vast a labour as the preparation of a strike was not so much the G.P.U. as the attitude of the mass of the workers.

" One can have no confidence in the worker. Today he is your brother, tomorrow he will betray you. He works with you in the same corporation, at the next bench ; he thinks and speaks as you do ; he sees that the workers have been let down, that their life is wretched, that they are being tyrannized. But tomorrow, as soon as he is given a little advancement, a little bone to gnaw, as it were, or a little rise, his speech will change and he will bray at meetings as if he had always been a bureaucrat. If he is spoken to as man to man, and is reproached for his conduct, he answers with insolence, ' I do as everyone else does.' Confide in those people ? You will lose yourself without advancing the cause in the slightest."

One question was tormenting this intelligent proletarian : where lies the origin of the curse that weighs on the working class ? After all these revolutions, there always seems to be someone left to exploit him, to benefit by his labour. In order to think things over together, to seek an answer to the essential question of our times, this worker was ready to run the risk of mixing with my comrades and myself.

As to this, I should like to tell of an incident of which I heard later, when I was already in prison. It had taken place in Moscow, in 1927, at the height of the struggle against the Left-wing Opposition. Most of the workers in a tanning factory were in sympathy with the Opposition and used to go with great pleasure to the forest-trips organized by this Opposition. To win the workers over to its own side, the bureau of the Communist Cell of the works acted as follows : it put up a poster asking workers to put in applications for the posts of jurymen. The ' strengthening of the working element ' in the administration was the order of the day and a promise had been made that three jurymen would be taken from that particular factory. It was obvious that this was nothing but a demagogic manœuvre, yet ninety candidates handed in their names, though there were only three places going. The Opposition trips were dropped.

In Leningrad I came across a similar case, only of greater complexity. Two Trotskyist workers were employed in the same factory. One of them, young and unqualified, suddenly enrolled as one of the 25,000 to be sent into the countryside. He communicated his decision to his comrade. The latter wanted to dissuade him from it, for, he said, the members of the Opposition should never endorse Stalin's policy. The young worker first made theoretical objections. The Opposition had demanded the offensive against the kulaks : it was essential therefore to join in whether Stalin was leading the offensive or not. Then he came to the immediate motives of his conduct : as a non-qualified worker, he found it difficult to feed his wife and child. If he went to the village, his wife would draw all his wages and he would be fed and would receive further wages in kind. Upon his return, the syndicate would send him to classes in order to let him perfect himself in his craft, or would even admit him to a school. He did not think he was deserting the Opposition ; he was giving himself some time until the day when conditions would be more favourable for a political struggle. As long as the masses remained inert, he saw no harm in improving his own lot.

A Trotskyist capitulater, an engineer of the Putilov factory, mentioned an interesting case to me in which the workers took a favourable attitude towards Stalin's policy of collectivization. One of the 25,000 had been killed ; ten volunteers offered to replace him. Among them was one of the oldest workers in the factory. My informant quoted the case to prove that the mass of the workers was supporting Stalin's policy and that the Opposition should do the same. This addition limited the scope of his statement, but the fact remained authentic. This example, together with those I gave before, shows how complex the situation was and that the workers' attitude towards Stalin's ' Left-wing policy ' was far from uniform.

Another story told me by the same engineer will confirm that. At a Communist meeting, an old worker declared, " We know that evil is spoken of those whose very policy is being carried out today. We shall support you, all the same. But don't think that we are ignorant of what is going on."

On the other hand, a large number of Leningrad workers expressed so-called peasant sentiments, i.e. sentiments of hostility towards the anti-peasant policy of the bureaucracy. " What does this policy bring us ? Hunger, and nothing else," were sentences often heard in the mouths of the workers. Sometimes social arguments were added : " Where is this famous alliance between workers and peasants, since everything is taken away from the peasants ? " or " That the kulaks should be tracked down, right ! But why the whole village ? "

I had a chance to see how the Russian social-democrats were fought within the factories. The case of which I knew was in the telephone factory, ' Red Dawn '. The factory workers were very discontented with the cost of living, the scarcity of goods and the deplorable wage-level. The bureau of the Communist Cell said that this discontent was kept alive by a group of skilled workers who at one time were active social-democrats and now were non-Party members. The bureau feared that the discontent might take the form of a strike. To avert this danger the help of the syndicate organization was invoked in waging a campaign to ' unmask the counter-revolutionary part played by social-democracy in the service of capitalism '. A meeting was devoted to this subject, as well as several copies of the wall newspaper. To my great astonishment, neither the articles nor the speeches of the official mouthpieces attempted to oppose the conceptions of revolution and reform. They limited themselves to forging lies adorned with the name of ' revolutionary truths ' to pit against the reformers. " Only counter-revolutionaries can say that the conditions of the working class are growing worse," the official orators proclaimed. It was the chorus of all speeches and all articles, yet this ' counter-revolutionary calumny ' was truth itself.

No refutation whatsoever, we said, was given of the principle of social-democrat reform. It seemed sufficient to call it demagogy and to utter direct threats against the social-democrat workers in the factory and to have recourse to the most repulsive forms of intimidation. Seeing these things, I felt the abyss separating us from the Communism of officialdom.

Here are a few more examples of the attitude of the foreign workers towards the Soviet system. K——, whom I had known for a long time, was entirely satisfied. Of peasant origin, he had been a manual worker and a member of the Comsomol. During the few years of his stay in Russia, he had succeeded as well as was possible in finishing his academic studies. Now he had become a teacher in a secondary school and had married a very charming young woman graduate of Moscow University. He had grown rotund and beamed with happiness. He had been through ' his ' social revolution and was full of a special kind of optimism : since he had made his way, why couldn't others do as much ? " All one wants is time and patience."

A young foreign worker astonished me by his incorruptibility. He did not wish to see anything wrong in Soviet Russia, but neither would he allow himself to be carried away. He was burning with the sole desire to return to Europe and resume the struggle.

A third, a convinced revolutionary, had a more critical spirit. One day he went to White Russia on business for the MOPR (International Association for Assistance to Revolutionaries in other countries). He could have crossed the border and gone into Poland. As he did not have permission to return to Europe, for he belonged to the Left-wing, the temptation was great, but he resisted it. On his return to Leningrad, he explained his attitude as follows : " The authority of Russia is stronger in the eyes of the Russian workers than mine is. I may be right a thousand times over, but whatever I may say, I shall remain suspect in the eyes of the workers if I run away from Soviet Russia."

A fairly well-known German engineer had passed through a stormy evolution. A sympathizer with Communism, he had come to Russia in 1923 after the German catastrophe. He was now a member of the Leningrad Soviet as a representative of the group of engineers and technicians of his trust. His stay in Russia had transformed his opinions. The numerous cases of bureaucratic conservatism, of negligence, waste and bad output which he had been able to observe better than anyone else, proved to him the inability of the proletariat to govern itself. He could not forgive the ' proletarian dictatorship ' for the humiliating conditions it had imposed on engineers and technicians. " At a meeting a workman will get up and shout and gesticulate, ' We workers . . .' It is perfectly obvious that the man is an ignorant fool, spouting forth utter nonsense ; yet one can't answer him, for he is the boss."

This situation appeared to him not only unjust but contrary to historical development. Social and economic evolution tend to reduce the importance of the proletariat in favour of the engineers and technicians. Aeronautics and chemical industry were no exceptions from this point of view, but models for all branches of evolution. Even the absolute figures of worker population were on the decline in America, and America was the vanguard of modern humanity. History refuted the *schema* of Marx concerning the continued numerical growth of the working class. The engineer ended by saying that the government of the world ought to belong not to the manual workers but to the engineers and technicians. Mentioning the faults of Soviet industry, he concluded : " If we were in power, we would do everything better and in a more economic and civilized way."

One day I found him bursting with indignation. " Look at your system ! " he cried. " The G.P.U. have sent one of the engineers of our trust into exile, an excellent man he is, and an excellent engineer. The G.P.U. asked him to become a spy and he refused. As a result he has been exiled for three years to a forgotten corner of Central Asia, near the Chinese frontier. He is condemned to rot there, just because he refused to be a *provocateur*. Show me an example of the proletariat behaving better than did their ruling classes ! "

He took great care of the affairs of his trust and seemed to live only for his work. The chairman of the trust, a Communist, filled him with admiration. " He is a fine boss, he holds them all in the hollow of his hand—economists, engineers, the chairman of the syndicate, the secretary of the Party Cell—he dominates them all. Without the revolution, he would undoubtedly have become a great captain of industry ; he was born to the part."

He entirely approved of the Five Year Plan, and patiently, with full conviction, explained the realist character of the industrialization plan to me. " It coincides with Russia's economic needs, and the Government will shrink from no sacrifice to carry it out. No doubt it will never be accomplished in entirety, but the essentials will."

During the last conversation that I had with this engineer, just before my arrest, I noted an interesting evolution in his opinions. " I see," he said, " that I wrongly accused the workers. They are the victims of the system just as much as we are. They are allowed to let off steam about unimportant details, but fundamentally they are deprived of all rights and all power, although all action is taken in their name. I had mistaken the rule of the Communist Party for that of the proletariat. That was the ambiguity of the situation."

To what did his new attitude amount ? To oppose to the workers' Communism bureaucratic Communism, or to make use of the workers' discontent in the struggle which opposes to the technical bureaucracy its competitor, Communist bureaucracy ? The latter hypothesis was probably the right one.

Here is another striking story. It deals with a German worker, a supporter of Brandler. He was an old social-democrat, who, since pre-War days, had shown Left tendencies. From the beginning of the revolution, he had belonged to the Communist Party. After 1923 he was sent to Russia to be cured of his ' Brandlerian opportunism '. He had worked at the Comintern for some time, then had gone into a factory. Working conditions in Soviet factories appalled him. These conditions were still worse than those he had fought against in Germany. What depressed him most was that all workers were systematically searched upon leaving the factory. " I felt this to be both for myself and for the Russian workers a humiliation such as I had never felt before. How we had to strive in Germany before this sort of thing was abolished." But he could not bring himself to protest openly, for, he said, " there really were cases when workers stole things ". Torn between the wish to protest against the system and that of justifying it by taking particular Russian conditions into account, he decided to return to Germany. He did not succeed in settling there ; he had lost the art of living as a simple workman, and apart from that he found the German Communist Party torn by internal dissensions. Abandoning the struggle, he returned to Russia. In 1930, in Leningrad, he occupied the post of factory director. It was his turn now to have the workers searched.

The Five Year Plan produced, at first, certain phenomena that seemed to indicate that Russia was really tending towards socialism. Books and newspapers sometimes asserted that money and the commercial exchange of merchandise were going to disappear. In a number of factories there were groups of workers, whole teams or even entire workshops that received collective wages which they then shared out in equal parts among the various workers. That was a sort of ' common pot '. It was hailed as the future method of liquidating the wage-problem, this ' infamous system of mercenary slavery '. But it was obvious that these were only ephemeral phenomena, for they were in flagrant opposition to the general tendency of Soviet society, the foundations of which were hierarchy and exploitation. In actual fact, a rapid end was made to these forms of initiative, and they were declared to be ' extreme Left-wing deviations '. Their temporary appearance says quite enough about the hopes and illusions bureaucracy offered the workers in order to turn the revolutionary and creative instincts of the masses to account.

X

THE DOMINANT CLASS AND ITS TRUE VISAGE

THE close contact I had with the Communist bureaucracy in Leningrad completed in a way my observations of the social conditions in Russia. This contact revealed to me, under the mask of official phrases, the true visage of bureaucracy and contributed to the formation of my definite judgement on Soviet society as a whole. It was not sufficient to know the life and conditions of the lower strata of that society. One could always explain away the oppression and the sufferings of the masses by having recourse to temporary and apparently ' objective ' causes. These explanations were patently false, but it was difficult to brush them aside before having studied the lives of the real instigators, the real masters of Soviet society : the bureaucrats, the high officials.

Observing the milieu in which I belonged in Leningrad was particularly instructive. My comrades and I, as I have already mentioned, were living at the Party House, where the Communist *élite* of Leningrad lived, to begin with Kirov, the Party secretary, and Komarov, the chairman of the Leningrad Soviet. Here Zinoviev had resided with his staff, some of whom were still living in the building. This Communist *élite* had installed itself in the Party House from the days of the October revolution. The immensity of the building made it possible for new officials to be put up there, without causing any inconvenience to the old ones. This again made it possible to study, as if in a laboratory, a ' pure culture of bureaucrats ' in successive stages from the revolution to the present phase. The number of bureaucracy's most typical representatives, each of whom showed a different stage of development, was a guarantee against all hasty generalizations.

I have no wish to show the private or sensational side of my observations, but merely their social aspect. In this milieu, all these families had something in common and belonged to the same social and psychological type. They formed an aristocracy of the ' new rich '. I knew, of course, that they belonged to the new privileged class, but what was new to me was that they were fully conscious of it and were permeated with the spirit of hierarchy and caste. That was an important detail which forced itself upon me from the beginning.

Most of these families were of working class or artisan origin. Their members, sprung from the people, retained, in their speech, manners and facial expressions, the imprint of their past, yet how cold and haughty was their attitude towards the workers.

They had consideration for none but those who occupied a dominant place in society. He who ' with us, in Soviet Russia,' had not succeeded in rising was an inferior being, a worthless man. A man's worth was measured by the elegance of the holidays he could afford, by his apartment, his furniture, his clothes and the position he occupied in the administrative hierarchy. The new privileged class was subdivided into strata that were invisible to the outsider, but that were carefully distinguished. It was not merely strict hierarchy. People belonging to the same hierarchic stratum were still differentiated in accordance with all sorts of criteria : their seniority, the way in which they had formed their career, their social and political biography. The solidarity that linked the members of each stratum was directed only towards the lower strata ; within the privileged class, the groups waged an insidious and malevolent strife. It reminded me of the heinous struggle described by Dreiser in his *Financier*, a struggle opposing the various groups of the upper bourgeoisie in accordance with their degree of wealth and the way in which that wealth had been acquired. Is it not astonishing that when the best writers of Europe and America, cognizant of the finest shades of hierarchic difference within bourgeois society, come to Russia, they fail to notice that these same social differences are bringing about a changed Soviet Russia ?

The differentiation of the bureaucratic *élite* was made on yet another plane : the husbands, the wives and the children constituted three groups, each with its own standards. The husbands had a developed sense of diplomacy, they were

not assertive and did not fail to remember to ' keep in contact with the masses ', nor to keep up proletarian and
revolutionary appearances. They expressed themselves in
cautious terms. The women had no such considerations.
Their only thought was to dazzle people with their clothes,
their box at the theatre, the elegance of their homes, their
descriptions of their holidays at such or such a watering-
place or of their journey abroad. They were conscious of
belonging to ' Society ', and lived only for their petty
ambitions. One of these ladies told me about her journey
to the Caucasus in the summer, and showed me photographs.
There she was, in the hall of the splendid hotel where she
stayed ; this photograph showed her at the side of Budienny.
Her face clouded. " Yes, you can only see Budienny there,
Voroshilov was absent that day." The tone in which she
said this ! How her face beamed when we came to the
photograph that showed her at Voroshilov's side. Another
of these ladies, married to a prominent People's Commissar,
was a member of the Perfume Trust ; this detail was entirely
in keeping with the style of Soviet ' high society '. There
were ladies who took part in social work ; they struck
attitudes at the Committee meetings of the MOPR, just as
in the past countesses did at Red Cross meetings.

As to the children, they were very shocked by their parents'
hypocrisy. They wanted to call a spade a spade. " We
are boss here, why hide it ? " " Why not always dress in
smart clothes ? Why may one do it on certain occasions,
whereas on others one must dress with mock-modesty ?
Why not go out in the car, as we have one ? Why does
So-and-so take the children to school in a car, whereas father
refuses to take us ? " Revolutionary phraseology grated on
them, they hated hearing the word proletariat used over
and over again. They very much disliked going to the
meetings of the Pioneers and the Comsomol ; most of them
did not even belong to these organizations, the activities of
which seemed conventional and tedious to them. A boy of
fifteen, whose father, an old Bolshevik and a member of the
Central Executive Committee, was one of the ten most
important people in Leningrad, spoke to me as follows :
" I am neither for nor against the revolution ; I am a
pacifist." He was a very thoughtful boy in some ways, but
he preferred offering flowers to a Leningrad actress to other

activities. The son of another equally important official showed such violent anti-Semitism at school, that, not without fear and trembling, the school authorities decided to complain to his father. Another boy, son of a high official, ten years old, having quarrelled with a boy who lived in the neighbourhood and whose father occupied a less important post, said with contempt, " Who is your father ? He has not even a car ; mine has two, one for his work and one for us."

I knew of only one case in which the critical spirit of the children of high officials was of a Left-wing Opposition type. A little girl refused to belong to the Pioneers. " You say yourselves that Stalin is a disgusting person, but at the Pioneers one has to respect him. I don't want to do that." Her parents were sympathetic with the Trotskyist Opposition ; at their place, during meal-times, the Party leaders were often roundly abused, Stalin in particular. The little girl had heard the talk and had benefited from it. But the parents could not get over it. " There we have been in the Party for over twenty-four years, and now our only child refuses to join a proletarian organization."

From the political point of view, this milieu divided itself into two camps. The one contained the relics of the Zinoviev group, the other the Right-wing men of Leningrad who had come into power after Zinoviev's fall. Genuine Stalinists were rarely met with. Stalin's emissary, Kirov, was, in those circles, considered a stranger sent by Moscow to keep them quiet and prevent them from reaping all the benefits of the victory over Zinoviev. Kirov reigned over the Party House and over the town, but remained in isolation, as a foreign conqueror who cannot pretend to either the love or the fidelity of the local administration. That did not prevent Stalin and Kirov from ill-treating the Right-wing Opposition in Leningrad, from removing some of its members from their posts and transferring others from their Leningrad ' hornets' nest ' to Moscow. Kirov was hated, therefore, with a hatred that was as fierce as it was impotent. Kirov's private life was the theme of all conversations at the Party House, and it must be admitted that this private life was not lacking its remarkable traits. I shall mention only one, because all Russia talked of it, and *Pravda* devoted an article to it. Kirov, going South, took two dogs with him ; he ordered the travellers out of one carriage to have it empty for his dogs. The article did not mention Kirov's name, and was passed by an oversight ; but the writer of it, Zoritch, lost his job on *Pravda*.

From where did the Communist bureaucrats get their means of existence ? Their salaries were relatively modest. They had therefore to devise another way. First they received payment in kind from the State. They paid a ridiculously low rent, and furniture, cars, holidays, theatres, books and children's education cost them nothing at all. Next they had introduced into the administration the tacit understanding that the shops should reserve for them the entire stock at their disposal of the first-rate goods from the factory or from the contraband confiscated in the harbour of Leningrad. When the food shortage began, this illegal but efficacious system spread gradually to foodstuffs. Later on the system was perfected and legalized by the creation of a distributive network reserved to the bureaucracy.

What struck me still more than the present life of the bureaucracy was what could be learned of its past, of its morals on the morrow of the October revolution. I could, by a stretch of the imagination, find a theoretical excuse for the abuses I could see at the moment, so many years after the revolution. But how was I to explain the abuses of the past ? The inhabitants of the Party House spoke of them now and again in tones of approbation, as if recalling pleasant memories. From the first days of the October revolution, the Communist leaders had shown a great lack of shame in these matters. Having occupied the building, they furnished it with the best furniture from shops that had been nationalized. From the same source their wives had procured themselves fur coats, each taking two or three at a time. All the rest was in keeping. Theoretically it was only the right of usufruct, but in my days it had been transformed into that of full ownership. If need be, the bureaucrats were now selling their extra furs and furniture. A short while after the revolution, the wife of a Communist leader received a diamond necklace for her birthday.

During the winter of 1930 fuel ran short and we had to do without hot water for a few days. The wife of a high official who lived at the Party House was full of indignation. " What a disaster to have this man Kirov ! True, Zinoviev is guilty of ' fractionism ', but in his day central heating always functioned properly and we were never short of hot water. Even in 1920, when they had to stop the factories in Leningrad for lack of coal, we could always have our hot baths with the greatest comfort."

Thus the leaders had managed from the very beginning, to the detriment of the revolution, whilst the masses, still full of energy, struggled and suffered for equality and socialism.

Another fact I had never before encountered made a very painful impression on me. At the beginning of the NEP, special ' triumvirates ' had been created to watch the improvement of industrial yields. One of the members of the triumvirate had to be a collaborator of the G.P.U., though usually appointed under another name. I was appalled. How could the work of the proletariat be organized with the help of the G.P.U., that is with the help of the police ? Had the G.P.U. been created to force the workers to work and, under the whiplash, increase their work ? Could the result not be achieved by normal means, that is by developing the workers' conscience, by making an appeal to their convictions, by setting up as examples the efforts of the best workers and the Communists ? I was all the more disturbed as this system of triumvirates was neither sporadic nor local. On the contrary, it had been instituted in virtue of a decision of the Central Party Committee with the approbation of both Lenin and Trotsky who were then at the head of the Government.

XI

THE OPPOSITION IN MOSCOW

THE great changes that had taken place in Russia in 1929 and 1930 did not fail to have their influence on our small Opposition group. We reflected in common on the experiment of the past year, on industrialization and collectivization, on the struggle that Stalin was leading against both Left-wing and Right-wing. Until the day of our arrest, we tried, between us, to extract the true meaning from events and to define to the best of our ability the new tasks that fell to the Opposition and to the Russian working class. And, be it understood, we did our utmost to act accordingly.

Our work was slow and difficult. Our total isolation, the entire absence of freedom of speech, writing, meeting and criticism were felt as severe handicaps. Finally, the inertia of the masses and the novelty of the problems with which we were faced were in themselves not less serious obstacles.

There are in Russia a great many small groups like ours, but they lack cohesion and hold the most diverse opinions. Russia digests her problems in secret, without causing the slightest movement of the masses. It is that which until now has enabled the Government to keep all this agitation away from public and lawful life.

The development and the fate of our group is but one particular example of that subterranean life of Soviet Russia, a subterranean life where are born the ideas and the new tendencies that will undoubtedly exert a great influence on the fate of Russia. Our own case may give the reader a fairly truthful picture of this less well-known aspect of Soviet life.

Out of the six members of our ' centre ', the Yugo-Slavs Draguitch, Heberling and myself and the two Russians Zankov and Glybovsky were advocates of a more energetic struggle against the Party leaders. The sixth member,

Deditch, was in favour of a more moderate policy. We, of course, had each our particular shade of opinion. Glybovsky had Right-wing, Zankov Left-wing sympathies, and Draguitch, Heberling and I occupied a more or less central position.

In April our respective positions had become firmer and we decided to act. On the 1st of May I went to Moscow with this end in view.

I first had some conversations with my friends of the ' centre ', then with those of cognate groups. It was decided that I was to draw up a thesis formulating the opinions and the aims of our movement.

The Moscow comrades were mostly in favour of undertaking large-scale activities in the factories, in publishing leaflets, creating extensive contacts among the workers and preparing strikes based on economic grievances, gradually introducing political slogans. On the whole, they preferred action to theory. There was only one comrade opposed to action. " We have demanded industrialization," he said. " Now it is being carried out we should not endanger it by strikes." We retorted that this industrialization was only strengthening the bureaucracy, that the re-establishment of a workers' rule was the preliminary condition for proletarian industrialization. He was not impressed by the argument. " I admit the shortcomings of the bureaucracy and the industrialization. But don't let us throw the baby away with the bath-water, don't abolish industrialization under pretext of abolishing bureaucracy."

In the end he left us. We felt the loss very much, for he was an excellent comrade and had a large apartment that he used to place at our disposal for our meetings.

All the others readily agreed on the necessity of taking action, of drawing up leaflets and preparing strikes ; but the difficulties began when we had to approach the question of a new Party and to define our attitude towards the economic problem and towards the Soviet State. Some of us thought that there still existed a dictatorship of the proletariat, though it had a bureaucratic slant ; others, that there was no real proletarian dictatorship left, but that there were relics of it or that the proletarian dictatorship was abolished but that its machinery, its methods, had been retained ; still others, that there was no dictatorship of the proletariat at all and that we were faced with a new social régime that was neither bourgeois nor proletarian. Opinions on Soviet economy were equally divergent ; socialist economy, transitional economy, typically bureaucratic economy, capitalist State economy. Everyone agreed about the necessity for a new Party, for experience had proved that the Russian Communist Party had become a mere instrument of the bureaucracy. Nobody had any doubts that the Party Congress that was to take place in July would unanimously reject the ' address ' of the Opposition. Most of us judged that that would be the moment to proclaim the slogan of the new Party. On the other hand, the minority believed in the necessity for waiting, for tactical reasons, as the mass of the Communist workers had not yet lost its faith in the Party ; the verdict of Trotsky and Radovsky had to be awaited.

Finally, our ' thesis ' formulated our attitude towards economy and the State and their class character in terms sufficiently general to be accepted by all, but yet containing the central points of the new Party as proposed by our majority. Stress was laid on the necessity for the organization of propaganda among the workers.

In that form, the ' thesis ' was adopted by our small group. Thus live, develop and work, each in its own field, the centres of opposition in Russia, groping their way along.

Having thus defined our task, we thought not only to become active in educational establishments, but also to influence the general organization of the Opposition in Moscow. To this end, Glybovsky and I, making use of our old contacts, went to see the representative of the Centre in Moscow. I expected to meet with great resistance because of our suggested radical reforms (new Party and strikes). But the representative, whilst reserving his final answer until the moment when the Moscow triumvirate should have examined them, declared he thought they were a basis for discussion. We also debated our favourite question of direct contact with Trotsky : one of my friends was shortly to leave for abroad and had agreed to place certain documents concerning the Comintern in Trotsky's hands.

Staying in Moscow, I had to call on certain officials. I had been suspended from the Party for one year only, and was soon to present myself before the Central Control Commission. " Do not imagine," they told me at the Comintern,

" that you will get away with it so easily this time. They will expect you to give them guarantees." I understood, then, that they knew more about me than I had thought.

I also went to see the representative of the Central Committee of the Yugo-Slav Party at the Comintern. I spoke to him of my approaching return to the Party and of my wish to go back to Yugo-Slavia. "The Central Committee is not keen on your return," he said openly, and then added, "Last year I thought your opposition concerned only the affairs of Yugo-Slavia, now I know that it concerns also the Comintern and the Russian Party. You are a Trotskyist." It was obvious to me that the storm was about to break over my head.

Next I went to an educational establishment where I had worked for some time in the past and where a group of my comrades had, for years, waged a determined fight against the bureaucracy and servility that prevailed there. The director of the establishment, anxious to avenge their 'offences', had persecuted my friends and had had them suspended from the Party for the sole reason that they had corresponded with our group. I therefore expected a somewhat chilly reception by the students. To my surprise, both students and staff greeted me with enthusiasm. It made me believe that people were really tiring of bureaucrats and directors.

I wanted to avail myself of the occasion to visit all my friends and acquaintances in Moscow. My 'business', it is true, did not leave me much spare time. Later, in prison and in exile, I often regretted my inability during this last stay in Moscow to see such or such a one of my friends with whom I would so much have enjoyed talking for a last time.

Those of my friends who worked in industry had apparently all agreed to talk to me optimistically about the progress being made by the country : industrialization was advancing with gigantic strides, but the Opposition would have none of it and limited itself to barren criticism. These Communists, by dint of admiring factory-chimneys, no longer perceived living beings and the social relations existing between them. One of them praised the G.P.U. "Just imagine," he said, "the G.P.U. keeps itself acquainted with all cases of workers' discontent, of conflicts with economic officials, of facts about *udarniks* (shock-brigaders), breakage of machinery, strikes, peasant demonstrations and village disturbances. The Politbureau receives weekly reports, giving a synopsis of all incidents throughout Russia. The heads of each republic receive similar reports about the territories that concern them. No small task that ! The Politbureau knows from week to week what happens throughout the country."

There was a lot of talk about Mayakovsky, who had just committed suicide. Communist circles had, at first, not attached very much importance to the fact. The official version of the suicide—due to reasons of a private nature— had been readily accepted. "But why had Mayakovsky turned his back on the revolution, and why had he attached so much importance to 'motives of a private nature'? " I objected to my informants, who refused to take my hint.

Mayakovsky's suicide was an event, and not the accident that the article in *Pravda*, written by Koltsov, made it out to be. But Mayakovsky's friends—Aseev and the others— hardly dared be more outspoken in their writings. It was Pasternak, the glory of the present Soviet Parnassus, a man in many respects alien to Mayakovsky, who acknowledged Mayakovsky's death with dignity and sorrow.

> *His shot explodes like Etna*
> *Over the plain of snivelling cowards.*

The suicide of Mayakovsky, the poet of the Russian revolution, made me doubt the veracity of the official account concerning the suicide of Yessenin, the greatest Russian lyric poet, and the version of Alexander Blok—the immortal author of *The Twelve*—as regards the revolution. I looked for a more plausible explanation in Trotsky's literary articles. But the latter merely reproduced the current version : Blok could no longer stand the difficulties of the revolution ; as to Yessenin, he expressed the peasant opposition to the proletarian revolution. Later I realized that, in actual fact, Blok had refused to sing the decadent revolution and that Yessenin had protested from his peasant point of view against bureaucratic oppression and in no way against the movement of proletarian emancipation.

Before I had been in prison and in exile, I had but rarely met with representatives, in Russia, of the old classes and the old Parties. All my interest had gone forth to the new order that was establishing itself throughout the land. On the occasion of my last stay in Moscow, I learned a few enlightening facts about the fate of the former aristocrats. I shall mention one which, by the way, is an example of the trouble into which a foreign Communist in Russia can run.

I visited a foreign Communist, a friend of mine, a kindly man, who did not go in for national politics. He had just returned from the South.

" A good thing you did not come to see me two days ago," he told me with a smile, " for you would have found two ' white ' ladies here."

" Don't joke," I answered. " Just what I'd need, to have myself accused by the G.P.U. of entertaining relations with ' white guardists '." After having talked about one thing and another, my friend came back to the topic that weighed on his mind.

" It happened because of an accidental galanterie. I was coming back by train from the Caucasus. We were arriving in Moscow, when one of the women travellers asked the guard at what time was there a train for Sverdlovsk. ' In a few hours' time,' the guard said. She seemed very pleased. ' You could have spent the night at my place, otherwise,' I said by way of a joke. Hardly had I spoken when two other women, after exchanging a glance, asked me whether I could put them up for two or three days. What could I do ? I agreed. They were going to Leningrad and had business in Moscow that would take them a few days. We got out together and took a tram. We were standing by ourselves on the platform, and as we passed by the Lubianka, they pointed at the G.P.U. building. ' That's where we have to go,' they said. I enquired whether one of their relatives was working there, going by their poor clothes and proletarian exterior. ' No, our husbands are locked up there ! ' What a shock it gave me, you can imagine. But I did not dare enquire any further and they remained silent. Anyhow, they were not guilty, for no one was after them and we must help one another in this life.

" We arrived home. I offered them tea and dinner, then, screwing up my courage, asked them questions.

" One of them began to tell me their story in an uncertain voice. ' Our husbands are imprisoned at Solovetsk, and we are going to pay them a visit. We first have to go to the Red Cross and the G.P.U. in Moscow to receive a permit. If we told you in the train that we were going to Leningrad, it was not to mislead you, but because we did not want to tell our story all round. What would people have thought of us ? But believe me, our husbands are innocent. . . .'

" I thought to myself : people in prison always are innocent. ' They are ex-army officers.' "

What innocence !

" ' They were arrested in 1927, after the murder of Voikov, and were exiled to Siberia for ten years, at Solovetsk. You know that to avenge the murder, they arrested as many as ten thousand officers and other ex-noblemen throughout the country. Those of them who had the slightest thing on their consciences were shot. As for those who were innocent, they were exiled for ten years.

" ' In the South where I've been, there are many ex-officers in the G.P.U. They were ' white ' officers before the Reds came into power, but as soon as they gathered that the Reds would win, they joined the other side. During these mass arrests, they showed themselves particularly ferocious, either to testify their fidelity towards the G.P.U. or to cover up their own misdeeds.

" ' My husband had a very good reputation ; he was a good worker and a supporter of the Soviet system. You see, he married me, although I was only an ordinary peasant girl, and he was a nobleman. At the G.P.U. they liked him, and knew that he was not against Soviet rule. But he had friends who were and who didn't hide their feelings. So the G.P.U. asked him to denounce them and report what they said among themselves. My husband refused, saying that it would not be honest towards his old friends, especially as he tried to reason with them every time they spoke against the Soviet Government.

" ' The G.P.U. knew it, but they kept on at him, " If you don't denounce them, it means that you are against us, too."

" ' In the end, they gave him ten years in a concentration camp.'

" The husband of the other woman had been a professor in a military academy, but had not fought against the Reds. He was automatically condemned to ten years' exile. Such condemnations are frequent. One of the women was a worker ; she was a syndicate member and showed me her card. The other was practically illiterate and had lived with her husband in a cottage with an orchard and a kitchen garden which had supported them. The first woman, though a peasant, seemed to possess an alert intelligence and even a certain culture. The other was more like an old man's governess than an officer's wife."

This story began to interest me more and more. I listened carefully.

"I naturally did not believe in the innocence of their husbands," my friend continued, "but their story appeared to me to be sincere. I had always thought the arrest of the officers perfectly justified. As they killed our Voikov, we must show ourselves unforgiving and thus convince white emigrants that their attempts do not frighten us. But seeing those two victims of our repression with my own eyes, I felt a certain pity. To hear those women talk, their husbands could not possibly have been counter-revolutionaries. By helping them, to argue as a Communist, I repaired in a way the damage caused by the error of other Communists. But on the other hand, what if the G.P.U. were having them followed ? What will it think when it knows I put them up ? But what can happen to me ? So many years in the service of the revolution give me certain rights, among others that of having a revolutionary conscience."

I looked at him with astonishment, still without saying a word.

"After three days, my guests obtained the necessary documents and left. On leaving me, they found it difficult to thank me enough. They had been touched by the hospitality given them by a stranger, a Communist, moreover. During the whole of their stay, they said not a word against the system. I was surprised after all that they had suffered. Indifferent to politics, they had but one wish : to better the lot of their husbands by their own submission. The men had already served three years of their sentence, and had only another seven to go.

"The labour they performed would reduce their sentence by a third ; and for all they knew, an amnesty might be proclaimed one day. On that note of hope they left me."

"My dear man," I told him at last, "do not tell anyone about this adventure."

" Do you mean to suggest that if the G.P.U. found out about it that it would make me pay for it ? " he asked with a worried look.

" Maybe the G.P.U. already knows. Do you really believe that it doesn't keep an eye on prisoners' wives ? But at the same time, the G.P.U. must also know the true motives of your hospitality——"

At these words, my friend's face beamed with joy.

" But that would not prevent it," I continued, " from persecuting you, if it wanted to, on account of your relations with white guardists, or even from calling you yourself a white guardist."

I shall now mention one or two other cases concerning pre-revolution groups and circles that came to my knowledge on other occasions.

Shortly after my arrival in Russia, I made the acquaintance of a lady who was related to Milyukov. She held a post in the Soviet administration, but the revolution had caused her to lose too many things for her to be fond of Communists. Moreover, she was still made to suffer a thousand petty annoyances. A bureaucratic member of the Party had, I don't exactly know how, succeeded in taking part of her furniture away from her. I was astonished to find that, after ten years of Soviet life, she still bore a greater grudge against Czarism than against Bolshevism. " It's that idiot Nicholas," she told me one day when she was in a temper, " who has burdened us with these Bolsheviks. If he had given us a timely constitution and made the necessary reforms, there would never have been either revolution or Bolshevism."

One of my comrades had, one summer holiday, made the acquaintance of a niece of Kerensky. She was a doctor and very outspoken in her views, liking to talk about Kerensky. She said, among other things, that Kerensky's career had greatly surprised his family. An aunt of his put that surprise into words by exclaiming, " What a revolution if Sacha is directing it ! " One must believe that the aunt changed her opinion after the October events.

But what to say of Stalin, who later sent the lady of the anecdote into exile for the sole reason that she was Kerensky's niece ?

I met another type of former aristocrat in the family of a Communist who had been a sailor in the Baltic Fleet and was now the secretary of an important Communist organization in Moscow. There were five or six guests. His wife, without taking the least notice of the guests, treated him as a parvenu might treat his servants. She was a former aristocrat and had married her husband so that she would not have to give up her dresses and her car. Yet she did not hide her contempt for her ex-sailor husband. As for him, he put up with it all with a humiliating patience.

Another former aristocrat who was trying to follow in her husband's footsteps was equally objectionable to me. She was the daughter of a rich engineer, had studied in Germany before the War and had married a wealthy aristocrat in that country. The War had broken up that marriage. At the time of the NEP, she married a well-to-do merchant. At the beginning of the Five Year Plan this man had been sentenced to five years in a concentration camp for speculating. After a year she left him in order to marry a Communist, an ex-workman, now an important Party-official. " One would no longer recognize her," her younger sister said. " When she was with her *nepman* she was so bourgeois that I had given up seeing her. I heard with joy that she had married a Communist, but today it suffices for me to speak one word of criticism against the system for her to jump down my throat. It seems strange to me. I have always been in favour of the Soviets. Shall I have to give up seeing her again ? "

That younger sister was also a fairly characteristic type of Soviet woman. She had been twice married, each time to an engineer. Having divorced her second husband, she went to the University at the age of thirty. Her brother was a Communist and occupied an important position. The lot of that family sufficiently shows how old-style bourgeois families belonging to the liberal professions have been able to settle in Soviet Russia.

The date of my departure from Moscow was approaching. Having completed my political task, I decided to spend my last evening in the home of an old, influential Bolshevik whom I had known in the days when I did not yet belong to the Opposition. In that family, intimately connected with several members of the Politbureau, I always had a chance of hearing the latest Party-news.

I found him in an excellent private hotel, in a comfortable

apartment, with tasteful furniture ; my hosts were kindly and cultured, their table served with the food reserved for the Kremlin people. At that time, the shops in the capital were empty, but here there was lack of nothing. One could have imagined oneself a thousand miles from starving Russia and from the fever of the Five Year Plan.

Apart from the occupants of the place, I met there a Communist acquaintance, the wife of a member of the Central Committee. She had just read Trotsky's book *My Life*, which had recently been published abroad, and with great malice she quoted the passages in which the present leaders were attacked by the author. My hosts, who had read the book themselves, added new details. What a situation ! All three were anti-Trotskyists, and yet they commented with obvious delight on Trotsky's attacks on their own anti-Trotskyist leaders.

My host was a Stalinist with a slight touch of toleration for both Right- and Left-wing elements. His wife was a rabid anti-Trotskyist. She hated Trotsky with an inveterate hatred. To her, he was nothing but an adventurer, but this did not mean that she admired Stalin. She was more a member of the old Russian radical democracy than a socialist or a bureaucrat. Her sympathies therefore went out to Right-wing Communism. The Right-wing elements, she said, were after all the most Russian of all groups, the most popular inside the Party. As to the lady who quoted Trotsky, she was a convinced Stalinist. Her hostility towards Trotsky was tempered with a touch of disdain ; she seemed to say : as an adventurer, he is unsuccessful ; he certainly does not fit into our age, and moreover he has had his day. She put all her heart into her hatred of the Right-wing, for, as an enemy, that Opposition was still alive and kicking. But she restrained her expression of that hatred in the presence of the master and mistress of the place whose political sympathies she knew.

Our hostess recalled to us a conversation she had recently held with a member of the Politbureau, concerning the Central Control Committee of the Party. This conversation had resulted from a few scornful words she had spoken on the subject of that institution. " How is your Old People's Home ? " Her friend of the Politbureau had taken no offence at the comparison. I interrupted her and asked in a tone of pleasantry, " The high Party authorities should therefore have the respect only of the masses, of the fools ? As to the leaders, they have the right to call things by their real names ? "

" That is so. There is a certain danger in this division of society into two layers to which belong two different aspects of the truth," my host said. " Machiavelli is fashionable. At present the bedside books of Voroshilov and Stalin are Napoleon's *Memoirs* and Machiavelli's *Prince*. Admittedly it is a good thing to learn from one's enemies, but all the same——"

He went on reasoning, mixing his ' admittedlys ' and his ' buts ' ; then he went on to the latest echoes from the Kremlin, the peasant risings and industrialization. All this over the sweets reserved for the people of the Kremlin.

At midnight I took leave of my friends and left for Leningrad, still under the impression that, in the depths of the Kremlin, Napoleon and Machiavelli had taken the places of Marx and Lenin. I remembered a phrase we had often repeated, Draguitch, Deditch and myself : Russia only climbed so high in order to fall still lower !

Book III

THE OUTCASTS

I

AT SCHOOL IN SOVIET PRISONS

I WAS arrested ten days after my return to Leningrad. From May 21st, 1930, until December 3rd, 1935, the day on which I crossed the Polish border, I was deprived of liberty. I spent more than three years in the Soviet prisons of Leningrad, Chelyabinsk, Verkhne-Uralsk, then again at Chelyabinsk, finally at Irkutsk and at Krasnoyarsk. As for the last two years, I spent them in exile in Siberia, first at Krasnoyarsk, later at Yeniseisk.

After having lived and travelled in Russia for four years in the position of a man belonging to the privileged minority, I had to suffer during five and a half years in the immense Soviet Gehenna, not so much as an observer but as an inhabitant of that arbitary empire. In the summer of 1935, a short while before my return to Europe, when I had lost all hope of getting out and was expecting to rot in Siberia, I wrote to a friend in Europe openly, for I no longer feared even the censorship. " It is easier to get out of Dante's Inferno than to get out of Soviet Russia."

They were hard years, especially the last two Owing to the insistence with which I made known my demand to leave the country, I went constantly in danger of my life. Those who have lived through such experiences know the indelible traces they leave. On several occasions I have physically felt the approach of death.

I now live in a land of liberty, in France, but even when I lived in the empire of the new Genghis Khan, in fear of execution, thinking of suicide as the only possible way to save my dignity, I never regretted having come to Russia. My thirst to know Russia to the bitter end was in my eyes the justification for all risks.

· The terror that prevails in Russia, its totalitarian rule, its revolutionary slogans mask the real life of the country from those who live abroad. Russia can only be thoroughly understood if one leaves the confines of its official and lawful life and goes to the world of the doomed, the prisons, the secret realm of the G.P.U. It is the only way to learn to know the real Russia, Russia without make-up, Russia as it was made by ' God and the G.P.U.'

Those who have not undergone the prisons, the concentration camps and Soviet exile, where more than five million galley-slaves are kept, those who do not know the greatest forced-labour camps history has known, where men die like flies, are beaten like dogs and work like slaves, they can have no idea what Soviet Russia and Stalin's classless society are.

If I had not been there myself, if I had not seen it with my own eyes, I would not have credited such things possible in our day or in the country of the October revolution.

When I knew it all, I put to myself a question that would never have tormented me to such an extent had I been free. How is it possible for the most audacious, the greatest of all revolutions, to have generated into this complete slavery ? How is it that in its first stages the Russian revolution shows the most modern social developments whereas in its next stage it exhibits the highest degree of exploitation and oppression ? What can explain so enormous a contradiction ?

The question is all the more difficult to answer as no civil war, no dated period of revolution separates these two stages. They are, on the contrary, linked by invisible and at first sight simple evolution. The revolution has at no time ceased to be ' victorious ', to maintain itself. The men and the organizations that stood at the head of the revolution during its first phase, its liberating phase, are, in the main, those who, during the second phase, defended and spread the rule of slavery and oppression. The outward forms have not changed ; but the realities of life teach that the change of front has been complete, and that social relations are developing in a sense diametrically opposed to that proclaimed by the October revolution. Nowhere can this be so clearly seen as in the Soviet prisons.

Over-simplified answers, affirming that nothing has

changed, that the great liberating tendencies of October have continued to prevail in Russia, or that this October revolution has never differed from the present Soviet reality, these answers could satisfy none but the blind or the prejudiced.

It is no answer, it is no ' dialectic synthesis ' to pretend that the character of exploitation of the Soviet rule has not been shown up so long as it is still clothed in certain socialist forms bequeathed to it by the October revolution. It is no answer to limit oneself to the statement that the inferior strata of Soviet society (as is the case in any society) aspire to emancipation.

The enigma of the Russian revolution that humanity and the international workers' movement must solve is exactly this : how has it come about that all that constitutes the October revolution has been entirely abolished, while its outward forms have been retained ; that the exploitation of workers and peasants has been brought back to life without reviving private capitalists and landowners ; that a revolution, begun in order to abolish the exploitation of man by man, has ended by installing a new type of exploitation.

But if a stay in Soviet prisons puts this problem in a particularly urgent way, it must be added that it also brings with it the rudiments of an answer.

All social layers of Russia are represented in prison. There one can at last get to know what really happens in the country and what people really think. It is very simple ; prison is the only place in Soviet Russia where people can express their feelings sincerely and openly. As to the danger of too great a subjectivity in these statements, it is eliminated by the very number and social diversity of the prisoners.

The attitude of the working masses and of the population as a whole is truthfully reflected in the opinions expressed by the political sections. All these are illegal and prohibited in Russia ; therefore they all find their way into prison with the sole exception of the one single section that reflects the opinions of the ruling bureaucratic *élite*. It is therefore impossible to know, except inside a prison, what has been the development of public opinion in Russia since October, 1917, and to know which are the lessons the population itself has drawn from the experiment of the Russian revolution. What can there be of greater importance to theory and to social action in our times than these lessons ?

How to separate the positive acquisitions of the revolution from its more threatening phenomena, how to guarantee social revolutions from the dangers of degeneracy—such are the problems passionately put by Russian public opinion, an illegal opinion that has been driven into prison.

Every day its importance to the international workers' movement increases. No nation by itself can solve the problem of social emancipation ; hence the world importance of the Russian experiment remains paramount in spite of its calamitous outcome.

And that is another reason why it has always seemed to me that what I learned in Soviet prisons was worth all the sacrifices involved.

II

IMPRISONED IN LENINGRAD

On coming back from Moscow to Leningrad, I took good care not to be followed. At first, I noticed nothing unusual. But after my arrival in Leningrad, I soon observed some suspicious indications. Every time I returned home, I came across a man posted near the house where I lived. It was of course possible that he was after someone else, but I soon felt that his interest was concentrated on me. During my absence from the University, a stranger had appeared there, and not having found me in had tried to glean information from the staff. He had even gone through the correspondence on my desk. Also, one of my acquaintances, whom I suspected of being an agent of the G.P.U., no longer came to see me at this time. This made me think that a friendly supervision was no longer deemed sufficient and that I was henceforward openly shadowed. I thought of going into hiding, and of returning to Europe by illegal paths.

In that frame of mind I returned home on the 21st of May, 1930, towards midnight. I was hoping to take away some of my belongings and to leave home for a few days as a precautionary measure. There was no one in the street, which I thought was a good sign. But as soon as I opened my door, I found a uniformed agent of the G.P.U. sitting in the passage. "A new chapter of my life in the U.S.S.R. is about to begin," I said to myself. I was convinced that the G.P.U. knew my secret activity in favour of the Opposition. It was therefore inevitable that my place should be searched and I arrested. But I could not guess from which source the G.P.U. drew its information concerning me. I decided to admit nothing before clear proof of my guilt was shown me.

"What's the matter?" I asked. By way of answer, the agent showed me both the search-warrant and the warrant for my arrest. The search had already been begun during my absence. The reason for my arrest was not indicated on the warrant, and the agent told me that he was unable to give me any explanation.

The search did not upset me in the least, for I had no compromising documents in my rooms. I soon left the agent and his assistant to continue the search and went to the kitchen that was at the other end of the passage. The service stairs led straight to liberty. I thought for a moment of escaping. First I should have to send away the housekeeper on some plausible pretext. The first of which I could think did not have the hoped-for result, and I found myself incapable of inventing another. My desire to flee met, moreover, with an obstacle within myself ; I believe that unconsciously I wished to go to prison and finish my study of Russia before returning to Europe. This impulse I understood only at a time when I was wishing much more ardently to leave the country and when this wish was much more difficult to fulfil.

Meanwhile the search had come to an end. The G.P.U. men took away all my manuscripts. I packed my clothes, including my winter garments. The G.P.U. men assured me that this was superfluous as I would soon be returning home, but I was fully persuaded that no return home was possible unless I ' capitulated ', and that I would never do. I told the G.P.U. men that I lived alone and had nobody in whose care to leave my belongings. A G.P.U. car was waiting outside ; we did not go very far, the car stopping next door at the Party House, where I saw my friend Deditch, also accompanied by a G.P.U. man. I was surprised, for Deditch, having disagreed with our group, had for several months no longer collaborated with us. We were not less pleased to meet one another and condoled each other on our bad luck.

We plied one another with questions. " What has happened to our comrade Draguitch ? He is so careful, so experienced, that he has no doubt succeeded in escaping arrest and reaching the frontier." Later we learnt that indeed Draguitch had succeeded in going into hiding, but was arrested three months afterwards. " And what about our comrades in Moscow ? They, too, must have been arrested. We shall meet them in prison." We made up our minds on the two following points : first of all, to make no statements that could be called capitulation and to admit only what the G.P.U. could patently prove. Secondly, to have our names given in their proper form. It was wise to let them know from now onwards that they were dealing with foreign Communists.

We soon arrived at the House of Detention in Chpalernaya Street. Our feelings were a mixture of anxiety and curiosity. Should we, in a workers' State, expect a different penitentiary system from that of a bourgeois country ? A workers' State must wish for the improvement and not for the punishment of the culprit.

We were taken to the gaoler's office. Everything resembled what I had seen abroad : the furniture, the voices of the officials, the creakings of a soulless machinery. " This is exactly as it is in bourgeois prisons," I whispered into Deditch's ear, and as a practical precaution I hid, on the off-chance, a pencil stump, as I used to do in similar circumstances in bourgeois countries.

After we had been searched, we were each taken to a cell. We were not to meet again for three months. It was already three o'clock in the morning before I walked into my cell somewhere in the basement. It contained two bunks, one of which was already occupied by a prisoner. He was asleep. I said to myself, " He must be an *agent provocateur* instructed to worm out of me those facts of which the G.P.U. is still ignorant." I could not fall asleep. Assailed by a thousand thoughts, I tried to envisage the fate that lay in store for me.

During the course of my third night in the prison, I was led before the examining magistrate. It is one of the principles of the G.P.U. to examine prisoners during the night. It is a more impressive procedure and, moreover, a man dragged from his sleep is not well prepared to defend himself. Psychology is a favourite science of the G.P.U.

The examining magistrate was no other than the G.P.U. official who had conducted the search of my apartment.

" Do you know why you have been arrested ? " were his first words. " No, you don't know ? In that case, will you tell me what hypothesis you have formed of the reason for your arrest ? "

A few months later in prison, I was able to read an article by the Bolshevist historian, Pokrovsky, on the subject of the Spanish Inquisition. I learned from that article that these were the classic questions put by the Inquisitors to their prisoners. Afterwards I often had the opportunity to be reminded of the Inquisition and Loyola's Order of Jesus in connection with events in Russia and the methods of the G.P.U.

In accordance with the policy I had thought out, I answered that my arrest could be due only to the intrigues of my adversaries within the Yugo-Slav Party.

" Oh, no, not at all," the magistrate interrupted me. " We are not concerned with the Comintern. We are interested only in your activities within the Russian Communist Party."

He was silent for a few moments, then fired the following question at me : " What do you think of the policy of the Russian Communist Party ? "

I answered in as offhand a way as possible, lying as is the custom in such a case in Russia.

" I entirely approve of that policy. My differences of opinion concern only the affairs of the Comintern in Germany and in Yugo-Slavia. I consider that the primary slogan in Germany should be ' Fascism is the enemy ' and not ' Social-democracy is the enemy '. As for Yugo-Slavia, I believe that Bukharin, Manuilsky and Gorkitch have betrayed the workers' movement in that country by handing it over to charlatans and adventurers, and that by so doing they contributed to the military *coup d'état* of January, 1929." Then I added, " I am not inclined to capitulate."

My declarations did not seem to satisfy the examining magistrate. He was concerned only with the Russian Party. I was led back to my cell.

Three days later I was once more interrogated, in the presence of P——, a Yugo-Slav comrade. He was a manual worker from Zagreb, a former militant syndicalist, who had been in Russia since 1923. In my capacity of secretary of the Communist Party of Croatia, I had been among those to send him to Russia. He had pursued his studies at the Sverdlovsk University in Moscow. He had not been allowed to return to Croatia because of his leanings towards Trotskyism from 1923 to 1926, but yet he had not been expelled from the Party. Of late he had been working in a Leningrad factory. A short while before my arrest, I had attempted to persuade him to collaborate in our clandestine activities and to insist on obtaining a permit to return to Yugo-Slavia. He had refused to do so, saying that the Party was carrying out Trotsky's programme, " and apart from that I have no desire to go to Siberia," he had added in an outburst of sincerity. Indeed, the struggle had nothing to tempt him ; he intended to spend the summer in the country with a Communist official employed in the administration. " Where we are concerned," I had remarked, not longer than two weeks ago, " we shall risk Siberia, sooner than give up the struggle."

I had scarcely realized the presence of P——, when the examining magistrate said to me, " You are not to speak a word, not a word, sit down ! " Then he began to read out a long statement made by P——. It contained everything, except the bit about Siberia. There was only one place where my thoughts were expressed more fully than actually they had been. At that point, P—— interrupted the reading and demanded that his statement be corrected. The magistrate wanted to protest, but accepted the correction. P—— apparently considered that there was no betrayal on his part provided that he truthfully recorded our conversation. As it stood, however, it sufficed amply to have me condemned. " We must go abroad to organize the struggle against the Comintern," I had said, for I was already an advocate of a new International. " The elimination of the Russian bureaucracy will take place in the end by violent means, for the bureaucracy will not willingly give up its privileges." All that was true, but what had made me say such things ? No doubt I had attached too much importance to P——'s old Trotskyist sympathies.

P—— approved and signed his deposition. As for myself, I declared that P—— had invented every word of it. In Yugo-Slavia he had belonged to the Right-wing, whereas I was a Left-wing Party member. All that was but a Party intrigue. In actual fact, I had reason to believe that P—— had not directly denounced me, but had reported our conversation to one of his friends, a member of the Right-wing section of the Yugo-Slav Party, and that the latter had communicated it to the G.P.U. Thus P—— had been forced to make a full confession under penalty of reprisals from the G.P.U.

The examining magistrate allowed P—— to leave, and had me led back to my cell. My third interrogation took place a few days later, in the presence of the examining magistrate and an unknown civilian. The latter asked me to draw up a written statement of my attitude towards the Russian Communist Party and Trotskyism. I confirmed my first deposition and added that I was ready to give all necessary explanations to Party authorities concerned, refusing to give them to the G.P.U. " The Party must decide on its own affairs, not the G.P.U."

" The Regional Party Committee," the stranger answered, " has instructed me to talk to you about all Party affairs."

" In that case, I demand to be immediately released and we shall talk. I refuse to discuss Party matters so long as I am in prison."

I thought that the G.P.U. had graver charges to bring against me than P——'s deposition, and I was unwilling to make any admission before it had come fully out into the open. But on the other hand, foreseeing proofs of guilt which would no doubt soon be produced, I was unwilling to commit myself by denying in writing my sympathies with the Trotskyist Opposition. At the end of the week, I was once more called to hear a document read concerning my activities in the course of my last stay in Moscow. This document described the conference of our small group and our attempt to send Trotsky documents relating to the Comintern.

" The whole of your Moscow group has been arrested ; all its members have confessed ; it is useless for you to continue your denials." But no statement made by any of the comrades was shown me, from which negative fact I concluded that the G.P.U. was still ignorant of many things. The only document that I was shown was the deposition of the representative of the Opposition Centre in Moscow, to whom Glybovsky and I had explained the plans and activities of our group. What struck me in that deposition was that the ideology had been treated in a very superficial way whereas details of organization had been reported with painstaking accuracy. " You see, once the man had been arrested, he confessed to everything."

It was clear to me that this was not the deposition of a prisoner but the report of an *agent provocateur* ; that would explain the peculiarity of the document's information.

The representative of the Opposition Centre had therefore been an *agent provocateur*, and we had walked neatly into the trap. That had been the cause of our failure. Afterwards I found out from the documents that I was shown that not only had the G.P.U. arrested my comrades in Moscow, but it had also seized the resolutions of our conference, part of our correspondence and numerous other documents.

It was useless to persist in my denials. I therefore declared myself to hold Opposition views. It was then immediately suggested to me that I should answer in writing the two following questions.

One : what are your political opinions ?

Two : what have your clandestine activities in the Opposition been ?

I was given pen and paper and allowed a few days to draw up my answer. I refused to reply to the second question and spread myself all the more on the first. I even took the offensive and expressed my political opinion with great freedom.

These were the essential points of my declaration. If the first phase of the Russian revolution, that of Lenin, teaches us how to act, the second phase, that of Stalin, teaches us how not to act. The Five Year Plan is progressive, but in no way socialist. If one were to judge merely by the number of factories, America would long since have been a socialist country. Socialism is not a factory but a system of human interrelationships. These interrelations in Russia are not of a socialist nature. Collectivization is not a struggle between socialism and capitalism but a duel between large State capital and small private capital. Stalin's struggle against the Right is attenuated by a great number of compromises, it is a struggle of the Centre against the Right-wing. In the long run, Stalin will come to an understanding with the Right-wing, as, in the past, Kautsky came to terms with Bernstein. His break with the Left-wing, on the other hand, is as definite as Kautsky's break with Rosa Luxemburg and Liebknecht was. As to Trotsky, though far from being a man of Lenin's stature, he is far superior to Stalin. In the domain of international politics, I accused the Stalinists of leading the workers' movement of the capitalist countries from defeat to defeat, and of treating foreign workers and Communists, not like equals and brothers, but like servants and lackeys.

In that same declaration, I demanded that I be allowed to depart abroad freely with my Yugo-Slav comrades. The workers of Yugo-Slavia had sent us to the U.S.S.R. to study the conditions there. We now wanted to report the results of our mission. " But," I said to finish the substance of my argument, " if instead of letting me return to the West, you send me to the East in your usual slave-driving fashion, know that you will not frighten me, for I shall find brothers out there."

I was interrogated no further after this declaration. My case was sent on to Moscow and I had to wait several months before my fate was decided. I had demanded on principle that I should be allowed to go abroad ; it was necessary to protest in some way or other against the offhand way in which the Russians prevented foreign Communists from leaving as if they were so many heads of cattle. While I was in prison in Leningrad, I learned through the newspapers that the Spanish militant syndicalist Nin had been sent abroad. Why should I not be treated in the same way ? I even thought of going on hunger-strike should I be refused permission to go. But I gave up this plan : was I not to carry out my resolution to study the whole of Russia to the end ?

In my behaviour towards the Soviet system, I adopted a much more hostile attitude than I would have thought possible a few months earlier. Solitude in prison was much more conducive to drawing conclusions than the daily excitements of a free life. As to my opinions concerning Lenin and Trotsky, they were still entirely ' orthodox '. It was much later that I conceived doubts concerning the parts played by them in the Russian revolution.

I spent five months in the House of Detention in Leningrad and did not leave it before October, 1930. The first months I was locked up in cell no. 11. It was small and gloomy, as were all the cells on the ground floor. During my stay, pains were taken to make it gloomier still by putting shutters over the windows. This was all the more cruel as my windows did not look out on to the street but on to a poorly lit yard. It had needed the abolition of Czardom and thirteen years of revolution for this old prison to lose the little light it had still had in the past. During the day, one had to climb on to the table, if one wanted to read, and keep the book raised as much as possible in order to catch a glimmer of light. My cell-mate and I did so in turns.

A few years before, so my cell-mate who had had previous experience told me, life in this prison was much better. It was even possible to talk through the window ; at night, when prisoners were shot, their names would be announced to all, and the condemned men could take leave of their more fortunate fellows and give them the addresses of their relatives, so that these might be informed of their death. Now there was none of this liberalism. A graveyard silence hung over the cells and corridors. The corridors, moreover, were padded so that the gaolers' footsteps were barely audible. Our daily walks were limited to ten minutes. Six cells, that is, twelve prisoners, were let out at a time. The pairs walked four or five paces apart, so that each prisoner could talk only to his cell-mate. All the same, we succeeded in exchanging a few words with the neighbouring pairs, those of cells nos. 10 and 12. We gradually learned the names of all those who walked with us, as well as the crimes of which they were accused.

My eleven fellow-prisoners were all accused of espionage in favour of Poland, Esthonia, Latvia, Czechoslovakia and Great Britain. The importance of each of the prisoners varied in accordance with that of the State he ' represented '. The one who had been accused of espionage in favour of Poland was a Polish craftsman, an earnest, thin-faced man, the father of a numerous family. A careless-looking young man, who kept on whistling softly to himself, represented Esthonia. He had already spent three years in Central Asia, accused of the same crime. On his return to Leningrad, he had once more been arrested. A wide-awake old man, apparently very skilled in the art of conspiring, had been accused of spying in favour of his former fatherland Latvia. As for Great Britain, she was represented by my cell-mate. He told me so himself, but I did not believe him, thinking he was an agent of the G.P.U. to whom had been assigned the task of watching me.

It seemed to me as if the G.P.U. had purposely imprisoned me among these people in order to terrorize me morally. The conditions of life were hard and the food was bad. In the mornings we received boiling water and slightly less than a pound of bread for the day. At breakfast we received some hot water with an occasional cabbage-leaf floating in it and a lump of buckwheat mash without butter. For dinner, the same ' soup '. In the prisons which were not under the G.P.U., treatment was worse still. The feeling of superiority connected with the G.P.U. covered all aspects of its activity and even demanded that its own prisoners should be better fed than any others. Later on, when we were moved into a common ward, I met prisoners who considered themselves lucky to be in a G.P.U. prison. Most of us had received permission to read books and buy newspapers. I, moreover, had been allowed to have pen, ink and paper.

My cell-mate received articles of food sent him by his relatives twice a week. Every time he insisted on my sharing with him. It only served to deepen my suspicions of him ; I mistook his kindness for a ruse of the G.P.U. But when in the course of my examination I was shown records of our Moscow group proving that the G.P.U. knew more than enough, I began to think that there seemed to be little need for sending a *provocateur* to me. But if I no longer suspected my fellow-prisoner of filling that part, I still thought him guilty of the crime of spying for which he had been arrested. "The G.P.U. would not torture an innocent man without reason," I said to myself, listening to his protestations of innocence.

All the same, the impression made by the story of his life, as he told it, did not fit in with that of an English spy. He was a very gifted man of a naturally cheerful temper, but fear had depressed him. He liked science and gave me a whole series of talks on physics and chemistry. He also loved the country and dreamed of settling there with a garden and beehives.

" Why didn't you leave Leningrad ? "

" The G.P.U. men were watching me and I was not allowed to leave without permission. But I was afraid to ask for it. I thought it better not to give a sign of life." Until recently he had been a specialist in a Leningrad municipal enterprise. He had studied civil engineering, but the War had interrupted his studies.

He had been a conscript under the Czar. When the Civil War broke out, he was living in the South and was mobilized in Denikin's army. He belonged to no Party, but during the struggle between Whites and Reds, his sympathies had gone out to the latter, for they were nearer the people. He had chosen a favourable moment and had gone over to the Reds. He served in Budienny's First Cavalry Corps. He fought throughout the Russo-Polish war and was the treasurer of his unit. During the retreat of the Reds, he got lost with all the money, but succeeded in joining his unit after two days' frantic search. He was mentioned in the army despatches for this proof of honesty. Today he bitterly regretted it.

" If I had only stayed where I was, the Poles would have made me a prisoner, and I would have escaped my present misfortunes."

After the demobilization, he found a modest employment in Leningrad. He married and was leading a quiet life when suddenly his troubles began. His sister, who was a teacher of foreign languages, had made the acquaintance of an English merchant named Hodgson, had married him and followed him abroad. When her brother came to live in Leningrad, she sought contact with him and gave him some help. Then Hodgson was appointed to a post in the British Embassy in Moscow, and returned to Russia with his wife. She called on her brother and invited him to the British Consulate in Leningrad. My companion took great delight in recalling the memories of the good wines and the cigars that had been offered him on that occasion. Shortly afterwards he was arrested for espionage. Then he was set free. A few years went by and now he had been once more arrested.

One day, after he had been before the examining magistrate, he told me the details of his interrogation.

" But they ask you to become an agent of the G.P.U., that is to say, to become a Soviet spy against England ! " I exclaimed. " That is what that magistrate means when he says : you have your entry into the British Consulate, you could be a very useful man and you would do well for yourself."

My cell-mate was very frightened by this suggestion and breathlessly tried to prove the impossibility of it. It was clear that I was right and that was what he feared most. His ' inability to understand ' cost him five years in the Solovetsk concentration camp. In the conflict between the Intelligence Service and the G.P.U., a man was made a martyr for having wished to remain honest.

One evening, my neighbour, listening hard, whispered, " Can you hear that muffled noise ? "

" Well, what is it ? "

" It is someone being tortured."

I was full of indignation. " It is all very well for these fables about the G.P.U. to be believed by the bourgeois and petit-bourgeois abroad, but in Russia, come on ! Do you think the G.P.U. is like the Czarist Okhrana ? The G.P.U. kills if necessary, it annihilates, but it does not torture."

My neighbour looked at me in despair, then concluded,

" I do not wish you a long enough stay in this place for you to find out what the G.P.U. really is. You foreign Communists are very ignorant. If a Russian Communist had spoken as you just have, I would never have talked to him again."

As I had complained to the magistrate about the light in my cell, I was transferred to the second floor, which was much lighter. My cell-mate there was a Soviet official. He refused to tell me of what he was accused, but I gathered he was supposed to have committed sabotage. Before the revolution, he had been an important official in the Ministry of Commerce and Industry. After the October revolution, he had taken part in a strike with other officials, but had given in when he learned that Lenin wanted a strong Government.

" I broke the strike and gave in to the Soviet Government. In its name, I worked out the nationalization of the mercantile marine. You see, I am a fifty-per-cent Communist."

I smiled. " You are not exaggerating the percentage ? "

" No, I assure you. I have always longed for the Government to control the national economy and to place itself above both workers and employers."

This man never offered me any of his food. Not even a lump of sugar. This conduct showed his non-Russian origin. He was the son of an Austrian-Slovak who had been a teacher of Greek in Russia.

The preliminary investigation of my case was drawing to a close. I was repeatedly called before the magistrate, who urged me to leave the Opposition and condemn its activities. He offered me my freedom in exchange. " How can I do that ? " I asked him. " I knew full well that you persecuted people if they took part in the Opposition. Now that I undergo the consequences of my actions, you ask me to give up my opinions and buy my liberty at that price. It would be dishonest of me. If I did so, I would lose all self-respect and give you the opportunity to despise me."

" Not at all, not at all, Anton Antonovitch," the magistrate answered. " It is not dishonest to admit one's errors. It often happens that a man loses his temper and makes a noise ; but when he sees where his behaviour is taking him, he changes his mind and quiets down."

On another occasion, when I demanded to be let free to go abroad, I began to accuse the Stalinist leaders of following a national policy instead of a proletarian and international one. The magistrate answered, "Anton Antonovitch, charity begins at home." He soon gave up his attempts to convince me and ceased conversing on abstract themes.

Towards the middle of July, I was transferred to a common ward in the main body of the building above the central gateway. There were three floors of wards. The conditions of life were very different from those in the cells.

The ward where I was put was arranged for twenty-three prisoners. There were twenty-three sail-cloth bunks which, during the day, folded up against the wall. But during the three months I spent there, there were never fewer than eighty people in the ward. On certain days that figure rose to 110. How did one manage to fit in ? There were two rows of tables in the middle of the room ; some of the prisoners sat down around the tables, others sat down along the walls, on the bunks or on benches. At night, the prisoners brought out their mattresses that during the day were kept at the end of the corridor. It was not easy to fit a hundred mattresses into the ward. Twenty-three people occupied the bunks, twenty-three others put their mattresses underneath the bunks, others put them on tables and benches, others again slept under tables and benches and in the 'empty' corners of the ward, beginning from the door and ending at the lavatories that were at the other end of the ward. The various places were occupied in order of seniority ; first one slept on the ground, then on tables and benches, finally on the bunks. The people who slept on the ground were a floating population ; those who were settled in the bunks represented the permanent residents of the ward. During my three months, I was never able to get hold of a bunk, although sometimes one would be ' on sale ' for five to twenty roubles.

Twice a month we were taken to the baths that were in the same building. It was a room with a few benches, less than a dozen wash-basins and hot- and cold-water taps. We were taken to the baths in groups, and were given twenty minutes for our toilet.

In spite of this overcrowding of prisoners, there were usually no lice. There were bugs, however, but we took no notice of them. The food was the same as in the cells. I then learned that political prisoners were entitled to a special diet. There is no equality in Russia, even inside prisons. As long as I was inside my cell, I never would have asked for better food, although it would undoubtedly have been given to me as a foreign Communist. Now that I had learned of the existence of a special diet for political prisoners, I demanded and obtained it. It consisted of soup with a large piece of meat. Moreover, I received two pounds of sugar a month, cigarettes, tobacco, butter and soap. That meant great wealth inside this prison and I felt somewhat ashamed to use my store in this place of misery and hunger. I had already grown accustomed to take my tea without sugar, so that it was easy for me to share my sugar with my new neighbours. But even when giving them half my meals, I felt better fed than before. A piece of soap, a little tobacco and a cigarette went a long way to alleviate the sufferings of my comrades in misfortune.

The large population of the ward was of very mixed composition. All provinces, all classes and all social strata were represented. It took but a short time to become acquainted with this Russia in little. The daily walk of a quarter of an hour brought together four or five wards each as overfilled as ours, which added all the more to the diversity of the social groups represented. Thus I learned not merely the lot of a few hundred individuals, but the conditions in tens of provinces and the feelings of tens of different social groupings.

This constantly renewed kaleidoscope reflected the life of the huge country, restless, turbulent and full of despair. Our wards rang with the echoes of anti-collectivist peasant risings and the moans of all Russia where mass executions of revolting peasants were taking place.

The prison contained many engineers and other prisoners accused of sabotage. Discontented workmen, sailors and Opposition Communists rubbed shoulders with speculators and priests. Almost every day some of the prisoners were shot. No journey through Russia could offer so rich a documentation as could a few weeks' sojourn in that prison.

THE ENGINEERS ACCUSED OF SABOTAGE

Prisoners in the ward formed small groups of three to ten people, in accordance with their social, political, cultural or religious affinities. The engineers and intellectuals constituted the aristocracy. A section among them even had a ward of its own, as large as ours, well-furnished and occupied by only sixteen to eighteen engineers. These spent their days working in the factories, to return to the prison at night. A few of them were still in the early stages of their interrogations, others had already been condemned. They received excellent food and were treated with respect. " They are engineers " or " We are the engineers " were phrases of particular significance ; even in prison, they exuded a feeling of superiority over the common run of Soviet citizens.

It was said that in certain factories in Leningrad, they had built special prisons for condemned engineers who spent their nights in them and worked in the factories during the daytime. It was also said that the G.P.U. indulged in the ' sale ' of condemned engineers, especially of those destined to go to Solovetsk concentration camp ; the G.P.U. let them out to the various trusts and factories all over Russia on the following conditions : half or two-thirds of the salaries of the engineers went to the G.P.U., one-third to the engineers themselves. The most amazing part of it all was that the men put up with it without too much indignation. They seemed to think, " It does not matter ; we have seen worse. We shall get out of it, for they can't do without us."

Those engineers who were in prison without working were not lodged in the common wards. They, too, were treated with consideration by the administration ; they were better dressed and received excellent food from outside. Among them were some who had confessed to acts of sabotage. It was with the greatest difficulty, and very slowly at that, that I learned some of their stories, i.e. the stories of their ' confessions '.

" I was kept for five months in the strictest solitary confinement," one of them told me. " I received neither newspapers, books, tobacco, nor parcels, and my relatives never obtained permission to visit me. I suffered from hunger and solitude. All the time the authorities insisted on my admitting having committed acts of sabotage I had never done. I refused. I was told : ' If you are in favour of the Soviet Government, as you pretend you are, prove it by your actions ; the Government needs your confession. Do not fear any evil consequences, the Government will take your frankness into account and will allow you to make good by your work. You will receive permission to see your family, you will receive parcels and newspapers and will be allowed to go for walks. If, on the other hand, you remain obdurate, you will be subjected to a merciless repression, and what is more, there will be reprisals against your wife and your children.' During those months I grew hardened, but in the end solitude became so unbearable that it seemed to me that nothing mattered, nothing could be worse. I became indifferent to everything, and I signed all that the examining magistrate wanted me to sign."

This man seemed very depressed and walked ceaselessly to and fro with a lost look. Many other prisoners who had confessed to imaginary acts of sabotage were in the same state. I shall mention a few more cases that took place at different periods and in different parts of Russia and with which I became acquainted through direct witnesses.

" I who have devoted the whole of my life to the development of the coal-mining industry, I have been forced to sign a confession that I wished to destroy that industry. What can I do ? For what else am I suited ? " one of the principal engineers of the Donets Basin said, in 1934, when condemned to spend ten years in the Ukht-Petchersk concentration camp on account of sabotage, where, incidentally, he was made to run the coal-mines and prepare some altogether new ones.

A young specialist, sent to the same concentration camp, was pursued by the following *idée fixe* : he wanted at all costs to solve the most incomprehensible of Soviet enigmas. Why should the Soviet Government wish him to confess to crimes he had not committed, and of what use could such a confession be to a Government sprung from the people and intended to bring truth and progress in its train ?

A metallurgist from Donets who used to occupy an important post met with a yet more tragic fate. The G.P.U. was dissatisfied with his hostility towards the present policy of the Soviet Government and decided to ruin him. To serve its ends, it availed itself of the services of the wife of the Communist director of the factory whose chief technical engineer he was. This woman, according to her instructions from the G.P.U., and unbeknown to her husband, played an amorous comedy by means of which all the necessary information concerning his opinions and conversations with other engineers was obtained. The G.P.U. found it easy to work up a case of so-called sabotage and send the engineer into exile at Solovetsk. Then came the second act of the drama. The woman was caught in her own snare and really fell in love with the exiled engineer. As her husband had just been transferred to another factory of the Donets, she persuaded him to have the exiled engineer recalled and to make him work in the new factory. The romance began afresh. But soon the engineer found himself in a very false position towards the wife of his director and towards his own family, and he found out also that he had been the victim of a well-staged machination. To escape this impasse, he committed suicide.

The demoralization caused by these trumped-up confessions sometimes amounted to cynicism. Here follows a conversation between agricultural experts accused of sabotage ; they were in the train taking them into exile. " I must tell you, Vladimir Nikolayevitch, that I have told terrible lies about you in my statement." " Don't worry, Ivan Pavlovitch, I have blackened you, too, for all I was worth."

After a few months spent in this atmosphere, it became clear to me that the sabotage cases engineered by the G.P.U. were cases of discontent or at most passive resistance on the part of the engineers systematically transformed into espionage and sabotage. The stories of the repentant sinners showed me the methods by which the sabotage was worked up to and proved. Only much later did I understand the political aim of these trials. It was intended to maintain a state of terror among the specialists, to demoralize them and thus restrain them from any inclination to link up with the peasants, an alliance which, at the time of the mass collectivization, might have become all the more dangerous to the Communist bureaucracy, as foreign capitalists would no doubt have given it their support. This terrorism was bewildering not only by reason of the lying character of its accusations and forced confessions, but by the material rewards given to the ' contrite '. After long months spent in prison in the company of these engineers, I was able to convince myself that this was not a cruel but honest course of action, but the vilest form of blackmail. The authorities seemed to tell their adversaries : ' Do what you wish, give us your honour and your conscience, admit to crimes you have not committed and in return you will receive all worldly goods.'

All this seemed a nightmare to me. What astonished me

most was the natural and orderly way in which it all happened. Thousands of people were arrested, they ' confessed ', they were condemned and sent into exile ; then they were made to work in various branches of production to purge their misdeeds, and finally they were re-established in their former rights. Some of these people perished along the road, dying a natural death or being shot, and the rapid current of Soviet life soon removed all trace of their existence.

GOLD AND TORTURE

In the Leningrad prison I was particularly shocked by the treatment reserved for those who were accused of hoarding gold. At that time, people throughout Russia were arrested on suspicion of possessing gold and precious objects. This is how it was done : at night, agents of the G.P.U. came to search a house and took away all valuables, from silver spoons to gold coins and *objets d'art*. Then, independently of the result of the perquisition, the suspect was gaoled and a payment was ordered for the financing of the Five Year Plan ; he was commanded to hand over all gold and valuables that he might have hidden. The demand was a legitimate one, but not so the methods of carrying it out.

These people were made to wait in batches outside the office of the examining magistrate. There they were left for whole days, without food or sleep, to force them to hand over their gold. Called before the magistrate, I had the opportunity of seeing them with my own eyes. Among them I recognized a young dentist who had been shut up in the same ward as myself. He had spent forty-eight hours standing in that corridor. His florid complexion had become grey and earthy. On one occasion one of them went mad and began to shout, " Blood ! look ! blood ! " The G.P.U. left him where he was for another twenty-four hours, to persuade the others to own up. One of my Trotskyist comrades was present, in a provincial prison, at the following episode. The G.P.U. knew that a number of prisoners who had been suspected of hoarding gold did not actually possess any. But there was one man among them who did. The G.P.U. called them all into the office but for that one and promised them their freedom if they could make him give up his gold. These wretches, taken back to their ward, began to shout in unison, " X——, give up your gold ! give up your gold ! " They kept that up for a couple of days and in the end X—— gave in.

Later, in Siberia, I met people, mainly old men and women, who had been made to suffer the terrible cold of Siberia for ten or twenty days to make them give up the gold they were supposed to have. After such tortures, those who had any gave it up. The Industrialization Fund grew richer by a hundred or two hundred million roubles throughout the U.S.S.R. ; but as the arrests were made in a haphazard way, as a rule on denunciations, most of those who were tortured did not possess any gold, but instead lost their health if not their life.

What was particularly odious about it all was the way in which this gold was handed in. The parties concerned had to sign a declaration to the effect that they had given such or such a sum to the socialist Industrialization Fund of their own free will. Besides this, those people who had been tortured were, at the moment of their liberation, forced to promise in writing never to tell anyone of what they had seen or undergone in prison. These Stalinist methods recalled to my mind the acts of the Spanish conquistadors and the analogous methods they applied to the unhappy Indians.

They were by no means the only category of prisoners to whom torture was applied. I know cases in which the G.P.U. subjected their prisoners to interrogations that lasted from sixteen to twenty-four hours. The prisoners were interrogated without a break, either by several examining magistrates or by successive magistrates, so that the prisoners were never allowed to relax. Moreover, attempts were made to demoralize prisoners by the following methods : my neighbour in the ward where I was put had been arrested for belonging to a religious sect, and came back after an interrogation of this kind. He was a man of frail health and the interrogation had left him entirely broken. He threw himself on the meal that had been kept for him, took off his shoes and dropped heavily on the bunk that was being reserved for him on this special occasion. Ten minutes had barely passed when there came a knock on the door and the gaoler called for him to undergo another interrogation from the examining magistrate.

All this was a terrible shock to me. I had, in the past, invariably refused to admit that such things were possible in Soviet Russia. I had a higher opinion of the G.P.U. Henceforward I could see that the degeneracy of Soviet rule—at one time revolutionary—had sunk even lower than I had thought. I was so surprised and disgusted at it that I availed myself of the first opportunity of protesting to the examining magistrate about all these horrors, these tortures, these false accusations and these not less false ' confessions '. " What are you doing ? " I asked him. " We abroad are standing up for you and you are carrying out atrocities that I would have thought impossible if I had not seen them with my own eyes ! You are compromising both the revolution and socialism, your achievement will be that all peasants, all urban petit-bourgeois and all non-Party intellectuals will become the mortal enemies of socialism and revolution." The magistrate, unable to deny the facts, answered to this effect : " You are not treated like it, nor are revolutionaries in general. As to the petit-bourgeoisie, we are forced to deal with them in this way, for the country is in the throes of the bitterest of all class-struggles." But in my eyes, nothing can ever justify the use of such vile methods by a socialist and revolutionary Government.

I soon learned that workers, too, were subjected to tortures worthy of the Inquisition. One day a sailor who up to that moment had been kept in the strictest isolation was transferred to our ward. He was a well-built young man. All the time he had been in solitary confinement the G.P.U. had done its utmost to force a confession from him concerning his participation in an imaginary plot against Stalin. The G.P.U. had used all means at its disposal. At night he had repeatedly been led out of his cell and told that he was going to be shot for his criminal silence. He was then taken into the courtyard and put up against the wall as if to be shot. Then he was taken back to his cell and told, " You are a worker after all ; we don't want to shoot you as we do any white guardist. But as you are a worker, you must confess everything openly." The sailor did not ' confess ' but became half-insane as a result of these tortures ; after that he was left in peace.

The most important aspect of all this is that it took place, not after the murder of Kirov in 1934 but considerably earlier, in 1930. I paid no attention at first to one detail in the story of the sailor. Now, after the three trials against

the Zinovievists, it assumes a sinister significance ; the
sailor was accused of belonging to the Trotskyist Opposition,
and an attempt was made to confirm this aspect of the
accusation by a ' confession '. In actual fact, the man was
a worker who was in no way politically minded. He had
sailed on Soviet ships that called at foreign ports and had
made a very good living ; he used to make little extras by
doing a small contraband trade, which was actually his sole
crime. He was happily married and pleased with his wife,
who was young and good-looking. Trotsky was to him the
glorious chief of the Civil War ; he had only the vaguest
notion as to what happened to Trotsky later on and he was
in no way interested in it.

The particular refined and ' psychological ' nature of the
tortures applied by the G.P.U. is very well illustrated by a
case described to me by a man with Trotskyist views. He
was imprisoned at the beginning of 1932 in the G.P.U.
prison in Moscow. He had been particularly struck by one
of his companions in misfortune, whose hair had gone
entirely white. From the man's own mouth he learned the
cause of this premature sign of age.

" As I did not confess to the crimes of which I was accused,
the examining magistrate threatened me several times with
capital punishment. Once, after midnight, I was taken out
of my cell. The G.P.U. man, as was customary, did not tell
me where he was taking me. He kept on telling me : straight
ahead, turn right, turn left, and so on. I soon gathered
that I was not being taken before the magistrate but sent
down into the cellars. My stomach rose. Everyone knows
they shoot people in those cellars, without telling them,
with a shot from behind. In that frame of mind, I was
walking along the corridors of the basement. I soon came
across an officer who appeared to be waiting for me. The
man who handed me over to him spoke these awful words,
' Can you manage him alone or shall I lend you a hand ? '—
' No, I can manage by myself.' We walked on. The footsteps of the officer echoed behind me, and I was prepared
to die at any moment. ' The door on the right ! ' he suddenly roared. I opened the door and was blinded by an
intensive light. ' That's the end,' I said to myself, remem-
bering a detail I had once been told : in the cellars of the
G.P.U. they killed their victims in a brilliant light to blind

them and prevent them from seeing the blood and the corpse-pit. But instead of the expected report I heard a new order, 'The door on the left!' Once more I came into a brilliantly lit room. 'This'll be the place.' But instead of death I saw a beautiful young woman dressed in white who smiled at me in an exaggerated way and said, 'You have complained about an aching tooth. I shall give you something for it.' Indeed, there was a small surgery down there and she handed me a small phial."

After this macabre comedy, the prisoner was brought back as if nothing had happened. But in the morning, his companions noticed that his hair had turned completely white.

THE RELIGIOUS PEOPLE

After the engineers, the most obvious group in our ward consisted of priests and members of religious sects. These, moreover, naturally grouped themselves into two distinct and even hostile camps, but they occupied places near one another and formed, as it were, a 'united front' towards the rest of the ward, who were either atheists or indifferent towards religion. The priests were subdivided into adherents of the 'recognized Church, governed by Serge the metropolitan, and adherents of the opposition inside the Church. What I learned at the time about the life and internal struggles of the orthodox church of Tikhon seemed truly incredible, but later events took it upon themselves to prove the truth of the facts. The orthodox Russian Church had gone through a profound crisis during the revolution. The sects that before the revolution had already been powerful had, during the revolution, gathered from 10 to 20 per cent of all believers and constituted a serious threat to orthodoxy. The hostility of the sects towards the ancient régime as well as towards the Soviet Government made them a very suitable vehicle for the expression of the discontent of the peasantry and the popular strata of the towns. As to the 'living Church', she represented a purely Soviet opposition to the orthodox Church and hence enjoyed the favour of the Government. But that did not endow it with life; it was still-born. The believing masses had remained faithful to their old Church, and inside this Church the most important struggle was taking place. At the moment of my imprisonment it had reached its greatest violence.

Most of the priests had linked up with the Stalin Government. To them the future of the Church was linked with that of the State, albeit a Soviet State. The task of the Church therefore was not only to spread the faith in God but also to spread the principle of submission to the powers that be. The policy of forced collectivization and the peasant risings did not alter their views. On the contrary, the Church supported the Government at its most critical moment, banking on the fact that the Government would remember this, and would later recognize the rights of the Church. The symbolic gesture that crowned this policy was the introduction into the Church services of a prayer for the Soviet Government.

" What ! " I exclaimed. " But is there no separation of Church and State in Soviet Russia ? "

" Certainly there is, but who is to stop the Church from praying for the State of her own accord ? "

A section of the Church was opposed to this policy and considered that, since the separation of Church and State was an accomplished fact, the Church should no longer take an active interest in the fate of the State. This opposition, which had arisen in various parts of the country, found its centre in Leningrad. Most of the members of the Leningrad Church joined the opposition and elected as their bishop of Leningrad the spiritual leader of the opposition, the bishop of Rostov. The minority in the Russian Synod also supported the opposition, whereas its majority, led by Serge the metropolitan, demanded the submission of the minority and refused the ecclesiastic communities the right of choosing their own bishops and other dignitaries without the metropolitan's sanction. Thus the question of the internal organization of the Church was added to that of her attitude towards the Government.

The claim of autonomy within the Church clashed with the principle of autocratic centralization. That constituted an unexpected analogy with the struggle inside the Communist Party. That analogy extended to yet other aspects : the ecclesiastic autonomist opposition consisted of two distinct groups, the Right-wing group composed of advocates of a restoration and opposed to all relations with the Government because the latter was Soviet ; the Left-wing group, desiring total independence of the State, to make this independence the starting-point of a struggle against the Government in favour of the masses of the people.

Then appeared the most astonishing phenomenon : the Government and the G.P.U. actively intervened in the conflict. When the majority of metropolitan Serge began to totter in the Synod, the G.P.U. arrested a few members of the Synod and sent them to exile and prison : the metropolitan thus recovered his majority. When the opposition became dangerous in the provinces, the G.P.U., without entirely destroying it, kept it down in the same way, to prevent its too rapid growth. Thus the bishop of Rostov, spiritual leader of the opposition, was allowed to go free until the moment when he was elected bishop of Leningrad. As this election was too direct a threat to metropolitan Serge, the G.P.U. decided to make the now dangerous bishop disappear, and had him arrested. Whereas on the Soviet stage, the comedy of the struggle against all religion was still being played, Stalin was entering into relations with the orthodox religion behind the scenes.

I never succeeded in finding out why the priests in my ward had been arrested ; they refused to tell me. I conjectured therefore that they had belonged to the opposition. A few among them were old popes of the typical fat and paunchy type. They assured me that they belonged to no opposition. " I have no idea why I should have been arrested. I am a supporter of Serge," the most educated among them told me. As to those who did not hide their sympathies, they belonged to various shades of opinion. The most uncompromising among them was a young monk, tall and spare, his eyes full of subdued fire, and with a full, fair beard. He looked like a fanatic from Byzantium. If he spoke little, his gestures were eloquent. One could feel that he hated and despised sinful humanity. To him, a church where one prayed for the Government was ' not a temple of God, but a temple of Satan '. He refused to officiate in churches that had thus—be it only once—been sullied by a prayer for the State.

An old *batiuchka* showed a curious mixture of extremism and conciliation. I first mistook him for a layman. He was not dressed in ecclesiastical attire and wore a cap that made him look more like a steward of a large estate. Then I heard that he was a priest in favour of sectarianism. The other priests, without excluding him from their midst, showed a certain reserve with respect to him. And, indeed, in the ward he occupied a place on the border-line of priests and laymen. He kept on saying that he was not in favour of the old régime, that he accepted the revolution as it had been invoked to improve the lot of the people, that the Bolsheviks had been right to get rid of the Czar, the great landowners and the capitalists. He added that even now he was an advocate of Bolshevism and that his own niece was a Bolshevik. These assertions made me smile. This drove him to greater sincerity. After we had spoken at great length of Russia and Europe, and after I had explained the aims of the Trotskyists to him, he asked me in a mysterious way, " And what do the anarchists want ? " I tried to explain this to him. Then he opened his heart. " You see, I approve of the Bolsheviks for having got rid of Czarism and for having thrown out landowners and capitalists, but I notice that the Government does no good to the people and that there is no justice. I see that all power, that of layman as well as that of ecclesiastic, brings with it nothing but violence and oppression. That being so, it seems to me that the anarchists are right."

When the fate of the priests was decided, I was no longer in that ward. But just before my arrival, another batch of priests had been condemned to various terms of imprisonment. One of them was even condemned to be shot. The accusation had been the same for all, the sentence differing according to attendant circumstances : those who had been priests before the revolution were sent to concentration camps, whereas the one who was shot had, before he became a priest, been an army-officer under the old régime.

Among the sectarians, there were evangelists and *tchurikovtsy*. They were peasants, craftsmen or sailors ; there were a few workmen also among them. The *tchurikovtsy* were the most active. Their sect was a Russian variant of evangelism or anabaptism. Its principal centre was Leningrad and the surrounding country, and it counted, so I was told, several hundreds of thousands of adherents. The chief of the sect, Tchurikov, was in prison at Yaroslavl. The members of the sect declared themselves in favour of Communism, but of a Communism that differed from that of the Bolsheviks. They told me the principal task of their sect was ' to help their neighbour and be useful to him '. In so far as I was able to understand it, one of the essential functions of their community was the upkeep of a rather ramified system of mutual aid that comprised all sorts of courses where sewing, domestic work and office work were taught. That organization covered those layers of the urban population which were not employed in factories and remained outside the field of Government and syndicate activities.

There was also a Tartar vagabond belonging to one of the radical sects most hostile to Soviet rule. Conversation in our ward came round to the extremist sects. It was said that there were certain sects, the members of which refused to have any relation whatsoever with the authorities, and would not allow their people even to talk to a Bolshevik. One of the prisoners who had been in Solovetsk told of a particularly fanatic woman sectarian who was detained there and had refused to countersign her own act of liberation, although she had been warned that she could not be set at liberty before she signed her name.

I must also quote the case of two prisoners who belonged to a section of ' religious people '. One of them, an old man, was a member of the Directing Council of a religious community. It was not easy to guess the reason for his arrest. Maybe the authorities thought that the communities were conducting their religious propaganda too openly and wished to intimidate them by making a few arrests. The story of this old man and of his family is worth relating. Before the revolution he had been the estate manager of a very wealthy prince. Owing to the prince's protection, two of his sons had become officers in the army of the Czar, which, however, had not prevented them from sympathizing with the revolutionaries and belonging to a secret Bolshevist organization. They had survived the Civil War, and under Voroshilov they occupied, in 1930, important posts at the Commissariat for War. As to the third son, he had been a hairdresser and had not changed his trade. The members of the community who had elected the old man had no doubt acted with calculation and foresight. It was customary to elect people on to the Councils of religious communities who had relatives or who were workers whom the G.P.U.—so they believed—could not easily touch, therefore.

It was no doubt the position of his two sons that led to the election of the old man. The family cycle had run its course : the sons who owed their career to their father were now his support in society.

The other case was that of a man of uncertain age, a member of the Council of a Jewish community connected with a synagogue. The G.P.U. had asked him to keep it informed of the opinions held by the members of the Council ; in other words, the G.P.U. wanted to make him one of its agents. Must we believe that if he had given a categorical refusal the G.P.U. would have left him in peace ? However that may be, he naïvely pretended, in order not to incur the anger of the G.P.U., to be lacking in the education needed to draw up such reports. The G.P.U. had then arrested him, no doubt to allow him to perfect his education in prison.

A LIVING CORPSE—' THE UNION OF WORKERS AND PEASANTS '

The people accused of speculating with silver money constituted a particular group in prison. At that time an active campaign was being conducted against speculation. Because of the inflation, the population had begun to hoard silver money. The following penalties were given out : those who had hidden more than five hundred roubles in coins to be shot ; the others to be sent to concentration camps for periods varying between five and ten years. Sometimes, by way of warning, a list of those who had been executed would be published. One day I was present at a terrifying scene. We had just received the morning papers when in the list of ' already executed ' we read the name of one of the men still in our ward. This man knew nothing as yet of his condemnation. All the ward and the corridor were horror-stricken. The prisoners who had already read the papers began to tear them away from the others in order to prevent them falling into the hands of the man who had in a way been buried alive. But somehow he felt that all this excitement concerned him. He grew pale and sank down on his bunk. After a few minutes the G.P.U. rectified its mistake : the man was called out and shot. The blunder was easily explained : the condemnation was of a group, the other members of which, imprisoned in Moscow, had been shot that night. But a complete list of the group had been handed out to the Press, inclusive of the name of the Leningrad prisoner who was to be shot only on the following day.

*   *   *

It was a long time before I learned the story of the prisoner Kozlov, accused of having organized the counter-revolutionary and terrorist group known as the ' Union of Workers and Peasants '.

This organization existed in a number of villages around Leningrad and had formed a small centre in Leningrad itself. Kozlov was a Communist, the son of a small employee in the Post Office of that town. He had fought in the Civil War and said that he had been the leader of a small detachment of irregulars who had fought against the English troops on the Northern front. He had studied at the Communist University of Leningrad during the NEP and, before his arrest, had been the director of a school in Leningrad. From the first days of collectivization, he had belonged to the Right-wing Opposition ; he considered himself a follower of Bukharin. A certain number of his friends in Leningrad and of his acquaintances in the villages shared his views, entered into closer relations and formed a group. After the leaders of the Right-wing Opposition had, in 1928–29, given up all active struggle against Stalin, the group seceded from the Right-wing Opposition to follow its own lines.

Apart from Communists and non-Party members, socialist revolutionary elements gradually joined them. The group, according to Kozlov, slowly took over their ideas and began to apply the methods of conflict proper to the socialist revolutionaries. In 1929 Kozlov misappropriated some Government funds to finance his organization, and the latter very nearly perished under it, for an inspector had unexpectedly arrived and had discovered the malversation. But the affair was settled, it was taken to be a private matter and Kozlov himself got out of it without too much difficulty. It is possible that the G.P.U. had already got wind of the conspiracy but wanted to give it time to develop more fully before unmasking it.

Indeed, the organization was growing and spreading, and was assuming an increasingly hostile attitude towards the Government. Already it was preparing itself to take part in the peasant risings. One member—it was later discovered that he was an *agent provocateur*—urged the group to take extreme decisions. He insisted on the drawing up of statutes and a programme ; they gave in to him and he himself drew up a project in which he wrote among other things that the organization was ready to answer by terror the terror which the Government used against the people. The draft statutes took into account that the organization would procure the necessary funds by means of subscriptions and gifts from sympathizers ' independently of their social position ' or even by ' expropriating ' public funds. Certain articles of these statutes gave rise to passionate discussions. While these debates were in progress, the members of the organization were arrested. The project in question, confiscated at Kozlov's place, was used as the basis of the accusation. The *agent provocateur* who was its author was arrested at the same time as the others, but was soon released. The organization had also drawn up appeals to the peasantry ; a few copies of these fell into the hands of the G.P.U. One of these appeals ended with the slogan ' Long live the Union of Workers and Peasants ! ' Thus the G.P.U. found a name for the organization.

Now that he was in prison, Kozlov was thinking over the past, wondering why the agent of the G.P.U. had urged the organization towards the Right rather than towards the Left. Kozlov wondered whether an attack on Stalin would not have been more effective if coming from the Left.

One night Kozlov was fetched away and he was told to take all his belongings with him. He had already lived a few days in expectation of some such event. Once he had left the room, he was put into the hands of an armed escort, the members of which walked revolver in hand. Then he was made to enter the car for those condemned to death, and was taken to the place where he was to be shot.

Later on, when I left Leningrad for the ' political isolator ' of Verkhne-Uralsk, the inspector of the G.P.U. who accompanied me told me that the entire Party in Leningrad had been told the story of Kozlov's group and its sad end, by way of warning.

MANUAL WORKERS, PEASANTS AND OFFICE WORKERS

A while later, two members of the Comsomol, who had worked in the paper mill ' the Zinoviev ', were brought to our ward. The other members of the same group were put up in the neighbouring wards. Their story was not without interest. At the meetings of the Comsomol one could neither discuss matters nor put questions. Therefore, a few of the factory workers, members of the Comsomol, decided to found a secret ' discussion circle ' where they could talk and work out problems in all freedom. This seemed all the more necessary to them as the material conditions of the workers were worsening, famine was approaching and it was necessary to be fully aware of what was going on and to look for solutions. But the G.P.U. heard of this unorthodox initiative and the entire group was arrested. The two members of the Comsomol, as soon as they had settled in our ward, started on an interminable argument ; before their arrest their sympathies had been slightly Right-wing, but by the time they were condemned to exile they had already become Trotskyists.

We also received a group of workers from a Leningrad factory, from the ' Vulcan ' works, if I remember rightly. They had gone so far as to show their discontent openly. Some ten workmen, considered to be the leaders, were arrested. Two or three of them were socialist revolutionaries, which enabled the G.P.U. to make the case a trial of a socialist revolutionary organization. The affair had a comic side to it. One of the arrested workmen had been a soldier in the Tsarkoye Selo ; this made him brag that he had seen the princess Tatiana there. To the great glee of our ward the G.P.U. turned him into ' a former lover of Tatiana '. The picture was not without colour ; a former lover of the Czar's daughter inciting the workers of the ' Vulcan ' factory against the Soviet Government.

During walks I had the opportunity to meet a group of workers from the Navy dockyards, who were lodged in another ward. They were accused of having sabotaged the loan for the Five Year Plan in certain workshops of the Dockyard. They were accused of Trotskyism ; some, indeed, were tainted with it, but most of them were plain non-Party workers. They assured me that the Dockyard workers had sabotaged the loan without anybody's prompting in order to protest against the continual worsening of their material conditions. These workers also told me that there was, in the prison infirmary, an important Trotskyist, former member of the Central Executive Committee (or even of the Secretariat of that Committee), who was being treated there after a prolonged hunger-strike on his part.

*   *   *

Among the prisoners there was a kulak condemned to three years' hard labour. He came from a poor peasant family in the Pskov region. He had been taken prisoner during the War and he had been made to work in a village in Hungary. There he might have married his employer's daughter and he bitterly regretted not having done so. Returned home after the revolution, he married a well-to-do Lutheran widow, and, to please her, he embraced the Lutheran faith. Most of his income was drawn from a dairy farm that sold its produce in Leningrad.

" What has brought you here ? "

" It's all my fault. I was drunk."

The whole story was very simple. The woman chairman of the village Soviet, a poor peasant woman, always ordered butter, cheap and on account, but she never paid her bill. One day, having drunk a lot at the village inn, he met his customer. " Drunk as I was, I asked her, ' Martha Ivanovna, when do you intend paying for your butter ? '—' You will have your money tomorrow.' " Indeed, she paid him the next day, but a couple of days later the village Soviet let him know that he was to hand over four hundred poods of corn to the Government. " I had hardly two hundred poods at home. I was unable to do it, and all my goods were confiscated and I was given three years on top of it. I am in the wrong, for if I had not been drunk, I would never have reminded her of her debt." He had yet another crime on his conscience. " We have no child, and it was very difficult for us to do all the work. In 1927 we had taken on a boy. Now the boy is in the Red Army, and has even sent a petition in our favour, but it has been of no use." He showed me the letter of his ex-farmhand, in which the latter complained of having been unable to do anything for him and in which he tried to console the man : it would all end well in time.

There was among us a Latvian barrister called Zaune, I think, who had also suffered in the peasant cause. He had been a socialist revolutionary, then a non-Party member.

During the War he had been an officer in a regiment of Latvian light infantry. This regiment had joined the Bolsheviks. Zaune had been in the Red Army throughout the entire revolution ; he told us episodes of the fight against Denikin with a wealth of picturesque detail. After the revolution he went to Latvia, but did not like it there and returned to Russia during the NEP. He settled in Moscow as a barrister. During the collectivization he specialized in the affairs of peasants who were robbed of their cattle. As this type of expropriation was contrary to the existing Soviet laws, he won every case that he took on. But it was this that led to his downfall. He was arrested in order to be repatriated to Latvia. In actual fact, he was kept in prison for months, both in Moscow and at Tver, finally at Leningrad. In the Tver prison he was present at numerous executions of peasants. This prison was not so well equipped with the cellars that made the G.P.U. so notorious. Prisoners were shot without trial in either the courtyard or in their cells. Two or three times a week there would be mass-executions ; the dull echoes of shots would ring through the entire prison.

The day before I left Leningrad the Latvian barrister had gone on hunger-strike to obtain the permission to be sent back to Latvia that had been promised him. His wife and two children had also been imprisoned, as they were all to be repatriated. Sometimes the barrister would succeed in exchanging a few words with his wife, for the courtyard where the women prisoners were exercised was not far from our window.

Still more painful was the fate of a former officer of the Red Army who had landed in our ward. He was a schoolmaster somewhere in the country round Leningrad and had been condemned to eighteen months' hard labour for his hostility towards Stalinist collectivization. But he succeeded in escaping and crossing the Finnish border. Having told his story to the Finns, he declared his intention of trying to go on to France. The Finns, having searched him, discovered that he had been a Red Army officer. Indeed, he still had his demobilization papers on him ; he had kept them as a souvenir of the heroic revolution days. The Finnish authorities refused to believe his story and thought him a Soviet spy. However, slightly shaken by his insistence, the Finns gave him the alternative of returning secretly to

Russia in the same way as he had come, without witnesses. Fearing that his return under those conditions would once more make him look like a spy—this time in the eyes of the Soviet authorities who might have accused him of working for Finland—he chose to be handed over directly. Now he awaited his verdict in prison. He told me that he belonged to no Party and had ' proletarian ' sympathies. The present state of affairs in Russia seemed an unintelligible nightmare to him. On the other hand, he had very distinct views about the past. " The NEP has killed the revolution, for it re-established money, trade and capitalism." On another occasion he said, " Women have caused the revolution to be lost. The Communist and the leaders of the revolution have married former Society women, which has caused a bourgeois morality to return first to the home, next to society."

" But you, too, must have had an aristocratic wife ? "

" Certainly, she was the wife of an officer. But we have long since parted."

Among the prisoners there was an official of the military administration. In the course of an inspection it had been found that the stocks under his supervision were not in order, and that part of the material had decayed owing to lack of care. The responsibility was that of one of his hierarchic superiors. But the G.P.U. had its reasons for not victimizing the real culprits but other highly placed people who had nothing to do with the whole business. The G.P.U. therefore arrested the official and insisted that he made statements along the lines indicated by it. The most ignoble procedure was followed : the prisoner was made to believe that his mistress had betrayed him and in his depressed state of mind he was made to sign statements which otherwise he would have repudiated. Upon his return to the ward he pulled himself together and sent a statement to the procurator in which he unmasked the proceedings of the G.P.U. examining magistrate. It is certain that had he been kept longer in solitary confinement, he would in the end have given in.

During my time in the prison, a large number of seamen, plain sailors or petty-officers, were there. They were nearly all condemned to three years' concentration camp at Solovetsk. Those sailors spoke but rarely of the accusations that were made against them. In so far as I could gather, they were based on letters exchanged with people in their own

villages on the subject of collectivization ; they were accused
of spreading propaganda in the Navy in favour of religious
sects ; to this must be added their discontent owing to the
constantly increasing privileges of the officers. One of them,
a paymaster with petty-officer's rank, was condemned to
three years at Solovetsk for having refused to recognize the
regularity of certain expenses made by the ship's captain.
The captain attained his revenge by accusing him of certain
breaches of discipline. Yet, notwithstanding their discontent, the sailors showed no counter-revolutionary inclinations,
neither before nor after their sentences were pronounced.

One of my ward-neighbours, an important official of a
light-industries trust, came back from an interview with the
examining magistrate one day in a state of great excitement.
The latter had demanded that he own up to certain acts
of sabotage. He asked my advice and reported the conversation he had had with the magistrate. " Did you perhaps think that we should limit ourselves to the heavy
industries ? "

" I conclude from this," the prisoner proceeded, " that
there never has been sabotage but that the G.P.U. invent
all these sabotage cases in the various branches of industry
from beginning to end, in accordance with a preconceived
plan." My informant was all the more surprised, as he
considered himself a good socialist and had belonged to a
socialist organization prior to 1918. Recently he had been
abroad a number of times for affairs connected with his
trust. Had he so wished, he might have stayed abroad, but
he had not done so out of solidarity with the Soviet cause,
though his parents were in Western Europe and he could
very easily have settled with them.

Official campaigns against such or such a group often
brought into our prison a number of victims belonging to
the category aimed at. Thus, after the Press had unmasked
malversations going on in State enterprises, our prison received
a large group of employees from the co-operatives. One of
them, put in our ward, told us openly, " How do you think
we could feed our families on one hundred roubles wages if
we did not steal some of the goods ? "

Later on, with the help of the flying squad of the Comsomol,
the way in which the Housing Committee distributed the
bread ration cards was checked ; as a result, the prisons

were filled with guilty managers. Some of them were Communists and vigorously defended the Government policy. After two weeks the managers were liberated and it was stated that the irregularities in the matter of the distribution of bread ration cards had been due to oversights. They were the only group of prisoners that got off so lightly.

THE ' ACADEMICIANS '

In my prison there was a group of professors, lecturers and academicians of Leningrad, the most notable among them being Professor Tarle and the academician Platonov. They had committed the crime of having failed to adapt themselves to the system and of having shown scepticism as regards the Five Year Plan. In prison slang they were always called ' academicians '. They enjoyed the privilege of special food ; alone among the non-political prisoners they were entitled to the food reserved for political prisoners.

There were two representatives of this group in my ward : Belayev, the director of the Pushkin House, and S——, lecturer in international law at the University.

Belayev was a Russian intellectual of the old school, cultured but narrowly academic. He was interested in Pushkin, in the history of literature and in the lives of the literary élite. The form of government, be it Czarist or Soviet, was totally indifferent to him. Planing over the peaks of learning, he looked down from a considerable height on the things of this life, and the people to him were but a negligible crowd. Even in prison he lived in his ivory tower, re-reading Sophocles, Cervantes, Thackeray and Dumas and speaking rarely to the proletarians in our ward.

Before his arrest he had been abroad several times for matters connected with his work. Had he wished, he need not have come back. The reason for his return was that he cared more for Pushkin House than for all the rest of the world put together. I particularly remember a talk I had with him about Gorky. Belayev told me that Gorky was not the naïve enthusiast that people generally liked to think him. Gorky was a clever *mujik* who did not overlook his own interests. But it had to be admitted that he was deeply and sincerely devoted to culture. His claim on the gratitude of the generations to come was that he had made use of his intimacy with Lenin and the other leading Bolsheviks to

173

save, in the days of famine and terror, a large number of the representatives of Russian culture. I learned from Belayev that Gorky had taken the initiative, immediately after the October revolution, of bringing about a *rapprochement* and personal contacts between the personalities of the old Russian culture, albeit princes, and the representatives of the new power, albeit Communists of the stamp of Zinoviev, who was then master in Leningrad.

S——, on the other hand, was a man of the Soviet type. He accepted the new régime in Russia as an ineluctable outcome of historic evolution. He was perfectly acquainted with the history of the international workers' movement. Yet one felt in his attitude a total absence of what seems to me to be the very ground of socialism : the feeling of an intimate bond with the lower strata of society. S—— belonged to the new aristocracy and limited himself to taking ' the people ' into account. From that point of view, this old student of Professor Tarle was a typical representative of the new Soviet intellectual *élite*. Even in prison he was not hostile to the system and aspired to one thing only, namely, to resume the place the new society owed him. It is very probable that today, after the Five Year Plan, S—— has been reinstated in his post and that he is a model ' non-Party Bolshevik '. From among the people of his type are recruited the best servants of Soviet Bonapartism. Moreover, Belayev, too, has now gone back to his place at the head of Pushkin House ; as to Professor Tarle, he has left his exile in Alma-Ata (where he taught in the new Kirghiz University) and having returned to the Leningrad University, he has already published a *Life of Napoleon Bonaparte*, in keeping with the spirit of the Stalinist period. The academician, Platonov, was too old to remodel his life ; he died in exile.

Platonov's two daughters were also detained in our prison. The women's recreation court was under Belayev's window, so that the academicians were acquainted with the latest news. Platonov's daughters were each condemned to ten years' concentration camp and were preparing themselves to leave for Solovetsk. But their departure was suddenly postponed. It was said that their sentence was going to be revised and they hoped for a more lenient one.

Platonov's daughters had as a neighbour a woman I did

not know, but whom I was to meet later in the political ' isolator ' of Verkhne-Uralsk ; she was the Left-wing socialist revolutionary, Sonia Lunin.

* * *

The campaign that was then being waged against Professor Tarle found a victim even among the Communist professors. The Cell of the Communist professors directed one of its members, Zakher, to open fire on Tarle. Zakher had drawn attention to himself during the years 1925–28, in the course of the fight against Trotskyists and Zinovievists by his bloody ' scientific researches ' against the Left-wing Opposition. In them he had justified the execution of Jacques Roux, Hébert and others, ' scientifically ' proving the ' counter-revolutionary *naïveté* ' of that Left-wing Opposition in the days of Robespierre. He was then already in favour of the execution of the members of the Russian Left-wing, which Stalin was unable to carry out before 1936. Not very desirous to enter into a struggle with Tarle, he thought himself very clever in writing a preliminary note to Tarle in which he told him that he was going to attack him, not out of conviction, but in obedience to Party discipline. This became known, and Zakher, accused of treachery, was expelled from the Party.

My neighbour was Zakher's uncle, an ex-banker. His gold had landed him in gaol. The G.P.U. suspected him of keeping large amounts for himself. He admitted to a certain figure which the G.P.U. deemed insufficient. Zakher's uncle received the largest parcels from outside and was the richest man of all the arrested gold-hoarders. He was also the only one among them who was not subjected to the torture of the magistrate's antechamber.

INDIVIDUAL CASES

Among those prisoners who had been arrested for crimes not falling within one of the already mentioned categories, I have remembered one or two cases that appeared interesting to me.

There was a page editor of *Pravda* who told me that Demian Biedny, the poet, received incredibly high pay and that his wife, a grand lady, occasionally came to the newspaper offices and drew advances of thousands of roubles on account of her husband's future earnings. He also spoke of the villa that Demian Biedny had built for himself on the shores of the Black Sea.

An engineer from a quarry near Lake Onega, where porphyry was extracted for Lenin's mausoleum, told me the speech he had made before the workers of the quarries (many of them deported peasants). " Every great period leaves great monuments behind. Today the world still admires the Pyramids, forty centuries old, although no trace is left of the Pharaohs who had them built nor of the slaves who perished building them. Lenin's mausoleum must become the unforgettable monument of our great epoch. We must spare no effort, no sacrifice, to erect it."

This speech was applauded not only by the workers and the deported peasants, but also by the representatives of Party and syndicate. Nobody discovered any subversive intentions in the allusion to the slaves of Egypt.

Later on, Opposition Communists told me of the discussions that had been held in Soviet circles concerning the mausoleum, especially in the *Consomolskaya Pravda*. The mausoleum had been built in the style of the royal tombs of ancient Persia. It was the incarnation of the ideas of eternity and autocracy. There had been no reply made to the protests of the Left-wing architects against this reactionary style.

A little greybeard told me some interesting details concerning the attitude towards Trotsky of the superior officers of the Czarist army who had passed over into the service of the Soviets. The old man belonged to a family of high Czarist officials and had been in the ministry of Post and Telegraphs, but his brothers and his friends were soldiers.

A general, a specialist in fortifications, found himself without occupation after the fall of the Czarist rule ; he did not attempt to enter service again. One day he was called before Trotsky, and the interview made the greatest impression on him. He had told my informant about it in the following words : " Trotsky received me with both affability and intelligence ; he spoke to me with so much authority and competence that after five minutes I was willing to follow this revolutionary Secretary for War anywhere." That, according to the old man, had been the attitude of practically all the high Czarist officers who had happened to come into contact with Trotsky.

Among the prisoners in the common wards there were many—three or four hundred—who were accused or suspected of espionage. The G.P.U. was conducting a vast campaign against the British Consul-General in Leningrad. The choice of suspects made one conclude that the G.P.U. was determined to lay hands on the entire spying system. The method was simple and probably efficacious ; all those who had or might have had the slightest contact with English people or with the British consulate were arrested ; the captains of all the ships plying between Leningrad and London, the chief officials of Leningrad harbour who by reason of their employment had had relations with British vessels, and so on. In short, in order to unmask about half a dozen spies, they had arrested about two hundred people who were all treated like spies and condemned to five years in concentration camps. One hopes that the true spies—even if their identity remained a secret—were amongst those who had been so condemned. It is not difficult to punish culprits when one can permit oneself the luxury of an entirely free hand regarding the fates of hundreds of innocent people, who can, moreover, be made to ' confess ' anything one likes. What I saw in the Leningrad prison made me wonder at nothing.

Every Soviet captain, I was told, who sailed to foreign countries had to leave a hostage at home, a member of his family, who would be responsible for what he said or did abroad.

* * *

The prisoners belonged to the most varied nationalities. Hardly more than 50 per cent were Russians. The others belonged to all the nations of the U.S.S.R. : Ukrainians, White Russians, Tartars, Poles, etc. There were many Jews. In my ward, apart from myself, there were only four other foreigners : the Latvian barrister I have mentioned ; a Chinese Communist, an ex-railway official ; a young German who had worked on the Turksib line ; and finally, a young Esthonian Communist, who was a political refugee. The latter's brother was detained in the next ward ; he had been a Communist deputy in the Esthonian parliament (the only Communist deputy, if I am not mistaken) who then had emigrated also to the U.S.S.R. There were in our prison a whole group of refugee Esthonian Communists. The reason for their arrest was that information had been received that among the Esthonian political refugees there was a batch of secret *agents provocateurs* of the Esthonian police. Unable to unmask them, the G.P.U. had decided to arrest all the Esthonian political refugees in a body.

As to their age, the prisoners were usually fully grown men, with a fairly large proportion of men past their middle age, and even of very old men.

* * *

After my transfer to the common ward, I had been able to gain information about the fate of my comrades Deditch and Draguitch. Deditch was in a ward that opened into the next corridor to ours. I never saw him during walks, but I was able to talk to him for five minutes at night when we were all going to the end of the corridor to fetch our mattresses. The ward where he was had originally been fitted up for fourteen men, but now held sixty-five. The examining magistrate had acquainted him with what the G.P.U. had learned through their *agent provocateur*, namely, that Deditch had for some time no longer belonged to our group. He had been promised his liberty if he would only ' sincerely reveal the names of the people who had been in contact with the group (of whom the G.P.U. agent was still ignorant). When Deditch refused to denounce those of his comrades still in freedom, the magistrate offered him his liberty provided he signed a declaration that our group was conducting counter-revolutionary activities and that Draguitch and myself were counter-revolutionaries. Deditch, as was to be expected, answered that, notwithstanding any disagreements he might have had with us, he still considered us to be his comrades and honest revolutionaries ; he refused to sign any declaration of the sort. That decided Deditch's fate. Prison was further to strengthen the bonds of friendship between us and to remove any divergence of opinion that had separated us.

As to Draguitch, I learned that he had been arrested and was in our prison, as the examining magistrate told me one day that Draguitch requested me to return a blanket of his that I had taken away with me upon my arrest.

In the neighbouring ward there was another Yugo-Slav, a Leningrad barrister called Duchan Semiz. He had studied at the University of St. Petersburg long before the revolution and had stayed in Russia. Of later years he had been a Soviet barrister in Leningrad and had been arrested on account of a trifling matter. The G.P.U. on some vague suspicion, had his home searched and had found a letter dated 1920, addressed to his wife, in which he bitterly criticized the Bolshevist policy of ' exterminating the intellectuals '. The examining magistrate availed himself of that document to accuse him of anti-Soviet opinions. Semiz answered that his opinions could not be ascertained by a private communication and that he could only be bound by his public utterances. He now waited for Moscow's decision as to his fate. As for his wife, she was first told by the intermediary of the Red Cross that her husband had been condemned to ten years' concentration camp ; later she was informed that his case was to be revised. Semiz was a native of Mostar in Herzegovina where I had spent my youth. Now, during our short walks, we recalled memories of that far-off land and the mutual friends we had left there. I was told by him that another man from Mostar, a Serbian, Professor Pitcheta, had been arrested during the trial of the White Russian university men, for the old man was himself a professor at the University of Minsk.

* * *

Sometimes the conversation in our ward would veer round to the diet in other prisons. There was a constant stream of new prisoners who had stayed in more than one prison. The conditions prevailing in the three sections of our own prison were compared, the starvation diet and relative freedom of the Kresty prison would be mentioned ; there the prisoners in civil law were housed. The Gorokhovaya prison near the G.P.U. headquarters was rarely mentioned ; prisoners who were wanted near at hand were kept there.

More frequent mention was made of Solovetsk—the arctic Guiana of the U.S.S.R. During the Five Year Plan, immense concentration camps had arisen throughout Northern Russia and Siberia, from the Finnish frontier to the Pacific Ocean, where several million men were packed together. Solovetsk owed its fame to the fact that it had been the first of its type. Moreover, most of the Leningrad prisoners were sent on to Solovetsk. There were among us several people who had been sent from Solovetsk to undergo a supplementary interrogation in Leningrad.

The convicts of Solovetsk were mainly employed in cutting and floating wood. On the islands and along the coast numerous camps had been built to house them. There were, however, not enough of these barracks. At night people were squeezed in like herrings in a tin. To get out, one had to walk on bodies lying on the hard floor. On coming back, one found one's place taken and one had to lie down on top of someone in order to acquire a little bit of floor-space eventually. Food was bad, clothing insufficient. The administration was composed mainly of convicts and was directed by condemned G.P.U. men ; they mercilessly robbed the prisoners and had discretionary powers over them. Inspectors had the right to knock down anyone displaying bad temper or making the least protest. During work in the forests, the inspectors made free use of this right. It was not only dangerous to escape, it was practically impossible. Prisoners who were unable to go on with it any longer mutilated themselves, simulating an accident at work. Cases of fingers chopped off with axes were very common, sometimes it would be a whole hand or foot. At first the G.P.U. used to liberate these invalids. Later, when voluntary mutilations were becoming too common, they were called acts of sabotage ; the culprits were executed. The women suffered most and were subjected to the greatest humiliations. Poor food, dirt and the overcrowding of prisoners caused periodic epidemics. From 1929 to 1930 these epidemics reduced the population of the islands from 14,000 to 8,000. When these catastrophes occurred, a G.P.U. commission would come down from Moscow and shoot half the administration, after which convict life returned to its customary horror.

The population of Solovetsk comprised deported peasants, ex-army officers, members of sects and all sorts of people persecuted because of their faith, especially ' nationalist ' Moslems from Central Asia, Ukrainian nationalists and White Russians. There were also some fifty or sixty Trotskyists at Solovetsk, one of whom had recently been a director of *Pravda* in Leningrad. Moreover, there were a few dozen Chinese students of the Sun-Yat-Sen University in Moscow, who had been deported for belonging to the Opposition. These Chinese were treated as prisoners in civil law. Soviet authorities had calmly handed over some of their comrades to the mercy of their enemy Chiang-Kai-Shek by forcibly putting them on board a ship sailing from Vladivostok to Shanghai.

One of the convicts from Solovetsk, who had for several years occupied a moderately important post in the administration there, still thought back with pleasure to the life he used to lead. In that inhuman and barbarous atmosphere there was nothing for the all-powerful administration to do but give itself up to drunkenness and debauchery. To anyone who cared to listen, our ex-officer from Solovetsk liked to describe his orgies, nocturnal outings and endless drinking bouts. There were no free women there, but the convict women were given over to debauch. Here is an example from one of his tales. Eighty new convict women were brought to the district centre. They were put in a row, the district administration reviewed them and, picking out the ten women most pleasing, sent the others off to the most distant camps. At the same time, the ten women of a preceding batch who had ' served ' with the administration would be sent off. Thus the women would be despatched from camp to camp as if they were mere slave-traffic. Power, bread, vodka, clean rooms, all these were monopolized by the administration and were sufficient to allure the most obdurate. " Any woman, be she the Holy Virgin herself, will become a prostitute at Solovetsk," the old gaoler declared with pride and, grinning, he quoted the case of a ' high-class ' woman, the niece of one of the best-known admirals.

This official from Solovetsk was a living example of what a man may become in such a convict station. He had reached the rock-bottom of corruption. Yet, at one time, he had been a worker in the engineering trade, a Bolshevik, and had distinguished himself during the 1917 revolution. In the Civil War he had been the president of the Cheka in one of the areas of the Upper Volga. Early in 1921 he had been political Commissar on board the cruiser *Marat* of the Baltic fleet. In that capacity he had joined the revolt of the Kronstadt sailors. He escaped execution, but was condemned to ten years' exportation which he had spent at Solovetsk.

This rebel from Kronstadt whom I saw here in the flesh seemed to me almost an antediluvian monster : every year counts in a revolutionary period. I did my best to get the details of the famous revolt out of him. He did not like to talk about it.

" What did the Kronstadt people want ? "

" No one knew much about it. It was not a revolt but a perfect chaos."

He knew a good deal more about the repression after the

revolt. According to him, most of the victims perished not during the revolt but after it had been quelled. More than ten thousand sailors were shot. Several thousands fled to Finland, then returned when an amnesty was promised them. But the Government did not keep its word and they, too, were shot. Now that Trotsky was no longer in power, my informant had no reason to hide his feelings. It was astonishing to find so much hatred towards Trotsky in a man so profoundly demoralized. Yet his hatred was as violent as it had been on the first day. To him, Trotsky was neither the hero of the October revolution nor the chief of the victorious Red Army, but only the bloody executioner who had subdued the popular revolt of Kronstadt. He did not like the Trotskyists and had no great liking for me.

How was it that this man had been brought to our prison ? At Solovetsk, he had occupied a post in the administration and consequently could go from place to place on service matters. He had even succeeded in surreptitiously coming to Leningrad once or twice, had been divorced there and had found time to get married again. But his first wife had denounced him and he was arrested during one of his clandestine visits to Leningrad. He was greatly afraid of being shot, but the G.P.U. showed itself indulgent towards the old Chekist and he was merely condemned to an extra three years, so that he was sent back to Solovetsk.

He had been head of our ward. The prisoners themselves elected one among them to that post, but the prison administration reserved to itself the right to confirm this election. As head of the ward, he was able to render various services to the prisoners either lawfully or unlawfully. He rendered such services to any who could pay for them—to the ' academicians ', to Zakher the banker, etc. This man who at one time had had people shot was now ready to humiliate himself for the sake of one or two roubles. By turning his headship into hard cash, he succeeded in raising a little capital and in buying some winter clothes and strong shoes. Gradually the prisoners began to envy him, then to fear him because of his relations with the G.P.U.

In the ward of my friend Deditch there was a well-known idealist Russian philosopher, who had been transferred from Solovetsk. The crime that had caused him to be deported was no other than ' counter-revolution in the realms of philosophy '. He had been made to work in the central offices of the camp. To the horrors of Solovetsk had been added a figment of delirium : in the midst of a typhoid epidemic, the prison theatre was filled with camp-beds on which the sufferers lay moaning, but on the stage, surrounded by the dying, those convicts who had been promoted to the role of actors were with great fervour rehearsing a play celebrating the success of the Five Year Plan and of Socialist Enthusiasm.

One day I stayed behind in the ward in order to read whilst the other prisoners went for their exercise. One of my neighbours who had also stayed behind drew near and sat down beside me. He had long ago attracted my attention. With visible interest he had listened to my violent but sincere criticisms of the prevailing system, but he had never spoken. His silence seemed due to fear of the G.P.U., though for all one knew he might have been a G.P.U. man himself, for there were always some in the wards disguised as prisoners. One had just been unmasked in Deditch's ward. At first, therefore, I showed great reserve. After having been silent for some time, my neighbour whispered to me, " Don't talk so violently against the Government ; last night, when you went out to get some boiling water, the head of the ward said that you ought to be shot. People like you might have a bad influence in these days. The head of the ward is a man of the Cheka, and he does not express merely his personal opinion. You must be careful with them."

My position in the ward was, indeed, somewhat peculiar. I was the only prisoner openly to criticize and declare himself against the present system. The others told what they had seen or suffered, and sometimes told of their interrogations before the magistrate, or of things that had incriminated them. But of the four or five hundred men I met in that prison, not one—with the possible exception of Kozlov (who was shot)—made himself out to be an enemy of the Government nor offered any projects of a possible struggle against the authorities. Even those who had been condemned to death were silent ; men taken out to be shot left the ward without a word, without a cry of revolt against the Government that put them to death. If such was the attitude of people in prison, what was there to be said of those who lived in liberty ? Those as a rule did not even venture to whisper about what they had suffered personally.

The fears of my companions were justified. Any man among them who spoke out would have paid for it with his life. In Russia no one has the right or even the liberty to speak the truth aloud ; and even in prison one is allowed to do so only if one belongs to the small group of ' political prisoners ', or rather to a small *élite* of that group. I, moreover, was a foreign Communist, which gave me particular privileges, for this appeared to be the reasoning applied to them : " They are still insufficiently Bolshevized ; they should not be treated as severely as the Russians ; when they have had more experience, they will change their opinions."

I began to wonder whether it was right on my part to avail myself of my privileges, and if it were not better for me by my silence to express my solidarity with these unfortunates, these victims reduced to enforced silence. In the past I had been in Italy among criminals in civil law—and what criminals ! —and everywhere I had succeeded in getting to know them and in sharing their lives, to the extent that, after leaving prison, I would send them a small sum of money with the words, " To my companions in suffering." Should I not act in the same way here and not try to single myself out ? Yet I could not succeed in keeping silence. All that was taking place in Russia—oppression, pillage of the innocent, torture of the prisoners—was opposed to Communism, and I could not be silent about it.

During the first days my ward mates had moved away from me as if I carried thunderbolts. Just think of it, I was publicly saying, " Is this Communism ? It is not, it is slavery ! The ancient tyrants have been removed, but the new ones are no better ; the bourgeois have been removed, but new bourgeois have been born within the bureaucracy."

Who could permit himself such utterances in Russia, under the very nose of the G.P.U. ? The very reason that the whole of Russia shared them made it absolutely prohibitive to express them publicly. At first I was suspected of being an *agent provocateur* of the G.P.U. Then, gradually, by listening to what I said, by comparing my words with my behaviour, people realized their mistake. They began to show me greater friendliness and confidence, and began to talk more openly of their affairs. On the other hand, there were several open supporters of the present system in my ward and with them I was often in conflict.

The ' academicians ' and the engineers sometimes behaved in a revolting manner. They put on airs towards the people at the other end of the ward. One day I could not help saying to them, " The Bolsheviks have oppressed you for twelve years now, and have done so successfully, since you are strangers to the people. The people resent your pride and remain indifferent to your fate." Although I was in constant touch with the intellectuals, I had decided, by way of protest against their haughty attitude, to range myself at the other end of the ward among the proletarians.

I tried to express myself in a schematic and simplified way in my attacks on the Government. Thus I spoke of a bureaucratic ' class ' that was in power, although in my heart of hearts I thought that the bureaucrats were nothing but a social layer that was developing into what later might become a class. The period in which we lived seemed to me to have all the signs of a period of transition, but I simplified all problems, taking my listeners into account. Later, having simplified all the finer points of my theory, I came to the conclusion that the explanations that had appeared ' simple ' to me at first were also nearer to the truth from the theoretic point of view. Complex and ' learned ' explanations often conceal falsities ; fundamental truths are simple. Simplicity in theory is like common sense in daily life in that it fits in with the truth. If this were taken into account, many works published on the Russian revolution would gain both in depth and in veracity.

The XVIth Party Congress was held during the time I was in prison in Leningrad. One of the ' pearls ' of the Congress must be mentioned here. Stalin, in his speech, stated that workers' salaries had gone up by 69 per cent in comparison with pre-War wages, when in actual fact they had been lowered by 50 per cent. This shameless lie was told before the whole country, before ten million workers who knew the truth about it. One may think Stalin a cynic, a criminal, a statesman of great magnitude. But what to think of the country, of the proletariat that heard this official lie spoken by the highest person in the State ? The country was unable to voice the slightest protest, worse still, it was forced publicly to sanction the lie ! Under these conditions, what could be expected of Congress ? Of all the speeches only that of Tomsky contained a note of human dignity :

" Certain comrades think only of repentance, of continual repentance. Let it be permitted to us to work and not merely to repent." Later on it was Tomsky, who, tired of Byzantine Stalinism, protested by committing suicide. One may say that his mode of protest was hardly efficacious ; but at least the whole world heard of it.

In his closing speech Stalin once more showed himself true to himself by throwing a few words to the Right-wing. " You have grown afraid of hypocrites ! " He expressed thereby not only the realization of his own strength, but his complete contempt for the life of the masses. The new general Line had caused the dislocation in the lives of 170,000,000 people, and had set tens of millions of people wandering from one end of the immense country to the other. A true migration of nations could be seen, accompanied by famines, epidemics and risings. This enormous population was in the grip of horror and despair, but to Stalin they were only ' hypocrites that had been forced out of their holes '.

In our ward there was great surprise at the election of the leaders of the Right-wing Opposition to the Central Committee ; Rykov was even elected to the Politbureau. " Had they not been torn to shreds during the Congress ? " I was asked by the prisoners who by now considered me as something of an authority on Party matters. I tried to explain the matter to them : " The Right-wing has the confidence of world bourgeoisie ; Stalin therefore, by allowing them into the Central Committee, wants to prove to the outside world that he is not as revolutionary as he makes himself out to be in his speeches. There is a Czech opera in which a village lad, disguised as a bear, begins to cry out, ' It isn't a bear, it's me, Vanka ! ' when the frightened villagers mistake him for a real bear. Stalin does exactly the same thing ! "

I was called several times before the examining magistrate. A high official of the G.P.U., who was present at one of the interrogations, tried to convince me that my opposition was merely the result of a misunderstanding. When I insisted on a complete democracy, I was right after all, but the thing was premature in Russia at the present stage of its development. He reproached me for looking at Russia with the eyes of the West. Moreover, the present system had not been created by Stalin but by Lenin. It was with Lenin's full agreement that the extremist representative of the workers'

Opposition, the old Bolshevik Miasnikov, had been arrested. To arrest members of the Party is undoubtedly a disagreeable task, but circumstances may make it imperative. Especially during the days of Zinoviev was there least democracy. It was he who had forced the Leningrad organization to back his Opposition policy.

Here is roughly what I answered : if Zinoviev was able to impose his will on the Party and on the Leningrad proletariat, it goes to prove that it is not the masses but the administration which decides, yesterday Zinoviev's, today Stalin's. It goes to strengthen my view that the working classes are oppressed or given second place both in the Party and in the country. I found it more difficult to answer the argument about Lenin and Miasnikov. " I know nothing about that. I am not sufficiently well acquainted with the affair. Anyhow, it is an isolated fact whereas today the persecution of Party members has become the rule."

Summer was drawing to a close. When should I spend another summer at liberty ? Discouragement swept over me, I thirsted for air and sun. September came. I grew disgusted with my walks of twenty minutes a day in a court-yard full of people in the rain or the Leningrad fog that pierced one to the bone.

As happened every autumn, the relations between the Government and the peasants were becoming more and more strained. It was the time of the wheat delivery, and the village, as usual, availed itself of the opportunity to express its dissatisfaction and offer a certain degree of resistance. As early as the 24th of August, *Pravda* had sounded the alarm. " Hasten to deliver the wheat " was the title of its leading article. " No more than 34 per cent of the August plan has been fulfilled." In September the situation grew worse. The peasants refused to be accommodating and preferred to slaughter their beasts rather than to deliver them up to the *kolkhosi*. From the new arrivals we learned that both bread and meat were lacking in the towns, especially in Leningrad and Moscow.

The state of over-excitement spread to the prison. The trials were conducted with a swing and executions became more frequent. The wards were in a constant state of emotion. But at the same time life there became more silent, everything was muted and one's existence seemed to depend on a mere matter of chance. On the 22nd of September we learned from the newspapers that the G.P.U. had laid hands on ' a counter-revolutionary organization sabotaging the workers' food-distribution '. From the communiqué one could conclude that all Food Departments—meat, fish, preserves, vegetable and fruit trusts, as well as the corresponding Organs of the People's Commissariat—were in the hands of the enemy. The reason for these exaggerated and sensational communiqués was only too clear : someone had to bear the burden of the responsibility of the alimentary crisis. It was obvious that this crisis was due to the general Government policy and the attendant class-struggle, but people chosen more or less at random were declared guilty. Suddenly the papers were filled with articles, resolutions and accounts of mass meetings all unanimously demanding the exemplary punishment of the culprits. What a cannibals' dance !

At last the curtain rose for the last act. On the 25th of October the newspapers published the G.P.U. communiqué : " Those guilty of the sabotage of the workers' food supply have been executed."

Forty-eight men had been shot. Our prison was riddled with horror. The workers were hungry and cried for bread —the Government threw them human flesh. This statement is more than a metaphor, and during those horrible days I had an almost physical experience of events.

A graveyard silence reigned over the prison. Everybody, but most particularly those who belonged to the category of ' deprived of civic rights ', felt death prowling round them. I thought in silence of what I could remember of the apogee of the terror in the French prisons on the eve of 9 Thermidor. I suppose the atmosphere must have resembled that in our prison.

Two weeks later we were condemned, Deditch and myself, to three years' political imprisonment in the Ural.

We took leave of our companions as if they were old friends. Misfortune creates a bond between men. " Now that your verdict has been pronounced and you no longer run the risk of having it made worse, tell us what you think of our future," the academicians were asking me. I could only repeat what I had said before, " The forces of revolution and of the Left are exhausted. The next historic stage will consist of an evolution towards the Right. What form it will take, I cannot say, and do not cease to ask myself."

III

ON THE ROAD TO EXILE

Deditch and I left Leningrad towards the middle of October. True to its principles, the G.P.U. kept us in ignorance of our destination. The examining magistrate told us merely that we would learn upon our arrival at Chelyabinsk.

There are two ways in Russia by which political prisoners are sent into exile. The first method is to take them in groups of ten or fifteen and add them to convoys of prisoners in civil law, which number from a hundred to two hundred men ; in that case, they travel from town to town, from prison to prison, penned in special vans. The journey takes months even if it is merely a transfer from the Ural or Central Asia to Siberia. Such a journey is worse than any prison. It is not surprising that ' politicals ' prefer an extra year in gaol to three months' travel, dirt, lack of space and bad treatment. The other method consists in sending them direct to their destination. In that case they travel in ordinary trains, though in special compartments, watched over by G.P.U. men. This mode of transport is reserved for the ' aristocracy ' among political prisoners : the Opposition Communists. It was the way in which Deditch and I were despatched.

As we were being transferred from the Leningrad prison to the station, we could not get accustomed to the streets and the people. We had spent six months in prison ; the large spaces of the town and the crowds in the streets seemed like an episode out of the *Arabian Nights*. At the same time there was something irritating about it. We had been in prison among thousands of other sufferers, and yet life went on unheeding. The bustle at the station, the departure— it was like a dream. An inspector and three G.P.U. soldiers accompanied us. The train went in the direction of the Volga and the Ural, on the Leningrad-Vitebsk-Tula-Samara-

Chelyabinsk line, that is, by making a detour round Moscow on the West and South.

During the journey we had occasion to become friendly with our guards and with the travellers in the next compartments. We had complete freedom of movement in the carriage, as if we were not prisoners. Throughout the world there exist closer relations between the prisoners and their keepers than the authorities imagine. But nowhere are they so close as in the U.S.S.R. Those who represent authority are sprung from the people ; their rise goes back only to the near past and they have not yet become fully conscious of their change of status. Both victims and gaolers are still in some confusion as to their mutual relations. The representatives of authority in the lower ranks feel themselves at fault and seem to say, " We know that we should not be friendly, but there you are, what can we do in the circumstances ? "

Our conversation with our guards soon left the field of trivialities to pass on to that of politics and Trotskyism. It was astonishing to hear those Red soldiers affirm that Trotsky wanted to ruin the peasants, whereas the Party wanted the union of peasants and workers, and furthermore, collectivization in moderation. Such was the success of clever propaganda linked with privileges given to the Red Army ! What Stalin did in the villages was a thousand times worse than Trotsky's programme. Trotsky had simply demanded an increase of taxation and a compulsory loan in the form of wheat. But the Red soldiers were convinced of the contrary.

As to the inspector, he thought our political disagreement with the Party temporary and unimportant. " In six months' time—say a year—you'll be back in Leningrad ; you will be reinstated in all your functions, and you may even get advancement. I know what I am talking about, for in the past I have once conveyed a whole carriage-load of Opposition Communists. They went making speeches and shouting slogans—but today they are all back in Leningrad, and they are once more living at the Party House and doing their work as before. When one is carrying out great things like the Five Year Plan, the Party must demand a rigid discipline ; it is not worth quarrelling about details. You'll see, you'll come back, I am telling you ; we'll meet again, in Leningrad."

His sincerity was disarming. On the whole, the inspector made an excellent impression on me. I answered him without bitterness. " No, I shan't come back. It is not in my character to go back on what I say. On the contrary, our differences with the Party will increase as time goes on. Moreover, we are foreigners and don't look at things in the same light as our Russian comrades do. With us, it is shameful to capitulate, with you it is an honourable act."

The inspector had been a miner in the Donets Basin. He was overworked at the G.P.U. and had dreams of educating himself to a better job. The good impression he created even persisted after a small incident in which he displayed the peculiar Chekist pride. During a stop, we had all alighted to go to the buffet and wanted to get back to the train via a gate of the station in front of which stood a little old man, an employee of the railway, who told us that the gate was not to be used because it was newly painted. The inspector threw the little man a glance such as one might cast upon an inanimate object and made a gesture as if to signify, " There are no gates locked against us," and passed through with great dignity, without saying a word.

In Leningrad I had nursed projects of escape which I might easily have carried out during my journey into exile. I had even fixed upon the place where I would hide after my escape. Now was the time to choose a favourable moment. It soon presented itself, for we had won the confidence of our guards who no longer closely watched us and now allowed us to go to station buffets on our own, where we sometimes spent as much as half an hour in liberty. But I did not have the heart to avail myself of the opportunity, for the inspector would have paid dearly for the confidence shown in us ; it would have cost him three years in a concentration camp. We weighed the pros and cons, Deditch and I, and came to the conclusion that it would have been inhuman on our part. Thus we abandoned all plans of escape and continued our journey towards the isolator.

After a few days of fairly uninteresting travel we drew near the Volga. The train ran on to a bridge ; it seemed as if we should never reach the other side. On the left and on the right stretched an immense, apparently boundless, sheet of water. After the rivers and brooks of Europe, the Volga seemed an ocean.

Having crossed the Volga, we began to climb the slopes of the Ural. On the steepest ridges, near Zlatoust, the train proceeded so slowly that one had the sensation of walking. We gazed out on the most picturesque parts of the Ural. Autumn was already well advanced and there was nothing to recall the warm and exuberant tints of the Caucasus ; but the fantastic accumulation of rocks and the severe mountain landscape stressed Nature's titanic force. Somewhere we passed a post marking the border between Europe and Asia. To a European, these two words call up pictures of two distinct and opposed worlds. Here, neither men nor things showed the least sign of change. It was neither Asia nor Europe, it was simply Russia. The people there were so fully conscious of it, that no one would dream of calling Siberia a part of Asia. To the Siberians themselves, Asia begins with Turkestan, China and Japan.

From the heights of the Ural, we descended towards Chelyabinsk. There we left the train. Our guards handed us over to the local G.P.U. and prepared for the return journey. We left them as friends, without any hostility and not without sadness. In their persons we seemed to say farewell to our illusions of the new Russia, of which we had dreamed so long. We felt a long and arduous struggle would be needed to create the Russia for which we had hoped and as for one instant we had seen it. The G.P.U. at Chelyabinsk acquainted us with our destination : the political isolator of Verkhne-Uralsk. But we had to wait until a special detachment came to fetch us, and meanwhile we were to spend a fortnight in the Chelyabinsk gaol. The vast prison was filled with peasants and prisoners in civil law. The peasants were there because of collectivization ; they were hungry, depressed and taciturn. We were put in a ward reserved for political prisoners who, on their way through Chelyabinsk, would often stay there a very long time. Our ward was open, and we could walk in the corridor ; the peasants' wards, on the other hand, were closed. Near the main prison building was a smaller edifice, which consti-tuted the Chelyabinsk political isolator. Various shades of socialists were kept there, but we never had any contact with them.

After a few days our ward filled with social-democrats who were being transferred from Tashkent to the political isolator of Verkhne-Uralsk. They were Israel S. Jakobson, Xenia S. Kuprianov, Ivan G. Rojkovsky, David Jmoud, Esther M. Levine, Olga Aspris, Dora Diamantstein, Elias Sokolovsky and a young man whose name I forget.

The first thing about these social-democrats that struck Deditch and myself was their appearance. They were tired, haggard and thin, like people who have not had sufficient to eat for a long time ; they were very badly dressed, too. They had the air I have so often seen in persecuted Communists in Europe. But in spite of it all, these people showed no signs of moral depression, and they seemed intellectually exceedingly alert. This immediately caused sincere and cordial relations between us to spring up. We were happy to have the opportunity of hearing the really competent views of Russian social-democrats on so many questions of burning interest. They, too, were pleased to meet foreign Communists, newcomers to the political isolator.

First of all, we mutually enquired about the ' affairs ' that had brought us there. The social-democrats had been condemned to three years' imprisonment for the following crimes : first they had read the *Socialistischesky Vestnik* (*Socialist Courier*), the organ of the Russian social-democrats abroad. Next they had sent help to other social-democrats in exile (these were in the extreme North, at Obdorsk, Narym, Turukhansk and were reduced to unemployment whereas the Tashkent group was in work).

Our new social-democrat neighbours had from eight to ten years' persecution behind them (which by now amounts to fifteen to seventeen years). They had been at Solovetsk, in the isolators of Verkhne-Uralsk, Tobolsk and Chelyabinsk ; they had been deported to the Ural, to Central Asia and elsewhere. Most of them were going to an isolator for the second time. Whatever our political differences might be, we could not but bow to people able to bear all that.

They told us how they had been caught the last time. A young worker from the Ural had one day joined them in their exile at Tashkent. He was a ' spontaneous ' Menshevik, typical of the rising generation. The old exiles received him with exceeding joy. Their cordiality was increased by the fact that soon after his arrival he had to go into hospital. The whole Menshevik colony surrounded him with attentions. Soon all were arrested. The young man had been an agent of the G.P.U.

As to our political conversations, I opened them by asking an exceedingly serious question in a light-hearted way. " I can understand the attitude of the social-democrats in Europe ; they do not like to go to prison, they do not want to risk a revolution, they have already secured a few good places in bourgeois society and are unwilling to lose them. But you, the Russian social-democrats, what do you want ? For the last ten years you have drifted from prison to prison. Is it to restore capitalism and the parliamentary republic in Russia ? It surely isn't worth while ? I cannot understand you."

They were very much taken aback at first by the way in which I stated the problem ; then one of them answered, " It would indeed be perfectly futile to wish to restore capitalism in Russia, for the good reason that capitalism, though in a modified form, exists there and has never ceased to exist. What we desire, what has led us into prison, is workers' democracy, the workers' right of freely organizing themselves."

That set the debate going. Rosa Luxemburg was quoted and her discussions with Lenin in 1903 and 1918 on the respective parts played by masses and leaders in the workers' movement. We were shown with abundant detail that the present system in Russia had preserved all the essential characteristics of capitalism : production of goods, wages, exchange markets, money, profits and even partial sharing out of profits among bureaucrats in the form of high salaries, privileges and so on.

Then we spoke of the problems of the day : the Five Year Plan, and the danger of Fascism in Germany. They all assured us that the great work of industrialization was going on throughout the land. Famine and terror had reached a high pitch, but factories were springing from the soil as if conjured up by a magic wand. They mentioned new constructions even at Chelyabinsk, which town they knew, having been there before : the electric-power station and the other factory buildings that had been built in a very short time. As to the *kolkhosi*, they were more sceptical and were inclined to think that this was a mad venture that would end in failure. All, however, but for one exception, feared this failure as they thought it might be the starting-point of the veritable counter-revolution. That one person thought that if the revolting peasants could overthrow the Bolshevist Government, the road would be open to a democratic republic. As to the German policy, they were all in favour of a co-operation between Communists and social-democrats, of a united front against the danger of Hitlerism. How different the opinions of these social-democrats were from those attributed to them by the Communist Press, which in this matter truly abused its monopoly.

In spite of all our differences it was comforting to find that people were able to retain their entire mental lucidity and to follow closely political events notwithstanding the years of prison and exile. In my opinion, Jakobson gave the best analysis of social and economic phenomena in Russia. With Rojkovsky, he represented the Left-wing of social-democracy. Jmoud and the young man whose name I forget represented the Right-wing; the women, being of a more conciliatory nature, occupied a centre position. Rojkovsky had fought in the Red Army during the Civil War, until 1921, having been mobilized by order of the Central Committee of the Russian Social Democratic Party. Later, at Yeniseisk, I met two Zionist socialists, Bernstein and Pfeffermacher, who had been decorated with the Order of the Red Flag for their heroic behaviour at the Civil War front. These were the 'counter-revolutionaries' who filled the prisons and concentration camps of the U.S.S.R.

At first our social-democrat neighbours appeared to Deditch and myself a compact group, very different from us Communists. The more we got to know them, the more differences we observed. At the end of a week, by reading the newspapers together and commenting on their contents, we were able to distinguish as many shades of opinion as there were social-democrat prisoners. Jmoud was the one to catch it most, for he was the extreme Right-wing man. One day he showed great satisfaction at reading that the strike in the Berlin metal industries, which had been organized by Communists, had failed. Jakobson could not conceal his indignation. "For the man to pass himself off as a socialist!"

When it came to criticism of the existing order, I nearly always agreed with the social-democrats; when they asserted the necessity of fighting for workers' democracy I could only concur. But as soon as we talked over a programme of action, an abyss sprang open between us. Fight for socialism in Russia ? Even the most sympathetic among the social-democrats, Jakobson, could only answer with a kindly smile, " Utopia, romanticism ! " What foolish assurance, I said to myself. Men and Parties afraid of daring, afraid of enthusiasm for Utopias, will never perform great deeds. If the social-democrat attitude had been adopted, the socialist Utopia would never even have been attempted. As to my own attitude, it was that if the Utopia had not come true, it followed that the struggle to bring it about had to be continued.

What appeared to me the greatness of the Russian revolution and the apogee of the social development of humanity, namely, the attempt at integral socialism of the first years of the revolution (known as ' war-time Communism ') inclusive of the abolition of money, was to the social-democrats the worst of follies. To them, the workers' democracy was but the means of achieving ' the possible ' ; to me, it was to be the instrument by which to achieve a total reconstruction of society.

We naturally spoke much of Trotsky. I shall quote two opinions. Elias Sokolovsky unsettled me by declaring that Stalin was a better man than Trotsky. " Stalin is a realist, Trotsky a fanatic. Stalin pursues his intentions until they lead him to the brink of a precipice ; then he makes good his retreat. As to Trotsky, he goes on to the bitter end, though the whole world perish. He has too much vanity to take anything into account. I know him well ; we are related."

Jakobson thought that Trotsky, in spite of all that separated him from the Second International, would finally come to agree with it in the matter of democracy.

As we were waiting for our transfer to Verkhne-Uralsk, a new companion arrived, an anarchist called Serge Tujilkin. He was a young electrician, a worker from Chelyabinsk who had conducted an illegal anarchist printing-press. It cost him five years in the political isolator. According to him, the anarchists were very active and entertained relations with anarchists abroad : indeed, the printing-press had produced foreign anarchist texts in considerable numbers. He also talked to us of the ideas and the organization of the

Soviet anarchists ; I learned that they had succeeded in founding a centralized and disciplined organization. Later on, I became acquainted with a group who wanted to create an ' Anarchist Party ' and even a ' transitional State ' or ' semi-State '. But the majority of the Russian anarchists rejected this revised form of classical anarchism.

At Chelyabinsk we also met a few Georgian social-democrats and an Armenian socialist. Having served their sentences in the Verkhne-Uralsk prison, they were leaving for exile in Siberia. They told us about the system at Verkhne-Uralsk.

We left on November 7th, the anniversary of the Bolshevist revolution—two Yugo-Slavs, eight Russian social-democrats, Tujilkin the anarchist and three prisoners in civil law—to proceed to the political isolator of Verkhne-Uralsk. From the windows of the train we could see demonstrations and feasts at Troitsk, Magnitogorsk and elsewhere, red flags and meetings, and we were being taken to prison. What contradictions ! The entire horizon was filled with buildings and factory chimneys in the course of construction, electric-power stations, giant factories. The construction of Magnitogorsk had commenced and the landscape was cut into segments by trenches and the accumulation of materials. A new America, immense and cruel like its elder, was being born on one-sixth of the land surface of the earth, the U.S.S.R.

That evening we were to arrive at our destination, Verkhne-Uralsk.

IV

VERKHNE-URALSK

THE railway line ended at Magnitogorsk and we had to continue our journey by car through the steppes of the Cossacks of the Ural.

Verkhne-Uralsk is a large village ; the political isolator is a few miles away in the midst of the steppe. The cars drew up outside the building, whilst from the windows the prisoners were making signs of welcome and shouting questions at us : " Who are you ? Where have you come from ? " —" We are the social-democrats from Tashkent, but there are some Trotskyists, too." The administration waited for us outside on the portico. Having recognized the social-democrats, the officials exclaimed, " Ah, it's you, Rojkovsky, Diamantstein ! Back again ! " The latter answered in their turn, " Ah, Biziukov, Matveyev ! Still playing at tyrants ? " On all sides there were cries of welcome.

First we were taken to be searched. Then our cards were filed and we were distributed over a number of wards. Deditch and I were taken to a ward near by. The door was opened and the gaoler roughly pushed us and our belongings inside. It was a very spacious room, with bunks all round the walls and a large table in the middle, round which some ten prisoners were seated. The room was very feebly lit by means of a very small light-bulb, so that faces could hardly be distinguished.

The prisoners were dressed in fur-lined jackets, overcoats and felt boots. It was cold and uncomfortable. The first questions once more were : " Who are you ? Where do you come from ? " As soon as they learned that we were not convicts and had been free a relatively short time ago and that we had come from the centre, they showed a greatly increased interest. All the thoughts of the prisoners were directed towards events that were taking place in the heart of the country, among the free. Their interest grew still more when they heard that we were foreign Communists. We sat down at the table and began to retail our story, telling what we had seen and heard whilst still free. Then we learned that two members of our Opposition group, Zankov and Glybovsky, had already been for six weeks at the isolator. That was due to the fact that there had been no need to discuss their fate with the Politbureau of the Yugo-Slav Party. Glybovsky was lodged directly above us. The news of our arrival was soon shouted out to them through the window. It quickly travelled along the three stories of the building. The gaoler knocked on our door. "Don't make so much noise, comrades!" But no one took any notice.

When we had finished the first part of our narrative, a signal was sent up from our ward via the chimney to indicate that the latest news was about to be sent up. Indeed, a few minutes a letter containing a précis of our story was going up that way. We were taken aback by the liberty that prevailed among the prisoners. In our previous prisons we had seen nothing like it. But greater surprises lay in store for us.

The following day comrades showed us papers published in the prison. What a diversity of opinion there was, what freedom in every article! What passion and what candour, not only in the approach to theoretical and abstract questions, but even in matters of the greatest actuality. Was it still possible to reform the system by peaceful means, or was an armed rising, a new revolution required? Was Stalin a conscious or merely an unconscious traitor? Did his policy amount to reaction or to counter-revolution? Could he be eliminated by merely removing the directing personnel, or was a proper revolution necessary? All the news-sheets were written with the greatest freedom, without any reticence, dotting i's and crossing t's and—supreme horror—every article signed with the writer's full name.

Our liberty was not limited to that. During the walk which brought several wards together, the prisoners were in the habit of holding regular meetings in a corner of the yard, with chairman, secretary and orators speaking in proper order. When the order of the day could not cope with all the business, debates were postponed until the next recreation-time. At these meetings the most dangerous and forbidden subjects were discussed without the least restraint and without any fear whatsoever. The invigilating inspector would sit down somewhere or walk to and fro. He no doubt made his reports in the proper quarters, but nobody seemed to be in the least concerned with that. At these meetings Stalin came off very badly, being called all sorts of names. I had seen many things in the U.S.S.R. but none so bewildering as this isle of liberty, lost in an ocean of slavery—or was it merely a madhouse ? So great was the contrast between the humiliated, terrified country and the freedom of mind that reigned in this prison that one was first inclined toward the madhouse theory. How was one to admit that in the immensity of silence-stricken Russia the two or three small islands of liberty where men still had the right to think and speak freely were . . . the prisons ?

After having made a summary acquaintance with the political life of the isolator, I first wanted to familiarize myself with its penitentiary system, which I will now proceed to explain.

Our prison consisted of a vast rectangular, three-storied building. Destined to be used as an officers' prison, it had been put into service as such on the eve of the War. Its main axis pointed north to south. Most of the prisoners lodged in the north wing, which was the coldest. The administration occupied most of the south wing. As to the living-quarters of the members of the administration, they formed a separate building. The prison was surrounded by a wall fifteen feet high, with occasional turrets for armed guards. The space between wall and prison was divided by transversal walls of the same height into five courtyards in which the prisoners took their exercise. The baths were also placed between the ring wall and the prison. The kitchens, the cells for prisoners in civil law who were made to perform the prison work, the food and clothes stores were all in the basement.

The prison counted sixty wards, that is to say, twenty on each floor. Ten of them had wooden floors, the others were floored with cement. There was central heating, but it failed almost entirely to heat the ground floor. As we were housed in the north wing of the ground floor, we could easily ascertain the truth of this. Throughout the winter we had to wear lined jackets and felt boots. The cold in the ward was such that every night a thick layer of ice formed on the inside of the windows. The one-man cells in the north-east were worse still. The cells for two overlooking the west were the best, but there were only six of them. The other wards were large halls for six to twelve prisoners.

The food consisted of the traditional poor *mujik's* fare : bread and broth morning and night, throughout the year. The only changes in this diet consisted of seasonal variations in the type of cereals that were used to make the broth : black wheat, millet or oats. Apart from that, a soup was given at breakfast made of bad fish, preserves or half-putrid meat. The same soup, but without meat or fish, was served at dinner-time. We had several conflicts with the administration on account of the rotten meat, the prisoners refusing their rations for several consecutive days. The daily bread ration consisted of 25 oz., the monthly sugar ration of 2 lb. 4 oz. Moreover, there was a ration of tobacco, cigarettes, tea and soap. Once a week we were given herring with cabbage and beetroot salad, and that was a real feast to us. As to the bread, it was black and poor in quality. Twice a year—on the 1st of May and the 7th of November—we were given a slice of white bread, which meant that during the three years of my stay I received six slices. Three times daily we were given boiling water for tea. All the serving was done by the prisoners in civil law.

The quantities in which this monotonous food was given were insufficient. We had to wage a bitter struggle not to have our meagre pittance still further reduced ; what was to be said of the struggles at the price of which we obtained an improvement of a few minor details ? Yet compared with the diet of the prisons of civil law, where hundreds of thousands dwelt in misery, and above all with that of the millions of wretches deposited in the Northern camps, our diet was in a way a very privileged one.

The furniture of the wards was scanty. Each prisoner received some trestles and a few planks by way of a bed ; also a small bedside table. Apart from that, there was a large common table in the centre of the room. Clothes and linen were partly provided by the administration, partly by the prisoners themselves. But there was a systematic refusal on the part of the administration to give us clothes or linen, on the pretext of insufficient stores. We had to suffer particularly during the last winter spent in that prison ; a large number of us fell ill owing to lack of clothes and footwear. Sometimes a proper battle had to be waged in order to obtain a single shirt. The sole exception was made in favour of foreign Communists. By special order from Moscow, the administration was to provide for all our needs without delay. When, after two years, Deditch complained to a Commission on a visit from Moscow, saying that the administration had failed to provide him with linen, Andreyeva, the chairman of the Committee, reprimanded Biziukov, the prison director ; the latter, greatly upset, replied, " But I provided Ciliga with all the linen he needed."—" You had been told to give the linen to all the Yugo-Slavs, not merely to Ciliga," Andreyeva went on. This little incident suffices to show to what extent Moscow was concerned with the smallest details of the penitentiary system and ruled the relations between prisoners and administration.

The prisoners went for their walks twice daily and these lasted one hour in winter, an hour and a half in summer. Four to five wards, that is to say from twenty-five to thirty-five prisoners, went at a time, and were allowed to do what they liked : walk, hold meetings, take exercise (football, tennis or *gorodki*, a Russian game of ninepins). In summer they were allowed to grow flowers or vegetables. Twice a month the prisoners went to the baths, and on those occasions sheets would be changed and body linen taken to the laundry.

The prison possessed a considerable library, the nucleus of which consisted of the books inherited from the Czarist prison (works from Russian, German, French and English literature). Many volumes, especially works on sociology, politics and history, were gifts made by prisoners at the time of their release ; moreover, the administration would occasionally buy books. Thus I was able to read some very new books : André Gide's *Voyage au Congo* and Traven's *Coton*. On the whole the library was not at all bad. Apart from that, some of the prisoners brought with them an excellent choice of personal books, often as many as a hundred or even two or three hundred volumes. A certain number of prisoners had new publications sent them by relatives. The use of these particular volumes was not limited to their owners, but all the owner's ward-mates and the occupants of neighbouring wards shared them alike. The prisoners, moreover, had the right to subscribe to any of the periodicals appearing in the U.S.S.R. As to the foreign papers, we were allowed only the central organs of the Communist Party, the *Rote Fahne*, *l'Humanité* and the *Daily Worker*, and then only one copy per floor of the prison.

Under such conditions, having enough reading material and not much physical occupation, the prisoners, who were mainly educated people, spent all their energy on the political life of the prison : the editing and publishing of news sheets, articles, the holding of meetings and debates. It is no exaggeration to say that the political isolator of Verkhne-Uralsk, with its 250 political prisoners, constituted a veritable university of social and political sciences—the only independent university in the U.S.S.R.

An important question was that of the communications between the prisoners. These communications, though prohibited, were actually tolerated to a certain extent by the prison authorities. There was a constant struggle concerning the ' internal postal service ', but both parties played this game according to certain accepted rules. Communications between the four or five wards of each floor were naturally easy. Less easy were ' vertical ' relations between wards on different floors. But they took place all the same : at a given signal a bag would be lowered from the higher floor in which the ' mail ' was placed. The warders had long poles with which they tried to intercept the bags. They succeeded on very rare occasions only, for it was impossible constantly to watch all windows, especially as there were prisoners brave enough to fend off the warders' poles with sticks. The rules of the game demanded that a victory was won as soon as the bag had been taken or raised again. The bars, with which the windows were provided, were far enough apart to allow all these manifestations.

The prison was subdivided by longitudinal and transversal corridors into three distinct portions : the north, the south-east and the south-west. It was much more difficult to organize regular communications between these three sections, but it was absolutely essential to do so, in order to ensure the political life of the isolator. The administration was using all its ingenuity to work out a system of walks by which contacts were made as difficult as possible. But the prisoners spared neither time nor trouble to succeed. A ' postal triumvirate ' was elected to be responsible for the smooth functioning of illegal communication throughout the prison. The ' postmen ' appointed by each group were under its orders.

The ' postal management ' was the only organization that all political prisoners had in common, Communists as well as socialists and anarchists. The prisoners had been housed in such a way that without this technical alliance, contact could not have been maintained between the different wings of the prison. All the other organizations of the prisoners were separate for Communists, socialists and anarchists among themselves. There were also two very distinct sections in the prison. The Russian Opposition Communists thought it was very humiliating to be compelled to live with the genuine counter-revolutionaries that in their eyes the socialists and anarchists were. The G.P.U. had forestalled their wishes on this point. This psychology evolved only gradually and equally gradually a common struggle that was waged against the G.P.U. for the general well-being of all political prisoners. The Communists formed the majority of the prisoners at Verkhne-Uralsk ; there were 140, a figure which later rose to 180. As to the socialists and anarchists of various shades of opinion, there were 50 at the time of my arrival ; later on there were nearly 80.

There were seven walking-groups of Communists and two or three of socialists and anarchists. Each of these groups had a common fund. The Communist ' minister of finance ' dealt with the money received by the prisoners from outside. He had a representative in each walking-group and fixed the sum which each prisoner was allowed to spend according to the state of common finances. The sum varied from two to five roubles a month. But we hardly knew what to do with even this modest sum, for there was nothing to buy at Verkhne-Uralsk except pencils and stamps (the administration supplied us with sufficient quantities of paper).

Correspondence was allowed only with one's nearest relatives. Communists were allowed to write or receive letters nine times a month, socialists and anarchists, being inferior categories, only six times. The prison censorship mercilessly blue-pencilled all concrete information concerning prison life or—if relatives were writing—about life outside.

Sometimes half a letter would be cut out with the scissors. Also chemical tests were applied. Yet, all these precautions did not prevent us from keeping certain contacts with people outside or even abroad. Thus we received not only letters, but even pamphlets from Trotsky, published abroad. From this point of view our prison was much better served than many others.

We Yugo-Slavs were not allowed to write to our relatives abroad, and as I had no relatives inside Russia, I was, throughout my three years' stay, never able either to write or to receive a single letter. What did it matter whether parents despaired for the life of their son, provided that it remained unknown abroad that he had been put in prison for disagreeing with the Russian bureaucratic régime.

Another peculiarity of the political isolator was that interviews with relatives were not permitted. The authorization could come only from Moscow and then in none but exceptional circumstances. I know of but two or three cases in which such authorization was given, yet there were more than two hundred of us in prison, and I was there for several years. A few wives of prisoners wanted to come and live at Verkhne-Uralsk to facilitate the despatch of food to their husbands and to help them feel nearer to them ; but the G.P.U. ordered them to leave the village within twenty-four hours.

In actual practice, the most important institution in the lives of the prisoners was that of '.heads of wards ' or ' elders '. Each ward elected an elder, who was to represent it to the authorities. His task was also to see to it that the internal regulations established by the prisoners themselves were adhered to. Several wards, forming one walking-group, elected two or three elders to exercise a similar function during recreation-times. Finally, the body of Communist prisoners elected three elders to form, as it were, the Supreme Instance of the Communist section of the penitentiary. These three elders were : one Right-wing Trotskyist, one Left-wing and one Extreme Left. There was a constant struggle with the administration to defend the internal autonomy of the prisoners and their right to be collectively represented by the three elders of the Communist section. The penitentiary administration, in other words the G.P.U., refused the *de jure* recognition of the elders of the Communist section and also of the recreation groups. Yet it carried out all discussions with these elders, stressing the fact that it dealt with them only in their capacity of ordinary prisoners. As to the heads of wards, they were recognized actually as well as by right. The anarchists and socialists were similarly represented. This compact organization of about two hundred prisoners, ready for the greatest sacrifices and with numerous connections throughout the U.S.S.R. and abroad, was a force with which the G.P.U. had certainly to reckon.

*　　*　　*

We had been at Verkhne-Uralsk for some time when, one evening, the door of our ward was suddenly opened and a new arrival was ushered in : Draguitch ! What a surprise ! We had thought him abroad, engaged in fighting for our liberation, or at least in hiding somewhere right across the U.S.S.R. Fate had decided that we set out together : in Yugo-Slavia, in Moscow, in Leningrad and now at last in Verkhne-Uralsk. He soon told us what had happened to him.

On the day of our arrest, the 21st of May, he had indeed succeeded in getting away, as we had imagined. He soon went to Moscow and there made contact with the members of our organization who were still at large, and with other friends. He had been able to see with what thoroughness the G.P.U. were annihilating our group and its ramifications. For weeks G.P.U. men would lie low in the homes of our friends. All suspects had been trailed by women. Draguitch himself had walked into several traps, but his great ingenuity had every time helped him to escape.

He had even been arrested to have his identity established, but owing to some faked papers he had escaped. On another occasion he had met a Yugo-Slav representative of the Comintern in town, but the latter showed such surprise that Draguitch had succeeded in making good his disappearance. He had even been able to talk to several Yugo-Slav labourers who had told him that immediately upon our arrest, all Yugo-Slavs in Moscow had been called to a meeting at which the information of our arrest had been communicated to them, with the mention that we were ' Trotskyist counter-revolutionaries '. At the same meeting, those of our writings had been read in which we had stated that the Russian

Communist Party had become a home for bureaucrats who had betrayed the cause of the workers and that a new Party should be created. It was also announced—which is not without its humour—that we were not in prison, but only under observation, under house-arrest or something similar. Draguitch also met Nin, the Spanish Opposition Communist, who was to become in 1936 a minister in the Revolutionary Catalonian Cabinet. He acquainted him with the arrest of our group and requested him to have it made known abroad. Draguitch's principal task in Moscow had been to prepare his departure for abroad, but preparations had of necessity to be slow, with the G.P.U. on his track. Leaving it to his friends to make these arrangements, Draguitch went into hiding in the provinces, and later in Leningrad. Then, hearing that everything was in readiness for his escape he went to Moscow. Not to be recognized in the capital, he wanted to procure a disguise, and to this end went to see a sympathizer, the same one with whom I was confronted on the occasion of my arrest. The man received him without great enthusiasm and pretended not to have the necessary clothes. As Draguitch insisted, he consented to help him late that night. When Draguitch turned up later, there was no one but a stranger who offered him a cigarette. Draguitch smelled a rat and left at once. The G.P.U. man—for he was one—followed him. Two others were waiting at the corner of the road. They came up to him and took his arm, saying,

" Greetings, Draguitch ! We were looking for you."

" You are mistaken. I am not Draguitch."

" Don't be a fool. Show us your papers."

He showed them. They were in the name of N——, a Yugo-Slav. The agents went on, " Open your mouth."

Draguitch had false teeth and these betrayed him.

" Yes, it is you. Come along."

Draguitch was led to the G.P.U. prison. It was midnight and the streets were deserted. As they passed through a dark alley, Draguitch succeeded in freeing himself with a jerk and he ran away as fast as he could. The two men pursued him, firing their revolvers at him. He began to zigzag, running faster still. The few passers-by, hearing the shots, hid in doorways. A few more paces to the street corner and he would have been free. But suddenly Draguitch found himself borne to the ground. A G.P.U. man who happened to be there had hurled himself at Draguitch's legs. Before he could regain his feet, the men were on him, had seized him, hailed a cab and he was taken to gaol.

Draguitch, like ourselves, was condemned to three years' imprisonment. He was sent to Verkhne-Uralsk under the strictest guard. He thought of escaping, but in vain. The two inspectors watched him all the time ; one of them with argus eyes did not take them off him. The other one, on the contrary, was more friendly, and Draguitch could not resolve to do him harm by escaping during the times of his supervision.

Gradually we learned the fate of our other comrades who had been arrested in Moscow. Some fifteen people had been seized, among them members of our organization ; a few were simple suspects or even innocent people, taken into custody on some vague suspicion. The people arrested were mainly Yugo-Slavs with a few Russians and one Swedish woman, a member of the Comsomol. Two of our Russian comrades—Zankov and Glybovsky—were already at Verkhne-Uralsk ; one Russian and one Yugo-Slav had capitulated. The Russian had thereupon been set at liberty in token of his ' sincere deposition ', the Yugo-Slav had been exiled to Narym. Another Yugo-Slav, Heberling, had also been exiled to the Ural.

V

POLITICAL LIFE IN PRISON

What most interested me in the isolator was its political life and thought. In the U.S.S.R., as long as one remained ' in freedom ', one could follow and discuss the political life of the country only in small groups. This was an arduous task, and it led to the raising of problems rather than to the solving of them, especially if one were a foreigner who had come to Soviet Russia ten years after the revolution. But to be among two hundred prisoners representing in uninterrupted development all the shades of opinion that are to be found in the immense country that is Russia—that was a precious privilege which allowed me to acquire a full knowledge of Russian political life in all its aspects.

When I arrived at the isolator in November, 1930, the era of capitulations, which had for the last eighteen months been demoralizing and disorganizing the Russian Opposition, was drawing to a close. But echoes were still to be heard of the storm that had carried before it four-fifths of the Opposition. ' Capitulater ' and ' semi-capitulater ' were still the worst insults one could fling at one's adversary in the course of a discussion. These echoes began gradually to die away, no new capitulations were heard of, and, six months later, those who had capitulated began to arrive at the isolator for not having shown themselves sufficiently enthusiastic supporters of the general Line.

The vast majority of the Communist prisoners were Trotskyists : 120 out of 140. There was also a Zinovievist who had refused to capitulate, sixteen or seventeen members of the ' democratic centre ' (Extreme Left) and two or three adherents of Miasnikov's ' workers' group '. Among the non-Communists there were three main groups of a dozen members each : the Russian social-democrat Mensheviks, the Georgian social-democrats and the anarchists. There were, moreover, five Left-wing revolutionary-socialists, a few Right-wing revolutionary-socialists, a few Armenian socialists of the *dashnaktsutiun* group and one maximalist. Apart from these, there were a few Zionists.

Such was the division into traditional Parties, but in reality each of these Parties comprised sub-divisions of various shades of opinion and even opposing sections due to deep-seated scissions. The reader will exclaim that twenty groups and sub-groups for two hundred prisoners seems ridiculous. But he must not forget that these prisoners were not ordinary prisoners but the representatives of all the Left-wing tendencies of a vast society, truly an illegal parliament of Russia. The burning problems put by the revolution, and in particular by the Five Year Plan in its present stage, produced the greatest animation in this circle and a state of ideological crisis singularly favourable to the breaking up of opinion into small sections. It was not until later, when the social and economic results of the Five Year Plan had clearly shown themselves, that a new political regrouping could take place in the isolator.

Five years of prison life and exile have closely linked me with the Opposition, be it Communist, socialist or anarchist, and I should like this book, not merely to serve as information, but also to rouse the conscience of democracy and of Western workers' movements in favour of the Opposition victims. Nevertheless, I consider it my duty to give a faithful and objective picture of this Soviet Opposition, and narrate what good and also what bad was contained in it.

* * *

The political groupings in the prison did not solely represent ideological tendencies, but were real organizations with their committees, hand-written newspapers and with recognized leaders, who might be either in prison, in exile or abroad. The prevailing system of repression, causing frequent transfer of prisoners from one prison to another, from one place of exile to another, ensured, better than could any system of clandestine correspondence, the clandestine contact between the members of a group.

What interested me above all was the Trotskyist Opposition to which I then belonged and which today is still the most important Opposition group in Russia. The Verkhne-

Uralsk isolator sheltered nearly all the most active members of the Trotskyist section.

The organization of the Trotskyist prisoners called itself the ' Collective of the Verkhne-Uralsk Leninist Bolsheviks '. It was divided into Left-wing, Centre and Right-wing. This division into three sections persisted during the three years of my stay, although the composition of the sections and even their ideologies were subject to certain fluctuations.

Upon my arrival at Verkhne-Uralsk I found three programmes and two Trotskyist newspapers.

(1) The Programme of the Three, drawn up by three Red professors, namely, E. Solntsev, G. Yakovin and G. Stopalov. It expressed the opinions of the Right-wing section, which at that time was the strongest.

(2) The Programme of the Two, written by Trotsky's son-in-law, Man-Nivelson, and by Aron Papermeister, was the credo of the small Centre group.

(3) The Theses of Militant Bolsheviks emanated from the Left-wing : Puchas, Kamenetsky, Kvatchadze, Bielenky.

They were documents of considerable length, consisting of five to eight different sections : international situation, industry, agriculture, classes in the U.S.S.R., the Party, the workers' question, tasks of the Opposition, etc.

The Right-wing programme gave a particularly elaborate survey of economic matters, the Left-wing programme contained good chapters on the Party and the workers' question.

Right-wing and Centre, between them, published *Pravda in Prison (Truth in Prison)*, the Left-wing *The Militant Bolshevik*. These newspapers appeared either once a month or every two months. Each copy contained ten to twenty articles in the form of separate writing books. The ' copy ', i.e. the packet of ten to twenty writing books, circulated from ward to ward and the prisoners read the notebooks in turn. The papers appeared in three copies, one copy for each prison-wing.

In 1930 the main subject of Trotskyist discussion was the attitude to be taken towards the Party-leaders, i.e. towards Stalin, and towards his new ' Left-wing policy '.

The Right-wing section considered the Five Year Plan, in spite of all its Right-wing or Extreme Left deviations, to answer the essential demands of the Opposition ; the official policy had therefore to be supported whilst submitting its methods to criticism. This section hoped for reform from above ; the increasing difficulties would force the Party and even the leaders to alter their policy. The Opposition would be re-established in its rights and would once more participate in the administration. As to making an appeal to the people and the masses, the Right-wing section thought this an extremely dangerous course to follow : the peasants were opposed to the dictatorship of the proletariat, they were ' against us ' ; the workers were undecided, the ' spirit of Kronstadt ' pervaded the land and the ' Thermidor front might well include the working class '. With what did the Right-wing reproach Stalin ? First, like all Trotskyists, it did not admit the rule Stalin had established inside the Party. Next it considered that Stalin was exaggerating the application of the Five Year Plan, that its rhythm was too fast and that the country would be unable to keep up with it. On the whole, it wanted the same things as did Stalin, but in a modified and more human form. It feared only one thing : that by his extreme policy, by his ' Extreme Left adventure ', Stalin would compromise the régime as a whole, the régime with the welfare of which it was above all preoccupied.

The section of the Militant Bolsheviks was very noisy and took up a position that was diametrically opposed to that of the Right-wing. Its essential idea was that reform should take place from below, that one had to expect a split in the Party and rely on the working class. The hostility shown by this section towards Stalin was in marked contrast with the attitude of the Red professors of the Right, and won it the support of workers and young people. The weakness of its programme consisted in the summary nature of its judgement of the economic basis of the Five Year Plan. It clung to a phrase of Trotsky that had only polemic value : " The Five Year Plan is nothing but an edifice of figures," and it declared that all Stalinist industrialization was mere bluff. As to the international policy, the Left-wing section not only denied the existence of a conjunction favourable to the revolution, but, in order to belittle Stalin, the existence of an economic world depression. All this showed the bohemian spirit of these Militant Bolsheviks, in particular that of Puchas, the young journalist. The more thoughtful members of the section were beginning to perceive that their programme should be founded on a more serious basis.

The Centre section considered it necessary to take both possible methods of reform into account : from above and from below. The Centre was soon strengthened by two Red professors : F. Dingelstedt, who arrived early in November from exile, and Victor Eltsin, who had formerly been considered to belong to the Extreme Right because of his insistence on the principle of out-and-out collectivization. Igor Poznansky, Trotsky's former secretary, was in agreement with Centre views, without belonging to any section.

It is interesting to note the five Red professors mentioned above : Solntsev, Stopalov, Yakovin, Dingelstedt and Eltsin, who in the past had collaborated with Trotsky in editing his *Complete Works*. Trotsky's organ issued abroad qualified them as 'young Opposition theoreticians '. (*Opposition Bulletin*, no. 19, 1931.)

The majority of the Opposition were therefore looking for a road to reconciliation ; whilst criticizing the Five Year Plan, they put the stress not on the part of exploited class played by the proletariat, but on the technical errors made by the Government *qua* employer in the matter of insufficient harmony within the system and inferior quality of production. This criticism did not lead to an appeal to the workers against the Central Committee and against bureaucratic authority ; it restricted itself to proposing amendments in a programme of which the essentials were approved. The socialist nature of State industry was taken for granted. They denied the fact that the proletariat was exploited ; for ' we were in a period of proletarian dictatorship '. At most they admitted that there were deviations in the system of repartition. I had thought as they did two years before, but how could one continue to think so in 1930 ? I attributed this time-lag in their views to their life in prison.

* * *

I made my début in the political life of the prison by writing two articles, ' A few theoretical premises in the Opposition struggle ' and ' The Theses of the Militant Bolsheviks '. In them I developed the following ideas : the moment has come to lay a more serious theoretic foundation to the struggle against Stalin's policy ; in the struggle against the Five Year Plan stress must be laid on his anti-socialist and anti-proletarian aspect instead of talk about ' bluff ' and criticism of details.

We members of the Opposition, I continued, had recognized in the Stalinist clique the Robespierre clique and had warned Stalin of the fate of his illustrious French predecessor. But we had been mistaken, for we had overlooked the fact that the ' Communist ' bureaucracy had a weapon at its disposal which Robespierre had not : the entire economy of the land. Unchallenged master of all essential means of production, the Communist bureaucracy was gradually becoming the nucleus of a new ruling class, the interests of which were as opposed to those of the working class as were those of the former bourgeoisie. Inside Russia should be organized an economic contest of the proletariat—demands and strikes—exactly as in any country with private capital. It was even necessary to link up with any socialists and anarchists one might find in the factories. The slogan of a new revolutionary workers' Party should be launched. The moment had come to abandon the attempts at reform inside the Party in favour of a revolutionary class struggle. This struggle should be provided with its theoretic background. " Without a revolutionary theory," I said by way of epilogue to my first article, " there is no revolutionary movement."

Whilst still at liberty, I had in vain sought the ' dictatorship of the proletariat ' in the U.S.S.R. ; all I had been able to observe was its slavery. But Thermidor remained equally absent and Stalin was still in power. What was the meaning of it all ? I learned what Trotsky's opinion on the subject was : the bureaucracy, skipping its Thermidor, was preparing its 18th Brumaire. " The Bonapartist preparations made by the Party are finished," Trotsky wrote on the occasion of the XVIth Congress, in his letter from Constantinople, dated August 5th, 1930. I began to see a first glimpse of the explanation I had sought everywhere. Other more radical groups I met in prison—the ' Decists ' of the Miasnikov group—asserted that Bonapartism had already triumphed. That seemed still more true to me. Stalin had a great likeness to an oriental Bonaparte. Did this not explain the magnitude of the crimes committed by the Stalinist régime ?

There was in my ward one Trotskyist from Kharkov, named Densov, a sound economist, former head of the Conjuncture section of the Ukrainian *Gosplan* (State Planning Commission). He was practically the only Trotskyist to consider Soviet economy as a form of State capitalism. He quoted several statements of Lenin on this subject, dating from 1918 to 1922, which Trotsky had failed to notice. Densov had arrived at Verkhne-Uralsk a week before myself ; he took a position in the Left-wing of the Trotskyists, without, however, linking up with the group of the Militant Bolsheviks. It was he who asked me to write the articles I have just discussed, in order ' to strengthen the position of the Left-wing.'

The nihilism of the Opposition and its small-minded attitude towards the Five Year Plan worried Densov. "The Opposition is about to find itself left high and dry for having failed to understand in time that the reproach to make to the immense Stalinist effort is that of anti-socialism. Today neither Solntsev nor Puchas can see anything else in the Five Year Plan but disproportion or bluff, but what will they say in two or three years' time when all the disproportions will have disappeared, when production will have improved, when the bluff will have become an undeniable economic reality ? During the spring Rakovsky was writing that in autumn there would be nothing left of the out-and-out collectivization. Autumn came and collectivization continued and grew in strength. What is Rakovsky to say now ? Certainly there are people who like nothing better than to contradict themselves, but other and more serious people will have a difficult time if they do not succeed in forming a timely and coherent picture of events.

Densov, while considering my conclusions somewhat hasty, was, on the whole, of my opinion. We therefore acted in concert ; while I wrote articles on political and sociological subjects, he wrote economic chronicles to back them up. The question whether the Five Year Plan was or was not a success was now a matter of everyday discussion in the prison.

My conclusions met with a favourable reception among the Trotskyist Left-wingers. The Right-wing and the Centre attacked me, however, declaring them to be premature, repeating the errors of the ' ultras ' (or ' Decists ', Miasnikov's workers' Opposition). One of my opponents wrote : " Richard (that was my pseudonym) has no need to discover America, for Columbus has already done so." " The light of the first floor North (where Densov and I were lodged) is not a beacon but a will o' the wisp ", another one wrote. Solntsev, the real head of the Right-wing and Centre, declared that " such ideas do not belong to our movement ".

To which I made the retort that "a movement cannot remain stationary; it must enrich itself by experience. Once the struggle against bureaucracy has begun, one must not pause half-way."

The Left-wing extremists were mainly of Solntsev's opinion. They considered the Trotskyist movement incapable of breaking entirely away from the bureaucracy, for it was nothing else but a 'Left and more Liberal wing of that same bureaucracy'. Tiunov, a supporter of Miasnikov, wrote: "It is an Opposition of high officials. In respect of the bureaucratic autocracy, Trotsky's Opposition is as rotten as that of Milyukov in the days of Czarist autocracy." The Decists argued that Trotsky still wavered between true revolutionary Bolshevism and its official and bourgeois carica-ture, just as he had remained undecided before 1917 between true Bolshevism and the Mensheviks. During the spring of 1930 the rumour that Trotsky had capitulated went round the isolator. One of the Decist leaders, V. M. Smirnov (not to be confused with I. M. Smirnov, the former Trotskyist, shot in the course of the Zinoviev trial, nor with A. P. Smirnov who belonged to the Right-wing Opposition together with Rykov and Bukharin), who was then in the isolator, and was the incarnation of the old immovable type of intellectual Bolshevik, had written: "Trotsky has capitulated. That is all to the good. This semi-Menshevik will now at last cease to hamper the authentic revolutionary movement by his presence."

It seemed to me that Decists and Miasnikovists were exaggerating. The Trotskyist Opposition was able, I thought, to evolve much more to the Left than the Right-wing Trotskyists and extremists of Decism and Miasnikov. Moreover, Trotskyism was the only Opposition grouping that carried any weight in Soviet society, the others being practically negligible. If Trotskyism continued incapable of expressing the needs of the working class, Russia would be condemned to pass through a period of 'political vacuum' until the day when the masses had once more elaborated a new movement, the nature of which was not yet to be fore-seen. It seemed necessary to me, therefore, to exhaust the possibilities of the Trotskyist experiment before throwing it aside.

*   *   *

To the struggle of ideas inside the Trotskyist 'Collective'

was added a growing conflict concerning the organization that was to relegate ideological differences to the second place. This conflict was so characteristic of the psychology and customs of the Russian Opposition that I shall here briefly record it.

The Right-wing and the Centre put the following ultimatum to the Militant Bolsheviks : either they dissolved their group and suspended publication of their newspaper or else they would be expelled from the Trotskyist organization. Indeed, the majority were of the opinion that the Trotskyist group was not to contain any sub-groups.

This principle of a ' monolithic section ' was, after all, no other than the one that actuated Stalin in the matter of the entire Party. But their principle also hid a calculation of a practical nature : once they could rid themselves of the ' irresponsible elements of the extreme Left, who had their doubts as to the socialist character of our State ', the higher-placed members of the Opposition would find it easier to come to an agreement with the Party leaders and, above all, with the Stalinist group.

Most of the Opposition personalities believed that the difficulties to come would force the Party to come to terms with the Opposition ; in order to be prepared for that eventuality, they tried to deal with the adversaries inside their own section and by methods that could only be called Stalinist. As to the Militant Bolsheviks, they refused to submit to the majority and thought it necessary to prove to Trotsky, by publishing their group-newspaper, that there was, inside the isolator, a strong Left-wing minority. They even sent Trotsky an article which the latter published abroad in his *Opposition Bulletin*.

A large number of the Left-wing Trotskyists, among whom I counted myself, were of the opinion that the theories of the Militant Bolsheviks were too flimsy and thus were in no way inclined to engage in solidarity with them. But at the same time, we protested vigorously against the ultimatum sent them, for we deemed that each group had the fullest right to publish its own newspaper. The arrival in prison of a well-known publicist, old N. P. Gorlov, strengthened our group which soon increased to some thirty members and hastened the *rapprochement* with the Militant Bolsheviks who numbered about twenty.

217

The ultimatum was discussed for months in all groups of the isolator. Debates, voting and resolutions followed closely upon one another. Our ' group of thirty ' proposed a compromise : one single paper would be published for the entire Communist section, but a new editorial committee would be elected containing a representative from each of the present sections. Up to the present, the editorial committee had contained two members of the Right-wing and one of the Centre, whereas the Militant Bolsheviks had not been represented at all. But the Right refused the compromise on the pretext that ' the majority has the right to decide on what it considers the best course '. This was Stalin's favourite gambit in his struggle against the Opposition : the dissolution of the Militant Bolsheviks was demanded while they were refused a place on the Central Organ. The people therefore who were in prison for anti-Stalinism could find nothing better to do than to indulge in Stalinism themselves while in prison. This absurdity was only apparent ; it merely served to prove that between Trotskyism and Stalinism there were many points in common.

In answer to this manœuvre our ' group of thirty ' decided that if the majority remained determined to exclude the Militant Bolsheviks, the ' group of thirty ' would break with the majority to found, together with the excluded members, a new and distinctly Left-wing organization.

This caused the centre (Dingelstedt) to waver. Poznansky (Trotsky's former secretary) openly accused Solntsev of provoking a scission with the criminal intention of engineering a reconciliation with the Party. But Solntsev would not be intimidated. The Centre gave way and the scission took place.

Thus, towards the summer of 1931, two distinct Trotskyist organizations existed : the ' Collective of Leninist Bolsheviks ' (majority) ; and the ' Collective of Leninist Bolsheviks ' of the Left. At the moment of the scission, the majority group counted between 75 and 78 members, the Left 51 or 52. A few comrades remained outside both of the organizations and formed a group preaching reconciliation between Trotskyists. Both groups underwent considerable modifications as to their numbers and their ideologies as time went on. The Left began to publish a new paper, the *Leninist Bolshevik*, edited by N. P. Gorlov, V. Densov, M. Kamenetsky, O. Puchas and A. Ciliga.

Whilst we quarrelled, the G.P.U. was at work. It first favoured the scission and, once that had taken place, did its best to widen the breach. Sometimes the *agents provocateurs* of the G.P.U. who lived among us would act with breath-taking effrontery. Thus an engineer from Moscow called Savelitch, who had joined our group in the exercise ground, began to prove with fiery enthusiasm that it was absolutely essential to exclude the Militant Bolsheviks. The part he played was so apparent that after two days I was able to declare that he was ' carrying out the mission that had been confided to him ' (by the G.P.U. was understood). A month later, when the scission had already taken place, we succeeded in unmasking him and he was chased out of the ward, for the G.P.U. consented to remove *agents provocateurs* once they had been discovered. On another occasion a member of the Opposition called Bagratian arrived, sent to us from Tashkent. He became an ardent Leftist. When a member of the Centre produced a humorous sheet, Bagratian lost his temper and provoked a scuffle between the Left and the Right, an occurrence entirely against prison ethics. He was allowed to go on as before, no one taking much notice of him, all Caucasians being supposed to be hot-tempered. A short while later though he was proved to be an *agent provocateur*.

Sournov, an old and rather well-known member of the Opposition, distinguished himself by his impetuous attacks on the Militant Bolsheviks. At a meeting he declared that ' if we were at liberty, they ought all to be shot '. That was unprecedented. Those of the Left demanded that Sournov be excluded from the ranks of the Opposition. It must be said that the Left-wingers had already begun to suspect him of being an *agent provocateur*. As to those of the Right, they called these suspicions ' Left-wing exaggerations ', attributed the words spoken by Sournov to the latter's lively temperament, and refused to exclude him. Sournov, by flattering Solntsev, soon succeeded in being elected to the Committee of the Right. The G.P.U. then had him transferred to the same cell as Solntsev and was able to get its information from a good source and at the same time influence the most important prisoner in the isolator. But Solntsev was not duped for very long. Sournov, understanding that he was soon to be unmasked, gave up the game, ' capitulated ' and had himself transferred to Moscow, there to be released.

One day, after the scission had taken place, two Trotskyist prisoners, one of the Left, the other of the Right, suddenly saw the door of their cell open. An inspector walked in, threw a roll of papers at them and walked away in the same dramatic way. The prisoners examined the roll of papers with great caution ; it contained old letters from Solntsev to Dingelstedt in which there was talk of expelling the Militant Bolsheviks and of sowing discord in the Left-wing camp. As the two correspondents lived in different wings of the prison and could but rarely communicate with one another, Solntsev had made an effort to be as full as possible and to omit no single detail of his plan of campaign against the Left-wingers. He had premeditated all of which the Left had accused him. The G.P.U. having intercepted the letters, put them aside and utilized them after the scission, further to widen the gap that was forming between the two Trotskyist groups.

* * *

It was an accepted rule among the prisoners that every new arrival was to write out a detailed account of the things he had seen whilst at liberty that might interest his comrades in prison. We Yugo-Slavs did as everyone had done ; consequently we were able to receive the latest information from new arrivals.

The news about the fate of the deported peasants was to us a revelation of a world of death and horror. When I was still free, I had heard talk about peasant risings and deportations, but I had never been able to imagine the actual immensity and ferocity of the repression. One comrade who came from the region of Narym told us that the previous autumn, one hundred thousand deported peasants had arrived there. All the buildings had been full, even the churches ; women and young girls gave themselves to the first-comer for a piece of bread. Then they left, in winter, for the most distant and desert districts ; it meant certain death to them. I could now complete the picture I had formed of collectivization. One hundred thousand deportees in the one region of Narym in one single season ! How many had there then been throughout the U.S.S.R. during the four years of ' dekulakization ' ?

Other prisoners narrated the misery of the peasants during their journey into exile. The peasants of the Ukraine were deported to Siberia in train-loads. The journey lasted some forty days ; they were packed into the carriages as if they had been cattle, forbidden as they were to get out at railway stations. They were given no food and often ran short of water. The provisions they had been able to take with them were insufficient for so long a journey. The people died in large numbers in horrible suffering ; the quick and the dead, stores and excrement, all intermingled. Despairing fathers had been seen to dash out their children's brains against the telegraph poles that were flashing by.

There were many reports of the excesses of the authorities in the villages. I shall mention one that came to us from Siberia. A group of peasants was being executed. The G.P.U. representatives forced them to dig their own graves. They carried out their task, made their farewells, were shot down and covered over with sand. Suddenly, to the terror of the people assembled, a hand rose and waved over the sand. In their haste, the executioners had failed to finish off one of the wretches.

But as we learned later, these horrors were nothing compared with those that took place in 1932.

*   *   *

During the first months of my term of imprisonment at Verkhne-Uralsk, two resounding political trials took place, directed against the ' industrial section ' of the engineers (beginning of December, 1930) and against the Bureau of the Menshevik Socialists (beginning of March, 1931). The two trials had their repercussions in our prison and it was not long before those who were convicted in the second trial joined us.

At the present time the entire world has been able to convince itself of the lying nature of the accusations. But the true meaning of the two trials has remained enveloped in mystery. Abroad it cannot be understood, in any case, how trials such as those of 1930 and 1931, nor those of 1936 and 1937, could have been staged, bloody and humiliating outrages to human dignity as they were.

Foreigners trying to solve this riddle by arguments of individual psychology arrive nowhere. Those who refer to crowd-psychology in general, or to the crowd-psychology of European or American society, are in no way more successful. The explanation can only be found in the extremely peculiar conditions of Soviet society. I have not set myself the task of giving a complete analysis of these trials in this book. I shall restrict myself to recounting what I heard of them in the circle in which I was.

The first trial arraigned a group of Soviet specialists, of whom Professor Ramzin was the leader. They were accused of having organized a vast network of sabotage and espionage for the benefit of the French Military High Command, which was preparing for the military intervention of France against the U.S.S.R. The accused admitted everything down to the smallest detail. To believe Ramzin, his group intended to install, in the place of the present Soviet Government, a ' Government of engineers '.

The accused were condemned to death. But the Government, ' taking the candour of their statements and admissions into consideration ', commuted the death sentence to various terms of imprisonment. Thousands of people throughout Russia were being shot for infinitely lesser crimes ; this unexpected clemency did, for that reason, strike a very suspicious note.

Our Trotskyist comrades in prison appeared very perturbed by the trial of the ' industrial section '. Most of them chose to remain silent. Much was written in prison ; yet, if I remember well, not one single article was devoted to the trial. The bolder prisoners who discussed it held the most contrary opinions. Some said the trial confirmed all the revelations that, at one time, had been made by the Opposition concerning the increasing influence of the bourgeois technicians. Stalin's clemency once more proved the affinity existing between him and them. Others said that this war of Stalin's against the specialists was nothing but a new manifestation of the ' Extreme Left Stalinist adventure ', in which, as in the collectivization, a retreat had to be called. Rakovsky, in a letter from exile, agreed with that opinion. As to Trotsky, who was abroad, he was more inclined to take the first view, but we, in prison, were still ignorant of his attitude.

There was a third group, to which I belonged, who argued that the present trials were in no way a manifestation of the struggle of the proletariat against the bourgeois specialists, but merely the competition of two bureaucratic groups. The only truth in the affair was the discontent of the specialists and their secret desire to see the Communists come to grief in a failure of the Five Year Plan, which would have left the road clear for the engineers, who would then have been called to power as a matter of course. All the rest of the accusations were lies ' and moonshine on the part of the G.P.U. Stalin, or rather the Communist bureaucracy, were in desperate need of a scapegoat on which to turn the anger of the famished masses, thus compromising their competitors, the technicians, and simultaneously frightening the masses. " If you do not support us Stalinists, it will be all the worse for you ; war will return along with private property owners, and Cossack hordes will carry out punitive expeditions." One of the accused, Ramzin himself, if I am not mistaken, ' admitted ' indeed that the engineers had decided, if necessary, to massacre the entire Russian proletariat.

Members of the Moscow Opposition who had been arrested after the Ramzin trial gave us further particulars. Ramzin had not even been sent back to prison after the trial, he had merely been ' confined to his own domicile ', an entirely fictitious type of arrest. Immediately upon the termination of the trial, that is, after a six months' interval, made necessary by the preliminary investigation, or rather by the setting of the stage, Ramzin resumed his lectures at the Institute of Thermodynamics, pronouncing the professors' ritual phrase, " We had left off at . . ."

What was much more interesting was the attitude of the workers in Moscow during the trial. The Stalinist Government had succeeded in provoking the bitterest indignation among the masses, whose nerves were on edge with hunger, against the engineers. Workers' demonstrations, which the Government organized on a large scale in Moscow, were not without a certain sincerity. The demonstrators demanded the death of the ' traitors ', the *saboteurs* and the ' spies '. But when the self-condemned culprits were let off with relatively light sentences, and Ramzin, the villain of the piece, had been set at liberty again, the masses, according to the tales of our observers, did not hide their bitterness. " We are being laughed at ; it's all a comedy," were the feelings of the people.

Gradually the whole prison took to the idea that the trials were essentially tendentious. A revealing passage in the statement made by Ramzin strengthened the belief that this was simply a struggle between two competing groups. Ramzin had stated that his group had no intention of abolishing nationalized industry nor of restoring private industry, but that it would have permitted private capitalists— be they foreign or Russian, inclusive of the former proprietors—to participate to a certain extent in the State industry. A year before, one of the chief members of the League of Ukrainian Emancipation (Ukrainian Nationalists) had made an entirely similar declaration, not hiding his sympathies with the Fascist régime. It seemed perfectly logical to me, from the technicians' point of view, that they should wish industry to retain its State character ; their social importance in such a system would have been much more considerable than in a system of private economy. The result was that the struggle between Communists and technicians was due neither to a class antagonism nor to two different conceptions of economics ; it was nothing but a quarrel over one and the same cake. That a section of the engineers should be in sympathy with the Fascist system shed much light on the true character of the struggle opposing Fascists and real Communists.

If that were so, the part played by the workers' demonstrations became clear. The Communist bureaucracy needed them to frighten the technicians, to prove to them that they were powerless, as at any moment the populace might be let loose on them. Was it not better to submit to the Communist bureaucracy and to receive in exchange those privileges that were allowed the technicians to the detriment of the masses ?

The fate of Ramzin was significant. According to the general opinion in Russia, Ramzin had consciously played the part of *provocateur* during the trial. After a very few years he was fully re-established in all his rights and was decorated with the Order of Lenin on a pretext of scientific merit. Stalinist authority ' does not avenge itself on culprits, it re-educates them ! '

I wish to mention a considerably less well-known trial that took place at Tashkent ; it enables one to form an idea of the way in which these trials were ' prepared '. Two Soviet engineers who worked in Central Asia had fled to Persia.

After some time they had returned to the U.S.S.R. of their own free will. They were tried. They told the story of their flight, due to their cowardice in the face of ' difficulties that must be surmounted during the building up of socialism '. Fugitives in the capitalist world, they had been able to see the deadly stagnation of it and its horrors. They had realized that Soviet life was made up of the joy of creation and of the conquest of obstacles. Thus they had returned to the U.S.S.R. of their own free will, to make good their default by honest work.

The whole of this touching story was told in public and then printed in the newspapers. But a few political prisoners who had been in the same prison at Tashkent had seen the reverse of the medal. As soon as the engineers had fled to Persia, the G.P.U. had arrested their families, children, babies and all. Communication was made to the escaped engineers that if they did not return to the U.S.S.R., the most merciless reprisals would be carried out against their families. The families were even then under ' special treatment ' ; one member of them died, another went mad. At that point the fugitives decided ' to return of their own free will ' to the U.S.S.R. and make ' sincere ' statements about anything the Government wished.

Three months after the trial of the ' industrial section ', the trial of the ' Bureau of Menshevik Socialists ' took place. The accused were men unknown in politics, who at one time had been Mensheviks, but during the NEP had become reconciled to the Soviet system and had obtained important posts in the economic structure and in the scientific institutes. It was difficult to believe that these men should have behaved in a fashion so humiliating and so dishonest as the technicians, who at least had the excuse of not having been renegades of a previous political opinion. But this was to deny the profound decomposition of Soviet society. The Mensheviks confessed to having adopted, in concert with the ' industrial section ', a whole programme of sabotage and armed intervention against the U.S.S.R. Furthermore, they admitted that their programme was that of Russian Social-democracy and of all other socialist Parties of the Second International.

The lie was flagrant. Today in a period of popular fronts formed by the Parties of the Second and Third Internationals, such confessions and such trials seem absurd. But at the time,

Stalin was still in a period of anti-socialist slogans : " Social-democracy is our main enemy ", " Social-democracy and Fascism are twin brothers ". Stalin was in need of proving that the objections raised by the Mensheviks against the Five Year Plan had degenerated into crimes against the civil law, into acts of treason against the country. The trial had no other aim than to furnish this proof.

The staging and the successful carrying out of the trials were the characteristic traits of the Stalinist era. Characteristic both of the society as of the rulers. Such trials are only possible if the rule of an immoral government coincides with a phase of profound apathy in society, tired of disinterested motives, tired of revolutions, with eyes left only for the immense economic development of the country. " The revolution has become materialist " was written by Michelet, to characterize an analogous phase of the French revolution.

In contrast with what had happened in our prison during the trial of the ' industrial section ', the prison verdict on the Menshevik trial was unanimous : we all thought it a manœuvre of the G.P.U. We also knew that the G.P.U. had not dared produce two men, deeply implicated in the affair : the social-democrat, Braunstein, and the old Bolshevik, Bazarov, translator into Russian of *Capital*, who since 1917 had belonged to no Party. The G.P.U. had not risked calling them, as it knew that these two men would categorically have refused to play a part in the comedy. Thus they were dealt with by administrative means, without any form of trial. Not one group inside our prison agreed with Trotsky, who was taken in and who seriously believed the ' confessions ' made by the so-called culprits.

A few months later the principal characters of the Menshevik trial—Groman, Sukhanov, Rubine, Ikov, Scheer, Ginzburg, etc.—arrived at Verkhne-Uralsk. The G.P.U. carefully kept them in isolation, forbidding them any form of mutual communication or of communication with any of the other prisoners. What could the G.P.U. fear, unless it were the revelations of the methods by which the trial had been staged ? But this was the point that exercised us most, and in spite of all G.P.U. vigilance, we succeeded in establishing contact with the sad heroes of the trial. One day I asked one of them how they had been able to make those monstrous statements. His answer was eloquent : " We ourselves don't understand it, it was all like a horrible night-mare."

A few years later Sukhanov (who by the way was the well-known historian of the revolution) had a copy of his appeal to the Government circulated throughout the prison, in which he demanded that they should fulfil their promises of " releasing those willing to make untrue confessions ". As a result of this incident the G.P.U. had Sukhanov removed ; but he was not released. Nobody knows what has happened to him since.

In the interval between the two trials there was a scandal inside the Party ; the opposition of Syrtsov and Lominadze was unmasked. Syrtsov was the Chairman of the Council of People's Commissars of the RSFSR (Russian Socialist Federal Soviet Republic). Lominadze was one of the foremost young leaders of the Communist Party. His opposition was remarkable for two of its characteristics that were never divulged. It systematically went in for hypocrisy, defending Stalin in public but conducting a campaign against him behind the scenes. For the first time there had been a coalition between Left-wing and Right-wing Opposition. Syrtsov, though not a member of the Right-wing Opposition, shared its views ; as to Lominadze, he was one of those Left-wing Stalinists who dreamed of a Stalin-Trotsky-Zinoviev coalition. The Syrtsov-Lominadze alliance had arisen from the growing economic crisis due to the frantic rhythm of the Five Year Plan and to the increasing distress of the workers. Syrtsov expressed himself in measured terms, " The country has light-heartedly entered into an economically dangerous zone ; the whole world talks of it with anxiety. The workers' initiative has been curbed. The wage-problem is becoming more and more acute." Lominadze dotted the i's. " The administration of the Party treats the interests of the workers and peasants in the manner of the old feudal ' barines '."

But Stalin was losing no time. Summoned to give an explanation, the leaders of the Right-Left coalition capitulated and were degraded to inferior posts in the hierarchy. Stalin availed himself of the incident to strengthen his position. Rykov was removed from the Chairmanship of the Council of the People's Commissars for the U.S.S.R. and was replaced by Molotov, whereas the industrial leadership was given into the hands of Ordjonikidze, an intimate friend of Stalin. As to Syrtsov and Lominadze's immediate collaborators, they were sent to prison or into exile. One of them, Riutin, former secretary of the Communist Party Committee at Krasnaya-Presnia, one of the pillars of the Right-wing section, arrived in our isolator.

Riutin in prison ! This same Riutin who, from 1925 to 1927, in the days of the Stalin-Bukharin coalition against Zinoviev and Trotsky, was the fiercest persecutor of Trotskyism, was now in prison, alone amongst his victims, delivered to their mercy. It was a great temptation. But since 1927 much water had flowed under the bridge, and it was no longer a question of 'widening the NEP' but of 'discussing the ultra-Left adventure' of Stalin. The prison therefore received Riutin coldly but calmly. That might have been taken to mean that the tension between the Right-wing of the Party and Trotskyism was diminishing, and on many points one could indeed speak of a *rapprochement*. As it was, Riutin was soon transferred elsewhere.

At that time I fell ill with rheumatism and was then able to make the acquaintance of a very important institution in the prisoner's life : the prison infirmary. This infirmary, as well as the doctor's study, was situated in a derelict church. The prisoners were often ill. The Communists had lived through years of Civil War and privation, anarchists and socialists through ten years in prison, concentration camp and exile. The G.P.U. knew the art of shattering the nervous system of their victims. It is difficult to imagine the state of morbid nervousness in which the prisoners were.

The infirmary was not the only refuge for tired prisoners. They would also rest, at times, by taking up their interests in literature when they grew weary of politics. On those occasions the most popular book would be the memoirs of an old Bolshevik conspirator, who since the NEP had become a Trotskyist—namely, A. K. Voronky's *Running Waters and Marshes*. With melancholy art he described the epic of the Bolshevik conspirators in the days of the revolutionary movements between the years 1903 and 1917. " Never again shall we meet, our dear old band, united and bold." It was a whole generation weeping for its lost paradise in these memoirs.

With the arrival of Gorlov, who in 1923 had defended Mayakovsky against Trotsky, I once more began to take an interest in the discussions on this poet and on literature in general. These debates did, as a matter of fact, go beyond the bounds of literature. I ferreted out Mayakovsky's review *The Left Front*, and the verbatim notes of the literary discussions which the Central Party Committee conducted in the days of the NEP, and finally the books of Trotsky and Lenin.

The Left Front breathed the spirit of battle in the deleterious atmosphere of the NEP. The manifesto of the Literary Opposition which Mayakovsky published in it will be part of the history of the Russian revolution with as much right as the manifesto of Trotsky's political Opposition in 1923 or the social Declarations of the workers' Opposition between 1920 and 1922. *The Left Front* fought against literary conservatism and the self-complacency of successful Communists, and recalled the fact that literature was not merely a mirror but also a weapon—all this at a time when compromise was the fashion.

It seems as if Trotsky ought to have seen an ally for his Opposition policy in this Literary Opposition. He might even have been able to change Mayakovsky's vague attacks into something more solid. But Trotsky, alas, recognized no such thing and opposed Mayakovsky. I was able to perceive clearly, whilst in prison, closely following the printed documents and the text of the discussions, that, in the way of literature, Trotsky was the most brilliant representative of the Centre-Right coalition against Bukharin and Stalin, notwithstanding the ceaseless political struggle he waged against that coalition. In literature he defended the reconciliation of the classes to which, in politics, he objected ; in this field he was nothing but an intellectual concerned with liberalism. Riazanov, at the Sessions of the Central Committee devoted to Communist Literature, did not mind turning his ridicule upon both Trotsky and Bukharin and accusing them of forgetting historic materialism in favour of a ' reactionary idealism '.

The Five Year Plan succeeded in confusing Mayakovsky. His ultra-Left slogans seemed to triumph in literature as for the rest in politics. But at the same time he felt that this was but lip-service and that the development remained reactionary, as in the past. He looked for salvation in death.

The tragic destiny of the great writers of ancient Russia

repeated itself in Mayakovsky's fate. Puchas, our comrade in prison, drew this analogy in an article devoted to the poet. But the sacrilegious comparison roused a storm in the penitentiary. " How can one possibly forget the essential difference between the U.S.S.R. and the Russia of the Czars ? " all the Red professors of the Opposition exclaimed with one voice. Poor old Puchas, an ignoramus in the field of theory, was very willing to agree to the ' essential difference ' and withdrew his article from circulation. Thus the members of the Opposition would no longer run the risk of having to meditate on ' the tragic fate of Russian poets from Pushkin to Mayakovsky '.

I have quoted this episode, for it was typical. In spite of the violence of its language towards Stalin, the Opposition was fundamentally conservative. As soon as it became a matter of criticizing the system, people were struck with unexpected timidity. They preferred to cling to words that were empty of meaning and to the clumsiest old parables, for the sake of evading the search for new ones. It was decidedly very difficult to observe any psychological difference between the Russian Communist Party and its Opposition.

" What ? You argue that we are no longer Party members ? But you argue like Stalin ! " kind old Gorlov exclaimed.

" Come on ! " I answered. " How can we consider ourselves members of a Party from which we have been expelled and which has caused the G.P.U. to throw us in prison ? "

But Gorlov continued to pretend that the All-Russian Communist Party remained ' our Party ' all the same, and that Stalin was nothing but a usurper, a vulgar crook. . . .

This attitude had one less objectionable side. One day, as I rejoiced on reading of a drop in the coal production in the Donbas, mentioned by *Pravda*, two Georgian members of the Opposition, Tsivtsivadze and Kiknadze, grew very angry with me. " It is our duty to be alarmed at any sign of weakening of Soviet power. We must certainly persuade the Party that Stalin is obnoxious, but we must not be defeatists as regards our own Soviet Government."

I tried to calm them down by explaining that my attitude was not one of defeatism, but that I merely rejoiced at the resistance which the workers of the Donbas had at last put up against the bureaucratic arbitrariness. This argument did not count with them. Any harm done to authority, even if done by the workers themselves, seemed to them a counter-revolutionary action.

I noticed, moreover, that the letters and other writings of Trotsky that reached us in prison kept silent on one point : Trotsky never spoke of organizing strikes, of inciting the workers to a fight against bureaucracy in favour of the Trotskyist economic programme. His criticisms, his arguments and his advice seemed all addressed to the Central Committee, to the Party apparatus. Mentioning the fall in the standard of living of the workers, Trotsky concluded in the tone of a good employer giving his advice to the workshop, " What are you doing ? You waste our most precious capital, the force of labour." The active body to Trotsky still remained ' the Party ' with its Politbureau or its Central Committee ; the proletariat was but ' the object '.

At this point it is worth noting that Trotsky's memoirs—*My Life*—aroused the unambiguous displeasure of the Opposition workers in Moscow. They complained, according to the latest arrivals from the capital, that Trotsky passed over the part played by the working class in silence, and in particular the part played by the Opposition. One of the most prominent workers' leaders, a former member of the Moscow Soviet, was even supposed to have been so disgusted that he threw the book aside midway through it. I can remember only one single favourable opinion, which I heard when free, from a Trotskyist from Kiev. As to the prisoners who came from exile, they had not read *My Life*, which was a banned book.

It should also be mentioned that all Trotsky's works, and those of socialists and anarchists that had lawfully been published in the U.S.S.R. before the groups that produced them had been forbidden, were in no way subjected to a G.P.U. ban, and were therefore not confiscated when in the possession of prisoners. We could lawfully read the works of Trotsky, Plekhanov, Martov, Kropotkin and Bakunin. But from 1934 onwards all these books, though lawfully published, were beginning to be confiscated. Bakunin's works, which at that time were being published under the editorship of Steklov, were not intended to be sold, but only to be circulated among a restricted group.

The letters of Trotsky and Rakovsky, devoted to the questions of the day, found their way into the prison and gave rise to ample commentaries. One could not fail to be struck by the spirit of hierarchy and submission to a leader which was permeating the Russian Opposition. A quotation from Trotsky had the value of a proof. Apart from that, both the Trotskyists of the Right and those of the Left used them for obviously tendentious purposes. The complete submission to Lenin and to Stalin that pervaded the Party could also be found in the Opposition, but then in favour of Lenin and Trotsky ; all the rest were the Devil's own.

I well remember the letter of March, 1930, in which Trotsky spoke of the ' intoxication of success ' and of the retreat ordered by Stalin, and in which he developed his own plan of retreat. In his letter of August, 1930, he pronounced his judgement on the XVIth Party Congress that had just terminated. One of his phrases, ' the preparations for Bonapartism inside the Party are now concluded ', became the basis of all reasoning and of all theses of the Left. As for the Right, it attributed to it only a rhetorical value without importance as to the general attitude adopted by Trotsky. The Left wished only to hear negative judgements pronounced by Trotsky on the political superstructure of the régime ; the Right listened only to his positive judgements as to the social basis : dictatorship of the proletariat and socialist character of the economy.

The real incoherence of Trotsky's attitude gave rise to two antagonistic groups in the isolator, both of which clung to one of the two contradictory aspects of the leader. In February of 1931 Trotsky made a passing reference to the economic successes of the Five Year Plan. Then there came an interruption of nearly a year during which none of Trotsky's writings reached us.

I have already mentioned Rakovsky's writings. Rakovsky occupied no separate place in the Opposition, for only Trotsky was recognized. Only in so far as he was Trotsky's representative was he listened to.

* * *

To finish this chapter I shall give a brief description of the men who for eight months had been my comrades in prison.

In ward no. 12, the first three bunks, starting from the

door, were occupied by Yugo-Slavs ; the fourth by a Right-wing Trotskyist called Akopian, former political Commissar of the Red Army. He came from a working class family and had a brother who was a Communist. Although he followed political discussions with keen interest, he did not take an active part in them, busily occupied as he was in improving his knowledge of mathematics, physics, etc.

His neighbour, the Georgian Chaliko Gotchelachvili, a member of the Comsomol and the son of an old non-Party miner, was a man of quick and sound intelligence, who studied the workers' problems with zeal and ability. One was all the more astonished to hear him obstinately defend the concept of a dictatorship by a minority of the *élite*.

The next place was reserved to Cherepakin, the only supporter of Zinoviev in our prison. A former Leningrad manual labourer, he had been a political Commissar in the Red Army during the Civil War. At the time of the action of the Zinoviev group, he was studying at the Tolmatchev Political and Military Academy in Leningrad. He argued that the dictatorship of the proletariat had been replaced by a ' democratic dictatorship of proletariat and peasantry '.

" A dictatorship, no doubt," I objected, " but in how far is it democratic ? Moreover, this dictatorship is not wielded by the workers and peasants but against them."

But, unshakable, he explained to me that the correct, dialectic analysis of events confirmed his theory. He read much philosophy, that of Hegel in particular. According to Hegel, Lenin and Cherepakin, there was, in Russia, a demo-cratic dictatorship of workers and peasants—which was hard luck on the facts.

In our ward there were also two Decists : Prokopenia and Fateev. The former had been a manual worker in Moscow, the latter first worker, then student. In the neighbouring ward was a third Decist—Michael Chapiro, a factory worker from Kharkov. The Decists, at that time, had split into two opposing groups ; the ' State capitalists ' who contended that the present system in the U.S.S.R. was State capitalism and that the bureaucracy was the ruling class, and against them the ' petit-bourgeois ' who considered Soviet rule and its bureaucracy the expression of a petit-bourgeois State. My Decist neighbours belonged to the second category. They were pleasant people, but in spite of many a discussion, I could not bring myself to understand how they could make their theory fit in with the obvious facts, with the open war of the bureaucracy against the petit-bourgeoisie (collectivization and ' dekulakization '). Thermidor, the petit-bourgeois counter-revolution, had triumphed, they said, at the moment when the Opposition had been expelled from the Party, that is, during the winter of 1927. Yet, two months later, the bureaucracy declared war against the peasants.

Vygone, a young sailor, former member of the Comsomol, was a Left-wing Trotskyist. Too young to stand so many years of privation, he left prison slightly unbalanced.

I have already mentioned the two Left-wing Trotskyists, Densov and Gorlov.

Khachtchevatsky, the official representative of the Right-wing Trotskyists in our recreation-group, was a complete pedant ; the bases of Bolshevism, daring and scope, were visibly absent from his nature. Another still more Right-wing Trotskyist was very different. He, Kiknadze, an old Bolshevik, had at one time been a revolutionary, whereas Khachtchevatsky had never truly been one. Another Right-winger who belonged to our recreation-group, called Tsivtsivadze, had at one time been the assistant head of the Georgian G.P.U., whose chief was the famous Kote Tsintsadze, who had since joined the Opposition. Tsivtsivadze had retained the haughty manner that belongs to the ex-representative of authority. He addressed the inspectors and gaolers with the severity of a superior, and I do not quite know why they put up with that attitude.

In the neighbouring ward, no. 11, the ' Centre ' set the tone, under the leadership of a Trotskyist from Kharkov called Abramsky, a quick-witted and cultured, yet fairly superficial man.

As for Antokolsky, a relative of the famous sculptor, and for Lobkovsky, former secretary of Rykov, they were modest, hardworking and self-effacing men. They occupied themselves copying out articles : Antokolsky for the Right and Centre, and Lobkovsky for the Left.

Among the seven workers of the neighbouring ward there was but one convinced Right-winger and that was Rappoport, a pleasant, ponderous tailor, forty years old and tubercular. Dorochenko, a Leningrad labourer, and Yoffe, an emigrant workman from Lithuania, belonged to the Left, but each in his own way. Dorochenko was always ready to make an outburst about something, whereas Yoffe considered everything with a serenity tinged with scepticism. Fomkin, a young textile labourer from Ivanovo-Voznesensk, was typical of the workman in revolt, not yet crushed by the heavy industrial machine. He belonged to the Left, of course.

There were still three other workers whose names I forget. One of them was from Leningrad, the two others from White Russia. The first did not belong to the Opposition, but had been condemned to a year in prison for having complained to a comrade, during the military manœuvres in which he took part, that the worker's life was difficult. The two White Russian workers took an active part in the discussions and disputes that arose during recreation-times. One question exercised them greatly ; why did the Opposition take so little notice of the workers' problems, why was it so imbued with the bureaucratic spirit ? These reproaches were well founded, but they bolstered them up with the most suspicious arguments. We understood later, when in exile, how that was : the two men were common *agents provocateurs*.

On the subject of *agents provocateurs* : one Right-wing Trotskyist, let us call him *N*, for I have been unable to remember his name, a former member of the Comsomol in the Ukraine and later a student at the University of Moscow, began to develop a theory according to which the *agents provocateurs* of the bourgeois police could not be compared with members of the Opposition who, after having ' capitulated ', reported everything they knew to the G.P.U. or even began to ' work ' in the Opposition in accordance with G.P.U. directions. Stalinists and Trotskyists were after all two sections of the same Party, which was not so in the case of Communists versus bourgeois authorities. Was it not normal that when a Stalinist joined the Opposition, he should tell us all he knew and sometimes even remain among Stalinists to keep us informed ?

This philosophy greatly moved my friend Draguitch. " This is a Bolshevism of spies ! It has nothing in common with revolution ! " he exclaimed. He was particularly repelled by *N*'s argument that ' this had, after all, always been done '. During the Civil War the same tactics were supposed to have been applied to revolutionary-socialists, social-democrats and anarchists. Draguitch declared war upon the theories of N and appealed to the old Opposition Bolsheviks, asking them to clarify the historical side of the dispute. They answered that in their time there had never been any talk about political evolution, and that neophytes were not asked to be common spies and *provocateurs*. As to the internal affairs of their former Party, they were not over-communicative. Certainly, there had been cases when deserters offered to continue to work in their former organizations for the benefit of the Cheka—the G.P.U. of that time —but these had been individual, rare cases. During the days of the Civil War there had been no established system of treachery and provocation.

After this rectification Draguitch demanded the exclusion of N from among the ranks of the Opposition, as his theories tended to demoralize it. The 'Right-wing Collective' to which N belonged refused, arguing that, though the opinions of N were false, they remained nevertheless within the limits of 'permissible deviations'.

One was fully justified in suspecting N of acting on behalf of the G.P.U. by spreading moral confusion among the Opposition. But nobody had any proofs—Draguitch any more than the others—nor even the slightest indication. After all, maybe N's opinions were perhaps only an abstract theory developed to its fullest implications. In any case, the episode explains many a thing in the life of the All-Russian Communist Party and that of its Opposition. Let us not forget that in those days 'capitulaters' and informants were not yet forced to give 'information' in the monstrous way in which they are forced to do so today.

Among the members of the Opposition who belonged to our recreation-group, there were two former factory-directors, both of working class origin. Lokhmatchev had been at the head of a large metallurgic factory of the Donbas, Marcus of a small factory in White Russia. The latter belonged to the Right-wing Trotskyists, but he was so permeated with the bureaucratic spirit that I was very surprised to see him in the ranks of the Opposition. I had been acquainted with him for several years before I was able to solve this enigma : Marcus was too human to accept the incredible sufferings which the Government imposed upon the workers. In accordance with his somewhat elementary views, the régime ought to have been able to make the interests of the bureaucracy coincide with those of the workers. This was the only motive that had driven him into the ranks of the Opposition.

As to Lokhmatchev, he belonged to the ' Workers' Opposition '. In 1929 the local group to which he belonged had shown signs of activity by joining forces with the Decists. This led Lokhmatchev straight to prison. Soon he ' capitulated ' and his term of imprisonment was altered into one of exile. Lokhmatchev's philosophy, like that of all the leaders of the Workers' Opposition, may be summed up as follows, " All is lost—the workers are silent—let us be silent, too."

In the spring of 1931 we saw the first batch of ' capitulaters ' arrive at the prison, those who had been unable completely to ' adapt ' themselves. Two of them, Sadovsky and Lozovsky, belonged to our recreation-group. They still considered themselves ' capitulaters ' and adherents of the general Line ; we therefore demanded that they be segregated, which was done. Their number soon rose from twenty to thirty, and they took their exercise by themselves. I was under the impression that a number of the ' capitulaters ' systematically practised hypocrisy ; having renounced open Trotskyist Opposition, they seemed to think it necessary to hide their secret activity by public display of solemn fidelity to the general Line. Those were the tactics of the I. N. Smirnov group.

VI

A HUNGER-STRIKE

THE peaceful course of our political discussions and of our new scissions and fusions was suddenly interrupted by an acute conflict with the administration that occupied all our strength for several months.

Towards the end of April the Ural snowstorms that made it impossible to walk even in a well-sheltered prison court-yard had ceased. The snow was melting, the days growing longer and the sun beginning to shine once more. Spring had come and prison-life was again becoming more bearable. Suddenly a few rifle-shots were heard. A Red Army sentry had shot at the prisoner Gabo Yessayan, who was standing at the window of his cell. Yessayan's lungs had been pierced. The isolator seethed with excitement and became as agitated as an ant-hill. All were immediately agreed that such an occurrence should not be tolerated. Indignation ran still higher when we learned the prehistory of the case, which showed that the attempt had been premeditated. Indeed, for a number of weeks the sentries had been constantly threatening to fire at the prisoners. The latter had sent their elder to complain to the prison director, whose answer had been, " It's the only language you people understand," an eloquent testimony that the sentries had acted only in conformance with the director's wishes.

One after the other the recreation-groups decided to go on hunger-strike from that night onwards, by way of protest. A strike-committee was elected, composed of the Right-wing Trotskyist, Dingelstedt, the Left-wing Trotskyist, Kvatchadze (who, suffering from dysentery, was later replaced by Densov) and the Decist, Sayansky. We proclaimed the aims of our strike : (1) Dismissal and punishment of Biziukov, the prison director. (2) Guarantees against new attempts on our lives. (3) Liberation of the wounded Yessayan in order to allow him to recuperate. (4) Improvement of the legal position of the prisoners, and better food.

The hunger-strike did begin that night. We handed back all the food in our possession to the prison authorities. The strike-committee was given dictatorial powers ; it immediately wired to Moscow and decided that some twenty comrades who were seriously ill should begin the strike only in three days' time. All private correspondence between prisoners was to cease. All possible measures were taken to inform the Opposition in Moscow of what was taking place.

More than 150 prisoners took part in the strike. A few prisoners on the sick-list went on strike too, out of solidarity. Three days later all the Communists, that is, 176 prisoners, were on hunger-strike. The socialists, too, made a protest against the abuses of the administration. A few anarchists took part in the strike out of camaraderie.

On the third day after the strike had been proclaimed, the prison director appeared, but we refused to see him. A few prisoners had fallen seriously ill : cardiac troubles, dysentery, etc. On this third day a sad occurrence moved the entire prison. One of the women prisoners, Vera Berger, at the end of her strength, went out of her mind. The next day she was removed to the lunatic asylum at Perm. One more victim. . . . The strike continued ; teeth were gritted, silence and good order were maintained. On the fifth day a second case of madness occurred. But it did not move us as did the first one, for the lunatic or so-called lunatic was Victor Kraini, who before the strike had already been a somewhat suspected person. Had this been staged by the G.P.U. to demoralize us and cause the strike to fail ? Kraini was removed, but we never heard whereto, which reinforced our suspicions. It is quite possible, of course, that the poor man was a victim and not an agent of the G.P.U.

There were eleven or twelve fasting in our ward. Some went on reading, talking or moving about, others remained in a recumbent position. I noticed that hunger depressed active and resolute people less than it did others. My further experiences of famine in the U.S.S.R. confirmed my belief that resistance to hunger is primarily a matter of will-power.

The administration had decided to temporize. After a week the director produced a telegram from Moscow, stating that a G.P.U. Enquiry Commission was soon to leave Moscow ; it would take at least a week to reach our forsaken corner, and the director suggested to us that we should cease our strike and wait for the Commission to arrive.

The proposition was almost unanimously accepted by the hunger-strikers. Only two or three suspected a clever move on the part of the administration.

Once the strike was over, we were put on a special diet before returning to our ordinary food. That brought us to the 1st of May, which we celebrated with songs and meetings, each recreation-group on its own. We put up portraits of Trotsky surrounded by all sorts of slogans. The inspectors objected to such heresy and we nearly came to blows in the courtyard, anxiously watched by other prisoners at their windows, but everything was amicably settled in the end. The various Trotskyist groups wished to send telegrams to our leader in exile, but the gaolers would not let us, saying, " We do not transmit counter-revolutionary greetings."

Socialists and anarchists also celebrated the feast of the revolution. All windows were adorned with red flags and the prisoners had manufactured red insignia which we wore in our button-holes. Paradoxes of Soviet life : one and the same feast, under one and the same flag, on both sides of the barricades !

The feast of the 1st of May passed, and the extra rations we were given on that day vanished too. Days and weeks went by. No Commission of Enquiry. The administration pretended that the Commission had been held up by un-expected business. After two months the prisoners lost their patience ; at the beginning of July we declared a second hunger-strike. To the amazement of the G.P.U. it was carried out with as much co-ordination as the first. The entreaties of the director who waved a telegram at us to the effect that the Commission was on its way did not cause us to waver. On the seventh day of the strike the Commission finally arrived, but we continued our strike nevertheless, firmly resolved not to interrupt it unless we were given satisfaction.

Two of our comrades—who were yet in good health—had ceased to participate in the hunger-strike of their own accord, and were excluded from our small society. One of them, Avoyan, finally ' capitulated ' ; the other, Assirian, promised that in future he would show exemplary solidarity and he was allowed to re-enter our Communist 'Collective' after three months.

The conduct of another prisoner, Kiknadze, is worth mentioning. Though not in agreement with the second strike, he behaved in an exemplary fashion and fasted like the others. Yet his wife had just come from Moscow to hand him a message from Ordjonikidze, his old comrade in arms. As a result of this message Kiknadze decided to 'capitulate', but he loyally waited until the strike should be over, and he participated in it until the end.

*　　*　　*

The Commission of Enquiry consisted of three people. Andreeva, the assistant-director of the Secret Political section of the G.P.U. 'College', had the last word in matters concerning political prisoners. Her particular gift was to remember the biographies of some thousands of militants belonging to the various Communist and Socialist Parties. She persecuted them with visible pleasure and went out of her way to separate, in prison and exile, husbands from their wives and children from their parents. The second member of the Commission was Popov ; he was chief of the Penitentiary Section of the G.P.U. His sweeping moustachios were in keeping with his functions. The third—I have not been able to remember his name—acted as a general Prosecutor. He was a Polish Communist, former railwayman, who distinguished himself from the other members of the Commission by his more polite, more 'European' manners.

Andreeva began by declaring that the G.P.U. did not recognize any collective organ representing the Communist prisoners and refused to deal with our Committee. Dressed in a Cheka uniform, with heavy boots, she walked bareheaded into the wards with a stern demeanour. But instead of entering into discussions with her, the prisoners referred her to the Strike Committee. The next day Andreeva changed her tactics. Elegantly dressed in a tailor-made of black cloth, perfumed, wearing fashionable shoes and flesh-coloured stockings, she attempted to enter into conversation with each of us separately. She was no more successful in this course than she had been the previous day and, giving up the contest, she entered into discussion with our Committee.

The discussions dragged through three days. Andreeva declared that most of our demands should be satisfied, but that we should first of all cease our hunger-strike as the G.P.U. could not give in to intimidation. Biziukov, the prison director, was not to be dismissed, but the soldier who had fired the shots was to be handed over to justice. She promised to issue an order allowing us to stand in the window-bays. She further promised a few other improvements of the system, in particular better nourishment. Finally, she promised that Yessayan should have his sentence commuted from prison to exile, and that he should be properly nursed.

The Committee demanded furthermore that it should be formally specified that no reprisals should be taken against those prisoners who had taken part in the hunger-strike. Andreeva made this promise verbally, but refused to give it in writing. A last question remained to be solved : were we to insist on the dismissal of the prison-director ? The Committee could not agree on the point. A census of the opinion of all hunger-strikers was made. The majority were in favour of a conciliatory policy ; the minority gave in and thus our second strike, which had lasted eleven days, ended in as disciplined a fashion as it had begun.

The G.P.U. kept the promises made by Andreeva, but had its own back in a different way ; six months later thirty-five of the prisoners who had been on hunger-strike were transferred to the isolator of Suzdal. Among them there were adherents of the three principal political groups in our prison : Trotskyists from the Right and from the Left, and Decists. The Trotskyists from the Left—who had shown themselves particularly resolute during the strike—suffered more than the others. The more notable among them were Densov, Kvatchadze, Puchas and Dvinsky. They were all transferred to Suzdal. Also the members of the Strike-Committee, but for one. As to Yessayan, the wounded man who should have been liberated, we learned later that he had merely been transferred to the political prison at Chelyabinsk.

Six months later the G.P.U. began to be active at Verkhne-Uralsk itself.

VII

POLITICAL REPRESSION IN THE U.S.S.R.

The hunger-strike of the summer of 1931 had fallen during a period of quiet and had met with a certain success. This was exceptional in the records of Verkhne-Uralsk. Attempted protests that had taken place earlier, in the summer of 1929 and in February, 1930, as also the one in December, 1933, which I still have to describe, were suppressed by force.

It might be useful to give the reader a general idea of the political repression that prevailed in the U.S.S.R. : the arrests of Communists represent only one stage in the history of that repression. The Communists, after all, were the victims of a system which they themselves had installed. The revolution had begun by destroying its enemies, the bourgeoisie and the great landowners ; then it had attacked its socialist and anarchist allies ; finally, it struck down its own children, the Communists.

*　　*　　*

I had been much surprised to learn that conditions at the penitentiary of Verkhne-Uralsk had been constantly worsening for a number of years. The socialists who had been imprisoned there for a first term in 1925 told me that at one time the cells had been open all day, so that prisoners could call on one another, go for walks in the courtyard when they pleased, and hold meetings there. The prisoners themselves controlled the use of their time, visiting hours and hours of silence. The prisoners had been cut off from the world, but had retained a certain liberty. It was on the whole, the same system as applied by Napoleon III at Belle-Ile, a system known to Blangin before his famous escape.

Then the G.P.U. had introduced the ' new system ' and had shut the doors of the cells. The socialist and anarchist prisoners had immediately gone on hunger-strike, but this was suppressed by violence. Stalin had showed himself less liberal than Napoleon III. But it was not due only to Stalin. Little by little, I learned that in the days of Lenin and Trotsky, the repression of socialists and anarchists had grown in severity in the same ratio as the country became pacified, and that, during the worst dangers of Civil War, the system had been much more kindly. It was from 1921 onwards, when the Civil War had come to an end and the NEP was launched, that the revolution, finally triumphant, had instituted the system of unlimited persecution. What is the logic of this inverted logic ?

The terms ' political repression ', ' political ' prisoners or exiles are, in the U.S.S.R., applied only to socialists, anarchists and Opposition Communists. They alone are entitled to the special treatment of political prisoners. But they are but an infinitesimal minority, a few thousands, a few tens of thousands at most, compared with the millions of prisoners and exiles all condemned for some political reason, though the authorities do not consider it as such. These millions are treated like criminals in civil law and are sent to do forced labour. If there is any attenuation of these rigours, it is applied only to intellectuals whose mission it is to direct the servile manual labour.

These prisoners can be divided into six fundamental categories : former aristocrats, people condemned for sabotage, peasants, ' religious ' people, members of national Oppositions whether they be democrats or Communists, and finally, manual labourers.

The first category comprises the members of ancient families belonging to the aristocracy, the bourgeoisie, the merchant class, ex-officers, ex-police inspectors, etc. During the Five Year Plan, a hundred thousand, or two hundred thousand, perhaps even more, were imprisoned. In any case, the figure I mention is the minimum.

The few tens of thousands of people condemned for sabotage were non-Party intellectuals.

The integral collectivization and ' dekulakization ' had resulted on the one hand in three hundred thousand *kolkhosi*, on the other in several million exiled peasant families. In our prison it was estimated that the number of exiled peasants was to be found somewhere between five and ten million. The real kulaks hardly constituted one-fifth of that number, the remainder being 'kulaking' peasants, that is, in actual fact middle or poor peasants who had shown their dissatisfaction in some way or other. This mass of people was greatly enlarged on the occasion of the 'clean-up' of the borders of the U.S.S.R. Right along the Western border, a zone of thirty-five miles in depth was almost emptied of its inhabitants ; along the Manchurian and Korean borders, the populations of entire regions were deported towards the Siberian hinterland.

During the Five Year Plan there were no mass movements of industrial labourers. When spontaneous demonstrations occurred in factories, the G.P.U. would seize the more active individuals and send them to forced-labour camps or to concentration camps, accusing them of 'economic counter-revolution', or of being 'bandits' or kulaks. Thus after the hunger-march organized by several of the textile factories in the district round Ivanovo-Voznesensk, Vytchug and elsewhere, the authorities limited themselves to exiling two workers, one of whom was the secretary of the Cell of the Comsomol and the other a non-Party member, and to transporting some twenty others to a concentration camp. As a precaution, the claims of the workers were met. *Izvestia* published a series of articles 'unmasking' the calumnies of the English newspaper that had dared speak of a hunger-march at Ivanovo-Voznesensk. Two months later we were to welcome comrades in our prison who had returned from exile and who with their own eyes had seen the poor wretches, condemned for their participation in that same march. The number of workers similarly exiled for 'individual crimes' may be estimated at several tens of thousands.

A foreigner can hardly understand the attitude of the victims themselves. In no way did they put themselves up as champions of a political cause, less even as adversaries of the system. On the contrary, they thought only of being taken back again into society, such as it was, of finding work, of earning money, and of deserving their liberation. This tendency led to the following paradox : the workmen and the peasants remained on the lower rungs, whereas the members of the so-called 'abolished' or 'hostile' classes received favourable treatment, enjoyed privileges and mixed with the representatives of authority.

Let me give two examples. In the concentration camp of

Ukht-Petchersk, those condemned on account of sabotage—engineers, doctors, economists and agricultural experts—lived in comfortable villas, side by side with the Communist authorities, and enjoyed a sufficient diet, though unvaried. The workers, miners and bricklayers, former peasants and prisoners in civil law, lived like cattle in huts with earth floors and did not receive enough to eat. They were overburdened with work and died off like flies from scurvy and other ailments.

Here is another example. In accordance with the ' last word in American technique ' a splendid car-road was being constructed across the terrible *taiga* or virgin forest, from the Bay of Nogaiev on the Pacific Ocean to the River Kolyma that runs into the Arctic Ocean. At the same time, the flow of the river was controlled and was being made navigable to ensure the connection between the two oceans. Engineers condemned on account of sabotage, supervised by the G.P.U., directed the work, which was carried out by deported peasants and by a number of free labourers. The engineers received high salaries ; thus in 1935, the chief engineer was paid three thousand roubles per month. The condemned engineers lived with the G.P.U. chiefs and Party leaders and formed with them an *élite* in the middle of this Arctic desert. This *élite* did not mix with the ' middle ' layers consisting of small officials and other convicts ; as to the humble workers of peasant stock, whether free or prisoner, they had no contact with their superiors.

After Kirov's murder, a group of former aristocrats was sent into exile to join this miniature world, and among them a few former princesses of the highest rank. They were all immediately received into the *élite* ; posts were found for them, as secretaries and typists ; they were invited to soirées and pleasure parties. Soon the famous singer, Utesov, arrived from Leningrad, condemned for reasons of an entirely private nature ; he soon organized a theatre with the assistance of the former aristocrats. This theatre absorbed the money laid aside for the ' cultural needs ' of the colony. Who were entitled to culture if not the authorities ? After five or six months most of the former aristocratic ladies had —for the third or even fifth time, maybe—been married to *saboteurs* or to G.P.U. or Party officials. One more year would entitle them to their liberty. After my liberation from Verkhne-Uralsk, I had occasion to meet one of those ladies.

She described to me, not without pleasure, the agreeable life led by the good company in that forgotten corner of the extreme North. But when I questioned her about the life of the peasants who worked there, she could tell me nothing, for she had never had to mix with them.

I did learn what interested me from the mouths of workers who had laboured from 1932 to 1934 upon the river Kolyma. One of them had been employed, with six hundred other exiled peasants, upon constructing a bridge across the middle reaches of the river. After two winters, only twenty peasants remained alive ; the others had died of cold, hunger and scurvy. There was nothing unusual in that ; in another sector, in the interior, nearly all the exiles had died, one winter, as the G.P.U. had been unable to provide the necessary food. That is what one refers to when saying, " The Five Year Plan is carried out under great difficulties." As to the free workers who had enrolled for the work of their own free will, they were systematically robbed of their wages, and their complaints remained without effect. It was because the administration was making profits out of the labour of these men !

As for the former aristocrats : it is plain that if, even in captivity, they found it possible to link up with the *élite* of Communist leaders and technicians, those in freedom must have had all the more opportunity of doing so. After what I have seen in the U.S.S.R., I can affirm that if one-third of the ruling class of ancient Russia has perished or has emigrated, two-thirds of it have amalgamated with the new dominating class born from the revolution.

But to return to our subject. The two other categories of prisoners to whom the appellation of ' political ' is denied are the ' religious ' people and the Nationalistic Oppositions. The ' religious ' people comprised priests, active members of religious communities and sectarians of every kind. There were a hundred thousand of them imprisoned during the Five Year Plan, for they were often deported on pretexts that had nothing to do with religion.

One must not forget that today there exist three organized social forces in Russia. (1) The Communist bureaucracy that governs the State, the military machine and the so-called workers' organizations. (2) The ITR or technical personnel, that is, autonomous syndical sections in which are found non-Party intellectuals. (3) The Church and the sects. As to the workers and the peasants, they have no free and autonomous organizations. After this, the importance of the Church in the social struggle will be readily understood. I have already mentioned the efforts made by Stalin to ensure the secret collaboration of the orthodox Church. The 'engineers', in the days when they reckoned on the fall of the Stalinist system, did exactly the same. One of the leaders of the orthodox Church, who belonged to the new generation and had served in the ranks of the Red Army in 1919, and had almost, so he said, become a member of the Communist Party, told me, when in exile, that an intimate friend of Professor Kondratiev had tried to approach him to feel the ecclesiastic ground. " He failed, for we are by no means inclined to put the Church at the disposal of a possible return of the bourgeoisie."

The same churchman told me an interesting episode of struggle the Church had had to wage in Moscow. During the Five Year Plan, the Church, to answer the suddenly increased amount of persecution, mobilized all its faithful for prayers that were made to last all day and brought together an imposing number of believers. The authorities understood the intention of this peaceful demonstration and lessened the scope of their persecutions. As soon as this happened, the Church discontinued the large prayer-meetings and returned to its usual less ostentatious services.

The Five Year Plan was a national catastrophe for a number of backward peoples in the U.S.S.R., the Bashkirs, the Kirghiz, etc., and it led the peasant races to the brink of disaster, the Ukrainians, the White Russians, the Turks of Azerbaijan. The most famous of all protests against this catastrophe was the suicide of Skrypnik, the leader of the Ukrainian Communists, an old Bolshevik and one of the founders of the Comintern. But there were also collective protests. Entire groups of democrats, socialists and Communists belonging to these nationalities dared openly question the official policy of the All-Russian Party. All these groups were crushed and deported, certain of their members shot. Those who had been convicted demanded that they receive the treatment of political prisoners, but the G.P.U. refused to grant them their request, not even giving way to their hunger-strikes that often ended fatally.

Declared counter-revolutionaries and monarchists—very few, on the whole—did not enjoy the privileges accorded to political prisoners. Those among them who had shown themselves at all active were mercilessly executed, and their ' sympathizers ' were shot on all sorts of pretexts. From 1928 to 1934, at a low estimate, a million men at least were sent to concentration camps and into exile, accused of speculation, unlawful commerce, etc. They were mainly artisans, small traders, members of the petit-bourgeoisie, in short. But among them were also manual labourers, peasants, office-workers, particularly office-workers from co-operatives and State commercial enterprises.

In our prison at Verkhne-Uralsk, we repeatedly tried to calculate the number of people arbitrarily dealt with by the G.P.U. Our estimates could only be very approximate. Towards the end of 1932, a recently arrived Trotskyist told us that, according to a statement made by an important G.P.U. official, condemned for reasons of professional errors, the number of arrests made in the course of the last five years amounted to 37,000,000 people. Even allowing for the majority to have been arrested a number of times running, the figure struck us as a hopeless exaggeration. Our own estimates varied from five to fifteen million. I must add that, when I was set free and was in Siberia, I was able to check the correctness of many an assertion that had seemed a fantastic exaggeration to me when I was still in prison. Thus I was able to verify the accuracy of the reports concerning the horrors of the 1932 famine, inclusive of the tales of cannibalism. After what I was able to see in Siberia, I consider that the figure of five million arrests is far too low and that ten million would be much nearer to the truth.

Westerners, used to relatively small and densely populated territories, with stable economic structures, will find it hard to admit that so large a mass of humanity could have been so rapidly deported. Russia's immense spaces do not seem a sufficient answer. It is by observing, with one's own eyes, the tumultuous ocean that was Russia during the Five Year Plan that one arrives at the belief that these migrations were not only possible, but even in harmony with the actual events. The gigantic achievements of the Five Year Plan were the outcome of servile labour. The situation of the theoretically free workers did not differ essentially from that of those workers who were not. The only difference was in the degree of enslavement.

Throughout the country millions of exiles were at work, but above all in the distant Northern regions, colonized for the first time ; there the hardest privations were borne such as would never have been freely accepted. Not only were the people exploited, but they were exploited in the most absolute fashion, regardless of the ' human capital ' they represented. From 1929 to 1934, the average lifetime of the Northern exiles did not exceed one or two years. But if the exiles died, the work of their hands remained.

Imagine a territory of six or seven thousand miles long by three hundred to fifteen hundred miles wide, from Solovetsk and the White Sea Canal to the shores of the Pacific Ocean, to the Kamchatka peninsula and Vladivostok. This territory, as well as the whole of Central Asia, was strewn at all crossroads with concentration camps and ' labour colonies ' (the latter being the name given to camps with a specific task to fulfil) and centres for compulsory exile. Of every two or three men one met in Siberia, at the office, in factories or in *sovkosi* (State farms), one would be an exile.

The colonization of the North is undeniably a task of world importance, but the way in which it has been effected calls to mind the former methods of colonization in America and elsewhere ; it is mainly the labour of slave workers. The forest industry of Northern Russia and Siberia employs servile manual labour, and the gold-mines employ it to a large extent. Similarly the coal-mines of Kuznetsk and Karaganda. The Balmach copper industry and the electric-power stations of Central Asia are the work of prisoners in the ' labour colonies '. Even in the Ukraine the factory for agricultural tractors has been built partly by forced labour. In the heart of European Russia, the cutting of the Moscow-Volga canal is done with powerful assistance from hordes of slaves. As to the enormous military and economic development of the Far East, with its railways, motor-roads and lines of fortifications along the Manchurian border, it is the work of an immense and constantly renewed army of convicts. I think it is no exaggeration to state that a third of the working class in Russia is composed of slaves. This servile labour, barely remunerated as it is, makes easier the task of keeping the wages of the theoretically free at a very low level.

There lies the true foundation of the Soviet economic victories, there the secret of the ' miracle ' of the technical revolution brought about by the first Five Year Plan. It is the duty of the working classes of Europe and America to obtain the emancipation of these millions of enslaved workers in the U.S.S.R.

* * *

The decisive date in the history of political repression in the U.S.S.R., as I have already said, is that of the introduction of the NEP in 1921. From that date onwards no further opposition was tolerated on principle, and the treatment of prisoners grew worse and worse. Before that date the intensity of repression had constantly varied, and the existence of certain Parties had been tolerated. Socialists and anarchists participated in Soviet Congresses and succeeded in publishing some of their books and periodicals. The dates when this toleration of socialists and anarchists was most marked are interesting to note : November, 1918, when the revolution in Germany seemed to forecast a very near European revolution ; October, 1919, when General Denikin camped under the walls of Orel ; summer, 1920, during the Polish-Soviet war. When Denikin was nearing Moscow, the Bolshevik Government gave socialists and anarchists the fullest freedom, linked up with Makhno's irregulars and allowed the drafting of Mensheviks into the Red Army.

But, as early as April, 1921, the promise made in view of the Soviet elections in Moscow of liberating the social-democrat prisoners detained at Butyrki was violated ; after being inhumanly beaten, they were transferred to provincial prisons. At that time occurred the first cases of outrages against political women prisoners. A year later began the first beatings of socialists in the prison of Yaroslavl. That year, 1922, saw the formation of the first concentration camp at Kholmogory on the White Sea, where a group of anarchists was sent.

At the beginning of 1923 this camp was transferred to Pertominsk, and various groups of socialists were held there. The system of this camp was so humiliating that, on the 22nd of May, the anarchists tried to commit mass-suicide by way of protest. After having drenched themselves with petrol, they were about to set fire to themselves when, just in time, the socialists prevented them from doing so. After that, 150 prisoners went on a hunger-strike that lasted seventeen days. The G.P.U. promised to set them free, transfer them to the Solovetsk islands and there create a kind of nordic paradise for political prisoners. In July it kept its word, but the paradise turned out to be a Guiana. The G.P.U. attempted to rob them of their last liberty, that of walking about inside the camp. The prisoners having protested, the director of the camp, on December 19th, 1923, sent some armed guards along who shot at them as they were peacefully walking outside their barracks. Seven prisoners—among whom were two or three women—were killed on the spot, others were wounded. A Commission of Enquiry sent down from Moscow reached no conclusion. Not before the autumn of 1924 was the Solovetsk concentration camp provisionally abolished, as a result of a new hunger-strike and, above all, of an intensive campaign of protest led by the Second International in Western Europe. As to the prisoners, they were transferred to prison or to exile on the mainland.

After the Solovetsk drama, five political isolators were devised, namely, at Suzdal, Yaroslavl, Tobolsk, Chelyabinsk and Verkhne-Uralsk.

That of Suzdal is the ancient and famous former convent of that name near Moscow. There the Menshevik trials were rehearsed before their final staging in Moscow. During the Five Year Plan some thirty or forty Trotskyists were kept there, among whom were Lado Dumbadze, former Chairman of the Tiflis Soviet ; Karpov, former director of the Caucasian Cheka ; Volkov, Trotsky's son-in-law ; this not counting the leader of the Decists : V.-M. Smirnov. That same Smirnov had, in October, 1917, at the head of an artillery detachment, dislodged from the Kremlin the officer-cadets who had entrenched themselves there. He had been the chief of the 1919 ' military opposition ' against Trotsky's bureaucratization of the Red Army. In 1935 Smirnov, having served his sentence, was allowed to spend two months at liberty, that is, in exile, at Ulala, near the Chinese frontier ; then he was arrested once more and sent back to the political isolator of Suzdal.

After the assassination of Kirov, the doors of this prison were closed on three notable foreign Zinovievists : the

Hungarian, A. Madyar, collaborator of the *International Communist Review*, the Pole, Domsky, one of the leaders of the Communist Party in Poland and the Yugo-Slav, Voya Vuyovitch, former secretary of the Communist International of Youth.

The isolator at Yaroslavl occupies an ancient fortress that had already been turned into a prison before the revolution. It was the worst of all penitentiaries. Three categories of prisoners were kept there : the ' religious ' people, political prisoners and prisoners kept in solitary confinement.

The religious people were the more numerous category. This prison was practically set aside for them. Orthodox bishops, leaders of sects, Catholic priests from the Western provinces of the U.S.S.R., were kept there. Professor Abrikosov's sister, a theosophist, was there for ten years. She was released only when dying. There were about a hundred political prisoners at Yaroslavl : Zionists, revolutionary-socialists, social-democrats, Opposition Communists and anarchists. During the Five Year Plan, three members of the Politbureau of the Hungarian Communist Party were also brought there ; although they were adherents of the general Line in the U.S.S.R. and the Comintern, they were opponents of Bela Kun within their own Party.

Part of the prison at Yaroslavl was strictly isolated and set apart for people who were put in solitary confinement. They were the people whom the G.P.U. wished to bury alive. They were allowed to communicate neither with one another nor with the outside world. Information about some of these unfortunate victims, however, filtered through. The name of Volkenstein, the revolutionary socialist, was mentioned, a woman who had been a scientific collaborator at the Military Academy and was said to have been five years in prison and there to have partly lost the faculty of speech. Another victim was supposed to have been heard to shout, " Tell them at the Persian Embassy in Moscow that I am Professor Mirza and that I am wrongfully accused of espionage."

Another particularly tragic case was that of the French radical socialist, Mallet. Here is his history. He had been attached to the French Embassy in Sofia. During the Terror that followed upon Tzankov's *coup d'état* in 1923, the September revolt of 1924 and the explosion in the Cathedral of Sofia in 1925, the French Ambassador did his best, as is known, to mitigate the hardships of the victims of the Terror, which was directed against the Peasant Party and against the Communists. Upon his return to France, Mallet, who had been greatly interested in these efforts, made contact with the MOPR (International Association for Assistance to Revolutionaries in other countries). He gave lectures on the Terror in Bulgaria and appeared at meetings of the MOPR. This organization sent him to Russia, where he made a lecture-tour. He was so full of confidence that he even let his mother come to Russia with him.

Suddenly it was demanded of him that he should testify that the explosion at the Sofia Cathedral was the work of the French authorities. With great indignation, Mallet refused to do this. The G.P.U. arrested his mother and told him that the fate of both himself and her depended on his words. Mallet refused all the more firmly. He was condemned to ten years at Solovetsk. All information about his mother was denied him, but Mallet did not give in ; he began a hunger-strike and demanded his freedom. Then— feeble and ill as he was—he was put in solitary confinement at Yaroslavl. Owing to his great tenacity and a fortuitous chance, he was able, some time in 1931 or 1932, to inform some other prisoners of his fate.

To understand the Mallet case, one must know that in those days the Soviet Government accused its victims (in particular those belonging to the ' industrial section ') of preparing armed intervention from abroad with the help of the French General Staff. Without Mallet's courage and honesty, which incidentally probably cost him his life, the world would have learned that the explosion in the Sofia Cathedral had been the work of the French police and General Staff.

The isolator at Tobolsk was no other than the famous convict prison of Czarist days. Dostoievsky was imprisoned there and described it in his *House of the Dead*.

In this isolator and in the one at Chelyabinsk, the Trotsky-ist prisoners predominated between 1928 and 1929. The ' capitulation ' crisis freed about half of them ; the others, who decided against ' capitulating ', were transferred to the prison of Verkhne-Uralsk.

This crisis not only broke up the Trotskyist Party along a line of political demarcation, but also along an age-line. The old generation ' capitulated ', exhausted as it was by the struggle, and more attached to the past than to the future. Budo Mdivani, former commercial representative of the Soviets in Paris—recently shot for treasonable activities—very well expressed the thoughts of the ' ancients ' : " I belong to the Opposition, that is clear. But if there is going to be a final break with the Communist Party, I prefer to return to the Party I helped create. I no longer have the strength to begin creating a new Party." And this was true : the 1900 generation of Russian revolutionaries had been through two revolutions, had been subjected to the blows of three reactions, had seen the shipwreck of two Internationals, and was worn to threads.

The members of the Communist Opposition who were transferred to Verkhne-Uralsk in 1929 were immediately in difficulties with the authorities. The G.P.U., in order to convince them of the fact that they were nothing but common counter-revolutionaries, answered their complaints with blows and hose-pipe drenchings, after which they were tied up and left lying for three days on an icy concrete floor, without food and unable even to go to the lavatories. In February, 1930, that is, in the middle of winter, this treatment was repeated ; a number of them fell ill, one of them—André Grayev—lost his eyesight.

Inspectors and gaolers were at that time recruited from among the local Cossack population ; they took an obvious delight in ill-treating this first batch of Communists that fell into their hands, especially as there were many Jews among them. Those Cossack inspectors really enjoyed themselves and shouted ' Dirty Jews ' at the prisoners they were beating. The prisoners returned insult for insult and finally asked the Cossacks, " You dirty bandits, wouldn't you beat even Stalin himself if he were brought to you here ? " To which the Cossacks unanimously answered, " Certainly, if those were our instructions." This gave the Communist prisoners a chance to send a regular protest to the Central Party Committee and to the high officials of the G.P.U. A short time later the Cossacks were removed and replaced by well-dressed men from the Cheka, sent from Moscow and mostly of working class origin.

The G.P.U. liked to boast of the working class origin of its henchmen. One day, in the Tobolsk prison, an Enquiry Commission answered the prisoners who complained of being ill-treated, " Our inspectors are not torturers, they are the sons of workmen and peasants." But a revolutionary-socialist, ex-Czarist convict, retorted not without humour, " You are wrong if you believe that in the days of the Czar the gaolers were recruited from among dukes and the executioners from among the princes ! "

The G.P.U. also liked, occasionally, to pretend that its dealings with the Opposition were in the nature of a Communist ' family row '. When socialists and anarchists protested to the prison director, Biziukov, about the bad treatment inflicted on the Opposition Communists, the director answered, " You do wrong to interfere with the domestic concerns of the Party ; it's none of your business."

More incredible still is the fact that Communist prisoners could be found who grumbled at the ' lack of tact ' shown by those socialists and anarchists and who called their protest ' inopportune '. A man of V. M. Smirnov's eminence, who considered that if the worst came to the worst one might have to link up with the anarchists, rebelled against the thought of linking up with Mensheviks to defend the prisoners' rights.

During the summer of 1930 the ebb of ' capitulation ' carried off some twenty or thirty prisoners from Verkhne-Uralsk. These men, a few months before, beaten and humiliated by order of Biziukov, left the prison shouting, " Long live Biziukov ! Long live the dictatorship of the proletariat ! "

As to myself, with my European ideas of a natural linking up of all Left-wingers in a common fight against the police, I first thought I had come to a madhouse. But common sense gained the upper hand. A year later, during our hunger-strike, no one showed either astonishment or indignation at the solidarity with socialists and anarchists in protesting to the administration. On the other hand, when two anarchists who had taken part in the strike were put in our ward, there was at first a considerable commotion. But the ice was broken. In the beginning of 1933, socialists, anarchists and Communists managed to act in concert when declaring a hunger-strike of twenty-four hours to protest against an abuse in the administration.

* * *

Although the prison inspectors from Moscow had been selected with the greatest care, the G.P.U. watched them by means of a twofold spying system. One of their branches, the ' political control ', was run by the prison director, the other was run direct by Moscow and kept an eye on the entire system, inclusive of the director ; the latter was ignorant even of the names of the people belonging to this secret service. They were *agents provocateurs*, recruited from among the prisoners and whose task it was to watch not only their fellow prisoners, but also their gaolers. But in spite of this wealth of precautions, it occasionally happened that inspectors, grown familiar with the prisoners, would render them a few services. In order to communicate with the outside world, we avoided as much as possible, however, having any dealings with the inspectors. I betray no secret by telling of one method by which we communicated with the outside world, for it was discovered by the G.P.U.

The prison charring was performed by prisoners in civil law. One of these convicts took it upon himself to transmit the correspondence given him by the social-democrats to their agent in Verkhne-Uralsk. The convict, being one of a band who had to cut down trees in the forest, used to bury the letters at a prearranged spot. All the agent had later to do was to come and collect them.

The prisoner's eternal dream—escape—haunted us too. But it must be believed that it was absolutely impossible to flee from Verkhne-Uralsk. I know of only one serious attempt at escape. One day painters had been called in to see to a prison wall. One prisoner, after having hidden himself during the walk, stole a painter's smock, seized some brushes and a paint-pot, and, thus disguised, walked towards the exit. The first sentry he met took no notice of him, but the second one challenged him : " Your pass ! " The prisoner did not lose his head. " My pass ? Here it is ! " And he began to search his pockets. " I must have left it behind."—" I am sorry, comrade, but my orders are very strict. Go back and look for it." All the prisoner could do was to return to his ward, where a dozen of his fellows were anxiously wondering what would happen when the inspector discovered his escape.

Contacts between the authorities and the prisoners were courteous as to form. But in every gesture, in every word, one felt a hidden animosity ready to flare up. It did indeed flare up from time to time : hunger-strikes, obstructions, blows and persecution, dousings, madness or suicides, or shooting at prisoners. After each outbreak, everything relapsed into silence for a few months.

The revolutionary-socialists decided, in 1928 and 1929, to have their revenge on an assistant prison director named Matveyev, who had caused socialist women prisoners to be cruelly beaten. This Matveyev made the acquaintance of two little sempstresses and liked them very much. He began to seek their company, but one day was met with revolver-shots. Severely wounded in the head, Matveyev managed to escape this well-deserved ambush.

In 1932 the Opposition Communists who had served their sentence were rewarded with a supplementary two years in prison. Nobody could tell when this game would come to an end, for Soviet legislation allows the G.P.U. to renew its sentences of prison and exile at its own discretion, without any justification. It is difficult to believe that such a state of affairs is possible. Yet it does exist, and the system of repression that has been in existence for sixteen years in Russia is based on it. The prisoners, weary as they were, did not immediately have recourse to a hunger-strike. But in May, 1933, it became obvious that no one was to escape a renewal of his sentence ; the prisoners therefore decided to warn the G.P.U. that they would call a hunger-strike if those prisoners who had served their sentences were not liberated.

By way of answer the G.P.U. transferred nearly half the prisoners from Verkhne-Uralsk to the isolators of Suzdal and Yaroslavl. This transfer took place in an attempt to break their resistance, but, before being separated, the prisoners agreed to begin the strike at a given date, wherever they might be. This plan was carried out, and the strike broke out simultaneously in three prisons. On the thirteenth day it was broken by violence : the strikers were forcibly fed and some thirty were transferred to other isolators or concentration camps.

The Strike Committee, consisting of Dingelstedt, Kraskin, Slitinsky and other comrades, was transferred to Solovetsk. There they found several hundred political prisoners : Georgian social-democrats, Moslems from Azerbaijan, Uzbek and Kirghiz Communists, who had defended their peasant compatriots during the Five Year Plan, revolutionary-socialists, Zionists, anarchists and Trotskyists. All these people had been scattered in small groups among the prisoners in civil law and were not given the special diet to which political prisoners were entitled. Central Asiatic Communists, guilty of national Opposition, were treated particularly badly. The newly arrived Communists from Verkhne-Uralsk soon took the initiative in the struggle to unite all political prisoners and to obtain the diet to which they were entitled. A few favourable results were finally won.

Another group was transferred from Verkhne-Uralsk to the concentration camp at Ukht-Petchersk. This camp covered an enormous area in the North-East of Russia, half as large as France. The population was very sparse, not more than 150,000 souls, mainly convicts. Great public works had been carried out there. Coal had been found, gold and petrol ; mines were dug, roads cut and forests levelled. The concentration camp of Ukht-Petchersk had car and river-boat services that belonged to it. It was a state within a state. The slave population was perfectly aware of this : the convicts of the region, as well as the free inhabitants of the neighbouring area of the Zyrians, gave the ' commander ' of the concentration camp the nickname of ' King of the North '. The Ukht-Petchersk camp had even newspapers of its own, as well as a central organ run by a well-known Ukrainian journalist.

The organization of the work there was very intensive. Every group was working under a ' brigader '. These brigaders were former bandit chiefs and they ran these groups exactly as they used to run their bands. The G.P.U. was interested in one thing only : for the work to be done. It left it entirely to the brigaders to organize the ' discipline of labour '. The famous re-education of the prisoners was sheer hypocrisy, from beginning to end. From time to time scandalous incidents revealed of what this re-education really consisted. Here is one that ended badly for the hero ! One of the chiefs of the camp noticed a deported young peasant woman and her family, and called her to his place under pretext of making her do the housework. As soon as he was alone with her, he tried to seduce her without losing any time. The young girl, terribly frightened, made such a noise that people came running to the house. It cost the chief three years in a concentration camp.

Attempts at escape were frequent but rarely successful.

The region was desolate and wild, and the nearest groups of free people were too distant. Usually those who escaped were driven back to the camp by hunger.

This slave population lived in complete isolation. The people knew that free life was hard, that famine and repression prevailed, that the ruling class was split by a thousand intrigues and that the men of the Kremlin often ended in concentration camps. But they ignored the true sense of these facts; they still had hopes and believed the wildest fables with the greatest credulity.

Here is an example. One of our comrades who was transferred to the camp of Ukht-Petchersk was met, at his first stop, by a crowd of convicts who told him the great news, "Three members of the Government, Yenukidze, Ordjonikidze and Bielov, the commander of the military region of Leningrad, have just arrived at the camp; they are being taken under escort to the centre." Our friend was taken aback. What was happening in Moscow? Were Stalin's most intimate friends being condemned? On the following day, at the next stop, he overtook a comrade from Verkhne-Uralsk, called Shemes, who had set out before him. "Do you know anything," he asked him, "about the arrival of Yenukidze, Ordjonikidze and Bielov, members of the Government?" The other began to laugh. "Yenukidze is our friend, the Trotskyist; Bielov is also one of us—he is the economist from Kharkov and not the soldier from Leningrad—but Ordjonikidze? He appears to be me!"

The story was simple. The population of the camp, having seen three comrades arrive, escorted by a dozen armed guards, which was unusual, and hearing the names Yenukidze and Bielov, had immediately embroidered a whole story round them and had believed that a palace revolution had taken place in Moscow.

* * *

From 1933 onwards, that is, from the beginning of the second Five Year Plan, more and more political prisoners and especially Opposition Communists were being sent to concentration camps in Russia, Siberia and Central Asia. The more Stalin went in for 'socialism', the more prisons there were in Russia and the more political prisoners were made to suffer.

VIII

AND NOW?

Whilst we were in prison spending our time discussing our views and struggling against the G.P.U., events in the country had followed upon one another with fast and furious speed. The Five Year Plan reached its highest points in 1931 and 1932.

Where was Russia going? Was she going to explode like a boiler, or was she going to win through the experiment and flourish under a new order? What were we to do? Were we to fight or to defend the existing régime? In the name of what? With what programme? The whole country and not only the Trotskyist Opposition was asking itself these questions.

In our prison the Trotskyists envisaged the question differently, since their scission. The 'majority', that is, the Right-wing and Centre, were interested only in the political aspects of the Five Year Plan. The Red professors proved, in innumerable articles, that such and such an industry should have been created in preference to some other, or that it would have been better to have begun with such and such a factory than with this other. They gave deep analyses of Year Plans and disputed certain percentages. All these reflections were devoid neither of earnestness nor of competence, nor of dialectic ability, yet they were pedantic and sterile. The country was at war : a social and economic war. What was the use of all these time-tables, in which everything was worked out for every minute? Was it not clear that a poor and backward Russia could not possibly carry out its revolution, unless it first of all by a superhuman effort built itself some essential bulwarks, ready to work out later the co-ordination of its economy from its advance positions? That was why the lamentations of these professors of economic science on the frightful disproportions of the Five Year Plan left me unmoved.

During the summer of 1932, when starvation descended

on the land, and the rhythm of industrialization had visibly transgressed the limit of possibilities, the theoreticians of the Opposition felt a new mission in their minds : elaboration of the plan of the retreat. They argued, " Since, in the past, the Party, in the person of Stalin, has borrowed the Opposition plan of industrialization, the Party will be equally dependent on the Opposition now that a retreat has to be planned." To believe them, the Stalinist policy was by no means determined by the social realities of the system nor by the necessities of its own development, but merely by Stalin's ' stupid short-sightedness '.

The elaboration of the plan of retreat caused a further split in the Trotskyist majority. The Right-wing, led by Solntsev, Jakovin, Melnais, etc., thought that the retreat should be slow and careful : methods of coercion against the peasants should be toned down, not abolished, otherwise the *kolkhosi* would be in danger of disintegrating, calling the old mercantile system of exchange back to life. On the other hand, it wished to collaborate with the Stalinists for tactical reasons. Their coalition was to prevent the petit-bourgeois elements from preparing their Thermidor with the friendly neutrality of the All-Russian Communist Party Right-wing—the Bukharin clique.

The Trotskyist Centre (Dingelstedt, Man-Nivelson, Aron Papermeister, etc.) supported, on the other hand, Rakovsky's slogan ' Return to the NEP ', a slogan on which he had expatiated in his letters from exile. Their specialist on agrarian affairs, Sassorov, the agronomist, went so far as to admit that the dissolution of all *kolkhosi* was necessary. In short, the Trotskyist Centre thought it expedient to perform a return at least as profound as Stalin's. As for the tactics of this retreat, it thought of forming a coalition with the Right-wing of the All-Russian Party. This coalition would force Stalin to form a Central Coalition Committee, that is, a Central Committee on which all Communist sections would be represented, and to establish democracy inside the Party. But it did not think of completely eliminating the Stalinist group, for it feared that such an action might well shatter ' proletarian authority ' and facilitate a return of the bourgeoisie.

As a matter of fact, the Trotskyist majority had no great programme to oppose to Stalin's official policy. But there was this, too : there was no attempt seriously to criticize the social character of the Five Year Plan or the Stalinist rule as a whole. If Stalin's workers' policy was criticized, it was on the score of the magnitude of the sacrifices it demanded, and not on that of the social principles which it violated. If Stalin's ' deformations ' and ' bureaucracy ' were attacked in details, this did not mean that no interest was shown in the percentage of socialism achieved in the U.S.S.R. on the basis of the percentage of success or failure of the Stalinist industrialization.

All these preoccupations of the Trotskyist majority left me indifferent. Their outlook was not very different from that of the Stalinist bureaucracy ; they were slightly more polite and human, that was all. All my hopes went out towards the minority, the members of which, in 1931 and 1932, were passionately discussing fundamental problems thrown up by the Five Year Plan and by Soviet rule as a whole. They did not limit themselves to judging the degree of the success of the Plan or the necessity of returning to the NEP. They clearly put themselves the questions whether there still existed a dictatorship of the proletariat in the U.S.S.R., whether the economic development was socialist by nature or whether it was a form of State capitalism or a transition stage.

The transfer of political prisoners as a result of the hunger-strike, during the summer of 1931, had considerably weakened the Trotskyist minority. The Militant Bolsheviks had lost Puchas, their ideologist, the ' State capitalists ' had lost Densov. The Trotskyist Left of our prison decided nevertheless to elaborate its own programme complete with its intransigent attitude towards the Stalinist bureaucracy. But soon it was found that the divergences inside the Left-wing were profound ; as a consequence, it was decided first to discuss certain questions, then to set forth a compromise in sufficiently general formulae to satisfy all the various conflicting opinions.

The first question to be discussed was that of the character of the Soviet State. Was it a socialist workers' State ? If not, what class did it represent ? The discussion lasted well over six months, for it was not easy to arrange the communication between the members of the minority, scattered as they were to the four corners of the prison. But we were unwilling to risk a new schism and remained patient. We also had one thought at the back of our minds that counselled us against all haste : we hoped that Trotsky would meanwhile cross the Rubicon and deny the proletarian character of the Stalinist State. Many of us were already persuaded that there was no trace of a ' dictatorship of the proletariat ' in the U.S.S.R., but thought it inopportune to proclaim this opinion in public before Trotsky had made up his mind. As to myself, although I agreed with the others in expecting Trotsky to make a decisive political gesture, a gesture made probable by his statement that ' the preparations for the establishment of Bonapartism within the Party have been concluded ', yet I thought with a few other comrades that it was better to speak up without waiting for Trotsky. Would it not be simpler for him to formulate the expected conclusion, if he already saw it spontaneously rising in the minds of the militants themselves ? Moreover, was it always necessary to wait for the ' leader ' to speak, as if we were common Stalinists ?

In the end, three distinct resolutions were put to the vote. The first one recognized, in spite of the many ' bureaucratic deviations ', the proletarian character of the State, for there remained ' vestiges of the dictatorship of the proletariat ' such as nationalization of private property and repression of the bourgeoisie. From this it followed that it was considered possible to re-establish the authentic dictatorship of the proletariat by a thorough reform of the system.

Those who denied the existence of a dictatorship of the proletariat in the U.S.S.R. could not agree among themselves, and put forward two distinct resolutions. The ones, guided by what remained of the Militant Bolshevik principles, found that there was no longer a dictatorship of the proletariat in the U.S.S.R., but that ' the economic foundations of the October revolution persisted '. They concluded that it was necessary to have a ' political revolution ' backed up by a ' thorough economic reform '. The present régime seemed to them to be above all classes, for, according to them, the bureaucracy in power was not a class, but merely a transitory social formation.

The other ' negators ', who included myself, believed that not only the political order but also the social and economic orders were foreign and hostile to the proletariat. We therefore envisaged not only a political but also a social revolution that should open up a road to the development of socialism. According to us, the bureaucracy was a real class, a class hostile to the proletariat.

Each of the three resolutions gained the same number of votes, that is, about fifteen each. In other words, the ' negators ' were in the majority. But the others threatened to secede if the point of view of the ' negators ' was proclaimed to be obligatory to all Left-wing Trotskyists. The difficulty was avoided by declaring that the question of the nature of the Soviet State should remain open.

There were lively discussions on the slogan 'Back to the NEP', which was finally rejected by an overwhelming majority.

The attitude of the prisoners as regards events in the land and as regards the Stalinist policy can be defined as follows, provided a certain schematic arrangement be allowed me : most of the political prisoners, whatever shade of opinion they professed, judged the Government's policy to be nothing but an absurd adventure violating the laws of evolution and betraying the lack of ability of the leaders. At every moment they expected a catastrophe to happen, followed by a complete change in the directing personnel, and this conviction stifled their every desire to investigate into the social meaning of events. But there were also prisoners, less numerous and more isolated, who had discovered ' a system in all this folly '. They thought their true task lay precisely in analysing and showing up the coherent elements in this apparent chaos of bureaucratic policy. They certainly did not lack subject-matter for their analysis !

During the year 1930 and part of 1931, the Government, in order to carry out its plans of industrialization and production, availed itself above all of methods of administrative coercion as regards the workers : obligatory ' emulation ' in the factories, forced exploits by the *udarniki* (shock-brigaders), abolition of the workers' right to leave the factory where he was employed, the ' right conferred on women and adolescent workers to work at night and in mines, etc. '. These measures caused a campaign abroad against the ' forced labour ', but the official phraseology caused the West to believe that the Soviet Government was in the midst of building up—be it by barbaric means—something resembling socialism.

The reforms that followed upon one another after June, 1931, revealed the true face of the régime. Stalin began by anathematizing one of the workers' dearest aspirations, one of the last conquests of October that had not yet been taken away from them : the principle of economic equality within the proletariat. By order of the dictator, a new gospel was introduced : the workers' hierarchy, the 'reform of the wage-system' in order to create 'greater differentiation in the remuneration of extreme groups'. This essentially capitalist principle was declared to be in accordance with socialism and Communism. The principle it replaced was stigmatized as petit-bourgeois levelling, against which a ruthless war was waged.

The worker was no longer to be stimulated to produce goods by collectivism, by, be it forced, solidarity, but by the old capitalist piece-work system, the contract with progressive premiums, long since abolished in the West owing to the workers' movement. Having thus doubled the administrative coercion of a new sweating system, the Soviet leaders declared that there were no limits to the intensity of the work ; the physiological limit that exists in capitalist production " is abolished with us ", they said, " in the land of socialism, owing to the enthusiasm of the workers ". The galley-slaves' rhythm, the chain-gang work of the capitalist countries, was henceforward to be exceeded.

If 'greater differentiation in the remuneration' of the workers was introduced according to their qualifications, what must I say of the abyss that was created between workers and officials, Communists and non-Communists ? The 'happy life' enjoyed by the upper layers of the population at the expense of the miserable masses did not fail to astonish the foreign tourist in the U.S.S.R. if he happened to look around him. This 'happy life' was legalized for the first time after Stalin's June speech in 1931. To add still further to the privileges of provisions and lodgings, a new network of closed 'distributors' was instituted and restaurants reserved for the use of high Communist or non-Party officials. Finally, 'State shops' were established for their exclusive use, where absolutely everything could be bought, but at prices well beyond those that the workers could afford. The relics of 'war-time Communism' which the bureaucracy liked to display at the beginning of the Five Year Plan were thrown on the dust-heap. All this was obvious class egoism, and the stories told by recent arrivals in prison confirmed the impression that this new policy corresponded to a deep and durable tendency. The people were not taken in by it, and the situation was defined by these bitter words. " There are no classes now, only categories." As a matter of fact, the entire population of Russia, from the point of view .of the standard of living, had been divided into five or six categories, that fixed the place of each individual in society. But at the period which we are considering, the label of ' dictatorship of the proletariat ' had not yet been replaced by that of the ' Soviet People '. The most favoured work-men still belonged to Category No. One ; the bureaucracy therefore modestly designated its privileged position by the anodyne appellation of Category No. Zero.

The switch-over was, however, so manifest and so brutal that the people outside prison could not be mistaken about it. A director of a Moscow factory who arrived at our prison in 1932 defined the position of the Communist personnel as follows : " During the daytime, we do propaganda work among our workmen in favour of the general Line, and we explain to them that socialism is about to triumph in our country ; but at night, among colleagues, we drink tea and wonder whether we are representatives of the proletariat or of a new exploiting class."

The tendency to consolidate the new order of things result-ing from the Five Year Plan was evident in a wish to con-ciliate the various elements composing the social *élite*. Non-Party specialists who, the day before, had still been mercilessly persecuted, were now becoming the proclaimed allies of the Communist bureaucracy. " There are striking symptoms of a changed attitude in intellectual circles," Stalin declared. " Those intellectuals who at one time were in sympathy with the *saboteurs* now support Soviet power. There are other symptoms : some of the former *saboteurs* are now beginning to collaborate with the workers." The middle stratum of intellectuals, especially the technicians, was put in the same rank as were the factory workers, and a short time later, in 1932, a solemn decree of the Central Executive Committee allowed the children of intellectuals equality of rights with the children of workers. The general barrister of the U.S.S.R., Krylenko, the main prosecutor in all the sabotage trials, thus commented on a speech by Stalin : " The factory workers have become the rightful owners of this country ; now, after a lengthy development of the relations between the Soviet Government and the leading technical personnel, the latter, too, must fully participate in the common thing on the same footing as the factory workers." In this way the foundations were laid for the future statute for ' non-Party Bolsheviks ', which was to lead up, in the 1936 constitution, to the granting of civil rights to non-Communist intellectuals. The Communist bureaucracy was preparing itself to share with the ' engineers ' the monopoly of power it held ' in the name of the working class '.

The ' new style ' of the Soviet towns, the reopening of elegant shops, restaurants and night-clubs, the generous and easy mode of life of the leaders, recalled the NEP to mind. But there was no private initiative, there were no merchants, no *nepmen*. The NEP without the *nepmen* seemed an absurdity to us in our prison, and the prisoners, imbued with out-of-date principles, predicted the certain reappearance of this indispensable personage. But there were also prisoners who attempted to understand the future other than with the help of the old oracles, and who said, " Certainly, the NEP without the *nepmen* is the symbol of modern Russia, replacing private commerce by State commerce, the merchant by the bureaucrat, the private NEP by the State NEP ! "

The letters Rakovsky sent us from exile were extremely useful in enabling us to understand this evolution. Rakovsky and Trotsky complemented one another in a sense, the first possessing a marked ability to grasp social changes though unable to draw political conclusions from them, the second suffering from exactly the opposite fault. It was a great pity for the Russian Trotskyists that these two men were unable to agree together.

From 1928 onwards, Rakovsky wrote a number of studies on the structure and function of the Soviet bureaucracy, the most important one of which *The Laws of Socialist Accumulation During the Period of ' Centre Rule ' of the Dictatorship of the Proletariat* remained unknown abroad. He brought out the parasitic and exploiting characteristics of the bureaucracy " which has transformed itself into a particular social order to the detriment of industrial labourers and peasants ". From that attitude to the conviction that the bureaucracy was nothing but a new ruling class was only one step, but Rakovsky was not bold enough to take it. At the decisive corner, he chose to " save what could still be saved " and to

" return to the NEP ". His policy, instead of drawing inspiration from the new needs of the proletariat, was dominated by the fear of a return of private capitalism. In the study we have just introduced to the reader, Rakovsky revealed one of the remarkable traits of the Soviet bureaucracy : the sacerdotal cult of two truths, the one, the esoteric truth, to quote Rakovsky, the real truth destined for the initiated only ; the other, the pseudo-truth for the needs of the crowd. He liked to compare this aspect with that of the Catholic Church as seen in the Jesuit and other religious orders. The bureaucracy " only administered " the means of production rightly belonging to the proletariat, as the Church administered the *patrimonium pauperum* for its benefit.

In our discussions in prison, industrialization did not by any means raise as many storms as ' total collectivization ' had done. If the Trotskyist Opposition had adopted a definite attitude as regards industrialization, that much could not be said as regards the peasant question. In the realm of industry, Stalin had done nothing but follow the road as indicated by the Trotskyist Opposition as early as 1923. In 1931 Trotsky was not wrong when he wrote that " all the viable elements of the official plan are but echoes of the ideas and slogans of the Left-wing Opposition ". We therefore only discussed the method by which Stalin carried out his industrialization plan.

The attitude of the Trotskyist Opposition as regards ' total collectivization ' was much more complex. It was not Trotsky—in spite of the current opinion to that effect—but Zinoviev who, towards the end of the NEP, favoured an intensified anti-peasant policy. The agrarian part of the policy of the Trotsky-Zinoviev coalition, in 1926–27, had been determined by the Zinovievists. When, in 1923, Trotsky first put forward the industrialization plan, he visualized at the same time an agrarian development on the lines of ' farming '. He very clearly expressed this thought in his famous speech of Dniepropetrovsk.

Stalin began by carrying out the programme of the Trotskyist-Zinovievist Opposition ; then, in the ardour of the anti-peasant offensive, he was led to proclaim ' total collectivization ' and ' liquidation of the kulaks as a class '. But if Zinoviev agreed to that policy, Trotsky furiously opposed it. To pass from ' the struggle against the exploiting tendencies of the kulaks ' to their complete expropriation, to push partial collectivization until it became ' total ', was in his opinion an anti-Marxist Utopia, in the light of historic conditions, and could only lead to catastrophe. In February, 1930, at the height of wholesale collectivization, Trotsky wrote that " until the end of the Five Year Plan, no more than 20 to 25 per cent at the most of peasant enterprises should be collectivized, lest the framework of reality should be overstepped ". Stalin, in his haste, had not even waited for the completion of the tractor-factories, thereby sharpening Trotsky's irony, " By putting together the poor hoes and the poor nags of the *mujiks* one no more creates large agricultural estates than one creates a large steamer by putting together a lot of fishing boats."

These opinions of Trotsky, which only penetrated the prisons about this time, made a great impression on the prisoners. Had not Stalin driven up collectivization to 50 and 60 per cent, and had he not introduced a very belated mechanized exploitation ? A number of us suspended our judgement, waiting for events to shape, others loudly demanded a return to the NEP.

The more recent writings of our leader, in which he had somewhat modified his position, had not reached us. Thus, confusion was at its height when, in the summer of 1932, we received Trotsky's latest writings. The main document, published abroad in April, 1931, was entitled *The Problems of the Development of the U.S.S.R.*, with the sub-title *Outline of a Programme for the International Left-wing Opposition as regards the Russian Question.*

Both the aim of this document and the name of its author conferred upon it a very special importance. Thus we decided to make it the subject of a discussion : was it not necessary for the Russian Opposition to pronounce on its own programme ? Yet the discussion lacked zest. Nobody appeared satisfied, yet all—except the Extreme Left—showed respect for the document, whilst showing reluctance to tackle it. Imbued with Trotsky's now obsolete views on the venturesome quality of Stalin's achievements, our Trotskyists found it hard to swallow the lavish praise conferred on them in the new document. Trotsky spoke of " the present really incredible successes " of " the unprecedented rhythm of industrialization which once and for all has proved the efficacy of the economic

methods of socialism ". As to the famous wholesale collectivization, Trotsky defined it as " a new era in the history
of mankind, the starting-point of the liquidation of village
cretinism ". He went so far as to admit that total collectivization might even be achieved " in two or three years'
time ". After this blow, those among us who in discussing
the Five Year Plan had spoken of nothing but " a mirage of
figures " and " Stalinist bluff " had nothing left but to
remain silent. All the same, Trotsky's new programme
called forth no enthusiasm. The Centre and Right-wing
Trotskyists considered that their leader exaggerated the successes of the Plan and that his attitude could be defended
abroad where the Plan had to be protected against the on-
slaughts of the bourgeoisie, but that it would not do in Russia.
As for the Left-wing, it was dissatisfied at not finding any
social and political criticism of the régime in this programme.

From the social and political point of view, Trotsky's
programme destroyed all hopes of the Left. Since 1930 it
had been waiting for its leader to speak up openly, and
declare that the present Soviet State was not a workers'
State. Now, in the very first chapter of his programme
Trotsky clearly defined it as a " proletarian State ". A
further defeat awaited the Left-wing in the treatment of the
Five Year Plan : its socialist character, the socialist character of its aims and even of its methods were vigorously
asserted in the programme. All Trotsky's polemics in the
social field had been reduced to a weak quarrel, " The
Soviet Union has not entered into the socialist phase as the
Stalinist group teaches it, but only into the first phase of an
evolution towards socialism." Further on, the Five Year
Plan, built on the extermination of the peasants and the
merciless exploitation of the workers, was interpreted as an
attempt made by the bureaucracy to adapt itself to the
proletariat. In short, the U.S.S.R. was developing " on
the basis of the dictatorship of the proletariat ".

It was henceforward an idle hope to expect Trotsky ever
to distinguish between bureaucracy and proletariat, between
State capitalism and socialism. Those among the Left
' negators ' who could not possibly see any socialism in what
was being built up in Russia, had no other course left open
to them than to break with Trotsky and leave the ' Trotskyist
Collective '. About ten—among them myself—took a de-

cision to that effect. As was customary, we gave the reasons for our resignations in a written declaration.

In substance we stated that Trotsky's positive attitude as regards the social phenomena along with his negative attitude as regards the political superstructure would logically lead to a purely political revolution. But, taking the most optimistic view of the matter, such a revolution would change the personnel of the bureaucracy and introduce a little liberalism without modifying the foundations of the system. It would be a mere repetition of 1830.

What annoyed me most in Trotsky's programme was that it might well strengthen the illusions of the Western proletariat as regards Russia instead of removing these. For, if Stalin said, " We have already carried out socialism," Trotsky merely corrected him by saying, " No, not socialism, but only its first phase. . . ."

Thus, having shared in the ideological life and in the struggles of the Russian Opposition, I ended—as so many others before me and after me—with the following conclusion : Trotsky and his supporters are too closely linked with the bureaucratic régime of the U.S.S.R. to be able to conduct the struggle against this régime to its final consequences. In his programme, Trotsky even underlined the fact that his criticism was not that of a hostile alien, and that he considered the problems of the régime ' from the inside and not from the outside '. To him, the task of the Opposition was to improve, not to destroy, the bureaucratic system, to fight against the ' exaggeration of privileges ' and the ' extreme inequalities of the standards of life '—not to fight against privileges or inequalities in general. Let these be somewhat mitigated, and everything would once more be right, under the auspices of the authentic ' dictatorship of the proletariat '. Those whom this would not satisfy were in danger of being called ' extreme Left-wing petit-bourgeois Utopists ', if not counter-revolutionaries.

Trotsky's later development was to bear out this prophecy. *The Revolution Betrayed*, published by Trotsky in 1936, remained true to the main lines laid down in the programme of 1930. Whilst criticizing certain aspects of Soviet society with wit and severity, Trotsky did not modify his general views on the U.S.S.R. as a ' workers' State '. He is still a contributing factor in the upkeep of the most mendacious and dangerous of all contemporary illusions in the minds of the international proletariat.

The inhuman methods of the bureaucratic exploitation to which the Five Year Plan owed its success were qualified by Trotsky as " socialist methods that have proved their worth ". He is silent on the exploitation of the workers, and only mentions the exploitation of the peasants to fulminate against the " learned economists in the pay of Capital " who dare mention it. It certainly is a noble task to unmask the advocates of private capitalism. But is that sufficient reason to make oneself an advocate of State capitalism ?

Trotsky is unable to see that the ' deviations ' and the ugliness against which he protests are but the logical and ineluctable outcome of the system which he vigorously defends in its entirety. Trotsky, after all, is nothing but the theorist of the régime which Stalin is carrying out in practice.

Bureaucratic or Proletarian Opposition ? was the title I gave to the article in which, in prison, I expressed my new attitude towards Trotskyism. Henceforward, I belonged to the camp of the Russian extreme Left-wing Opposition : ' democratic Centralism ', ' workers' Opposition ', ' workers' group '.

What separated the Opposition from Trotskyism was not only its way of judging the régime and of understanding the present problems ; it was, before all, the way in which the part played in the revolution by the proletariat was being considered. To the Trotskyists it was the Party, to the extreme Left-wing it was the working class which was the mover of the revolution. The struggle between Stalin and Trotsky concerned Party politics and the directing personnel of the Party ; to one as to the other the proletariat was but a passive object. The groups of extreme Left-wing Communists, on the other hand, were above all interested in the actual conditions of the working class and the part played by it, in what it actually was in Soviet society and what it should be in a society which sincerely set itself the task of building up socialism. The ideas and the political life of these groups opened up new perspectives to me and confronted me with problems unknown to the Trotskyist Opposition ; how should the proletariat set about conquering the means of production taken from the bourgeoisie, efficaciously to control both Party and Government, to establish a workers' democracy and safeguard the revolution from bureaucratic degeneracy ?

IX

LENIN, ALSO . . .

The extreme left Communist groups of the extreme left were not afraid to grapple with the whole revolutionary experience in Russia, contrary to the Trotskyist Opposition, in the eyes of which the Lenin epoch remained sacrosanct. Morevoer, all these extremists groupings came into being as early as 1919–1921 in more or less sharp opposition to Lenin's policy.

The role of Lenin in the revolution was the subject of heated discussions during the time when I was incarcerated in the Verkhne-Uralsk isolator. In its discussions with others as in its own meetings the Trotskyist Opposition defended the view that Lenin was always right. In order not to run counter to this dogma, Trotsky had long 'recognized' the correctness of Lenin's position in all the disputes that had set them at logger-heads in the past. Trotsky also approved Zinoviev's proposal to called his oppositional group, 'Bolshevik-Leninists'. Still later, Trotsky reinforced the dogma that the correct position in regard to the permanent revolution (and of all Trotskyist concepts, that is certainly the one of most value) was not his, but Lenin's. In reality, Trotsky added, Lenin was in fact a proponent of the permanent revolution, and that was why their disagreement was purely formal and of no great importance. This led the Trotskyist Opposition to develop this new theme: disagreements between Lenin and Trotsky had never been very deep; Lenin and Trotsky had always been in agreement on basic issues and disagreements bore only on points of detail. The Trotskyist Opposition reconciled Lenin's past with that of Trotsky. Refusing to adopt a critical attitude towards either, it smeared a bureaucratic veneer over the most hotly debated aspects of the two tendencies. To the myth fabricated by Stalin, it did not oppose a serious study of the facts, but another myth.

On the other hand, some Trotskyists, those of the 'V.B.'

group (*Voinstvuyshchii Bolshevik* — Militant Bolshevik), the '100% Trotskyists', went even further, declaring that if the disagreements between Lenin and Trotsky had always been very grave, it was Trotsky who had always been right. A characteristic fact — the Trotskyists, who loved quotations, nearly always referred to Trotsky, and only with rare exceptions to Lenin.

The Democratic Centralist group found itself in a very different position when Lenin was in question. Unlike the Trotskyists, the group had its origins in the Bolshevik old guard. Consequently, as much in its general conceptions as in the way its members expressed them, it was 'Leninist'. At its origins in 1919 and 1921 it represented the local apparatus. 'His Majesty's opposition', against the centre. In the name of "democratic centralism", it was opposed to the bureaucratic centralism of Lenin's Central Committee. Hence its name. Deeming that Lenin had departed from his own programme, or that he did not see where his policies were heading, the group had been set up to defend Leninism against Lenin. Without wishing to admit it to themselves, they set the Lenin of the revolution's decline against the Lenin of its rise. They criticized the policy of Lenin in power, taking their stand on the Leninist principles of *The State and Revolution*. But, profound as that 1917 work of Lenin's was, nonetheless, it did not supply all the answers to the new problems raised by the course of the revolution. Finally, the group had dithered for ten years (1919–29), now capitulating to Lenin's ultimatum, now supporting the Trotskyists in their struggle against Stalin. Its orientation, 'more royalist than the king', proved to be sterile. The Five Year Plan shook the group to its foundations. The majority, like the majority of Trotskyists, capitulated. They justified their capitulation by saying that from the moment when NEP and the bourgeoisie were liquidated socialism was being built and they were in the wrong.

If the condition of the workers is wretched, that is because one cannot make an omelette without breaking eggs; before the complete construction of socialism a final difficult stage has to be traversed—that of the liquidation of the last capitalist class, the petty bourgeoisie. That is how Timofei Sapronov, leader of the group and one of the best-known worker Bolsheviks in Russia, explained the standpoint of the 'capitulators'.

If one holds to Leninist principles on this, the attitude of the capitulators is not lacking in logic. Lenin's whole strategy after October rested on the thesis that the petty bourgeoisie and private capitalism alone menaced the proletariat and socialism. Lenin castigated with an iron hand all the oppositional forces that spoke of bureaucratism and State capitalism as a danger threatening the working class. Following the course laid down by Lenin, the *Decemists* (Democratic Centralism group), on the eve of the Five Year Plan, spoke only of the victory of the 'petty-bourgeois counter-revolution' and the transformation of the U.S.S.R. into a 'petty-bourgeois State'. The Leninist conception admitted of no other counter-revolution . . . And thereupon comes the Five Year Plan, which wages war on the petty bourgeoisie and liquidates it. One had to choose: either remain faithful to the Leninist thesis and recognize that the Five Year Plan was realizing socialism, or bow to reality and recognize what even Lenin might have said, the triumph of the 'third force'—the bureaucracy and State capitalism. Those *Decemists* who did not capitulate chose the second course . . . But this re-evaluation which in fact rejected all the post-October ideas of Lenin, and put in question even those of pre-October, was effected only slowly, step by step. And the small group of *Decemists* in our isolator split on this occasion into three or four fractions.

Some continued to think that Lenin, after October, although making some small mistakes, had a correct attitude, and that the line only began to deviate with Stalin. Others considered that already in Lenin's time, with the establishment of NEP, the bourgeois-democratic structure of the revolution had got the upper hand of the socialist structure and that Lenin himself did not realize what he was doing. The third fraction declared that in spite of all proclamations, the socialist structure of the revolution had always been weaker than the petty-bourgeois structure. The revision of Leninism consequently bore no longer only on State capitalism but also on the dictatorship of the proletariat. In the beginning, when Lenin, in 1920, upheld the thesis of the single party and the dictatorship, the *Decemists* had approved and had then broken with the Workers Opposition, who at once denounced them. Experience of the dictatorship of the party led them to reject their original views. They now began to understand that there could not be democracy within the party without workers' democracy. The reassessment of Lenin's political ideas was more rapid than of his economic ideas. During two years of exile the opportunity was given me to follow all these twists and turns. The end result of this was a critical, not to say hostile attitude towards the practice and the theories of the post-October Lenin.

In the criticism of the Lenin of the revolutionary period the tone was set by the Workers Opposition of 1920, more accurately, by its left wing, which took an organized form in 1922, under the name of the Workers Group. In the language, then current, members of the group were called 'Myasnikovists', from the name of their lead, Myasnikov, a well-known worker Bolshevik.

He was one of the most outstanding figures of the Bolshevik revolution. The Workers Opposition and the Workers Group were, in origin, from the Bolshevik old guard. But, contrary to the *Decemists*, they criticized Lenin's course of action from the beginning, and not on details but as a whole. The Workers Opposition denounced Lenin's economic line. The Workers Group went even farther and attacked the political regime and the single party established by Lenin prior to the NEP. In the person of Serge Tiyunov, the Workers Group in our isolator possessed a highly educated, very active, uncompromising representative. Moreover, according to some reports, he was not devoid of Nechayevist* traits.

Having put as the basis of its programme Marx's watchword for the Ist International — "The emancipation of the workers must be the task of the workers themselves", the Workers Group declared war from the start on the Leninist concept of the 'dictatorship of the party' and the bureaucratic organization of production, enunciated by Lenin in the initial period of the revolution's decline. Against the Leninist line, they demanded organization of production by the masses themselves, beginning with factory collectives. Politically, the Workers Group demanded the control of power and of the party by the worker masses. These, the true political leaders of the country, must have the right to withdraw power from any political party, even from the Communist Party, if they judged that that party was not defending their interests. Contrary to

---

*The jacobin anarchist Nechayev—the disciple of Bakunin and inspirer of his "revolutionary catechism", was the typical nihilist of the Tsarist epoch. It was he who inspired Dostoyevsky's celebrated novel *The Possessed*. (Author's note.)

the *Decemists* and the majority of the Workers Opposition, for whom the demand for 'workers' democracy' was practically limited to the economic domain, and who tried to reconcile it with the 'single party', the Workers Group extended its struggle for workers' democracy to the demand of freedom for the workers to choose among the competing political parties of the worker milieu. Socialism could only be the work of free creation by the workers. While that which was being constructed by coercion, and given the name of socialism, was for them nothing but bureaucratic State capitalism from the very beginning.

In 1923, during the largest of the strikes led by the Workers Group, they appealed to the Russian and the international proletariat through a *Manifesto*, in which they set out their views, clearly and without beating about the bush. Here they stigmatized the nascent tendency of Bolshevism to base itself, not on the working class, but on the 'cult of the leader'. This *Manifesto* is one of the most remarkable documents of the Russian revolution. Its publication at the moment of the internal collapse of the Russian revolution had the same significance as Babeuf's *Manifesto of the Equals* at the moment of the internal collapse of the French revolution.

For a long time in the isolator I abstained from participating in discussions on the role of Lenin. I belonged to that young Communist generation that had been raised on the idea that Lenin was sacrosanct. For me, it went without saying that 'Lenin was always right'. The results—the revolutionary conquest of power, and holding it—spoke in his favour. Thus, I and my generation concluded that the tactics, and the means, too, were justified.

When I arrived at the isolator, it was in this sense that I intervened. So I was not a little put out to hear the *Decemist*, Prokopenya, give me this ironic advice: "Useless to get heated, comrade Ciliga, about Lenin's struggle against the bureaucracy. You rely on one of the last articles he wrote before his death, the one on the reform of the Workers and Peasants Inspection. Did he call on the masses to organize themselves against the bureaucracy? Not at all. He proposed the creation of a special organ with a well-paid staff, a super-bureaucratic organ to combat . . . the bureaucracy!"

"No, foreign comrade," Prokopenya continued, "At the end of his life Lenin lost confidence in the worker mass. He banked on the bureaucratic apparatus, but, fearing that it would overdo things, he sought to restrict the evil by making one part of the apparatus control the other." After a moment's silence, she went on: "Obviously, there's no point in shouting this from the rooftops; that would only give Stalin additional arguments. But it is no less a fact."

If I felt little inclination for a study of the discussions and quarrels of the past, it was because I was overwhelmed by the problems of the present. To the extent that historical problems interested me, it seemed to me that these groups over-estimated the importance of their old differences with Lenin. The fate of the revolution, in my opinion, was decided by the relationship of class forces, and not by the formulas or theses upon which this or that internal tendency had been able to agree.

As the fulfilment of the Five Year Plan progressed, so the question of organizational, political, and economic formulas again became correspondingly immediate. Problems that one might have thought long since settled by history were suddenly once again on the agenda, and with added force. The suppression of the petty bourgeoisie and of private capitalism made it plain that within the social arena there were no other forces but the bureaucracy and the proletariat. And now it was at the level of organizational forms that one had to seek the solution to problems such as the mutual relation of these organizational forms themselves, and "what is socialism, and how can it be achieved?" Technical questions of organization revealed themselves as social questions. The struggle of the labouring masses against the bureaucratic tyranny could henceforth only be against the organizational forms that the bureaucracy had given the economy. But these forms had not been invented by Stalin. They had ben bequeathed him by Lenin. The Russian revolution, in spite of its antagonisms and internal strife, is an organic whole. And Lenin cannot be exonerated.

Applying himself to the study of these new questions, the *Myasnikovist*, Tiyunov, wrote an essay on the historical dispute over the bureaucratic or the socialist organization of production. His work was based on a critique of the military measures taken by Trotsky to organize production during the period of war communism. The young *Decemist*, Jacques Kosman wrote a brilliant historical study on what was called 'the trade union question'. He reached the conclusion that the manner in which Lenin organized industry had handed it over entirely into the hands of the bureaucracy. And the direct consequence of that recapture of the factories from the proletariat meant that they had lost the revolution.

Another *Decemist*, Misha Shapiro, wrote a refutation, supporting the traditional viewpoint of the *Decemists*: the disputes over the diverse systems for organizing production had no principled significance. According to Shapiro, the Workers Opposition did not represent the interests of the proletariat, but those of the trade-union bureaucracy. And if the demands concerning the transfer of the factories to the trade unions had been satisfied, the only difference would have been the management of the factories by the trade-union bureaucracy in place of the party bureaucracy.

To be able to fight the bureaucracy the proletariat needed freedom: freedom to organize, freedom of the press, freedom of assembly. But that led to the argument of freedom to choose one's party, upheld by Myasnikov, and condemned formerly by Lenin, by Trotsky, and by the *Decemists*. And even then the major part of the *Decemists* and almost all the Trotskyists continued to consider that 'freedom of party' would be 'the end of the revolution'. "Freedom to choose one's party—that is Menshevism", was the Trotskyists' final verdict. "The proletariat is socially homogenous and that is why its interests can only be represented by a single party," the *Decemist* Davidov wrote. "And why should not democracy within the party be coupled with its dictatorship outside?", the *Decemist* Nyura Yankovskaya wanted to know. "The Paris Commune succumbed because over there they had too many parties. But with us there is only one. How, then, has it happened that our revolution, too, has succumbed?", Dora Zak retorted to Davidov. The young *Decemist* Volodya Smirnov even went so far as to say: "There has never been a proletarian revolution, nor a dictatorship of the proletariat in Russia, there has simply been a 'popular revolution' from below and a dictatorship from above. Lenin was never an ideologist of the proletariat. From beginning to end he was an ideologist of the intelligentsia." These ideas of Smirnov were bound up with the general view that the world was steering straight towards a new social form — State capitalism, with the bureaucracy as the new ruling class. It put on the same level Soviet Russia, Kemalist Turkey, fascist Italy, Germany on the march to Hitlerism, and the America of Hoover-Roosevelt. "Communism is an extremist fascism, fascism is a moderate communism", he wrote in his article, *Comfascism*. That conception left the forces and perspectives of socialism somewhat in the shade. The majority of the *Decemist* fraction, Davidov, Shapiro, etc., considered that young Smirnov's* heresy had gone beyond all bounds, and he was expelled from the group, amid uproar.

Grasping the importance of bygone problems for the understanding of new problems, for a precise assessment of future tasks, I set myself to studying them seriously. The nuances in the interpretation of these questions by the extreme left milieu favoured critical examination and self-determination. And, studying them after an intense revolutionary experience, I approached them in a state of mind obviously different from that of comrades who ten years before had found in them reasons for splitting. I had behind me fifteen years of the history of the revolution and could judge the past with a mind both clearer and more aware than theirs.

But in subjecting the 'Lenin epoch' to a critical analysis I entered the holy of holies of Communism and my own ideology. I subjected Lenin to criticism, the leader and the prophet, crowned by the immortal glory of the revolution, and even more by the legend and the mystification of the postrevolutionary myth. And, in spite of the critical spirit of the surroundings in which I lived, I entered the sanctuary on tiptoes, so much did I find myself guilty in listening to that inner voice saying to me: "To understand the experience and the lessons of the revolution one must shrink from nothing and show oneself as pitiless as the revolution itself, that also shrank from nothing."

And the farther I penetrated into the sanctuary the more, day after day, week after week, month after month I asked myself the fundamental question: And is it, perhaps, you also, Lenin? Were you not great only so long as the masses and the revolution were great? And when the force of the masses declined, did not your revolutionary spirit equally decline, decline even more?

"Could it have been possible that, to retain power, you could have betrayed—you, too—the social interests of the

*It is not difficult to see in Smirnov a precurser of Burnham. *A.C.*

masses? And that what had seduced us, we, the naive, had been the decision to retain power? And that you had preferred the bureaucracy victorious to the defeated masses? And that you could have aided that new bureaucracy to bend the neck of the Soviet masses? Is it possible that you could have crushed the masses when they did not want to accommodate themselves to the new order of things? That you could have slandered them, that you could have distorted the sense of their rightful aspirations? Lenin, Lenin, what weighs the most, your merits or your crimes?

"I set little store by the motives that inspired you: it was, you thought, better that the bureaucracy should be the ones to bend the neck of the masses than to see again the former exploiters, the bourgeoisie and the landlords. It is possible that the bureaucracy considered the matter important, but for the masses who bowed their heads it mattered little . . .

"I set little store also, Lenin, by the arguments of your defenders: subjectively, your intentions were the best in the world. It was you yourself, Lenin, who taught us to judge people, not according to their subjective intentions, but according to the objective significance of the latter, according to the social groups in whose interest their activity operates and on whose behalf they speak. And besides, in your own justifications—very cautious, it must be said—I find proof that you have yourself subjectively accepted the regime you were objectively bringing into being. Worse still: just when the dictatorship of the bureaucracy was becoming stronger you consciously (proof of this exists) slandered the worker masses resisting the triumphant bureaucracy. Yet that resistance—feeble as it was, crushed as it was by the bureaucracy—is the supreme testament of the revolution. And a new revolution, truly freeing, socially freeing, the lower orders, can arise in Russia and elsewhere in the world, only by realizing the programme of the annihiliated Workers Opposition. It is in this return, in this continuity of the history of mankind, that its progressive tendencies will be carried forward . . ."

The sun sets in the distance, over the Urals, casting on the desert steppes, the mountains and the prison, the last rays that lighten my cell. It is the third year of my imprisonment. And it is hard . . . Through the bars I look with intense yearning at the mountains, the sun, the sky, freedom, freedom. I am alone in the cell. My cell-mate is in hospital. My soul is desolate . . . I am in mourning for Lenin.

"What have I just done? Have I not gone mad, a prey to the delirium of prisons?"

Let us look at this more closely.

In 1917 it was obviously a question of who would go farthest, the quickest, be the strongest, the masses or Lenin. Like a hurricane that devastates everything in its path, they overthrew everything in Russia and the world that was old, corrupt, deceitful. Truly these were 'days that shook the world'. Russia was making world history. And because Lenin had known how to make the heart of humanity beat at that moment of its magnificent, liberating explosion; because in those days when one saw the grand audacity of that triumph of the popular masses, he had known how to be one with them and to lead them, Lenin has forever taken a place of honour in the hearts of the workers and in the Pantheon of history. And that place is forever assured him, even if he must, like Cromwell, settle accounts with the masses for his crimes or those of his successors after the downfall of the revolution; even if, at some moment of history, his corpse is delivered on the streets of Moscow to the popular fury, as Cromwell's corpse was hoisted on the gallows.

But from the moment when the old edifice collapsed and Lenin took power there began the tragic divorce between him and the masses. Imperceptible at the start, it grew, and finally became fundamental.

The worker masses instinctively achieved their complete freedom, entirely achieving their aims. And it was for that that they made the revolution. Everything and all at once. Now or never. And it is that which distinguishes the epoch of revolutions from that of reforms. Going beyond the bounds of the old socialism of 1905 in order to create the new, the labouring masses of Russia, in 1917—18, went farther than Lenin initially desired. And the impetus was so powerful, and the situation so tense, that the masses swept Lenin up in their wake. Such were the relations between the leader and the masses at the culminating point of the revolution.

And the facts speak for themselves: after the October revolution Lenin did not want the expropriation of the capitalists, but only 'workers' control'; control by the workers' shop-floor organizations over the capitalists, who were to continue to retain management of the enterprises. A fierce class struggle ensued, invalidating Lenin's thesis on the collaboration of the classes under his power: the capitalists replied with sabotage and the workers' collectives took over all the factories one after the other . . . And it was only when the expropriation of the capitalists had been effected *de facto* by the worker masses that the Soviet government recognized it *de jure* by publishing the decree on the nationalization of industry.

Then, in 1918, Lenin answered the socialist aspirations of the workers by opposing to them the system of State capitalism ('on the model of wartime Germany'), with the greatest participation of former capitalists in the new Soviet economy. Lenin was not a partisan of the total destruction of the old economic order, but of a kind of equilibrium of the old and the new, for their co-existence. Lenin, who had shortly before attacked 'class collaboration', is now its apologist. Holder of power, he has begun to feel the influence of the diverse forces of society, and no longer, as formerly, that of the working class alone. He has made himself the apologist of the momentary status quo and no longer of the dynamic of the epoch.

The growing civil war came to correct once again this phase of Leninist philosophy of the revolution. The collapse of the German and Austro-Hungarian empires gave fresh nourishment to the maximalist tendencies of the popular masses, and the case for the immediate achievement of socialism received official sanction. The year 1919 began. It is the apotheosis of the Russian revolution, its own '1793'. And, as one has seen, it is once again on the initiative of the masses and not that of Lenin.

From revolutionary apotheosis to bankruptcy is only a step. And at this historic conjuncture it is Lenin who has the saddest role. If the period of social upsurge, of revolutionary exaltation, was characterized by the fact that the masses succeeded in drawing Lenin behind them, the decline and bankruptcy of the revolution revealed the antagonism between Lenin and the worker masses, and his victory over them.

What then was at stake in the battle? The very principle of socialism, the fate of industry wrested from the hands of the bourgeoisie. It is that which causes the divorce of Lenin from the proletariat. It is there that one must seek the key to an understanding of the duplicity of Lenin's role in the revolution.

The workers had become masters of the factories and had introduced the principle of collective production. But the

284

liaison between the various factories depended on the bureaucratic apparatus. And this was already a symptom of the danger threatening the proletariat. The fate of socialism in Russia depended on the workers having the possibility of ensuring the overall control of production. To achieve a socialist organisation of society, to reorganize the agrarian economy by the socialist method, the proletariat had above all else to realize the socialist organization of its own place of abode—industry.

It would seem that it was a question here of a compelling truth. Yet it is always forgotten when the destinies of socialism and the revolution are investigated. Lenin, placed at the summit of the apparatus, looked at the problem through the eyes of the apparatus. And that is what a worker delegate to the Tenth Congress of the Communist Party, Milyunov, pointed out. saying: "Lenin's attitude is psychologically understandable. Comrade Lenin is president of the Council of Commissars; it is he who directs our Soviet policy. It is clear that any action, from whatever quarter, that embarrasses that direction can only be regarded as petty-bourgeois and particularly harmful." In fact, during the civil war the central bureaucracy had not ceased to spread, and had taken over the factories. The management of the factories, at first nominated by the workers and employees, was now more and more appointed by the centre. At the same time the original management had gradually become a one-man management. The factories had begun to slip from the hands of the workers. And that had happened on Lenin's initiative, and in spite of the stubborn opposition of the entire workers' fraction of the party, of all the leading worker Bolsheviks. For his opposition, Tomsky was exiled by the party to Turkistan; as in the past Sapronov was sent to the Ukraine for his 'democratic centralism'.

With the end of the civil war, the struggle between the bureaucracy and the proletariat for the mastery of industry was resumed with renewed force. It entered upon the decisive phase. And it was precisely that struggle which shattered the system of war communism. "In our industry there are two powers, that of the workers and that of the bureaucrats. And that is paralysing production. The only way out is a radical decision: a single power, either that of worker socialism or that of State capitalism." It was in these terms that Shlyapnikov, theoretician of the Workers Opposition, denounced the conflict in an article published by *Pravda*, during the pre-congress preparatory period for 'trade union discussion'.

What was Lenin's attitude then? He also stood for a no compromise decision, like Shlyapnikov, but with the difference that he was for sole power to the bureaucracy. And Lenin himself confessed that, under the guise of 'trade union discussion', there was indeed the question of withdrawing control of the factories from the working class. He declared: "If it is to be to the trade unions, *that is to say to the nine-tenths of the non-party workers*, that management of industry is confided, then of what use is the party?" So therefore the party had no more than one-tenth of the working class, in the shape of worker Bolsheviks, who demanded the same thing as the non-party workers. So the class line on this decisive question was very sharp: on the one side the workers (members of the party and non-party), on the other the bureaucrats (members of the party and non-party); behind the workers—socialism; behind the bureaucrats—typical State capitalism.

To compensate for the violation of the factories Lenin promised the workers the right to strike. As if the workers had made the October revolution for the right to go on strike!

Characteristic are Lenin's relations with the 'liberals' of his own bureaucratic camp. Standing halfway between the Workers Opposition and Lenin, the Trotsky, Bukharin, Sapronov groups proposed a slackening of the unique power of the bureaucracy by the addition, in a consultative capacity, of the workers' voice in the organization of production. Lenin opposed this in the most categorical manner and applied the most energetic organizational measures against them (at the Tenth Congress of the Party in 1921) for the 'wobbling' they displayed.

He, Lenin, certainly did not 'wobble'. Making himself the spokesman of the Soviet bureaucracy (non-party as well as Communist), with unshakeable firmness he wrested the factories from the workers (Communist and non-party) wrenched from them from their essential conquest, the one weapon they could use to take another step towards their emancipation, towards socialism. The Russian proletariat became once more the wage-earning manpower in other people's factories. Of socialism there remained in Russia no more than the word.

And what, many will ask, about 1921 and Krondstadt? The

fate of industry, that is to say, the fate of socialism, was settled well before. The suppression of the Krondstadt revolt was the bureaucracy's reply to the attempt of the proletariat and the peasantry to unite against it. Lenin and his bureaucracy were very frightened by this. After the suppression it was NEP, and the conclusion of the alliance of the bureaucracy and the peasantry against the proletariat. It was only at the time of the Five Year Plan that the strengthened bureaucracy turned on its provisional allies—the middle peasants and the kulaks.

Having liquidated socialism on the economic domain, having liquidated workers' power in the factories, the bureaucracy had still one more task to accomplish—to liquidate the political power of the proletariat and the toiling masses. The organ of that power was the great mass organization that surged up during the revolutionary process—the Soviets. To the mass political organisation, the Soviet, as to the mass economic organization, the trade union, the bureaucracy opposed the organization in which the participation of the masses was the weakest but where it was itself the strongest—the Party. To suppress all possibility of battle in favour of the masses, both within the party itself and without, the decisions of the Tenth Party Congress were, on Lenin's initiative, as follows: suppression in the country of all parties except the Communist Party; suppression in the Party of any opinion and any group opposing the bureaucratic summit of the Party. The Party was transformed into an auxiliary organism of bureaucratic Caesarism, just as the Soviets and the unions had been transformed into auxiliary organisms of the Party. The bonapartist dictatorship over the Party, the working class and the country had taken shape.

I was dumbfounded when I discovered that the Communist Party leaders themselves were fully aware of this. In his book, *The Economy of the Transition Period*, (Russian ed., 1920; cf. p.115), Bukharin formulated the theory of 'proletarian' bonapartism ('the personal regime'). And to this passage Lenin made the note: *"It is true . . . but the word is not to be used." (Lenin's Collected Works*, Russian ed., Vol. XI; 1930.) One can do it, but one must not say it—there is all the Lenin of the time when he left the proletariat for the bureaucracy. Lenin also knew how to disguise the bonapartist character of the bureaucracy. "It is not possible to realize the dictatorship of the proletariat through an organization including it in its entirety", he wrote, "for the proletariat is still too divided,

287

too humiliated, too easy to bribe." And that is why the dictatorship of the proletariat "can only be realized by the vanguard, which gathers to itself all the revolutionary energy of the class: the Party". Subsequent experience would demonstrate all the bureaucratic reality of that theory of the dictatorship, of that theory of the dictatorship of the party over the working class, of the dictatorship of a select minority over the 'backward majority' of the proletariat. Once again history would demonstrate the soundness of that phrase from the old revolutionary song:

> *There is no saviour supreme,*
> *Neither God, nor Caesar, nor tribune,*

the soundness of the watchword of the workers' movement: The emancipation of the workers is the task of the workers themselves.

The liquidation of the political power of the proletariat nevertheless required a solid 'ideological basis'.

An oblique approach had to be made, for it was impossible to call things by their right names. In a revolution initially made in the name of socialism, it is not convenient to say bluntly: "It is now we who are the new gentlemen, the new exploiters." It is so much easier to call the seizure of the factories from the workers —"a victory for the socialist mode of production"; the grip of the bureaucracy on the workers—"the strengthening of the dictatorship of the proletariat"; and the new exploiters—"the vanguard of the proletariat". Since the landlords had been 'the protectors of the peasants', the bourgeoisie 'the vanguard of the people', the bureaucracy could well be 'the vanguard of the proletariat'. The exploiters have always considered themselves the vanguard of the exploited.

Lenin justified his new policy by the weakness of the proletariat. Confiding the revolution to the hands of the bureaucracy, he asserted that he was safeguarding it for the workers. Tomorrow's rewards would justify the sacrifices of today. These rewards are now before our eyes and we know what they are worth. It must be said, to the honour of the Russian proletariat, that it sensed immediately, in spite of its weakness, what was being hatched. It understood that Lenin was acting as if he had said: "You others, you workers, you are not logical. You want the immediate introduction of socialism, and you have not the strength to do it. Since you cannot be the masters of society, you must be the servants: it is the law of the class struggle in a society of classes. If you resign yourselves to the inevitable, we will give you all that is possible to give you."

The workers had their own conception of the struggle and they acted as if their reply to Lenin had been: "No, it is you who are not logical, comrade Lenin. If we are not strong enough to be the masters of the country, then we must pass over to active opposition. A class does not surrender, it fights."

The spontaneous opposition of the proletariat to the encroachments of the bureaucracy was indication enough that the proletariat was not as weak as Lenin asserted. And if he had been heart and soul with the proletariat, he would have supported the opposition of the workers that manifested itself throughout the country. But he thought and acted in the spirit of the bureaucracy, in the spirit of his power. That proletarian force appeared to him as a menace, and he applied to the proletariat the laws of the class struggle: a class that does not surrender must be crushed by the victor. Amid the plaudits of the whole of the country's new bureaucracy, Lenin, closing the Tenth Congress, exclaimed: "Now we are finished with the opposition. We shall not tolerate it an instant longer." Effectively, that was the end of the legal opposition. The doors of prison and exile opened before them, while they awaited the arrival of the execution squads.

In spite of fundamental transformations, the revolution continued to be called, as in the past, 'proletarian', 'socialist'. Even more: Lenin himself showed how necessary it was to marry the habitual phraseology with the actual subjection of the proletariat. When the workers, veritable victims of bureaucratic pretensions, set themselves to protest against the bureaucratic mystification of socialism and demanded satisfaction of their true interests, Lenin dismissed them *en bloc* as 'petty bourgeois', 'anarchists', 'counter-revolutionaries'. The interests of the bureaucracy were, on the contrary, characterized as 'the class interests of the proletariat'. He established in the country a totalitarian and bureaucratic regime that dubbed 'counter-revolutionary' everything that had politically and socially a progressive character. He ushered in that era of lies, of falsifications and distortions in which today, in its completed and reinforced Stalinist variant, the whole of Russia lives, and which poisons the entire social life of the international workers'

289

and democratic movement.

On hearing the resolutions and the speeches of Lenin on the Workers Opposition, Shlyapnikov exclaimed at the end of the Tenth Congress: "Never in my life, and after twenty years in the Party, have I ever seen or heard anything more demagogic and more vile." These words of Shlyapnikov echoed those of Thomas Muenzer, who called Luther 'Dr. Liar' (Dr. Lügner), after his pamphlets in support of the protestant princes against the protestant peasants.

"And that is exactly what you became, Lenin, at the close of your historic career," I said to myself . . .

I looked fixedly and with animosity at Lenin's portrait on the table of my cell. Before me there were two Lenins, as there had been two Cromwells and two Luthers: they climbed with the revolution and then they slid back down the slope, crushing the minority who wished to go on.

And the whole of that crucial evolution took place over two or three years, in the Russian revolution as in the others. Whilst we, the contemporaries, like those of the former revolutions, still continued for ten, twenty or thirty years to argue about whether that crucial evolution had ever taken place.

"And your opposition, Lenin, in the last year of your life, to ravenous Stalinism—tragic though it was for you—had no more political significance than that of a wavering between Stalinism and Trotskyism, that is to say, between the ultra-reactionary and the liberal variants of the bureaucracy."

The fate of the Bolshevik Party, the fate of Lenin, and of Trotsky, shows yet once more that the most advanced parties and the greatest leaders are limited in their character by the circumstances of time and place. And that is why it is inevitable that at a given moment they become conservatives, heedless of the new demands of life.

The legend of Lenin appeared to me no more than a lie designed to cover up the crimes of the bureaucracy.

"To destroy the tyranny of the bureaucracy created by your own hands it was also necessary, Lenin, to destroy the legend of the infallible sage of the proletariat. At the hour of supreme danger, instead of stretching out your hand to the proletariat—you struck it down.

"If the world has still need of this lesson, you bear it out: when the masses are incapable of saving the revolution, no one can do it for them. Your experience, Lenin, tells us that the only means of saving the proletarian revolution is to carry it through to the end, to the point where the toiling masses are totally emancipated. If the revolution is not carried through to the end, the day inevitably arrives when a new privileged minority exercises its tyranny over the majority of the workers. Contemporary revolutions will achieve complete socialism, or they will one day inevitably be anti-proletarian, anti-socialist. They will become counter-revolutions."

"Neither God, nor masters", a voice said from the depths of my subconscious, but not the less audible, firm, commanding. The portrait of Lenin on the table of my cell was torn into a thousand pieces and thrown into the litter bin . . .

The cell was dark. Outside, night had fallen. The Urals and the steppes were plunged into an ominous stillness. And I was ill and sick at heart. For six months I could not open my mouth to speak, could not write a single word on politics, on my new conclusions about the great revolutionary leader, so depressed I was, so much I suffered in separating myself forever from the myths of Lenin that I cherished so much.

X

THE FIRST TERRORIST TRIALS AGAINST THE COMMUNISTS

IT was during the winter of 1932, and not during 1936 nor even following upon the murder of Kirov, that the first Communists were tried on charges of ' terrorism '.

At first, the trials were held behind closed doors. When, in 1933, we saw the first batches of convicted ' terrorists ' arrive at Verkhne-Uralsk, we could not believe our eyes : a plot against Stalin ? A palace revolution ? What an hallucination ! In the West one is, even today, ignorant of most of these early trials.

The people concerned were fairly unimportant members of the Right-wing Opposition, former members of the Government and of the Central Party Committee : Riutin, Uglanov, Tolmatchev, Eismonte and a few younger Communists. The papers had announced that they had been expelled from the Party for having tried to form ' counter-revolutionary organizations of bourgeois and kulaks ' in order to ' restore capitalism and kulaks in particular in the U.S.S.R.'

It was only after these prisoners arrived that we learned that there had been other charges which the Press had not mentioned at all ; they were supposed to concern a plot to bring about a palace revolution and the assassination of Stalin. This was already more serious than the first accusations.

Riutin was the central figure at the trial. He was accused of having, during the summer of 1932, unlawfully published a programme of 160 pages in which he demanded : (1) An economic retreat, a slowing up of the rhythm of industrialization and the abolition of enforced collectivization ; (2) Democracy within the Party ; (3) Stalin's dismissal. The author of this programme was in favour of a coalition of the Right-wing and Trotskyist Oppositions, for, so he wrote,

" the Right-wing has proved correct in the economic field and Trotsky in his criticism of the system inside the Party ". The programme attacked the leaders of the Right-wing Opposition—Rykov, Tomsky and Bukharin—for having capitulated to Stalin. A whole chapter was devoted to Stalin himself, who was described as " the evil genius of the Party and the revolution ", and compared to the worst despots of history.

The accusation considered this document, and in particular the chapter on Stalin, to be the ' ideological basis ' of a terrorist plot. But where were the elements of the plot ? As Riutin, a former army officer, had been editor of the military newspaper *Krasnaya Zvesda* (*The Red Star*), he was accused of having organized among the students of the Military Academy of the Central Executive Committee where officers were trained for the higher ranks, a group of plotters who were to kill Stalin.

Tolmatchev and Eismonte, members of the supreme organs of the Government, were accused of having prepared a palace revolution. One of the prisoners who arrived at Verkhne-Uralsk—named Alferov, if I remember rightly—a man who belonged to the Right, had, as his only crime, pronounced the following significant phrase amongst a circle of intimates, " The only thing to do is to get rid of the boss."

Two things struck one in this first terrorist trial instituted against Russian Communists. First of all, the appearance of a fleeting desire for terrorism in the leading circles and not at the periphery of power or in Opposition circles, in prison or in exile, where one might have expected to find Stalin's bitterest enemies. Never did I, in prison or in exile, encounter the slightest propensity towards terrorism among the members of the Opposition. The second peculiarity of the trial was that the prisoners belonged to the Right-wing Opposition. It is true that Zinoviev and Kamenev, too, were implicated, but they were only accused of not having denounced the existence of the Riutin programme, though criticizing it, to the right quarters.

There were, it was said, grave dissensions within the Politbureau when the penalties to be applied were discussed. Stalin had insisted on the execution of the principal prisoner, Riutin ; the majority of the Politbureau were opposed to it, probably considering the charges insufficiently proved, and hesitating to open yet another chapter of bloody repression in the inside history of the Communist Party.

This entire story of terrorism seemed so absurd to me that I did not even take the trouble to look for the slightest truth in it. Rumours that came from Moscow were not calculated to remove suspicion, however. They were increasingly fantastic. Blucher was supposed to be implicated in a plot against Stalin; an ambush had been prepared opposite Lenin's Tomb and there a noted member of the Opposition was to have made an attempt on the life of Stalin in the course of a demonstration. But when I left prison, in the summer of 1933, I was soon able to convince myself that I had believed Stalinist authority more firmly established than it really was.

It was not the only point on which I held mistaken views whilst in prison. The horror stories I was told about the famine, the cannibalism and the fearful mortality, I thought were all exaggerated Opposition stories. I had to give credence to them when Opposition groups from Central Asia arrived at Verkhne-Uralsk, composed of men absolutely worthy of belief who reported frightening tales about the famine. In one prison the Kirghiz peasants had been devouring the legs of their dead comrades; elsewhere, corpses had been kept hidden for a week, in order that their six-ounce ration of bread might be secured. I believed them to be isolated, exceptional cases, but once I was out of prison, I was able to convince myself of the contrary. The extent of the famine, the typhoid epidemics and the mortality surpassed anything that the greatest pessimists among us had imagined. Hundreds of thousands of human beings were roaming through the land, homeless and famished. In the small Northern provincial towns, the police would every morning collect some eight or ten corpses of these wretches, who had starved to death in the streets. Typhoid fever completed the work of hunger. The whole country was panic-stricken. One unspoken thought galvanized the masses: " It can't last much longer ! " Conscious of their inability to act, the masses wished for a change ' from above '. " If Stalin will not yield to necessity, let them put him aside." In silence the whole country demanded a palace revolution. When I first realized the existence of this current, all the more intense in that it was subterranean, I understood that the thought of a *coup d'état* might well have arisen in leading circles, in spite of the police terror. If members of the Right-wing Opposition were to be found among the plotters, it was because there the strongest supporters of a ' retreat ' could be found. In any case, one could logically ascribe to the Right-wing the view that Stalin ruined the country and the revolution, and that it was therefore necessary to get rid of him.

But in January, 1933, Stalin did sound a retreat. At the last minute he adopted the programme of his opponents, after having taken every precaution to place the latter behind lock and bar. Persuaded as I had been that Stalin was perfectly able to call a retreat, I had been unable to believe that he would first of all have led the despairing country to the brink of the precipice. As soon as the retreat had been carried out, the country began gradually to calm down. The year 1933 went by in hesitation and waiting : was there a real change of policy, or merely a brief respite, destined to herald a yet more exhausting effort? In 1934 one was already able to talk of stabilization. Things began to accumulate, in so far as I could judge in my lost corner of Siberia, famine was on the decrease, and a few concessions were being made to the peasants. The Communist and non-Party bureaucrats began to live ' in joy and comfort ' : such was the slogan.

Suddenly, on the 1st of December, 1934, Kirov was struck down by Nikolayev. The wireless gave out that " a white-guardist had struck the blow ". Obviously a white-guardist, I said to myself, as most others did, how could it be anyone else? But after a few days public rumour soon confirmed that the assassin was a well-known member of the Comsomol belonging to Zinoviev's Opposition ; he had been a propagandist in the Viborg district where the secretary of the Comsomol Commissariat was Kotolynov, a member of the Central Committee of Communist Youth and one of the ideological chiefs of the Comsomol Oppositions. These details proved to us political prisoners to what extent we had lost touch with reality. Whilst our moderates thought of a peaceful reform of the system, and our extremists of a popular revolution at some vague time in the future, the representatives of authority were already face to face with individual acts of terrorism which we had not foreseen.

That Nikolayev's gesture had had great political importance was proved by the postponement of the trial of 30,000 Communist and non-Party workers in Leningrad. They and their families were sent, in large convoys, into the depths of Siberia. The workers commented on their lot as follows, " At first the peasants were ' dekulaked ', now it is our turn." A few thousand of them were driven into the Yenisei province, where I was in exile after I had left prison. They told me that the life ' in joy and comfort ', proclaimed by Stalin, had caused a silent but profound irritation among the workers. Stalin's slogan had been interpreted as the final consecration of the bureaucracy's triumph over the hoodwinked and oppressed proletariat. The assassination of Kirov seemed to assume the character of a protest against such an end to the revolution. It was nothing but the protest of a modest bureaucrat, himself guilty of many a crime against the masses, but they had been crimes committed in the hope of a better future. The life ' in joy and comfort ' had dashed this hope.

Was Nikolayev's act isolated, or was there a whole organization behind him ? I was unable to find out. The sending into exile of tens of thousands of workers proved nothing ; Stalin might have thought simply of making sure of the future.

As a result of Kirov's assassination, all the principal leaders of the Zinoviev group were sent to Verkhne-Uralsk, namely, Zinoviev himself, Kamenev, Kuklin, Zalutsky, Unchlikht's sister, Vuyovitch's wife and others. The chiefs of other groups arrived : Chliapnikov and Medvedev, the leaders of the former ' workers' Opposition ', Timothy Sapronov, an old worker, the leader of ' Democratic Centralism ', and finally, Smilga, a very well-known former Trotskyist—and I must be forgetting others. Half the Kremlin had moved house to Verkhne-Uralsk between 1917 and 1927. . . . The Zinovievist leaders spent eighteen months there, and then were allowed to return to Moscow for the trial that was, to end in their execution. Abroad the whole of their prison life has remained a secret, for which reason I shall recount a few episodes of it.

That the Chairman of the Third International should walk in the prison courtyard seemed a symbolic occurrence. A slouching old man, walking in shirt-sleeves and bare of foot across the hot sand, such was Zinoviev during the summer of 1935. Was he already aware of what had been reserved for him : a bullet at the base of the skull ? In any case, he had already been terrorized and feared to pronounce the least opinion. Kamenev seemed more at ease. One day, he ventured to say that he agreed with Stalin on ninety-eight points out of a hundred in matters of policy. But so much independence was soon punished : he was locked in a ward with twelve prisoners, whereas Zinoviev was allowed to enjoy the use of a cell shared with but one other person.

Kuklin, the third important Zinovievist, thought that ' all was lost ' ; the Russian revolution, the Party, the International. . . . It was to be begun all over again. Then he added with the condemned man's grim humour, " As to Stalin, I shall swindle him ; he won't be able to make me serve my ten years' sentence, and I am very glad of it ; for I am sixty years of age and I shall certainly not live to be seventy." This argument seemed to have prevailed, for Kuklin was the only Zinovievist leader whose name did not appear at the public Moscow trial. It is not improbable, though, that unsuccessful attempts were made to make him ' confess ', but I do not know whether he is still alive.

Zinoviev's and Kamenev's transfer to Moscow in August, 1936, which was to end in their deaths, was not their sole journey. They had already been taken to Moscow once, during the summer of 1935, but that time they escaped with their lives. This became known, for, upon his return, Zinoviev managed to shout through his window that all had gone well in Moscow.

The trial of the summer of 1935 has remained practically unknown abroad. Zinoviev and Kamenev were accused of hatching a plot against Stalin. More than thirty prisoners appeared at the trial—people of slight personality and often of doubtful reputation, low officials, Kremlin servants and women of the former aristocracy, now wives or mistresses of the accused. Two of the prisoners were shot : one collaborator of the G.P.U. and one officer of the Kremlin guard. The others escaped with sentences ranging between five and ten years.

Kamenev's brother, Rosenfeld, the painter, was in a way the hero of the whole affair. He declared that it was only owing to his arrest that the catastrophe, that is Stalin's assassination, had been prevented. But Kamenev denied everything, and this 'obstinacy' caused five years to be added to his sentence. Zinoviev, on the contrary, ' admitted the possibility of this criminal affair ' and thus, as leader of the Opposition, took upon him part of the responsibility. For this he received his reward. Not only was his sentence not increased but, upon his return to Verkhne-Uralsk, his prison diet was considerably improved.

The trial of the summer of 1935, though kept rigorously secret, was mentioned without any explanation in the verdict of the public trial in August, 1936.

* * *

In August, 1936, a new wave of terror swept the country ; it has not yet spent itself. What is its meaning ?

First, two trials were held of former members of the Left-wing Opposition, who had long since capitulated to Stalin. A few among them, especially Radek, were already profoundly demoralized and dishonoured men. Why pronounce judgement on these political corpses ? No doubt to strike at those who were not yet in that state.

After that, the leaders of the Right-wing Opposition were arrested : Bukharin and Rykov. But their trial did not take place. One must suppose either that they refused to enact the required comedy or that they were protected by forces which the dictator had to take into account.

Then followed the trials of the Red Army chiefs, Tukhatchevsky, it would seem, was but the forerunner, the lieutenant of the men of the morrow : Blucher, Voroshilov or some other man. The execution of the men of the Left-wing Opposition or even of Yagoda, chief of the G.P.U., might be considered as the liquidation of the past, the removal of phantoms. But that could not be said where Bukharin-Rykov were concerned, still less in the case of the Army chiefs. In their case, it was a struggle with the living, a contest between the real masters of the land.

What were the stakes of the game ? The official version, according to which the victims wished to restore the power of capitalists and landowners, is a monstrous lie to tell of people who had spent years of their life in prison to defend diametrically opposed ideas. It was a foolish lie to tell about people who, up to the last minute, had themselves been at the summit of power. No, the dilemma was not whether to restore the old régime or to defend the new. The stakes were to be found within the present régime ; the supremacy of one of the two competing groups to the exclusion of the other. In the duel between Stalin and the generals, the Party dictatorship was at war with the army dictatorship. The whole question was to know whether, by his bloody repression, Stalin succeeded in averting a Soviet 18th of Brumaire. But to be able to answer this question, several fundamental facts must be borne in mind.

The revolution is over. The Five Year Plan is finished. The Soviet volcano is cooling and, in cooling, seeks its equilibrium. The masses are disappointed in a revolution from the benefits of which they are excluded. The bourgeois and landowners have been replaced by the bureaucrats. " We have suffered and struggled in vain " ; this is the final word of all shades of Left-wing Opposition. But the disappointed masses are politically passive, whence the total lack of strength of the Left Opposition. One can argue that the more Left a group is, the weaker it is. Not that the people is entirely inert ; on the contrary, in *kolkhosi* and factories, a daily struggle is waged against the system, an obstinate but silent struggle to better the ' details ' of life. This struggle, however, does not yet rise to the height of a political movement.

Very different is the position in the camp of the ' masters '. They fight for the inheritance of the revolution. The masters —that is to say, the two groups of Communist and non-Party bureaucrats. The former have the Party and the workers' organizations at their disposal, they have a predominating influence in the administration and in the army. The non-Communist bureaucrats, consisting of intellectuals and technicians, direct the production and command the workers in workshops and heavy industries. They direct a highly centralized, corporate organization, the ITR or technical personnel ; this is very important in the State apparatus and in the army, and has the support of one of the most powerful and most secret forces in Russia, the Church. For one must never forget that the important strata of the people who no longer believe in the revolution have faith in the Church, which has succeeded in modernizing itself.

In the eyes of the people, the Communist bureaucrats are worse exploiters than the ' engineers '. Now that the NEP, the bourgeois and the kulaks have been liquidated, the bureaucracy can no longer avail itself of these abolished classes for its scapegoat. Thus this Communist bureaucracy is in an entirely isolated position in the country. The new Stalinist constitution was an attempt to remedy that isolation. Beneath the mask of ' general equality ', the constitution was to reconcile and bring together the two bureaucracies, by giving them the new rights whilst keeping the workers and peasants in their former subjection. The reconciliation with the intellectuals was to make up for the estrangement of the masses. But until now this attempt seems to have met with no success. The article of the Constitution which ensures the monopoly of the Communist Party at every stage of social and political life has revealed to the non-Party bureaucrats that the Stalinist concessions are nothing but a fiction. But the Left-wing Opposition perceived the abandonment of Communism in it. Stalin therefore hoped by crushing this Left-wing Opposition to kill two birds with one stone, for the trials that annihilated this Opposition were, in his opinion, to serve as a warning to the non-Party malcontents.

In actual fact the very opposite happened. The Moscow trials brought the Communist Party into disrepute and stimulated the appetite of the non-Party Bolsheviks. These circumstances naturally brought the army into the forefront. The army is sufficiently connected with the revolution to defend the Communist bureaucracy against any reactionary attack ; it is sufficiently ' above all Parties ' to reassure all non-Party bureaucrats ; it is, in short, the incarnation of the new national ' classless unity '. Such might well be the roots of a Soviet Bonapartism. External dangers increase the chances of such a development.

By assassinating the generals of the revolution, Stalin has by no means triumphed. The young army-chiefs—for one cannot just abolish generals—may show themselves more enterprising than their predecessors. To prevent a military dictatorship, all Stalin has to do is to succeed in reconciling the two bureaucracies with one another and with the Church. But to carry out that task, even Stalin may be too compromised by reason of his revolutionary past—too Trotskyist, in fact.

The murder of the generals meant that the military dictatorship was ripening in Russia. But whether it was already mature, whether it had reached the concrete form of a plot, it would be difficult to say. It would be more prudent to say that the trial of the generals, as all the Soviet trials between 1929 and 1937, had a preventive character. What might happen was to be prevented. The accused were guilty of potential crimes. The accusations were put in the most convenient forms each time, and contained what Stalin deemed useful as charges against his enemies.

Such, it seems to me, were the shares of truth and lie in the famous Moscow trials and in the new Soviet Terrorism.

XI

TOWARDS DEPARTURE

AFTER our incursion into the realm of the Moscow trials, we must return to Verkhne-Uralsk. During the summer of 1933 the prison was becoming passionately interested in the two great events of the day : the ' retreat ' Stalin had just announced, and Hitler's accession to power.

Now that Stalin's ' retreat was there, the Trotskyist Opposition could no longer discuss its ' programme of retreat '. Sections and scissions had lost their object. It became necessary to take up a new position in the face of present-day realities.

The Right-wing Trotskyists realized that there was no chance now of a ' reform from above '. The promoters of the 1931 scission, Solntsev for the Right and Kamenetsky, the former militant Bolshevik, for the Left, became champions of reunification. After a certain amount of resistance, the Trotskyist unity was re-established in the autumn of 1933, on the following bases : freedom of opinion and propaganda inside the Opposition and struggle against the Stalinist bureaucracy (modified by a few timid democratic claims). The number of ' negators ' was increasing, all denying that Stalin's régime had the character of a proletarian dictatorship. It is curious to note that these ' negators ' first appeared in the former Right, whereas the small group of Trotskyists from the Extreme Right, known as the M.B.M. (after the initials of the names of its three members : Melnais, Barkine and Milmann), demanded a ' more loyal ' criticism of the Stalinist policy, whilst considering that the U.S.S.R. was passing through a ' monarchic phase in the dictatorship of the proletariat ', after having been through phases of class, Party and oligarchy.

The Trotskyists were visibly relinquishing their bureaucratic pride in favour of a more democratic attitude. I was very rejoiced at this, wrongly perhaps, for all this was merely Opportunism. As in the past there had been a demand for a NEP tinged with democracy, so there was now a demand for a State capitalism tempered with democracy. The thought that democracy should be the very foundation of socialist evolution remained foreign to Trotskyism. Was it the—deeply bureaucratic—tradition of the Trotskyists that was responsible for this, or was it their petit-bourgeois origin ?

The new situation equally facilitated the unification in the Extreme Left camp. The Miasnikov group, the Decists, a few former Trotskyists, altogether some twenty to twenty-five prisoners, formed a ' Federation of Left-wing Communists '. This Federation was instituted after my departure from the isolator, but I was able to take part in the ideological discussions that preceded its formation.

There was no agreement on the definition of Soviet State capitalism : was it ' relatively progressive ' (according to me), ' purely parasitic ' (according to Tiunov) or did it represent a ' new period of civilization ' as V. Smirnov would have it ?

Tiunov demanded integral socialism in industry, and the re-establishment of the NEP in rural economy. He approved ' integrally ' of historic Bolshevism, the programme of the ' Workers' Opposition ' and the ' Worker Groups ' of 1920 to 1923. I, on the other hand, considered that the new workers' movement had to benefit from the experience of all Left-wing groups, that is, of Russian Bolshevism, of the German Party of Rosa Luxemburg, of French and American syndicalism, etc. It was obviously also necessary to take into account the transformation of the Russian revolution and the victories of Fascism over the old workers' movement. V. Smirnov, on the contrary, swept the board of historic Bolshevism and did not take foreign Communism into account at all, for he could see no workers in it. In the end, it all led to long arguments *in vacuo*.

* * *

The German crisis, beginning with the elections for the Reichstag, in September, 1930, passionately interested the prisoners. At each election, at each step in the rise of national-socialism, we wrote articles, we drew up comparative tables and organized discussions during recreation-time. The *Rote Fahne* was the only German newspaper we were allowed, which meant that we read it until the paper on which it was printed wore out. In spite of all our divergences, we were unanimously agreed on the tremendous international importance of the events in Germany. This led us to study the problem in its general aspects : what is Fascism, what is its place in modern society ? We minutely analysed the programmes of the Fascist parties and the Soviet and foreign works that dealt with it. (I don't know how we managed it, but we had somehow succeeded in obtaining even the foreign books !)

Hitler's accession to power caused a veritable panic among the Trotskyists. They awaited the ' inevitable ' aggression of Hitler against the U.S.S.R. with the assistance of England and France. " Hitler and Stalin will agree in the end," I remarked to Trotsky's son-in-law, M. Nivelson. " Impossible, Hitler would not have it."—" In that case, Stalin will agree with France." Nivelson and the other Trotskyists could not bring themselves to believe that the laws which governed the foreign policy of bourgeois States also ruled that of Russia. These were the somewhat short-sighted patriots of ' our Soviet State ' that Stalin was to accuse of collaborating with Hitler. . . .

After the collapse of the German Communist Party, a group of intransigent Decists spoke of forming a Fourth International. The Verkhne-Uralsk Trotskyists were opposed to it, for they still hoped for a reform of the U.S.S.R. and the Comintern. The Left-wing Trotskyist leaders, V. Yenukidze, Kamenetsky and Jak, published a manifesto accusing the Decists of spreading an untimely and demagogic slogan. Moreover, ignorant of Trotsky's views on the matter, the latter's supporters at Verkhne-Uralsk preferred not to move from their positions. When they learned that their leader was in favour of a Fourth International, they were not opposed to it, but did not know how to interpret the fact that the French Trotskyists had joined the socialist Party, a section of the Second International.

Zankov and Tiunov, from the Extreme Left, were against a Fourth International for other reasons. They feared that it might be nothing but a new version of the Third. V.

Smirnov made a half-turn ; considering that in the circumstances a new International and new workers' organizations
would be pure Utopia, he saw no issue but in a fusion of
social-democrats and Communists. The former would ensure
the participation of the proletarian classes, the latter—
revolutionary initiative. My comment on this to Smirnov
was that " the union of two corpses would never produce a
living body ! "

* * *

I availed myself of my last few months in prison to document myself on the non-Communist groups.

The Russian social-democrats, who numbered about
fifteen, edited a paper, several articles in which I still remember. In the one it was shown that in 1917 and during the
Civil War the Bolsheviks had relied on the lower levels of
the working class, but, during the NEP, on its higher levels.
In an article on the results of the Five Year Plan, a Right-
wing social-democrat denied that there had been any sub-
stantial economic progress, whereas the author of another
article, belonging to the Left-wing, deemed the results of
collectivization satisfactory. Finally, I remember an article
entitled *Hitler in Power*, also written by a Left-winger, in
which the absence of a united popular front was denounced
as the primary cause of the victory of Fascism.

The Georgian social-democrats, in so far as I could discover, both in prison and in exile, were mainly petit-bourgeois ; there were but few genuine social-democrats. But
let this not prevent me telling the truth about the suppression
of the 1924 insurrection in Georgia. The suppression was
carried out with unbelievable cruelty, mingled with provoca-
tions and mass-executions, with no form of trial ; people
who had been in prison a long while and had nothing to do
with the insurrection were suddenly shot. This blood-bath
was organized by Stalin, Ordjonikidze and Bela Kun.
Numerous Georgian Opposition Communists whom I knew
at Verkhne-Uralsk told me the truth about it, which they
knew by having seen the suppression or by having played
a part in it.

There were only five revolutionary-socialists at Verkhne-
Uralsk, but I met a few more in exile. Their opinions were
very like those of the Communist Opposition. Some of
them, led by M. A. Spiridonova, the legendary heroine of

the Russian revolutionary movement (she spent twenty-five years, that is, nearly half her lifetime, in exile), almost held the Trotskyist views. Another group, led by Kamkov, former revolutionary socialist People's Commissar in 1918, was closely allied to the Extreme Left-wing Communists.

The Right-wing revolutionary-socialists were few in number and very hostile towards those of the Left.

The Armenian revolutionary-socialists who constituted the *Dachnaktsutiun* Party, were almost exclusively interested in national emancipation.

The Jewish Zionists belonged to various shades of socialism and were, above all, interested in the Jewish national problem in Palestine. But they were not altogether uninterested in the Russian and international workers' movements.

There were not many anarchists at Verkhne-Uralsk, though in exile I came to know quite a number, two of whom were famous men : Jonas Varchavski and Barmach. If in prison, the humanist element was contributed by the social-democrats and the revolutionary principle by the Communists, one might say that the anarchists contributed the spirit of chivalry. They were always ready to support any group in a struggle against the administration. If there was a hunger-strike, the anarchists usually had the greatest number of dead. There were generally in Russia quite a number of former Communists and members of the Comsomol, who, at the end of the Civil War and at the beginning of the NEP, joined the ranks of the anarchists.

The working masses in Russia, manual workers as well as peasants, prefer, as I have already stated, passive resistance to an overt struggle. The time of the ' Workers' Opposition ' of 1920 to 1923 was past, the mighty social opposition of the extreme Left, created by Russian workers. This situation was accurately reflected in the social and national composition of the Verkhne-Uralsk prison, which was Russia's main political prison, at the time. There were not more than 15 per cent of workers among the prisoners. Those workers did, on the whole, ' capitulate ' fairly rapidly. I have heard some who said, " What's the use of rotting in prison ? The time of action will come when the people rise, but not before."

The social aims and national composition of the various political groupings was approximately as follows : the most numerous group, the Trotskyists, who could count on the sympathies of a large section of the Communist apparatus, consisted—in prison—of a majority of young Jewish intellectuals and technicians of petit-bourgeois origin, from the Jewish zone of the Ukraine and White Russia. There were also many Georgians and Armenians of peasant origin. Among the Trotskyists there was a strong group of former military men and Chekists, a fair number of whom were Russians.

The Russian and proletarian elements were relatively stronger in the group of ' democratic centralists ' (the Decists) ; they predominated in the Miasnikov workers' group. To judge by its members who began to arrive in prison from 1933 onwards, the Right-wing Opposition could be called purely Russian. Thus the two extreme wings of the Communist Opposition were Russian by nationality with the peculiarity (which has a symbolic value) that the Extreme Right-wing was much stronger than the Extreme Left-wing.

In the entire body of prisoners there were, according to the statistics drawn up by our ' Council of Elders ', a Communist body composed of 43 per cent Jews, 27 per cent Caucasians, the other 30 per cent consisting of Russians and a few other nationalities. The joke at Verkhne-Uralsk was that the Russians were nothing but a national minority. There is not a doubt that this situation, though very honourable for the Jewish, Georgian and Armenian peoples, constitutes a weak spot in the contemporary Opposition in Russia.

Most of the social democrats (Mensheviks) spring from the Bund, the former Jewish Workers' Party from before the War. One can say that the Right-wing Bundists have turned into social-democrats, the Left-wing Bundists into Trotskyists.

The main body of revolutionary-socialists and anarchists is composed of Russians.

ANOTHER HUNGER-STRIKE

On the 22nd of May, 1933, Deditch, Draguitch and myself were to be set free. Two months before we had sent a declaration to the Central Executive Committee and to the highest authorities of the G.P.U. in Moscow, in which we demanded that we be allowed to leave Russia after having served our sentences. In case of refusal, we wrote, our intention was to fight with every means at our disposal. All the prisoners supported our demand, and the 'elders' of the Communist group even sent an official telegram to Moscow. It was an act of solidarity on the part of our comrades, who moreover desired us to acquaint the world of workers abroad with the situation of political prisoners in Russia.

When the G.P.U. realized that the dispute was an organized one, it decided to remove us from Verkhne-Uralsk on a plausible pretext, which was done on the 18th of May, 1933. We were told that we were going to Moscow. The director of the prison told us that he believed it was 'in connection with discussions concerning your demands'. All the prisoners gave us their best wishes, wondering whether we were not merely to be transferred to another prison. Two cars took us away. Soon the one containing my two friends was lost in the dust that rose from the road. I never saw them again. I travelled all day. At night we stopped outside the political prison of Chelyabinsk. As soon as my name was entered in the books of the prison, I lodged a protest, declaring that I had been purposely separated from my comrades and that I considered this treatment as a refusal of my demand to leave the country and that I was immediately going to begin my hunger-strike. Dubnis, the prison director, answered that under those conditions he could not take me in charge and would have me sent back to Verkhne-Uralsk. I was put in a car and taken, not to Verkhne-Uralsk, but to a basement of the prison for criminals in civil law, in the charge of the police. My cell was cold, damp and dark. Even in the middle of the day electric light was needed. I was to spend two months in that cellar, without one minute's walk, sun or fresh air.

As soon as I arrived I went on hunger-strike. I knew that wherever they were, my comrades were doing the same, as this had been arranged between us. A special G.P.U. man was set to watch over me, for though I was in a prison for civil law cases, the G.P.U. had taken over the care of my person. I had already a certain practice in the matter of hunger-strikes. Half-undressed, rolled in a blanket, I remained stretched on my bench for days on end. The hours passed, long and monotonous.

On the tenth day after midnight—the G.P.U. likes to act

at night—a group of Cheka men entered my cell. Among them were Dubnis and a few local men, but also some old acquaintances : ' the Commission from Moscow ', citizen Andreeva, the woman, and citizen Popov. . . . The third member of the Commission, the prosecutor, had preferred to be absent. It was better that the affair should be dealt with in his absence, for it was too blatantly infringing all the laws of the land !

" Citizen Ciliga," Andreeva declared, " I have been instructed to communicate to you that both the ' College ' of the G.P.U. and the Central Executive Committee of the U.S.S.R. have refused to comply with your demand. By decision of the same ' College ', your detention will be prolonged by two years. The G.P.U. refuses to take your hunger-strike into account. From tomorrow onwards you will receive artificial feeding. The doctor has been instructed to that effect."

I answered with calculated coolness, " Hunger-strike and artificial feeding are henceforth matters of secondary importance. You want to make me your prisoner and slave for always. I have only one means of protest left, and I shall use it, namely, suicide. Let them know in the West what you are doing to foreign revolutionaries who refuse to become your slaves. I shall communicate my decision to Moscow."

" People who decide to commit suicide don't usually tell other people about it."

" My death would please you, provided you could not be held responsible for it. I am waging a political fight with you and you are responsible for anything that happens to me and to my comrades. That is what I have to tell Moscow : to make you responsible for my protest-suicide."

" We shall prevent you from killing yourself ! " Andreeva answered. " Two of our men will be left in your cell. Take his things away from him ! "

No sooner had she spoken than her orders were carried out. Nothing but a few indispensable objects were left me, but a brand-new blade that I had acquired at Verkhne-Uralsk was among them. I could therefore truthfully say to Andreeva, " There are no obstacles in the way of one who wishes to do away with his life."

Andreeva now began to use persuasion. " The Politbureau of the Yugo-Slav Communist Party has agreed to the prolonging of your sentence. I can show you their written statement."

"Don't bother! Your henchmen have no power over me, be they Russian or Yugo-Slav. I do not recognize the present Politbureau and I am no longer a member of your Communist Party."

On that, the Commission took its leave. The next day I sent a telegram to Moscow. The prison doctor was becoming anxious. "I am being held responsible for your life. Commit suicide or cease this hunger-strike, but do make up your mind."

Then four days later, on the fourteenth day of hunger-strike, Dubnis came into my cell. He announced the arrival of a telegram from Moscow. My two supplementary years in prison had been commuted to three years' exile at Irkutsk. Dubnis thought himself a good diplomat by explaining the difference to me, "Irkutsk is a large town; it isn't like Chelyabinsk; you will be in a better position there to solve the problem of your departure."

"Thank you," I answered. "I want to return to Europe at once and not go on a journey round the world to Irkutsk. But as they no longer talk of keeping me in prison, I am willing to drop my threat of suicide whilst continuing my hunger-strike."

I fasted another nine days. On the twenty-third day of my strike, Dubnis turned up again and produced another telegram calling me to Moscow. I demanded written proofs. These were procured and I ended my strike.

At the end of two weeks I was able to walk once more. I must say that Dubnis was feeding me very well, no doubt actuated by his 'international, revolutionary' conscience, but also by a wish to win me over. Moscow, however, was out of the question. I was told that there had been a typist's error, I had not been called to Moscow, but the possibility of this being done had been adumbrated. A few days later I was informed of the fact that there was no other choice for me than to go to Irkutsk.

I once more declared a hunger-strike. But, one night, a group of G.P.U. men burst into my cell. An order to transfer me by force was shown me. My trunks were packed, I was put in a car and taken to the Chelyabinsk railway station. Thus, on the 20th of July, I set out for Irkutsk with a strong guard.

What could I do? Nothing. Once I had regained my strength in exile, I might look for an occasion to take up the struggle once again. I ended my fast and began to take notice of my surroundings. This was the first time for three years that I had seen ' the world ' . . .

THE G.P.U. ATTEMPTS TO ' RUSSIFY ' ME

At last I arrived in Irkutsk, with its dirty roads and its low, wooden houses, and was taken to the central prison of the town. It was a huge ancient building, built on a vast scale, yet too small to cope with the needs of the Five Year Plan. Its two thousand or two thousand five hundred prisoners were three or four times the maximum number provided for in Czarist days. I spent six weeks there, waiting for the G.P.U. to decide on the place of my exile.

The prison was a sort of barracks where the prisoners of the whole province were concentrated, to await their transfer to the innumerable concentration camps of Transbaikalia and the Far East. Every week from two to three hundred people, sometimes as many as six hundred, were sent eastward. The frontier fortifications, the new railway lines, the car-roads, the Northern colonization, all were the work of this vast slave-population.

All classes, all social groups were represented : peasants, office-workers including those belonging to the Party, soldiers, manual labourers, former aristocrats, engineers, bandits and thieves. There were wards reserved for those who had been condemned to death. They contained from sixty to eighty prisoners. Half of them would be shot, the others pardoned after keeping them in the torture of uncertainty from four to six weeks. Their reprieve was commuted to ten years' concentration camp. There were many women and children, even infants in arms.

There was hardly any food in that prison, but the prisoners considered themselves fortunate, during the 1933 summer, now that the desperate famine of the previous winter was over. Only from seven to ten prisoners a day were dying instead of the average of forty in February. There were still some survivors of that atrocious winter ; they looked like shrivelled skeletons and were slowly dying.

In this prison, as in all Soviet prisons in civil law, one could communicate with people outside prison and also more freely inside, than one could in political prisons. The contrast was so striking that, from the moment of my arrival at Irkutsk, I had the illusion of freedom.

In spite of hunger and overcrowding, the prison was a beehive of activity : courses, lectures and propaganda. The illiterate were taught the alphabet ; courses in mathematics, geography, physics and so on were organized for those who had a modicum of instruction. There were orchestras and a theatre, the musicians and actors being recruited from among the prisoners. Films were shown. The prison library provided books and newspapers for every cell. I was asked to give a course of Latin classes to the infirmary staff. The young people followed all these classes with avidity and showed no despair at all. All that mattered was to survive. After that one would be all right ! What struck me most, after what I had seen in the Leningrad prison, in 1930, was that here prisoners were not afraid to speak up. Nothing was said directly against the Government, but about life in freedom and in prison there were no reticences. Terror itself had ceased to impress.

At the beginning of September I was sent on to Yeniseisk. It was frightening : having started from the shores of the Adriatic, I was to go to the Arctic regions ! At Krasnoyarsk my journey was suddenly interrupted by my falling seriously ill. The doctors diagnosed several simultaneous complaints : anaemia, rheumatism, sciatica and a few others. Not in vain does one spend years in prisons and cellars. I was left at Krasnoyarsk to be nursed.

Hardly had I recovered, when the local colony of exiles had a conflict with the G.P.U. over the bad treatment that a sick exile had received. The classical remedy, the hunger-strike, was applied, and out of solidarity I joined in. It was not easy after all I had just suffered. At the end of ten days a compromise was reached. The G.P.U. promised not to carry out any reprisals, but it avenged itself all the same by immediately transferring to more Northern stations a number of sick strikers who had been granted permission to stay until summer and to go to their destination by way of the river. The vengeance consisted in sending them off at once, by sledge, which was a very painful mode of transport. I was among those ordered to go, and protested to the G.P.U., for there was no means of recuperating at Yeniseisk. Upon my categorical refusal to leave, the G.P.U. official shouted at me, " We shall see who has the last word ! "

" Indeed we shall ! " I answered.

I was sent back into the hall before they attempted to put me on a sledge by main force. There was no hesitating now. I drew forth my precious blade and cut the veins of both my wrists. But some people, happening to come by, gave the alarm ; in a few moments I was surrounded by officials who tried to bandage my wrists. I resisted as much as I could, but I was soon overpowered and taken to the hospital, where, in spite of my desperate efforts, my wounds were closed. I once more began to fast and refused to enter into negotiations with the G.P.U. After a few days I was told that I would be kept at Krasnoyarsk, that I would be placed in an ordinary civilian hospital and would be given a chance to work. I decided, not without hesitation, to accept this proposal and to put off the decisive struggle for my departure abroad.

After about two months I was progressing so well that I was able to begin work. I was given a post as economist at the Prombank (Industrial bank). I familiarized myself with the technique of industrialization, and, with an interest increased tenfold by my years in prison, I began to watch an aspect, new to me, of the life of an immense area inside Russia.

Later, at Yeniseisk, when I worked at the forestry trust ' Sevpolarlies ', I was struck by two facts, the one social, the other economic. On the one hand, the Communist and non-Party bureaucrats were closely allied in fact and in law ; there existed, between them and the workers, a veritable moral and material barrier. On the other hand, the economic processes of production and development astonished me greatly. I was able to measure the immense practical difficulties Soviet economy had to conquer. It seemed at any moment as if the development were coming to a standstill, as if production itself were going to cease ; the shortage of raw materials and capital was permanent. Yet, in spite of all these obstacles, development was taking place, though often in a way which in no way corresponded with the Plan.

Six months passed. I was in perfect health once more. In the early summer the G.P.U. decided to act yet again. On June 3rd I was told that I was to leave for Yeniseisk by first boat. Yeniseisk ! Had I not received the formal promise that I should not be exiled to a more Northern spot than Krasnoyarsk ? I used the last legal means at my disposal : I applied to the Italian Embassy, asking for a passport.

Here I must explain that although Yugo-Slav by nationality, I was born in one of the provinces of Austro-Hungary that had fallen into the hands of Italy. Therefore, since 1918 I was officially an Italian subject, and whilst I worked at the Comintern in Vienna, I had taken out an Italian passport. I had a few scruples to overcome before I applied to the Italian Consul, although this country had just signed a treaty of ' amity and neutrality ' with the U.S.S.R. But in the end, I decided that, if I had been able to avail myself of a passport of Fascist Italy in the days when I had not yet broken with the Comintern, there was no reason why I should not again do so now, provided the passport was given me unconditionally. On June 7th I sent a telegram to the Italian Embassy in Moscow : " Italian subject Anton Ciliga requests passport to leave the U.S.S.R." On November 1st I received my papers from the Embassy, entirely unconditionally.

The G.P.U. had not foreseen this. It had hoped that I should obtain it with conditions that would compromise me from the political point of view. These hopes dashed, the G.P.U. was not long in interfering. It first tried to circumvent me : it proposed that I should buy my departure by signing a declaration in favour of Stalin's policy ; next, it was suggested that I should ask for permission to give up my Soviet citizenship, a quality I had never possessed, nor asked to possess ! Obviously I refused. The G.P.U. then asked the Italian Embassy to withdraw my passport and to deprive me—retrospectively—of my Italian citizenship. The Embassy, though refusing the second point, consented to concel my passport and thus enabled the G.P.U. to hold me in Siberia.

On the pretext that my passport wanted a visa, the G.P.U. took it from me and returned it to the Embassy. As for me, I was arrested and sent off to Yeniseisk, some 250 miles north of Krasnoyarsk.

Winter had come. The journey in sledges lasted five days through the boundless snow of the *taiga*. I felt as if we were traversing the interstellar regions. We drew up at rare villages lost in the midst of the immense icy waste. These villages gave one the impression that the system of *kolkhosi* was now more or less functioning. The peasants no longer believed in themselves and considered that only a war in which the U.S.S.R. would be beaten could bring a change. We also drew up at a MTS (Machine and Tractor Station), which loomed over the peasant dwellings like a mighty fortress.

Winter at Yeniseisk was horrible. A leaden, unbroken sky was stifling me. The intensive winter cold that lasted seven months almost robbed me of the wish to live. I had no exotic appreciation of the Arctic. My teeth and gums were painful and I noticed the first symptoms of scurvy. The North was killing me. What finally depressed me was that my relatives abroad were unaware of the situation ; some were advising me, in view of the reaction and unemployment prevailing in Europe, to ' come to some sort of agreement with my comrades in Russia ' ; others thought they were being helpful by sending a letter direct to Stalin begging him to allow me to return home !

During May, 1935, the G.P.U. prepared another surprise for me : my exile at Yeniseisk was prolonged by another three years.

" What have I done to deserve this prolongation of my sentence ? " I asked the chief of the G.P.U. at Yeniseisk.

" I know nothing of it. I was not present at the meeting of the Moscow ' College ' at which the decision was taken. Anyhow, the G.P.U. are not supposed to account for their actions."

But one of my comrades in exile showed himself a greater philosopher, " You are lucky, Ciliga ! You are left at Yeniseisk ! I was convinced that you were going to be sent higher north to punish you for your pig-headness."

FAREWELL, RUSSIA !

THE situation seemed hopeless. I was advised to resign myself until better days should come. Sometimes I felt inclined to agree with my advisers. But I could not subdue my indignation against this Government that pretended to champion the oppressed and yet was keeping millions of people in slavery. In any case, could I stand another winter ?

I decided upon a final effort. I must leave, at all costs, or end my life. I wrote a violent protest against my new sentence to Vyshinsky, the Public Prosecutor of the U.S.S.R. This protest, I considered, would force them to get rid of me, either by killing me or by telling me to go. The executions of Communists had not yet become a common practice, and I had a chance of escape. In my protest I refrained from giving the arguments of Stalin's Right-wing opponents. I also sent a copy of this document to the Italian Embassy in Moscow. At a later date I was to learn that this latter document never reached its destination.

My letter based its arguments on a decision of the Council of People's Commissars and the Central Executive Committee of the U.S.S.R. of November 5th, 1934, by which the function of the G.P.U. had been clearly defined. Section 4 of this decision stipulated that the G.P.U. could apply only one single sanction to foreign subjects : ' to deport them beyond the borders of the U.S.S.R.' I was therefore able to state that in my case the G.P.U. was violating the laws of its own country.

Once my protest had been written and sent off, I waited. What would happen ? Would I be allowed to go, would I be sent farther north ? Was I to rot where I was ? What was I to do in such a case ? Fly ? I spent two anxious months.

Suddenly, on the 31st of August, I was told to leave by river for Krasnoyarsk.

" What is the matter ? "

" You will be told there."

More than a hundred comrades in exile, belonging to all Parties, saw me off to the boat. It was both sad and joyful at the same time. I was torn between hope and fear.

The voyage on the Yenisei lasted five days. There were stops at small river stations, lost on the edge of the majestic forests. Everywhere was an atmosphere of poverty, yet there was also the air of power, the breath of a growing giant. I saw a new continent opening to life.

At last I arrived at the Krasnoyarsk G.P.U. " In accordance with a decision of the ' College ' of the G.P.U., you will be "—I held my breath—" deported beyond the borders of the U.S.S.R." I was saved. But I had not recovered from this information before I received a new shock.

" The date of your departure will be communicated to you at a later date."

" In ten years' time ? " I joked, with sinking heart.

" No, no, you will leave in a few days' time, but there are still a few details to be settled."

I spent two months there, suspended between heaven and earth.

Krasnoyarsk had changed somewhat since the previous year. The entire country was rapidly changing. Soviet Russia is animated with a dynamism unknown in Europe. In nine years I had known three distinct Russias : the land of the NEP, the land of the Five Year Plan, and that of State capitalism, or, as it is called nowadays, of the ' life in joy and comfort '. Such a country, whatever may happen to it, will not go under.

I took my leave from this land with its multiple face, that put so many an anxious enigma to the world. It is a land of youth and strength. The cruelty of its power is compensated at the other pole of the social life by warm cordiality that makes up for all suffering.

The last recommendations, given me by my acquaintances, simple working people, were twofold.

" Anton Antonovitch, when you are back in Europe, tell the truth, and tell all you know of the life of the people. Do not tell lies as do the writers who, after having been here, and having seen everything, go back to write nothing but praise ! "

Others said, " Be careful when you are across the border ; ' their ' secret agents might gently push you out of the train ! "

*   *   *

On November 26th the G.P.U. announced to me the date of my departure and arrested me by way of farewell. I spent my last night in prison. On December 3rd an escort of G.P.U. men conducted me across the border.

I left behind me the hardest years, yet the richest in experience and emotion, of my life.

PART TWO

SIBERIA:

LAND OF EXILE,
LAND OF INDUSTRIALIZATION

HOW STALIN HAS BECOME THE PRINCIPAL REPRESENTATIVE OF RUSSIAN NEO-IMPERIALISM

IN PLACE OF A FOREWORD

The Russian Revolution took place in two waves. The first, from 1917 to 1921, realized the partition of the large landed estates and the confiscation by the State of Russia's feeble industrial plant. Workers and socialist tendencies were suppressed in favour of bureaucratic dictatorship and State capitalism.

The second wave, from 1928 to 1933, under the unchallenged domination of the bureaucracy, manifested itself in the forced industrialization of the country and the stratification of the agricultural sector, modernised in its turn.

My book, *The Russian Enigma**, was devoted to an analysis of the second wave and an explanation of its organic connection with the first.

These two waves, from 1917 to 1933 (eliminating the transitional period of NEP from 1921 to 1928) created Soviet society as we have known it from 1933 until today.

This is the subject of the present book.

Of the ten years spent by the author in Russia, the three last belong to this contemporary phase. The Second World War, which has played a capital role in Soviet external expansionist policy, has brought no essential change in the social and political structure of the country.

This book was written between 1938 and 1941. Begun before the war, it was finished under the German occupation (the end of the last chapter carries the date 21 August 1941). Those were the days of the triumphal march of the Germans into Russia. But the reader will find no echo here of the menace of Hitler's *Greater Reich* to Russia and to the world. For that Greater Germany full of horrors was in my eyes no more than a vast bubble of soap that, although filled with poisonous gases, was doomed to vanish into nothingness. Its doom was as

*See copyright page at the start of the book. We have retained the title of what was the first volume of a two volume book for this edition of the book in its entirety.

321

inevitable as it was imminent. From my perspective I saw Germany already prostrate in the dust under the heel of the conquerors.

On the other hand, the great expansion of Russia and her direct threat to Europe were profoundly felt and presented in my book. Today these prognostications may appear as prophetic as they were unbelievable in December 1935 and even in August 1941. I must, however, recognize that I did not think the menace and amplitude of Russian expansion would be so immediate. I did not anticipate that the situation in 1945 and now would arise for another twenty years, and even then I thought it would affect Europe alone.

In my presentiments faithfully recorded in the following pages there was, however, another and much more important error of judgement. It would have been a simple matter to suppress or modify this passage before the present publication of this book. But I had no desire to change a single word, although I have eliminated various passages devoted to details of daily life that have been out-dated by the passage of time. I have not cut the particular passage in question because it is not simply an individual error and because of the problem that follows from it.

Confronted with the German advance of 1941, I expressed once more in my book the opinion I came to concerning the Russia of 1935, published in 1938: "Such a land, whatever may happen, will not perish."

The country, but not Stalin, I thought.

I assumed and I wrote that Stalin and the top layers of the Bolshevik Party, who had behind them the horrors of the Five Year Plan and the desperate discontent of the entire Russian working people, would not be capable of assuring national defence and victory over Germany. My opinion was that the war, and the defeats already suffered and still to come, would overthrow the power of this group by opening the way to the Soviet army leaders. I assumed that the establishment of a national military dictatorship was inevitable, and that it would be this new government that would lead the war to final victory over Germany. (The aims of Hitler's war against Russia did not in my opinion permit a separate compromise peace.)

I was convinced that the Stalin regime "is absolutely incapable of undertaking a large-scale offensive ... it is incapable of conducting even a defensive war of long duration".

This, then, is the question that is posed in a different form to the whole world: how did this miracle happen? Why did the

Russian people, terrorized and martyrized by Stalin and his regime, and mortally hating them, yet support them in war and permit them to remain so strongly entrenched after it?

Stalin's apologists advance the following argument: "This support proves that the Russian people are happy and love Stalin and his regime." This is totally false. The testimony of hundreds of thousands of Russian DPs proved it to the entire world, and my own eyes and ears constantly gave me evidence against the Stalinist argument during all the time I was in Russia.

The second argument: "The Russian people are born slaves, they support and admire their tyrant, their Red or White Tsar", is no less false. This people, slaves during certain periods, have been great rebels in others. The problem then arises: why did they consent in the critical phase between 1941 and 1943 to be slaves and not rebels as in the winter of 1916—17?

The 'fault' is Hitler's, says the third argument. According to the most widely held opinion of Russian emigres and foreigners, it was the abject treatment of Soviet subjects by Hitler and Rosenberg that compelled the people to rally to Stalin. At the beginning of the war the Russian soldiers allowed themselves to be taken prisoner in hundreds of thousands and millions, but after the horrors of their 'welcome' by the Germans, what could they do? This argument has its weight without any doubt, but it is not decisive. It contains part of the truth, but not the most important part.

When a people confronted by an implacable enemy sees itself delivered over to an evil government, which it hates with all its heart—and such was the situation with regard to Stalin and his government in 1941—42—it is by no means obliged to rally to it. It may take advantage of the situation, make use of the difficulties of the government in order to overthrow it and, under a new regime, wage implacable war against the external enemy. The history of all countries, including Russia, offers many examples of such action.

Stalin was well aware of the danger. His famous toast on 24 May 1945, after the victory: "Thanks to the Russian people who were patient, who did not disown us at the difficult moment", testifies, with Stalin's characteristic humour, to his real fear during the years 1941 and 1942.

The Hitler terror might well have prevented Red Army soldiers from giving themselves up as prisoners, but it could not have prevented them from getting rid of Stalin and the

G.P.U. when the Germans were marching on Moscow, on Stalingrad, on Leningrad.

That was exactly how the question was posed, whether in the Politbureau, the Government or in the Army. On this critical moment in the German-Soviet war there exists in the West a great many reliable witnesses. I will quote one of the latest—Lt.-Col. K.D. Kalinov, a wartime member of the Soviet General Staff who fled to West Berlin after the war. He writes on this subject in his memoirs: ". . . the main thing, in the consciousness of the Politbureau, was that the three great forward sectors (of the Western Front) had been seriously broken. The Politbureau feared that the concentration of troops in great masses might serve the schemes of a possible Bonaparte, and frequently referred to the example of General Russky, the Commander of the North-East front during the First World War who, with his troops, had forced the Tsar to abdicate. 'We do not want another Russky', Voroshilov declared one day to the Generals of the Supreme War Council." (*Le Figaro Litteraire*, no. 185, 5 November 1949.)

The question of a Soviet Bonaparte was thus openly posed in the upper circles of the Politbureau and the Army. In a broad instinctive manner it was no doubt also posed throughout the Army and the country. The supercession after the war of the victorious marshals, with Zhukov at their head, is an irrefutable proof that everyone can appreciate of the existence of profound antagonism between the Politbureau and the Generals. That circumstance once more confirms the soundness of the analysis of the ruling class given in this book. That class contains four basic groups: the Party, the Army, the non-Communist intelligentsia, and the Church; the Politbureau and the Generals being the most active and direct rivals.

But why, in that rivalry that was doubtless very fierce at times, did Stalin and his Politbureau emerge victorious and not the army generals and marshals? What was the 'imponderable' that decided the issue? For, from all the evidence, the question was on the order of the day.

The principal reason for the victory of the Politbureau in that struggle must be sought in the birth of Russian neo-imperialism, in the way it established itself in the contemporary world.

Stalin said, or hinted, to the Russian soliders and people: "You are not only going to defend Russia from German pillage, but you are going to pillage the homes of the Germans. All the German goods will belong to you, all the women of Germany and of Berlin will be yours"—and he kept his word.

Stalin said to the generals and the non-Communist intelligentsia: "We shall not let the Germans make the Ukraine their agrarian colony, but on the contrary we shall make industrial Germany our colony; we shall transport German industry to Russia and that which remains in Germany will work for us. We shall make of Germany a vassal State and we shall create a magnificent German army to serve us. Free Germany shall be our Germany. Von Paulus, our enemy at Stalingrad, is already under our orders. Wtih the Russian army and command at the centre, with the German army in the West and another Sino-Japanese army in the East, with the workers of the West as our allies behind the front, we shall enter upon the inevitable Third World War against the West for the conquest of the world. Between our socialism and their capitalism there can be a provisional but never a lasting peace. To secure that it is necessary that the world be transformed in our image and under our leadership."

One must recognize that Stalin has also kept that promise—by partly realizing it and partly preparing it in the future.

What alternative programme could the Soviet generals counterpose to the imperialist designs of Stalin? What were their possibilities? Could they counterpose a more imperialist plan? Assuredly not. Could they counterpose an anti-imperialist programme calling for a truly democratic social union of the peoples of the world? Even less.

So all that was left to them was a programme of more restrained imperialism and nationalism. But, among imperialisms, universal imperialism is—in our 'One World' age—more realistic than the 'provincial' imperialism of the division of the world, characteristic of the nineteenth century, of the pre-1914 epoch. Faced with the choice between these two imperialisms, the Russian soldier and the Russian people gave preference to Stalin's more dynamic and more realistic one.

In the soul of the Russian people there are two very distinct sentiments: one, hidden in the depths, is that of rancour against the advanced, proud, rich and senile West on which they look:

> . . . with avaricious eyes
> like those of the Vandals and the Goths,
> the day they came upon Rome,

as Blok, the great national and revolutionary poet, said in January 1918, shortly after the October Revolution.

The other sentiment, less veiled and even apparent on the surface, is of hatred against Stalin and the Communists.

In noting these two sentiments I imagined in 1935, and still in 1941, that the latter—the feeling of rancour against Stalin and the Communists—would prevail in the current phase, and that the rancour against the West would only come uppermost in the succeeding phase under the leadership of a post-Stalin and perhaps a post-Communist Government.

But Stalin, by appealing to the instincts of rancour against the West, to imperialist urge and the desire for loot, and by simultaneously unleashing a ruthless terror against all opponents, was successful in relegating to second place the hatred he inspired in the breasts of the people. By these means Stalin and the Communist Party succeeded in maintaining the leadership in the national war and the subsequent neo-imperialist expansion. There was nothing left for the generals to do except resign themselves.

Although rivalries and antagonisms undoubtedly continue to exist, neither the generals nor anyone else among the new masters sees any immediate chance of wresting the government of Russia from the hands of Stalin and the Politbureau. Only a Stalinist and Communist Government can today assure the functioning of the immense fifth columns in existence in all parts of the world. And it is precisely in the nationalist and imperialist interests of Russia to preserve those fifth columns. Difficulties facing the ruling class now find expression in the heart of the Politbureau and not in tension between the generals and that body.

This strengthening of Stalin and the Politbureau, this elimination of any immediate possibility of a nationalist government more to the right than that of Stalin, has however a positive result. It opens the way to the possibility of the creation in the immediate future of a popular, left-democratic, internationalist opposition, the birth of which appeared to be relegated to the distant future. There is a more than adequate basis for its foundation, and it will open up quite fresh perspectives to humanity.

To orientate oneself towards a Soviet opposition from below—the workers and the kolkhozniki—instead of looking to combinations and antagonisms in high places—this is the real and urgent issue.

The fact that the sovereign and separate national State has outlived its time, that world union is on the order of the day—whether that union be imperialist or fraternal and egalitarian—

that fact paralyses the anti-Stalinist generals, but it invites the Russian people to act. The catastrophic menace of atomic war, which will spare no country, which will safeguard no country, is a strong reason for the Russian people to have done with imperialism, to repress the desire for pillage and conquest so assiduously fostered by the regime.

That applies equally, on the international plane, to the other peoples of the East and the West.

It is not in the name of any imperialism, any Western egoism; it is not in trying to make Russia another Germany and Magnitorsk a second Ruhr, that Stalin and Soviet imperialism can be effectively fought, and the peoples of Russia and Asia and the workers of the West detached from their allegiance to it. That can only be done by demanding, on the contrary, world union on the basis of the brotherhood and equality of all peoples, of universal social solidarity, of the liquidation of all imperialism—and not only demanding it, but realizing it.

Paris, December 1949   *Ante Ciliga*

I

FROM THE URALS TO THE PACIFIC

It was by accident and against my will that I came to know Siberia.

"Citizen Ciliga, you are leaving immediately for Irkutsk. This is an order of the G.P.U. and it will be executed whether you agree to it or not."

No sooner had the Governor of the Prison pronounced these words than four G.P.U. men burst into the cell. It was nearing five o'clock in the morning. I was lying on my bunk, half undressed, hunger-striking. Silently, with a stony politeness, the G.P.U. men immediately began to carry my things out to the car waiting in front of the prison gates. Without a word I rose, dressed, gathered together my few remaining trifles, including the little box of dried oatmeal in which a razor blade lay hidden. Not for shaving . . .

Five minutes later I was in the car with my G.P.U. escort and speeding towards Cheliabinsk station. Cheliabinsk is situated on the eastern slope of the Ural mountain chain, near the frontier dividing Europe from Asia. The hands of the station clock stood at 3.10 Moscow time, which is standard throughout the U.S.S.R. railway system. The two hour difference from local time reminded me sharply of how far away from Moscow I was. And in Irkutsk this difference in time, proportionate to the 5,339 kilometres [3,337 miles, *Ed.*] distance from Moscow, would be fully five hours! How many thousands of kilometres separated me then from everything for which my soul yearned—from Vienna, from Yugoslavia, from my native village in Istria on the shores of the azure Adriatic!

Thus was my fate decided. My hunger strike, my threat of suicide, instead of achieving my return to Europe, had won me merely release from prison—and exile to Siberia.

What must I do? Bow quietly to fate? Take what I had gained and regard it simply as the first stage in the struggle? End my hunger-strike and try from the depths of Siberia to contact my relatives in Europe . . .? Or here and now end it all with the blade?

Only a few minutes in which to decide.

But here I was after three years of prison, of the strictest isolation from society, from life, and now once more I was coming into contact with the world of men and with nature. The sun smiled a welcome in the East. Why hesitate? Why lose this chance of seeing Russia after her great and terrible re-moulding? Of observing with my own eyes the results of the Five Year Plan, at whose launching three to four years ago I had been so deeply stirred? Let me immerse myself once more in this mysterious land, this heroic step-child of contemporary humanity. Time enough later to think of escape ... or death ...

I decided to stop my hunger-strike and began to gaze avidly at everything about me. In one day I forgot weeks of self-imposed hunger and years of prison. On to Siberia!

The train was packed full to overflowing; the station crowded with pale-faced, emaciated, poorly-clad people. Not a single good-looking, cheerful face among them. Was this the impress of the Five Year Plan?

From Cheliabinsk we rolled eastwards through the boundless West-Siberian Plain. It was a four-day journey to Irkutsk. It was July and summer was at its height. In the fields stood combine-harvesters, threshing machines, sheaves of grain, huge stacks of harvested wheat; then a landscape covered with the stunted trees typical of that part of the country sped past. Siberia welcomed me in her most attractive dress: in summer she resembles the countryside of Central Europe. The immensity of field and steppe seemed to be awaiting only the machine for transformation into a new America. At that moment I was inclined to view the results of the Five Year Plan optimistically. The vastness of Siberia completely conquered me. I was bewitched by its very immensity that had somehow to be grasped, comprehended. "From the Urals to the Pacific", said the guide-book and map that I had bought at the railway station. The title itself was a challenge. Enthusiastically, as though now realizing a long-cherished dream, I plunged into the study of this land.

Siberia! One and a half times the size of Europe East and West; thirty times as large as France; each of its four great rivers 3,500 kilometres in length! Yesterday I was hardly sure of their names or where they ran—tomorrow I should be near them. And the railway line upon which I was travelling—

Moscow-Vladivostock—is nine and a half thousand kilometres long. Compare that with the celebrated New York-San Francisco line's six thousand kilometres cutting across the entire North American continent!

Of this enormous distance I was, within the next few days, to cover only the 3,273 kilometres separating Irkutsk from Cheliabinsk. What a pity that I had not been sent to the Far East! To be on the Pacific Ocean, in Kamchatka, in the Arctic, on the Lapland Islands, on the river Indigirka; to peer into all those remote corners of the globe where at that very moment the 'Conquest of the North', policy, singularly reminiscent of the opening-up of America, gripped everyone in its feverish turmoil.

Yesterday I was ready to threaten suicide in order to force my return to Europe. And today, no longer having this possibility, I am complaining at being sent only to Central Siberia and not to its farthest outposts! Already I am ceasing to regret that the G.P.U. has exiled me to Siberia and not to Central Asia, although on my way from the prison to the station it was the thought of Siberia that made me despair. If it be exile, I thought, then let it be Central Asia with its scorching sun, its motley southern colours, its luscious fruits. To be in the Samarkand of Tamerlaine, in the Bactria of Alexander of Macedon, to trace the desert paths along which Marco Polo had passed on his way from Venice to Peking; to see all those Parthians, Persians, and Uzbeks whose ways of life had so enthralled me in my youth; there on the very spot to investigate the traces of the empire that still fascinated historians, the empire of Genghis Khan ... I had found it infuriating that instead of the splendour of this oriental tale I was to face, thanks to a caprice of the G.P.U., the savage, frozen lifelessness of Siberia. The very word made me shudder. Yet here I was in Siberia, and it was—at any rate for the moment—a sunny, smiling land. Not till later was I to become familiar with its terrible winter ... Turning these thoughts over and over in my mind for the hundredth time, exhausted by the emotions of the last few nights, it was not long before I fell asleep.

The sway and clatter of the train and the clamour of conversation awoke me. It might have been nine in the morning. The train was descending the Ural mountain range, crossing a wooded landscape to the Siberian plain. There was a promise of a fine cloudless summer day. Colour bathed the world, colour my eyes had not beheld in years—green. Now not only the sun smiled at me through the carriage windows, but the foliage also, gay and dancing. The train slowed, stopped. In the midst of the all-embracing green appeared a neat little house, an isolated signal station. It was built of wood, with decorations and carving in the traditional Russian style. How did this charming little house, with its air of calm peace, come to be here, in this land where for sixteen years the Revolution had raged, overturning everything? It seemed a part of the green wood whose arms embraced it tenderly. After the damp, sad, grey walls of the prison this was the fairy-tale cottage found by the two little children lost in the forest. And all around was fairy-like too: the bare-footed, merry children and the country-costumed peasant women who had taken up their stand on the clean path alongside the station and were displaying for sale pats of fresh butter wrapped in cabbage leaves, roasted chickens and game. Against the glorious background, how close, how intimate a contact with nature this scene expressed.

The passengers, the G.P.U. guards and I left the train and strolled around, buying what we could afford of these rare delicacies. We brought boiling water back with us and when the train started began breakfast. My four guards and I shared our provisions, offering what we had around the compartment. I was allowed to move freely in the carriage and even to leave it at the stations, but I was closely guarded, two of my escort following me everywhere like shadows. At times this became almost comic. Even when I go to the water-closet I am followed. I want to shut the door, but no, the two enter with me. "Look here, how can I get away? I can scarcely jump out of the window!" "Those are our orders. We can't leave you for a single minute. We are personally responsible for you."

Towards evening we approached the fertile grain region of Omsk. Animated chatter among the passengers: we were coming to a station where bread was sold on the free market. White bread? On the free market? In the Russia of 1933 a miracle indeed. At the station itself, set in the midst of the steppe, peasant women competed for business, offering fresh flat loaves at 20 roubles apiece; but, taking the advice of one of the passengers, who assured me that at the next station bread would be far cheaper, I resisted the temptation. And so it proved to be: at the next stop the price of a magnificent white loaf weighing one kilogramme (2.2 lb) was only ten roubles. I sacrificed a tenth of the 120 roubles I had on this then extremely rare luxury.

During the night the train suddenly came to a halt in the middle of the steppe. Out of the darkness came excited cries of "Accident!". Panic! People started jumping from the carriages. However, it did not take long to find out what the trouble was. It was not our train that had suffered but a goods train ahead, one that had been delaying us all day. While the line was being cleared of wreckage, and the twisted metal and broken sleepers piled alongside the embankment, I took a look around. The monotonous sweep of the steppe was broken here and there by the bell-like tents of the nomad Kirghis. By administrative decree this part of Kirghisia, near Omsk, had been incorporated into Western Siberia, but the enslaved descendants of Genghis Khan continued to regard this as part of their homeland and to roam it with their herds. Their camels vividly recalled other lands, other cultures, even another age. But how miserably poor now were these descendants of the great conqueror—or poor as wandering gypsies. What a caricature of the splendid pageant of the East their shabby clothes, a patchwork of city shoddy and homespun rags! What melancholy irony that the new culture should here be represented in the cheap city-made brooches pinned on the dresses of the young Kirghis belles who came to look at the train!

The next day I went through the papers carefully to find an account of the accident, as it could hardly have been without casualties. Not a word . . .

However, we were rewarded a hundred-fold for the shock and the broken night's rest: for at the next station a white loaf cost only five roubles, and milk and vegetables were also to be had. The kingdom of bread, alas, lasted but a day or a day and a half. Approaching Novosibirsk we were already entering upon the majestic but hungry kingdom of industry. From afar the skeletons of half-constructed buildings drew our attention. The foundations of Novosibirsk had been laid as late as 1893, during the construction of the Siberian Railway. It had grown so rapidly that within two years it had acquired the nick-name: 'The Chicago of Siberia'. After the Revolution it became the centre of Western Siberia. With the Five Year Plan it grew miraculously, in step with the huge coal and metal region, the Kuznetsk Basin, encircling it.

Observe the rhythm of growth of this Siberian Chicago. In 1893 the first few houses; in 1911 a population of 64,000; in 1926—120,000; in 1939—406,000: the largest town in Siberia.

Nearing it now across the mighty river Ob, the town looks from a distance as if a recent and disastrous earthquake has hit it. All its houses seem half destroyed. In fact, however, the entire town is caught up in a feverish construction boom—the bustling, lusty scene of Roerich's painting, 'Building a Town', is here brought to life. Stacked timber, gashed earth, everywhere heaps of sand and cement, the stark walls rearing up; machines, men, shouting, thud, clangour, rattle and ring of metal; everywhere a jumble, an apparent chaos and confusion; over all an unbelievable tension. At the Novosibirsk station throngs of people milling to and fro, their faces strained. Workers seeking jobs or leaving to find something better, travelling with their families and all they possess. The shouting of the men mingles with the anxious voices of the women, the crying of children. A fierce fight for seats in the train, for 'a place in the sun'. In startling contrast with this agitated human ant-hill, a few well-dressed men and women—leather coats, suit-cases, silk scarves—more with leisurely unconcern towards the carriages with reserved seats.

* * *

No matter what surprises the majestic and treacherous Siberian land might have in store for me, I had gained one impression that would never be effaced. Having traversed this enormous, marvellously fertile, West Siberian plain, this Siberian Ukraine, and pondered over the connecting links uniting the Urals (Magnitogorsk, Cheliabinsk, Sverdlovsk) and Siberia itself (the Kusnetsk Basin, Novosibirsk), my former conception of Siberia as an icy, desert waste was gone forever. No, from every cranny, from every pore of the earth gushed forth a fecund and impetuous life; it forced its way through, not from immediately beneath a thin layer of soil, but from some inexhaustible reservoir of treasure in the deep heart of the land. At every point two torrential streams of energy intermingled: above, man's feverish activity transforming the face of the land in a furious constructive effort; and, welling up from below, from the very womb of the earth, an elemental power re-moulding entire zones of a virgin continent. And all that I saw and experienced later in the course of two and a half years in Siberia only strengthened this first impression.

Our train moved on slowly, with many halts to make way for opposing traffic or to let train-loads of Red Army units pass: artillery, cavalry, tanks, and airplane parts *en route* for the Far East. A whole year had gone by already since the Japanese invasion of Manchuria and intensive military movements all along the line from Novosibirsk to Irkutsk bore tacit witness to the degree of tension on the Soviet-Manchurian frontier.

At one of the main stations, I think it was Omsk, we stopped not far from a goods train loaded with peasants, 'ex-kulaks' on their way to Siberian deportation. Through the half-opened doors of the trucks the peasants looked like cattle doomed to slaughter. A cordon of Red Army men stood guard over them, allowing no one to approach. Yet the peasants somehow managed to exchange a word or two with the crowd of onlookers, one or two of whom, thanks to the tolerance of the guards, even managed to throw across the odd hunk of bread, and bottle of water.

In Novosibirsk this heart-rending picture of the people's lives was temporarily forgotten as a motley crowd of students came storming into a carriage. Mostly twenty-year-old youths, but with here and there one of forty or so, they were all students of the Krasnoyarsk Forestry Institute returning from a course. My escort quickly made friends with the newcomers, and we were all soon at ease, chatting quite freely and offering one another food. Even drinks appeared. The new arrivals appeared to regard me as on a level with my escort and not at all as a prisoner. The conversation went over from general topics to politics, and—although superficially—we discussed Lenin, Trotsky, Stalin, collectivization, industrialization—all those matters in which officialdom was at that time keenly interested. Then the students started to sing. The latest numbers intermingled with traditional revolutionary songs. I asked them to sing that one about the Volga, which had seen "So much of the sorrow of the people":

> *Volga, Volga, in the spring o'erflowing,*
> *Not so deep on our fields*
> *As the people's sorrow*
> *That drowns our land.*

"Why that song?" one of the students demanded, half-challengingly.

"Well, it seems to me so very characteristically Russian; really of the people," I replied.

"Ah, down with this intellectual rubbish," protested the student. "That's a thing of the past. Russia is now accomplishing miracles; the time of sorrow and lamentation is past and gone. Just wait a bit—the sixth will trump the lot," he boasted, hinting that Russia, one-sixth of the world, would soon become a first-rate Power. Then, as though to substantiate his optimism, he went on to speak of himself: "Look at me, for example. I'm thirty-six and for several years now I've been sitting at a desk like a schoolboy. I used to be a carpenter, but in a year from now I'll be a forestry expert. I'm just writing my thesis; not a bad one either."

Behind Novosibirsk, like a fairy palace set in the midst of the jungle, we saw Taiga Station's glittering windows and brilliant blue paint. From there a branch line led north to Tomsk, 88 kilometres away. The whole appearance of the station and its surrounding buildings advertised the fact that this was the gateway to 'The Athens of Siberia', Tomsk, home of the first University of Siberia and of the celebrated Technological Institute. What a contrast Taiga Station made to the gloomy, dust and dirt-laden stations of Anzhersk and Sudyanka, those vitally important centres of the great Kuznetsk coal region to the south!

It was long past midnight when our students left the train at Krasnoyarsk. Fate decreed—I will tell of it later—that I should meet my proud student once again, but then his attitude would be somewhat less heroic . . .

Another day and a half's travel past hills and forests, through the Cheremkhovsk coal area, and at last we pulled into Irkutsk, our destination.

II

IRKUTSK IDYLL

BETWEEN FREEDOM AND PRISON

Both Irkutsk Station and the people around it had a workaday air about them, but they were orderly, tidy. This at once made me feel hopeful. And right away I encountered my first free Soviet citizen from the town, a boy of twelve or thirteen years who was cleaning boots.

"I'm not a loafer or a hooligan," he explained, stowing away my fifty kopecks in his pocket. "Look I'm a real scholar—here's my school certificate. I work during the holidays to save up for winter cloths."

My escort thought I had given him too much; the 'norm' was supposed to be twenty kopecks . . .

But indeed I had given him too little. For in this little boy radiating zest for life, freedom had given me a welcome. It was a beautiful summer day, three to four in the afternoon. And so what if he really was a hooligan, as the G.P.U. men maintained! Was not Yesenin the 'first hooligan' of the new Russia?

My guards phoned from the station for a car from the district office of the G.P.U., and off we went. On the streets, as at the station, there was none of the haste and turmoil characteristic of the era of the Five Year Plan. Irkutsk, a large administrative centre both before and after the Revolution, had at this time no large enterprises under construction. It gave the impression of a drowsy town. Its outward appearance in the summer of 1933 could hardly have differed much from its pre-revolutionary aspect, perhaps it had even looked the same in the time of the Decembrists*. It was still the same small Asiatic town of civil-servants and merchants; the streets wide, dusty and dirty; the houses low and built of wood. That is Russia—a single step from the most frenzied activity to the most profound slumber. It is true, nevertheless, that even here, though the Five Year Plan had not succeeded in changing the

---

*The conspirators against Tsar Nicholas I who had lived there in exile one hundred years earlier.

336

face of the town, it had thoroughly transformed its social life and the souls of the people.

I sat in the regional G.P.U. till late at night, awaiting some chief who was supposed to regularize my liberation. But he never showed up and at midnight I was sent—"only until tomorrow"—to the central Irkutsk Prison . . .

I knew immediately that nothing would come of this promise and that I would now have to sit for a month or two in Irkutsk Prison waiting for the routine to finally allot me a place of exile. This, of course, would be in a province, far from any main centre.

So once more the G.P.U. had failed to keep its promise. But this time had I not myself to blame? I should not have stopped my hunger-strike *en route* here . . . In this ceaseless psychological struggle, this cruel war of nerves waged by the G.P.U. against its victims, in this gamble for life or death, I had missed the moment; the initiative was now theirs . . .

At that moment I had no idea that, although in a great prison, I should be as close to life as on the outside. What, in a normally ordered society, could only have appeared as a catastrophe, or at the very least a most painful burden, turned out under Soviet conditions to be a return to life and a breathing space between two perilous journeys. Such the country—and the times!

* * *

In the prison office next morning I was registered as an inmate.

"Anton Antonovich Ciliga."

"Date of birth: 1898, 20 February."

"Born: Shegotichi, Province of Istria, formerly Austria, from 1919 Italian."

"Passport: Italian."

"Nationality: Yugoslav-Croatian."

"Former member of the Communist Party of the Soviet Union from 1926 to 1929; before that member of the Yugoslav Communist Party since 1918."

"Arrested in 1930 for Trotskyism. Then sentenced to three years imprisonment under Article 59 of the Criminal Code."

"At present does not belong to any political organization. Left the Trotskyist group in 1932 and did not join any other, refraining from political activity in the U.S.S.R. Having finished his sentence, demands permission to return home, abroad."

"Your new sentence?" continued the clerk.

"Exile for three years to eastern Siberia, the town of Irkutsk," I replied.

"For your return home, abroad," said the clerk with a grin, "you'll have to wait awhile. For the moment you will go into the political section, corridor 9; you'll find a couple of your comrades there. Your cell will be open all day. You will be able to walk around freely and do some sunbathing. You will receive 'political' rations; you've got nothing to complain about. Better than in Italy," concluded the clerk, with a slightly mocking smile.

I did indeed find two political prisoners there: Tatë Shusish-vili, a Georgian Social-democrat, and a young Zionist, Boris Rusak. They took me for a walk in the garden and acquainted me with the general lay-out of the prison. We politicals were given free run of the yards and some of the buildings. The same privilege was also permitted those who 'worked' and in general to all who were well dressed and looked like 'intelligentsia'.

The Central Irkutsk Prison was, as the name implies, not the only prison in the town, but it was the main one. A large, old, rambling affair—a whole little town to itself. For Great Russia, great prisons. But to tell the truth, even this prison proved too small for the epoch of the Five Year Plan. Its 2,500 population exceeded by three or four times the norm anticipated by its Tsarist architects. The main part of the prison consisted of a vast square building of two storeys, a sort of barracks, with a large courtyard in the centre. A part of this yard had been converted into a small garden, where there were fir trees, some grass, a path with benches along it. Here those prisoners who were not restricted sat, walked and chatted. Here also there was sunbathing when the grass was cut. Only about twenty of the prisoners could in actual fact spend the whole day in this garden: the politicals and a few others enjoying special privileges. Besides these there was also a category of those working within the prison who were allowed to spend about two hours there. The rest spent their non-working time in the cells or other parts of the prison and for exercise were permitted to walk round in a circle for half an hour.

The other part of the prison consisted of an enormous square with several buildings, each with its own little courtyard On the left, surrounded by a small walled-in yard, was a two or three storey 'villa'—the isolator, which was under a special G.P.U. guard. There was no communication whatever with this building, in which were confined 'particularly important prisoners, under investigation or, more accurately, being groomed for criminal status . . . In the middle of the last yard was the prison bath-house and laundry. The politicals and the other privileged ones could, of course, use the bath-house every day; the rest took turns. One had to pay the prison administration for laundering, which was done by the women prisoners. The bath-house was the centre for gambling specu-lation and crime. A sort of prison 'Stock Exchange'.

THE ARMY OF FORCED LABOUR

My acquaintance with the army of forced labour began with the prison elite. The old man Shushiashvili, with obvious pleasure and an oriental politeness, undertook the role of master of ceremonies. The prison garden served as the 'salon' where the introductions were effected.

"Anton Antonovich Ciliga," said Shushiashvili, addressing the old-timers, "foreign communist, professor, Comintern functionary. I spent three years with him in the Verkhne-Uralsk isolator."

"Ivan Petrovich, Chief of X Railway Station (a large junction near Irkutsk), communist. Sentenced to death by shooting for the loss of railway trucks and contents. Sentence commuted to ten years of concentration camp."

"How did it happen?" I asked my new acquaintance, a nervous-looking, still young man. He told me that the authorities considered him responsible for the loss of many trucks full of goods. He himself, however, blamed the transport difficulties between Moscow and Vladivostok, bureaucratism, robbery in transit . . . The sentence of death had given him a great shock; he had taken leave of life (though he did submit an appeal to Kalinin). When, after four weeks of painful suspense, he was called out at night "with his belongings", he thought it was the end, that he was being led out to be shot. But in the Control Office he was informed of the commutation of the sentence and straightway transferred to the free cells. Now he was waiting to be sent to work on the construction of the Baikal-Amur railway (BAM), where he would probably be given a responsible job as boss on some construction site. In Russia he who has once been a boss can be relieved of that responsibility only by death. In all likelihood this man, after the completion of BAM, would stay on there to work in his former capacity; and should he be amnestied before its completion he will still settle down somewhere in the neighbourhood: once an affair has passed off without shooting, the incident is closed.

"Nikolai Ivanovich, director of the Irkutsk Branch of the Zernotrest (Grain Trust), communist, recently arrested together with his staff. Here they are: his deputy, his chief accountant, chief agronomist, and other non-party specialists. Their crimes: non-fulfilment of plans, loss of grain; the non-party experts are accused of deliberate sabotage and wrecking activities, and the communist director of negligence, of having shown too much trust in them. Their 'case' is in its initial stage; the G.P.U. has just started to 'organize' it. And they are all very scared, very cautious; especially the director. Their wives bring them wonderful parcels from home, which help temporarily to relieve their precarious situation.

"Fedor Mikhailovich, chief accountant of the Irkutsk Branch of the Sovpushnina (Soviet Fur Trust), non-party. Accused of misappropriation, in being party to the exchange by his Trust of furs against goods from another Soviet organization."

"How was that? That surely entailed no loss, no theft?"

"No, but there was an infringement of the regulations for planned economy, and this is called speculation and misappropriation."

"What do you expect to get?"

"Well, I'll have to work two or three years for nothing as an accountant on some G.P.U. job or other. A couple of hundred roubles a month . . . There's only one consolation—the G.P.U. feeds one fairly well."

"And how much did you earn in the Trust?"

"Seven hundred roubles basic salary; with bonuses it came up to a thousand a month."

"A thousand roubles! But that is a fortune! And in addition, I suppose, a fair amount of stuff at special prices from the Trust supply department," I said in amazement.

"Yes, I and my wife did not live badly. We had a nice apartment, new furniture, good clothes . . ." (he was the best dressed man in jail).

Fedor Mikhailovich was worried about retaining his flat and furniture until his release. The G.P.U. might install someone in it. I therefore suggested that he should let me a room if I were allowed to stay in Irkutsk as promised. No sooner proposed than accepted. He immediately wrote a letter to his wife instructing her to let me a room. But since I was not given freedom to stay in Irkutsk I never found out how Fedor Mikhailovich settled his affairs.

340

Igor Maximovich, a Muscovite, tall, lean, around fifty, a construction engineer by trade. Apparently a big shot in his Trust. A man of wide knowledge, with amazingly portentious gestures and aristocratic manners. Probably a nobleman by birth, one of those who were called the 'elite of the Russian intelligentsia'. He has fallen because of his wife, who is a Latvian. In 1916 her family fled before the Germans from Riga to Moscow. After the war her brothers returned to Latvia. For corresponding with them, especially since one of them was an officer in the Latvian Army, she was arrested, and her husband also, on a charge of espionage. Sentence—ten years of concentration camp. They are on their way to BAM.

"The G.P.U. has decided, since I am an expert in machine construction, that I am also able to build railways. Well, why not . . . perhaps I shall learn," he remarked pensively.

Igor Maximovich is being sent with a whole party of condemned experts, thirty to forty men, despatched with all speed under a special escort direct from Moscow to the town of Svobodny (ironically enough the Russian word for 'free'); it is precisely this town that had been made the clearing centre for forced labour on the BAM project). This party was held up in Irkutsk for only a day and a half. They had been allocated a large open cell on the second floor above us, the politicals. There they settled down as though in some club converted for an overnight stay. I did not enter their cell—they were afraid to invite me in—but left them at the entrance.

"BAM needs experts. That's why the G.P.U. is recruiting them. Nobody will volunteer to go into such a wilderness, and in any case one would have to pay fantastic sums to the few who did volunteer. Now we are going there for nothing, and, into the bargain, are glad not to have been shot," said one of them, a young chemist, indicating with a wave of his hand the spectacle presented by the cell, a noisy, animated human anthill. The chemist himself had suffered because he was the friend of an arrested professor.

Igor Maximovich's wife, Yelena Eduardovna, was in one of the women's cells of the same prison. They came out together for the walk, or, more exactly, to see the doctor. That's how I met her. I must here add that there was a considerable number of women in our prison. They were lodged in separate cells, but since the majority of them were working they moved around as freely as the men.

Yelena Eduardovna gave the impression of being more scared than her husband. Instantly I read in her eyes the question: aren't you an agent of the G.P.U.? But she soon forgot her caution and I actually learned the greater part of their story from her. She was consoling herself with the fact that the food at BAM was excellent, especially for the *spetsy* that is, the experts. Vegetables and butter such as could be found nowhere else. "To the 'shock' workers—'shock' rations!" She was repeating the current slogan. She had obviously moved in the highest circles of the non-party intelligentsia in Moscow. Presumably they had suffered as a result of the purges carried out in those circles. After a time I also got to know some of the Moscow news and gossip from her. For a while I even felt as though I were in Moscow again.

" 'The Merry Fellows' " *(Vesolye Rebyata)* has made a hit all over the Union, but its author has been exiled to Siberia for a 'counter-revolutionary' joke he told at a social gathering . . . Also exiled is Kluyev, who now, instead of writing poems, works as a carpenter and soaks in drink somewhere in Siberia..." After mentioning the latest plays she had seen, Yelena Eduardovna went on to behind-the-scenes political gossip. Still a topical subject at that time was the sudden, unexpected death of Stalin's wife, Allilueva.

"She committed suicide, that is quite definitely known," she assured me.

"But in our Verkhne-Uralsk isolators", I ventured to say doubtingly, "all Georgians were unanimous in asserting that Stalin had poisoned her."

"No, no," insisted Yelena Eduardovna, "she poisoned herself. It was like this. Stalin and Allilueva were on a visit to Ordzhonikidze; it was during the October celebrations—the 7th or 8th of November. When they were about to leave a quarrel started. Allilueva reproached Stalin for his affair with X (I confess that I have forgotten the name she mentioned). Stalin, who had been drinking heavily, barked furiously: 'Well, now I'm going straight to her.' Allilueva went home alone and took poison."

Later, in Siberia, I heard a third version. Allilueva was said to have taken poison as a moral-political protest against Stalin's perfidy. Of Allilueva's modesty and decency I happened to have already heard during my stay in Moscow in 1928—29. At the beginning of the Five Year Plan Allilueva enrolled as an ordinary student at the recently opened Industrial Academy *(Prom Akademia)*. Anyway, her death, sudden, mysterious, and never quite cleared up, served as a basis for popular legend in the U.S.S.R.

Of exceptional interest to me were two arrested officers of the Red Army. Both were approximately forty years of age. One, who seemed the elder, a stout and gloomy man, began to organize parties of prisoners for work outside the prison and for transfer to the Far East; he also drilled them as though he had recruits in front of him. A year later I met him again in Krasnoyarsk. He looked radiant and seemed to have become younger. Now released, he was engaged in army drilling instruction.

The other officer, slim, supple, with a small pointed beard and with a stick in his hand, often accompanied us on our walks in the garden, recounting all kinds of military adventures. Judging from his simple manners and his speech, I concluded that he was an officer of post-revolutionary vintage. But I was mistaken. He proved to have already been an officer under the Tsarist regime. Becoming closely acquainted with him, I noticed several things that convinced me he was indeed a man of the old culture. Yet how he had changed. Life and revolution had created a curious synthesis: the old habits had put on a new cloak; it had already become difficult to distinguish him by his speech and manners from an officer risen from the people. It will not be easy for Communists to compete for popularity with these 'non-Party Bolsheviks'. Those of the old ruling class have shown themselves more tenacious of life than it is customary to think. Before his arrest he had, it seemed, been the commander of a battalion, but that was all I could squeeze out of him. Much as the story of these two officers (their political convictions, their attitude to the government, etc.) interested me, I could get nothing out of them. They were seasoned men and had gone through the hard school of life. Taciturn and strong-willed, they managed to get what they wanted without superfluous words. The second officer had two young friends sharing his walks and his cell. One was an employee of the frontier customs office; the other the director of a teachers' training college. I never discovered what the charge was against the custom's employee, but the director, a communist, was accused of tolerating chauvinism in his school. The students were of three nationalities—Russian, Tartar, and Tungusian. There had been perpetual conflicts among them on the national question and this had finally led to the director's arrest.

Among themselves the prisoners talked openly, and far more freely than had been the case in the Leningrad prison when I was there in the spring of 1930. One partial explanation

of this was that here were confined only those already sentenced, and not those awaiting trial, as in Leningrad; a second
explanation was that the Five Year Plan had been completed,
and the all-pervading terror had abated. Of course, people
spoke with caution, for the most part only of what they had
seen and heard. Nevertheless, I did on three or four occasions
hear open and direct criticism of the government. One of the
most outspoken in this respect was a young student from
among the specialists. He declared that he had been imprisoned
"on account of a counter-revolutionary organization in the
electrical industry". The public trial of this case took place, if
I remember correctly, in Moscow in the spring of 1933. Apart
from the Russian accused there were also some English engineers
on trial, who were freed after being sentenced, and extradited
at the request of the British government.*

This young fellow's story struck me not only because of its
outspokenness against the government, but also, and particularly, because of his detailed account of the 'counter-revolutionary organization'. According to him the affair was far more
serious than had been made public by the Court proceedings.
The government, he thought, did not want too many revelations, and deliberately conducted it as a wreckers' case, whereas
it was in fact a real conspiracy. He asserted that the organization
had a complete plan to plunge the whole of Moscow into
darkness at a moment's notice and to blow up the Kremlin and
other strategically important points in the town by means of
some mysterious rays. The blowing up of the Kremlin would
result in the overthrow of the government and its replacement
by one composed of specialist-technicians.

"Only by means of modern technique and only with the aid
of technicians and specialists can the communist be overthrown," the young fellow declared, repeating one of the
clichés fairly widespread in Soviet circles.

The conspiracy had apparently been exposed quite accidentally. One of the chief engineers of the 'Electric Combinat' in
Moscow, a leader of the plot, while taking some papers from
the safe in his office, had inadvertently dropped a map of
Moscow with the points to be blown up marked on it in front
of the nose of a communist who happened to be there. According to the student, he himself was a close relative of one of
the principal accused, but had contrived to escape immediately
the first arrests had taken place. With false papers he had

*The 'Metro-Vickers' Trial, 12—19 April, 1933. —*Translator.*

344

managed to get taken on at a ship-building yard on the Baikal, and thought that having travelled so far he was no longer in danger. However, after six months he had been traced and arrested.

"When arresting me the G.P.U. addressed me by my real name. I realized then that further denial was senseless and I admitted everything. I was threatened with shooting of course, but on account of my youth I got off with ten years in concentration camp."

The whole tale sounded fantastic, incredible, pure conceit and boasting—if not worse. I mention it only because this was the sole case where an accused assured me that the accusation of wrecking was not a frame-up but the truth. It goes without saying that I cannot vouch that this young man had really been accused of the things of which he told me. One thing, however, was undoubtedly true. He came from the technical-intelligentsia circles of Moscow, and yet he did not look like a son of the old-style bourgeois-intelligentsia. Even he was a product of the times, uniting the traits of the intelligentsia with those of a student risen from the people. In a certain sense he was the embodiment of 'Our Soviet Students' of the post-revolutionary era—democratic in his habits and manners, in his inmost thoughts contemptuous of the people and a worshipper of 'Technique'. Aside from this he was an excellent sportsman, self-possessed, without principles, ready for anything . . .

Imagine my astonishment when a few days later I saw that he had joined the work of the 'political education department' of the prison as a propagandist among the prisoners working in the local brick factories. It was this student's task, in speeches and in writing, through explanatory lectures and wall-newspapers, to convince the half-starved men engaged on hard manual labour that their work was "a matter of honour and of conscience—for the cause of Socialism". It was he, this freebooter, who was called upon to instil them with socialist enthusiasm.

"Good lord," I could not help exclaiming, "only just recently you were setting out to overthrow the Soviet Government and now you've taken on the job of sweetening the slave labour of these wretched men."

"Well, it can't be helped. One has to look after oneself," he replied, not in the least embarrassed, and smiling in a completely natural unforced manner.

The fashionable Moscow sports jacket, somewhat the worse

for wear from the stormy adventures of the last months, blended with the strong, healthy neck of this sportsman, on whose sinewy wrist a leather strap held a metal watch, the most favoured emblem of the 'young man' of the Soviet high society. Work as a propagandist had many advantages: it freed him from hard physical labour, secured him extra rations, and also opened the way to an amnesty. In addition, if this young man really had serious intentions, he could occasionally put in a word against the regime too. How he will finally mould himself it is difficult to say. His motto in life is—"Get on in the world, stay on top!" If it seems to his advantage he will take part in a move to overthrow the regime; if not, he will remain within it. Inwardly this Soviet *condotierre* accepts both variants.

Among the prison elite might also be counted a young komsomolka (girl member of the Young Communist League), sentenced to ten years of concentration camp for embezzling socialist property. In her spotlessly clean frock, her fresh face unclouded by any sorrow, with her two naive looking pigtails hanging down her neck—not beautiful, but youthful and pretty—she seemed like the spoiled daughter of some provincial civil servant or merchant strayed into prison by accident. From the look of her one could not possibly give her age as more than fifteen, although to judge by her sentence she must have been at least seventeen or eighteen. In the prison she worked on internal guard duties, that is, she stood at the entrances to corridors or other premises. (All internal duties were carried out by the prisoners themselves, selected by the administration.)

"How did you manage to 'earn' ten years?" I could not help asking her.

"I worked as a shop assistant in a model Komsomol Co-operative. The manager was stealing goods. We Komsomol employees did not report this and so now we are all doing ten years."

"Well, why didn't you report him—if you weren't taking part in the stealing yourself?"

"I was afraid. The manager was also the secretary of the Komsomol cell and a member of the town 'Active' of the youth. One could get into trouble for reporting a man like that."

The neat little doll appeared to be more calculating than at first appeared. On another occasion she whispered to me secretively:

"The prison Governor told me that I ought not to talk to you politicals—it might spoil my chance of an amnesty. The administration is putting my name forward for one."

I have little doubt that she was in fact amnestied after a year or a year and a half, without her having even left Irkutsk. Not for nothing was she the little aristocrat of the prison, and experienced in the ways of Soviet opportunism.

THE PRISON PLEBS

The great mass of the prison population, the plebians as it were of that world, was made up of the most varied categories. In the first place there was a group of two hundred employed on all sorts of work inside the prison; attending to and supervising the other prisoners, looking after the bath-house, working in the hospital, running the ambulance service, working in the kitchen, the store-rooms, the barber shop, in the prison office and the various 'cultural' departments, cleaning the cells and doing internal guard duties. There were only a very few paid workers from outside—in fact, only the Governor, the heads of the various departments, and the doctors.

A few of the women cleaners lived in the cell adjacent to ours. The youngest among them was an eighteen-year-old peasant girl, Tatiana. In spite of her name she did not in the least remind one of the classical, fair-haired type of Russian woman. With her dark complexion and yellowish-grey skin she much more resembled a Kalmuck girl. She was the daughter of a wealthy peasant from the Manchurian frontier region. Her father had been 'de-kulakized' and the whole family sent to forced labour in Central Siberia, in a timber mill in Yeniseisk. But there they had been so starved that after the weaker children had died of hunger Tatiana resolved to escape and return to her native village in the faint hope that kindly people might feed her better than the State factory. This she succeeded in doing. But the village Soviet, learning of her 'illegal' return, had her arrested, and now she was again on her way to Yeniseisk. In spite of her city misadventures, she remained a typical peasant girl—shy, restrained, with even in her gait something of an animal far from its native haunts, treading warily through the forest thickness, at every step fearful of a trap.

Another of nearly the same age, but a bold lively girl, was the daughter of an Irkutsk factory worker. She had worked as a cashier in a bank and had received a *chevronetz* (ten roubles, i.e. ten years) for the theft of 1000 roubles. She assured me that she had not stolen this money but had overpaid 1000 roubles in error when handing over large sums to factory cashiers for wages.

A friend of hers who worked as cashier in a co-operative found herself in prison as the result of a forced entry with theft, in which deed she was suspected as an accessory. Judging from her numerous experiences of criminal prisons, this suspicion seemed to me not unfounded. She too had received ten years of concentration camp, but she was hardly likely to have served it—tuberculosis was eating her away before our eyes. Always feverish, constantly spitting blood, she lay on her bunk for hours eagerly devouring Mamime Sibiryak's tales of the Siberian 'Wild West'.

The last in this group was a young woman of about twenty-five. She had come from somewhere around Novosibirsk and was being sent to an eastern concentration camp for three years. Her husband had already been sentenced at the beginning of the first Five Year Plan, first in Mariinsk, then in the Kuzbas Basin (part of the Kuzbas coal mines worked by prison labour, for which purpose a concentration camp had been established nearby). Her husband had been lucky and had managed to become a supervisor there. It was to this camp that she was on her way. She herself, after her husband's imprisonment, had taken accountancy courses and become a book-keeper in a sovkhoz (State Farm). I was very interested to hear about life in the sovkhoz; I wanted to know if they were 'catching on'. From her stories it was hard to get any precise impression; she narrated a mixture of good and bad, of successes and failures. Clearly this question did not greatly interest her. She had landed in prison as a result of a visit to relatives. Finding them in a difficult situation she decided to help feed them by trading: going to a place in Omsk where goods were cheaper and selling them in her part of the country at higher prices. For this 'speculation' she got three years. In addition, there were amongst the imprisoned women a dozen or so with small children.

Murders are sometimes committed in the prison. Today, for example, my comrade, the Georgian Social-Democrat Shushi-ashvili is overcome with grief. One of his compatriots, a young Georgian from Tiflis condemned for speculation, has just been killed. He worked as assistant to the bath-house attendant and was killed in a quarrel that flared up there during a gambling session. His partner, an expert in the art, stabbed him right through the heart and he dropped dead on the spot. By the time Shushiashvili arrived on the scene, the murdered man had been stripped as well; all his belongings, money, even his clothes, had vanished. The lion's share of the spoil had been acquired by the dead man's boss, the bath-house attendant. Shushiashvili was particularly concerned at the loss of his friend's sheepskin coat, a first-class thick Siberian-style fur coat.

"Since you are his countryman, I will give you first refusal of the coat and will let you have it cheap—one hundred roubles. Outside you'd have to pay at least three hundred," said the old attendant. Shushiashvili agreed. Now he was equipped for his forthcoming transfer to Siberia.

The second group of prisoners consisted of those working outside in local industries, in particular in a brick works. There were two detachments of sixty men each. Their situation was the worst of all. Most of them were peasants. They received starvation rations and were compelled to do ten hours of exhausting physical labour day after day. Those unable to fulfil the prescribed 'norm' were subjected to additional punishment. Going to work and at work they were under the close surveillance of numerous guards (themselves prisoners, apart from their chief). The guards had the order to fire on anyone making the slightest attempt at escape. When in the evening a party of these brick workers returned—covered with dust, in rags, exhausted—they looked as though they had crossed the Sahara on foot. When one speaks of the low price of Siberian bricks, this is the other side of the medal!

Only those condemned to death were sadder and more apathetic than these brick workers. There were about sixty to eighty of these, confined in a special block. They were exercised, under special guard, for half an hour each day. During this time the whole yard was cleared of other prisoners. But it was sometimes possible to exchange a word or two with them from the windows of the prison. There was also a secret correspondence with them. The youngest among them sometimes roused themselves from their apathy, smiled, and even went so far as to send love letters to some of the women prisoners.

Half of those condemned were actually shot. The rest, after four to six weeks of waiting, had their sentences commuted to ten years of concentration camp. To judge by appearances, the real criminals amongst them amounted to less than a third. Taking the prison as a whole, however, the criminals were far fewer; about one-tenth only. They were not given employment in the prison. Together with the majority of the other prisoners, they were sent to forced labour in the Far East.

About one half of the whole prison population consisted of peasants. Nearly all were condemned under 'six-eight'.

"Six-eight? Whatever is that?" I asked in bewilderment.

"Oh, that's Stalin's decree of the sixth of August last year (1932), on the safeguarding of 'holy socialist property'," I was informed.

This decree provided for only two punishments: shooting or ten years of concentration camp for the smallest crime against State property. Pilfering of kolkhoz (collective farm) potatoes or grain came under this decree. The crimes of many of the peasants consisted precisely in that, faced with the hunger of their families, they used to go into the kolkhoz fields at night to dig for potatoes or to pilfer grain. There were occasional cases of peasants being sentenced for gleaning, the Government claiming that the kolkhoz peasants deliberately left a lot of grain in the fields in order to collect it afterwards on the sly. In general one can say that the law of Tsar Boris Godunov's time against those 'godless thieves', the peasants who resisted the landlord's yoke, has found a strange revival in the 'socialist legislation' of Stalin.

All these peasants were on their way to forced labour in the East. If the prison elite supplied the 'officer corps', the common people furnished the 'rank and file' of this enormous army of slave labour.

I met only a small group of peasants (four or five people) accused of active resistance to the regime. This was the 'catch' after the series of peasant risings against collectivization in the Bratsk District (north of Irkutsk). The known participants in this movement had long ago been arrested, and shot or sent to concentration camps. These men arrested later were accused of having aided the rioters. This they denied. But from their stories I gathered the impression that they had given a certain assistance to the rebels hiding out in the woods.

I managed to get interesting details of the mood of the peasants in Siberia from an arrested communist, a former guerilla and village leader in the fight against Kolchak and the Japanese. He was working in the prison office. He assured me that the Red partisans in Siberia had all without exception been arrested.

"Why?" I asked.

When the forced collectivization came the Siberian peasants approached them, their old defenders. They responded to the appeal, worked up an agitation and began to come out before the Party and the Soviet organs as their spokesmen, demanding that collectivization should be carried out in a "reasonable and just manner". Because of this they themselves became suspect. My informant, however, considered that all this was simply due to a misunderstanding.

"We are far away from the centre ... These are local abuses ... You see, Yaroslavsky recently came to Irkutsk as a special envoy of the Central Committee of the Party with full power to deal with these abuses and to correct the work of the Irkutsk Party leader, Leonov ... Look, after all, Yaroslavsky, Voroshilov, Stalin himself—they are all also old partisans ..."

The main function of the prison was the transfer of prisoners to the Far East. Every week parties of two hundred, three hundred, or even six hundred were sent off. They were replaced by the hundreds of new candidates from the District prisons, sent for despatch to the innumerable concentration camps of the Trans-Baikal and Far Eastern regions. This whole process represented a kind of unique general mobilization of the working population, including also some experts—engineers, technicians, accountants, etc., for forced labour.

The number of those to be sent to the East was in no way determined by the prison stock, but by telegrams from Chita, Khabarovsk or some other clearing centre. Cost what it might, the numbers demanded had to be found. Telegrams were sent from Irkutsk to provincial prisons for them to despatch their prisoners at once to the Irkutsk Central Prison. The provincial prisons in their turn brought pressure to bear on the Courts, demanding rapid trial and sentencing of the cases pending, in order to satisfy the demands of Irkutsk. They sent the sick, those due for release ... And if all this was not enough, round-ups were made in Irkutsk itself, and all the arrested 'suspects' were automatically included in the parties destined for the Far East. The required number just had to be sent, and if half of them proved to be unfit for work that was no longer Irkutsk's worry.

A great deal of the internal life of the prison was reminiscent of a barrack mobilization centre. The way the parties heading for the Far East filed on to the yard in columns, their appearance, their military formation, their little suitcases, and with their supervisors in some kind of military uniform—all this vividly reminded me of life in the Austrian barracks during the First World War.

The prisoners were sent to concentration camps close to large construction works. For example, the wide line of fortifications along the Soviet-Manchurian frontier, with its block-houses, underground hangars, etc., the Soviet Maginot Line as it was dubbed, was built by slave labour. With their help railways and roads were also being built. It is they, my prison comrades and their brothers, who have built the Khabarovsk-Vladivostok motorway. It is they who have laid the second line of the Verkhneudinsk-Khabarovsk-Vladivostok railway. It is they who were constructing BAM, the Baikal-Amur Railway, a new double track line running one hundred to two hundred kilometres north of the Manchurian frontier (along which the old Siberian railway runs) from the northern end of Lake Baikal to the Amur estuary. This new line runs across the 'taiga', a hundred-metre-wide belt of which has to be cleared to accommodate the double track and the adjacent road.

How many thousands, tens of thousands, have parted with their lives there? And how many hundreds of thousands, perhaps millions, throughout the whole of Siberia and Northern Russia? The timber industry, which characterizes this region, is based almost entirely on slave labour. It is also on this type of labour that the famous 'Conquest of Siberia', carried out by the Soviet conquistadors, is based. It was my nameless comrades from cells neighbouring mine who were sent to Nogaev Bay 1, opposite Kamchatka, to build a motorway from the bay to the Kolyma river, terrible but rich in gold. Gold! This is the god of Eastern Siberia that mercilessly devours the bound slaves cast by the Government into its maw. If African gold is stained with the blood of Negro slaves deprived of all rights, Soviet gold is soaked in the blood of the allegedly free workers and peasants.

In this gigantic process the prison system served as the conveyor belt along which the stream of raw material—slaves, officers and rank and file—is delivered to the construction sites. Thus our prisons seem to resemble not so much jails as mighty mountain passes over which a new Ghengis Khan leads his army of countless thousands—but this time for the conquest of the East, not the West. Two thousand years ago nature's treasures were being torn from their earthy beds by the toil of slaves. But then, in Aristotle's time, slavery was called by its right name. Is this revival of slavery following in the wake of the Russian Revolution perhaps the revenge of the ancient world imposed on the workers for their having dared, in the flood-tide of revolt, to attempt to raze to the ground the very pillars of slavery in contemporary society?

COURAGE AND DISASTER

Prisoners are always interested in their mutual affairs and somehow manage, even in the most unfavourable circumstances, to exchange a few words and looks eloquent of meaning. They form at all times something in the nature of a closed society, more precisely, a brotherhood.

A peculiarity of our barrack-prison was the fact that one could sit for hours at a time with a considerable number of the inmates of the various blocks, talking as though one were at liberty—no, even more frankly than one would have done if free, since in the U.S.S.R. free men are more afraid of frankness. Our talks took place in the two gardens and the three yards. One could also drop into a neighbouring cell, visit the hospital, the rooms housing the cultural institutions, and stroll through the various corridors.

Looking into the prison library one was sure to encounter from five to ten readers and two or three assistants, all 'our' people, that is, prisoners. There one could stay and browse. I discovered several books published during the first years of the Revolution and long since banned: the most original of Trotsky's writings, *The Balance and the Prospects—The Moving Forces of the Revolution*, in which he first formulates his theory of 'permanent revolution'; the works of the Russian anarchists Kropotkin and Bakunin; the publications of the Workers Opposition, in particular Shlyapnikov on the Revolution.

Library regulations allowed two books a week to each cell. During the week books could be exchanged between cells. Those who were at liberty to circulate within the prison could go to the library and take out books.

From ten to fifteen copies of the local daily, *Irkutsk Worker*, were distributed free of charge, one or two to each section of the prison. But that was a drop in the ocean. From time to time Moscow papers were distributed. Those with money could buy them every day.

In charge of the library was a young communist, formerly employed on the Chinese Eastern Railway, which was later sold by the Soviet Government to Japan. According to his story, he had undertaken to deliver a letter from a Siberian to his friend in Manchuria. For this action he had been arrested and charged with espionage.

Several courses were organized in the library. The illiterate were taught to read and write, and for the literate there were courses in arithmetic, geography, the natural sciences. Text-books especially published for this purpose were used. I had a look at them. Some were graphically and interestingly written. Both pupils and teachers were prisoners. Arithmetic was taught by a little old man, a former merchant from the Ukraine who after the Revolution had worked as a book-keeper in Soviet enterprises. In prison, after a bout of dysentry, he became very weak, and in order to obtain an additional 200 grammes of bread (approx. ½lb) and 20 grammes of sugar a day, he took on this work. I came to his aid from time to time and gave him something from my privileged 'political' rations.

We had also a drama circle, an orchestra, and a weekly cinema show. For all these 'cultural activities', as one calls them in the Soviet Union, a whole block was allocated, taking up the space of six to eight large cells. Half of them were occupied by the 'cultural workers' and the musicians. They were the best cells in the prison.

The organization of the entire cultural work was entrusted to the communist director of the teachers' college, whom I have already mentioned. The political leadership was also held by a communist volunteer; his official title was 'Head of the Political Education Section of the Prison' (P.V.C.H.—the title itself indicates that this cultural work was permeated with the political propaganda necessary to the regime).

He was a young fellow recently demobilized from the Army. His original trade had been that of a sailor on the ships of the Lena River and the northerly Far East. He displayed great interest in the life of workers abroad and often questioned me about the workers' movement there and the work of the Comintern. He used to ask questions with a real interest, modestly, without being opinionated. He knew, of course, why I was in prison—that I had long since been expelled from the Party for oppositional activities. But he considered this of no great significance. When a forest is being cut down, splinters are bound to fly. He thought that the differences were in essence not so fundamental and that in time all things would be ironed out. Anyway, all the things that were wrong in Soviet life were only trifles accompanying the period of transition, the results of purely objective difficulties. He was firmly convinced of the identity of interest of the Soviet Government and the masses, and sincerely sought to reconcile them. In his small way he tried to help every prisoner he could. Over-crowded prisons? That was the result of the kulak's resistance, petit-bourgeois, capitalist encirclement of the working class striving towards socialism. He was unshakably devoted to the Government, believing that in this way he also remained loyal to the working class from which he sprang, and which he was then about to leave: for he was preparing to enter a University and dreaming of an academic career. He had made his choice and I did not even attempt to dissuade him.

"Why did you join the Political Education Section and not go straight to the University?"

"I had no money and did not win a scholarship. This year I shall buy some clothes, shoes; study a little. And my work for the P.V.C.H. will, of course, make it easier for me to get a scholarship."

He had made up his mind to get on in the world and the regime was offering him the chance to do so. That was how an understanding was achieved between him and the regime. The bureaucratic machine is not only a press that squeezes, it is also a snare that entraps the best of the potential leaders of the people. Amid all this slavery and misery he was radiant with the vision of his future, in spite of the fact that things did not 'quite' accord with his socialist ideal.

"Whatever comes, will come; but there will be no return to the past. We the youth will not permit it." These were his farewell words to me when I left Irkutsk prison for exile. He wished me luck and a happy return to my home abroad. He was disarming in his frankness, his enthusiasm, his working-class origin, his utter unawareness of his own crimes. Without being conscious of it he was, with the whole of his being, psychologically and sociologically, 'on the other side of the barricades'. The liquidation of the Old Bolsheviks—then still in the future—will have now opened up to him and others in his age group new opportunities, which without doubt they will have seized. That is how revolutions perish, eaten away from within.

In comparison with this singleness of purpose, this drive of the post-revolutionary tops, the masses, broadly represented in the prison by the peasants and all kinds of 'little people', not excluding the workers, seemed somehow inwardly adrift, victims of violence and hunger. Yet there were exceptions, some sparks of a new fire, even among these. Once I met a young worker in the prison yard, really just a youngster, an apprentice from the Irkutsk gold refining works. He had been picked up by chance during a night round-up and was with us for only a day. He had no more than a contemptuous smile for all the Soviet slogans.

"Their freedom—death by starvation.

Their socialism—the enslavement of labour."

I was staggered by the precision of these formulations, which was a sign that it was not the thought of an individual but the outcome of many discussions. Even more striking were his eyes and his voice. His voice—dispassionately calm: everything is clear, there is nothing to argue about. And his eyes seconded: whom do 'They' really think they are kidding! There was even a hint of defiance: 'We' will not yield to 'Them'!

In the Soviet ocean of humanity one meets this type of youngster comparatively rarely and only individually, but one does come across them in all corners of the land. We shall have occasion to confirm this later. Here I will only allow myself a slight digression in order to relate an incident that happened at another time.

I was once in the corridor of a G.P.U. building, waiting to see an official. The decision that was about to be pronounced on me was, I knew, a hard one. I was desperate and gave vent to my feelings without restraining my tongue. In the corridor I was guarded by a young soldier from the G.P.U. troops.

"Abroad we risk our lives for you and here you treat us like dogs. Not enough that you behave vilely to the workers and peasants of Russia, but in addition you don't want anyone abroad to hear about it. Hypocrites, traitors . . ."

After a cautious look around the young soldier suddenly turned to me and in a voice trembling with emotion, said:

"But . . . explain comrade . . . if you can, why . . . why are the people being tortured . . .? how much . . . blood . . . workers' blood has been shed within these walls during the year of my service here. It is terrible . . . Explain comrade . . . why is this being done . . . is it really necessary for the workers' revolution . . .?"

What must have been the inner conflict of this youngster that he dared to speak with me like that—and there of all places. He was the son of a worker and himself a young worker who had volunteered before his time for the Red Army when seventeen years of age. Because of his proletarian origin he had been promoted to service with the G.P.U., and it was there that he had found the doubt that was torturing his soul. Our talk, the whole meeting, did not last more than ten minutes. I had never seen him before, I have never seen him since. But I think it worthwhile to have suffered a year of imprisonment to have met such a youngster in Russia.

The isolated, disunited, protesting voices of Soviet youth! Each, for the time being, but a tiny drop. But those solitary drops together are a sea of tears expressing the unvoiced sympathy of millions. Later, in Siberia, I became aware of the enormous popularity enjoyed by Nikolayev, the assassin of Kirov. Sooner or later this silent sympathy will find its voice. A drop can wear away a stone . . . Only it is difficult to uncover the processes at work below the surface, in the depths of Soviet society, under the steel armour of the regime. I desire passionately that the workers of Europe and of America, that all honest folk who are striving for the triumph of the new, and who have grasped the nature of Stalin's tyranny, should turn their eyes to the depths, to the lives of the Soviet people, and think on these isolated signs of protest . . .

PRISON PARIAHS

My many meetings and long talks in Irkutsk prison were for me a return to the realities of Soviet life. After three years of strict isolation in the political prison of Verkhne-Uralsk, where one stews in the juice of professional politics, and where, in the midst of the most absorbing discussions, one is suddenly attacked by the feeling that one is after all very removed from real life, this abrupt plunge into a world buffeted by contrary winds invigorated my whole being. I felt much more free, here in prison, than I was later to feel at liberty, in deportation. This sensation arose not only from my freedom of movement within the prison, but also from my free contact with the outside world through the continual flow of thousands of prisoners bringing with them the living spirit of the country.

Even direct contact with the outside world was not lacking. There were among us not a few who worked individually in some outside institution or who were permitted visits from relatives. Since they were subjected to hardly any searching when they returned to prison, it was possible to receive and send letters. There was also an authorized correspondence. There was even a post office within the prison, next to the administration office, and it was open to all of us for normal postal transactions. Censorship was more a matter of form than of reality. This was not a G.P.U. prison, that is, a political prison with its draconic severity, but a common 'criminal' prison belonging to the People's Commissariat of Justice, with almost the atmosphere of 1917. This was one of the oversights of the People's Commissar, Comrade Krylenko, who was later taken out of action, perhaps even out of life. He was liquidated and his successor made a better job of things.

But during my time in this 'blessed' criminal prison one could write openly to friends abroad, just as one could from any part of Russia. I then and there wrote several letters to my friends in Russia and to relatives abroad. This for the first time in three years, since throughout that time the G.P.U. had forbidden me to correspond with anyone.

In the Irkutsk prison I chanced to make contact in a certain sense with the world abroad through the person of a Viennese worker. He was a mechanic, operating the cinema in our prison, and had been sentenced to three years of concentration camp.

"What for?"

"Allegedly for neglecting the machines," he replied smiling. "In fact, however, for opposition activity, for too open criticism. But that is their way—not to implicate a worker in a 'political affair' but to deal with them on economic or technical charges, and when this won't wash, then they are 'hooligans'. There are quite a number of German workers who have been sentenced in the same way as me," he concluded.

The films the Viennese comrade had to show were romantic, Soviet-heroic tripe. But even worse than the films themselves was the technique; the film often broke, intervals were then announced and the film would be run again from the beginning. The usual audience in the small cinema room was between one hundred and one hundred and forty. Again these were the same men and women who worked within the prison, a small select group separated from the plebian mass. Between the 'elite' and the mass this group that went to the cinema, that had employment, that was in general the most active in the prison, formed a kind of middle class—the 'Shock Workers', comprising about ten per cent of the whole. In distinction from the 'elite', whose social origins linked it with the upper strata of Soviet society, this group came from the people and had become separated from them only in prison. Class differentiation could here be observed in the process of working itself out. Emerging from the mass on the basis of its small earnings and able to develop culturally because it was socially active, this class, determined not to fall beneath the wheels and eager to push itself up, to a certain extent set the tone in the prison and, in spite of all set-backs, radiated a contagious optimism in striking contrast with the mass below. These consisted for the most part of peasants older in years, radiating an atmosphere of doom, utter impotence and resignation to fate.

This mass, which made up the majority, could not move around the prison but remained locked in cells awaiting transfer to the Far East. It had the right to only half an hour's exercise. Here the occupants of one block, between 100 and 150 people, would form up into columns of two: men, women, old, young, children; the sick and the well; those with footwear and those without; the ragged and the not so ragged. They walked in a circle, a long nightmare procession. According to the regulations, they were not permitted to leave the column and sit in the garden around which they walked. Occasionally I would go into the garden and contemplate for a long time those hunted-looking, sad faces round which the unkempt hair hung from bowed heads. Sometimes I managed to exchange a few words with one of them. Today, for example, one of them takes from his pocket a small drinking mug, and looking at me says in a timid, pleading voice: "Perhaps you would like to buy that?" I did not need the mug at all and I had very little money, but it was impossible to refuse. How much? Two roubles.

In prison things were generally speaking cheap; only food was dear. For a piece of very bad, soggy black bread weighing 400 grammes (approximately nine-tenths of a pound), our daily ration, one paid five to six roubles. One could buy a fairly good suitcase for from ten to fifteen roubles. Whoever had money would buy supplementary food, mainly herrings, from the prison canteen. Sometimes one could buy direct from the outside; and there, or even in the bath-house, vodka could also be bought. But this was primarily for those with 'pull'. To have 'pull'—this is the first and foremost requirement in the U.S.S.R.

Once an old woman who could hardly walk came out of the procession and sank down on a bench.

"Tired, mother?"

"I'm worn out ... Perhaps you could give me a little something to eat, something hot? ... God will repay you."

Shushiashvili went off to look for a drop of soup. He heated it in the kitchen and brought it to her. The poor old woman had lost the sight of one eye in prison and could hardly see with the other. She seemed like a living corpse, decomposing as she breathed. She came from Viatka, where her husband had been a craftsman with his own small house.

"We were suddenly arrested, everything taken away, and we ourselves sent to concentration camp. It was there that my husband died. I was sent back to prison. I am only waiting for death, but God doesn't send it."

"Have you any people?"

"I have a daughter and a son, but where they are I don't know. They were also driven off to some concentration camp."

I met other 'living corpses' in the garden. They were so emaciated that no food could ever help them again. From these walking skeletons work was no longer demanded, there was no intention of sending them anywhere any more and no one paid them any attention, neither the administration nor their fellow prisoners. As though buried alive these miserable wretches felt the ghostly emptiness close around them. They were not prevented from walking around, but together in a group, like shades from Hades, they kept to one small corner of the hospital garden. They would sit there during the warmest hours of the day, huddled together, silent. The old woman from Viatka soon joined them. I remember also among this group a Ukrainian woman from the Kuban, not quite so old as the one from Viatka. She had been required to deliver to the State 450 poods of grain. She had given all she possessed—150 poods. For "non-fulfilment of the quota" all her family had been sent to prison or concentration camp. For a time she had continued to receive news of her family, then it had stopped coming altogether and she did not know if they were still alive. She spoke haltingly and looked at me questioningly, as though trying to read in my eyes what I thought—whether she would survive or leave her bones there.

Of about the same age as this woman was an old and dying man, also from the south. His most cherished dream was an appeal for mercy to the Chairman of the All-Russian Central Executive Committee, Kalinin. "They say he helps." When one reminded him of the number of appeals he had already sent without avail, he replied: "They must have been written badly, and perhaps the paper wasn't good enough." And turning to me he begged: couldn't I help him to get some good paper? The little people in prison without money found it very hard indeed to get even a sheet of paper. When they did get hold of a piece, they hung on to it with superstitious reverence; it was like a pearl of priceless value. I managed to get hold of some for the old man, of course, without his having to pay for it, and wrote the appeal for him. News of this at once went the rounds and then came others, equally doomed, and I wrote

360

appeals for them also. All, I knew, fruitless, completely fruitless.

It was a hungry place, our prison. Twice a day we were given hot water on which floated a few cabbage leaves or barley grains. On top of that we received three or four hundred grammes—I forget the exact amount—of bread per head per day. Several times a day boiling water was dished out. No tea, of course, and no sugar either. Besides this, those who worked received an additional ration of 200 grammes of bread and 20 grammes of sugar. There were also a few other privileges, but these were unofficial. We politicals, for example, got an extra so-called 'hospital' ration, from the infirmary kitchen. Even this was not a staggering amount, but it was of better quality. Thus we three politicals received enough for us to be able to help out one or two of the ordinary prisoners.

The prisoners considered the ration then (July—August 1933) really magnificent in comparison with that of the previous winter (1932—33), a winter of terrible hunger when the bread ration had fallen to 200 grammes and even that irregularly distributed—that is, there were days when there was simply no bread at all and the soup was hot water pure and simple. This starvation brought typhus and dysentry in its train. But now the death rate had fallen considerably; now there were only seven to ten deaths a day from starvation, while in February of that same year the death rate had reached forty a day. The 'living corpses' of whom I have told were the last survivors of that time.

When the authorities resolved to act and were able to improve the food situation (after Stalin's general retreat in the spring of 1933), they did so with all the propaganda theatricality characteristic of the U.S.S.R. The Chairman of the Irkutsk Soviet 'accidentally' encountered the forty corpses being removed from the prison. At once he demanded to know what was wrong, waxed highly indignant—"This is disgusting", and so forth . . . He then and there ordered the dismissal of the prison Governor and summoned a meeting of the prisoners. In Soviet Russia everything is done in an 'organized' manner.

The horrible famine of the winter of 1932—33 swept across the whole of Russia and its monstrous trail was to be seen not only in our prison. There were cases of cannibalism in the Ukraine and Central Asia. The wife of an engineer who came from Omsk prison, told us that there she had encountered a group of sixteen from the Ukraine guilty of cannibalism. They looked, she said, terrifyingly repulsive, and yelled as though demented. Among them was a mother who had eaten her own children. "I don't understand why they were sent to Omsk. They are supposed to be shot on the spot for cannibalism," she concluded.

I TEACH THE PRISONERS LATIN

In order to be registered for the 'hospital' ration we had to report in person to the director of the hospital before collecting our rations from the kitchen. This gave me the opportunity of getting to know the conditions in the hospital and the level of medical science there at close quarters.

There were three medical centres in the prison: a) two or three rooms reserved for medical treatment, serving those employed in the prison and the slightly ill; b) in our block, the ninth, a small sanitary post where those in quarantine were cared for; and c) the hospital proper, a small one-storey building. There was also a wing for contagious diseases in this building. The rest of the establishment contained a dispensary, a kitchen, visiting room, and all kinds of other services. On the first floor were seven or eight rooms for the patients.

Presenting myself to the doctor on the first day of arrival, I asked him to grant me a special diet instead of the ordinary hospital one, since I had just finished a prolonged hunger strike and felt very weak.

The director, who was also the head doctor, was a robust looking Tartar of about forty. He looked at me with surprise.

"No, there's nothing I can do about it. You didn't go on hunger-strike here and you broke it before coming to Irkutsk. I have ten people here dying daily from starvation and you, you healthy ones, you want rations even better than the hospital gives! . . . No, impossible!"

He likewise refused my request for a mattress or at least for a blanket. Since our cell was damp it was no joke to lie all night on bare planks without cover. But here again the doctor had weighty arguments.

"I haven't enough bunks for the sick. Many of them lie on the floor, and even for those I have no mattresses or blankets. You politicals are not my responsibility but the G.P.U.'s. Let them give you mattresses and blankets, they are richer than a poor *Narkomyust* prison hospital (*Narodny Komissariat Yustitsii*—People's Commissariat of Justice).

The head doctor's assistant was a woman of thirty-five, formerly a nurse, who had been sent to the Medical Faculty during the First Five Year Plan and had recently finished her studies.

The entire subordinate personnel of the hospital consisted of prisoners.

A day or two after my arrival, whilst waiting for the distribution of the rations, I strolled into the dispensary, which was opposite the kitchen. An old man from Dvinsk, Abraham Moiseyevich was in charge. Tall, lean, red-haired, he had lived a long time in Siberia. After the 1905 revolution he had been confined in the Schluesselburg Fortress for three years and afterwards deported to Siberia. Here he had been caught by the war and the revolution of 1917, but preferred to remain rather than return to his native town. He had married when already old and had two small children with whom he played touchingly, like a grand-papa. In spite of his impressive political past (three years in Schuesselburg!) he had never really engaged in politics. He had been sentenced simply for rendering the revolutionaries a service—he had stored a bomb for them.

His assistant was a young, neat woman of about twenty-two to twenty-four, always dressed in a spotless white uniform. She was one of the prisoners, formerly a student in the Irkutsk Workers' School. (*Rabfac*—'Workers' Faculty', giving workers and peasants a four-year course prior to entering University or a High School.) She had been sentenced to five years' concentration camp for selling bread which she had received on her student's ration card on the market. She had sold part of this bread in order to buy a little meat, which was available only on the market and then only at a very high price.

"What kind of speculation is that? The sentence is a judicial error and Nadia will soon be freed by the Amnesty Commission," said Abraham Moiseyevich with animation.

Nadia looked at him with a shade of adoration, as one looks at a teacher and benefactor.

"And how is she getting on with pharmacy?" I asked.

"Excellent," said the old man enthusiastically. "She will soon be a real pharmacist. When she is freed she will come to me in a voluntary capacity."

She loved her work. Her dream had been to become a doctor, but now after her arrest, even if she were amnestied, she would not be taken back into the Workers' School; so since she had had to abandon her dream, she devoted herself all the more eagerly to pharmacy.

"Yes," she said, "I already know everything here by heart. There's only one drawback, I don't know Latin and cannot read the prescriptions and the names of the medicines, although I know exactly where to find everything."

"Well, that's nothing serious," I replied. "The Latin language and script are not the most sacred mysteries of the Lord. If you like I will teach you these in the few weeks I have to spend here."

Thus I obtained my first pupil for my future Latin circle. Nadia was the daughter of a Siberian peasant, a member of a religious sect rejecting the authority of the clergy, who had joined the Kolkhoz from its inception but obstinately refused to accept any leading or paid office in it, or in the village Soviet. "I don't recognize any priests and it's not for me to put myself in the position of one."

This obstinate, determined heretic had three children: a son who worked as a book-keeper in the Irkutsk Sovkhoz and two daughters, of whom Nadia was the elder. Both of the daughters had joined the Komsomol and gone to live in town. They worked at first in a dress factory and then, through the Komsomol organization, they were nominated for the Workers' School. Then the paths of the two sisters began to part. Nadia resolved to leave the Komsomol: "Too much injustice, dishonesty; nothing but crawling—I can't stand that." The younger was more opportunist. "One has to take people as they are. Without the Komsomol—no University; no University—no completion of our studies." But fate had made its own plans for the sisters. So it came about that the younger had to quit her studies sooner than Nadia. The previous autumn (1932) they had been so starving that their bodies had begun to swell and they had had to return to their village to save life itself. But when they had both somewhat recovered, Nadia wanted to go back to town and tried to coax her sister to accompany here. The younger, however, had been so frightened by her experience that she categorically refused and Nadia had to return alone. In the Workers' School she married a worker student. After her arrest her husband thought it advisable to disappear. This roused the suspicions of the G.P.U. and they conducted an investigation. They found out that Nadia's husband was really the son of a Siberian factory owner and that he had almost completed his secondary education during the Kolchak period. During the Sovietization of Siberia his family had emigrated, but he had stayed behind, taken a false name, become a worker, established himself as 'worthy of trust', and been recommended for the Workers' School. From there he had intended to enter the University and thus, in this roundabout way, to regain his old position in the world. The fact that he had succeeded in passing two years' examinations in the first year of study, and proposed, had Nadia not been arrested, to do the same the following year, was regarded by the G.P.U. as confirmation of its suspicions, which were in all probability aroused in the first place precisely by his unusually rapid progress. Nadia, for her part, insisted that she knew nothing of her husband's past. He was the comrade of her studies; there was much she could learn from him and he had gladly helped her, and so she fell in love with him. But this explanation did not satisfy the G.P.U. To punish her for her husband's flight, they gave her ten years' concentration camp. In prison Nadia did not give way to despair. She started work in the kitchen and the pharmacy, thus securing better rations and the goodwill of the administration, whose opinion carried great weight with the Amnesty Commissions. The Amnesty Commissions periodically visited the prisons and the prison administrations prepared lists of those recommended for amnesty. Candidates for amnesty came firstly from among the 'activists', the so-called 'enthusiasts for socialism' re-educated in prison; secondly from those obviously sentenced in error; thirdly from the gravely ill whose upkeep cost far more than could be covered by any possible unpaid labour they might be able to do. The Amnesty Commission is the 'deus ex machina' which, aided by Death, adjusts the scales of Soviet justice.

It was not, after all, so easy to teach Latin. The first stumbling-block was where to obtain a text-book; even the doctors did not possess one. While a search was being made I began to teach Nadia the Latin script from a little volume of Balzac's tales that I happened to have with me. My pupil's progress absolutely staggered me. She mastered the script in one day, so well that I could dictate a French text to her (reading it in the Latin manner) and she would write it down with hardly a mistake. It seems to me that in our epoch it is only among the Russian youth that such extraordinary talent can be found.

Soon a fresh difficulty arose. The prison authorities decided that individual tuition was not in accord with Soviet principles. But a way out was offered me: the organization, under the general supervision of the P.V.C.H., of a Latin study circle for the hospital personnel. Normally politicals refused to collaborate with the administration in such activities, but I regarded myself as the guest of the Soviet Union. Aside from that, another motive played a decisive role in my agreeing to to this suggestion: the desire not to miss a single opportunity of getting to know the people of this immense unexplored land. The administration received my agreement with evident satisfaction.

"The P.V.C.H. will at once get the Latin text-books you need," I was informed.

Within a week the six or seven members of my course already had three copies of the text-book issued specially for those preparing for the medical profession. Nadia continued to study with avidity and to make the same fantastic progress. During the month and a half that I spent in Irkutsk prison she succeeded in assimilating two-thirds of the elementary grammar, that is, declensions and conjugations, ordinal and cardinal numerals, and so on; material that, in my opinion, normally takes at least a year to learn. I was slightly teased on her account by my friends among the prison 'elite'.

"Your pupil has been looking for you," the former customs employee would say to me with a sly twinkle in his eye.

"Which one?"

"Don't pretend you don't know. Always the same one, the plump little one from the pharmacy, of course."

I tried in vain to convince him that she was completely wrapped up in her studies.

We used to study in the evening, three to four times a week, on the hospital premises in a room containing a gigantic boiler. Apart from Nadia, none of the circle had any particular ambition in the matter—it was enough for them if they could read the prescriptions and the labels on the bottles of medicine, and all but one achieved this.

In the room where our class was held lived the superintendant of the boiler, a Ukrainian woman of around twenty-five, tall and stately, with breasts and hips as though moulded from steel. But the sad, perplexed brown eyes looked down on this blossoming body as if to say: "Don't pleasure in this body, life has dishonoured it." Thrown out of her native village, together with her whole family, for refusal to join the kolkhoz, and losing all those dear to her on her prison pilgrimages, she was now alone, utterly alone. Her youth had faded on these pilgrimages through prison. She had had many passing affairs, but never found her heart's desire. To lose oneself in grief or seek the calm of resignation? To accept life as it is or to reject it? A bewildered soul brooding constantly over this problem, unable to bring herself to put by the dreams of youth, she had fallen into a state of profound melancholy.

My pupils were a mixed bunch. One young girl from the

isolation ward was the daughter of a highly skilled worker in the Irkutsk Gold Trust refining works, where her brother was also a skilled worker. She belonged, so to speak, to the Soviet aristocracy of labour. She herself had worked as a shop-assistant in the Co-operative. She, her mother, and her sister-in-law had each been sentenced to ten years' of concentration camp for the theft and illegal use of ration cards. The sister-in-law had worked in the Irkutsk Town Soviet, in the rationing department. She had got hold of a considerable quantity of ration cards and, together with the two other women, re-sold the goods obtained with them. An Amnesty Commission had freed the mother on account of her age, and the other two were also hoping for an amnesty. Having learned that I was imprisoned for 'political reasons' she expressed a sincere astonishment.

"What do you get out of it? What is the value of it? From prison to exile, from exile to prison, and so on, endlessly."

Her work-mate in the isolation ward was a lively young Komsomol. He had left his mother in some remote corner of Siberia and come to Irkutsk to study and try his luck. From there he had been sent as leader of a special Komsomol brigade to the gold fields of Aldan. He had been very satisfied with the life in that place. Memories of strenuous labour in the taiga mingled with visions of the immense virgin country, with thoughts of 'striking it rich' and all kinds of romantic notions. Sweat, gold, pleasure—gushing forth and streaming together to some frenzied can-can tune. "Ah! That was real life there!" he cried with a challenging flash in his eyes. His tales of the life of the Aldan gold prospectors conjured up visions of the American gold-rush fever. But it was on the Aldan that the lucky star of our Komsomol suffered its first eclipse. During one of the frequent debauches a furious sleigh ride ended up in a fight and the exchange of revolver shots. The sleighs damaged, the State horses injured—nabbed! . . . that was the finale. *En passant* the trial revealed what was an open secret to everyone: the trading in vodka that was carried on in spite of its being forbidden in that district. Not only the prospectors, but the Komsomols themselves obtained this contraband in exchange for illegally held gold-dust that should to the last speck have been handed over to the State in return for paper 'Gold Bonds'. For his crimes our young hero was expelled from the Komsomol and given ten years. But he was not down-hearted; a grin full of the joy of life never left his face. By assiduous work in prison and concentration camp he reckoned to obtain a remission of his sentence and an amnesty. In any case, he calculated on being at liberty in two or three years, even if he had to risk an escape.

"And then?"

"Then?"—a wily look crept over his face. "Then I'll get some papers and join the Komsomol again under a false name, resume my studies and return to life . . ."

The siren song of Gold seemed to dominate the entire life of Irkutsk. From casual remarks and conversations between prisoners one gained the impression that it was the passion for gold and the profit from it that kept the town alive. Everyone there had direct or indirect connection with the gold industry.

The youngest and least accurate of my pupils was the fifteen-year-old Lidochka, who worked in the dispensary. 'For prostitution' she was being sent to the 'labour colonies' in the East to be 're-educated'. But even in prison she continued to occupy herself with prostitution. Our class was held after working hours. Who was it turned up late or not at all? Little Lidochka!

The greatest fame among the women of doubtful reputation belonged to the 'typist', Marusya. Suddenly she materialized as it were on the scene. One fine morning there stepped forth from the long procession of those walking around the garden, the figure of a young woman, fashionably dressed in a gay flowered material, with hair dyed blonde and 'Soviet permed'. In those prison surroundings of drabness and neglect, where darkness and gloom dominated, she seemed to us like a princess out of a fairy tale. Like a flash of lightning the news zipped round: a Soviet 'typist-miss' in the prison! A week later came a new sensation. Marusya had joined up with a notorious gang of bandits and thieves who were confined in a special cell, but in the same block as Marusya's. One day after the exercise period she hid herself in the gangsters' cell, put a kepi on her head, covered her shoulders with a man's overcoat and thus evaded the evening control. A wild orgy went on throughout the night in the cell and Marusya's deception was discovered only in the morning. As punishment she was put into solitary confinement. A few days later she hung herself there, but was taken down in time—the administration even asserted that she had been play-acting. Whatever the truth of the matter, hanging is certainly a rare phenomenon in a Soviet gaol. As their most radical form of protest political prisoners resort to cutting their veins; more frequently they go on hunger-strike, which often ends in death. As for the criminals: their means of struggle is a deep cut in the belly with a knife. It is said that this is a grave but not a mortal wound.

Let us turn back to the last two members of the class: a forty-year-old woman thief and a thirty-four-year-old railway engine driver, both working in the general hospital ward.

The woman thief not only had a very stormy past but also a life stamped strongly with the Soviet impress. The daughter of a cab-man in the suburbs of old Petersburg, she had early drifted into the underworld, becoming a member of a daring and wealthy gang with contacts abroad. This gang's speciality was cat-burglary, and the woman became an expert drain-pipe climber. Everything went well and in the intervals between 'jobs' our heroine lived either in Russia or abroad in Paris and Nice, like a well-to-do, distinguished lady, maintaining several establishments under various aliases. Even when caught she always served her sentences under a different name. Then, having served her six months, she would resume her comfortable, luxurious existence under another alias. But once she was caught in a particularly serious affair and had to do three years in Tsarist penal servitude. Her authority in the underworld was merely enhanced by this.

She continued to ply her trade under the Soviet regime. In the twenties she was apprehended in a big affair and sentenced to be shot as an habitual criminal. However, she was offered a pardon in return for a promise to abandon her old life, and given twenty-four hours in which to think it over. After a day of hesitation she yielded. "To tell the truth, I just got the wind up." Then she was taken in hand. She was taught cutting and dress-making, given a job in a dress factory, became a forewoman and a member of the Party, which entrusted her with the task of re-educating a group of young thieves. All the newspapers advertised her as a model example of successful re-education. But still she was unable to hold out against temptation. She was exposed by one of the old criminal police, who surprised her with a member of her former gang. When, after her movements had been watched for a long time, she was at last arrested, the police official said to her: "Well, you dug yourself in very nicely—member of the trade union and the Party, and a forewoman to boot. It was quite a job to get at you."

From the Examining Magistrate she demanded proofs. Not caught in the act, therefore not a thief, said she. But he informed her: "That was under Tsarism. Under the Soviet regime things are different. Now, if we know someone is a thief, then he is a thief."

She got three years and could not grasp it at all. "How is it possible? They didn't catch me stealing, yet they give me three years . . ."

The engine driver had received five years of concentration camp for a train accident. This was the second time since the launching of the Five Year Plan that he had been condemned on the same charge. Now he had firmly decided to change his occupation. "Railway work is the worst there is. The engines are good for nothing, the lines completely rotten, and the driver has to take the blame for everything that goes wrong. It's true that after the show trials we are soon freed. But all said and done one doesn't like having one's head continually in the noose. I'm going to get a less dangerous job—I'll become a hospital attendant, that's much less exciting."

The engine driver was among the most enthusiastic of the 'activists' within the prison. He wrote the most hard-hitting articles in the wall-newspaper, *The Sun of Labour*, on such subjects as 'The Victory of Socialism in our Great Land', 'The New Man Re-educated by Labour', and so on. Of course all this activity, which he simply regarded as a meaningless formality, secured him a speedy release. In my study circle he was looked on as a sort of P.V.C.H. trusty. As a proletarian, it was his job to see that the work of the circle proceeded smoothly and, in particular, that neither I nor anyone else covertly propagated anti-Soviet views.

THE FINAL DAYS

Time does not stand still, even in prison. About two months passed in observation, in conversations, meditation and study while I waited for a place of exile to be allotted me. At last the day arrived when I was informed that this was to be Yeniseisk.

"A pity," said the woman doctor, "you would have been better off in Turukhansk, in the real north."

I said nothing. My two cell companions, Shushiashvili and Rusak, were leaving at the same time. Shushiashvili, the old Georgian Social-Democrat, who had commanded the Social-Democratic 'people's guard' of his district, was a thick-set peasant, a democrat and a poet. He also was going to Yeneseisk. He suffered not a little on account of his children having sided with the Bolsheviks and joined the Komsomol. It is true that in return for that they had received the right to go on with their studies and carve out careers for themselves. Later I met Shushiashvili in Krasnoyarsk and in Yeniseisk and we lived together in friendship throughout the period of our exile.

Boris Rusak, young, intelligent, an insatiable reader, and a Zionist, was sent to Turukhansk. His parents were both in exile in Tashkent, also for their Zionism. Until recently young Rusak had been together with them, but the G.P.U. came to the conclusion that he visited the other exiles just a little too often and interested himself too closely in the problems of Soviet life. So, as a punishment for his curiosity, they transferred him to exile in the far north, to Turukhansk, fifteen hundred kilometres from a railway. Two and a half years later, when he had finished his term of exile and was returning from Turukhansk via Yeniseisk and Krasnoyarsk, we met again and spent a few days together.

Such is the life we lead. The political exiles in Russia feel themselves to be members of one great family dispersed across the land in the most sinister prisons, the most forsaken places of exile. Many years of suffering in the prisons, of pilgrimages on the roads of this huge country, develop in them their own peculiar habits and attachments: spending some time in prison as comrades they become attached to one another for the rest of their lives. And since the G.P.U. in spite of all the refinements of its imagination, is nonetheless limited in its choice of prisons and places of exile, those who have once lived together find themselves re-united after two, three, or five years of separation. Meeting thus, one plunges at once into questions and animated discussion, quickly recounting all that has happened in the interval of separation, exchanging information of events within the country, telling of friends, relatives, acquaintances, and finally speaking of what one has heard from abroad—of Trotsky, the Second International, Palestine, the Georgian and Amenian emigrés. With a delay of a year or even two one sometimes picks up very interesting news, such as is not known even to the free world abroad. Thus the author of these lines brought to Paris at the beginning of 1936 the information on the first secret trials of Communists accused of terrorist attempts on Stalin's life.*

---

*Author's note: The trial in the winter of 1932—33 of Ryutin and Tolmachev, whom I met in prison; and the secret trial of Zinoviev and Kamenev, which took place in the summer of 1935, a year before the public trial that ended in the notorious executions.

Shushiashvili and Rusak were being sent into exile with a whole group of young criminals in goods trucks. To me, as a Communist—in particular a foreign Communist and a former functionary of the Comintern, the G.P.U. was more generous, allowing me to travel by ordinary passenger train, accompanied by two G.P.U. guards.

The day of departure came round. I was to proceed later on my own and I therefore looked in on some friends during the morning, to tell them that I should come and say goodbye later, when the departure of the other columns had made things easier.

In my cell I bagan to busy myself getting my things together. My joints pained me and I had a stiff neck. I attributed this to the hardness of my couch. Suddenly I heard someone call me. It was Nadia.

"I will come and say goodbye to you in the afternoon as I promised . . .", I began, but she interrupted me.

"I've brought you this letter."

She turned and went off hurriedly, leaving the letter in my hand. Here it is:

"Anton Antonovich,

There's no need for me to repeat what I've already told you—how grateful I am to you for the lessons you have given me. I feel that with you I could learn so many things and so easily. That is why I am now asking you to give your consent to my joining you in your exile in Yeniseisk after my liberation, which—everyone tells me—won't be long delayed. I know that it is not considered the thing for a woman to be the first to show her feelings towards a man. But that is the old way of looking at things. Now we have made the Revolution. A woman has equal rights with a man, and I think that you, as an advanced person, will agree with me. I will go with you wherever you wish. I am used to work and not afraid of it. I hope that I can be of use to you in your life and in your struggle and I love you very much. I shall not be admitted to the Workers' School any more, my husband has left me and disappeared and I consider myself completely free. We could lead a life of study and work together. I hope for a favourable reply.

Nadia."

As I read these words, embarrassment mingled with admiration for her courage. But there was the difficulty—however much I liked Nadia as a personality, I was indifferent to her as a woman. And yet . . . how was it possible not to love such audacious, vigorous youth? Carried away by her spirited determination I for a moment thought—why not? Perhaps we really could settle down together somewhere. She could come to Yeniseisk and we could live together. At Igarka, on the Yeniseisk River, foreign ships called for timber ... who knows ... perhaps she might succeed in smuggling herself into the hold of a ship, escape abroad and from there come to my aid through the intermediary of my relatives ... But at once I pulled myself up. What right had I to involve her in such a risk? No, our paths were not destined to merge.

And so it was. I was sent to Yeniseisk and she, in a few weeks, went with a large party urgently needed for construction work on BAM. There, I learned later, she again managed to establish herself in the hospital, became friendly with a young exiled doctor, stayed on after her release and soon after married him. But at that moment of my departure it was very hard for me to leave her lonely. We promised to write to one another and just before I left I went to see her for the last time.

It was then that I had an encounter that left a deep impression on me.

Nadia lived together with six or seven women who worked as cleaners in the hospital, in a small room under the staircase near the kitchen. The little room was scarcely lit by a tiny window. At first on entering it I found no one there and I sat down to wait. After a while a young girl came in, a child of about fourteen who worked as a dishwasher in the kitchen. She had been sentenced to concentration camp for vagrancy and for stealing bread from the market. She came into the room with a book in her hand. Without noticing me, she settled down on her bunk opened her book and in a half-whisper began to piece together the syllables of some story printed in the large type of a spelling primer. Her voice as she spelled out the words became louder and louder with obvious emotion.

No, I said to myself, resolving the riddle that had perplexed me when I had seen her previously in the yard, this is no lost creature, no vagabond, even though she had wandered in the depths, beset by pitfalls. I had never spoken to her. But now in her thin face one could sense her soul. She looked more like a young boy than a girl. The large eyes of this fair-haired child had a slightly timorous expression; they were sad, remote; she gazed into the distance, the far-off distance. But one did not see this face at first glance; the incredible jumble of rags and tatters that was her clothing prevented one from noting it. She was as ragged as David Copperfield when he came to his aunt. But the rags of Dickens' little hero were at least the sorry remnants of clothes that had once upon a time been made for him, whilst this poor child had everything off someone else's back. Her thin legs stuck out from impossibly big boots like frail reeds. She was clad in the cast-off frock of a tall stout woman. She looked indeed forlorn in all that rubbish.

Seeing her now so agitated over a book I forgot all this ragamuffin exterior, divining the other world concealed by this outward disfigurement.

The story she was reading dealt with the hard life of women workers in the textile factories of India. She finished her reading, and unable to control her emotion, said aloud:

"Poor women, poor people! How they have to suffer . . ."

There is little in life that has moved me so much as those simple words spoken in the very lowest depths of human existence. On the brink of concentration camp; having no single close or dear person to her in the whole world; having instead of David Copperfield's kind aunt—the G.P.U., instead of a brother—the Siberian frost, instead of a roof over her head—the savage taiga; in the midst of this, she forgot her own self, she became agitated over, suffered for the workers in Bombay . . .

Not from prophets, not from theoreticians, but from out of the mouths of children, from the simple people, one makes the final test of the truth that is socialism.

In an hour I had gone. My comrades of Irkutsk prison became memories. The names of most of them, as of this little child, I do not even know. But I see them again before me. I see again those numberless, nameless people of Russia wandering across the endless icy wastes . . . The Twelve of Blok . . . the rebels of the October night caught up in eternal Siberian bondage . . .

III

PROVINCIAL SOVIET LIFE

We arrived. Black night and the sleeping town. Behind me was Irkutsk and all that had gone before—seven years of Soviet liberty and Soviet prison. Ahead lay an intimate acquaintance with provincial Russia, with those who make up nine-tenths of the country, although the fact is not advertised.

My former brief sojourns in the provinces of 1927 and 1928—in the Crimea, the Caucassus and the Ivanovsk districts, with hasty visits to the villages of those areas—could not be compared with my present situation. Then it had been a holiday affair, the tour of a distinguished foreigner who himself sat among the mighty in Moscow. Now it would be a long stay, the hard life of an exile amid the similarly hard lives of ordinary common citizens. I was now better prepared to take in this workaday provincial life.

After a long telephone call from the station my escort managed to obtain a car, more precisely a lorry, which took us to the Krasnoyarsk G.P.U. headquarters. I was received by the officer of the guard and locked up.

"The official in charge of political exiles will ask you to report tomorrow and afterwards you will be free to stay in the town, where you will wait for the next ship to Yeniseisk, your place of exile."

Of course I stayed in prison not one night, but three days. In Krasnoyarsk itself, before I left for Yeniseisk, I fortunately spent not a week but a whole year. The machinery of Soviet life does not always move quickly.

I was examined by a minor official of the political department of the G.P.U., a local inhabitant named Minkov.

"In 1932, when in Verkhne-Uralsk, you left the Trotsky group. Why?"

"Why? Hm . . . well, because although in many respects he is better than you, fundamentally he is just the same bureaucrat as you."

"Indeed! So then you are against the Party—you are against both Stalin and Trotsky."

"To me it is not important who controls the Party, Stalin or

375

Trotsky. What interests me are the rights, or rather the lack of rights of millions of workers. Because it is not you with your G.P.U. but they, and they alone, these Party or non-Party workers, who can build socialism."

"That means that you are an adherent of the Workers' Opposition."

"That would not be quite accurate. As you know, I have not belonged to any political group since 1932. As for the Workers' Opposition, its old programme does not in my opinion embrace many aspects of present-day life; in general it does not take into consideration the whole range of experience, the lessons of the Russian Revolution. But twelve years ago, when it first came on the scene, it was basically right."

"Well, well, Comrade Ciliga, you go rather far; the Workers Opposition was already at that time condemned by Lenin for its anarcho-syndicalist tendencies. Think a little over the road you have travelled: you started off as a 'Bolshevik-Leninist' criticizing Stalin and now you have got to Lenin. Comrade Lenin was right in saying that small deviations if persisted in lead to grave errors."

And he rambled on and on ... Finally he got back to practical matters.

"In a week or two you will go to Yeniseisk. We shall have to get a move on because in a month's time the river Yenisei will be frozen over. We have to make all the use we can of these last trips."

"And in the meantime where could I stay in Krasnoyarsk? Could you give me the address of an exile here?"

"That can be done ..." He dug into his papers. "Here, here you are—Ivanov. The Street of Labour, no. 12."

"Ivanov? I don't know him. Isn't there anyone here I might know from the Verkhne-Uralsk isolator?"

"From Verkhne-Uralsk? ... H'm ... yes, there is—Davidov, 97 Bograt Street."

"Davidov, Davidov here? Splendid! I'll go to him."

Davidov was an outstanding young publicist of the Democratic Centralism Group (an oppositional grouping more to the left than the Trotskyists). I had become friendly with him in Verkhne-Uralsk.

On saying goodbye Minkov gave me my ration cards. At that time everybody in Russia was rationed and the exiles received their cards from the G.P.U. Although it was assumed that I should be staying in Krasnoyarsk for only a week or two Minkov, as an expression of his goodwill, gave me coupons for a whole month.

Leaving my luggage for the time being in the G.P.U. head-quarters, I went in search of Davidov.

It was autumn; September drawing to a close. In the still-warm midday air there was already a touch of dampness. Leaving Minkov and the G.P.U. I found myself on a large square.

At last I was alone. Nobody with me; nobody behind me. I could go where I liked, speak to anyone I wanted to, and breathe the fresh air of liberty. Free! Free! I was free! And yet not free. I could not believe it. When one has sat in prison for three and a half years, shut off from the world by the walls of the cell and the keys of the warder, freedom seems some-thing impossible, unreal. The space one walks in appears limitless. From force of habit I moved cautiously, looking back to see if I was followed, half expecting a shouted command to halt. I alternately quickened and slackened my pace. But no, nothing happened. No one tried to stop me. Each passer-by went his way absorbed in his own thoughts, knowing nothing of the turmoil within me. Their indifference at last communicated itself to me and calmed me down. I forgot about myself; I turned my gaze outward, to the streets, the people, the town.

On what an enormous deserted square the G.P.U. building stood! It was more like a steppe than a square, and right in the centre of the town at that! The only houses to be seen were away in the distance. How boundless everything is in this Russia. Only gradually does it dawn on one that the square is not completely empty. At different points dots can be seen, whole groups of dots. These are wooden huts serving as shops, tea-rooms, co-operatives—all poor, wretched, higgledy-piggledy. On one side of the square is a stone arcade of State trading establishments. They even give the impression of doing quite a brisk business.

In the middle of the square rises a stone church, the quondam cathedral of the town. Its architecture recalls more the Catholic Baroque than the Byzantine style characteristic of Russian Orthodox churches. Externally it gives an impression of neglect, almost of ruin. For twenty odd years it has presumably no longer been kept in repair and from a distance its cupolas look like the remains of some ancient towers. Now the church serves as a garage for some Soviet transport organization. The altar and all religious objects have long ago been removed and lorries are now parked in the interior.

Dreamy and quiet in the midday hour, the square at morning market time had a quite different aspect, when a mixture of State, Kolkhoz and private speculative trade was carried on. Then, directly facing the G.P.U. building, the traders with their one or two baskets of wares lined up. Onions, carrots, eggs, milk, cabbages were to be found there in modest quantities. The buyers complain in chorus of the high prices; but the goods sell like hot cakes just the same. Small wonder, since half a year ago, at the end of the Five Year Plan, there was nothing at all to be had. Behind the Kolkhoz market stood the booths of the State organizations. There, a noisy and chaotic 'service of the needs of the population' was carried on: a barber-shop and a pub, a gawdy poster advertising snap-shots while you wait, a bookstall, a merry-go-round. All this little changed since Gogol's time; maybe it had become slightly livelier, in spite of the appalling poverty.

On the other side of the square on certain days, I think once or twice a month, a cattle market was held where around two dozen lean cows and ten or so not too mettlesome horses became the object of animated discussion and minute inspection on the part of the rare buyers.

"Where is Bograt Street?" I asked a passer-by.

"Bograt Street?—there at the end of the square is Marx Street, the first side-street is Mutual Aid Street, and the second or third along that is Bograt Street."

From Marx Street, dusty and calm in spite of its resounding name, I turned into Mutual Aid Street, on which no activity whatever was to be observed. The road was not paved. Here was the realm of wind-blown dust and sand, and, after rain, of impassable mud. Not at all like a town, more like a village street; the houses mostly one-storey, very infrequently two-storey; built of wood from which the paint had peeled, and which time and neglect had blackened and warped. The houses were surrounded by high fences hiding the yards from the eyes of passers-by. The planks were of the same solid timber as the houses but had long since lost their once impressive air; they leaned drunkenly, here and there were broken or missing altogether.

The complete absence of traffic, of any movement; the air of desertion; the silence (and what silence!), gave me the feeling that I had accidentally wandered into a dream world. At long intervals in the midst of this forest of wood rose a house of stone. But in this spell-bound provincial realm nothing astonished me so much, nothing seemed such a striking embodiment of the traditional ancient *Rus* as the pavements of these streets. For the sand piled in front of the houses, here hardly above the level of the roadway, there a full yard high, was paved with plain planks of wood. These were laid two by two, with gaps of earth and grass between, and reminded one of shaky little bridges thrown across ditches. Where it was not held by grass, the sand had sifted down from the sides; the wooden planks were badly worn, in parts quite rotted away. For the first time in my life I beheld a pavement of wood, and in what a sorry state! Well, well, well! So that is how it is! Thousands of times one has read of wood-built *Rus*; one looks at Russia oneself for many years; but it requires a trifling detail like this—the rotten planks of a provincial pavement—to truly understand for the first time the wooden heart of this enormous land. The poverty, the wretchedness of Russia came to me almost at once, from the first days, the first hours of my arrival in the country. I saw it in the rough Moscow roads, the pavements, the houses, the clothing, the looks of the people. But the wooden heart of the land, the soul of ancient thousand-year-old *Rus*, came to me only then, in the seventh year of my pilgrimage through the Eurasian spaces of the U.S.S.R., from these time-worn planks flung down with careless, slap-dash indifference to form the pavement of this Siberian provincial town. So this is how they are, I thought, the provinces of Holy Russia upon which October crashed down with such ruthless force. So it was out of these depths of poverty and despair that the passion and anger of this mighty world arose. I was so moved that I involuntarily halted. There on that pavement, still spell-bound in the dusty dream of centuries, I felt blow over me a wind from far-off oceans. I felt that I had suddenly grasped something new about the Russian Revolution, its sources and its future.

The Russian Revolution was not only a revolt of the province against poverty, it was also the dearest child of the province. It was not chance which willed that the greatest Russian revolutionaries, those who needed a century to come to ripeness, Chernychevsky, Bakunin, Lenin, were sons of the distant province. Everyone is aware that the roots of the Russian Populists were planted in the black soil, but one often forgets that the Bolsheviks too, long before they conquered the cities, grew and matured on the Volga and in the Urals. Revolution, I said to myself, trying to shake off the provincial torpor surrounding me, is always a revolt of the nation against itself, a decisive hand-to-hand battle of its own spiritual and material forces, the triumph of the traditional, century-old peoples' opposition over the traditional and century-old oppression of power. Outside of this struggle there is no real peoples' revolution; there are only putsches, palace revolutions.

How ignorant and pitiful are those who do not want to understand that the October Revolution had its roots deep in the people, who try to represent it as the expression of foreign ideas and intrigues! Russia had often had rulers of foreign origin, but its riots and revolts have always been manifestations of the elemental spirit and genius of the people.

In the womb of the province, in the depths of the peasant land; that's where one has to seek the roots of the Russian Revolution in order to understand its two characteristic features: the gigantic sweep of its internal impetus and the almost incredible weakness of its international programme. Because—there is no need to hide it or be silent about it—the Russian Revolution, profoundly national, truly Russian, did give itself at the same time international aims. It has the right to lay claim both to Stenka Razin and to Marx, to Pugachev and Robespierre, to Avakhum and Cromwell. This roll-call of names and epochs is not a revolutionary agitator's flight of fancy, but expresses the essence of a really popular revolution impregnated with the desire to liberate all humanity. The proletarians of Gracchus, the slaves of Spartacus, the fishermen of the Lake of Galilee, the *sans-culottes* of Paris, the craftsmen Levellers and the simple Diggers of England, were the highest synthesis of the national and international ideas and ideals of their time. So with the simple Russian workers and peasants of 1917. This eastern Revolution was carried through under the ideological banner of western Marxism adapted to their conditions. Therein lay not only a tribute from the East to the great creative merits of the West, but also an effort towards a synthesis with the West, their fraternal union as free and equal members of one single human community. A union not in words but in deeds: the replacement of the capitalist system of national egotism and social exploitation by a new socialist system based on international solidarity and freedom. What a Utopia! And yet what an absolute, matter-of-fact necessity for Europe and the world, for the East and the West! But this creative audacity, the sole progressive programme of our age, has suffered a defeat—whether episodic or epochal time will tell. In Russia, as elsewhere, national egotism has come out on top.

The West remains faithful to imperialist unification with the East; indeed it counterposes the metropolis to the colonies, the civilization of the western exploiters to the barbaric but oppressed East. The East, including Russia, has entered upon the road of national-capitalist development, counterposing its young barbaric egotism to the senile egotism of the West . . . We do not need western oppressors, since we can be ourselves oppressors, cry Russia, China, India and the entire East.

Between 'barbaric' *Rus* and the 'decadent' West yawns the old gulf. But it does not follow that the world has stood still. An epoch of reaction is equally as rich in changes as that of revolution. Bolshevism has now become the bearer of social and nationalistic reaction, but it continues to realize—by virtue of its initial revolutionary impetus—the greatest technical and economic changes in the country, thus bringing Russia closer to Europe and America from another direction. The Five Year Plan is no more than the first of the great undertakings of the new conquistadorial oppressors.*

But where, in this lost corner of Siberia, are the results of the Russian revolt against backwardness and poverty? Where are the traces of October and the Five Year Plan? Standing on this pavement I do not see them yet. I have still to discover them.

This thought brought me back from historic speculations to immediate reality, the purpose of my walk along this wooden pavement: where then was Davidov's apartment? Would I learn from him the fate of other exiles? I quickened my pace . . .

Not yet initiated into the mysteries of Siberian locks and bolts, I had some little difficulty in opening the small door into the yard of no. 97. I knocked on one door, on a second, on a third. Not a soul about. Finally, a man of about forty slipped out of the last door.

"Excuse me, doesn't the political exile Davidov live here?"

"Oh yes, here, in this room."

"There is no one in?"

"No, he must be still at work."

It was already dusk when Davidov got back. We embraced, delighted to see each other once more. I followed him into his room. Damp, cold, topsy-turvy . . . Davidov had been famous throughout the isolator for his untidyness, which was in marked contrast with his methodical, even pedantic ways when working.

---

*The victorious march from Stalingrad to Berlin, epic of the Second World War, was the second; others are in preparation, their recent beginnings are seen in China and the discovery of the atom bomb. *A.C.*

After being some time together with him in exile I was able to appreciate highly his patience and his organizing abilities at work. But, unfortunately, these qualities did not reveal themselves in the domestic field; here he had in some way an organic ability to be unconscious of disorder. To excuse himself, he hastened to assure me that for all practical purposes he did not live there but spent most of his time with an exiled friend, Comrade Plomper.

In the course of conversation, I suddenly noticed that he limped. He had not limped in the isolator. It turned out that since our separation he had contracted typhus on the way from Irkutsk to Krasnoyarsk, a journey he had been compelled to make with a party of 51 criminal prisoners. He had been taken to Krasnoyarsk hospital, having managed to contract a severe form of the disease. But for his strong heart he would not have pulled through. The limp remained as a souvenir.

"Actually I was scheduled for exile in Turukhansk but because of my illness the G.P.U. decided to leave me here. It's an ill wind that blows no good."

Poor Davidov! To his tuberculosis, which periodically became acute, he had now added lameness. That is the road that revolutionaries in Russia must travel: persecution, illness, poverty, death. But Davidov was not at all despondent. On the contrary, he was full of energy and the joy of life, qualities that had more than once served him in good stead.

"Well, but how did you get my address?"

"From Minkov, in the G.P.U."

"How does he know I'm here? I am still registered as living with Plomper, and I've only been sleeping here two days," he asked in surprise.

Still talking of the never-sleeping eye of the G.P.U. we made some tea and strengthened ourselves with bread and butter. Observing my wolfish appetite, Davidov decided we should go right away to see the Feldscher, Ivanov, who was a family man and fond of visitors. Over supper in the family circle we should be able to talk to our hearts' content about our friends and our affairs.

No sooner said, than done. Ivanov lived in the Street of Labour. As we turned into it I noticed a large two-storey building enclosed by a high fence.

"That's the prison," explained Davidov.

"Couldn't they find a better spot for it than the Street of Labour?"

"It would be more correct to ask: couldn't they find a more

appropriate name for the street—the prison has been here since Tsarist times."

Ivanov indeed met us with great hospitality. At one time he had ben a worker in one of the large chemical plants in Petrograd. There he had been dangerously poisoned and compelled to give up the work. But that was already during the Revolution, and he had been able to go to the *Rabfac* and from there to the Medical College. He had almost completed his studies when, in 1927, he had been expelled from the Communist Party for belonging to the Trotskyist Opposition. In 1929 he capitulated and returned to Leningrad, but, for resuming his old 'connections', he had been re-arrested and in 1932 sent into exile. Here he had obtained work in his profession and as he was a good worker he had soon settled down as a Feldscher in the Krasnoyarsk hospital. After a year he had already earned the title and the work of a doctor. His wife, the daughter of a railway worker, was secretary of the Agricultural Commission of the Executive Committee of the Regional Soviet. She was a Communist Party member and had never joined the Trotskyist Opposition, but had gone voluntarily into exile with Ivanov. True, a year later, during the Party purge, it was precisely for this reason that she was expelled, since it does not do for a Communist to go into exile with a husband who is a Trotskyist and a counter-revolutionary.

Ivanov had a flat of two rooms and shared the kitchen with his landlady. Since both he and his wife worked they lived without hardship. After supper, drinking tea with biscuits and jam, we began discussions that lasted till midnight. We spoke of common friends, of events in Russia and abroad. This was one of those 'pouring out one's soul' talks that are so typical of Soviet exile life in provincial isolation: talks that like flames flickering in the wind momentarily light up the long hard road of the exile. Alas, already on the morrow the G.P.U. had a detailed account of this conversation . . . As we learned, later, Ivanov, still posing as a Trotskyist, was in fact a G.P.U. informer.

The first thing I did the following day was to go to the post office and send off letters and telegrams abroad. In a semi-conspirative form I also sent news to friends in Russia. The visit to the post office took me to the centre of the town, to the main street—the only paved and well-kept one in Krasnoyarsk—with its large number of two and three-storey stone buildings that to some extent modified the impression of provincialism so striking in the neighbouring streets. In these stone buildings were situated the Soviet administrative institutions, trusts, banks, shops, the cinema, theatre, the schools, the hospital and the dispensary.

On the outskirts of the town there were two settlements and a railway station, one of the largest stations on the Siberian line. The southern settlement housed the railway workers, and had at one time been known as 'Nicolayevka', but was now called 'Third International Settlement'. The northern one, where the smaller fry lived, had been re-named 'Paris Commune Settlement'.

The days passed and little by little my picture of the town took shape. For a long time the re-naming of streets and settlements had been almost the only change brought to the outward appearance of Krasnoyarsk by the October Revolution. It is worth while to pause on this, because, with the exception of Leningrad, I have not come across another town in Russia having such a calculated symbolism in the naming of its streets.

In the distant days of the Revolution's birth the central artery of the town, the main thoroughfare, had been called Soviet Street, because the leaders did not then wish to sanctify it with the name of either a living or a dead revolutionary leader. But the two parallel streets were called Marx Street and Lenin Street. Then came the minor gods, streets and lanes bearing the names of lesser revolutionaries of all-Russian or only local fame—the Bograts, Lebedevs, Pernsdorfs and others. Considerable tribute was paid to international socialism. In addition to Marx Street, there was a Lassalle Street, and the streets of the Paris Commune, of Marat and Robespierre evoking memories of the great French Revolution. This encounter with Marat and Robespierre did not, I admit, arouse my irony, but only respect for the heroic years of the Russian Revolution, for the time when Alexander Nevsky and Peter the Great had not yet been thought of as having revolutionary connotations. There was another peculiarity about this collection of names: I did not see one street there bearing the name of Stalin. One assumes that today's rulers of Krasnoyarsk have by now attended to this 'grave negligence' of the first years of the Revolution; presumably Stalin today dominates the former Soviet Street, with Marx and Lenin on his right and his left.

Among the streets of all Soviet towns there was always a black sheep—Trotsky. What town could in its time refuse the honour of naming one of its main streets after the leader of the victorious Red Army? Later all these streets had themselves to experience the vicissitudes in the destiny of revolutions.

During the fierce struggle with the Left Opposition, Trotsky Street in Krasnoyarsk became Mutual Aid Street (from the co-operative situated there). This was effected without a sharp polemical thrust: "Because we are now against the deification of leaders". But later, when there was a pressing need to express one's indignation at Kirov's assassination, Mutual Aid Street became Kirov Street.

Subsequently I was able to plot the course of the Revolution in the street-names in Yeniseisk, my second place of exile. There, no tribute whatever had been paid to Soviet ideas as such, or to internationalist traditions, but instead the changing *status quo* had been honoured: the main street being called Lenin Street, the next Trotsky Street, and the remainder distributed among the local heroes of the Civil War. Trotsky Street was successively re-named Red Street and Kirov Street. There, by the way, I also found a Stalin Street—the very last street on the outskirts of the town. The re-christening had apparently been undertaken during the first years of Stalin's rise, when someone among the new 'fathers' of the town wished to mark the appearance of a new star in the firmament by thus naming a hitherto nameless street on the edge of town. During the period of Stalin's greatness the fact became embarrassing, since it was hardly possible to re-baptize a street of medium importance in the name of Stalin, and on the other hand it was not yet, in 1935, permissible to change the name of the main one, Lenin Street . . . How quickly the symbolism of revolution ages. How quickly it falls back into the proud sad past. Only life—be it good or bad—preserves the eternal present.

There was another way in which this symbolism was not fitting. The revolutionary audacity of these street-names, these challenging declarations of the new, contrasted sharply not only with the social realities of the Stalin epoch, but also with the external, the physical appearance of the town. It was still the same old pre-revolutionary Krasnoyarsk—only shabbier, more ramshackle. Even all the large houses in the centre, with perhaps one exception, were of pre-revolutionary origin. Neither the October Revolution nor even the Five Year Plan had left its mark on the architecture of the town. Against the flood of the new people, plebian in its essence, they seemed like genteel relics bearing the blows of fate not without dignity.

In this connection I heard an amusing and revealing little story. The people of Krasnoyarsk roared with laughter when they saw in a copy of the MOPR (International Red Aid) journal, intended for distribution abroad, two photographs of Krasnoyarsk: one showing part of the town as it was, under the caption 'Before the Revolution', and another showing the centre of the town built under Tsarism, with the caption 'Krasnoyarsk After the Revolution'.

As I saw later, the only building that had been done was on the other side of the Yenisei, where during the Five Year Plan a new industrial town, or rather the skeleton of one, arose amid a mass of new factories and giant stacks, looking in the distance like the funnels of great ocean liners under construction and still surrounded by scaffolding. Near the factories sprawled the rather mean-looking houses for the workers, still uncompleted: the building of communal dwellings was then still in its infancy.

Conceived on a grandiose scale, the industrial city attracted a horde of people to Krasnoyarsk and the population grew during the first Five Year Plan from one hundred thousand to one hundred and sixty thousand. The old roofs had to shelter thousands of additional lodgers, and even the offices of powerful Soviet enterprises were given temporary accommodation under them. The lack of capital did not permit the housing programme to keep pace with the speed of industrialization, so that the deep changes wrought in economic life were in fact not noticeable in the outward aspect of the old town.

The general appearance of the people was in keeping with that of the town: poverty on the one hand, and poverty on the other. But during my two-year stay in Siberia important changes took place. The second Five Year Plan got under way. It ended with the series of Moscow Trials (1936–38). But in its initial stages it functioned as a process of smoothing out, softening the hardships of the first Five Year Plan. In its economic aspect the second was essentially conceived as inaugurating the period of 'mastering' that which had been achieved with blood and sweat during the first. The emphasis was placed on the daily life of the people. The second Five Year Plan was to become, in contrast with the suffering and militant asceticism of the first, the incarnation of the 'gay and well-to-do life'.

"Life is easier, comrades; life is gayer." It was 'He' himself who said it. In these words was an admission, and a justification of, and encouragement to those who had risen during the first Five Year Plan. It was their political passport for the voyage into the "happy life amid plenty".

The Soviet provinces, and particularly Krasnoyarsk, decided

to live up to the demands of the times. Shops, restaurants with orchestras, and cafes open till the small hours sprang up like mushrooms after rain; a variety of spots where one could 'make a night of it': quite elegant establishments, even with a pretence of luxury, catering for the higher-ups and others, more modest, for the common people.

When I first arrived in Krasnoyarsk there were only two shops in which one could buy 'everything'. Second-hand goods were to be found in the pawn-shop where the *ci-devant* went to realize what they could on their remaining possessions, while all new goods were sold in Torgsin for gold and foreign currency. In the course of one year there appeared, in addition to these shops, seven 'Gastronomes' (delicatessen shops), two of them really very large establishments. In these 'Gastronomes' paper roubles were accepted, but the prices were 'commercial', that is two, three and sometimes even five times the prices of State-rationed goods. At these 'commercial' prices one could obtain 'everything' in the way of food and drink. Commercial clothing shops were also opened but these were frequently short of supplies.

One curious thing to be noticed, typical of all these new developments, was the eagerness, the passion almost, with which people tried to make the new resemble as much as possible the 'old': even chocolates were sold in paper wrappings labelled 'Chanticlère', 'Bon Gout' and so on, recalling pre-revolutionary times. It was the same with the wines and the white 'French' bread. To strengthen the resemblance, a commissionaire stood at the entrance, decked out in pre-revolutionary livery complete with kepi and gold braid. And only the profoundly plebian atmosphere within, and the manners of the commissionaire, clashed with this old-regime spectacle.

Here for the high 'commercial' prices one could buy everything one desired. But this 'everything' was accessible only to a very small circle of the privileged. The ordinary folk had to content themselves with window shopping, or at best with some crumbs from the tables of the rich. For example; I knew a woman worker who twice a month, on her pay days, used to buy a hundred grammes (about 3½oz) of butter for her sick child.

It was not long before the new trend towards the 'cultural' and 'well-to-do' life began to show itself on the streets as well, where the contrast between the appearance of the well, sometimes even elegantly dressed minority and the majority clad literally in rags became more blatant. Important Communists could be recognized at a distance by their fur hats and their good quality fur coats. The non-Party experts preferred clothes of a European cut and wore collars and ties. Between the wives, daughters, and sweethearts of the Party members and the 'non-Party Bolsheviks' there was less difference in dress: they all paraded in beautiful furs and Moscow style silk dresses (Moscow style is a rather original mixture of European and Russian). They were all devotees of the permanent wave, lipstick, nail-varnish, and so forth. They remained true Siberians only when it came to their boots.

It was at the railway station that another stratum of the population could best be studied. The newcomer is always staggered by this conglomeration of poverty endlessly waiting for trains. A crowd of two to three hundred always throngs the two waiting rooms, where the people lie huddled together. Still more unfortunate and miserable are those who crowd the street outside the entrance to the station. They wait for trains two, three or even five days. The train arrives already overcrowded, takes on a dozen or so more passengers and departs, leaving the rest to wait patiently for the next. Men, women, children, babies dressed in all kinds of indescribable rags; their scanty belongings stowed away in bags, boxes, all sorts of queer objects—it was a picture of utter poverty, misery, and eternal resignation. Unforgettable!

The higher-ups do not sprawl on the floor and they do not even need to wait for a train. The majority of them when they travel are on official business; they go to the capital on a mission or to the Crimea or the Caucasus for a vacation. Their seats are reserved. Tickets for these seats are sold in a special booking office so that those who require them do not have to queue up with the common people at the general booking office. Even those who cannot produce a leave permit, or a document stating that their journey is on 'State' or 'public' business succeed in getting away by the first or second train: contacts, bribes, or just the fact of being well dressed open all doors to them. They travel, of course, free of charge, or at the expense of the organization that sends them, and in the 'soft' class, mostly by express. Not everybody has a hard time in Russia . . .

The second Five Year Plan brought another novelty. During the first Plan the town was blacked out at night—why should electric power be wasted? With the inauguration of the second Plan, the Krasnoyarsk Town Soviet decided by a stroke of the pen that the town should be lit at night, at the expense of the people of course. Under threat of a heavy penalty for non-compliance, every householder was required to wire a lamp to the outside of his house. Nobody dared to protest.

The Red Army occupied a certain place in the life of Krasnoyarsk. The sharpening of Soviet-Japanese relations produced a military flood. Tanks and guns rumbled along the streets; squadrons of planes thundered overhead. When the military came to the town they took the best there was to be had of everything for themselves. The best restaurant was converted into an officers' mess, the best building became the House of the Red Army. The military uniform now set the tone on the streets and the officers behaved towards the civilians with full consciousness of their superiority. Their manners and their language indicated very plainly that they did not so much ask as order, without recognizing the right of refusal. One sometimes had the impression that an enemy army had occupied the town. Noting all this, inevitably one thought: militarism is true to itself—Red or White!

Krasnoyarsk was indebted to the army for the town bus service. From one stop to the next cost ten kopecks; the fare from the railway station to the other end of the town was one rouble. That was not cheap, but the inhabitants were glad of it just the same. The small buses held only sixteen passengers and there was thus always a queue of far more people than there were empty seats. Moscow sent only three buses, including one reserve. That was not a large number, especially if one takes into consideration the fact that one, and sometimes two buses were held up for repairs.

The town had a considerable number of lorries, about a dozen cars of the Ford type, and two good limousines. The latter were used—as the whole town was aware—by the secretary of the Krasnoyarsk Party Committee and the Chairman of the Regional Executive Committee. Once, when about a dozen of us ordinary citizens were waiting on the main square for the second, maybe the third bus, one of the women there could no longer restrain her feelings when she saw one of these limousines pass.

"They drive their cats about in those cars, and us—we can't even get in a bus. Yes, yes!—I know what I'm talking about all right, I work as a cleaner in the vet's place and only a few days ago the Chairman of the Committee brought his cat in for treatment by car."

Neither by word nor gesture did anyone in the waiting crowd express the slightest comment on the woman's remark.

I could not help being astounded at her boldness, and I indicated with a movement of the eyes the G.P.U. building right opposite where we standing. A grim silence ensued; then the people began to drift away without waiting for the bus.

How does Krasnoyarsk earn its living? What is its principal activity?

Krasnoyarsk is one of the largest stations on the Trans-Siberian Railway and one of the main stopping places of the parallel Moscow-Khabarovsk-Vladivostok airline. But even more important to the life of Krasnoyarsk is its role as a relay point between North and South, a role assured by its position on the Yenisei, the natural north-south route. The town is therefore on the junction of these two basic lines of communication. Down from the mighty Sayansk ridge, sweeping for fifteen hundred kilometres through the black soil land, rich in timber and gold, the River Yenisei reaches Krasnoyarsk, and then flows on for a further two thousand five hundred kilometres to pour its waters into the Arctic Ocean. The Yenisei is Krasnoyarsk's great master and bread-giver; it is the Arctic Nile. One goes to Krasnoyarsk by rail and one leaves it by river. And it is not only visitors who journey on; the local people are also used to travel. Ask anyone you like. Everyone has been or intends to go to the mysterious 'down-river', looking for work, trying his luck. This amazing 'down-river' means in the direction of the North Pole. We Europeans would say 'up-river' and, realizing as we said it that it meant moving from the temperate climate of Krasnoyarsk into that of the Arctic, we would shiver involuntarily, feeling on our bodies the frosty fingers of the North. But the people of Krasnoyarsk reason otherwise: together with their foster-mother the Yenisei, flowing down from the Sayansk mountain range, they go 'down' to the Arctic.

The Yenisei feeds the town only by its traffic, for it is not in itself rich. Throughout its entire enormous length it is poorly stocked with fish, except at its estuary, where they come in from the open Karsk Sea. it is there that the numerous fishing fleets go in the early spring, remaining till the autumn and the ice. The fishermen go there with their entire families, women children and all, and they salt the catch themselves on the spot.

But the main trade of the Krasnoyarsk region is not in fish but in timber. The banks of the upper and middle Yenisei and those of its numerous tributaries, particularly the mighty

Angara, are covered with splendid forests. At various points spread over the whole length of its enormous river and most of its tributaries, that is, over a distance of from seven to ten thousand kilometres, there are timber camps. The first timber sawmills are at the foot of the Sayansk mountains on the Chinese frontier; the last in Igarka on the threshold of the Arctic Ocean, the new town built during the first Five Year Plan on the bones of thousands upon thousands of deported peasants, in the belt of eternally frozen earth, the tundra.

This entire timber industry, enormous in its scope and volume, is in the hands of a complete system of organizations, partly independent, partly linked together. Aside from the purely economic, there are also two scientific bodies: the Scientific Research Institute of the Timber Industry and the Timber Technical Institute. The first devotes its labours to the classification, geographic and economic, of the forest wealth of the Yenisei basin; the second trains specialists for the timber industry. When I knew it, there were about eight hundred students enrolled. But this Institute had only been established during the first Five Year Plan, and it has without doubt a great future in store. It was at first located in the former Girls' Secondary School, then moved to new quarters in the only new building constructed in the centre of the town since the Revolution.

The new factories on the other bank of the Yenisei were primarily connected with the timber industry: wood-working, railway carriage construction, paper making. In addition there were 'secret' plants, i.e. military enterprises, in particular chemical plants, and an engineering factory for the gold industry.

The Yenisei Gold Trust had its central office on the river bank in a new, not particularly remarkable wooden building. The gold workings were distant and the role of the Yenisei centre consisted in supplying them with labour, transport, tools and food.

Each organization had its own means of transport; these, however, were never sufficient for its requirements. But a number of transport organizations also existed, with cars and lorries, and there was the Yeniseisk Shipping Company, with its own school—the Waterways Technical Institute.

In the life of the town an important part was played by G.U.S.M.P.—the State Administration of the Northern Ocean Route. This world-famous organization dealt with all matters concerning the 'conquest of the Arctic', navigation between

Murmansk and Vladivostok across the Arctic Ocean, and navigation of the estuaries of all the large rivers. The charting of the seas as well as the entire Arctic shoreline, the building of harbours near ocean settlements and their provisioning, the organization of an Arctic industry—this in a few words was the broad outline of the work embraced by G.U.S.M.P. The organization of air transport between the extreme north and the rest of the country also came within its province. This powerful organization, a kind of State within a State—the East India Company of the North,—is the real ruler of the Arctic. It was enough to enter the building in which G.U.S.M.P. headquarters were located to feel the breadth of its power—and its arrogance, too.

The main route into the Arctic runs between Krasnoyarsk and Dixson Island (at the estuary of the Yenisei where it flows into the Karsk Sea), a distance of two thousand three hundred kilometres. Hydro-planes fly at least every other day, if not every day. In Krasnoyarsk one talks of Dixson Island and Igarka as though they were neighbouring villages; the whole life of the town centres around this axis between these distant poles.

In winter the gold and furs are transported from the Siberian continent by air. For this purpose branch airlines have been set up, stretching as far as the tiny settlement Tara, fifteen hundred kilometres west of the Yenisei. Thus into the northern desolation the airplane and the wireless penetrate to places where the railway has not yet ventured and where ships call but rarely and with trepidation.

IV

ROOM NO. 14

My stay of a year and a half in Krasnoyarsk did not pass without a few incidents expressive of the times and the place. The first and perhaps the most harmless of them was my illness.

My broad, though not thorough exploration of the town was involuntarily interrupted. Fate willed that I should for a time concentrate my attention upon the small closed world of the inmates of the hospital, and become intimately acquainted with some results of the Five Year Plan, not from books, not from statistics, but from what harsh Soviet reality itself had written on the bodies and souls of one small group of its victims. And it so happened that I even took part in their struggles, their friendships and enmities, which endured right to the very door of death—and sometimes even beyond.

My new comrades-in-misfortune were non-Party and Party people: workers, peasants, employees, and students. With the exception of two or three more exiles like me, they were all free. Even before meeting them I had seen many victims of the Five Year Plan—I was one myself—but these were all people whom I had met in prisons and here I met the subjects and the objects of that gigantic experiment who had been allowed to live and die in freedom. These had a different psychology; they expressed through a different structure of the soul this merciless struggle that had been unleashed within the country.

Illness had been stealthily and relentlessly creeping up on me. I was queuing up in the corridor of the G.P.U. headquarters with the other political exiles. Suddenly I felt such an attack of weakness that I asked to be given a chair.

"Lean against the wall; you'll manage all right without a chair."

I did so, but after a few minutes collapsed. I was taken into the fresh air and my temples rubbed with alcohol. I came to but could not move my limbs. Only then did I recall how my joints had ached in Irkutsk, how painful it had become, on the journey and in Krasnoyarsk itself, to turn over at night. From the dampness of the cells, the hunger-strike, the nervous tension, and a general exhaustion of the organism I had a whole series of attacks of rheumatic fever. The G.P.U. gave me a note for the Town Hospital, my comrades straight away hired a cab and we drove to the hospital, where I was placed in the general ward, room no. 14.

The hospital was a small town in itself, consisting of a great number of single and two-storey buildings. On the first floor of our building was an operating theatre, and on the ground floor were the rooms of the general ward. Room no. 14 was at the end of the corridor, with windows looking out on the western and southern aspect of the inner court of the hospital. In addition to the beds ranged round the walls, there were several in the middle of the room. There were two doctor's visits a day: a thorough examination in the morning and a cursory visit in the evening with the standard formula—"Anything special to report?".

"You are lucky, you've got muscular rheumatism. It will pass off without any after-effects. Had it been rheumatism of the joints there would have been a danger of it affecting the heart."

Thus was I consoled by the capable young doctor from Leningrad, himself an exile through being mixed up with some social democrats. He insisted that there had been a misunderstanding and tried in every way to demonstrate his loyalty; he was an eager subscriber to every government loan and an active participant in 'social activity', speaking at all meetings of the hospital personnel; he had married and was altogether solidly rooted in the local life. The G.P.U. took note of his zeal and did not bother him.

The head of the general ward was a woman doctor of about forty-five, one of the general practitioner type of the old school. Most of the senior doctors in the other departments were the same. I was surprised that hardly any of them knew a foreign language. It seemed somehow strange—a capable and well-trained doctor who yet did not know any language except Russian. Sometimes they would ask me to translate an article from a German or French periodical; but they assured me that in view of the abundance of medical literature in Russian translations it was possible to manage perfectly without a knowledge of foreign languages.

The patients were looked after by men and women nurses of three or four categories. To an outsider they all appeared to belong to one and the same group of junior personnel, but there was among them such a jealous emphasis of the microscopic differences between their ranks, that I could not help thinking to myself: this is the foundation, and the real strength, of the entire hierarchical system—particularly the strength of the upper and really privileged strata; this is what lies at the bottom of it all, this urge to stand a little higher in the social scale than one's petty colleague.

A group of young girls in their last year of study at the Medical College also came to the hospital for practical work.

The food was completely insufficient and those who did not receive parcels from relatives or friends were literally starving to death.

The room seemed quiet, calm, and the patients gave the impression of being simply tired, not ill. But this was a sad illusion. Death hovered close over most of the beds, and the dying were rent by fierce animosities.

One of the first events that I remember from my hospital days was the discharge of a peasant who was still a sick man. He was an exile and the G.P.U., without waiting for him to recover, sent him further north to forestry work. He could hardly move; but argument was useless—one just had to obey. Collecting his few belongings together, he asked nobody for anything, but complained aloud of having no soap and no food. I wanted to show solidarity with a sick comrade and an exile by giving him a bit of soap and some bread and fat.

But would the G.P.U. not look on that as a political act, I pondered. Ah—to hell with the G.P.U. I'll do what my conscience tells me is right and see what happens afterwards.

Apparently the G.P.U. did not get to know about it. But the entire room—something I had not at all expected—looked on my action as an outspoken political demonstration. The hearts of the Communists boiled with fury; the hearts of the non-Communists were filled with a timid affection for me. But I did not know this all at once; I became aware of it only from what came out in the course of other happenings.

Soon two more peasants left before being cured. A kolkhoznik was sent home because his kolkhoz refused to pay for his upkeep any longer (social insurance does not apply to kolkhozniki). The other went back home to die. He was a young Kirghis. Chance had brought his family to Krasnoyarsk and he, a nomad son of the steppes, had become a worker on some building site. But that climatic and social upheaval, those hunger years of the first Plan, had undermined his health and given him galloping consumption. When his family saw that the hospital could do nothing for him, they decided to take him home.

During my stay there only two patients left the room cured: an old man, a book-keeper; and the middle-aged secretary of some industrial organization.

The first death was that of my left-hand neighbour. He was a quiet old chap whose body was all swollen up from starvation. At night he stole bread and other food from the other patients. He was not the only one to do this, so all those who received food from relatives or friends hid their treasure carefully each evening, dividing it and hiding it in various places, in the hope that if anyone were tempted it would not all be discovered. The old man died as quietly as he had lived.

The second death was more tragic. This was the death of a young student of about twenty-two, who lay at the end of the row of beds to my right. He had come to Krasnoyarsk with his young wife a year before, to study. But 1932 had been such a terrible year of famine that he had had to abandon his studies and look for work in order to survive. Too late—galloping consumption had already taken hold of him. His wife escaped unscathed and managed to get a job as cook on the 'Elite' State pig farm and send him food.

She came to visit him in hospital only a week ago, riding the twenty kilometres into town on one of the horses belonging to the farm. She came striding into the room in high boots, short skirt, a whip in her hand, her cheeks glowing from the ride; a finely built woman radiating health and energy—a Siberian Artemis returning from the hunt. But a few days after this visit her husband began to have difficulty in breathing, to gasp for air—and now he is a corpse. She comes again today, the same attire, the same glowing cheeks, but now she is agitated, her former self-possession gone completely. She is not weeping; she approaches the body without a sound. But bending above the body of her husband for a last farewell, she suddenly collapses and falls down upon it, and there come not tears alone but such deep, rending sobs that we cannot bear to hear her. It is as though two lives, not one, had suddenly ended here. Even in this waiting-room of death the loss of this young, unblossomed life was dreadful for us to witness.

To the beds thus vacated came new patients, again from among the common people.

My right-hand neighbour was a forty-five-year-old Communist, a highly skilled worker, a 'shock brigader' and a foreman. Ivan Grigorievich. He had come from the north, from Igarka, suffering from scurvy. He looked a sturdy man, cut all from one piece and strongly sewn together, inspiring confidence. Drawn to him by an instinctive sympathy, I became frank with him, opened my heart to him and told him that the G.P.U. refused to allow me to go home abroad, in spite of the fact that I had already served my three year prison sentence and that no new charge had been made against me; that, in any case, I had come to the U.S.S.R. only temporarily, as a visitor, to learn from the experience of the Russian Revolution, and that therefore I had every right to return home when I pleased. I was speaking of these things to him when he brusquely cut me short: "It's quite right for them not to let you go. You'd only start anti-Soviet propaganda abroad."

I tried to discuss with him, to convince him: the working class should know the truth; international solidarity did not mean that the Soviet bureaucracy could hold as life-long prisoners those foreign workers and revolutionaries whom they considered undesirable. I spoke to him of the fate, similar to my own, of my comrades Dedich, Dragich, Heberling—Yugoslav workers who were languishing in exile or in prison, God knew where. It was no use. Ivan Grigorievich stuck stubbornly, doggedly to his point of view, though without anger, and continued to defend the actions of the Moscow Government. Our discussion ended up by involving the whole room. A second Communist, director of the Oxygen Factory in Krasnoyarsk and himself a former worker, came to the support of Ivan Grigorievich. The Five Year Plan had left him with a legacy in the form of severe tuberculosis. He spoke in a sharp, squeaky voice and, as his bed was at the other end of the room, he had to shout his comments the whole length of it.

"Let you out of the country! So that you could reveal State secrets to the bourgeoisie! No! Never!"

"What nonsense are you talking! In the first place I don't know any State secrets; and, secondly, if I did I wouldn't give them to the bourgeoisie. I haven't broken with Stalin in order to pal up with the bourgeoisie."

"That's not true! Look at Trotsky—he got abroad and revealed all the secrets to the bourgeoisie."

"Well, tell me a single secret which Trotsky has given away. No—of course you can't! And the reason is simply because Trotsky hasn't revealed any State secret. I am not a member of the Trotskyists' organization and therefore cannot answer for Trotsky—but the truth is the truth. He hasn't given anything away, and I know that for certain because I've read what he has written abroad. He doesn't hesitate to criticize Stalin pitilessly, but when he comes to the social order in the U.S.S.R. he doesn't expose it for what it is, he embellishes it rather. For, in Trotsky's opinion, the evil lies more in Stalin's person than in the bureaucratic nature of the Soviet regime."

"Ah, so Trotsky writes too little about the Soviet regime for your liking—you'd rather he slandered it a bit more ... and after that you want to be allowed abroad! All of you oppositionists, whatever you call yourselves, Anarchists, Mensheviks, Trotskyists—you're all traitors, agents of the world bourgeoisie!"

On his inflamed face could be read his final judgement: you ought to be shot, all the lot of you! But he did not say this out loud: since the Party does not do it, therefore it must not be spoken; the duty of a Communist is to defend the Party and the Government and not to anticipate policy ...

After such a heated discussion silence would fall on the room, the conspiratorial silence of the people against the Communists. The Communists had done their duty—they had defended the Government; the people did theirs—they remained stubbornly silent. Not expressing any opinion, their very silence was a condemnation. The rhythm of their breathing, the attentive stillness of their bodies, the way in which they strained their necks and held their heads so that not a single word should escape them, their impassive faces—all expressed the verdict of the people. And these sick people understood better than I that the particular asperity of the Communists was not caused so much by my demand to leave the country, as by my demonstration of solidarity with the exiled peasant whom the G.P.U. had sent further north ...

But it cannot be said that my polemic with the Communists had won the complete confidence, the real sympathy of the patients. The very fact that I could afford to openly contradict the Communists, openly criticize the Government, separated me from the people, put me above them as it were. I could do this because I was a foreigner and a communist, although an oppositionist—and the masses have an attitude of reserve towards people like that.

Who can fathom these Communists? Who can trust them? Today they quarrel among themselves, revile each other—and tomorrow perhaps they will again be united together against us ...

It would be rash on my part to affirm that the Russian working people are mistaken to think like that ... A new, really popular opposition can arise only from the mass of the fresh youth unburdened with the general struggle of the previous decades. The Communists of the older generation, those in the government and those in opposition—from the viewpoint of socialism and the proletariat, are only the exhaust system of the locomotive of history.

There was a slight re-arrangement of the room. Ivan Grigorievich had a relapse and was placed nearer to the door, where it was more convenient for the nurse to attend to him, and his place was taken by a newly arrived Communist, the director of some distant State farm. He had come to Krasnoyarsk to talk over some business matters with the Grain Trust and had suddenly been taken ill. Next to Ivan Grigorievich was a labourer.

Ivan Grigorievich and I had found many things to talk about. After the Revolution of 1905 he had, while still a young fellow, emigrated to Germany, where he worked in Berlin, learned German and took an active part in the social-democratic movement there. Even now, twenty years after, he still spoke with enthusiasm of Bebel's meetings. With the same enthusiasm he recalled how, going to work one early morning, he had read in his *Vorwaerts* the previous day's speech against militarism made by the young Liebknecht. The war caught Ivan Grigorievich unawares, put him out of action, but in 1919 he succeeded with great difficulty in making his way back to Russia through Poland. During the Civil War he worked as political commissar of a Red Army Division. During NEP he had several times occupied important economic and administrative positions; but nowhere and never could he settle down comfortably in the apparatus, and he periodically took up his old trade again. He worked in a motor factory in Moscow, then in Central Asia as the chief of a transport unit on supply work for the construction of the Turksib Railway, and afterwards in the same capacity on the strategic highway to the Pamir. For a year now he had been working as foreman of a G.U.S.M.P. engineering workshop on the Igarka. In spite of his steady defence of the Party bureaucracy, one sensed in him a good comrade, and we talked a great deal together about life abroad, about the paths our lives had taken. I became even more attached to him when the doctor told me that what was the matter with Ivan Grigorievich was not scurvy at all, but general alcoholic poisoning, particularly of the liver.

"His days are numbered and only his iron constitution is delaying the inevitable."

A different attitude was taken towards Ivan Grigorievich by his other neighbour, the young agricultural labourer, who came to hate him with a burning hatred. Ivan Grigorievich strained every nerve to convince him, to win him over, educate him. But this merely increased the hostility of the entire non-Communist part of the room—including the nurses—towards him. Throughout the world the labourer on the land has always been the most down-trodden section of the proletariat; and this applies also of course to the Soviet Union. Clever and deceitful propaganda can conceal this fact, but cannot change it. This day labourer had been through the gamut of Soviet experiences. Of late he had worked on some State farm. In our room this representative of the lowest layers of Soviet society became the spokesman for the only legal opposition in the U.S.S.R., an opposition that did not attack Communism or the Communist Party, but aimed its barbs against individual communists, criticizing them as persons.

On the surface this land worker did not appear to be ill at all; he looked in fact quite robust. But he displayed a greed for food that was extraordinary even for our room. He continually quarrelled with the nurses, accusing them of not giving him his full ration of food. The nurses received rations for the whole room and distributed them, not forgetting themselves or their people at home in the process. That was why he was perpetually at loggerheads with them. The nurses were very poorly paid and lived in dire poverty. Their guilt was relatively speaking not really so very great. But the land worker knew no pity. He would throw himself on the leftovers of some dying patient who had no appetite to finish his modest portion. He gave the impression that he was ready to kill anyone who might dare to challenge his right to these leftovers. Yet the doctor had prescribed a starvation diet for him—rusks instead of bread and no other solid food.

"He's all swollen up from hunger and the first essential is to reduce the swelling. But I'm afraid he's been starving too long. He's liable to go off any minute," the doctor explained to me when I expressed my surprise at such a diet for a man suffering from malnutrition.

In the meantime quarrels between Ivan Grigorievich and the land labourer arose on the most trifling pretext and developed every time into fierce exchanges of insults.

"Scoundrel, cannibal!" the labourer would call Ivan Grigorievich.

"Fool, idiot, beast — —!" the other replied immediately.

"Ivan Grigorievich, don't insult the man. Look, he doesn't get any parcels," the whole room would cry in chorus.

"I don't get any either; and if someone does bring me anything, it's from my own money, earned with blood and sweat," Ivan Grigorievich would defend himself. Then he would turn over in bed, muttering to himself: "Counter-revolutionary . . ."

Yes, it was "counter-revolutionary" all right. When the land worker called him scoundrel and cannibal, this did not so much refer to Ivan Grigorievich personally as to Communists in general, to the Communist Party, which, for the sake of its Five Year Plan, was sucking the blood of millions of workers and peasants. This the room understood very well, and that was why all were so united—although for differing reasons— in their support of the agricultural worker. The fact that all this on the surface took the form of personal hostility towards Ivan Grigorievich alone, gave a 'legal' cover to the expression of their quite 'illegal' feelings.

All the same, it was astonishing that this general anger against the Communists was directed at Ivan Grigorievich and not at the other two Communists, the directors. Why? In what respect were they better than Ivan Grigorievich? Strange as it may seem, these two Communist directors were impervious to this outburst of feeling because of their estrangement from the people. They were too contemptuous of the people and this contempt was their armour, it made them unassailable. They felt themselves so much above the others in the room that they ignored them, did not deign to argue with them. The rest of the room were vaguely aware of this, felt that they had no way of grappling with these two. And the unfortunate Ivan Grigorievich—who was continually trying to convince them that the Communists were their brothers, one with the people, fighters for a common cause—still belonged to the old guard of the Revolution, when no gulf had existed between the Communists and the people. And by this fact alone Ivan Grigorievich, a living wreck of the past, opened up old wounds without meaning to, and so drew the people's wrath down on his head. Nothing of all this was of course expressed in so many words; it came out in the expression of the face, the gesture, the uncompleted innuendo, silence. All of which showed the intensity of feeling, the degree of 'heat' reached by the internal frictions hidden deep below the surface. When Ivan Grigorievich, in order to defend himself, went over to the offensive, his opponents' anger became rage. In order to avoid any further trouble, Ivan Grigorievich was finally transferred to another room. In the whole of this episode of injustice towards Ivan Grigorievich one could not but feel the great urge of the working people for social justice against the Soviet bureaucracy, against the Communist Party.

Of the two Communist directors, my neighbour, a sovkhoz director, particularly distinguished himself by his coldly contemptuous aloofness. He had a certain right to this—nobody received so many parcels and such rich ones as he did. His visitors, members of the Regional Grain Trust, were not only the best dressed, but they also distinguished themselves by that peculiar dignity pertaining to those conscious of their importance and their superiority to the small fry around them. Amid the poverty of our waiting-room of death they looked like men from Fifth Avenue strayed by mischance into the slums. There was even something unseemly in the fact that such influential Soviet men, occupying such exalted positions, should have to lie in such a room or even visit it. The situation intrigued me, and I learned that it was a purely temporary state of affairs, because at that moment there were only a few cases of illness among the 'responsible workers'. The previous winter a special building had been set aside for them and they had received better medical treatment and better food.

My neighbour, the sovkhoz director, was a young man full of strength, energy and ambition. He had just crossed the threshold of his fourth decade and had already succeeded in making a remarkable career, and was probably still on his way up. That, at any rate, was his profound conviction. It was this certitude that made him so reserved, so haughty. Not without difficulty, very gradually, and chiefly from personal correspondence, papers and documents left after his death—yes, the black chasm engulfed him too—I pieced together his life story.

He was the son of a Ukrainian peasant settler in the Far East. During the Civil War he had been with the partisans in the Vladivostok area fighting the Japanese. He had distinguished himself by his courage and intelligence and had joined the Communist Party. Then he began to study. Towards the end of the NEP he was already working as secretary of some District Party Committee in the Far East. During the Five Year Plan he became an organizer of collective, and later of State farms. His energy and organizational ability were highly appreciated by the Siberian authorities and he was sent to All-Union Conferences in Moscow. He knew his own value: the

Party, the Soviet Government, Communism, and he himself were in his imagination one. The Organization and Idea were important, and he served them as their prophet; but they in their turn served him.

I did not enter into any political arguments or discussions with him. But there were certain things I wanted to know from him.

"Why do the sovkhoz not fulfil their plans? Why are their crop and grain deliveries fifty per cent or even more below the Plan figures? Why do they regularly fall behind schedule? (The facts were known to everyone; it was the end of September and the local newspaper 'Krasnoyarski Rabochi' was full of complaints against the State farms and the slow tempo of their work.)

"Shortage of labour," was his laconic and obviously ready-made reply.

"How is that?" I persisted. "A large percentage, almost half of the peasants are still outside the kolkhozy; they have little land because most has been taken by the kolkhozy; all these individual cultivators consequently need supplementary earnings . . ."

"They are good for nothing," the director interrupted. "They are incapable of disciplined work, they are die-hard saboteurs who would rather starve to death than work as they should. The only ones who work properly are the kolkhoz workers. If the State farms were guaranteed labour from among the kolkhozniki I would fulfil the entire programme!" he almost declaimed, as though he were addressing the Chairman of the Grain Trust and not me. Then he added more thoughtfully: "But for the time being this is not possible, since the kolkhozniki cannot yet cope with their own work. That's how we have to struggle with difficulties. We can't overcome them all at once, but only gradually, step by step."

For the first few days after his admission to hospital my neighbour the director felt well, and after a few days appeared to have quite recovered. He was already making plans for his departure from Krasnoyarsk, thinking of being once more in charge of his State farm, when his condition took a sudden turn for the worse. I looked at him in dread: was he going to die? Then I should be the sole survivor of all the beds along my wall.

Somehow he suddenly sensed it; it broke on his consciousness like an awful flash of lightning illumining the void—tomorrow will be the end. He, the Prometheus of Communism, who was destined to liberate, or at least to conquer almost the whole globe—he must vanish into nothing! The inevitability and the senselessness of such an end oppressed him with equal force. His face darkened with the shadow of black thoughts, becoming a dull grey. He tossed and turned, his forehead beaded with sweat. He, who held so firmly in his worker hands one-sixth of the globe, must give in, yield to a trifling illness? Stay, O Sun! Earth, cease to turn!

That inner struggle, however, was soon over; not so much through his reason, already clouded by the grave malady, as through instinct. He accepted death. The doctors busied themselves. The Grain Trust spared no expense: visits, examinations, consultations, injections—a ceaseless struggle to save him. The last reserve of oxygen was used up to prolong his life for a few hours. But it was in vain: a tumour in the lung had suddenly burst.

The sick man was already indifferent to all the tumult around him. He knew that all this fuss was not at all in order to save him, but merely to emphasize his social importance: let the people see that here dies a valuable, important Soviet citizen. And in the face of death his Communist aristocratism failed. Now when the final balance sheet was about to be drawn up, all his contempt for the people, instilled into him by the bureaucratized Party, the Soviet Government, and his own practices, disappeared. He looked at the other occupants of the room with new eyes, in a kindly, almost a guilty manner. From his store of food he began distributing gifts to those to whom a few days before he had not condescended to speak a single word. As his strength ebbed he asked me to carry on with the distribution, continuing to follow it with his eyes. And more expressive than this sharing was the look in those eyes. "Brothers," they said, "dear ones, People—forgive me for betraying you; forgive me for making you suffer, shedding your blood, forcing you to go hungry while I lacked nothing . . ."

Had this director been an aristocrat by birth, sucking in the hierarchical tradition with his mother's milk, the consciousness of his class superiority would not have crumbled within him on the threshold of death, he would have taken this contempt for the people with him into his grave, he would have said in self-justification: so it has been, so it will be, and so it must remain. But our director was of a different mould. And now, his life career so unexpectedly shattered, he remembered suddenly that it was not for the sake of this that he had taken up arms in his youth, when the Revolution itself had been young.

He remembered his parents; remembered his neighbours and contemporaries, whom later he had driven into kolkhozy and concentration camps, into slavery, into the grave; and thinking on all these things, weighing in the balance of his rebellious youth and what he had later made of his life, he turned to the poverty around him in that room, turned back to the man he had once been, and asked for pardon with his eyes.

His eyes spoke—but his lips remained silent. Life had left its indelible mark on him: he was a disciplined member of the Bolshevik Communist Party. And as such he died.

He died during the day in sight of everyone. All had raised themselves in their beds. What was to be done with his treasures, with the milk, jam, honey, biscuits, and butter that had accumulated in such considerable quantities? The agricultural labourer dared not claim that he was the sole heir . . . At any moment the nurse might enter the room, and that meant that everything would be taken away. We were faced with a delicate, ticklish problem that might even result in fisticuffs. There was a moment of indecision, as though we were considering: can the share-out be peacefully accomplished or is a squabble inevitable?

As the dead man's neighbour I possessed certain rights, and I decided to use them.

"Hold on a minute! I'm doing the sharing."

Everyone held his breath. The agricultural labourer gave me a furious glare, which said plainly enough—"Robber, scoundrel!"

And I realized that the share-out would be without a fight only if I myself took nothing . . . Goodbye to any jam, honey, butter, I thought sadly. But the squaring of the circle was accomplished. From that time on the labourer became attached to me like a child, although I had not given him the largest share, for the first and largest portion had had to be given to the nurse. The labourer had quietened down generally. He had become thin, that is, the swelling had gone down, and under the yellow skin his large bones could be seen. He lay quietly and became only slightly agitated for short periods during the distribution of meals. One morning, a few days after the death of the director, the nurse approached his bed.

"Oh, he's already quite cold. He must have died last night."

So the agricultural labourer, representative of the lowest class in Soviet society, departed this world quietly, unremarked. There was no fuss around his bed. His corpse was thrown into the common pit for the homeless.

Three weeks had already passed since my admission to hospital. I was getting better and could already move. But I was—how to express it?—emotionally, psychically exhausted. At my request I was transferred to a smaller room, no. 9, where I stayed for another week, but did not have to witness any more deaths.

There were four of us in room no. 9, but I can recall only my two immediate neighbours. One, a Ukrainian peasant deported to Krasnoyarsk, where he worked for the Timber Trust, was a strong, thick-set man, except that from having constantly worked in water his skin had taken on a glaucous tinge, the colour one imagines a water-sprite must be. I believe he was recovering from scurvy. His one aim in life was, by diligence, to gain the goodwill of his boss, get better food and a reduction of his sentence. If he had a grudge against the authorities, he had buried it somewhere deep down in his soul, and no complaints, no recriminations came to the surface; there was only an impassive reserve, a hard shell. But this hard shell was itself suspicious. He only once became excited, when telling me that, after a long interval without news, he had received a letter from his home village saying that the harvest this year was better and that now there would be no starvation. But when I asked him about the famine, and the suffering it had caused in his village, he said, with his usual cold impassiveness: out of three hundred families there now remained only fifty; the others had either perished or dispersed, scattered in all directions. These figures, and given with such impassive calm, so staggered me that I repeated my question. He repeated the figures, with the same imperturbability, in the same level tone, as if to emphasize his unwillingness that they should convey any judgement on his part.

My other neighbour was a young lad, a Komsomol, apprentice journalist on the staff of the local paper. During the summer he had been sent by his newspaper to the Krasnoyarsk State farm to organize several wall newspapers. One of his duties was to stimulate production.

In hospital he received visits from his young sister and his mother, an elderly, provincial woman dressed in black and giving the impression of having belonged to the bourgeoisie. There were only these three to the family and the young man was obviously its pride and hope. I do not think that he will have disappointed the hope placed in him, for his character was a strongly knit unity of lively intelligence, ambition, and an aptitude for keeping in step with the times. He had acute rheumatism and walked around the room on crutches. He had contracted this after some weeks of living in the open, in the fields of the State farm. When still in room no. 14, I had met another youngster with the same complaint, an agronomist on the Krasnoyarsk State farm. This gave me an indication of the actual conditions on that farm and the meaning of the slogan under which work there was carried out: "Overcome all obstacles no matter what the cost!"

I was very interested in what he told me about the strict division of food supplies into five categories. The food on the State farm was distributed already cooked, and the differences were therefore particularly noticeable. But the discrimination was firmly insisted on and there were no exceptions to the rules. The decisiveness and ruthlessness employed by the new regime in the execution of its technical-economic plans, is also employed in both implanting and fostering the social differentiations necessary to a complete hierarchical system. This phenomenom appeared to my young neighbour as perfectly normal. He spoke of it matter-of-factly, giving detailed replies to my questions, as if it was all part of the natural order of things.

At last came the day of my release from hospital. But during my illness I had made new friends and after my discharge I continued to pay them visits and listen to their gossip. Thus I learned that the director of the Oxygen Plant, who had been released while I was in hospital, had been re-admitted; but this time he had not managed to get on his feet again. They gave him a splendid funeral in town, and the *Krasnoyarsk Rabochi* carried a high-flown obituary on the death of an "untiring fighter for the victory of world Communism who burned himself out at his post".

A different fate was accorded my friend Ivan Grigorievich. He felt very, very lonely.

"Anton Antonovich, come to see me. We'll have a chat together. Be a pal and bring me a pound of white bread, the paper says the free market is open now."

During one of these visits I mentioned in the course of conversation the word 'system'. It proved to be the key that released a flood of pent-up emotion.

"Aw, system, system!" he burst out heatedly, "this cursed system. That's all it is with us, system, nothing but system! and the working man hasn't a chance to breathe!"

He could no longer restrain himself. There poured out in a boiling flood the bitter words of a working man against the

Soviet bureaucracy and its contempt for the working people. Now all at once everything became clear to me: why Ivan Grigorievich had not been able to settle down in the apparatus, why he had taken to drinking, why he approved of my forcible detention in Siberia, why he had become friendly with me, and why he had quarrelled with the agricultural worker, that intransigent rebel . . .

Ivan Grigorievich expressed the revolutionary traditions of the older generation, the best part of it; the part that knows much, understands much, but sees no way out; that perishes silently, hugging to itself the pain of its disillusion and defending the established order from fear of aiding counter-revolution, but also from fear of an insurrection of the popular masses leading to chaos.

The next time I went to see Ivan Grigorievich the nurse told me he had died.

"Where is he buried?" I asked, for I wanted to visit the grave of this obscure worker-revolutionary who had left his class but could not bring himself to join its enemies.

"His body lay in the mortuary for three days, but as nobody came for it he was buried in the common pit."

Ivan Grigorievich's body was buried with those of the homeless, those who had no family to claim them; in the same pit where earlier the body of his enemy, the agricultural labourer, had been thrown. Two representatives of two different categories of Soviet workers, who did not know how to unite in life, were now united in death.

V

THE MASTERS OF THE LAND

The U.S.S.R. is proudly proclaimed the land of the 'dictatorship of the proletariat'. From time to time Moscow still sounds this 'challenge to the old world'—the workers of the U.S.S.R. are 'the masters of the land'.

Yet here in some 'room no. 14' in the remote provinces, in the lives of men like Ivan Grigorievich and the agricultural labourer, one sees the age-old destiny of the workers still fulfilled, the ancient curse not yet lifted. But are these two exceptions, or are they characteristic of the fate of the workers in contemporary Russia? A reply to this legitimate question will perhaps be given by continuing my recital of my encounters with Soviet working people.

But—it may well be asked—can one get to know the life and thought of workers in a country where the G.P.U. is all-powerful and where counter-revolution has long ago overwhelmed and crushed every free expression of opinion? Yes, one can—and more easily than is commonly supposed.

It is practically impossible in present-day Russia to conduct a *political* struggle against the Government, to create anti-Government *organizations*, but it is very easy to get to know the living conditions and the thoughts of the people one meets, of the local population among which one circulates freely. In this respect a political exile is even in a privileged position: for he has nothing more to lose and his situation in itself creates a certain confidence in him.

If the Russian people are prevented from *publicly* discussing their situation and their aspirations, and are unable to *generalize* their experiences, this by no means signifies that they keep silent, still less that they accept as true all that the Government tells them without grasping the truth of what goes on around them. No, the position is quite otherwise. There exists an enormous, really staggering gulf between the public, so to say official, silence of the Russian people, and their private opinions and conversations.

Life is stronger than political terror. The G.P.U. has succeeded in *narrowing* the possibilities of expression by the mass of the

409

people, but it has not destroyed them. It is not such a rare occurrence to hear even generalized oppositional opinions privately expressed. And there is no end to the tales of individual grievances—one's own or other people's—with a barely concealed point to them. The whole of Siberia, and presumably this applies also to the rest of the country, is inundated with anecdotes aimed with greater or lesser precision against the regime.

Indeed, there is no counter-revolution, no restoration even, that could completely tame the revolutionary element, completely root out and exterminate the creative instincts of the people, so powerfully aroused by the upheaval of the Revolution. In spite of all the shifts and changes of the ruling clique, the rich fruit of that tremendous seed-time will live for decades, for centuries in the souls, the thoughts and the feelings of the people.

Even now—under the jack-boots of bureaucratic reaction—one is more than surprised at the acuteness of observation, the profundity of judgement evinced by the Russian working masses and expressed *sotto voce* in their own circles.

Looking at Russia from a distance, people must often ask themselves: How does this country, how do these people endure everything, keep silent about everything? But when one has lived in the midst of this country and this people, the question is rather: How does this regime maintain itself, when literally everyone and everything is against it, when not even the Communists believe what they preach? And here one inevitably reminds oneself of certain peculiar features of Russian history and the general traits of all great revolutions in their period of decline.

So what is the life, the grey everyday life of the working people, of the 'average' worker of the Soviet land twenty years after the Revolution and the famous, much-trumpeted Five Year Plans? What are his most intimate thoughts and aspirations? How does the Soviet worker see himself? How does he regard the existing regime and the ruling clique? What does he do and what does he think of doing? These apparently humble, trifling questions are of world importance, not simply because of Russia's vastness, but even more because of the greatness of the 'Russian experiment', which is, as it were, the culminating experience of three Internationals, the century-long experience of the entire European working-class movement, reaching back to the Chartists of England and the insurrectionary weavers of

Lyons. These are great questions, and the material that can be gathered for answering them, the documentation to be obtained even on the spot, at the very source, is meagre, partial, and difficult to come by. However, in this epoch of might conflicts the rare and precious information needed is only to be found hidden in the hearts of the people. Let us then obstinately and patiently pursue our search.

In September, 1935, towards the end of my stay in Siberia, I was left without accommodation and went to live for a few weeks in the home of one of my worker friends. For getting to know the life of the workers, a better opportunity than this intimate, informal, common life together could hardly be found, and I shall therefore begin with this experience.

My friend was a forty-six-year-old mechanic who had worked at his trade for over twenty years and been through the World War of 1914—18. For the last ten years he had worked in the Krasnoyarsk railway workshops, one of the largest and oldest established enterprises in that town. For thirty years these workshops had been a stronghold of the proletariat. In 1905 they had made themselves famous throughout Russia for their revolutionary deeds. One of the first Soviets in Russia had been set up here and it was in Krasnoyarsk that, with the active participation of the soldiers returning from Manchuria, a local revolutionary government had been established—the Krasnoyarsk Republic of Workers and Soldiers, later bloodily suppressed by General Rennenkamp.

Thus it was in no petty provincial enterprise that my friend was employed. But for all that he was no better off. He worked intensively on piece work for ten to twelve hours a day and earned from 180 to 220 roubles a month. He had a wife and three children, two small ones still at school and one grown-up son who was a mechanic in the same workshops.

The whole family lived in one basement room, which served as living room, bedroom and kitchen. It was of medium size, with two small windows looking on to the courtyard. Adjoining their room was a small, dark cupboard room whre they kept all sorts of family belongings and their food. In the middle of the living room was a stove on which they cooked and which heated the place. There was a large table ranged against the wall under the windows, and against the other three walls were three beds: one for the parents, one for the two children, and the third for the grown-up son. I shared the son's bed. Each bed had a mattress and a blanket, but no sheets. To keep ourselves warm at night we put all our clothing on top of the blanket: sheepskin coats, lined jackets, wadded suits. Almost every night the room gave shelter to a few more people: peasants from collective farms who had come in to town to trade. They passed the night sleeping on the floor. The mechanic's wife was herself a peasant woman and the peasants who slept there were relatives or friends from back home. They did not pay for their lodging but gave the family food or let them have it at cost price. Sometimes the peasants brought meat or vegetables to trade and the family would help them to sell their merchandise among the neighbours; in this way they avoided having to take it to the official market.

The mechanic and his son used to go off to work very early in the morning. Before leaving they had a hearty breakfast. Rising even earlier, the housewife prepared some soup, cooked potatoes or sometimes pies, and two or three times a week they had a piece of meat or bacon. The other members of the family, who remained at home, had tea and bread every morning. The two who went to work took only a snack to eat at midday and had a good meal when they returned in the evening. The food was pretty monotonous: soup, potatoes, gruel, tea. The family only bought meat from the peasants who came to stay with them; they were not able to afford the prices in the State shops or on the 'commercial' market. About twice a week the town slaughter-house sold offal. Since this was the only meat accessible to the majority of the population, the demand was always greater than the supply. In order to obtain it one had to rise at three in the morning and queue up at the gates. The mechanic's wife did this twice a week. At six o'clock one of the children would take her place in the queue and she would hurry back home to prepare breakfast for her husband and son. She then returned to the queue. The sale of offal did not begin until eight o'clock. The front part of the queue got their full allowance of just over two pounds; those further down the queue received just over a pound, and the remainder went away empty-handed.

The eldest son was a little better dressed than the rest of the family. This was because he had recently returned from the Soviet colony in Mongolia.

In Siberia I often had occasion to note that those who do not fear very hard toil and terrible cold, and who want to earn money quickly, go to the far north, to the shores of the Arctic Ocean, where the pay is high; but those who want to replenish their wardrobes or buy things of foreign origin (bicycles, leather clothing, tools, etc.) go to Mongolia. In discussing these matters the workers and employees showed no hint of any concern for the welfare of the Mongolian people; they spoke solely in terms of their own enrichment. The mechanic's son earned, as a fitter in the Krasnoyarsk railway workshops, somewhat less than his father, around 150 roubles a month. Thus the monthly income of this family of five, with two bread-winners, was about 350 roubles. How the family lived on this money, how it ate, what living space it occupied, we have already noted. The food and clothing prices made it impossible for them to live any better. Here are the prices for that period: a kilo (2.2 lb) of black (rye) bread, 1 rouble; a kilo of white bread 2½ roubles; a kilo of potatoes 1 rouble; a kilo of meat 8 to 12 roubles; a kilo of sugar 5 roubles; a pair of boots 150 to 200 roubles; a pair of felt boots 80 to 120 roubles; a half-length sheepskin coat 150 roubles; cotton working overalls 80 to 150 roubles; a woollen suit of medium quality 500 roubles.

My friend's qualifications and the nature of his work showed that his earnings represented the average workers' earnings, perhaps even a little above. This can also be established from other observations. I myself worked in a bank in Krasnoyarsk and on one occasion I had to investigate some inaccuracies in the wage payments at one of the Timber Export Trust yards. This organization had large stocks of timber on the banks of the Yenisei, but the staff of permanent workers was not very large, only about 110 people. Here are the wages and salaries I found there: the Communist director received 600 roubles a month; his deputy, a specialist, 700 roubles a month; about a dozen employees received from 400 to 600 roubles; then came a sharp drop to between 220 and 250 roubles for about a dozen of the highest grade workers; then another fifty workers receiving from 150 to 200 roubles, twenty others from 120 to 150 and the rest, about fifteen, earned less than 100 roubles. To this last category belonged in particular the old men and women.

It is a cruel fate that has befallen these old men and women of the Soviet proletariat.

I once travelled into the town with one of these old men. He worked at the Timber Export Trust as a cab driver and was driving me home, for the enterprise was located out of town. On the way I asked the old chap how much a month he was getting. It was 40 roubles. He ate only once a day, in the works canteen. His supper consisted of dry bread and hot water.

Here are the views of another old worker.

Late one night going home, I stopped to sit on a bench on the main street of the town. An old night-watchman came up and sat next to me. He started to talk about living conditions.

"It's hard for a working man to make a living nowadays," he said. "It's true, before there was the bourgeoisie, the rich capitalists. They took the best of everything for themselves. But now a working man doesn't get any fats at all, and without fats one hasn't got any strength. Yes, no strength . . . Before a working man could at least buy a little bit of fat."

That is how the old people of 60 and 70 years struggle along—as night watchmen, porters, cabmen.

Women workers are in general badly paid. At the Krasnoyarsk Timber Mill no. 2, where I was once sent by the bank to investigate some over-payment, I saw groups of four to six women engaged in very heavy work. They were dragging tree trunks from the river on to the banks with long poles. They were all women of about thirty, but were so emaciated and had such yellowish, waxen faces that they seemed twice that age. Their clothing looked like the rags of a tramp. But how could they look better? They earned under 100 roubles a month (as the book-keeper at the mill informed me in reply to my questions). At the local 'Spartak' boot factory, where only women were employed, the situation was no better. In the home of a local doctor whom I knew there was a servant working part-time. She undertook this extra work because an eight-hour day at the 'Spartak' factory brought her only 105 roubles per month.

The new 'classless' Soviet society has given birth to a new theory on servants. Here it is as I once heard it expounded. "There is no exploitation in keeping a servant, since the labour of a servant creates no surplus value and cannot give rise to private property. On the contrary, since a master gives his servant part of what he receives from the State for his own labour, the hiring of a servant is rather a sacrifice on his part."

The data on wages can be summarized as follows: the monthly wages of an unskilled worker are around 100 roubles, of a skilled worker 200 roubles; the monthly wage of an employee around 400. These figures are sufficiently eloquent in themselves. The facts are well known to those who received them. If at congresses in Moscow they can cook up a common hash—'the average wage'—out of these striking differentiations in wages, that deceives no one in the U.S.S.R.—for everyone knows well enough that he receives not an 'average wage' but his own particular wage, and everyone is fully aware of the category he is in and how much it differs from the other categories.*

One must here mention another, not unimportant fact: the higher employees as a rule enjoy free living quarters and communal services (electricity, water, heating), and their quotas of supplies in kind (food, clothing, linen, footwear) are higher and of better quality than those of the workers. It is not for nothing that the campaign against 'petit-bourgeois egalitarianism' was launched and pressed forward with such noisy official clamour; it is not for nothing that resolutions are passed for 'increasing the differentials in the scale of earnings'.

I shall say more about the employees later; for the moment let us return to the workers, their mentality and their methods of struggle. Let us return to the mechanic's family. It is a typical family, not only in its income and in the qualifications of the chief breadwinner, but also in its general outlook and the methods employed to improve its conditions.

In order to obtain an increase in his wages our mechanic used regularly to go to the head of the workshops and complain that his money was insufficient. The manager would express his full understanding of this complaint, but refuse an increase on the grounds of lack of funds and the instructions of higher authorities forbidding wage increases. In his turn the mechanic would express his appreciation of the manager's difficulties. But his work reflected his reactions in another manner: he carried out repairs to his manager's car in such a way that, instead of requiring an annual overhaul, it broke down nearly every week. Passive resistance, silent and continual sabotage is a mass phenomenon in Russia. It is the general, almost the only means of bringing pressure to bear on the bureaucratic apparatus by the mass of the workers, robbed of freedom and legal forms of struggle. The mechanic did not appeal to his trade union. That would only be a waste of time, he said, the trade unions serve the bosses, not the workers.

In such conditions the mass of the workers, in order not to starve to death, are compelled to resort to all kinds of manoeuvres and subterfuges, which not only injure the bureaucracy but are also demoralizing to themselves. Take the case of my mechanic's workmates, the railwaymen employed on the

*Events have since altered these figures, but not the relationship between the categories—*Translator.*

trains. This was one of the worst-paid categories. The engine driver of the Manchuria-Moscow Express, on which I returned from Siberia to Europe, received 120 roubles a month. How do these men manage? They buy food and goods where they are cheapest and, since they are able to transport them free of charge, sell them where they are dearest. Trading is even carried on in the trains themselves.

In the factories the workers often help themselves by pilfering goods to exchange with peasants and middlemen for food. In order to get more food they even sell some of the issue of working clothing they receive.

Politics in the narrow sense of the word did not interest my mechanic. Neither he nor any other member of his family belonged to the Party. Any thought of taking any *action* against the Communists, against the regime, was far from them, but the whole *attitude* was unfriendly in the extreme, even hostile. In the eyes of that family the Communists were the bosses, the exploiters, the police. Rank-and-file Communists, including workers, they looked on as careerists, chasing soft jobs in the apparatus, acting as stool-pigeons, denouncing their work-mates, trying to speed up the work to an inhuman pace. Whoever imagines that this attitude was exceptional and isolated is making a grave mistake. A deep gulf yawns between the Communists and the mass of the Russian working people. Some day, somehow, the world will become aware of this gulf—and will be shocked by its awful depth.

There was something rather patriarchal about the mechanic's family life. The children gave absolute, submissive obedience to their father. Even the eldest son turned over all his earnings to the family. The wife was crushed beneath a load of work and household worries. The only time I ever saw her relax was at the little family parties she sometimes organized. Her husband did not deny himself the pleasure of sometimes getting drunk. With his wife he was at once rough and yet attentive, even occasionally tender.

On his days off the mechanic liked to give a party, which was held on a 'bring and share' basis. In that basement living room there would gather from fifteen to twenty people, members of the family, visiting peasants with their wives and daughters, and workmates with their families. Cakes were produced, vodka bought, tea made, and the fun began: talking, singing, dancing. In spite of all their poverty and the bareness of their lives, the Russian people are full of the joy of life, their vitality is truly astonishing. I, the intellectual and foreigner, was welcomed into their midst without distrust; there was no wall dividing us. The masses retain from the Revolution the consciousness that there is nothing about the upper classes which need awe them. A salient feature of the Soviet world is the democracy of its everyday life. Toward those of another, non-Russian nationality, whether from within the country or abroad, the working people have an exceptionally hospitable, brotherly, and egalitarian attitude. One may hate this regime, this power, but one cannot but love the people of Russia once one has come to know them.

An incident at one of these social gatherings stands out in my memory because of its peculiar combination of crude frankness and good-natured pleasantry; it would be unthinkable anywhere in Europe. At this particular party there was a woman of about thirty-seven years of age, who danced and sang ravishingly. Her partner in these songs and dances was a young man of twenty—her lover, not to mince words, her gigolo. He did not work but lived at her expense. And here was this woman worker not in the least embarrassed to call him "my parasite" in the presence of the others, at the same time explaining why she called him this. All in a tone of friendly pleasantry, without the slightest trace of irritation or malice.

Everything that comes from the Russian working people, both the good and the bad, breathes such freshness, simplicity, inexhaustible joy of living, natural force—that one cannot help being convinced that this people has not yet said its last word in History, that it is somehow only just beginning its life, its bold and daring career.

But it is not easy for this people to live. We have looked at the workers' wages and the prices of goods. Let us now, having seen the mechanic's home, visit the other homes I entered. The picture will be more complete and its objectivity unquestionable. The general characteristic of these homes is over-crowding.

A family of three, four, or even five people living in one room is not exceptional but quite common. Moreover, these rooms are often communicating rooms. In this respect the house in which I lived in Krasnoyarsk during the winter of 1933–34, before I moved in with the mechanic's family, was a typical one.

Before the Revolution it had been the residence of some merchant, but after the Revolution he and his family had vanished without trace. The house then belonged to 'Gorkomkhoz'

(Municipal Economic Administration) and was already occupied after the Soviet manner. Where once a single family had lived there were now six. This is who they were and how they were distributed.

The aristocrat among all this over-crowding was of course a 'specialist', an agronomist earning from 600 to 700 roubles a month and enjoying the privilege of a 'special quota living space' as a member of the Scientific Workers Organization. This family had the two best rooms in the house, constituting in fact one-third of it. The agronomist's wife had decided that her husband was not after all so absorbed in his scientific work as to require a separate study. So she, her husband, and their child occupied the larger of the two rooms, which had three windows in it. Part of this room she partitioned off to form a bedroom. The remaining room—slightly smaller, although also a good one with three windows—she let unfurnished and unheated to an engineer for eighty roubles a month. Such sub-letting, although not quite legal, is winked at. The sub-tenant quarrelled with the director of the factory in which he worked, lost his job, and took the case to court. He took me in as a lodger in order to help pay his way.

In the remaining three rooms, two of which were communi-cating rooms, lived three families from the non-privileged section of Soviet society: a *ci-devant* family of four (two widows and two children); the family of an old man who worked in the hospital office, his wife and her young niece, a working girl; and the family of three young sisters who worked in a factory. To get to their room, the sisters had to go first through the kitchen, then through the rooms of the other two families.

The youngest of these three sisters worked at the 'Spartak' boot factory. The eldest, a twenty-five-year-old widow left with a three-year-old child after the death of her husband in the typhus epidemic of 1932—33, worked as a cook in the Water Transport Workers' hospital. A year after I went to live in this house, the third sister married a chauffeur. The sisters' room was then divided into two by a curtain, one half for the newly wedded couple, the other for the widow, her child, and the unmarried sister. Thus four adults and one child were crowded into a single room. But that only proved the truth of the saying—the more, the merrier. I was invited to one of the three social evenings organized in celebration of the wedding. The room was crammed full with relatives and friends. Every-one, of course, had brought something to eat or drink. What a crush! How poor these people were, and yet what spontaneous, unforced gaiety! Where does it really come from? Does it spring from the conviction that in a few years' time everything will be well—a room of one's own, a better life, or simply from sheer youthfulness? I will not undertake to answer. But this social gathering radiated freshness and self-confidence.

At the back of the house was the common kitchen, used by all—the battle-ground of continual disputes.

Our house had a cellar basement. Here live a labourer's family of four, in a state of permanent under-nourishment. I have rarely seen such emaciated, wan faces as those of this worker's wife and children.

The differences in situation between the workers and the employees, obviously all in favour of the latter, could be observed even in the basements. We have noted the two worker families' basement homes. Now here are two employees' homes.

The first was that of a family of former craftsmen, quite recently returned from European Russia. It was composed of the father, who worked in an office of the administration of 'Northern Ocean Route', the mother, and a twenty-five-year-old daughter, widow of a doctor killed by bandits during the famine of 1932. They possessed a kitchen and a large room with three windows. The room was barely furnished but very clean.

The second family—mother, grown-up son and two daughters—possessed an entire basement flat consisting of three rooms and a kitchen. It was a family of former industrialists from Irkutsk, formerly very wealthy. Now everyone worked in Soviet industrial organizations, with the exception of the head of the family, who had been shot by the G.P.U. at the beginning of the Five Year Plan because he had not furnished a certain quantity of gold demanded of him in the belief that he had it hidden away from former times. The daughters were married, one to a Red Army officer, the other to an engineer.

The fifth—and last—basement flat I saw (I am citing all those I saw and not making a tendencious selection) belonged to a working-class family: a cleaner employed in some Soviet institution, who in addition took in washing in order to scrape a living for herself and her children. She had a basement room that she had divided into two with a thin wooden partition, behind which lived two mechanics. Since the room possessed only one window, after the partitioning there was only half a window to each portion and the air in the room was consequently very unhealthy. The woman was forty years of age and had two sons. Her husband had abandoned her for another woman.

Her small eight-year-old son was consumptive. A lively and intelligent youngster, he was popular with the teachers at his school, which often sent him to a sanatorium. "But what is the use of it?" said his mother. "He improves, is sent home again, and then two months later gets laid up with a high temperature. He won't live to be twenty." Indeed, how could he get well in that airless hole, and always under-nourished as he was. Through the school doctor the mother was able to get milk at a reduced rate, one rouble a litre instead of two. The rest of their food consisted simply of potatoes, bread and cabbage. They had meat only once a month. Often there was not even a rouble left to buy milk for the sick child. They still drank their tea with sugar, but it was kept locked up so as not to lead the kids into temptation. Sometimes the elder got hold of the bread on the sly and ate it. Then what a storm of abuse broke over his head if he was detected; abuse justified enough, for it meant that they all went without bread for half a day, perhaps a whole day.

On pay days, twice a month, the mother bought a hundred grammes (about 3½ oz) of butter at the 'Gastronome' for the sick child. The elder boy slept on a mattress on the floor; the younger had a bunk with a mattress. Once I found the little lad cleaning his teeth with the air of one performing a solemn act of devotion. His mother explained that the teacher had impressed on them in school that they must clean their teeth every day without fail, and the lad had pestered the life out of her until she bought him a toothbrush and toothpaste.

So they clean their teeth, but have nothing to put into their mouths.

In the next room of that same basement lived a carpenter, with his wife and a babe in arms; and in the end room was another family of husband, wife, and twelve-year-old daughter. These last lived the best of all: they had a room and a separate kitchen, decent furniture, not bad clothing, and good food. I ventured to ask the charwoman how this family managed to do so well for themselves.

"Oh, they steal," she replied. "The husband works as a night-watchman in a big warehouse and steals all he can safely get away with."

On entering the bare, comfortless room of the charwoman, a yard-high, gaudily coloured, full-length reproduction of a well-known Soviet artist's portrait of Maxim Gorki hit one in the eye. This, and the newspaper always lying on the table, indicated the dominant passion of the elder, seventeen-year-old son. He was in his way a bit of a character. His mother complained, not unreasonably, of his aversion to work. "But read—he likes that all right. And he has to have his paper every day—not just the local paper, it's got to be the big Moscow *Izvestia* or *Pravda*. He has to know everything that goes on in the great world—America, Germany, England—and not just here in Siberia. And if I can't give him the money for these fancies he scrounges it from neighbours or friends on some excuse or other."

He was a sober youth and spent money only on newspapers, books, and, occasionally, food. But he really had a strong aversion to work. His mother had placed him in various enterprises so that he could learn a trade, but he always managed to lose his job. He had at that time just been thrown out of his last job as a painter in the shipbuilding yard, and one day, as his mother was reproaching him for this in my presence, he burst out with: "Their work! Work like a horse and die of hunger! That's the wages you get! That's their freedom! And even then they keep you waiting for your money!"

I was absolutely dumbfounded to hear such outspoken words—"*their* work", "*their* freedom" in the mouth of that Siberian youngster. Where did he get these expressions from? His mother, a meek drudge, was shocked and bewildered: "How does he get to be so anti-Soviet, living here at home with me?" For, in her eyes, whoever criticized the bureaucracy must be 'anti-Soviet'.

Systematic delay in paying out wages is a scourge of the Soviet worker—and it creates a rich reserve fund for industrialization. I had heard rumours of this when I was in Moscow, but at that time I was too far removed from the lives of the people and from industry to appreciate it properly. I had my first lesson in these matters immediately on my arrival in Krasnoyarsk.

While waiting for my friend Davidov to return from work, I got talking to his neighbour. He was a carpenter in the repair shops of the Yeniseisk River Fleet and earned up to two hundred roubles a month.

"That's not very much," I suggested cautiously.

"Of course it's not much. And the worst is, even that is not paid out promptly. Either the bank hasn't got enough money or the credits from Moscow haven't arrived—there's always some excuse—and we're left without money."

"But how do you live then?"

"We get an advance on what's owing to us—ten or twenty

roubles a week. Then we do a bit of work on the side—one thing and another. We get credit from the factory co-op. Now they've promised to pay all the back payments on November 7th" (that would be in two months' time).

When, later on, I worked at the bank and then at one of the Timber Trust departments, I had to learn and utilize, like it or not, all the finesse of this intricate, double-dealing system of delaying wage payments for one, two or even three months. Accounts were settled up only twice a year, on May 1st and November 7th, when the 'liquidation of wage payments due' was carried out. 'Economies' thus effected freed not a few million roubles, which went to the speeding up of construction and the prompt payment of salaries to the administrative staff and the cadres.

Aside from the hardship this involved, what humiliations the Soviet worker has to endure just to get what is owing to him!

I remember once being sent to one of the four Krasnoyarsk Timber Mills for the purpose of checking whether certain construction work had in fact been carried out to the extent shown in the report of the enterprise. I was in the director's office, together with some other employees, when a worker of about thirty-five years of age came in and, very humbly and timidly, asked the 'comrade director' for the balance of his wages, or at least the greater part of it, as he had some special personal expenses to meet, which the small payments on account then being made to him were not enough to cover. The director, a young man of about twenty-five, corpulent and beefy-complexioned, a former G.P.U. man, did not even look up at the applicant, treated him as though he were an inanimate object and not a human being. Enunciating his words slowly and emphasizing them with light taps of his pen on the inkwell, he said: "For your in-for-ma-tion—I ad-min-i-ster pro-duc-tion. The wages are paid out by the Ac-count-ant. Make your ap-pli-ca-tion to him." This, of course, is simply an excuse; but there is nothing for the worker to do except leave. We also leave shortly after, the director and I, for his pleasant little house with a garden, near the factory. There we dine well, listen to the wireless, to music, in company with a superb bust of Stalin placed square in the middle of the newly furnished lounge.

Another case. Into the Accountant's Department of the Trust where I was working, a rather elderly worker came several times to see a cashier, who was under my orders, in order to claim some money, which was always refused because of 'lack of cash'.

"And how much is it he wants, Mikhail Petrovich?" I finally asked the cashier politely.

"Twenty roubles, Anton Antonovich. It is for social insurance. It is for a child who has died. Death benefit for funeral expenses; but we haven't received any social insurance money from the bank for a long time . . ."

The worker looked at me hopefully but said nothing.

"Yes," I said to him, "the bank put us in an awkward position, not paying out the money. But twenty roubles is not a large sum. Mikhail Petrovich and I will try to get it for you tomorrow. That will be possible, won't it, Mikhail Petrovich?" and I turned towards the cashier.

"Of course, if it is possible, Anton Antonovich, we'll gladly help a working man," replied the cashier obsequiously.

The next morning, about an hour before I left home for work, the old chap came to see me. He was anxious to assure me of the justice of his claim. He told me that he was a night-watchman in the Trust buildings and the father of a numerous family and that it was already two months since his child had been buried and still the insurance money remained unpaid. And finally he came out with the following significant remark:

"I very nearly told you all this yesterday at the Trust, but I was afraid. Perhaps I might have offended someone and done us both harm . . ."

There it is—the freedom of the Soviet worker.

There is another aspect of Soviet affairs that reveals the abasement of the workers with particular clarity: in the hiring of labour, especially when it is a question of some coveted employment. The directors of large, and even medium-sized enterprises themselves select only the cadres, the commanding staff: technicians, accountants, foremen (in so far as these are not directly engaged by a higher authority). This staff in its turn engages the requisite number of lower employees and workers. How the workers are obliged to humble themselves, kow-tow, and even make presents and stand rounds of drinks in order to be taken on, is an eye-opener.

Inevitably the question arises—Who then are the masters and who are the servants? Does the bureaucracy serve the workers? —as official theory proclaims; or do the workers serve the bureaucracy?—as the facts indicate.

Once upon a time 'wage slavery' was regarded as an attribute of capitalism; now it has become an integral part of the 'socialism' advocated by all the theoreticians of contemporary socialism, whether of the 2nd, 3rd, or 4th International.

One sometimes comes across contrasts of a truly symbolic character.

A few days before my departure from Siberia into western Europe I met a young woman acquaintance. She had recently married an engineer.

"Come round to my place", she invited, "and see what a fine home we have. I'll give you something nice to eat and we can have a last chat before you leave."

I accepted the invitation. As soon as I entered the lounge of her apartment I stopped short in astonishment: parquet flooring, carpets, a divan, a heavy oak table and oak chairs, table cover and curtains of rich heavy cloth, a piano; the room brilliantly lit with pleasant indirect lighting. My hostess herself had on a very pretty silk dress. In Krasnoyarsk I had occasion to mix with the 'cream of society', and I had seen more spacious and more elegantly furnished apartments, but this one particularly impressed me because it was located immediately over the basement home of the poverty-stricken, starving charwoman's family. The same house, only one floor higher, that was all. And what a different world! If I had wanted to intentionally 'slander the Soviet power' I could not have found a crueller contrast than this one offered by life itself ... And throughout my visit to this charming, inoffensive wife of a bureaucrat, I could not tear my thoughts away from this contrast—these two households, these two lives in the 'workers' fatherland', the 'land of socialism'.

Yet in parting she did not fail to express the longing felt by all of her circle: "Ah, Anton Antonovich, how I envy you going to Paris! Ah, Paris!"

What a vast gulf between the aspirations and the cares of the basement and those of the first floor in the U.S.S.R.!

The workers, they too, felt very sensitively and acutely the existence of the 'different categories', and understood the true role and the actual social position of each of them. The charwoman's son was not the only one on whose lips I heard the angry "We" and "They". "They" is the distinctive term applied by the working class to the Communist clique in power. The lower levels of Soviet society are deeply conscious of the social antagonisms contained in this "We" and "They".

But the formula is not new. It is the traditional definition, which has existed in the popular language and consciousness for thousands of years, ever since the division of society into classes, into upper and lower, into people and government. By reviving this formual "We" and "They", those at the bottom of Soviet society merely make public the fact that, in spite of the initial promises and actions of the October Revolution, in reality "nothing has in essence changed", the eternal "We" and "They" has remained.

Nevertheless, the Soviet workers are not so unimaginative and passive as to be content with old formulae. The creative fantasy and irony of the people have found fresher and more adequate expressions to characterize the new juridical forms, the specific vestment assumed by the old social relationships of "We" and "They". Before my arrival in Siberia, when I was still in the Verkhne-Uralsk isolator, I was told by my fellow prisoners that the people had coined the following formula: the land is "ours", the wheat is "theirs"; Baku is "ours", the oil is "theirs"; the factories are "ours", what they produce is "theirs".

Then in Siberia I heard workers say bluntly:

"We are now no longer the workers, but the bosses. The workers are Stalin, Kaganovich, Molotov, Ovchinnikov" (this last was the dictator of Krasnoyarsk).

Developing this line of thought, the Krasnoyarsk railway workers have invented some very telling expressions. For example: on the arrival of the Trans-Siberian Express, which carries only the bureaucrats, specialiasts and their families—the new aristocracy—the workers say, "The workman's train has arrived." And when the workman's train—filthy, over-crowded, loaded to the steps—pulls into the station, they say: "The bosses' special has arrived."

Other ironical expressions are even more barbed.

"I just had an interesting encounter," an exiled comrade said to me one day. "Not far from the station I met a peasant with his cart. He was standing in the middle of the road, looking about him uncertainly. Seeing me, he came up and asked: 'Citizen, where is the Central here?' ('Central', i.e. the central prison). 'How do you mean, Central, brother? There's no Central here; there's only the municipal prison, over there ...' 'No, no, I'm not talking about the prison—I mean the railway workshops; that's what they're called.' "

That then is the name given by the people to these celebrated workshops, once famous throughout Siberia, throughout Russia, as 'The Citadel', for they were truly a stronghold of the Revolution.

The elevation of the Soviet bureaucracy into a new ruling class over the proletariat became particularly obvious after the Five Year Plans. The extinction of the last traces of private enterprise, the existence of which during the NEP period served to blur the outlines of reality, sharply exposed the new class antagonism between the proletariat of the factories, the collective and State farms, and the bureaucracy. They now stand face to face, as it were in battle array on an open plain. One is the privileged, ruling; the other is the exploited, ruled. The menace of a 'third force' (the private owners) has now vanished for both of them.

Under these conditions, the official verbal fiction that the working class is the ruling and privileged class, can only appear to the workers as bitter mockery.

This general conviction that everything is lost, that the final result of the Revolution has led to a new enslavement of the proletariat—this, in my opinion (arrived at on the basis of my observations between 1926 and 1936), is what profoundly and fundamentally distinguishes the Soviet proletariat of the post-Five-Year-Plan period from that of the NEP period, when the proletariat still had doubts, hopes, illusions ("perhaps something will come of it after all") on this basic question: what are the final results of the Revolution?

But these acid pleasantries of the Soviet worker about "who is the boss" express their impotence, their inability to conduct any immediate mass struggle. An oppressed class preparing to pass to the attack does not speak of the enemy in an ironic tone, but rages, foams at the mouth. The present state of the Soviet proletariat is as follows: it is perfectly aware of *what is*, but is not in a position to launch any open offensive. Why is this? Why does their talk express only bitter disillusion? Let us try to penetrate a little deeper into their psychology.

Well, struggle for what? A new revolution to what end? Only in order that everything should be repeated all over again? That is what the Soviet worker, utterly disillusioned by the results of the October Revolution, asks himself . . . We have shed our blood, we have gone hungry; and others reap the fruits, others benefit from the results of our sufferings . . . No, we won't be fooled again . . . Once is enough.

It is not simply a matter of physical and psychological weariness due to the proximity of the Revolution (although the weariness is an important factor). The trouble is that the masses see above them and against them, not the old ruling

class they knew so well—the bourgeoisie and the land-owners—
but a peculiar new class—the bureaucracy of Communists and
specialists—which has partly sprung from their own ranks, the
workers and the peasants. Private ownership has been replaced
by State ownership. This is a completely new historical phenomenon, a historical situation without precedent. The masses
must have time to acclimatize themselves and adapt their
psychology to it. A new conception of the future social order
and a new programme of action must somehow or other arise to
confront this new situation. Misery alone does not impel the
masses to struggle; they must have some positive understanding
of what they are fighting for, what the precise objective is.

The working people feel this; but subconsciously. Only
isolated individuals try consciously to grapple with the problem.
I came across a really moving example of this.

In the room of a young worker I saw many books. And on
the wall and the table were portraits of Belinski, the passionate
Russian critic of the thirties and forties of the nineteenth
century, epoch of the worst Tsarist reaction. This worker was a
carpenter, a skilled maker of fine furniture. He liked his work and
earned good money, which was also able to augment by private
work. The new leaders of Soviet society thirsted for comfort and
a good carpenter need never be idle. After a while I succeeded in
learning the reason for his admiration for Belinski.

"Everything printed today is lies and humbug. I can't
stomach the rubbish. But with Belinski—well—one feels that he
loved the truth, that he was sincere. That's why I love him."

He had bought himself all Belinski's books; various uncol-
lected editions of the thirties and forties, and the complete
works issued at the end of the century.

This young worker was filled with intense hate for the
Soviet bureaucratic regime. What most excited his fury was
the manner in which the bureaucrats played up to the workers,
affecting their dress and speech, while everything they did was
directed against the workers. He could describe at great length
and in minute detail how the director of a factory behaved in
front of the workers, and how he changed his attitude, his
dress and his speech, at home in his own circle. Or how the
secretary of the Party Cell, a forty-year-old man, bought over
and seduced young and pretty women workers by promising
to use his influence on their behalf. Or how the entire administration (director, chief engineer, secretary of the Party Cell,
chairman of the Factory Committee) 'organize' themselves
apartments at the expense of the factory, and so on. A burning

passion to reveal 'what is' consumed this young man and made him akin to the 'frenzied Vissarion'* who so fiercely stigmatized the hypocrisy and deceit that characterized the reign of Tsar Nicholas I. If in this book the reader finds some evidence of the life of political exiles in Siberia, it is thanks to this worker's love of the truth: for he secreted these pages between false boards in my wooden suit-case, so that they could pass the frontier control of the G.P.U. He was always prepared for any sacrifice in the struggle against the ruling bureaucratic regime. "As with the bourgeoisie and the land-owners, so with the bureaucrats—down with them!" That was his battle-cry. He saw no essential difference between the old and the new masters. But what to put in place of the bureaucratic machine, once it was destroyed—that he did not himself know. His great originality—what, in my opinion, made him such an exceptional character—was that in the midst of the prevailing general apathy he was clearly aware of the need for a new positive programme; this was what constantly occupied his thoughts. Needless to say, he did not even want to hear of a return to the old capitalist society. But merely to limit oneself to accusing Stalin of deviations from, or betrayal of Marxism-Leninism seemed to him insufficient, not serious. "If the bureaucrats are able to quote Marx and Lenin in their defence, that means that the latter are guilty in a way . . . Didn't Lenin himself say that a leader is responsible not only for himself but also for his co-workers, and Stalin was after all his nearest . . .", he was fond of repeating with a sort of naive obstinacy. And proceeding from this thought, he concluded that it was utterly useless to keep on mechanically repeating the old formulae and programmes of Marx and Lenin, no matter how 'pure' these might be. The new revolution demanded a new programme: after a new experience, new deductions.

All this was obviously very far from a positive programme. But the very existence of such passionate and creative groping, exceptional though it was, demonstrated to me that after the Five Year Plan something new had entered into the political atmosphere of Russia.

Other manifestations of this spirit that I came across were not so striking ideologically, but no less symbolic, for they arose on the practical plane.

In one of the large Krasnoyarsk factories a worker conducted open revolutionary anti-Government propaganda

---

*V.G. Belinski was so called by the contemporary intelligentsia.

among a group of thirty to forty people in his workshop, organizing illegal meetings; in summer out of town, in winter at one of their homes. He sometimes took part in official meetings. These workers furnished people living underground with false papers, so that they had the possibility of travelling and so on. I watched this work going on for over a year and this worker was never denounced. At the time of my departure from Siberia he was still carrying on.

At another factory the workers of one department organized a strike, or rather—as they put it to the G.P.U.—"decided not to work until the dispute in question had been cleared up".

One oppositionist living underground hid for two weeks on a State farm. He was there concealed by the workers, both young and old—most of them Komsomols or Communists, or even students of the Agronomical Institute. No one gave him away; they kept him in food and supplied him with false papers when he moved on.

The oppositionist living illegally on this State farm was a Trotskyist of very moderate views. For him Stalin was still a 'comrade' who was simply pursuing an incorrect policy, who was not paying sufficient attention to the needs of the working masses. He was therefore stupified to discover that the workers on the State farm did not even want to listen when one spoke of 'improving' official policy, or reforms, or replacing individuals. "The axe to the roots", was their attitude. For them the Communist leaders were not comrades but a new ruling class. But he was even more staggered by the conclusions they drew from their utter rejection of the existing regime: "Not division of the State farms into small peasant holdings, but the creation, in place of the present State slavery, of a really friendly and comradely large-scale collective economy." The Russian workers want to go forward, not back.

In the nineteenth century France was the 'fatherland of revolutions', which followed one on the heels of another, and the intervening reactions appeared merely as interludes of preparation for the next, socially more profound revolution. Will not Russia become the same fatherland of revolutions for the 20th century? Will not the world see the next social revolution, far deeper and more radical than the Revolution of 1917, again take place in Russia?

I do not venture to assert this, but I should like to develop this thought a little. The social aspirations of the masses that showed themselves with such force in the years between 1917—20 have not yet been satisfied; the Russian workers' will to live and their vital energies are so enormous, so powerful, so inexhaustible—in spite of the terrible strain and suffering of the last twenty years—that they must find an outlet. The new technique brought into existence by the Five Year Plans can prove the economic basis for a new, creative social venture on the part of the masses.

The rejection of the present bureaucratic regime by the masses is as widespread as is their passive endurance of it in practice. The inner storm of discontent, of which we have seen only isolated instances, glimpsed only portents, can rise up and overwhelm—much more rapidly than may appear from the social surface—this calm of stolid endurance. Passive rejection can pass over into active opposition. For the time being the evolution of the Soviet leaders is towards the Right, and there is no doubt that it will continue to go further to the Right, deeper into reaction. But at the same time, at the other end of the social scale, among the working masses, new forces gather and mature for new historical battles. The time, the forms, and the perspectives of the new clash between these two extremes are secrets that belong to the future. But even in face of the apparently omnipotent Soviet bureaucracy one should not forget that the alteration of storm and calm is just as much a law of social development as it is of nature

In my encounters with the workers of Siberia there were occasions when I asked myself, not without reproach: Was I not, after all, seeing the social heart of contemporary Russia in too sombre a light; was I not in my generalizations mixing the colours too dark . . .?

Among the local officials of the Krasnoyarsk G.P.U.—with which, as a political exile, I had sometimes to deal—was a particularly unsympathetic, unlikeable, degenerate young man. Here, I said to myself, is a one-time member of the oppressed classes who has found a suitable place for himself. My conviction was strengthened when I learned that he wrote plays for the local theatrical clubs, that he composed verses, lyrical poems . . . And then fate, always more capricious in the U.S.S.R. than anywhere else in the world, brought me for a day or two to the home of this G.P.U. official. In addition to him there were three women in the household. Two of these, his wife and sister, turned out to be minor Soviet employees, modest, unpretentious creatures; simple women of the people and therefore pleasant in spite of the narrowness of their outlook. The third, the mother of the G.P.U. man, was an extraordinarily cordial, intelligent and attractive woman.

She had formerly been a worker in the Krasnoyarsk Railway Workshops, where her late husband had also worked. And yet this profoundly honest and intelligent woman was the mother of this G.P.U. abortion; lived in the same house with him; reconciled herself to his disgusting trade, i.e., accepted it . . . Or else—the whole system, including the G.P.U., could not after all be so loathsome if such a worker could accept it? I was puzzled, perplexed. The existing regime I knew only too well— yet my confidence in this working-class mother was absolute.

When I came to the home of this G.P.U. man his mother of course knew that I was a political exile, a foreign communist. Later on I told her my whole history, my life abroad and in Soviet Russia; some of the story when the others were present, but in more detail when we were alone. And once when we were alone and talking like that she suddenly, on her own initiative, broached a topical subject. "I don't know why there are so many exiles in Siberia now," she said straight out. Then after a moment's hesitation, as though she were recovering from the first plunge, she went on in a low voice: "And altogether I can't understand how it is that now, under the Soviet Government, it is so hard for poor people to live. My late husband and I, we were always poor, ever since 1905; but even now life is no better for the poor."

She began then to talk about the low wages and the bad living conditions of the workers at her former place of employment, the Railway Workshops. Then she reverted to her personal life.

"Why, when my husband died I couldn't even get a pension, although according to the law I was entitled to one. I only got it when my son entered the G.P.U."

Here she paused again, considering. Should she tell something more, something that it was apparently difficult to say. At last she said: "I wanted him to stay in the factory, but several of his friends were already working in the G.P.U. Well, they talked him into joining." There a hint of apology in her voice . . . Yes, that was the answer to my riddle.

Regarding the face of this honest, kindly, working-class woman, hearing her sorrowful confession and the social judgement she made, all the thunderous clamour made by the Kremlin bosses with their innumerable congresses, their resolutions, their newspapers, speeches and broadcasts suddenly appeared to me ludicrous, trivial, empty of meaning. Humanity and History alone can weigh them in the balance; and when they do, her quiet voice will have greater weight than all their propaganda, all their millions of 'unanimous' resolutions.

VI

AND THE DAYS PASS . . .

CLASHES WITH THE G.P.U.

On my discharge from hospital a double conflict with the G.P.U. awaited me. Firstly on a personal matter: whether I should remain in Krasnoyarsk until the completion of my treatment or be sent further north immediately, to Yeniseisk. The question was urgent, since the Yenisei River would be frozen over shortly, and all shipping would cease.

The second conflict arose out of a general action of all the Communist-Oppositionists in exile in Krasnoyarsk against the G.P.U. in support of their sick comrade, the Trotskyist Plomper. He had been brought from Yeniseisk because of illness, an acute nervous disorder, and ought to have been sent away for special treatment. The G.P.U. was holding up his departure and even hinting at returning him to Yeniseisk. The colony of exiled Oppositionists therefore sent a collective resolution to Moscow, categorically demanding that Plomper be sent away for medical treatment, and threatening to go on hunger strike unless this demand were conceded. The time limit for a reply was set at one month. At the moment of my discharge from hospital the deadline was already near. On both sides—the exiles' and the G.P.U.'s—preparations were being made. As in a real war, force, cunning, and—on the part of the exiles—self-sacrifice were brought into play.

On my discharge from hospital the senior doctor had given me a certificate stating that "Citizen Ciliga has been under treatment from September 9th to October 10th, 1933, for sciatica, rheumatism, and neurosis . . . His state of health on discharge had improved . . . he requires further treatment with electrical apparatus for a period." They possessed this apparatus in Krasnoyarsk. There was none in Yeniseisk. That was why I refused to go there. I felt that in taking up a stand on this shaky ground I was at the same time defending the dignity and the elementary human rights of man against police terror. If I yield now on this question of medical treatment, I thought, how can I ever win the right to leave the country? On its side the G.P.U. did not, as might have been expected, at once proceed to my forcible removal to Yeniseisk.

"We are sending you before a competent and impartial medical board. They will decide whether you are in a condition to leave or not. And in the meantime continue your treatment here and get completely cured . . ." the G.P.U. chief, Denisov, said to me.

This Denisov at the same time gave orders to one of his commissars that I should be granted, in addition to the normal ration, a supplementary ration. The half litre of milk per day and the 3¾ oz (approx.) of butter per week that I thus received were in those days real luxuries.

But my good fortune did not end there. My comrades in exile, some of whom were well paid and well provided for, took turns in inviting me to their homes. What a spread there was! I still recall those magnificent Siberian 'piroshki' made of white flour, butter and cream-cheese, filled with red-currant jelly, with meat or honey. After three years of black prison bread can anything in the world be more delicious? . . . It was not simply the usual cordial fellowship always displayed by exiles towards each other; they wanted also to express their international solidarity, because I was a guest from abroad. Perhaps it is only in adversity and bondage that the human heart can display such warm tenderness and staunch brotherly love.

A week after my discharge I was called before the medical board. It had a rather long title: Expert Medical Control Commission of Social Insurance for the Krasnoyarsk Region. Here too the realities and the necessities of Soviet life found expression. For what Commission in Russia can resolve a problem contrary to the wishes of the G.P.U.? Yet at the same time one has to save face, one has to demonstrate the conscientiousness of the medical profession and maintain professional solidarity with the hospital doctor who had diagnosed my case. It was therefore necessary to establish both that the G.P.U. had the right to deport me and that the doctor had been right in prescribing treatment for me with apparatus that Yeniseisk did not possess. I was curious to see how the medical board would extricate themselves from this dilemma. They succeeded all right. This board evidently had wide experience in discovering solutions that would satisfy all concerned—at the expense of the patient. In such disputes between science and the police, the patient is, of course, the weakest and most defenceless.

After a thorough examination by several doctors the medical

board reached its decision. It reiterated the diagnosis given by the hospital doctor, even filled in the details—"traces of inflammation of the right sciatic nerve; rheumatism, neurasthenia, anaemia . . .". It upheld the principle of further treatment regarded as indispensable by the hospital, only with this slight difference: where the hospital had written "requires" it wrote "is desirable". This did the trick. If—to quote official jargon—"in the hard struggle for the fulfilment of the socialist Five Year Plans necessities must sometimes be renounced", then there could be no question of what was "desirable".

The medical profession gave the required scientific basis for the carrying out of justice by the G.P.U. It was even stated without equivocation, in the third phrase of its report: "there are no special obstacles against a departure from Krasnoyarsk". The medical board doctors were conscientious men. They did not say that there were "non-special" obstacles, or that there were no obstacles at all. Still less did they assert that I could live or be cured further north, somewhere in Yeniseisk or Turukhansk. No, they very modestly and conscientiously took responsibility for only one thing—that I would survive the journey. Where the patient went—further north or to the south, to be cured in the Caucassus or to rot in the Arctic (a matter of some importance to the patient)—this did not come within the scope of their scientific competence. The board's decision was handed to me dated October 16th, 1933 (I still have it in my possession, together with the hospital certificate). It carried the stamp of the board, the signatures of the Chairman and the secretary, and was on official paper. Everything official and correct—give the devil his due! Yet all the same there was a very characteristic little detail. In the column relating to the nature of treatment the words "And requires . . ." were printed. It was precisely this word "requires" that should have been replaced by the less categorical "is desirable". But the medical board thought otherwise. To make such an alteration appeared to them like open flouting of medical principles in compliance with the wishes of the police. They therefore simply treated this "and requires" column as if it was not there, and made a new column with the words "Electrical treatment is desirable".

It is far from my desire to reproach this medical board. To be honest, the doctors who composed it were not at all anxious to send me to the Arctic and finish me off. They were only concerned not to come up against the G.P.U. themselves. Such is the law of the Soviet jungle: if you don't want to perish yourself you must assist in the destruction, or at least in the enslavement of others. That is the price to be paid for Stalin's "gay and well-to-do life".

Even after this unequivocal decision of the medical board I refused to leave for Yeniseisk. But my dispute with Denisov over the correct interpretation of this Pythian text was interrupted by the new, collective conflict over Plomper. Around the twentieth of October the one-month time limit fixed by the exiles expired, and they decided to begin their hunger-strike. I also had to take part in this, and even a very active part, although at that moment, after so many years of prison and hunger strikes, I longed more for peace and quiet than for battle. The comrades elected me leader of the strike. Well, I thought, if one must fight, let it be a good fight.

This is how the hunger strike was carried out, under the normal Soviet conditions of lack of any civil liberties (press, the right to meet, etc.). The Communist-oppositionists in exile in Krasnoyarsk were not numerous—seven or eight in all—but none of us had a large enough room to hold us all. It was agreed that a core of five or six men should come together in N's flat (I forget his name), a lawyer. Each was to bring his bed so that the strike could be carried out lying down. Two others, Plomper and Davidov, who lived together, would fast in their own room. At the last moment a complication arose: one of the comrades discovered a note-book of N's containing items headed 'Information', which were clearly reports to the G.P.U. That meant there was an agent of the G.P.U. among us. The evidence in the note-book was plain and irrefutable. We decided to expel him from our ranks—but not until after the hunger strike; in the meantime let the mangy cur starve with us. But we put him under close observation. Any correspondence of those on strike would be sent unsealed through the medium of the leader of the strike.

At eight o'clock in the evening we were all to meet at N's place, send a telegram through the G.P.U. to Moscow informing the authorities of the commencement of our strike, and spend the night in the lawyer's room. This N, and the *feldscher* Ivanov, whom we also had under a certain suspicion (a year later it turned out that this was justified) were to be the last to be informed of zero hour. I had an appointment with them after work, in a small pub at five-thirty on the decisive day. It was arranged that I should inform them in the course of conversation that we were to start at eight o'clock. I stood them a bottle of vodka; they were both fond of drinking, which in itself was a bad sign. But to hell with it, I thought, they're human beings, even if they are stool pigeons. If they're so keen on it, let them have a good drink before they start.

We left the pub together and I would not let them out of my sight for an instant. We went first to Ivanov's to get some of his things and say goodbye to his wife, and then on to N's place. The others were already assembled. At eight o'clock in the evening all food and drink, except water, was taken out of the room. Out of comradely solidarity, Trotsky's son-in-law, Volkov, who was then living in exile in Yeniseisk and had just come to Krasnoyarsk on business for the North Pole Timber Trust, joined us. Everyone wrapped himself in his blanket and lay down on his bed. The hunger-strike had begun.

The G.P.U. took no action against the strike or the strikers; our telegram to Moscow was accepted; but it refused to send a doctor to observe the strike officially. To the G.P.U. this was our 'private affair'. Whoever heard of men not in prison going on a hunger-strike! Apparently the G.P.U. hoped that, with the assistance of the stool-pigeons, it would collapse from within. The lawyer did indeed try on several occasions to make 'demoralizing' remarks, but every time I cut him short. "Mind what you're saying! You know well enough that it is to your interest not to talk too much." "What sort of language is that . . .?" he protested the first time. But he didn't go far with his protests; he stopped short each time, like a scared rabbit afraid he would be discovered. As a provocateur he was a miserable little specimen.

In order to have some kind of 'official' observation of the strike, and to watch over the health of the strikers—especially of the two weakest, Davidov and Plomper—we invited the doctor of the Town Soviet's Health Department to visit us daily.

Through the doctors, and neighbours and friends, the whole town got to know of our strike. The other exiles, socialists of various tendencies and anarchists, came to see us and express their moral support. Even some 'capitulators' visited us. Through letters written by one person or another, other places of exile also heard of the affair. Some colonies in western Siberia, in Pavlodar and elsewhere, sent a protest to Moscow against the "unspeakable treatment of the comrades in Krasnoyarsk". In the course of one week the hunger-strike became an event of considerable public interest. The attempt at sabotage had been unsuccessful and the strike proceeded smoothly and unitedly. The local G.P.U. grew very anxious. As long as a year after one of its chief men said to me: "Well, you certainly cooked up a nice lot of trouble then."

Through 'unofficial' channels, the wives of the exiles, the G.P.U. gave us to understand that it would raise no objections to Plomper's immediate departure, at his own expense, for special treatment. In practice, that meant at the expense of the exiles, since, of course, Plomper had not sufficient means of his own. But this concession was already a half-victory, and we hoped by holding out a day or two more to achieve complete victory. However our plan did not succeed. On the tenth day the *feldscher* Ivanov broke the strike. The doctor had given Plomper injections against stomach cramp, and Ivanov declared that he knew very well that these injections contained nutritive elements and that in consequence he was no longer prepared to carry on.

"We went on hunger-strike for him and now he is taking food. No, I am not going to be made a fool of one moment longer . . ." he declared firmly and obstinately.

It was obvious that the injections were only a pretext for him to give up. What possible nutritive value could they have?

But the ensuing argument, coming at the end of the tenth day of the hunger-strike, immediately created a basis for about one half of the strikers. The excuse of someone else's 'treachery' made it easier to rationalize the desire to retreat, to give up. The others declared in favour of carrying on, and thus two factions were created. In such circumstances a split is always a portent of demoralization and defeat. There was therefore nothing to be done except end the strike at once, but in the same organized and united manner in which it had so far been conducted, in order to benefit, if possible, from the half-victory already wrested from the G.P.U.

After a brief discussion they all agreed with my suggestion, and I was given full powers to negotiate with the G.P.U. In order that the latter should not discover that the hunger-strike had already in effect collapsed through the Plomper-Ivanov incident, all correspondence, and even conversation with visitors, was banned until my return.

A cab was called and for ten roubles I was driven to the G.P.U. headquarters. It was already nine o'clock at night, dark and cold, but in my state of feverish excitement I felt neither cold nor tired. The chief of the G.P.U. received me immediately.

"According to medical opinion the health of Plomper and Davidov is seriously endangered. The doctor has been obliged to give Plomper an injection. I consider it necessary, and I am authorized by the others, to bring this to your notice, since the responsibility for anything that may happen falls upon the G.P.U., which has broken its promise to Plomper."

"What are you saying, Ciliga? The G.P.U. has nothing to do with it. This is entirely your own affair. Who in the world ever heard of people organizing a hunger-strike outside of prison? Maybe Ghandi in India . . . but after all we are revolutionaries, not pacifists. The G.P.U. can therefore have nothing whatever to do with it. Carry on if you want to. Stop if you want to. You have only yourselves to blame for any injury to your health."

"We are not free men, Citizen Denisov, but exiles. We are in your hands, exactly as if we were in prison. We have not the possibility of using the printed word, still less of calling a meeting of protest. That can be done by the International Red Aid abroad, but not by exiles here. In these circumstances a protest hunger-strike is one of the few means of self-defence left us. And since you, the G.P.U., do not keep your word, there is nothing left for us to do but continue the struggle to the end—to death if necessary."

"You are making wild accusations, Ciliga. The G.P.U. always keeps its word."

"Oh? How? . . ."

"We have never objected, and we do not now object to Plomper going away for special treatment to Irkutsk or Tomsk. But we are not wealthy; the proletarian State is devoting all its efforts and making the greatest sacrifices in order to build up socialist industry and at this critical time some Communists prefer to occupy themselves with aiding the counter-revolutionary activity of the class enemy, rather than help in the construction of socialism. Let them cure their bad nerves at their own expense."

I did not enter into a discussion on the subject of building up socialism, but at once took up the question of Plomper's departure.

"You know perfectly well, Citizen Denisov, that Plomper has no means whatever. How can he go?"

"We will give him two weeks to get ready and you will manage to collect the necessary funds among yourselves."

"All this is not so easy to arrange," I said slowly and in a firm tone. "But on this basis one might perhaps come to an agreement to end the struggle. But there are also some other details to settle."

"What?"

"After enduring a ten-day hunger-strike we shall need a

438

special diet for a time—light, nutritious food, milk, butter, flour, semolina . . ."

"You will get it . . ."

"Then another matter. There must be no dismissals from work or other reprisals by the G.P.U."

"The G.P.U. will, of course, have to investigate your behaviour," Denisov began cautiously. "But I do not think that it will be necessary to punish you more than you have already punished yourselves by this senseless hunger-strike. As to victimization, I do not think that the G.P.U. will ask for anyone's dismissal from employment. But I cannot demand that the directors keep people at work either; and your comrades have after all absented themselves from work for ten days."

"No, we won't reach an agreement like this," I replied. You yourself have declared that the G.P.U. considers our hunger-strike a private matter and in that case there is no room for 'investigations' and reprisals. As to work, no director will dismiss an exile without the consent of the G.P.U., especially since the participants in the strike informed the administration at their place of work that they would not come in for a few days for reasons of health."

"Ah, well," Denisov said "let us consider that everyone stayed away from work owing to illness; and the G.P.U. will not take any sanctions against those who hunger-struck. Does that satisfy you?"

"Yes, on that basis, Citizen Denisov, I am authorized by my comrades to inform you that the hunger-strike is ended."

Upon Denisov's request I immediately drafted a telegram in this sense, signed by myself and carrying the names of the others, and handed it to him for despatch to Moscow.

When the chief of the G.P.U. got hold of this his face cleared, brightened with relief and pleasure. It was evident that our struggle had worried him not a little, and that we had been within an ace of complete victory. My first impression was even that we had perhaps missed a still greater opportunity.

I returned to my comrades, who were tensely awaiting the results of my talk with the G.P.U., and informed them that the strike was over. Convinced that we had carried off the victory, we drank our first cup of tea.

For once the G.P.U. appeared to have kept its word: the promised food supplies were given us in full, no one lost his job, and nobody was arrested. Three or four weeks passed. The river Yenisei was already frozen over; shipping had ceased and with it the transfer of exiles further north. We prepared for the winter; some seeking work, others getting in fuel and food. The hard Siberian winter was on the threshold. I went regularly for electrical treatment and was gradually getting better ... One could breathe a little easier. An undisturbed winter, a good warm room, work, the possibility of corresponding with friends abroad and in Russia—all in all my situation was much better. I got into the habit of going to the town library, of visiting the theatre and the cinema.

However—the exile proposes, the G.P.U. disposes. It likes to give first hot and then cold showers. And no sooner was one conflict ended than another blew up ...

One morning I went to the G.P.U. to see the secretary of the Political Section, our supreme chief. He had been holding up my permit to buy wood in the co-operative (where it was cheaper than on the open town market). He was young, a functionary with plenty of 'pull' and much given to priding himself on his 'culture'. He was always very amiable, but I had already seen him two or three times on the matter without result. It was the same that day.

"Comrade Ciliga," (it was unpleasant to hear this title on his lips, but I let it pass), "I'm very sorry, but I really am terribly busy today. Come tomorrow and I'll see you have it without fail."

In response to my protests his amiability increased.

"Comrade Ciliga, I give you my Bolshevik word of honour. Come tomorrow at ten o'clock and you shall have the permit right away. Look—a day won't make all that difference. Come, we'll settle the matter tomorrow and have a chat together. You know I regard you with particular respect and esteem as a foreign comrade and because you were a trusted man of the Comintern. The G.P.U. keeps a record of people . . ."

It was not difficult for him to give his "Bolshevik word of honour" since he knew that tomorrow I would not be there. That very same night two agents of the G.P.U. came to my room, got me out of bed, searched the place, and took me away with them. As usual, not a word was said about the reason for my arrest. I was taken to the waiting room of the G.P.U. headquarters. There I met about ten other exiles— Mensheviks, Anarchists, Zionists. I was at first the only one of those who had participated in the hunger-strike, but later they brought in Volkov. Some of the exiles had already been interviewed by the chief of the secret police; the others were awaiting their turn. Everyone was told the same thing: that he was leaving immediately by lorry for Yeniseisk. Two lorries were already standing ready for us in the courtyard. A few had already gathered up their belongings and got into a lorry. Such movements by road, in cars or sleighs, cost the G.P.U. far more than by river, and for that reason all transfers were normally suspended when ice interrupted navigation. In this case expense was apparently of no moment. Probably revenge was being taken on the hunger-strikers. Others were being thrown in together with them to make up the weight, so to speak.

My turn came. I was received by the affable young representative of the Political Section.

"I am terribly grieved, Anton Antonovich" (no 'comrade' this time) "but I am obliged to inform you of the instructions of the G.P.U. Regional Administration for your immediate transfer to your place of exile, Yeniseisk."

"You know very well," I began solemnly, "that from the moment of my departure from Irkutsk I had accepted in principle to be exiled to Yeniseisk. I was prepared to go there immediately upon the completion of my cure, which, as the G.P.U. is aware, cannot be effected in Yeniseisk because of the lack of the necessary apparatus. Moreover, Denisov promised at the conclusion of our hunger-strike that there would ne no reprisals whatever."

"This is not a reprisal. We are simply carrying out an old instruction. Your allocation to Yeniseisk was arranged already in Irkutsk. I am extremely sorry, Anton Antonovich, but I must carry out without question the orders of higher authority."

"I should not count on that. In no circumstances will I submit to this order for my departure now."

"We shall see," he said, his tone now far from friendly.

"We shall see," I replied sharply.

I went back into the neighbouring room, where I was to await being put on the lorry—forcibly, since I did not intend to enter it of my own free will. It was clear that I was to be punished for the hunger-strike. Me first, the others later. Again I thought: if I yield now, goodbye to my chances of getting out of the country. My six months' battle with the G.P.U., beginning with the twenty-three days' hunger-strike in the cellar-prison of Chelyabinsk in May, was approaching its climax there in that room where I awaited forcible loading on to the lorry. I had to resort to extreme measures—to slash my veins. It was time to make use of the razor blade that I had kept by me for six months. Slowly and painfully my nerves had to adjust themselves; my mind had to accept the idea of cutting my own flesh. My blood would flow, but the G.P.U.

would not gain the victory. It would learn that its victims were not docile cattle. I sat down in a far corner of the room, cautiously took out the razor blade and, grasping it in my right hand, cut the veins of my left wrist. I then cut the veins of my right wrist. I had taken my handkerchief to conceal the operation as much as possible and to soak up the blood. It was not without emotion that I made the first cut. When the cold blade first touched the warm, it seemed to me the almost burning flesh, an icy shiver passed through my whole body. I felt that I was bidding a last goodbye to life. But once the first cut had been made, once the blood had begun to flow, the pain ceased, and I experienced an indescribable feeling of satisfaction in thus slashing my veins with the blade. The paradoxical sensation surged wildly within me that the more I mutilated myself the more blows I dealt the G.P.U. I experienced a feeling of real triumph. When one of my neighbours looked at me questioningly, noticing that something abnormal was happening I gave him such a ferocious look that the words he was about to speak froze on his lips. But his sharply checked half-movement in my direction ran like an electric shock along the row of men seated on the bench. One after another the heads turned towards me, and, meeting my answering glance, turned quickly away in frozen immobility and silence. The sudden hush and the tension did not pass unnoticed by the two G.P.U. men standing by the door.

"Hey, you! What's going on there in the corner?"

"Nothing, nothing at all," the reply came quickly, too quickly and excitedly to satisfy the G.P.U. guards.

Quickly they were at my side, and others with them. The blood jetting from my gory hands and the pool already formed on the floor spoke for themselves. In a flash the blade and the handkerchief were torn from me. But in vain the agents and the *feldscher* summoned from the first-aid post tried to bandage my wrists and stop the flow of blood. This shift of the battle from the moral to the physical plane—slashing my veins and engaging in a hand-to-hand tussle with the G.P.U. men—gave me a strange pleasure and the strength of ten. To overpower me they threw me on the floor, trying to keep me down by lying on my chest, my arms, my legs. I resisted desperately. A savage struggle ensued. Furious and weltering in blood we milled around the floor.

"You don't want me to be cured," I yelled. "You want us to die . . . all of us. All right . . . but not your way . . . not a slow death . . . not the 'natural' death you want . . . You invite us to Russia . . . foreign communists and workers . . . to the so-called workers' country . . . and when we see through your fraud . . . you won't let us out of the country . . . But you fraternize with the foreign bourgeoisie and the Fascist States . . . Hypocrites! Scoundrels! . . ."

I shouted and struggled. They did not say a word but stubbornly and viciously bore me down. We wrestled desperately but did not lash out. Life and death, liberty and slavery, honour and dishonour struggled together according to the rules of the game—as though at a sports contest.

My strength gradually exhausted itself; my limbs grew numb; they bandaged my wrists, put me into a car with a G.P.U. man on either side. But now I was not going to Yeniseisk but to the Krasnoyarsk Prison hospital, where a doctor, aroused from his home by the G.P.U., awaited to stitch my wounds. I had not yet quite calmed down, not yet exhaused all my strength. but the G.P.U. overcame the remnants of my resistance without much difficulty. I was forced on to the operating table and my arms pinned down while the doctor sewed up the cuts. Then I was taken into an isolated cell and laid on the bunk. One agent remained with me. Exhaustion overcame me. I slept.

It was morning when I woke. Breakfast was brought in—a glass of milk and a snack. I refused to eat or drink. I had no strength left to re-open the wounds, tear off the bandages, break the threads holding the flesh together; but I had enough to refuse any nourishment. I no longer felt any will to live. Somehow in the course of the struggle a transformation of values had taken place. The struggle with the G.P.U. had been for life and not for death: so that I could bear witness abroad to all that I had seen in Russia, and tell the truth about the cruel and barbarous regime masquerading under the guise of 'socialism'. I had accepted the risk of death in order to save my life. The subsequent Moscow Trials of 1936—38 proved that I had been right in so doing. But in the heat of the battle I lost sight of my main objective for an instant, and death, which had been no more than a weapon in the struggle, became an end in itself. It was necessary for me to die in order that my relatives, my friends abroad, the workers of all countries, should know from my death the truth about Russia. Perhaps this was the best evidence I could give them.

Half an hour later the warder again brought me the glass of milk and some breakfast.

"The G.P.U. doesn't recognize your hunger-strike, so if hunger-striking isn't going to help you, you might as well eat."

"That isn't important. I didn't ask you to telephone the G.P.U. and inform them. I don't need their authorization. I don't need anything from them."

I fasted the whole day: tranquilly, calmly, alone. The G.P.U. man had moved into the corridor, where there was a little more animation.

The next day I had a visit from the secretary of the Political Section, still as affable and hypocritical as ever. I refused to speak even a single word to him. The following day Denisov's deputy, Valaev, chief of the Political Section, came in.

"Comrade Ciliga! What are you doing? Why are you trying to kill yourself. You know perfectly well that neither the G.P.U. nor the Party desire your death. If we are sometimes compelled to resort to the use of forceful measures, we do so as Communists, as the armed unit of the Party, by order of the Party, by decision of the competent Party organs, towards groups of individuals who have broken Party discipline, Party decisions. We always take into consideration the possibility that those oppositionists who have descended to fractionalism may come to their senses and again become useful members of the Party. We know you have done a great deal for the Party abroad. It is not necessary to go to extremes, to become desperate. Now tell me, what are your concrete conditions for putting an end to this hunger-strike?"

"Valaev," I said "I have no more demands whatever to make to you. You know all there is to know. Everything has already been said. What is the use of repeating it. I have nothing more to say."

It was not long before he put in another appearance.

"I come on the instructions of my chief, Denisov, to inform you in his name, Anton Antonovich, that in view of your injuries and illness the G.P.U. has decided not to send you to Yeniseisk or farther north. In view of your serious state of health, Denisov will support before the higher organs of the G.P.U. your application for transfer to a locality with a warmer climate than Krasnoyarsk. In anticipation of such a transfer we will help you to find work here so that you will be better nourished and get well again."

Should I content myself with this result? Again to accept this breathing space before once more raising the demand to be allowed to leave the country? Or right then and there to take the bull by the horns: departure or death?

In my war with the G.P.U. I was once again faced with this fundamental strategical question and once again I decided that the time was premature for the final battle. My relatives abroad had only just learned the facts of my situation; it was necessary first to await the results of their efforts on my behalf.

"What you tell me of Denisov's decisions are of course important, but I can only consider them when at liberty. As long as I am in prison I cannot go into any discussions and cannot stop my hunger-strike," I replied.

"As soon as you are in a fit condition to walk, you can go home."

"Good, but I shall not take any food as long as I am here instead of in the municipal hospital," I said distrustfully.

It was already night (at that time of the year it got dark early) when I was indeed transferred to the municipal hospital and put in a room already prepared for me in the Opthalmic Ward and not in the Surgical Ward, where, according to my state of health, I should really have been placed.

But, as I later learned, this was no accident. The G.P.U. put me there because that was the most isolated part of the hospital. I was there as a person under arrest, although I did not know this, and was not supposed to know it. A G.P.U. man was placed at the entrance to the Ward, with instructions to check all those entering and to prevent anyone from visiting me. I myself could not get out of bed and did not even think of putting my head outside the room. Orders had been given the hospital staff not to accept any messages or letters from me to my friends in town, or rather, to hand them over to the G.P.U. and give me replies in accordance with instructions of the G.P.U. In short, the G.P.U. had played me another malicious trick. It thought to let me stay a few days in hospital, until I recovered sufficiently to be put on the lorry for Yeniseisk. During this time I was told that my friends had been informed of my transfer to hospital and that they would shortly visit me. Although I was surprised that on the second day of my hospitalization no one had been to see me, I did not suspect that the G.P.U. had gone to such lengths of duplicity.

But the G.P.U.'s plan nevertheless miscarried. However great its power, the Soviet people's hatred of it was greater. As I had recently spent a month in this same hospital, albeit in another ward, I had made many contacts and friendships there. So my friends outside were informed of my presence. They immediately came to visit me, but the agent guarding the entrance refused them entrance to the ward. They then went to G.P.U. headquarters to lodge a protest. The dirty game was exposed. And this time the G.P.U. really retreated. My comrades received permission to visit me and two weeks later I was discharged and returned home. Valaev helped me to find work. Since the trick had not succeeded Valaev and Denisov did their best to make me forget about it.

My companions of the night of November 27/28th were taken to Yeniseisk. The tale they had to tell there aroused a lively response. A number of the Yeniseisk comrades knew me personally, having shared prison life with me in Verkhne-Uralsk, and after a thorough discussion it was decided to send a resolution of protest to Moscow, to the Procurator of the Republic, Akulov, who controlled the activities of the G.P.U. In addition to supporting the struggle of the three Yugoslav Oppositionists (Dedich, Dragich and myself) for the right to leave the country, the resolution protested against the whole system of reprisals taken against the Russian Communist Oppositionists. Referring to the events of November 27/28, they concluded with the following words:

"Bringing these facts to your notice, we draw your attention to the fact that although his attempt at suicide failed, Comrade Ciliga's life is in constant danger, so long as his fundamental demand is not granted. Placing upon you the responsibility for the system of provocation established by the G.P.U. with the object of exterminating communists, and of which Comrade Ciliga is a victim, we warn you that the entire responsibility for Comrade Ciliga's fate falls on you.

"We bring to your notice the fact that the life of Comrade Ciliga and of other Yugoslav comrades is in danger. Also, in spite of the remoteness of the places of exile to which the treachery of the ruling clique has sent them, the international working class will be given a detailed account of these matters. We demand that the G.P.U. put an end to its systematic torturing of Comrades Ciliga, Dedich, and Dragich, and that they be allowed to leave the country, since they are forcibly and illegally detained in the U.S.S.R."

Thirteen of the Yeniseisk exiles: Bibinski, Volkov, Gurovskaya, Dzhinashvili, Shapiro, Ida Lemelman, Plomper, Rappoport, Simbirsky, Plotnikov, Kordina, Fedorov, Chikin, signed this resolution and sent it off. This act of comradeship and international solidarity placed them in danger of grave reprisals; but they did not hesitate. (The full text of this document was published in Western European and American periodicals soon after my return from Russia in 1936—A.C.)

The reply of the Prosecutor and the G.P.U. to this protest was not long in coming. Not only the thirteen signatories, but over sixty of the Yeniseisk exiles, among them not only Communist Oppositionists but also socialists and anarchists, were arrested. They were accused in the first place of counter-revolutionary agitation; secondly of illegal meetings; and thirdly of participation in drawing up the declaration of the thirteen. The counter-revolutionary agitation and the illegal meetings consisted of the discussions and meetings of the exiles among themselves. As the Stalin Comintern was at that time campaigning in Europe for its 'Popular Front' policy, the arrested socialists and anarchists were released after a few months' detention. But the G.P.U.'s hands were not thus tied in regard to the Communist Oppositionists, and thirty of them—not just the thirteen—were given fresh sentences and sent to new places of exile. They had to pass through Krasno-yarsk on their way to remote, lost corners of the land: some to the burning sands of Central Asia, to Alma Ata, Petro-pavolsk, Tashkent; others to the Urals, to Tymen, Ishim; the rest to the frozen regions of Eastern Siberia, to Narym, Obdorsk, or to the shores of the White Sea, to Archangel.

In the most forsaken places along the rivers of Siberia, the colonies of Soviet exiles have replaced the exiles of Tsarist times. The burning deserts of Central Asia, the savage Taiga, the islands of Solovietsk, there the persecuted exiles live out their lives. It is in these places that the immense concentration camps are to be found, worse than in the time of the Tsars. From prison to exile, from one place to another, the immense army of political exiles wander, year after year, across one-sixth of the land suface of the globe.

THE DAILY ROUND

The after-effects of that night of November 27/28th were with me for a long time. In the course of five years of prison and exile nothing had so drained my strength as this severing of my veins. It was as though with the blood I had lost not only physical energy but also psychological force. In comparison, my hunger-strikes, so long and oft repeated, appeared simply a game.

An impalpable but non the less real barrier shut me off from the world, as though a wall of glass enclosed me. I walked the streets of the town, went to work, to the theatre and the cinema, visited friends; but for a long time it seemed that another person than I did all these things. The barrier around my spirit divorced me from the living world, prevented

447

its keen winds from buffeting me, its warm sun from caressing me.

Painfully and slowly, over a period of months, I recuperated.

My first joy came to me with letters from relatives, from the shores of the far off Adriatic, bringing a breath of the sunny south and memories of my carefree childhood.

My mother scolded me: "My dear little son, it is seven years since I had a letter from you, and it is I, who cannot write, who must write the first . . . When will you return? When will you find tranquillity again? Will you be always like the waves of our sea, never knowing rest? . . ."

I also heard from old friends. What joy after eighteen years to receive a letter from a friend of one's youth! My relatives and friends sent me money as well. My food was already assured by a registered letter from Switzerland containing thirty dollars. For foreign currency and gold one could buy food of the best quality in the special 'Torgsin' shops.

This privilege weighed heavily on me sometimes. I was sitting in my landlady's kitchen one morning having breakfast: cocoa, and egg, white bread and butter. In the hungry Russia of that time these things were fairy-tale delicacies. An old woman entered the kitchen, begging a morsel of bread. I was too ashamed to give her a bit of dry bread. I gave her bread and butter and an egg. The poor old woman burst out sobbing.

"The good God keep you!" she said. "I used to live like that myself once. I had all I needed. Now I have to beg for a crust of bread. Forgive a poor old woman."

Another incident was still more painful. I was going through the market place with a large loaf of bread under my arm, when suddenly a man stepped in front of me, begging a piece of bread. He was covered in rags, filthy and unshaven; his skin the colour of earth. A scarecrow. But the most striking thing about him was that he appeared only recently to have fallen into that state, that it was not long since he had known better times. This man had suffered some sudden overwhelming catastrophe; he has plunged in one instant from the heights of the social pyramid to the depths. Has he only been stunned by the fall, or is he completely broken?

I shared my bread with him and added ten roubles. He looked at me in stupefaction, his very soul in his scared eyes, then without a word flung himself on his knees before me, his eyes brimmed with tears. I fled without staying to question him.

Passing through the doors of a *Torgsin*, the Soviet citizen

entered the special world of the legalized Soviet 'black market'.
It was fed by two sources: the Leviathan-State and the Pariah-
Citizen. Gold, in its raw or worked state, and foreign currency
constituted the medium of trading. Torgsin was organized as a
State commercial Trust, strictly centralized and with branches
in all the main towns of the U.S.S.R.

Goods were not sold directly for gold or currency. Before
any purchase could be made these had to be exchanged at the
cashier's office for bonds of corresponding value in 'torgsin
roubles' or 'gold roubles'. One paid with these bonds. One
dollar equalled 1 rouble 11 kopecks. A special office changed
foreign currency against torgsin-roubles or weighed and valued
the gold and silver objects brought there. The gold-dust and
nuggets of the Siberian prospectors were also accepted.

The Torgsin bonds were in the nature of letters of credit.
The amount they represented could be spent all at once or in
portions. They were not made out to a particular holder and
the Government thus tacitly recognized their re-sale. It was
here that the Citizen-Pariah entered on the scene. In the shop
itself, right by the side of the exchange-office, there were men:
on the one hand those who changed their gold or currency
against torgsin-bonds, on the other those who offered roubles
in exchange for these bonds. The rate of exchange rose and fell
just as on a stock market. At that time, that is to say during
the winter of 1933—34, the rate of exchange oscillated around
forty paper roubles for one torgsin gold rouble. In the spring
of 1933 the rate held regularly at fifty roubles. The previous
winter, when the famine was at its height, the rate had gone up
to sixty. In 1935, just before the closing down of Torgsin, it
fell to thirty.

The trade in these bonds was carried on through the intermediary of professional speculators.

Besides this, foreign currency was sold publicly. The Chinese,
for example, readily purchased dollars, either for illegal
transmission to their relatives at home, or for the smuggling
of all sorts of goods from abroad, including opium. In the
'land of socialism' opium smoking was quietly indulged in by
many people. There were also less exotic enterprises to be
found, such as gambling houses with roulette wheels, card-
sharpers, and so forth. Their clientele was made up of Soviet
administrative personnel, the chairmen of co-operatives, heads
of stores, cashiers, accountants. I was always surprised that no
one feared the G.P.U. and even more surprised that the G.P.U.
tolerated these things. I knew, for instance, of one opium den

and gambling house that functioned without interference during the whole of my stay in Siberia.

Having bought a suit-length in Torgsin, the question then was—how to get it made up? Not an easy matter in Soviet Russia. There were few skilled tailors left from former times, and the new ones did not know their trade.

Where could I go? I learned that the large State enterprises (the Railway Workshops, etc.) and Government administrations (The G.P.U., the General Staff, etc.) had tailoring workshops that accepted outside work. I went therefore to a military tailor.

The military workshop was situated on the second floor of a large building. My order was accepted for the sum of about two hundred roubles. I saw large quantities of finished and semi-finished clothing, and many bales of cloth lying around. There were very few civilian suits. Almost half of the clothing consisted of uniforms and coats for Red Army officers, and nearly the same quantity consisted of coats and costumes for their wives, some of whom were there, alone or with their husbands, trying on clothes or handing over material to be made up.

My eyes were attracted to a large bale of black cloth, near which stood two men dressed in semi-sportive, semi-military fashion, in short leather jackets, black trousers, black kepi, and high boots. These were two members of the Political Section of the railway (Politodel—a kind of Party police). They were ordering about twenty uniforms for members of this body. This is where one must look to discover those 'ameliorations in living conditions for the worker personnel of the transports organizations'.

The atmosphere of the place was redolent of quiet comfort; a pleasant spot where members of the ruling class in process of formation could come together to fit themselves out for their new roles. They felt at home here, among their own kind. There was no risk of encountering ordinary workers or soldiers having a uniform made or ordering a costume for their wives.

The basic wage of workers there was small: a military man would pay 50 roubles for what they were charging me 200. But skilled craftsmen of former times worked in such places with pleasure. Firstly, because it gave them a certain security, not only against taxes, but also against arrest; secondly, because they received better rations than the rest of the population; and thirdly, because they could take advantage of their right to accept outside orders and so augment their incomes. A little wangling did not do any harm either. Supposing, for example, an officer's wife has not enough silk lining material, and no gold with which to obtain the necessary Torgsin bonds. It would be embarrassing for her to buy the bonds or the silk direct from the dealers or on the 'black market'. The tailor is thus the natural intermediary. Of course, he gets his cut; and the lady's husband has only to close his eyes to such dealings.

As a matter of fact, Red Army officers are not exactly care-worn, in spite of all the 'responsibility of their status'. Let us take Captain Mikhail Grigorievich, for example. One day he said to me:

"Tonight, Anton Antonovich, we'll go on the spree."

His friend Eleonore Alexandrovna gaily seconds him: "Oh yes! Let's all three go to the *Gorodsky*." (This was the most exclusive of the night clubs in town.)

"What's come over you, Mikhail Grigorievich? Go to a restaurant with an Oppositionist! You'll compromise yourself!"

"Pooh!—You've hit the bull's-eye! You're scaring me! Tell me, who is Trotsky? Who is Stalin? First one leader of the Red Army, then another. But the Red Army stays the same. Party quarrels pass but the Soviet power remains. True, eh? Besides," he added, " I've only to put on an overcoat over my uniform and even if a military patrol should come in, they're our own people, they won't say anything."

I have to fall back on a last argument.

"Well, if you're not compromised, I shall be. It isn't proper for a political exile to be seen together with a public figure in a restaurant."

The Captain and Eleonora Alexandrovna are Soviet society *en miniature*. He, a son of the Ukrainian steppes, child of simple peasants; she, a nobleman's daughter, her parents ruined by the Revolution. The two are at this moment in the middle of an ardent love affair. A few days before they had such a wild orgy in the young woman's apartment that the whole neighbourhood is still talking about it. At the moment, I notice, there are still bottles of vodka and strong liquor on the table.

They are both about thirty. The beginning of their conscious life, the riot of their youth, coincided with the end of the Civil War and the victory of the Reds. He had run away from home when still a youngster to join the Red Army; that was the beginning of his rise. She, with all the ardour of eighteen years, was enchanted by the new rulers and their ideology. Thus the Revolution had lessened the social distance between them. During NEP she so to speak turned back on her path, divorced her first husband, a Communist, and married a non-Party specialist, with whom she went to Siberia. Her husband is a colleague of mine and has recently left Krasnoyarsk for the North, on a mission of several months duration on behalf of his Trust. Eleonora Alexandrovna has in the meantime made the acquaintance of Captain Grigorievich and started an affair with him. In the fierce embraces of this son of the people she seeks, it seems to me, not so much the flame of a new passion as forgetfulness. There is something feverish in her passion, something of anguish. She is tired of life and of the Revolution. She clings to life still, it is true, but she is no longer sure of the future.

With him it is quite otherwise. His rise is steady and continuous. For him she is a real prize; a social, cultural, and physical conquest. Behind him and before him on life's road he sees nothing but victories. He is indomitable, as sure of himself as the mettlesome horse on which he has ridden ten kilometres from barracks into town. He rides in a devil-may-care style, ties his horse to a tree in the courtyard, and lets it stamp and neigh there to the great scandal and annoyance of all the neighbours and the families of her husband's colleagues in the Trust. Mikhail Grigorievich and Eleonore Alexandrovna have shut the door of the apartment. It is the middle of the day, but they close the shutters; they are not at home to the rest of the world. They live recklessly, for themselves alone.

During my stay in Krasnoyarsk a 'change of power' took place in eastern Siberia. Moscow dismissed the old leadership headed by Leonov, because of 'weak development of the kolkhozy and agriculture in general' and 'lagging behind in industry'. The new leader was Razumov, who came from Kazan (capital of the Tartar Autonomous Republic). In this change Moscow, and Razumov as executor of its instructions, leaned primarily for support on the Communists of the G.P.U.

The replacement of the local authorities in Krasnoyarsk was accompanied by a noisy campaign against the former Chairman of the Party Control Commission. Eventually he was even expelled from the Party. In addition to his normal political sins and his bad manners, the Press particularly attacked him for getting the Invalids' Co-operative to make him a pair of boots from chrome leather originally allocated for another use. Since there was an acute shortage of leather and footwear the charge was especially effective with the public. But the first thing I learned about the new Chairman of the Party Control

Commission (from a Communist member of this Co-operative) was that he had himself just ordered a pair of boots of chrome leather. Apparently he feared that there would be no leather at all in the immediate future and was therefore in a hurry to place his order.

The Siberian winter arrived and settled down. The snow froze and crackled underfoot. It covered the streets, the houses, the fences, the trees, the fields beyond the town, the woods, the mountains—the whole world.

And it will stay like this for seven months. Everything will be frozen whiteness, still, unchanging; a boundless immensity, a horrible monotony.

The Yenisei can now be crossed on foot; the ice supports not only pedestrians but even heavily loaded lorries.

On days of strong frost one has the impression that even the air is freezing, thickening, solidifying; one moves through it with difficulty, as if ploughing through icy sand. Oh where are you, sun of my native land!

But nostalgia possessed me only for brief moments. The winter is long, very long, but in Krasnoyarsk it is still endurable, even for a southerner. This is actually still southern Siberia and the temperature does not often fall below twenty degress of frost. The average temperature of a Krasnoyarsk winter—15 below freezing point—when there is no wind, and one has enough warm clothing, is even rather pleasant, invigorating, as the air is dry, clear and clean, healthy. It seems to knit together and strengthen the whole organism.

Moreover, everything seems to go well with me. The G.P.U., which supplies the political exiles with their warm winter clothing (an old tradition inherited from Tsarism) and usually gives only half of what is necessary, gave me everything without any argument: a short sheepskin coat, felt boots, wadded trousers and jacket, a fur cap, and even underwear. It also helped me to find my first job. All the exiles together were like one big family. My relatives sent me a second sum of thirty dollars from abroad. The local Siberians, among whom one has to live and upon whom one has to depend, opened their doors wide and were extremely considerate to me. The cordiality and generosity, simplicity and open-heartedness of the Russian people—whether it concerns the cultured section or the broad popular mass—is astonishing, unsurpassed. This Russian character charms, seduces, conquers everyone and everything. Because of it all the rest seems secondary, unimportant; one forgets it. It is largely this wherein lies the secret of the Russification of this enormous country, from the Baltic to the Pacific. Among the mass of the Russian people, in worker and peasant circles, there is no trace of that racial and national arrogance that erects such barbed psychological barriers between the peoples. Instead of that arrogance there is an innate feeling of equality and brotherhood with the other peoples of their common Eurasian territory. One may argue that this is because of the low level of civilization of the Russian masses, which have after all not risen so far above the culture of the Bashkirs, Tadzhiks, and so on. That may be so; but this aspect of the Russian character still remains a highly significant factor in the destiny of one-sixth of the globe stretching from Leningrad to Vladivostok, from Tashkent to Murmansk. And in this the psychology of the Russian people profoundly distinguishes itself from that of the German and Anglo-Saxon peoples.

After eight o'clock in the evening one walked the streets of Krasnoyarsk at the risk of one's life. Not because of the cold, but because of bandits. There was no night without a robbery with violence, and murders were frequent. Since the population was so poor, robbery consisted in most cases of stripping lone pedestrians to their underwear. After a visit to the cinema, the theatre, or to friends, people hurried home in groups, avoiding lonely streets as much as possible. I myself ran into danger twice but managed to extricate myself without any particular unpleasantness. As a rule the bandits did not belong to the local population. They were either professionals who had been exiled to Siberia, or had come there of their own free will to carry on their trade, or were the children of peasants deported to the Siberian taiga.

One day a high official of the G.P.U. was a victim. He was killed early one evening, only a few yards round the corner from the G.P.U. headquarters, before he had even time to cry out. The G.P.U. took this as a challenge and replied with due dignity: from criminals already in prison and suspects arrested in a special raid, about a hundred were selected and shot, in order that bandits should also appreciate the difference between ordinary mortals and officials of the G.P.U. In fact the G.P.U. was not at all sure that the crime had been committed by ordinary criminals, being inclined to believe that it was the work of some undercover organization connected with Japan and was therefore anxious to show itself capable of action. About half a year later, the G.P.U. attributed to the same cause the huge forest fires that broke out south of Krasnoyarsk, near the Mongolian frontier.

Of course, I do not know how much truth there was in these suspicions, but it was clear that Russia was then going through a period of acute diplomatic tension and that the disaffected populace placed great hopes in Germany, and even in Japan. It does not matter from what direction deliverance comes, so long as we are rid of Stalin and the Communists—that was the mood of the greater part of the non-Party intelligentsia and the almost unanimous mood of the peasantry. The workers did not lay their stake on the interventionist card, but gravitated rather towards the notion that in the event of war they would be armed and might be able to turn things to their own advantage and set up a new government.

Summarizing, it may be said that between 1933 and 1935—when I was able to observe matters on the spot—all classes of Soviet Russia, with the exception of the Communists, wanted the war with Germany and Japan that then appeared imminent. They wanted it in the hope that the Stalin-Communist regime would suffer a defeat similar to the defeat that had finished off the Tsarist and Kerensky regimes. I knew of a group of Red Army soldiers, of Siberian peasant origin, who had agreed among themselves to go straight over to the other side as soon as war broke out. I spoke with one of these soldiers personally.

I was shocked by the sympathy displayed towards Hitler by the members of the old liberal intelligentsia who had formerly stood on the basis of bourgeois democratic opposition to the Bolsheviks. I even encountered convinced Fascists among the younger elements of the intelligentsia. One of these was a former leader of Siberian partisans, who had occupied a very high position in the Soviet apparatus after the defeat of Kolchak and had for a short time even belonged to the Communist Party. He had left both the Party and the partisan organization (which he then referred to as an "organization of bandits"). He called himself politically a fascist and philosophically a mystical-idealist (in opposition to Marxist materialism). He was a man whose nerves had completely gone to pieces. He contracted typhus and did not survive the illness. The example of the opera singer S. was very characteristic of the mood of the intelligentsia. On the stage he sang what was expected of him by the authorities. But when on a visit to relatives in Krasnoyarsk he fell ill of typhus, and in the delirium of the malady shouted out all the rankling bitterness he felt towards the Soviet regime. He instantly acquired enormous popularity and his funeral was attended by all the intelligentsia and all the non-Communist employees of the town.

My interlocutors would have liked to receive from me, a foreigner, confirmation of their prognosis on foreign affairs, but I was obliged to disappoint them, since I was convinced that no one, including Germany and Japan, would wage war on Russia, and that Stalin, knowing the weakness of his regime in the event of war, would seek to avoid one at all costs.

"Japan gravitates more towards China than towards Siberia, to the south rather than to the north. The climate there is more favourable; the country has abundant natural resources, riches accumulated over thousands of years, and a population of hundreds of millions for exploitation. Moreover Stalin himself, in order to stave off the danger to Russia, will do his best to facilitate Japan's expansion in this direction. At the beginning of the Sino-Japanese war Stalin had, in the name of 'neutrality', refused the use of the Chinese Eastern Railway—then belonging to Russia—for the transport of Chinese soldiers; but had afterwards agreed to its use by the Japanese, putting only one condition—that payment should be made in gold."

"But Germany, Hitler?" My interlocutors spoke as though this were their last hope.

"The national interests of Germany and Russia are complementary rather than contradictory. This is a permanent fact and the present ideological contradictions are secondary, temporary. Therefore Germany and Russia will not only not wage war with one another, but will together wage war against western Europe. Of course, for such a joint war the political regimes and ideologies will first need to be brought into alignment with each other. This will take time, and that is why a European war, a world war, is relegated to the fairly distant future."

The war that broke out five or six years after these conversations had not been expected by me before ten or fifteen years. Under-estimating Germany's strength and over-estimating that of France, I considered that Germany alone, without the active support of Russia, could not risk a war against France and England. And since Russia, judging from what I had observed, would still for a long time be incapable of waging an offensive war (not to speak of the lack of a common ideology of the two regimes), I concluded that a European war was a long way off. I also under-estimated the rivalry that could spring up between the two regimes on the question: Who is going to organize Europe: Hitler or Stalin? Finally, I said to myself, not only Russia's vastness but also the undoubted strength of the Red Army, resulting from the advance of heavy industry through the Five Year Plans, and the manoeuvring skill of the new ruling class formed since the Revolution, were factors ensuring that war against Russia would not be lightly undertaken. Contemporary Russia is not contemporary China. It would perhaps not be difficult to defeat Stalin, but it would be difficult to defeat Russia.

As the experience of the Second World War has shown, I was a bad prophet as far as Germany, France and England were concerned, but not such a bad one about Russia; and it was this aspect of the problem that most interested my interlocutors, and most depressed them.

"If the other countries won't fight Bolshevism, then we shall perish," the peasants said to me.

"If over the next ten years the outside world does not put an end to Bolshevism in Russia, then it will fulfil its Five Year Plans and, possessing allies in the workers' organizations in all countries, c conquer the world," said the intellectuals despairingly. "Yes, yes, in that event the whole world will be enslaved by Bolshevism," they insisted passionately in answer to my sceptical smile.

For myself, I thought that as a result of the Five Year Plans the strength of Russia would increase but the strength of Bolshevism would decline, wither, decay at the roots. In my opinion Russia moved towards national expansion in foreign affairs, and internally towards the liquidation of Bolshevism.

No theoretical prognosis can map the unforeseeable course of life itself. And in those days Moscow itself, and not the Siberian population alone was jittery. It had good cause to be. Japan's penetration into Manchuria and Hitler's coming to power had undoubtedly created a new international atmosphere and one sensed the advent of a new and ominous phase in the destiny of the world. What if the struggle should begin with the U.S.S.R.? . . . The negotiations in May, 1933, around a proposed 'Four-Power Pact' (England, France, Italy, Germany) perhaps marked the high-point of the danger of Russia being isolated. But the projected Agreement was never concluded. In France and Great Britain the tendencies opposed to essential concessions to Germany predominated, resulting in an attempt at *rapprochement* with the U.S.S.R. Stalin seized upon this both through Soviet diplomatic channels and through the Comintern, propagating an alliance with the democracies and the creation of a united anti-fascist front. But, at the same time, Russia and Germany did not completely break off relations with each other. Trade agreements were renewed and fresh credits granted. And not only this. The big political trial in Leipzig against the Comintern (Reichstag Fire Trial), which took place from September to December, 1933, ended in a compromise between Moscow and Berlin, with Dimitrov's release and his return to Russia.

However, there was no lack of signs indicating a development in the opposite direction. On 15 October 1933 Germany left the League of Nations, and on 15 September 1934 Russia entered it. The population was completely stunned by this new and unexpected turn in Soviet foreign policy. Some grew hopeful, others were completely cast down. The Government attentively followed the reactions of the population, gauging its mood; while the G.P.U. kept check on the reactions of the political exiles.

"What do you think of the entry of the U.S.S.R. into the League of Nations?" Valaev asked me point-blank one day during a routine visit.

The question was so unexpected that I had to ponder some time how to reply to it.

"What do I think? That it is a natural, logical step. Day by day you move farther away from socialism and the proletariat in your domestic policy. It follows that you must do the same in foreign policy. One begins by talking about the 'peaceful co-existence of two systems', proceeds to alliances, and ends up with a war waged in common. You will support each other and wage war side by side. But . . . well, life has a logic of its own . . ."

"Oh, come now, Anton Antonovich, you and your logic! Do you really think we've changed. No, we don't forget for an instant what the League of Nations really is, nor what Lenin said about it. Us fight for the bourgeoisie! No! Never! We didn't join the League of Nations to take part in an imperialist war, but in order to safeguard ourselves from war. We shall not let them make use of us. On the contrary, we shall make use of their quarrels in the interests of proletarian policy . . ."

To discuss Geneva, war or peace in Europe, the life or death of the West, was for us, watching Stalin's international double-game from this Siberian seclusion, like talking of another world, somehow unreal, fantastic.

Siberia has horizons peculiar to itself. There one stands on the banks of the Yenisei and looks along its course to the

Arctic, and it seems that one can stretch out a hand and touch the North Pole; and on the right, away off to Mongolia, China, Japan, the entire north Pacific, it is as though one can reach out and touch San Franscisco. This mighty triangle—Krasnoyarsk, San Francisco, the North Pole—is close to you, your neighbour; *this* is your world, *this* is the atmosphere you breathe. The West fades far behind you, into the remote background; even European Russia is something else, different. In the language of the Siberians "Russia" is always and only European Russia. "I am leaving for Russia"; and, "I have come from Russia", they say. In their thoughts and in their language Siberia is not Russia.

But if European Russia seems today so remote to the Siberians, all the more reason for western Europe to appear like another world, almost another planet. Siberia looks towards the north and the east—the extreme north and the extreme east; and it calls upon distant Russia to look that way too.

AT WORK

Three circumstances help the political exiles to obtain work: their knowledge—they are on the whole better educated than the local population; their solidarity—if a new arrival obtains work with which he is not familiar he will certainly be assisted by his comrades in exile; their honesty—they do not steal and do not engage in any speculation on the side. But to obtain a job it is not enough that the director of one or another enterprise or institution be willing to engage you. The director must also have the consent of the G.P.U., and this is not always granted. Such intellectual work as teaching, literary work and journalism are barred on principle. All creative work of the spirit must remain the monopoly of the orthodox conformists. Labour in factories is also barred—for the working class must be safe-guarded against any dangerous influences. There remains only office work: planners, book-keepers, cashiers. Because of the bureaucratic character of Soviet economy such jobs are usually plentiful.

Walking along the bank of the now frozen and consequently deserted Yenisei, I came upon a little wooden house with the sign: 'Siberian Station—River and Lake Fisheries Branch of the National Economy'. I went in to try my luck.

"Yes, I will gladly give you work if we have anything suitable, and our small budget will allow it," said the director, a young man with a sallow complexion and tired eyes. "Do you know foreign languages? Perhaps you could help to put our library in order."

It was agreed that I should call again in three days' time for a definite decision. I was then informed:

"The G.P.U. has no objections. They even urged that you should be given work if it could be managed within our budget. I cannot give you a permanent job but I can lay out 500 roubles for you to catalogue the library."

My work continued for two and a half months and my earnings consequently were 200 roubles a month. I was not familiar with the fishing industry and its literature, but it relaxed and soothed me, turning the pages of these tranquil books and journals. I classified them according to categories and languages, preparing a card-index for each with a resumé of the essential contents.

Turning the pages of books and journals in Polish, Czech, Yugoslav, Bulgarian, then in Italian, French, German and even Spanish, I had the impression that in this little, lost corner of provincial Siberia I was somehow re-establishing contact with the outside world.

Over half of the books consisted of American luxury publications, beautifully printed on magnificent paper. Here, too, America wanted to be 'ahead of and better than anyone else'. These signs of her achievements, her ambitions and her challenge penetrated with forceful vigour even to the depths of Siberia.

Since Russia is a land of beautiful simplicity, I was quite free to attend meetings of the station employees, where plans and programmes of future work, as well as reports of completed studies, experiments, and expeditions were discussed. There were in all five or six stations like ours on the territory of the U.S.S.R., each linked to the co-ordinating Institute centred in Moscow. Our station was in active contact with another located on the lower Volga even more than it was with Moscow. The entire organization had been inherited from Tsarist times.

The finances of the station and the tasks assigned it were regulated least of all through the Moscow centre, to some extent in the form of contracts by the Siberian Soviet author-ities but lastly, and mainly, by the powerful Siberian economic organizations—the wealthy State Trusts that for one reason or another were interested in the study of fishery resources on their territory. The preparatory work and the final collation of reports was done at the station itself, in Krasnoyarsk; but the collection of material and the studies were done in the field, and one, two or three men would therefore spend several months at lake Baikal, in the tundra, in Buryat-Mongolia, at a canning factory in Ust Port (in the Arctic on the Yenisei estuary), on the Taimyr Peninsula by the River Khatanga. They would recruit assistants on the spot. These expeditions were the most interesting and absorbing part of the work. There were several of them each summer.

The permanent staff consisted of some twenty people, divided into two categories, according to the level of training: scientific workers, assistants, and students. There were two age categories: pre-revolutionary and post-revolutionary. The work itself was split into four or five departments.

In charge of the natural science department was a woman of about thirty to thirty-five years of age; of noble birth, simple but not without a quiet elegance. She was unmarried and lived alone in a furnished room rented from some local intellectuals. She suffered from tuberculosis. At work she seemed passionately and exclusively devoted to ichthyology, but I fancy that at home she gave herself to literature and music. Of Central Russian origin, she had studied at Moscow University and spoke both French and German. In this department there was also an old man, a former teacher, big, stout, with Tolstoyan beard and views; a self-taught enthusiast. There were also a few young men.

At the head of the chemical department was a specialist of around forty who before the Revolution had studied in Germany. With the mass arrests of the intelligentsia he too had been imprisoned. He had only recently been released and was of course particularly reserved.

The department of national economy was headed by a rather young specialist, the deputy-director, around thirty-two years of age, with considerable scientific capabilities but still more self-conceit. He was a shining example of the latest type of Soviet careerist—the 'non-Party Bolshevik'. He was of bourgeois origin but had received his training under the Soviet system and used the official Soviet jargon and quasi-patriotic phrases as well as any Communist. It would be wrong, however, to assume from this that he was simply spineless; on the contrary, his enthusiasm was nicely calculated and did not spring from lack of backbone. In his capacity as deputy-director he was very strict towards his colleagues. Neither the non-Party specialists nor the Communists liked him, but everyone feared him. He treated even his immediate superior, a Communist, as the nominal rather than real director. The behaviour of the director himself encouraged him in this attitude. A decent man, the Communist-director felt that his nomination to this post by the Party had been premature. Neither his theoretical training nor his practical experience justified such a promotion. But he was a Communist, and his two predecessors, men renowned in their field throughout Russia, had both been arrested and vanished into some concentration camp or other.

There were not many Communists at the station—the director, a member of the intermediate personnel, and four or five Komsomols among the students. The middle and upper posts of scientific workers were all firmly in the hands of non-Party people, and they missed no opportunity of emphasizing how superior they were in knowledge to the Communists who had been placed in authority over them. This was especially evident when the progress of the work and reports on expeditions were under discussion. As in all Soviet enterprises, here too there was a concealed but sharp antagonism between the two top categories of Soviet society, which betrayed itself whenever an exchange of scientific views or a discussion of practical methods took place. Only once did I observe the station temporarily united in a common sentiment—their sincere grief when the old Tolstoyan, the former teacher, the self-taught ichthyologist, died in the following spring.

By that time my work had already come to an end and I only occasionally visited the station out of habit. I was again walking the streets of Krasnoyarsk in search of work.

I obtained employment at the Krasnoyarsk branch of the Industrial Bank of the U.S.S.R., as an auditor of the financing of capital construction in the timber industry of the Krasnoyarsk region, with a monthly salary of 300 roubles. I had never before done work of this nature and I had to begin from scratch: learn how to write out a cheque and see that those of others were correctly signed.

The Industrial Bank occupied three rooms: the director's office, the auditors' office, and the book-keeping office. In still smaller premises along the same corridor was the Communal Bank and the Bank of Socialist Agriculture. The latter, the smallest of all, financed the State farms, the Machine Tractor Stations, and Collective farms. Actually these three banks were not even really independent but rather autonomous branches of the State Bank, the 'Gosbank'. All money transactions, all financial operations were made through the 'Gosbank', where each had an account. But the 'Gosbank' controlled their operations only externally, that is, verified signatures, checked current accounts, etc. Otherwise they transacted business quite independently; they were responsible only to their superior authorities, the Central Regional Office in Irkutsk and the Central Administration in Mocow. The Industrial Bank had very little to do with Irkutsk, instructions being received in ninety cases out of a hundred direct from Moscow.

Only the State Bank really looked like a bank. Only there were financial transactions carried out; only there did one see the milling crowds and feel the feverish excitement and tension characteristic of financial establishments. Between ten and twelve o'clock in the morning the large hall of the State Bank resembled a Stock Exchange. As the Government had started its deflationary policy at this time, the bank never had enough ready money, and the representatives of the various organizations waiting for cash pushed, struggled, and shouted for attention; their frantic activity recalled the agitated, jostling crowds associated with Stock Exchanges.

The State Bank occupied premises corresponding with its status: two whole floors, with numerous offices for its various departments; and it employed more than one hundred people. Its director was a young, energetic and strong-willed Jew who had presumably risen from the poor quarter of some small Jewish locality. He was, of course, a Communist, appointed directly by Moscow. He was later replaced by an Old Bolshevik, a very cultured Latvian with even slightly aristocratic manners. At the moment of my return to Europe this Latvian had just been suspended because he had at some time in the past belonged to one of the Party oppositions.

At the head of our three specialized banks were local Communists, ex-combatants in the Civil War. The *curriculum vitae* of the director of the Industrial Bank was as follows: member of a peasant co-operative before the Revolution; soldier in the Tsarist Army; Red partisan against Kolchak. In banking matters he was shrewd, even intelligent, but his knowledge was not profound. He compensated for this in two ways. First, he surrounded himself with capable colleagues, in particular with an able deputy who, in fact, directed operations under his control and supervision. Second, his Party activity served to strengthen his position. The Krasnoyarsk Party Committee regarded him as one of the irreplaceable specialists in village work. Every spring and autumn he was sent on a month's tour of the villages with the taks of persuading and compelling the collective farmers first to plough and sow, then to harvest the fruit of their labour and deliver it to the State. Occasionally he went into the country for a week's hunting, the favourite diversion both of the old landlords and of the new Communist squires. In summer—like the rest of the new nobility—he lived with his wife and fifteen-year-old daughter in a summer resort near Krasnoyarsk, in the midst of woods on the sunny left bank of the Yenisei. This had formerly been the summer resort of the merchants, and in order that no one could say that the workers gained nothing from the Revolution, three of the thirty to forty houses in this resort were allocated to the trade unions as 'Rest Homes' for workers who were ill or on holiday. There the workers and lower employees spent their two weeks crowded into rooms like hospital wards, with each bunk almost on top of the next. The Communist bureaucracy lived a little more comfortably, one family often occupying an entire house, and never less than a whole floor— 'petit-bourgeois egalitarianism' had certainly been liquidated here.

The Industrial Bank in fact financed only new industrial constructions: the erection of new factories and the enlarging of old ones, i.e. all fresh investments of capital. Since industrialization of the country was then in full swing, this activity was of course considerable.

The entrance to the bank led from the corridor into the office of the auditors, who more than any other employees came into direct contact with the clients. The furniture as well as the whole equipment of the bank was extremely simple— tables, chairs, filing cabinets all cheaply and crudely made, in no way corresponding to one's usual conception of a bank. Only in the director's office was there a proper office desk, but even that was of pre-Revolutionary make and very worn and shabby.

The bank financed three industrial sectors: heavy industry and gold mining; the timber industry; and local industry. Each sector was administered by an accountant, all of whom worked under the orders of a fourth, the chief accountant, who in particular checked and controlled the accounts of those enterprises requiring credits, auditing the bank's accounts, and editing our notes on the accounts of the various individual enterprises financed by us.

This is how the financing was carried out. Every enterprise, whether a new one in course of construction or an old one being extended, had to have its annual 'licence' *(titulny spisok)* approved by Moscow: either by the Trust administration, the department of the People's Commissariat, by the Commissariat itself, or the Government (i.e. the Council of People's Commissars), according to the size and importance of the enterprise in question. In this 'licence' was entered all the stock and all the capital investment of the enterprise in the course of the calendar year. If the new constructions extended over several years, as was usually the case with large new projects, then the 'licence' contained, in addition to the column for permitted expenditure for the current year, a column for future expenditure approved for the whole period of construction in question. The 'licence' not only laid down the total overall expenditure, but divided this into the sums to be spent on the various basic items—construction materials, machines, administration expenses, wages, etc. A series of further instructions laid down the method and volume of expenditure of each enterprise for the current year, for each quarter and sometimes even for each month. In order to obtain payment of bills and other expenses by the bank, each enterprise had to fill in a mass of forms and comply with a host of regulations. If these regulations had been adhered to one hundred per cent no enterprise would have received the cash required in time. Incidentally, the amount of actual cash received was relatively small, amounting to twenty-five or thirty per cent of the total credit—for wages, administrative expenses, petty cash. All other expenditure was effected by a simple book-keeping entry-transfer on the books of the amount in question.

But it was not sufficient to have a 'licence', project approval, construction plans and other documents. It was also necessary that Moscow should release the credit for the enterprise concerned. The two transactions did not always coincide in time. In order to avoid inflation, Moscow · was manoeuvring; and credits, instead of being granted at the beginning of the quarter, were often released only in the middle and sometimes towards its end; and, instead of in the middle of the year, at the end of it.

Since Moscow manoeuvred, we also had to manoeuvre, but often in opposition to Moscow. To know how to manoeuvre without too blatantly conflicting with the regulations, and ensure the necessary credits for the enterprises—*this* was our task. It was actually for our skill in doing this that we were paid. But there were situations when we were faced with the dilemma—either a gross infringement of the regulations or a grave delay in, perhaps a total stoppage of the construction work ... It was then that we, the small cogs in the great bureaucratic machine, handed the matter over to the director. The Communist directors of individual enterprises and institutions have the right to break any Soviet regulation or law if they consider that this is necessary in the interests of the business entrusted to them. Fulfilment of the task is everything, the highest criterion. The old adage: "Russia is despotism tempered by anarchy" has not lost its validity.

But since the leading Communists are personally responsible for such breaches of the law, they do not take these steps lightheartedly. Sometimes the whole problem consists in how to carry out an illegal transaction under a spuriously legal form. Under instructions from the director we did this from time to time. If the matter was too complicated he would consult with others, the director of the 'Gosbank', the secretary of the Party Committee, etc. After all, every one of them was concerned that Krasnoyarsk should carry out the plan one hundred per cent. If in order to achieve this objective other ways and means than those strictly allowed by the law had to be used, then of course Moscow need not know about it. The main thing, both for Moscow and for us, was that the plan should be fulfilled, that the Report Sheets should glow with figures, that on paper everything should look fine and above-board. And that was why we employees of the bureaucratic apparatus were paid better than the workers—not just for our work, but also for our ability to 'manoeuvre'. Lying and deceit are as much part of the necessities of the Soviet State as work itself. The result is that a semi-slave society can be represented to the outside world as a workers', socialist society. The most terrible thing, in my view, is not that many honest folk abroad accept this fiction for reality but that slave labour and oppression—even in this epoch of boasted civilization—can still achieve truly great economic and technical progress, thereby safeguarding the national independence and increasing the international weight of those countries utilizing such means. The fact that even today slavery can serve as an enormous social force for tremendous economic progress and a vast expansionist foreign policy is the saddest page in the history of contemporary humanity. The world is deafened with the voices shouting one against the other, proclaiming—we are free, we are democratic, we are socialist; while each in reality is sunk up to its neck, its ears, its eyes, in the rottenness of slavery.

Let us return from this great problem to our small world of the Krasnoyarsk Industrial Bank. Here are two examples of our activity. The first concerns the business of subscribing to State Loans. The procedure is as follows: one fine day the Soviet press abounds in resolutions from workers' meeting in large factories, beseeching the Government to issue a new loan "in the interests of strengthening socialist industrialization". A day or two later the Central Executive Committee of the People's Commissars of the U.S.S.R. "meets the wishes of the workers" by issuing such a Loan of three to five milliards of roubles that the "workers will lend to their State". The functions of the bank permitted us a slight advance warning of this touching *mise-en-scène*. This was how I saw it.

In the first days of April all Krasnoyarsk banks received a circular from their central administrations stating that a Loan would be issued in the near future, preliminary preparations for which had to be carried out within ten days. The staffs of the banks were instructed to prepare for the launching of the loan in collaboration with the trade-union leaders and the heads of enterprises. Within ten days each enterprise had prepared premises and a staff and the requisite forms for the collection of the subscriptions. On April 15th the press published the workers' resolutions asking for the issue of the Loan, and shortly afterwards announced the Government's compliance with this request. The subscription was opened and in two or three days the "greatest proof of the readiness of the workers for any sacrifice in the interest of strengthening their State" had been given.

Among the papers I smuggled out on my departure from Siberia to Europe is a sheet of figures relating to the Annual Report of the largest new construction in Krasnoyarsk (Krasnoyarsk Heavy Machine Construction Plant for the Gold Industry). On this sheet are data only for the year 1933. Our audit of the Report for this year gave the following results:

The capital construction plan was fulfilled to 64.9%, i.e. 6,257,200 roubles against a projected expenditure of 9,639,000 roubles.

Purchases of 892,900 roubles were made, against a quota of 1,699,500 roubles, i.e. 52.6% of the planned purchases.

Temporary buildings erected reached 82.4% of the plan, i.e. 2,132,300 roubles against 2,585,300 roubles.

Thus the planned total of capital investment for all these was fulfilled to 66.7%, i.e. 9,282,200 roubles against 12,920,000 roubles.

Financing of construction was carried out to 84.9% of the plan, i.e. 13,243,900 roubles against 15,598,800 roubles. Production has reached 48.3% of the planned figure.

And so on, and so on . . .

With the aid of all possible accounting devices, the Report of this enterprise showed that credits had been exceeded by only 604,200 roubles. The task of our bank had been to discover the truth: that the actual excess had really been twice as much. In relation to the original plan the excess in the cost of construction had been at least 17%. This acquired greater significance because during that year the Government had issued new instructions revising the cost of construction down by 15% on the figure of the original plan. Thus the real excess was 32% over the revised figure of the plan.

This case of the Krasnoyarsk Machine Construction Plant was not exceptional; it was typical of the development of new enterprises during the Five Year Plan. Price increases and other obstacles delay such constructions, and although officially declared open on the planned date, they are in fact rarely completely finished, some departments lagging behind others, and there is often a delay of three, six, or even twelve months before full production can begin. Two years later this plant in question was in full swing, and served in fact two purposes: heavy machine construction for the gold industry and railway-waggon building.

The financing of this plant and the supervision of the work in progress was, in so far as it concerned our bank, in the hands of the chief of the finance department for heavy industry, Ivan Stepanovich. He was the most colourful personality among the employees of the Industrial Bank. A former worker and a mechanic in the Baltic Fleet before the Revolution and during the Civil War, he shared the general hostility of those newly risen from the ranks towards the old leaders of society. On the other hand, having remained a non-Party man, he looked askance at the privileges of the Communists "who had no qualifications other than their Party tickets". The chief butt of his attacks was his immediate superior, the chief accountant, who was of noble origin and until recently had occupied a high position in the Moscow 'Gosbank'. He had been exiled to Siberia after the Menshevik Trial of 1931 because he had had friendly relations with one of the accused, a colleague in the 'Gosbank'. Ivan Stepanovich and the chief accountant were both non-Party men and therefore from the Communist point of view neither was "one hundred per cent

Soviet". But this did not prevent either of them seeking to prove before the trade-union commission (to which their dispute was finally referred), that he was a hundred per cent loyal Soviet citizen and the other of more than doubtful loyalty. Each supported his case with lengthy memoranda. Ivan Stepanovich's criticism of Party members who did not know their business was more cautious, but it was stubbornly persisted in, and it concerned, of course, our director. Ivan Stepanovich himself was a very capable and energetic man, but he had technical knowledge rather than a broad grasp of economic questions, and his pretensions were consequently not proportionate to his capabilities.

The financing of the timber industry was in my care, and the department dealing with local light industry was presided over by a young woman, Tasya Nikolaevna. She had risen painfully from a lower-middle-class family, had attended a financial-economic course in the small Siberian town of Biisk, and handled the work entrusted to her with difficulty.

There were three people working in the book-keeping department: two old professionals, typical pen-pushers, and a quite young girl clerk, Valya. Ivan Stepanovich helped her and trained her for the work. The result was a romance. Ivan Stepanovich was already married, with a ten-year-old child, and his wife, a former nurse, was on the point of finishing her studies at the Medical Faculty of Tomsk University. The affair ended with Ivan divorcing his first wife and marrying Valya. Thus our little establishment sailed the ocean of Soviet life.

I worked for half a year in the Industrial Bank. I left towards the end of the summer, "of my own accord", as one says. But it came about in this way: I discovered irregularities in two of the timber mills that I had to control. One of them had spent twenty thousand roubles on transport of logs, instead of the five thousand allowed by the plan. The other, worse still, had borrowed five thousand roubles from the bank for repayment of wages and had used them for making purchases. Our director hailed this discovery as manna from heaven.

"To Court with them," he shouted, hoping to gain moral capital from the affair by demonstrating his vigilance to Moscow. Such a prospect did not please me at all. For a trial would necessitate my presence as accuser or chief witness. But in reality there had been no crime. The expenditure of twenty thousand roubles on transportation of timber was normal, but the factory had deliberately named a lower sum in the estimate it submitted, fearing that otherwise it would not receive permission to extend its workings. On the other hand, the mill had not expended other sums provided for in its plan, so that the sum total of expenditure had not really been exceeded. The other factory, which took five thousand roubles for wages payments, had in fact been authorized to do so by the plan although it did not need them for this purpose, but had dire need of money for purchases. I explained this to the director and he finally yielded. The affair was settled without a scandal, but in the course of our sharp exchanges of views on the matter the director let fall the remark: "So you don't want to bring them to trial—then I'll bring you to trial!"

A dangerous person, I thought to myself. I shall have to leave him. Two days later I gave notice.

During the time I worked for the bank I met an interesting person at one of the factories. He was a night-watchman. Before the Revolution he had been a wealthy merchant in European Russia, with a capital of 250,000 gold roubles. During NEP he had worked as chief accountant in a large Soviet institution. Swept into the whirlpool of the Five Year Plan, he finished up as an exile in Krasnoyarsk, working as a night-watchman. He had no desire to be anything else.

"Here I don't get in anyone's way. No Communist director can lay the blame for unfulfilled plans on me."

He was one of the few representatives of the dispossessed classes that I met.

"I sincerely desired to work with the Bolsheviks. I adapted myself to the NEP period and did all that was demanded of me, but nothing came of it. I bore the stigma of a bourgeois and I was doomed."

This is how he viewed events:

"It is the eternal alternation of the wolves and the dogs. The old ruling classes of Russia had indeed become senile; they lived too well and their vigour was sapped. But then out of the depths of the people came the wolves to take the place of the dogs grown fat and useless. No matter—the wolves too will become domesticated and senile in their turn."

His consolation and pleasure in life was now Machiavelli. In Stalin, Hitler and Mussolini he saw the modern incarnation of the ideals of Machiavelli's Prince, and he was sincerely enthusiastic about them.

"That's politics. They are smart. They know how to keep the people in hand; the people are sheep."

But with all his worship of Stalin he could not wholly forget his 250,000 roubles.

"One more Five Year Plan and there will be full socialism in Russia. No trace of capitalism will be left."

"What socialism?" I objected. "There's not an atom of socialism left in Russia right now."

"Well, what is it then?"

"State capitalism."

"Well, what's the difference? In any case, I shan't get my 250,000 roubles back."

Somewhat better was the fate of a member of a famous Russian family of merchant-manufacturers, the Morozovs. He owed his more enviable position to two circumstances—that his wife was French and that part of his capital was abroad. At the start of the Five Year Plan he passed through Krasnoyarsk on his way to exile in the Arctic, in Turukhansk. He made a proposition to the Krasnoyarsk Soviet: that the latter should obtain the G.P.U.'s permission for him to stay in Krasnoyarsk, in return for which he would instruct his relatives abroad to transfer sufficient monies from his capital to present the town with a circus. The deal was concluded: Morozov remained in Krasnoyarsk, Krasnoyarsk got its circus.

The resourceful G.P.U. thought to obtain a further advantage from this situation. It demanded Morozov's signature to a document assigning all his foreign capital to the Soviet Government. Morozov signed, but his relatives in Paris and the French Government declared the signature invalid because obtained under duress, and the Soviet Government did not get the capital it coveted. All this time Morozov and his wife received one hundred gold roubles monthly, which enabled them—and their two little dogs—not only to survive the lean years of famine but also to help their neighbours by selling them goods cheaply. Apparently wanting to get their own back on Morozov, the G.P.U. tried to persuade his wife to go back to her native land, to leave the icy Siberian wilderness; but nothing would induce her to leave her husband, and they were eventually permitted, after the first Five Year Plan, to go to Rostov, in southern Russia.

A deputy of the Second Duma whom I met in Krasnoyarsk could be called a pre-revolutionary personality of some standing, although not a member of the ruling classes. I was looking for lodgings and went to an address recommended to me. The owner of the place was a man of about fifty, a robustly healthy, typical man of the people. I did not take the room, but we started to chat.

"Have you read in the papers of the award given to Henrikh

Grigorievich?"

"To whom?"

"Why . . . to comrade Yagoda!"

Indeed, Yagoda, supreme chief of the G.P.U., had that day received a high Soviet Order. My interlocutor was foreman on one of the G.P.U. building sites in Krasnoyarsk (a war factory being erected largely with the labour of deported peasants).

Looking around the room during the conversation, my attention was drawn to a large photograph of a man with an intelligent face, with a big beard like Tolstoy.

"Whom have you got there in the place of honour?" I asked.

"That's Muromtsev, the President of the Duma. Not a Bolshevik, of course, but he was a good man . . . You know, I was also a member of the Duma; elected by the peasants. I belonged to the Trudoviki and Muromtsev presided over the Duma at that time."

He also showed me photographs of peasant deputies from the Minusinsk district, which is south of Krasnoyarsk, and from where he had been sent as representative to the Duma.

"And what became of them?"

"During the Five Year Plan they were sent to concentration camps as Kulaks. They were well-to-do peasants."

"And how did you keep out of trouble?"

"Well, after the February Revolution I became active in the Co-operative movement. I immediately joined a trade uion and was left in peace throughout the Revolution."

When I later told someone in the town about this encounter, he laughed.

"He forgot to tell you the most essential thing about himself. When Lenin was in exile in 1898, in a village near Minusinsk, he lived in the house of that peasant's father. That's what saved him."

The wreck and the rescue of the *Chelyuskin* expedition happened during that spring. In the middle of June the expedition was on its way from the Far East to Moscow, and had to pass through Krasnoyarsk. The trade unions organized a grand demonstration to welcome them at the station. Attendance by all workers and employees was made compulsory, just as on the 1st of May and the 7th of November. For a month and a half the Soviet press filled columns every day on the *Chelyuskin* affair. This use of an heroic episode for propaganda purposes had unforeseen results.

"They wrecked the ship on purpose, so as to have something to make a noise about and pull the wool over our eyes", commented the people of Krasnoyarsk.

Half a year later a new type of 'Chelyuskin man' arrived from Russia. To join us in Siberia came a worker from Leningrad, guilty of singing a song that began:

> *"Comrade Schmidt has scuttled his ship;*
> *For this he got some money.*
> *Oye, Oye, we do live gaily . . ."*

It appeared that in Leningrad this song was all the rage, in spite of its strict prohibition by the G.P.U.

A family I knew had a thirteen-year-old daughter. One evening she told me:

"Oh dear, tomorrow we have religious instruction and I haven't done my homework."

"What's that!? Religious instruction in the schools?" I cried, stupified.

That spring there had been a new 'reform' in Soviet schools, which re-introduced a number of ranks and titles. The heads of schools were again to be known as 'directors' and 'groups' of pupils referred to as 'classes'. The gradual re-introduction of uniforms for pupils was also announced. Some years later a new 'reform' liquidated one of the greatest acquisitions of the October Revolution—free schooling with free supply of text-books and other scholastic requisites.

But I had nowhere read or heard of the re-introduction of religious instruction. The child's explanation was no less astonishing than her remark.

"No," she said, "in school we call 'religious instruction' our lessons in historical materialism, in Marxism-Leninism."

On another occasion I saw a group of pupils, boys and girls, stop in front of a poster advertising Kolkhoz socialist agriculture and amusingly poke fun at it. Their words showed that they knew to perfection how delusive was the mask and what really lay behind it. How do children educated in the new schools, entirely subject to official propaganda, orientate themselves so correctly in the maze of deceit and falsehood around them? Whatever the explanation, the fact is that they do.

The children's spirit of opposition assumes another form: bandit romanticism and the romanticizing of brigands. The lower and middle forms abound in pupils' 'gangs' organized in fun—but sometimes in earnest. The song about Marusya, the bandit who is killed by her lover because when arrested she betrays the gang to the Cheka—this song resounds in all Soviet schools in spite of all prohibitions and punishments.

In the universities, and particularly in the Krasnoyarsk Technical Institute for Forestry, there were during my stay in Krasnoyarsk repeated cases of political unreliability, resulting in student arrests. Whether these cases were echoes of old disputes or symptoms of new political struggles I do not know.

But one episode rather inclines me to favour the first view. This affair concerned the student with whom I travelled part of the way from Chelyabinsk to Irkutsk—as narrated in the first chapter—the great optimist who prophesied that the Soviet 'six' would soon become an ace and decreed that the present was no fit time for nostalgic songs . . . A few days after my arrival in Krasnoyarsk I met him on the street. A penetrating autumn rain was falling and our student was in a tearing hurry to attend a lecture. But one sunny day half a year later I met him again; or, more exactly, he approached me and greeted me cordially. He started to chat and then without any preamble began to abuse—Stalin.

"That Koba (i.e. Stalin) is leading us all to the devil. It's a dog's life."

He invited me to visit him. I was interested in the change that had come over him, and felt disposed to accept the invitation. To persuade me, he added:

"Do come round; there will be some other comrades. They are equally disturbed over what is going on in the Party."

Some other comrades, I thought, pricking up my ears. That means a group? An organization? No, that doesn't sound so good; that smells of provocation. I did not go to see him.

I do not know if our heroic optimist had fallen so low as to accept the role of agent-provocateur. But shortly afterwards a group of students at the Institute was arrested and the G.P.U. made great efforts to prove its connection with exiles.

WEEK-END IN THE TAIGA

"You don't know the Stolby? . . . Well then, you haven't seen the most interesting thing in Krasnoyarsk . . . Go on Saturday for the week-end. You'll have plenty of company there and it'll be friendly and jolly. Do go, Anton Antonovich."

So my friends at work and in the town repeatedly urged me.

It was strange to hear this English word 'week-end'—they pronounced it just like that: ooeekend—here in the heart of Siberia, of northern Asia.

I went off alone one Saturday morning. The decrepit little

ship of the Yeniseisk Shipping Company was crowded to capacity with trippers; it dated from before the Revolution and barely made any headway against the current. It took two hours to cover ten kilometres.

The mighty river, its sparkling silver waves only rarely marred by black dots—a rowing boat or barge; overshadowing both banks the dark masses of forest seemingly untouched by human hands . . . Our tiny ship was enclosed in the serene grandeur of virgin nature, but had no part in her elemental harmony; she stood aloof from the agitations of the nervous little creature man, as though saying that all her primordial strength and beauty is not for him but for herself alone.

We were sharply reminded of nature's hostility when we disembarked at Lialino, on the right bank. It began to rain, and in a few minutes the downpour was furious, tropical. A premature night fell; a prehistoric gloom lay on the world. What to do? There was the empty harbour; not even a cabin in which to pass the night. Before us the taiga, and through it the eight to ten-kilometre-long narrow pathway leading to the large clearing where lay the Stolby camp.

The stream of people coming off the ship did not pause to reflect but without hesitation took the pathway, shouting, laughing, and singing. I went with them. In the pitch darkness, under the pouring rain, the men and women, old and young, marched like a horde of vikings, teasing and helping one another as they stumbled; falling into groups, walking arm-in-arm, or in single file as the way dictated. Soaked clothes becoming too heavy, one took them off, rolled them into a bundle and tied it to one's rucksack, and carried on in shorts. The more daring took off their boots, since it was easier to walk barefoot in the black muddy soil. It was past midnight when we reached the camp, soaked through and starving hungry, but in excellent spirits and not at all exhausted. Those who had arrived before us, undeterred by nature and her thunderstorm, had lighted huge camp-fires. The rain passed over and we warmed and dried ourselves around the fires. Our dried clothing served to cover us in the huts where we slept, for the nights in the taiga and in Siberia in general are cold even in mid summer. The women made tea and heated up some food. The provisions each had brought were put into the common pool and shared equally with friends and strangers as we sat round the fires. Week-end brotherhood, brotherhood of the taiga.

In the morning we crept out of our lairs, bathed in the fresh springs, breakfasted round the communal fires, and then made up parties according to common tastes and sympathies, either to go walking, or to gather the abundant berries and raspberries, or to climb the famous Stolby rocks that rise there high above the surrounding landscape. Washed by rains and winds the sandy obelisks stand like stone idols raised by nature to her gods. Here and there they look like human faces and figures silhouetted against the sky. It is from these columns of rock that the whole district takes its name, Stolby (The Pillars).

As soon as the first rays of the morning sun broke through the mists the effects of the previous night's storm were rapidly dispelled. It became warm; the sun sparkled on the dew-drops; arrows of golden fire shot through the foliage. But again clouds rolled up over the sun. Out of the taiga the hostile elements of nature pressed in upon our little clearing with demonic force: dampness, darkness, the impenetrable tangle of the jungle. It seemed, standing there, that everything wrested with great effort from nature and subdued to the aims of man might, in one instant, at a single stroke, be re-conquered by all-powerful nature, and humanity vanish into nothingness as though it had never been.

Between four and five in the afternoon two-thirds of the excursionists returned in groups to the harbour and the ship. Nature smiled again and they went gaily in the sunshine, skipping and hopping over the puddles left by the previous night's rain. But two steps from either side of their path the taiga, a solid wall of trees and fallen trunks and twisted undergrowth, watched them with relentless hostility, like a wild beast.

Those who remained in Stolby were returning home either on the Monday morning, walking the twenty kilometres to town through the beautiful chestnut trees to which the taiga gave way, or taking the evening ship. There are the 'professional Stolbyists' who go regularly every week and the amateurs who pay only occasional visits. The place had a certain amount of organization and one might perhaps even say comfort. Apart from the large, barrack-like house for the excursionists and the two or three small buildings belonging to the Observatory, there were a dozen or so huts sprinkled here and there on the edge of the taiga. These huts were either the personal property of the excursionists, or belonged to trade-union organizations (railwaymen, banking employees, etc.). But no one was tied down to a particular spot or particular company. Yet in spite of this happy-go-lucky disorder a marvellous blend of freedom and harmony was achieved.

Over all this, like a father exercising unquestioned authority, ruled Mikhvas.

"Mikhvas? Is he a Latvian? How did he get here?"

"No, that's Mikh-Vas, a nickname abbreviated from Mikhail Vasilievich, a real Russian and a great scholar, but he has escaped from Russian and Soviet reality into the Siberian wilderness."

Mikhail Vasilievich lived here as the director and sole employee of the Observatory and guardian of the Stolby, which were a kind of State preserve. He was not a city lover and hardly ever went there but his friends from the town would bring him food.

Since their house was not big enough for all comers, and was generally considered rather dreary, the excursionists usually preferred to make use of the small buildings belonging to the Observatory, where all the rooms and floors were put at their disposal by the hospitable Mikhvas. Everywhere was choc-a-bloc with sleepers. Mikhvas had a friendly welcome not only for those who liked to stay on his domain, but also for those who slept elsewhere. He always paid them a visit to see that they were comfortably installed. It must be admitted that besides enjoying a chat, he was also fond of taking a drink with the more convivial of the holiday-makers. This was his consolation for his solitude.

In spite of the very free-and-easy life at Stolby, I did not see any dissoluteness. The calm grandeur of nature induced an atmosphere of sanity and simple jollity, soothing to the soul.

There is no excursion without its minor incidents: either it pours with rain; or one is too late to catch the ship, or it leaves too early and one has to walk all the way back; or it breaks down and one has to stay the night on shore around fires. But the good humour and buoyant spirits of the excursionists never deserted them. A day in the heart of the country braces one not merely for any minor discomforts of the return journey but for the workaday cares of the following week.

Given a week-end of undisturbed sunny weather, it is really magnificent there. Then one can climb the highest, most dangerous of the Stolby—not, of course, alone; it is impossible even for the strongest, the most skilled and experienced to do this. Parties are made up, led by young, trained climbers, and the ascent begins. The unpaid, but not the less considerate guides give advice, lend a helping hand and at the most risky and perilous places even carry the amateurs. Owing to lack of sportswear one has simply to make do with old clothes, and all, of course, men and women alike, wear trousers. Most of the climbers are satisfied to reach some tolerably high shelf; only the most experienced or the most daring go on to the highest peaks. Never having been an alpinist, I surprised myself at the risks I took to gain the top.

From the height of the Stolby a vast horizon opened up before one, covered with the impassable taiga. Seen from those heights it is no longer a forest but an ocean, the swaying tops of the dense tangle of trees surging southwards towards the Sayansk mountain range.

But here in Stolby was something that stirred me more than the fascinating panorama of the surrounding landscape. That was the brotherliness, the friendliness, the simplicity and kindliness of the people. One felt that even the modicum of civilization existing in Krasnoyarsk was sufficient for men to feel the need not only of physical but also of moral regeneration in contact with nature. And it was amazing how quickly one fell into the mood of the place. It seemed to newcomers to the camp as though they had at last escaped from hell. The new atmosphere enveloped them instantly and easily; social distinctions went by the board, vanished as if by magic; men became brothers—no longer wolves, but men.

A little of this moral regeneration we took with us back to town. But alas, only a little. Meeting by chance on the street, we recognized each other with difficulty. We were different. And it was not merely the starched collar and the well-pressed skirt—the soul too was stiff and ironed. We were once again creatures bound by the conventions of a hierarchical civilization.

Ah! it is a great experience—a week-end in the taiga!

You should go there some time.

PSYCHOLOGY OF A COMMUNIST

Summer brought not only joy: the vigilant eye of the G.P.U. sleeps neither by night nor by day, neither in winter nor in summer.

On June 3rd, 1934, Denisov stunned me with the information that I must leave for Yeniseisk on one of the first ships. The G.P.U. takes care that even in these out-of-the-way, monotonous places the exile shall not lack variety.

"Yeniseisk again! But you promised me in winter that you wouldn't touch me any more."

"We promised to support your request for transfer to a more suitable place. This we have done. But since no reply has been given and there are no fresh instructions regarding you, we have to carry out the old order."

It was, however, only after a further six months' delay at the end of November, that the G.P.U. finally succeeded in carrying out this order, and transferred me to Yeniseisk by land. The battle I waged revealed certain mechanisms of the Soviet machine, and aspects of Communist manners and psychology, till then unknown to me.

This episode presents a particular interest: it reveals the specific forms and the peculiar rhythm of the struggle that was, and partly still is, conducted between the Communists in power and the Communists in prison; it may help the reader towards an understanding of the preparation of the Soviet Trials, with their 'spontaneous' confessions and their executions . . . My own adventure ended with a temporary triumph for the G.P.U. A year later, at the end of November, 1935, the situation was reversed: the G.P.U. had to bring me back to Krasnoyarsk, then to the Polish frontier, which I crossed on December 3rd, 1935.

I was sent to Yeniseisk when it seemed that at any moment I might be sent home; I finally broke free when it seemed that all was lost.

By warning me on June 3rd of the proposed departure to Yeniseisk and leaving me at liberty, the G.P.U. apparently wanted to emphasize that it intended to use only legal, normal methods in my case. This caused me to behave in the same way—to make use of the as yet untried normal, legal way of getting out of the country. That consisted in reclaiming the passport that had been in my possession when I entered the country, and, with this in hand, demanding an exit visa from the Soviet authorities. I hoped, with some justification, that the authorities would respect the juridical argument of bourgeois law more than they did the ethical argument of international working-class solidarity and socialism.

Asking an Embassy for a passport is a most simple, trivial thing, something that is done by thousands of people every day in dozens of countries and something that I myself had often done when abroad. But in the circumstances it became for me a complicated psychological, juridical, and political act. One false move and I might destroy myself morally or physically—or both.

Yes, everything is logical, justified, clear, I argued with myself. But, just the same, I was going to turn away from the Soviet Government and appeal to the bourgeoisie, to fascism. Although for a long time I had lost the last vestige of any illusions concerning the 'Workers' State' and socialism in the U.S.S.R., and although I had long ago broken with the Comintern, the old Party discipline, the old views, the old prejudices, the fetish phrase 'Soviet State' were still so strong in me that I suffered spiritual and mental torment in deciding the question: did the situation I was in justify my appealing to the Italian Embassy? Logic and the spirit, reason and the heart, do not like to march in step—one or the other always lags behind. At last I persuaded myself with the argument: if I could approach the Italian Embassy in Vienna, when I was a member of the Comintern and accepted Moscow's policy (before going to Moscow I lived in Vienna, working as a member of the Balkan Bureau of the Comintern), why can I not now, when I have broken with the Comintern and the Soviet Government, do the same thing with the Italian Embassy in Moscow? So on June 7th I sent the following telegram to the Italian Embassy: "Italian subject Dr. Ante Ciliga requests passport purpose of leaving the U.S.S.R. Address Krasnoyarsk, 41 Marx Street." (I am actually a Yugoslav, a Croatian. I lived and worked mainly in Yugoslavia, in the Yugoslav Communist Party, but I was born in Istria, between Trieste and Fiume, a district that became part of Italy after 1919, thus making me an Italian subject.)

In my telegram to the Embassy there was not a word of my

being an exile, no complaint against the G.P.U. I hoped that with the receipt of a passport the question of my being an exile would automatically fall.

In a state of extreme tension I awaited the reaction of the G.P.U. and the reply of the Embassy. Would the G.P.U. stop the telegram at the Post Office and arrest me, or would everything proceed peacefully, legally? Would the Embassy not give me the passport this time, or would it suddenly put forward some political condition, for example a declaration, that I approved the policy of fascism, which I should have to refuse and which would mean that I would henceforward be irrevocably delivered into the hands of the G.P.U.? Not a simple business. But he who would save his life must not shrink from risking death.

However, the actual course of events, at any rate in the beginning, was smoother and more favourable than my fevered imagination had pictured.

A week later the Embassy telegraphed: "Steps for issue of passport taken." That meant that the G.P.U. had let my telegram go through. I was not only not arrested, but nothing more was said about Yeniseisk. After a few weeks I received through the Soviet mail a request from the Embassy to fill in a form, a purely routine matter without any questions about my politics. But a month later I received a telegram with the tricky question: "Where do you intend to go, to Italy or another country?" I intended to go—as indeed a year and a half later I did—to Paris. I wanted to look at this capital of western Europe, to rest a little there and write my book on all that I had seen during my ten years sojourn in Russia. Then, if possible, I intended to go to the place that had never ceased to call me, to the shores of the sunny Adriatic, to re-visit my Italian and Yugoslav relatives. But I was also prepared to take a chance, should there be no other way out, of going first to Italy, in the secret hope that it would be easier to get to Paris from there than from Siberia.

The politely diplomatic question of the Embassy gave me not a few headaches. Instead of themselves posing their conditions, they gave me the seeming possibility of choosing where to go. But that freedom might be only appearance, and dangerous appearance. Translated into plain language, the sense of it was: we prefer and advise you to go to Italy, but we do not insist on it beforehand. There was no indication from the telegram that they had agreed in principle to issue me a passport, and that it only remained for me to say where I

481

wanted to go. Yet the issuing of the passport might depend precisely on my choice—and the choice was left to me.

In 1920—21 I had as a young student taken part in the anti-fascist struggles in Istria during University vacations. But from the second half of 1921 I had no longer any connections with the political life of Italy. My status there had for a long time, even before my departure for Russia, beeen quite legal. But I had not the slightest desire to go to Italy. Although I had broken with the Comintern, I had never had anything at all in common with fascism. As a Yugoslav, I could have a lot of trouble in Italy on national grounds. I did not want to furnish my former friends of the Comintern and the Communist Party —now my enemies—with any demagogic arguments. Finally, I did not want to run the slightest risk of endangering my projected book on Russia. I wanted to write a critical work, in complete freedom, free from the slightest censorship. For this I had to go to Paris.

Taking all this into consideration I decided to reply to the Embassy in the sense that I was ready if necessary to go direct to Italy, but would prefer first to go elsewhere. Written in the same diplomatic language as the question, my reply read: "I intend to visit relatives in Italy and Yugoslavia. Would request that the passport be issued as before for all European countries."

The Embassy regarded my courteous reply as indicating a somewhat independent spirit. It cost me a delay of two months in the issuing of the passport. But—something I had not at all foreseen—it almost cost me my life. At any rate it led to my transfer to Yeniseisk and another year in Siberia.

The situation at that time changed radically and often, as a result of three factors: the course of my correspondence with the Embassy; the course of my negotiations with the G.P.U.; and the course of negotiations concerning my affair between the Embassy, the G.P.U. and other Soviet bodies.

At the end of September or the beginning of October I received the long-awaited telegram: "Your passport ready. Shall we send it to Krasnoyarsk or will you collect personally in Moscow?" I replied: "Leaving for Moscow within few days. Will collect passport there."

With the Embassy's telegram in my hand I went to see the head of the local G.P.U., Denisov. He declared that without instructions from Moscow he could not give me, an exile, any permit to leave Krasnoyarsk. After this I sent a telegram to Moscow, to the Central Executive Committee of the Soviets, and a copy to the Collegium of the G.P.U., demanding that my illegal detention in Siberia should end, and that, since I possessed a foreign passport, I should be given the possibility of going to Moscow to obtain a visa and leave the country. A few days later, one Sunday morning, a special messenger came from the G.P.U. asking me to report immediately to local headquarters. Freedom or arrest? What awaited me?

I was received by Denisov.

"Tell me, Ciliga, what is this statement you have sent to Moscow?"

The question was not very clear and I replied guardedly:

"Well, I have sent many declarations demanding permission to leave the country."

"Yes, yes, I'm talking about the one in which you give notice of your change of opinion."

"It is not the first time that I have stated my disagreement with you. That is why I want to leave the country."

"And no other declarations?" Denisov asked. "I have received the following telegram from Moscow: 'Why do you further keep the foreign communist Ciliga in Krasnoyarsk in spite of the change in his views?' "

"Well, that's good. They are asking for me. Then why don't you let me go? Moscow knows what it is doing."

"No, I can't do it like that. Only if I receive from you a declaration that you approve of the Party policy under the leadership of Comrade Stalin. Then you can leave immediately for Moscow."

This was the cunning way in which I was invited to sign a declaration of my capitulation. That would be equivalent to simultaneously losing both honour and freedom. Whoever renounces his views, whoever yields himself up to Stalin's mercy—or lack of mercy—immediately becomes the helpless and pitiful tool of Stalin's machiavellianism. It goes without saying that I refused.

"You accuse all capitulators of double-dealing, of dishonesty, of betraying the Party, and you want me to say that I agree with Stalin, that I submit to his decisions?"

"But it is not the same thing with you. We have full confidence in you. We know that if Ciliga declares his submission to the Party, he will not go back on it."

"You do me a great honour, Denisov. And I am going to show you that you are quite right in thinking that with me words and deeds are the same. As I do not agree with Stalin's policy, I will not make a statement saying that I approve of it."

The matter dragged on. No news came from Denisov. My repeated telegrams to the Central Executive Committee in Moscow remained unanswered.

I then telegraphed to the Embassy: "The local Soviet organs illegally detain me in Siberia and prevent my going to Moscow." The reply was encouraging: "We have intervened at the People's Commissariat for Foreign Affairs, speedy regulation of the affair promised." Still the permission to leave did not come, and the Embassy asked me for the third time if my passport should be sent to Krasnoyarsk. At the same time I had a number of fruitless conversations with Denisov and other representatives of the G.P.U. Apparently the Embassy wanted me to have my passport sent to Krasnoyarsk. I decided to agree, in the hope that matters would be speeded up. I sent a request to that effect and on 1 November received my passport by registered mail. In a covering letter the Embassy explained that in accordance with their information from the Soviet authorities, I should apply to the foreign department of the Town Soviet of Krasnoyarsk for an exit visa. The letter ended by saying, that in order to ensure a satisfactory settlement of the matter, *ad ogni buon fine,* I should inform the Embassy by telegram of the day on which I made this application.

The passport and the letter seemed to me like a kind of Charter of Liberty. I straightaway telegraphed my relatives abroad and my friends in Russia that I should be leaving for home within a few days. This news was very comforting to my Yugoslav comrades in exile. I had yet to learn that the G.P.U. had not shown me all its tricks.

In the foreign department of the Town Soviet I was told to "come tomorrow". The following day I was informed that my application could not be accepted as I was not registered with them as a foreign subject. Beside myself with anger, I went to the G.P.U.

"Listen, Denisov, what sort of joke is this you're playing! The foreign department of the Town Soviet refuses to accept my application."

"Presumably they have reasons for that. We will look into the matter. There's no need to get so excited, Ciliga."

I had plenty of reason to be excited! I at once went to the post office and sent off an acid telegram to Kalinin, President of the Central Executive Committee of the Soviets, against this "unspeakable cynicism on the part of the Soviet authorities". On reading this telegram the post office clerk received such a shock that he at first refused to accept it. His hands trembled;

his eyes said—"You will not only ruin yourself, but me too." I calmed him down. "There's my address on the form. I take complete responsibility. I am a foreign subject and have the right to tell the Soviet authorities that they are acting illegally if that is the case."

After a few days of "looking into the matter" the Town Soviet "met me half-way". Now they suggested that I make application not only for the exit visa but also for permission to change my Soviet citizenship to Italian.

"Are you crazy? I have never renounced my Italian citizenship, I am not and never have been a Soviet citizen. I have never made the slightest move towards applying for Soviet citizenship."

It was evident from this, after the suggestion about capitulation, that another attempt to catch me by trickery was being made. They wanted me to give colour to something that was completely false, by signing a document that would make me out to have been a Soviet citizen. I did not know what I should be more furious at, their insolence or their stupidity.

The G.P.U. defended the action of the Town Soviet.

"The foreign department keeps to the law; that is its duty. Two years ago the Krasnoyarsk Town Soviet passed an order to the effect that foreign subjects must attend with their passports and register within one month. All those failing to do so, automatically lost their foreign citizenship and became Soviet citizens. You failed to do so and you therefore became a Soviet citizen."

"Since when, citizen, has the unilateral act of a local authority been able to regulate matters of international law?"

"We have Soviet democracy which gives a wide initiative to local authorities."

"Hm . . . granted. But it so happens that I was in any case not in Krasnoyarsk two years ago."

"You did not register with the Town Soviet when you came here, and you have been here for over a year."

"But when taking lodgings I immediately registered with the militia as an Italian citizen and nobody told me that I had to register with the Town Soviet."

"Well, you know, anybody could do that. What's to prevent me, Denisov, from going to Kislovodsk tomorrow—incidentally, I've been wanting to go for a long time for a cure but my work does not allow me—registering as a Chinese citizen!"

"Of course. But for making a false declaration you could be held responsible and it would cost you dear. You are not

Chinese, but I *am* an Italian citizen and I am registered as such not only with the militia but also with you, the G.P.U., who hold my special exile's file. When I was brought to Krasnoyarsk from Irkutsk your official Minkov filled in my questionnaire and wrote in the appropriate column that I am an Italian citizen. And you never questioned the fact. Even two years ago when the Town Soviet was passing that democratic order on the compulsory and automatic acquisition of Soviet citizenship by foreign subjects, I was registered as an Italian citizen in the files of the Verkhne-Uralsk political prison where I then was. No, the Soviet authorities are putting themselves in a ludicrous position by trying now, *a posteriori*, to deny my foreign citizenship."

I already felt myself the stronger and Denisov went over to th defensive.

"Good, but in Moscow you were registered as a Soviet citizen and not at all as a foreigner."

"Oh, so that's the way it is! That's the pretext for trying to deprive me of my foreign citizenship! Naturally, like the other Comintern workers from countries where the Communist Party was illegal, I lived in Moscow with a false passport, under an assumed Soviet name, as a Soviet citizen. But nobody loses his citizenship through using a false passport or living under an assumed name. You have all the less right to refer to this now, since the Soviet authorities knew all about it at the time and themselves arranged it. It was they who provided me with Soviet papers, knowing that I held an Italian passport. How then, can you assert that I have ever been a Soviet citizen? Do you really want, by denying my Italian citizenship, to transfer the question to Moscow and make it a matter of dispute between the People's Commissariat of Foreign Affairs and the Italian Embassy? Do you want me to have to explain to them why I lived in Moscow as a Soviet citizen, that is, to tell them how the Comintern workers live in Moscow? In that case the political responsibility will fall entirely on you. In my fight to leave the country I have used, and I intend to continue using, only politically and morally honest means, but I have firmly and irrevocably decided to use all my legal rights and possibilities as a foreign subject in order to get out."

It seemed that this conversation helped. In the Town Soviet my application for departure was accepted without any question of my applying to 'revert to' Soviet citizenship. They took the passport. They said that they had to send everything to the foreign department of the Regional Executive Committee in Irkutsk. After ten days I could expect a reply. In this instance the powers of the local democracy did not prove after all to be so great.

While waiting, I had several interviews with the G.P.U. I thought of them as the final interviews, conversations more of farewell than of confrontation. These took place either with Denisov alone, or with one of his deputies, or in the presence of a whole bunch, consisting of Denisov and several representatives of the Irkutsk Regional administration of the G.P.U. During these arguments I felt free and easy, as I was absolutely convinced that my departure was a foregone conclusion, and that it was a matter of only parting shots before I was allowed to go. I was already mentally drawing up the balance sheet of my life in Russia, and I spoke with the Communists of the G.P.U. as though we met on neutral ground and on an equal footing. These conversations may not be without value for an understanding of the psychology of Russian Communists, of the forms and methods of their inner-party struggles.

"Why, Ciliga, are you now so particularly energetic in trying to secure your departure abroad?"

"A strange question. I came to the U.S.S.R. after all, not as a permanent resident, not as a refugee seeking asylum, but on a temporary visit and for particular Party work, after which I should naturally have returned abroad, where all my activity and all my interests are concentrated."

"Yes, but now—you have broken with the Party and the Comintern."

"It is very sad, of course, that I have not found things in Russia as I imagined them to be and as I should like them to be. I should myself prefer to be enthusiastic about you rather than disillusioned. Having defended you for so many years, I feel after all a certain share of the responsibility. But I never gave an undertaking to praise everything that I might see here. When I came to Russia I hoped, as you did when you allowed me in, to be able to praise and not to criticize—but I made no promises, nor did you ask any of me. And if you had done so when I left Vienna for Moscow I should have refused and not come here. So I never lost my freedom of judgement. If—to my own great regret—my judgement has proved unfavourable, that does not mean that I have thereby lost the right to go home, or that you have acquired the right to detain me."

"And where do you intend to go?"

"To Paris," I said, after a moment's hesitation.

Maybe my frankness here helped the G.P.U.'s game, its

manoeuvres with the Embassy.

"To Paris!" my interlocutor exclaimed. "But that is the centre of anti-Soviet propaganda."

"I understand what you mean by that," I replied. "But there is something else also in Paris—it is the centre for your People's Front propaganda. And there is another aspect of Paris—for me the most important: it is the most suitable place in which to study the western world, which I shall be entering for the first time. Of course, what's the use of playing hide and seek, the first thing I shall do in Paris is to settle accounts with you."

"There you are! And you want us to let you go!"

"Allow me—a husband and wife can separate, and politicians can do the same. They do not lose their liberty because of that. For both of us—you and me—this separation is not pleasant. But it is a fact. The whole question is: which is the lesser evil for us both—to let me go peaceably or to be forced to it after a long and painful struggle that can only end in my victory and your defeat. Morally, I have already won and you have already lost. You may or may not appreciate this. But in any case I shall achieve my objective; in fact, I already have achieved it. That is, unless you kill me."

"Now really, Anton Antonovich, you know very well that we do not kill Communists." (This was a year and a half before the Moscow Trials, when Stalin began to shoot oppositional Communists.)

"Why, Ciliga," I was asked on another occasion, "is it precisely *now* that you so energetically insist on your departure abroad? The hunger-strike, opening your veins, appeals to the Embassy. Yet in 1930 when you were arrested, and when, as you are aware, it would have been easier for us to let you go, you did not resort to any of these extreme measures, but restricted yourself to appeals to the Central Executive Committee."

"I had then infringed your laws; I had taken part in an illegal opposition, and I knew that I ran the risk of arrest for it. Since I had done this, it seemed to be natural that I should accept the consequences, although from the standpoint of international workers' solidarity your repressive measures were inadmissable. But now it is different. I have now on my side not only ethics but also law. Then you condemned me to three years' imprisonment. You yourselves considered that sufficient punishment for my 'sins'. I have served those three years, consequently we are quits, the account is settled. I no longer participate in the political struggles in the U.S.S.R.; I have not belonged to any political organization since 1932. Therefore you have no legal basis for repressive police measures against me; they are simply arbitrary, and that is what I am rebelling against. (However freely I talked with the G.P.U., I still kept silent about my other motive. In 1930, Russia and the Russian Revolution confronted me with a challenging riddle, but now in 1933–34 the enigma appeared to be solved.)

"But we are in the first place proletarian Jacobins, and only afterwards jurists," replied Denisov.

"From the proletarian standpoint you never had any right to detain me forcibly in Russia and put me in prison."

"And what about the decisions of the proletarian Communist Party and the Comintern? After all, we in the G.P.U. are only carrying out the decisions of the Party and the Comintern regarding punishment of Communists."

"The decision of the Party and the Comintern are binding on the members of those organizations, and on those former members who desire to return to the fold and who recognize their authority. But it is a long time since I recognized their authority. Moreover, for workers and revolutionaries there is always the final resort: an appeal from the organization to the class, to the masses. For example, when the Party and the majority of the Central Committee opposed the Brest Litovsk peace treaty at the beginning of 1918, Lenin declared that he would appeal to the workers, that he would go to the factories, to the whole mass, Party and non-Party, to the class. The deeds of the great are an example to the small. The class, the people is the last and highest judge, not the Party. Let the Yugoslav workers who sent me and my comrades Dedich, Dragich, Heberling and others to Russia—let them decide their attitude towards our criticisms of Soviet Russia."

"But listen, Ciliga, you know very well that the Soviet Union is at the moment isolated, an island besieged by capitalism. We are responsible in the first place to her. *Salus rei publicæ suprema lex,* Plekhanov said of the dictatorship of the proletariat when he was still a revolutionary. Our responsibility is too great for us to afford the luxury of the broad democracy of which you dream. Abroad your criticism of the Soviet regime would not benefit the proletariat but the bourgeois and fascist counter-revolution. If the Revolution of 1918 had spread to Germany and the rest of Europe then, of course, with the support of the more highly developed West, our regime would be better, more ideal, life would have been easier, criticism more free, democracy less restricted. But we have remained alone in the most difficult circumstances."

"I understand you—you have remained alone and you have become nationalists. The interests of the State over which you rule are for you higher than the interests of the working class and the international workers' movement. The G.P.U. examining magistrate in the Leningrad prison told me the same thing in 1930, only in plainer words: "the shirt is nearer than the jacket". You regard yourselves not as *part* of the international working class but as its masters; it is they who must serve you and not you them. That is your idea of internationalism. The internationalism of the Second International meant that the proletariat of each country had to serve the national interests of that country. Your internationalism means that the proletariat of all countries and the peoples of all countries have to serve the national interests of only one country—the Soviet Union. I understand you; you have remained alone and you have ceased to be socialists. The forces of socialist revolution in Russia were exhausted towards the end of the Civil War, in 1920—21. Left without direct support from the West, you were faced with the alternative—either to liquidate the modest beginnings of socialism in Russia yourselves, or to be swept away by the Whites, who would introduce the counter-revolution in their own way. You decided that it would be the lesser evil for you to organize reaction yourselves; that it would be only a 'manoeuvre' on the road to socialism . . . This was the essence of NEP. In reality, however, in the course of your struggles, your 'manoeuvres', you changed yourselves. It is impossible to bring about reaction and to escape becoming a reactionary.

"You", I continued, "are reactionary in relation to socialism, to October, to 1919.* But you are progressive in relation to Tsarism and the February Revolution. Even now, with your industrialization and collectivization, you are accomplishing deeds of enormous national and even world importance."

"There you are then. You recognize yourself that we are right. Full socialism and real democracy will come with the next step."

"Yes, it will come with the next stage. But not on your initiative, not with your aid, but in the struggle against you, against all your privileges, which you foster, which you defend, which you embody," I argued hotly. "I see a better future for Russia not in the failure of the Five Year Plans, but in the struggle of the factory workers and the rank and file of the

*Foundation of the Third Communist International — *Translator*.

490

collectives against you, the new bosses. And in a way I am speaking to you at this moment in their name, in the name of these future fighters who are being born in the ranks of the disinherited of the U.S.S.R.

"But you have one excuse before History," I went on. "You have degenerated, but you have carried through a revolution, a great revolution. You have degenerated because you exhausted your forces and did not receive sufficient support from other countries."

"But what do you expect of us—you foreign workers and revolutionaries? That we should approve and support your anti-socialist, anti-worker policy, when you haven't done anything serious, haven't achieved the revolution in your own countries?" he demanded.

"You withered after a glorious blossoming. And you demand that we shall wither without ever having flowered. You have no strength left for any revolutionary action? Well, peace be with you! But leave us alone, leave us to do our work, to carry on in a certain sense the old work for which you yourself have no more strength left.*

"The old world does not threaten you, neither do you threaten it. You are blood brothers. If not Stalin, then Voroshilov or some other from among your leaders will do the little still required for your final reconciliation. By supporting you the workers are not devoting their strength to their own cause. And you can manage without them."

"You keep harping on our *rapprochement* with the League of Nations, Roosevelt's recognition of the U.S.S.R."

"It is not only a question of that, but of everything else. The bourgeoisie, fascism, the Popular Front, Roosevelt, Hitler, you juggle with all these as it pleases you, to suit your convenience. You change slogans and alliances, but you remain constantly selfish and reactionary.

"Your victims," I told them, "are always the same—the working class and the international workers' movement. So long as they have not freed themselves from your influence, from your leadership, they will go from one defeat to another, and the reaction—the bourgeoisie, fascism, imperialism—from one triumph to another.

---

*Of course, let it at once be added that to carry on the "old work" does not mean to repeat Bolshevik history. History does not repeat itself. "The same" a second time must assume new forms and find new formulae. But the author is here recording the conversations as they took place—A.C.

"I understand you perfectly, but I do not approve of you. Still less do I want to be used as a pawn in your game. Your work is finished; let us begin ours."

On another occasion one of the higher officials of the G.P.U. told me in a confidential tone (the question whether he was being sincere or using 'tactics' is here not important):

"We know very well, of course, that you oppositionists are not counter-revolutionaries and that you on your side don't really regard us as 'red policemen', in spite of the fact that these are the terms usually employed in our polemics.

"Do you really think", he continued, "that the Party has such a short memory that it does not, for example, remember Trotsky's services in the Civil War? The revolutionary exigencies of the moment compel the denial of all merit, demand defamation. But the memory of the Party is more faithful, it does not forget anything. Moscow has not forgotten your long years of Party work and I am sure that nothing dishonourable will be asked of you. You will be allowed to go abroad, but, as I see it, they want some guarantee about your future activity there."

He did not go into details on the guarantees expected of me, but switched to another subject.

"Well, what really separates us fundamentally at the moment, after the successful progress of the Five Year Plan, when it has become possible to introduce a number of relaxations in the undoubtedly very severe regime of the first Plan?"

"What separates us? ... Some things in the past, many things in the present, everything in the future. The decisive aspect of our separation is that we are moving forward upon two diverging and opposing paths. What separates us today is nothing to what will separate us tomorrow. Of course, if you were still what you pretend to be, what you still partly believe you are, we could go forward together. But as I know you for what you really are—from now on we shall never again be united. Sentimentally, one would prefer it otherwise. Subjectively, no doubt, we do not feel ourselves so far removed from each other as we are objectively. Memory, the remembrance of common battles in the past, to a certain extent conceals the new reality from our consciousness. It is easier for me, a foreigner, to recognize this. I have fewer personal ties than a Russian has. Stalin and Trotsky never liked each other. Even the secretary of the Ukrainian Communist Party, Kossior, has a brother in exile as an oppositionist. Yagoda's niece is the wife of the exile Pevzner, whom she followed into exile; the

492

head of the local G.P.U., Denisov, has a brother in exile in Archangel, and his best friend in the Sverdlovsk* Institute is here as an exile. Coming up the stairs to see you I thought a little about all this, because I had just seen the latest issue of your wall-newspaper *On Guard* exhibited in the corridor. Its editorial is entitled 'For the defence of the prisoners in the capitalist prisons'. It sheds tears over the fate of those imprisoned in Sofia. And at the same time you hold us in prison here."

All these talks reinforced my conviction that departure abroad was a matter of days, if not of hours. Another incident made me even more certain. At the home of some friends I met a young woman, very pretty and very well dressed. We were introduced. When she heard my name she cried:

"Ciliga! Oh yes, my husband has spoken to me of you. You are the foreign Communist exile who is soon to go home abroad."

Her husband was one of the leading officials of the G.P.U. She herself had only just arrived in Siberia from European Russia. According to her husband and the local G.P.U., she said, I should be leaving in a few days. We spoke about this without constraint, as though we were speaking of a third person not present. Then we went on to talk of domestic matters. Her husband's salary, like those of G.P.U. officials in general, was not high. But on the other hand, they obtained their provisions at the G.P.U. Co-operative at pre-war, pre-Revolution prices. For a kilo of sugar, meat, and butter they paid some six, ten, and seventeen kopecks respectively, while we ordinary citizens paid at least as many roubles, that is, one hundred times as much on the market or in the State commercial (official 'black market') shops.

At last I was summoned to the Town Soviet.

"Your exit visa has been refused, since the Soviet authorities regard you as a Soviet citizen."

"We'll see about that! Give me your refusal in writing so that I can immediately send it to Moscow."

"I cannot give you anything in writing."

"Ah! So that's it. You're afraid to give your 'reasons' in black and white, because you know the decision is illegal and won't stand examination. Well, we'll do without it. Where is my passport?"

"Since you are a Soviet citizen the passport cannot be returned."

*The Communist University in Moscow—author.

"What! So now it's stealing! Hand it over at once! Or give me a receipt for it!"

"We cannot possibly give you anything in writing—neither confirmation of the refusal nor a receipt for the passport. We are only authorized to give you an oral answer."

"You're not overburdened with courage. Like petty thieves caught picking someone's pocket and yelling 'It wasn't me!' when caught in the act. Why don't you behave like real gangsters who at least come out into the open and take a risk when they rob someone. You sneaked the passport from me with the pretence of giving me a visa and now you're too scared to give me a receipt confirming your bravery. Petty, cowardly sneak-thieves! And you call yourselves a 'Great Power'! "

"Citizen, this is no place to shout. Calm yourself. Otherwise I shall be compelled to have you removed," a young man in a black leather coat, probably a G.P.U. man in civvies, interrupted me.

"Why shouldn't one shout", I rejoined, a little less vociferously, "when one is being robbed in broad daylight!"

In the following days my interviews with the G.P.U. became more tense.

After exhausting all the old arguments I wrenched out of myself yet another.

"The retention of my passport, Citizen Denisov, is an illegal act of the foreign department not only with regard to my person, but also with regard to the Italian Embassy. The passport is the property of the Embassy given into my keeping. Theft of the passport is a crime, and if this is committed by a State organ of another country, in this case by the foreign department of the Krasnoyarsk Town Soviet, then this is a violation of the Soviet Government's international obligations towards another State with which the Soviet Government has normal diplomatic relations."

"The passport will be returned to the Italian Embassy, which is in agreement with our action," Denisov curtly and almost brutally interrupted me.

That was a bombshell! A pact between the Soviet Government and the Italian Embassy would mean that I was tied hand and foot and delivered up completely to the G.P.U. But th bomb did not explode; it had no effect on me, because I simply could not believe that such a pact had been made. Even before receiving the passport I had considered such an agreement unlikely, and after receiving it there could be no question of an agreement.

494

For his part, Denisov did not press this point, but came out with a new proposition.

"Actually, Ciliga, there's no need for you to get worked up about this: in six months your term of exile will expire and you will presumably receive a 'clearance' (meaning, that is, that there would be no arbitrary prolongation of my sentence) and you will be free to go where you like, to European Russia or abroad. But let me give you a piece of friendly advice: do not approach the Embassy again."

That "do not approach the Embassy again" meant that no agreement with the Embassy existed. Perhaps the only object of the whole business was the desire of the G.P.U. to save its face, its prestige? Or was it just another trap?

"I do not take the slightest pleasure in asking aid of the Embassy. Greater than my bitterness over the three years of imprisonment you inflicted on me, is my bitterness towards you for forcing me to appeal to the Embassy. All along I have been pleading with you to let me go peaceably."

"Ciliga, the problem of your departure must be looked at from the political and not the personal angle."

"So then, for ten years we have worked together abroad and in Moscow. For years I've been risking my freedom, my neck, for the Comintern and the Soviet Government, and now that we are politically at loggerheads, a simple human attitude, a minimum of respect for my conscience and my elementary rights would be 'impolitic' but your gangster attitude towards me—that is an act of high-level politics."

"You are a strange person, Ciliga. Why is it that you don't want to understand hard reality, the painful truth: one can't build socialism with kid gloves."

"And still less can one build it with filth and lies. Yes, Denisov, that is the worst part of it—no man can put his trust in you, because you don't know the meaning of honour. You have derided and rejected bourgeois honour, but not in order to replace it by a purer proletarian honour, but for a total absence of any honour whatsoever. You have exchanged bourgeois morals for no morals at all. But let's go back to what we were first speaking about. You said that if I did not approach the Embassy any more I should be allowed to go abroad at the expiration of my term of exile. In principle I am prepared to accept this. The world is not particularly awaiting my advent in Paris. In order to part without strife—even if this is only a last-moment peace—I am prepared to serve out another six months' exile. But, in the first place, I have still another year and a half to go and not just six months."

"No, no, Ciliga, you were sentenced to two years of exile."

Denisov straightway called the official in charge of the exiles' dossiers. My control card was found. We looked at it: three years.

"It's a mistake," Denisov declared. He searched in his desk and in the filing cabinets, and finally produced a document: an order of a special Session of the G.P.U. condemning me to two years of exile.

Where the truth lay, whether this was trickery or indeed an error, I had no means of knowing. But there was the apparent fact—I had gained a year. The official document established that my term of exile was for only two years.

"All right," I said. "I am prepared to wait another six months. But where is the guarantee that after this time you won't prolong my exile, since you need only a stroke of the pen to do it? The 'clearance' is given to some exiles but not to all. Where is the guarantee that I shall fall in the first category and not the second? Personally, I can see only one safeguard. That is the return of my passport. As it is valid for a year, I could wait another six months. If you should not keep your word I could apply to the Embassy again. But if you don't return the passport that means that even now you are thinking of trickery. In that case I have no other course than to apply at once to the Embassy."

Denisov and Valeyev forwarded my reply to their proposition to G.P.U. headquarters in Mocow. On the morning of 26 November I received their reply. This time Valayev's secretary, Smirnov, received me. Not a very favourable omen.

The moment after I had entered the room it filled up with G.P.U. agents, and I felt their eyes on me from all sides, watching my every movement.

"Citizen Ciliga," Smirnov announced, "you are leaving at once for Yeniseisk, your place of exile."

He paused. The hands of the G.P.U. men surrounding me moved as though they were making ready to grab me. God knew what they thought I might do. Try to commit suicide again perhaps . . . I looked at them with a bitter smile . . . No, gentlemen, not today, it isn't on the agenda now.

"I am taking you there myself," Smirnov continued. "We shall leave today in a comfortable car. You will receive a new winter outfit: felt boots, a warm suit, a fur jacket, and for the journey a fur coat and a thick travelling rug. You won't feel the cold at all. I cannot let you return to your lodgings. Our men have already gone there for your things and they will be brought here for you to take with you to Yeniseisk. You will have dinner here in the canteen."

And that was how it went. I demanded an interview with one of my exiled comrades, so that I could send them all a farewell and tell them what had happened. The meeting took place in Valayev's office. But my comrades believed, as I learned later, that I was not going to Yeniseisk but to a remoter and worse place.

Before my departure I handed the following telegram to one of the guards for despatch to the Italian Embassy: "Arrested today by the G.P.U. Illegally and forcibly deported to Yeniseisk. Please inform my mother in Shegotichi, Diniano, Istria, that I hold the Soviet Government responsible for anything that may happen to me."

A few minutes later Valayev burst into the room in a state of great excitement, waving the telegram in his hand, with an agent at his heels.

"Anton Antonovich, why do you send such a telegram!? What are you hinting at here? that we are going to kill you?" He concluded his questions on an offended note.

"I do not say that. But I know that with you anything can happen, that you are capable of anything, and I am warning my relatives."

The telegram was despatched. I paid the charge and the G.P.U. guard brought me the receipt. I had no means of knowing whether the telegram would reach its destination. But the behaviour of the G.P.U., in spite of the retention of my passport and my removal to Yeniseisk, somehow indicated that it did not feel itself complete master of the situation. That meant that all was not yet lost. Yeniseisk would be only a stage in the battle and not the final issue of the question—to the West or to the North?

VIII

THE ROAD OF "6001 GRAVES"

> *There are many roads in Russia;*
> *Every road—a grave,*
> *Every verst—a cross.*
> *It is six thousand and one graves*
> *To the Yeniseisk lands.*
>
> Yessenin

It was half past three in the afternoon when our car, loaded down with luggage and passengers, left the courtyard of the G.P.U. At a signal the guard opened the large gates and the car slipped out into the street, paused like a dog sniffing the air, and turned right—to the north. It was November 26th, already winter, and night would soon be falling. The road before us to Yeniseisk was four hundred kilometres long.

And so, my friend, since the finger of the G.P.U. beckons and fate commands, you will not fail to see the Yeniseisk lands.

But now this road is marked not only by the six thousand and one graves of Yessenin—proud poet who committed suicide in 1924, throwing his life contemptuously in the face of the Revolution's *nouveau riche*—it is marked also by the numberless peasant graves of Death's great harvest from 1929 to 1933. Over them the grass has only just begun to grow and the snow to settle. One no longer saw the dead but the stench of the corpses seemed still to hang in the air, and the deserted huts cast a gloomy shadow on the mind. It is the decay of the old life that nourishes the new grass. It is from soil drenched in the blood of the people that the new life pushes up cruelly towards the sun.

The car crawled along. It was surprising that it moved at all, for the road was covered with a thick layer of hardened snow. Under the broad blanket of snow the road, in any case primitive and worn out, could hardly be distinguished from the surrounding fields, and we were continually going off it, skidding into ditches and bumping into frozen mounds of snow. We had driven some fifteen to twenty kilometres and my escort, who in Krasnoyarsk had still been worried about what I might attempt in my despair, had now relaxed, and sat talking to one another, ignoring me. Wrought up by the disaster that had overtaken me, and yet fascinated by the experience ahead, I remained silent in my corner.

We have passed the first village and are approaching the next. The way becomes even more difficult, the snow deeper and deeper, the ditches more treacherous.

"We'll leave the car at the next village and go on by sleigh. We thought we might do half the journey by car, but it won't be possible, there's too much snow," one of the G.P.U. men says.

To make matters worse it has become dark. We lose the road again and the chauffeur cannot get back on it. We are all compelled to alight, but even this does not help. The G.P.U. escort aids the driver. Heaving and pushing they try to shift the car, but to no avail. They take off their coats. In spite of the frost they are sweating. But it is no good.

"Let them sweat," I think to myself, standing aside and regarding their efforts with a kind of malicious pleasure.

One of my guards is a captain, the other a major. Smirnov, who is, I believe, a former student, went through the Civil War as a political commissar. The other, Khlebnikov, is a former metal worker from Krasnoyarsk, active in the underground movement during the Kolchak regime, and now head of the Krasnoyarsk G.P.U. Prison.

Senior police officers don't sweat like that in Europe, I think to myself; work is not one of their strong points. Although these fellows have degenerated into political scoundrels, they haven't altogether forgotten they were once workers . . .

Standing aside like that I begin to feel a little embarrassed, as though I were a parasite with others working for me. Yes, but after all, I can't help them to weld the chains around me. That car is the symbol of my bondage . . .

No . . . one must have respect for work. That car is like a boat from a shipwreck. We all have to row. We can settle accounts later, I argue with myself. No, I am not going to let 'them' enjoy a perverse pleasure, say to themselves: "We G.P.U. men are not afraid of work, we don't shirk simple labour; while you gentlemen of the opposition look at it with the disdain of aristocrats." So I go and give them a hand.

Betwen the Communists in power and the Communists in prison there still at that time existed a rivalry on the question —Who are the better revolutionaries? Things have changed a lot since then.

But we did succeed in shifting the car, and the G.P.U. men decided to turn back to the village. The driver would take the

499

car back to Krasnoyarsk and we would hire horses and continue on sleighs.

In the present-day Soviet village one cannot hire horses direct from the peasants but only through the new bosses, the kolkhoz administration or the village Societ. We were informed that the horses would not be available before midnight. While waiting we made ourselves as comfortable as we could in the hut of the village Soviet, stretching out on the wide benches ranged along the walls and wrapping ourselves in our sheepskin coats and furs. In one corner, seated around a table on which stood a paraffin lamp, were some peasants, members of the kolkhoz administration with their book-keeper. They were apportioning some taxes among the various households belonging to the kolkhoz, arranging the compulsory deliveries of potatoes to the State, distributing the salt and paraffin received from the State, and checking the number of 'labour-days' to be accredited to the kolkhoziki.

This rough and ready sharing out, recording of 'labour-days', and bartering, is part of the kolkhoz system—the last word in social progress! Bizarre! Outside the circle of light thrown by this little lamp, beyond this hut, the village and the kolkhoz, are the snowdrifts, the vast deserted icy fields, the boundless taiga, and the black night. Thousands and thousands of kilometres not only from Europe but even from Moscow, this hut seems to me like the winter quarters of some Polar explorers who, menaced at every moment by the frozen wastes of silence that encompass them, battle with Nature on the roof of the world, intent on subduing her to the will of man.

When we were awakened late at night the peasants had gone from the hut. We mounted the sleighs, wrapped ourselves up and, dozing, sped smoothly on the ocean of snow through the deep night to the tinkling music of the horses' little bells.

At the next village we pulled up at the postmaster's place. It was long before dawn when we arrived. Everybody was fast asleep, but without standing on ceremony the G.P.U. men roused the family. Half-dressed men and women, young and old, rose from some kind of mattresses placed on bunks, on the floor, on the stove. It looked more like the scene of a bivouac than a settled home. They put on the samovar and we had hot tea and something to eat and went to sleep on the mattresses left vacant. In the morning there was a two-hour delay negotiating over horses, which the village Societ refused to let us have. Owing to collectivization the number of horses had decreased to one-fifth of its former figure. In addition, this was the day on which deliveries to the State—a priority matter—had to be made.

"First we must fulfil our kolkhoz tasks and then we'll see what we can do for you . . ."

I was simply staggered to hear the village Soviet talk to G.P.U. men in this manner. Later I saw that this was a common occurrence all along the way. Moreover, something I had not anticipated, the G.P.U. had to pay the village Soviet or the kolkhoz for the use of the horses, just the same as any ordinary traveller.

My escort discovered that there was a sick horse on the kolkhoz, barred from heavy work by the vet. This horse could therefore take us to the next stop, they said, since pulling a sleigh was easy work. But it appeared that the sick horse also had its kolkhoz task to perform—taking the children to school. A fresh obstacle. But eventually it was discovered that for some reason or other there was no school that day and we could use the horse after all.

It was a brilliantly sunny morning. The landscape was flooded with such dazzling light that it seemed the snow must surely melt. I was surprised to see so much sunlight in the far north. But there was something of an optical and psychological illusion about it, due to the purity and stillness of the air, and the glittering whiteness of the all-embracing snow. In actual fact the strength of the sun was insignificant. The mantle of snow did not melt but resisted unyieldingly, like an adamantine wall . . . and soon the sun's rays fled and the grey northern day returned, as it was when we had left Krasnoyarsk the day before.

Towards midday we approached a large village. On both sides of the road stretched the peasant huts, many of them deserted, the windows and doors nailed up or sometimes simply torn from their hinges to reveal gaping emptiness. It was a depressing sight. From there on, those nailed-up deserted huts were frequently encountered. The peasants of various villages told me that one-tenth, sometimes even one-fifth of the peasant households had been destroyed; their occupants dead or deported scattered throughout the land.

At the end of the village a bustling crowd of people, and machines and buildings could be seen. On one side of the road was a large courtyard around which many sheds were scattered, the whole surrounded by a solidly constructed wooden fence. We drove into the courtyard through a wide gateway with heavy iron bolts, above which was the inscription 'M.T.S.' (If my memory serves me right it was the Mindarlinsk Machine

Tractor Station.) We drove right across the courtyard to a small newly-built house—the Political Department of the M.T.S. We were received by the chief of this Department, also a G.P.E.er, and a good friend of my escort. The G.P.U. men exchanged greetings and news. Then the conversation turn to me.

"Daily Herald or Daily Mail?" the chief of the Political Department asked my escort. (That is, what was I—a social–democrat—Daily Herald—or an oppositional Communist—Daily Mail. The Soviet press was at that time making a great to-do about an article of Trotsky's that had appeared in the Daily Mail—*author's note*)

"Daily Mail" was the reply.

Following these elliptic words, my guardians were given a note to read.

"Yes, yes—all right," they agreed after reading it.

The solution of this particular riddle came immediately after. The G.P.U. men went off to dine with the higher staff of the M.T.S., in a canteen on the other side of the road, while I was sent to canteen No.2, used by the tractor drivers and mechanics. There was a third canteen reserved for the unskilled workers.

In canteen No.2 the dinner was not at all bad: cabbage soup, mutton, cabbage and potatoes. Considering the times, it could even be called excellent! Meat! I ate at the table of the apprentice mechanics, young peasants. One could see from their faces that they were children of the people. Strong, large-boned, iron-framed children of the people hardened to toil. Maybe a little too restrained, too serious, too intent for their age. They were dressed simply, but not in rags like the rest of the village population. I did not enter into conversation with any of them, but I listened attentively to their talk, looking at their eyes and their faces and finding what I later heard expressed more explicitly. I will tell of it now.

It was a question of the contrasting destinies of two brothers, both member of the same kolkhoz. The younger, married but without children, seized the first opportunity that presented itself to leave the kolkhoz, to abandon all his belongings and go off with his wife to the town as a worker. Being a good carpenter he soon settled down comfortably, even becoming a foreman. He blessed the day when he had been able to free himself from the serfdom of the kolkhoz. His brother, who had a large family, dared not risk such a venture and stayed in the kolkhoz. He had come to pay a visit to his younger brother one day, and in spite of my presence he fell to describing life in the kolkhoz in the gloomiest colours: under-nourishment, serfdom, chaos—above all, chaos, bureaucratic chaos. The sixteen-year-old daughter of the elder brother listened to all this, and one could see that she knew it was true and agreed with her father's words. But at the same time, it somehow did not seem to concern her. She did not utter a single word on the subject. It was all secondary, unimportant for her. It had in any case no longer anything to do with her future life. In the Kolkhoz she went from house to house collecting the milk that had to be delivered to the Co-operative in town. But now she was about to leave for a six-months' book-keeping course on which the kolkhoz was sending her. This course was free, but she had to find her own clothing, and there would be no harm in taking a little something extra to eat as well. So now both families were pooling their resources in an effort to equip the gifted daughter for her new career. The uncle gave her new felt boots, for among the numerous family of the Kolkhoz father there apparently was not a single pair of presentable boots. The young girl is radiant . . . She will become, so it seems to her, a very educated person. True, she will have to serve the kolkhoz for two years afterwards as a book-keeper, but then she will go to town and become a book-keeper in a factory and eventually an accountant—and who knows what besides . . . She will be independent. An interesting career opens up for her, and she is absorbed in dreams of the mysterious future; waking and sleeping she lives only for this new life. What her father and uncle speak of is true, but of no importance. One must seize the opportunities given one, and not cry over those lost.

The young trainees of the M.T.S. seemed to me to be of the same mind as this young girl, tempered with a certain masculine hardness.

After dining I returned to the Political Department, but my guardians were not there. I was alone and under no restraint. (In these remote places there is no fear of a prisoner escaping, for an escape would only be possible after long and careful preparation.) I went on a reconnaissance of the M.T.S. It gave the impression of a boyar's stronghold. The wooden palisade and the low wooden buildings with all kinds of auxiliary sheds used as workshops, strengthened this impression of a landlord's fortress dominating the peasantry of the surrounding country-side. But the old intermingled with the new. The simple wooden structures housed tractors and the most modern agricultural machinery, and in this same courtyard there was a post office with a telephone and telegraph. There was also, of course, a wireless, a club, and a library. In short—a little island of contemporary civilization set in the Siberian wilds.

Having inspected the M.T.S. and compared it with the surrounding village with its isolated, wretched huts, I was very forcibly impressed by the superiority of the first over the second. It was a brutally convincing proof that the new system of Soviet agriculture really existed. I saw with my own eyes that the Machine Tractor Stations, the kolkhozy and the sovkhozy were not articifial transplantations doomed to wither away, but the basis of a new economic order, a new social development, and moreover, a new social struggle. This social struggle was inevitable because the new system was based upon the exploitation of the broad masses dominated by, and subordinate to the new rulers. Even during this brief tour of inspection I came upon evidence of this new social antagonism.

I entered one workshop. It was the smithy, and a miserable enough place it was. Adjoining the workshop was a small room in which the smiths lived. It was low-ceilinged, gloomy, and contained several beds, a table, and some wooden chests. This being the dinner break. I found the smiths there and started to chat with them. When they learned that I was a political exile, and a foreigner to boot, they readily began to talk.

"We thought at first that you were one of 'them'; we went by the spectacles, and also because you sat on your own in a sleigh, wrapped in a gentleman's fur. But when you got up and took off the fur and got out of the sleigh, we noticed your sheepskin coat was tied with a piece of string" (Indeed, when I left Krasnoyarsk I had tied a piece of string round my waist to hold the warmth in, as in the hurry of the departure my belt had been left behind.) "Then we said to ourselves, this one isn't the same as the others, he isn't one of 'them'." I was struck by this unambiguous workers' distinction between 'them' and 'us', by their notice of the 'gentleman's' fur coat and the interest they showed in trying to discover which camp I belonged to—'ours' or 'theirs'.

They replied to my questions in a free and unconstrained manner; it was clear that no one feared denunciation by any of the others. However, they avoided definite, precise formulations and spoke in a round-about way: for we were, after all, on the territory of the M.T.S. and my G.P.U. escort might turn up at any moment. But the sense of their replies was clear enough: we live badly, life is hard; before there were the landowners, now there is the M.T.S.; formerly one kind of gentleman, now another.

Then they asked me point-blank:

"Tell us the truth, how do the working people live abroad, better or worse than we do?"

The question spoke for itself. And in the tone of their voices could be heard their conviction that the workers abroad must live better than they, that it was impossible for anyone to live worse than they did . . . I recalled at that moment the false idea that the workers abroad have of the life of Soviet workers, and I replied:

"Abroad the workers think—'There in Russia the workers really live well', and here in Russia one thinks the same thing about them. And how is it in reality? In fact, life is hard for the workers both here and there."

"Ah, yes. Yes, that's true enough. Yes, that's how it is," they answered in chorus, not in tones of resignation but spiritedly, almost militantly.

The strength of the new system lies not only in the G.P.U. but perhaps even more in that it draws up into the leading cadres the most energetic part of the youth. But the majority, the mass of the working people, who remain at the bottom, who carry the whole weight of the system, also recruits its strength and ideas in the same manner . . . And even among the youth who rise to the top there are some who remain at heart in sympathy with those at the bottom.

The new landlords have not only better dining rooms, better houses, better clothing, not only the political and economic power in the M.T.S., the kolkhoz and State farms, they also have, as becomes a ruling class, the privilege of culture and entertainment. Here is a small example of this. When living in Krasnoyarsk I called on some friends to discuss renting a room from them. But their free room had just been let. To whom? "To some ladies of the Political Department of a certain Machine Tractor Station." The ladies in question visited the theatre in Krasnoyarsk once a week and required a room in which to stay overnight.

"The ladies of the Political Department"! What a phrase! How symbolic! Of course, the former landlords when visiting town did not rent rooms, they had whole apartments or even houses at their disposal. But the principle is the same.

As so often happens in life, on my journey from Krasnoyarsk I learned many things from the end and not from the beginning. I got to know the heights of the new agricultural system before the depths, the Machine Tractor Station before the State farm, and the romanticism of the road before the tale of horrors committed on it. Only on the second half of my journey did I come close to the bedrock of Soviet life, hearing words and learning facts that seared the soul. Sometimes the most tragic stories of the fate of men and women, of the bones of little children scattered along this road during the Five Year Plan, coincided with such magical beauty of landscape that these facts seemed a vile calumny on mankind; such naked cruelty could exist only in the depths of the ninth circle of hell.

It will not be out of place here to briefly explain the differences between the State farm (sovkhoz), the collective farm and the Machine Tractor Station.

The status of the sovkhoz (abbreviation of *Khozayistvo Sovietskoye*—State Farm) is clear and simple. This is a farm, including machinery and livestock, that belongs directly to the State, which appoints a director to administer it, in the same way as in the bourgeois world an agent might be appointed by a bank or finance company to manage a farm belonging to it. The workers here are hired labourers paid directly by the State, just as workers in a factory, with the difference that a large part of the sovkhoz worker's earnings are paid in kind and not in cash.

It is an entirely different matter with the kolkhozy and the Machine Tractor Stations. Legally the kolkhoz is a joint State-peasant economic unit, in which the respective rights of the two parties are not clearly defined and vary according to place and time. The land is the property of the State but has been granted for use 'in perpetuity' to the peasants who farm the kolkhoz. The land (except the vegetable allotments), as well as most of the livestock and the best of the buildings, constitute the 'inalienable fund' of the kolhoz, that is to say have been definitively separated from private peasant ownership. If the peasant leaves the kolkhoz he has no claim to any part of this fund. Part of the administrative personnel is elected by the peasants, part of it is appointed by the State. In actual fact the owners of the kolkhoz are the bureaucrats of the official 'Land Departments', who have the right to change the administrative personnel by appointment or by holding new elections. They also lay down or confirm (depending on circumstances) the plans for sowing and the work of the kolkhoz in general.

The peasant is neither the master nor the hired labourer of the kolkhoz. Herein lies the cunning mechanism of the system. For in this way the State can impose a mass of obligations on the peasant without giving anything in return. The kolkhoz (that means the peasant) is compelled to deliver the greater part of its harvest to the State (that is, the Government). The State itself determines its share of the harvest, as well as the prices to be paid and the delivery dates. The peasants have no legal possibility—not even formally speaking—of expressing their views on these matters. They have simply to carry out instructions received from above before they even think of taking a share of the harvest. Then, it is the M.T.S. that presents its bill. The balance of the harvest—money income included—is then finally shared out between the 'collective needs' of the kolkhoz as a whole and the individual peasants, in accordance with the 'labour days' credited to them. In this way the State takes for itself the lion's share. The peasants naturally 'sabotage' this; they do not want to work for the State for nothing. But since the Government neither pays the peasants any wages for their work, nor guarantees them anything at all, they must keep at their work on the kolkhoz in order to gain a few pence or simply in order not to starve to death.

The Machine Tractor Station is an additional weapon in the hands of the Government for compelling the peasant to work and for safeguarding the State's control over, and domination of the kolkhoz. The basic work on the farms is performed with the aid of machines—tractors, combine harvesters, and so on. The State produces these machines in its factories but does not hire them out or sell them to the kolkhoz. It retains them as its property, under its administration, organizing in each district one, two, or three Machine Tractor Stations. These are centres, bastions, where all the machines serving the Kolkhozy of a given region are concentrated. For work performed the kolkhoz has to pay the M.T.S. in kind, always at rates unilaterally fixed by the State. An M.T.S. has no land of its own and a kolkhoz has no machines of its own. This is the basis of their collaboration. The tractor and combine drivers and other workers handling these machines are members of the M.T.S. and not of the kolkhoz; they are paid by the former and not by the latter. So, possessing all the machines through the M.T.S., and, through the kolkhoz, three-quarters of the land, livestock and buildings, the State assures itself a decisive role in the new agrarian system.

It is the kolkhozy and the Machine Tractor Stations that play the key role in Soviet agriculture. The role of the sovkhoz is comparatively small. I myself have not been on a sovkhoz, but a friend of mine, a former farm worker, who was wanted by the G.P.U. lived on one of them illegally for two months. I have already mentioned this in another connection and I quote here a further part of his testimony, dealing with relations between the administration and the workers. The director of the sovkhoz, he told me, today possesses the same rights as were formerly enjoyed by the country police chiefs (*zemsky nachalnik*) and the owners of the serfs. If a worker did not work to the director's satisfaction, or if he in some way incurred his displeasure, the director issued an order removing his name from the food distribution list for one or more days. Since bread and other food is distributed daily, and there are no villages in the neighbourhood this simply meant that the worker and his family had nothing to eat. And that would in fact be the case if the other workers did not always give a little of their rations to help their comrade in misfortune.

The attitude of the workers to such a regime is understandable. "The mass of the workers", said my friend, "regards the Government and the present regime as completely alien and hostile to them, as something that cannot be changed by a trifle, by reforms, but must be torn up by the roots. The directors, technicians, agronomists, the chiefs of the Political Departments, etc., are their enemies, a new ruling class that exploits them, which they must rid themselves of in the same way as they disposed of the landowners and the bourgeoisie in 1917."

It is remarkable that it was not only the older workers but also the youth that thought like this—whether komsomols, or Communists or non-Party people. They hid my friend. In the sovkhoz it was social position that made the dividing line and not membership of the Party. On the one side, the management, Party and the non-Party; on the other side, the workers, Party and non-Party. Among the Komsomols who helped to conceal him from the G.P.U. were students of the Agronomical School who had worked in the sovkhoz and whose families belonged to it.

We did not stay long at the Mindarlinsk M.T.S. Soon after dinner we moved on, using M.T.S. horses. The next village, Shilo, was not one of the most docile. There the peasants had not long since hung up a hen on a pole one night, outside the hut of the village Soviet. A note attached to the hen read: "Have hung myself—unable to fulfil the task". (The compulsory delivery in kind per hen per annum was thirty eggs and one kilogramme of flesh). Naturally, the sarcastic peasants of Shilo were not handled with kid gloves by the Stalin government. During collectivization the village had lost two-thirds of its horned cattle, four-fifths of its horses, and nine-tenths of its pigs. More than fifty of its five hundred houses were deserted and nailed up.

Late in the evening after hours-long negotiations, marked by much shouting and cursing, two pairs of horses were finally ready. In the first sleigh sat the two G.P.U. men, in the second I with my baggage. We drove the whole night. Silence, a light snow falling, the temperature at freezing point or a little below. The dryness of the climate and the warm clothing made this a pleasant temperature. Had the temperature fallen twenty or thirty degrees below zero I should, of course, have sung a different tune; but in those conditions the journey was fantastically beautiful.

The sleighs glide silently along the white ribbon of the road winding between the black masses of the forest. The slowly falling snowflakes give to the whole scene a magic, mysterious grandeur. Shutting the eyes one feels for a moment like a Jules Verne traveller speeding through interplanetary space; opening them again, one floats through an enchanted wood in a poem from Torquato Tasso:

> E sovra e intorno a lui la selva annosa
> Tutte parea ringiovenir le spoglie.

I think to myself: this is the most romantic voyage in the whole of my life—if only I don't leave my bones here. And the farther north I am taken, the more my thoughts turn to the south; the more snow around me, the more passionately I dream of the sunny mediterranean, of the forest of Tasso:

> La s'apre il giglio, e qui sponte la rosa
> Qui sorge un fonte ivi un rescel si scioglie.

I read those verses long, long ago, in an Italian prison, after a bloody clash with the fascists. And now they come back to me, in the deep night, under the falling snow, as I pass through the virgin Siberian forest . . .

Around four o'clock in the morning we reached Bolshaya Murta. Here there was a G.P.U. post and we drove straight to it. We found only a subordinate officer there, who lived on the premises with his family. He had been a worker in Krasnoyarsk and was a personal friend of one of my escort, so quickly made ourselves at home. We stayed there the whole day and the wife of the local G.P.U. man gave her distinguished guests a good dinner: a chicken, pancakes, and drinks. There in the depths of the province, in the home of a former worker, there was a different atmosphere from that of the M.T.S. and I was invited to dine as an equal with the others.

We left at two o'clock in the morning and towards morning reached another village, where we stopped at one of the better-looking peasant huts. It was large but poorly furnished. its occupant was a kolkhoz 'brigade leader', an elderly man. His wife prepared breakfast for us: tea, sauerkraut, and potato salad. We had our brown bread and sugar with us (distribution of sugar was infrequent and irregular in the countryside, and bread was also scarce). I was anxious to learn something concrete about life in the kolkhoz from this brigade leader, its organization and method of work, etc. "Two-thirds of the village", he told me, "belong to the kolkhoz. One third have remained as individual farmers." According to him, now that everything was going smoothly they all wanted to join, but the kolkhoz farmers were not prepared to accept them. Now in 1934—35, after two bad harvest years, better times had come. This peasant made only scant and cautious reference to difficulties and seemed bent on boosting everything of a positive nature. What was his motive? The presence of the G.P.U.ers, his position as a brigade leader, or some other reason? But judging from his remarks and the food offered us it did appear that the kolkhoz system there, although still creaking a bit, was moving forward.

Once more on the road. Two more fine days. the horses are fresh and we drive at full pelt. The snowflakes envelope us; the forest rushes forward to meet us. At considerable distances apart we come across huts, small hamlets. In some places the road appears to have completely vanished and driving is difficult. We overtake other, more heavily laden travellers; whole families of gold prospectors or workers traversing the taiga with all their worldly goods. These are a peculiar 'nomad' people. Work in the taiga is no laughing matter. They travel in a special kind of cart like a covered waggon, which is called a *kibitka*. They are small carts on high wheels, enclosed with a felt covering stretched over hoops. These families take one, two, or three weeks to reach their destination, and during this time they make these tented carts their homes. From time to time we encountered other travellers making in the opposite direction, for Krasnoyarsk.

Towards the evening we reached a village in the hollow of a

valley. On either side of the road were huts to the number of about twenty or thirty. All around were the hills and the black forest. The pure air was as though it had never been tainted by human breath; one had the feeling of standing at the beginning of things, lost on the edge of the earth. We stopped at a large house whose spacious rooms were filled with travellers. This was an old inn, now owned by the kolkhoz. The charge made for staying there was paid into the kolkhoz fund, those who ran the place being credited with one 'labour day' for each overnight guest. Each family, or group of travellers is allotted its corner and given hot water for tea, and everyone settles down and makes himself as comfortable as he can for the night. No food is to be obtained at the inn, so we all scatter through the village. When we return I note with pleasure that the peasants had not been keen to sell anything to the G.P.U.ers, whilst I had been able to get a dozen eggs. Of course we shared what we had.

We spent the following night in a large village, in the home of a kolkhoz 'brigade leader'. His house was large and well furnished, and there were even some dwarf palm trees in the rooms. This was the best and richest peasant home we had come across on our journey. The numerous members of the family were well dressed and slept in several rooms on comfortable beds. There was a generous supper for them and for us. The entire surroundings indicated that we had arrived at the home of a rich, cultured peasant—a kulak of the highest order. How had he managed to survive? Why had he not been mown down in the collectivization drive?

Well, it was evident that he was still firmly on his feet. Our host was even a member of the kolkhoz administration. it was he who directed the agricultural work. In addition, he was an enthusiastic apiarist, attended to the kolkhoz bee-hives and also went to neighbouring kolkhozy to supervise their bee-hives and teach the art to the youth. For this he was paid a fee. He was a non-Party man but appeared to be in complete support of the kolkhoz system. He was attracted by the broad opportunities for activity that the new system of farming offered him. He gave a little the impression that he felt himself in the position of a small landed proprietor in the midst of *his* kolkhoz and *his* region.

On the way I had two encounters that, so long as the Kremlin power remains unchanged, I consider it necessary to relate without specifying the exact place and circumstances. The first was with a young peasant who opened his heart to me as though it had been a matter of life or death for him. After the initial daring and outspoken charges that he made against the regime, I began to be alarmed for him.

"Careful! Don't rely on the fact that I am an exile. I won't denounce you, but there are other kinds of exiles. And, after all, here you are confiding in me after a five minutes acquaintance, after meeting me for the first time in your life."

"Well, one gets to know how to figure out what sort of person one is dealing with," he replied self-confidently.

This peasant had just returned from his Red Army unit stationed on the Manchurian frontier facing the Japanese. He and all his comrades had been firmly persuaded that war would break out there, and several men of his unit had agreed among themselves that as soon as they went into action they would go over to the Japanese. This was the only way they could think of in which to free themselves from the Communists, who were ruining the peasants with their collectivization. But the war had not broken out after all, and he wanted to know from me, a foreigner and therefore one who could find his way in the international situation better than a Siberian, whether one could count on war or not. It was plain from all he said that he hoped to have from me confirmation of his own views.

"By making concessions on the one hand, and arming on the other, the Communists will avoid war with Japan. There will most certainly not be a war now," I told him.

"Then we are all lost," he said categorically, as if resigning himself to the inevitable. He then went on to describe in detail the destruction that collectivization had brought to his village, concentrating with a particular venom on the machines and the tractors.

"Curse the tractors! We peasants hate them more than we do the Communists. Without the tractors we would have put paid to the Communists long ago."

I asked him if there was a difference in the life of the village then, in comparison with the time when collectivization was just beginning.

"Yes, now it's a little better; we suffer less from hunger now," he replied.

"Would the peasants reconcile themselves to the kolkhoz and work in them conscientiously if the Government let up on them a little, and left the kolkhozniki enough to live on?"

I awaited his reply to this question, a basic one for the future of the new system of economy, with some emotion.

"Yes, probably," he answered slowly, reluctantly. "You see one doesn't really know what to do. If one began to re-divide the land there would be fighting in the village and more bloodshed than during the Civil War, when everyone was denouncing, slandering and ruining everyone else . . ."

The other peasant I met spoke to me in a very hostile manner.

"You a prisoner? An exile? But you travel like a gentleman! . . . in a fur coat, with enough to eat, in comfort. The Ukrainian peasants who passed through here last year were treated differently. They were piled into sleighs like cattle, half-naked, starving. Whole droves of them were taken into the taiga, on the other side of Yeniseisk; to cut timber it was said—but in reality to die. They were driven into these deserts and more than one perished on the way . . ." And he began to tell me of a particular case.

"A woman was being deported together with her children. The husband had been sent to a concentration camp elsewhere. They were allowed to take only what they could carry. But what can a woman with four or five children carry (I cannot today remember whether he said four or five children). On the road a severe frost set in, and as they were starving and poorly clad they began to freeze. The woman sees she is going to lose all her children. She undresses the eldest and with her own hands throws him out of the sleigh. Then she covers the youngest with his clothes. There were only two children with her when she reached her destination . . ."

It would be wrong to think that this was an isolated case. One heard of similar tragedies at every step. In Yeniseisk, while waiting my turn at the bath-house, I met an exiled peasant, two of whose children had died on the journey. A third had become an incurable invalid. A comrade arriving in Yeniseisk from exile in Voronezh told me:

"In the famine winter of 1932 a peasant boy from the Ukraine appeared on the streets of Voronezh. 'Why did you run away from home?' he was asked. 'So that mum and dad shouldn't eat me . . . They ate Mikula (that was his brother) . . . and then it was my turn. But I ran away.' "

One day a G.P.U. man was brought into the hospital in Turukhansk. He had typhus. "Bad luck," he remarked to the woman doctor. "We were taking along seventeen peasants when typhus broke out among them. Well, we thought to ourselves, they will all get it now and infect us too. The road was long and deserted. No doctor, no medicine . . . So after

513

the first one pegged out we 'liquidated' the other sixteen. But we woke up to things too late. Tough luck. I got it too . . ." he concluded. The disease had robbed him of full control of himself and he had blurted out the truth. The doctor, however, was an intrepid woman who was not afraid of getting into trouble, and she told the G.P.U. man what she thought of him and related his confession to other exiles.

There was a family I knew in Yeniseisk that employed an elderly invalid peasant woman as a domestic worker. She had been exiled and her husband and son deported to some concentration camp, where the husband had died. The son had been transferred to a more distant place and she had had no news of him for a year.

"And where did your husband die?"

"On Medvezhya Gora" (i.e. Bear Mountain), she answered, as West Europeans after World War I used to answer a similar enquiry with the words: "At Verdun". Medvezhya Gora has a horrible reputation all over Russia as the gruesome place where mass death awaited the prisoners who worked on the construction of the Baltic-White Sea Canal.

But in Russia it is "every road—a grave, every verst—a cross", and there are "Bear Mountains" all over the country. To one such place, not far from Yeniseisk, 120,000 deported peasants were brought one autumn. Eighty thousand of them had perished by the spring. Even in Yeniseisk itself, where the authorities made every effort to keep up appearances, the militia made the rounds of the streets every morning, during the winter of 1932—33, to collect the corpses of homeless old people who had died of hunger and cold during the night. Every morning they found about a dozen bodies . . .

Who knows this, who has seen the victims, and realizes that they must be counted in millions, will never forget that the bones of these millions of workers burden the Stalin regime with an unredeemable debt. On the path of Stalin's Five Year Plans, his industrialization of the country, his collectivization and mechanization of agriculture, lie not thousands, not hundreds of thousands, but millions of graves. Whatever the positive achievements of the regime, whatever its partial successes, its skilful manoeuvres, its concessions to the people, it can never free itself of the bloody burden of those perished millions.

The immense majority of these victims came from the working people. A power that arises on the basis of a popular revolution and constantly refers its claim to rule back to that revolution, can, without danger to itself, shed the blood of the old classes against whom the revolution was directed; but not that of its parent, its progenitor—the people, without whom it would not have come into existence. If the development of social contradictions leads to a degeneration of the revolution and the emergence of reaction, inevitably demanding a bloody suppression of the people, then an overthrow of the supreme power is only a question of time. A government arising from the revolution and officially conserving its ideology can, it is true, itself introduce a certain measure of reaction. But after a period of strengthening and consolidation, genuine reaction will in turn replace this already debilitated 'revolutionary' power and its ideology. A pseudo-revolutionary dictatorship always gives way, in one manner or another, to an openly reactionary dictatorship. The mechanics of the decline and strangling of a revolution becomes clear immediately one looks into the eyes of these victims of Stalin's Five Year Plans.

The road to Yeniseisk in November 1934 brought me into close physical proximity with those frightful sacrifices of the immediate past, scarcely two years gone, when death struck pitilessly at every moment. I could also observe with my own eyes the practical results to the peasants of the concessions made since Stalin's retreat in the spring of 1933. In the villages, the kolkhozy, and the Machine Tractor Stations, could be seen the living effects of all those efforts and struggles to introduce the new agricultural system. The rank-and-file kolkhozniki, the brigade leaders, the agronomists, the directors, the tractor drivers, the mechanics, the apprentices passed before me in the intimacy of their daily lives. Most of them expressed their views on the general situation. To this broad picture must be added the detailed observations, the isolated facts accumulated over a period of two years, the time I spent in Krasnoyarsk preceding my journey and the time in Yeniseisk after it.

For a just moral and social judgement of Stalin's work, the victims demanded by it and the methods it employed (based on social antagonisms and a new hierarchical system) must be taken into account. But for practical life, for the future destiny of the country and the working people, the last word will be spoken by other factors. First, by the actual state of this system—its capacity to function effectively; second, by the physical and moral condition of its human foundations—the peasant population, the kolkhozniki.

"Yes, now it's a little better; we suffer less from hunger now."

These words of the young peasant who hated with all his soul collectivization and the Communists, and who intended to desert to the Japanese at the first opportunity in case of war, correctly described the situation at that time. It would, however, be a grave mistake to think that the life of the kolkhoznik had become 'gay and well-to-do'. Two years before people were literally dying of starvation; now they were assured an existence in which famine would be no more than episodic. That was the essence of the improvement.

What did this mean in practice? In 1934—35, in the Yeniseisk and Krasnoyarsk areas, the kolkhoznik received for one 'labour day' from three to eight kilogrammes of bread (depending on the particular kolkhoz), double that amount of potatoes, and a small quantity of vegetables. A grown man had, on an average, around one hundred 'labour days' to his credit per year; women and children proportionately less. This was not much, but it guaranteed a certain minimum, however low. When I asked the secretary of a District Communist Party in the Krasnoyarsk region (who secretly sympathized with the opposition and therefore talked to me quite openly) if this modest minimum promised in Stalin's grandiloquent boast to "make the kolkhozes Bolshevik and the kolkhozniki wealthy" was just bluff, he replied:

"No, this is a serious and settled policy. Stalin is now trying to gain the confidence of the peasants and watches closely to see that his promise to improve their position is kept. Formally, the old slogan regarding the priority of grain deliveries to the State remains in force, but in practice it does not operate. We have received a secret Party circular to the effect that the minimum of three kilogrammes of bread per 'labour day' must first be assured, and only then must the State grain deliveries be considered. In practice this is done by working it so that an excess delivery from one kolkhoz with a good harvest can make up for the deficit of another."

The degree of exploitation of the kolkhoz peasants by the State can be seen from the following figures: for one kilogramme of unmilled wheat the Government paid seven kopecks; for one kilogramme of bread the Government charged 2 roubles 50 kopecks (in Krasnoyarsk for two or three months in the autumn of 1933 the price even rose to 3 roubles 50). Since the 'grain delivery plan' was applied with such ruthless vigour in the villages and even the kolkhozniki themselves were left without grain, the peasants had to come into town to buy bread. A small improvement in the pay for kolkhoz work and an increase in the price for the produce represented one side of the changed situation; the other side was the permission granted to work small household plots, which received the official title of 'family exploitation'. On the half hectare of land given him the kolkhoznik could grow whatever he liked and sell the produce freely on the market. He was also allowed to possess one or two cows, about a dozen sheep, and poultry. The produce he could either keep for himself or sell, in the same way as he was free to dispose of what he received from the kolkhoz in payment of his 'labour days'. Of course, this change did not affect the fact that the greater part of the land and livestock remained kolkhoz property. The new situation was sanctioned by the 'father of the people', who characterized it as 'a combination of the general interests of the kolkhoz with the particular interests of the kolkhozniki'.

This amelioration of the peasants' situation brought a diminution of their passive 'sabotage'. But they continued to regard the kolkhoz work as a form of serfdom. The ideal for most of them remained a return to private farming. Even if they despaired of ever achieving a return to the past it still remained their dream. An absolutely hopeless dream, it seemed to me—and I remain of the same opinion—for no government that might replace Stalin could afford to dissolve such a profitable system as that of the kolkhoz, combining the highest degree of exploitation of the people with the introduction into agriculture of the latest technology.* It was precisely the fact that the kolkhoz, while intensifying the exploitation of the peasantry, also led to a general raising of the cultural level in the countryside, that assured its eventual success. On the one hand there is the terrible fact of the countless victims of collectivization. On the other hand there are: (a) the new bureaucracy of the kolkhozes, which is on a higher cultural and technical level than the top strata of the peasantry under Tsarism and NEP (the landowners were too remote from the people and relatively too few in number for their high cultural level to essentially alter the low general level of the village; and moreover the technical level of the landowners' husbandry was on average not very high); (b) the army of tractor drivers, transport workers, mechanics, book-keepers, clerks, agronomists drawn from the village youth and giving a completely new social-psychological imprint to the

*The experience of the last war has thoroughly confirmed that prognostication. The German occupation forces in the Ukraine maintained the kolkhozes the better to exploit the country—A.C.

village; (c) the schools, clubs, radio, cinema, and M.T.S., which have transformed the general cultural and economic aspect of the village.

To sum up: I think that the social struggle in the Soviet village is moving away from the line of destroying the new State capitalist system and a return to the old system of private capitalism, and is instead moving towards the line of a struggle for the social-political rights of the workers within, or more correctly on the basis of the new system. The net result of the opposed forces within the kolkhoz system led to the following: that although it still creaked a good deal, the system functioned, and was becoming stronger as time went by. During the year I spent in Siberia after my journey to Yeniseisk, what struck me most forcibly was how, through the gap that Stalin's tactic opened up to the peasant, new life poured through like a spring flood. With how much energy, even passion, did the peasant seize upon the opportunity given him by even this small concession. Russia—the limitless plain across which a year or two before gaunt hunger had stalked, and hundreds of thousands, millions of people had sunk into despair—again began to mantle over with the green of fresh young leaf and on every side new life welled from countless springs, as though all the terror of the past had never been.

How cruel is nature. How unjustly forgetful the grass that grows on the graves of those who perish. But what lusty vigour, what biological and social health of a people capable, after all it has gone through, of rousing once more into such boisterous life. Let the machines, the kolkhoz, remain—this is a people that will yet defend its social and political rights even within the framework of this system. Let the system crash and the machines disappear—which I think highly improbable—this people and this country will not perish in our epoch. Whatever changes and cataclysms may shake the heights, the vitality of the Russian people tells us plainly that their history has only just begun.

In Russia more than in any other country the strength of the government and the strength of the people are two different things. This outward show of governmental power and the hidden strength of the people is one of the mysteries of Russia. Oh where does this strength of yours spring from, Russia—this secret strength of your people? . . .

IX

IN THE KINGDOM OF THE SOVIET TRUST

I have only a very confused impression of the fifth day of our journey, no doubt because of tiredness. We went through the villages at a steady pace, stopping here and there at small G.P.U. posts. At last we were running along the bank of the Yenisei, its more than a kilometre wide expanse of frozen waters like a vast avenue bordered by chestnuts and plane trees.

"We shall be in Yeniseisk today," the G.P.U.ers announced. The sun came out for a while and comforted me a little.

At last the town appeared on the horizon. The snow became less deep. We approached the first houses of the suburbs; then a timber mill and two rows of small, one-storey, wooden houses surrounded by fences against which the snow had piled up. We crossed a little bridge over a tributary of the Yenisei. As we advance towards the centre of the town the houses improve in appearance. In a deserted square, in the former palace of the governor of the town, we find our old friends the G.P.U. Having relieved me of my fur coat and travelling rug, the G.P.U. set me at liberty, ordering me to report the following morning to fill in a questionnaire and receive some clothing. I had the address of an exiled comrade, an old friend of mine, and I went straight to him.

"Glad to see you again. Everyone will be pleased. Of course, it's a great pity you didn't manage to get out of the country, but don't be too down-hearted. You'll be able to get employment right away with the Trust. All of us here work for the 'North Pole Timber Trust'. You can look for a room later; in the meantime you'll stay here with me. Now have a good sleep and in the evening we'll go and see the other comrades," said my friend.

One day passed; another . . . two weeks, and it did indeed seem that this programme would be followed out. But fate decided otherwise.

On the day of my arrival in Yeniseisk, 1 December, 1934, Kirov, the 'governor' (as a writer called him), member of the Politbureau, and one of the ten highest dignitaries of the Soviet regime was assassinated in Leningrad. We learned of this only two or three days afterwards, from the Moscow radio, and it was not until more than two weeks later, on December 17th—on the very day that the papers announced a "great victory on the socialist front", the "fulfilment of the year's production plan of ten million tons of pig iron, compared with the four million tons produced before the Revolution and the 6.6. millions of the previous year"—that it was officially stated that Kirov's death was not the work of some White Guard or non-Communist, but of a former Komsomol member, a one-time oppositionist, Nikolayev, who belonged to the "scum of the Zinovievist opposition". It was the first political *attentat* within the Communist ranks, effected by a member of the Party in the seventeenth year of the Revolution. An unprecedented, staggering event. It was to have its repercussions on the whole of my life in Yeniseisk, although I did not at once fully appreciate this and instinctively fought against its having any connection with my fate.

Indeed, what possible connection could there be between this murder in Leningrad and life in such a remote, lost corner of Siberia as Yeniseisk? And for a man who had never in his whole life even met Nikolayev? None whatever, I thought; and so thought the other exiles. But no sooner had the wave of consequences resulting from this murder abated and we had calmed down than another wave rose up and broke upon our world. Even at the moment of my triumph over the G.P.U. and return abroad, the consequences of the Kirov affair—the blood ready to flow from the Moscow Trials—still threatened to submerge me.

"In the face of this ten million tons of pig iron, what significance has this Zinoviev opposition, all that is left of the opposition groups?" Radek indignantly demanded in *Isvestia* on December 21st. But in spite of this weighty barrier of pig iron, wave after wave surged out from the Kirov affair, overwhelming even Radek himself, and sweeping almost the entire old Bolshevik guard over the precipice of death.

And when one day Stalin goes, whether he dies or is assassinated, the Kirov affair will be spoken of again, and fresh aspects of this drama and its consequences will be brought to light.

December and January proved to be hard months for me; not so much from the financial viewpoint, for, although after the Kirov affair no new exiles were taken on by the Trust, I was nevertheless given work to do at home on piece-work rates. It was the end of the year and the Trust had many balance sheets and plans to make out and the normal staff could not cope with all this bureaucratic scribbling. Moreover, those who worked there did their best to help out those who were unemployed. Thus a group of six exiles, of which I was one, were given a large batch of work to do. We finished this within three weeks and my share of the proceeds came to six or seven hundred roubles. On this one could live in Yeniseisk for two or three months, or even four if one were very careful. I also found myself a room.

From the moral and intellectual viewpoint I found this period not without interest. In this little town there were always from two to three hundred political exiles, and at times this number rose to from fifteen hundred to two thousand. Among them were to be found some exceptionally agreeable companions and extremely interesting personalities. My spirit relaxed in enjoyment of the warm, comradely atmosphere that these people, persecuted, hunted, and buried in the depths of Siberia, had created around themselves. In the evenings or on their free days groups gathered in one or another place, particularly, of course, where there was a family circle. Our conversations were never about petty matters. Thus when we gathered together to discuss it was as though we were at the very centre of events themselves, and not removed from the world.

This was true not only of Yeniseisk. In the isolated settlements along the great Siberian rivers and along the shores of the Arctic Ocean—Vorogovo, Imbarskoye, Tara, Turkhansk, Dudinka, Norylsk, Ordersk, Narimsk—in places not even marked on the map, in dens where man's inhumanity to man rages unchecked, live the best of Russia, tormented yet surviving, and striving to develop their thought, to expand their creative faculties. Nearly all of them came from the metropolitan centres and their intellectual level was above the average even there. I have been present when they discussed Verlaine and Stendhal, Lucien and Joyce; democracy, fascism, communism, anarchism, and totalitarianism; the evolution of world economy and the structural changes in contemporary society, the sociological foundation of classes, on problems of contemporary philosophy ... The thoughts there expressed would have been listened to with respect by the clearest and most instructed of minds in any capital in the world. It would obviously be absurd to suggest that no great and fascinating personalities have been left in the metropolitan centres of Russia. It nonetheless remains true that some of the most gifted and capable men of Russia are to be found in those waste lands of the distant north.

Yet in spite of these circumstances, in spite of their interest and the profit I gained from them, the months of December and January were a terrible experience for me. I felt that my whole organism was breaking up, that I was dying on my feet. The nightmare Arctic winter was killing me. When the temperature fell to thirty or forty degrees below freezing point—and there were times when it stayed like that for weeks—my internal organs almost ceased to function. My mind remained quite clear, and I could note the numbing of my body as though I were observing the decomposition and destruction of an organism in a test-tube. It seemed to me that every cell, every organ, was slowly losing its vitality, its suppleness and elasticity, and becoming cold, hard, heavy, insensate. The predominant impression was of a freezing numbness, as though the whole of my organism were decomposing into petrified portions and cells.

The streets are dead, inert, deserted; only now and then does a hurrying solitary figure pass. No human voice breaks the silence. No ray of sunlight falls. For one and a half or for two months this grey nightmare stillness presses down on you. And yet the true Arctic night does not touch Yeniseisk. The sky is simply leaden; a dull, dead, impenetrable grey. The sky and the landscape, the streets and the whole town remain in spellbound immobility.

Two months of such a life sufficed to affect my health for the rest of the year. The warmth of summer could not overcome all the consequences of that terrible winter and restore me to health. I knew that another one or two such winters would put me in my grave. Better death than a life like that.

What would have become of me if the G.P.U. had sent me, as the woman doctor in Irkutsk prison had hinted might be the case, another 1000 kilometres farther north, to Turukhansk where the true Arctic night reigns!

My Russian friends and the other exiles stood up to the Siberian winter infinitely better than I. But even among them I encountered several young women of from twenty-one to twenty-five years of age who had returned from Turukhansk after two or three years of exile there and whose nerves were shattered, raw-edged, in spite of the fact that their wills remained unbroken and their intellectual faculties unimpaired. Young men returned from exile in Turukhansk with grave rheumatic illnesses. One of them, a former student of Moscow

University, at one time a Komsomol member and later an anarchist, came back from there to join his wife, herself an exile in Tashkent. Two weeks later he was dead.

In June, the Yenisei at last began to break up. "The ice is going!" the cry shocks like an electric current, rousing the entire town to its feet. The long-awaited day has at last arrived! The river stirs. The link with the outside world is restored, the long winter sleep is over. Everyone stops work. From offices, shops, and houses the whole population pours out and makes for the river bank, to watch in delighted fascination as the huge masses of ice crack, rear up, grind and clash together with thunderous clamour, thrusting forward through the icy armour ahead. The whole town celebrates: summer and life have arrived! Every day more and more kilometres of the Yenisei are freed; from one week to another more and more towns are linked together. In six weeks the whole river is in movement and shipping from Minusinsk and Krasnoyarsk to the Arctic, to Igarka and Dixon Island, calls at Yeniseisk on its way. Brief but intensive, developing rapidly in movement and growth, there begins the northern summer. It is only now with the re-opening of navigation, that people, races, and things begin to move.

* * *

In former times Yeniseisk was not only the central point on the old trade route but it was also the administrative centre for the entire middle Yenisei area. But the population of Yeniseisk has remained at its once considerable figure of 10,000, whilst that of Krasnoyarsk has grown to 100,000; a sufficient demonstration of Yeniseisk's relative decline.

The fishing industry gives a living to part of the population, but for very rich catches one has to go two thousand miles to the Arctic Ocean, which is too distant to benefit the town.

There remains the timber industry.

The two timber mills in Yeniseisk are the basis of its industrial life. But it is not these mills themselves, situated in the suburbs, that give the town its tone; it is the 'North Pole' timber export organization, whose numerous offices are spread out all over the town, particularly along the riverside.

This Trust controls the entire timber exports of Central Siberia. Its turnover figures make it the second most important timber organization—next to Archangel—in the U.S.S.R. Since the timber industry is the main economic activity of the

Yenisei Basin from Krasnoyarsk to Dixon Island, the 'North Pole' directs the entire economic life of this enormous area. Most of the timber goes to export. There are two main sections to this work: one for obtaining the raw material, the other for working it. For the first there are about a dozen centres spread out over enormous distances throughout the middle Yenisei Basin, notably along the Angara River; and for the second there are five mechanized mills: two in Yeniseisk, one in Malakhavo (or its environs), and two, ultra-modern and immense, in the extreme north of Igarka.

The annual turnover of the Trust was 140 million roubles. In reality the turnover was far greater, this modest figure being arrived at because the Trust passed over to the State all foreign currency received from export, at the official rate of exchange, of course. Thus the State obtained foreign currency at the best rate, while the Trust always had a deficit, in spite of its enormous resources and the sweatshop wages paid to its workers, mostly deported peasants. This deficit accounted for the delays in paying out wages, for the Trust never had enough ready cash. Payment of wages in remote timber camps was sometimes two or three months behindhand, and while waiting the workers had to ask for small advances, or borrow, or make do in whatever way they could. But somehow or other the central office personnel were always paid on time. I knew this from experience, for as soon as the first wave of repression following the Kirov affair had died down, and the Trust again began to recruit personnel from among the exiles, I obtained a job as an accountant in the 'construction and repair' section. Its annual expense budget was 7½ million roubles. When on one occasion the employees of the department were paid on the Monday instead of on the Saturday I was given a very unpleasant time.

I do not remember the total number employed by the Trust but it must have been somewhere between twelve and twenty thousand. On one of the two sovkhozes belonging to the Trust, that at Vorogovo about a hundred kilometres north of Yeniseisk, there was a solitary free worker. (This farm was called 'Yenukidze', after the close friend of Stalin, who was deported to this district in Tsarist times. When Yenukidze fell into disgrace in 1935 the farm was re-named 'Molotov'.) All the other workers there were deported men, and even the lone free worker was an imprisoned merchant's son who had avoided his father's fate only by taking this job. Only the mills in Yeniseisk employed any considerable number of free workers.

Deportees working in the Trust enterprises had, of course, no right to leave their jobs, but the Trust itself could 'transfer' them elsewhere if it thought fit. On the eve of my departure abroad I had to deal with the financial arrangements for the transfer to Igarka for the summer season of 150 deportees working in Angara. They were loaded on two special barges, like cattle or slaves; all they lacked were chains. They were not permitted to leave the barges *en route*. Of course they had not been consulted about the transfer, and, more than that, they were compelled to leave their families behind in Angara to await their return. The only human note in this painful business was that the officer in charge of the convoy did his utmost to provide them with satisfactory food on the way. The reason for all these transfers was always the same: shortage of man-power in Igarka. Formerly all deportees had been sent to Siberia, but in 1935 the great, steady flood of deported peasants had already ceased.

At one time a decree had been published restoring civil rights to deported peasants after five years had elapsed. Then this decree was given more precision by an addendum: "the restoration of civil rights does not carry with it freedom of movement". And lastly there was a secret instruction to the effect that civil rights could only be restored on a recommend-ation by the local G.P.U. concerned. Deportees working in factories lived in nearby barracks under the supervision of the G.P.U. Those employed in lumber camps in the depths of the forest had a special G.P.U. commandant over them, with a few guards and a small prison for any eventuality.

During the first Five Year Plan the G.P.U. confiscated part of the wages of these deportees. By a decree of 1935 it was laid down that they were to receive their wages in full and that they were to be equal to those of the free workers. But the wages were so low that no free workers were prepared to accept work in these concerns. Hence the Trust operated mainly with forced labour.

The monthly wage of an unskilled worker was from 100 to 120 roubles; of a skilled worker from 200 to 250 roubles. The average salary of an employee was 300 to 400 roubles. In the department of capital construction where I was employed the chief engineer received 1100 roubles; the head of the planning bureau 700 roubles; the director of the department (a Com-munist) 700 roubles; the chief accountant and the chief cashier 600 roubles each; the pay clerk (that was me) 500 roubles; the two book-keepers 400 and 450 roubles; clerks 175 roubles; a woman office worker 120 and a cleaner 80 roubles. (The cleaner was a peasant woman whose husband had been sent to a concentration camp, and she had four small children to care for. In addition to her wages she had the use of a room free of charge.) In the head office of the Trust the salaries were, of course, higher. The Communist director received 1,500 roubles, the chief engineer 2,500 roubles, and the commercial director 3,000 roubles (these were the highest salaries paid by the Trust). The heads of the Trust had, in addition to their salaries, free apartments, services, and the personal use of the motor-cars and motor-boats belonging to the organization. In the whole town the Trust alone possessed cars and motor boats. But it was not only through these cars and motor-boats that the Trust people set the tone for the town. For just as the best seats in the theatre and cinema were reserved for them, so they were to the forefront in the whole life of the town.

The Trust possessed two co-operatives: one for the workers, the other for the employees. This division was necessary so that the workers should not be incensed by constantly seeing the better rations and superior goods, particularly textiles, available to the employees. The head office also had two dining rooms: one for the administrative personnel, the other for the workers. The first was well equipped and clean, with curtained windows, table-cloths, good crockery and cutlery. The second was dirty and gloomy, with long, bare tables. True, meals in the workers' canteen were only half the price of those in the employees' dining room, but on the other hand the two menus bore no comparison. The workers got cabbage soup and gruel, the employees had in addition a meat course and dessert.

The Trust was housed partly in old, long-since nationalized buildings, partly in premises specially constructed for it. Occasionally it requisitioned property still belonging to Yeniseisk people, who were expelled without ceremony and their homes 'nationalized' and taken over by the Trust. The local Soviet did the same.

I had the opportunity to witness such an expropriation with my own eyes. It concerned the house in which I lived during my first few weeks in Yeniseisk; a good house, although built of wood, as were all private houses. The owner was the widow of a former merchant and she made a living by letting four or five rooms. An official of the local Soviet found himself without suitable lodgings and took a fancy to this little house.

So the old woman suddenly received from the Finance Department of the Soviet an order to pay 2,000 roubles special tax within two weeks. Of course she was unable to pay. "And even if I could, what would be the use? I should pay two thousand roubles and in a month they would demand another two thousand." Two weeks later the house was confiscated for "non-payment of taxes" and the bureaucrats of the local Soviet drove out both the owner and her lodgers. The old woman did not dare to complain to the Court of this clearly illegal, selfish bureaucratism. "They might send me somewhere to the north, and in any case I shouldn't get my house back."

Early in spring the G.P.U. shook us up with a fresh event: the mass arrival of the Leningraders into exile. Whole caravans of sleighs arrived from Krasnoyarsk, bringing about 150 people at a time. Over the course of a month and a half more than a thousand gathered in Yeniseisk. When shipping was resumed in summer over half of them were sent by ship farther north, to Turukhansk, to the platinum ore mines of Narymsk, to the oil wells and coal mines of Khatanga. Others were sent north direct from Krasnoyarsk. In the Yenisei Basin there must have been concentrated a total of several thousand Leningraders, deported in entire families: wives, children, sisters, the parents and even the grandparents.

Groups similar to those in the Yenisei Basin were sent to other districts of Siberia, Central Asia and the Urals. During the mass 'purge' that took place in Leningrad after the Kirov assassination about forty thousand suspected Communist workers were exiled. They went from Leningrad in whole trainloads, just as in their time the 'de-kulakized' peasants had gone. The Leningraders jested about this bitterly: "We laughed when the peasants were de-kulakized—now it's our turn." Everyone against whom the top men had ever had a grudge was taken. Since the days of the defeated Paris Commune there has never been such a mass punishment as was then inflicted on the workers. When the first sleigh-loads arrived in Yeniseisk the exiles were accommodated in public buildings and in the large basement of a printing works until such time as they managed to settle in with local people. I paid a visit to this basement. It was packed with men, women, children, and baggage. Each family or group of friends had settled down on its own tiny island. In the midst of all this I came face to face with the chief of the local G.P.U., who had also come to see for himself how the newcomers had installed themselves.

We looked at one another without a word, like the representatives of two hostile worlds. He represented the State power, and I the proletariat abroad. We confronted one another for a brief moment, as though weighing each other up, and then parted without speaking.

The G.P.U. did not recognize the Leningraders as political exiles, and they received no allowances. Those who had previously held good jobs and had brought their savings with them were not destitute, but the majority found themselves in a terrible situation, and there were many heart-breaking scenes of old folk dying and children starving.

The majority of those who had once belonged to the Zinoviev group humiliated themselves in order to gain the goodwill of the G.P.U. and obtain some improvement of their situation. The workers, on the contrary, displayed a grim resentment and conducted themselves with an innate dignity.

On May 1st the fallen bureaucrats of the alleged 'Zinoviev Group' themselves proposed to the G.P.U. that they should take part in the official celebrations, but they were 'advised' to abstain.

Immediately following the Kirov assassination one had the impression that the consequences would affect only the former adherents of the Zinoviev opposition. The press of the capital referred only to them, and when the wall-newspaper of the Trust published an article in which Trotskyists were coupled with Zinovievists, this mention of the Trotskyists was deleted upon the demand of one of the employees, an exiled Trotskyist.

One one occasion a local commissar of the G.P.U. was galloping by on a horse. As he passed an exiled worker shouted out: "What's the hurry, Gordeyev? Trying to catch up with Kirov?" From this little remark sprang a series of police discussions about the 'terrorist mood' of the exiles. The aggrieved Gordeyev even complained to me of this. I was highly amused and could only reply ironically: "Listen, Gordeyev, I am surprised at you, an educated man, making a mountain out of such a molehill. If that had been shouted at you by an exiled intellectual, then an ulterior motive might be suspected. But a young worker simply blurts out what he thinks, and you are making yourself ridiculous creating such a fuss about it."

That was enough at the time to shut him up. But a few months later the situation would have been quite different.

Certain of the exiles, such as the sister of Zinoviev, the sister

528

the sister of Kuklin, the sister of Medvediev, the widow of the executed Shatsky (one of the fourteen shot together with Nikolayev, and the only one who had refused to confess), and Rumyantsev's widow, behaved in a manner above all praise. Before exiling Shatsky's widow the G.P.U. had taken away her children and sent them to an institution. For months she did not even know where they were. The two Rumyantsev brothers had been executed at the same time as Nikolayev, but the circumstances in which the elder brother was executed were particularly revolting. He had been an officer in the Red Army and had never belonged to any kind of opposition. He was arrested immediately after Kirov's death. With great difficulty his wife managed to obtain from Kyshinsky, then State Prosecutor, the information that her husband had been arrested on the charge of having once served in the White Army. She at once told him that this was false, that her husband had been a Komsomol member from the beginning of the Revolution and had later joined the Red Army, and that she could furnish written proof of this. When she went to the Prosecutor with these documents she was informed that her husband had already been shot. Her anguished protest met with the heartless reply that it was her own fault, she should hve brought the documents sooner.

Following this she was ordered to report to the G.P.U. There she was told that there was nothing against her personally, that she was free to do as she liked, but that it would in the circumstances be desirable, to avoid gossip and for her own peace of mind, for her to leave Leningrad "on her own initiative and for a place of her own choosing". She was requested to think the matter over and return in a few days with her decision. When she went again to the G.P.U. to tell them that she had decided to leave for the provinces, she was given a statement to sign, saying that she was leaving Leningrad of her own free will. Before she had time to leave, however, she was again called to the G.P.U. and informed of the order banishing her to Siberia . . .

According to the new arrivals, several dozen officers of the Red Army had been shot after Kirov's assassination. This was about a year and a half before the infamous, bloody Moscow Trials began. The rumour went round Yeniseisk that the widow and the mother of Nikolayev, the assassin of Kirov, had passed through the town by sleigh on their way farther north. The name of Nikolayev enjoyed a remarkable popularity among the people of Siberia. People who never read a newspaper, who were not in the least interested in politics, pronounced the name as though it were that of a very close friend. One frequently met men of very ordinary mental calibre who spoke of Nikolayev in terms of such intimacy, such tenderness, that one did not at first grasp which Nikolayev they meant. Among the mass of the population there was only one reproach heard against Nikolayev: "Ah, that wasn't the one he should have killed."

One day a cry rang through the Trust, through the whole town: "The saw-mill is on fire!" For a small town like Yeniseisk this was an event; for the Trust it was a catastrophe, since the loss of one saw-mill meant non-fulfilment of the annual plan. The excitement was intense and telegrams flew thick and fast to Krasnoyarsk and Moscow.

The main question to be resolved was whether to re-build the half-destroyed mill or begin the construction of a large new mill, which the Trust had had in mind for several years. Two factions arose from this problem and waged a sharp battle over it. A conference was called to decide the matter. About a hundred people attended: the entire personnel of the head office and the administration of several lumber camps. Discussion went on for hours. The director of the damaged mill took the floor and was followed by the technicians, the accountants, the director of the Trust, the chairman of the trade union, and all sorts of influential persons, Communists, non-Party specialists, and even political exiles occupying important posts as economists, statisticians, planners. Everybody had his say. Everybody, that is, except the workers. But that was only because no worker had been invited to the meeting.

A cursory glance over this meeting is enough for one to realize that here is the elite of Yeniseisk society. With the exception of a few from the outlying camps who are not properly shaved and are carelessly dressed, all those participating have taken great pains with their toilet. The women even have their finger-nails painted. But the presence of the workers is not considered necessary. It is not even necessary to call them together in a separate meeting to hear their views on the question. The result of the deliberations will be passed on to them in the form of a cut-and-dried resolution. Some will perhaps find this rather singular for a land calling itself socialist. But in effect this particular episode gives a very precise reply to the question: "Who are the real rulers in the U.S.S.R.?"

It is enough to enter any factory, to investigate any plant, in order to see the same picture. All questions of production, all construction plans are decided by the director, his assistant the chief engineer, with the more or less active participation of the other heads of departments and non-Party specialists. Only when problems connected with an increase in the productivity of labour are on the agenda are workers' meetings called for the purpose of acquainting them with their new duties.

A close, detailed understanding of Soviet life and its inner mechanism leads to two series of corrections of the picture officially drawn. In the first place there are the corrections, fairly well known, to be made to the picture of the relationship of the Communist Party to the workers. If one is to believe official documents and the Soviet Constitution, the whole wealth of Russia is 'nationalized' and belongs to the people: the U.S.S.R. is the land of 'the dictatorship of the proletariat'. But a very slight study of Soviet reality is sufficient to show that all this does not belong to the proletariat as such, but to those who give themselves out to be the *representatives* of the proletariat, that is to say, to the Communist bureaucracy, the directors of factories and trusts, the secretaries of Party Committees, chairmen of trade unions, Soviets, etc. These are allegedly simply the servants of the people, but that does not prevent them from living in palaces, controlling all production and all public organizations, and in general leading a well-to-do and cultured life. On the other hand, the proletariat, the so-called masters of the country, inhabit basements, work under the whip in factories and elsewhere, live poorly and find access to any kind of culture difficult. The Communist bureaucracy is organized in a strictly hierarchical manner, similar to the Jesuit organization of the Catholic Church, as Christian Rakovsky wrote from his place of exile. The present head of this bureaucracy, Stalin, holds the post of Director General of the combine formed by all the trusts in the Soviet Union; he plays the role of the ideological, political, and economic Pope in the Soviet oligarchy.

This contradiction between fiction and the reality of Soviet life is fundamental, and is fairly well understood, even abroad.

The other difference between fiction and reality is less well known. The monopoly of the Communist bureaucracy is neither so absolute nor so unlimited as appearances would seem to indicate. Whilst on the surface of public life—in the press, at meetings, in political bodies, in the Government, etc.—there does exist a monopoly of the Communist bureaucracy, below the surface, in the daily functioning of social life

—and so on—the Communist bureaucracy is everywhere compelled to share its power, as we have seen in the course of this book, with the non-Party specialists and intelligentsia.

Science, literature, and the arts are those domains in which a division of power is spontaneously brought into existence. Thus the factory worker has two sets of masters over him: the Communist director, the secretary of the Party organization, the chairman of the trade union, etc; and the specialist, the technician, the foreman. It is the same for the peasant on the kolkhoz; it is the same in any Soviet administrative body, in offices, in trusts, and even in the armed forces.

The strictly hierarchical organization of production and of all administrative, scientific, and social work in Soviet Russia gives these specialists enormous power over the workers, the producers. The Communist bureaucracy and the specialists thus share the power in the factories, the trusts, the Machine Tractor Stations, the kolkhoz, the schools, the law courts, and in every administrative and scientific institution. If in the political field there exists a monopoly of the Communist bureaucracy in the economic, and even more in the social domain, there is a dual power of Communists and non-Party specialists. The factory workers and the kolkhozniki simply take orders.

The two bureaucracies, Communist and non-Party specialist, also share the good things of life between them. They live together or as neighbours, in good houses; they sit side by side in the boxes or the front rows of the theatres; they buy fine books; their wives drive out together in their cars; they are everywhere conspicuous for their well-dressed appearance; they are the most valued clients of the commercial shops; they visit the best summer resorts in company. In a word—they are the real masters of Soviet society.

Of course life has introduced subtle nuances between them. From the financial viewpoint the technical and scientific specialists are in the best position. The so-called 'liberal' professions (doctors, teachers, etc.) are, or were until recently, the worst paid. They eke out a reasonable livelihood with additional jobs, doing two or three hours extra in this, that or the other place.

Such, in the social sphere, are the new rulers of Russia. But in the political sphere they comprised two different groups, like two factions of one and the same class. One, the Communist, enjoys enormous political privileges, amounting to almost a complete monopoly of political power.

Over many years the policy of the ruling Communist bureaucracy towards the non-Party specialists, was to compensate them for their lack of political privileges and full rights with higher incomes and all kinds of material advantages. At the same time the Communist bureaucracy concealed its own material privileges under a mask of austerity. During the years of my life in Siberia, after the first Five Year Plan, a change became noticeable, tending towards a levelling out of the two standards of life. The 'gay and well-to-do' life meant the achievement by Communists and non-Party specialists alike of equal social rights: material privileges were no longer hidden but openly displayed.

Moreover, between these two groups there was also a political levelling out of rights and privileges. Stalin's characterization of the Soviet specialists and non-Party intelligentsia in general as 'non-Party Bolsheviks'—later confirmed in the new Constitution of 1936—expressed a completely new political phenomenom in the history of Soviet society. The new Constitution proclaimed the principle of political equality for both groups of the bureaucracy. Proclaimed it, but did not realize it in practice. It was window-dressing; a programme but not reality. The struggle for the conversion of this letter of the Constitution into reality constitutes one of the characteristic traits of present-day political life in the U.S.S.R. Before sketching the perspectives of this struggle we will first see how this duality of power showed itself in our Trust.

The director of the Trust was a Communist. Like every director, of no matter what enterprise, he could not undertake any expenditure without the written consent of the chief accountant. At the same time no instructions could be given regarding production without the signature of the chief technicians responsible. These were all non-Party specialists. The control or participation of the workers in the administration of production has, of course, long ago been excluded by the introduction of one-man control. Production is directed by the Communist and non-Party specialist cadres, working together through the skilfully organized hierarchical links. But more than this, and strange as it may seem, the Communist director is directly dependent on the non-Party specialist. A few examples from actual life will help to make this clear.

For example, the director of a trust decides to make a tour of branches spread over a wide area, or he is called to a meeting at the head office in Moscow. Such journeys are a legal excuse for dipping into the cash box of the enterprise, and are the chief ways in which salaries are augmented. The director receives an advance from the chief cashier. Upon his return the director presents a list of his expenses, with documentary evidence in support of his claim. These expense sheets offer scope for considerable wangling: inflating the figures or even entering false items. The money is paid out only after the chief accountant has certified the expenses as correct; he checks the account presented with the aid of his assistants. I know of this from my own experience. That is when the haggling begins. The chief accountant strikes out the sums that seem to him too fantastic and reduces them to more reasonable proportions. He suggests that certain expenses that are difficult to pass should figure under another item, and some days later the duly 'rectified' expense sheet is presented and the director paid. It is obvious that the director cannot remain indebted to the chief accountant for these favours and sooner or later will seek to return the compliment. The situation applies equally to the chief engineer. In one way or another the bureaucratic apparatus is constantly robbing the State. But certain unwritten laws exist governing these matters. It sometimes happens, dependent upon the position of the interested person, that someone oversteps the mark. The culprit is then severely punished. I witnessed the following instance of this in Krasnoyarsk. The director of a factory, a Communist, and the chief engineer, a non-Party man, systematically submitted for a second and even a third time expenses for construction work that had already been paid. The money was paid and the two split the proceeds fifty-fifty. The affair eventually came to light and they were sentenced to several years of forced labour. But they served their sentences in the same factory, occupying the same posts, although, since this was punishment, at reduced salaries. In a similar case the director of a Krasnoyarsk factory served his sentence as the director of a much more important factory run by the G.P.U.

Within the trade unions the specialists have their own autonomous organization, the I.T.R. (engineers' and technical workers' section). Soviet law relating to this recognizes special privileges for the members of this section raising them above the ordinary trade union member. These privileges are material, and originated in the need to win over the 'socially foreign' but, from the technical viewpoint, indispensable elements. No privileges were recognized for the Communist chiefs, as such, and during the first years of the Revolution it was even specifically laid down that Communists must not use their power to gain material advantages not accessible to the mass of the workers ... But in real life the rule was not adhered to. The Communists in positions of power began very early on to acquire certain privileges, at first in secret, and later quite openly. They abandoned the celebrated principles laid down by Marx and Engels in their book on the Paris Commune, that the income of socialist officials should not exceed the average income of the workers. Certainly, the Communist leaders have the greatest possible respect for Marx's works, but they reserve the right to interpret them in their own fashion.

One of the ways devised for legalizing these privileges was the admission of Communists into the I.T.R. Officially, the salary 'fund' allocated to I.T.R. members in any given concern is 10% of the total wages fund for the workers employed. In practice it amounts to more than 20%, and provides individual salaries from three to five times as high as those of the workers. By becoming members of the I.T.R. the Communists are automatically entitled to their scale of salaries and are no longer bound down to the old 'Party maximum'. Thus by a simple stroke of the pen a whole social grouping is transferred surreptitiously and without creating any fuss to a materially privileged category. Formerly these privileges of the I.T.R. members were justified by the necessity to 'buy' these 'socially foreign elements', who had the monopoly of knowledge; now that I.T.R. embraces only 'non-Party Bolsheviks' and, even better, leading Communists, these privileges are justified by the argument that higher qualified workers must be given better conditions in order that their valuable labour shall become still more productive.

The inclusion of Communist production chiefs within the I.T.R. was a discretely conducted manoeuvre, effected by a single circular sent out by the All-Union Central Council of Trade Unions. The specialists were of course compelled to accept this influx of Communists into their organization, but while doing so they made them aware of the value of the service rendered. The entry of the Communist chiefs into the I.T.R. speeded up the process of *rapprochement* and inter-dependence of the two groupings: the non-Party specialists gave their trade union, and the Communist managers in return covered up the cheating of 'the firm'.

Another aspect of these privileges should not be overlooked. Education in the U.S.S.R. is in theory available to everyone and is the same for everyone. But in actual fact, in each district and in each small town there are schools where only the children belonging to Communist and non-Party high society are admitted and where the tuition and the teaching staff is far better than in the schools attended by the children of workers and lower employees. These two classes of schools differ from each other in everything, from the school buildings themselves right down to the equipment in the class-rooms. The privileged schools lack nothing and teach foreign languages. I recall another detail: the children of two families, political exiles who were friends of mine, attended one of these privileged schools in Yeniseisk. There was a social basis for this: the intellectuals among the political exiles, although completely devoid of rights the same as any other exile, had nevertheless retained a certain social position as economic planners, finance advisors, accountants, and so on. They belonged in the ranks of the new social class from which the leaders of society were drawn.

When a socialist competition was organized in the privileged school in Yeniseisk, it was somehow natural that the best pupil should turn out to be the daughter of the secretary of the Disctrict Party Committee, Comrade Iskra, the highest political authority in the town. The prize was an airplane trip from Yeniseisk to Krasnoyarsk. It received a good write-up in the local press. Comrade Iskra himself, who was after all only secretary of a District Committee in an isolated corner of Siberia, had difficulty in finding a vacancy at the Caucasian spa where he wanted to spend his annual holiday. But the nationally important 'North Pole Timber Trust' was in this respect in a better position. Every year it had many reservations at this spa. And so—'you scratch my back and I'll scratch yours', as the saying goes—a 'warrant-voucher' was presented to Comrade Iskra.

Comrade Iskra has other and more important irons in the fire. Comrade Stalin has given out the slogan of a 'gay and well-to-do' life and in the shops there are some excellent but expensive goods. Our secretary's Party salary, however, is not sufficient for him to live up to the new style. Still, there is a way out of every quandary. From the Town Co-operative he orders suiting, silk, cotton, and more mundane things such as sugar, tinned goods, etc., on credit. He has an account in all the shops. But who among the managers of those shops would care to remind the secretary of the Party Committee of his debts? It is possible, of course, that there is a note on these imposing sums in his G.P.U. dossier, so that, if ever it should be necessary, he may be reminded of them. But even if such an unpleasant occasion should arise, it would be wrong to suppose that Comrade Iskra's situation would be hopeless. For he in his turn has some information about the chief of the G.P.U., Comrade Strelnikov, whose son-in-law is in charge of construction control for the 'North Pole' and has incurred some expenditure not completely accounted for on the books.

Working in a large Soviet Trust in daily contact with its workers and employees, one sees a picture in miniature of the social structure of Soviet society.

There is a struggle between the ruling class and the working class, and there is a struggle between the various groups within the ruling class.

These two lines of struggle have not only a different social significance, but also a very different rhythm and intensity. The mass of the workers is disillusioned with the results of the Revolution and is sunk in political apathy. Its desires and its moods are expressed almost entirely in the form of a passive resistance; it wages the fight against the new privileged on a petty scale in each branch of industry, without contact with analogous movements elsewhere. No demand is raised to the level of political struggle.

An essentially different situation exists in the camp of the new social leaders. There a sharp, direct, and sometimes bloody, though for the most part secret struggle is waged. This conflict takes place over the inheritance left by the Revolution; over this booty the Communists and the non-Party specialists confront one another. To appreciate the scope and perspectives of this combat it is necessary to weigh up the respective forces of these adversaries. Through the one-party system the Communist bureaucracy dominates the trade unions and the other mass organizations; it occupies first place in the whole State apparatus and holds the key positions in national economy. The monopoly of political power is firmly in its hands.

The non-Party bureaucracy is composed of various cadres of the intelligentsia and its foundations are formed by the technicians. This is very important, for it means that this bureaucracy plays a predominant part in the management of production. The factory workers are directly under the orders of the non-Party foreman, technician and engineer. In science, literature and the arts the non-Party intelligentsia also occupies the front of the stage. In its autonomous trade-union sections, the I.T.R., it has created its own corporative organization, and the initials I.T.R. have in the U.S.S.R. of today almost as challenging a ring as the word 'Soviet' once had. Europe and America will one day be aware of this. This non-Party bureaucracy occupies an important place in the whole State apparatus, even including the Army. It can count on the support of one of the most powerful organizations in the new Russia: the Church and the ecclesiastical hierarchy.

The Orthodox Church in contemporary Russia is somewhat in the shadows; hence her strength and the political role she will be called upon to play in the years to come are underestimated. In my opinion there are in Russia three powerful, autonomously organized forces: the Communist Party, the I.T.R., and the Church.

In spite of the official apolitical attitude of the Church, and even its willingness to co-operate with the Stalinist regime (ten years before official recognition by the Soviet State, the Patriarch Sergius re-introduced the prayer commending the established power to the Lord), it undoubtedly stands closer to the non-Party bureaucracy than to the Communist bureaucracy, and at some time or other this will publicly manifest itself. One must also take into account the fact that the influence of the Church has grown in proportion to the increasing disillusionment of the masses in the Revolution and the concomitant adaptation of the Church to Soviet reality.

What is the attitude of the masses towards this rivalry within the bureaucratic heights? So far as the peasants are concerned, the answer is clear. Since the liquidation of the landowners and the definitive victory of the new regime, the Communists have become the arch-enemy of the peasants. But with the workers the matter is less simple. During the NEP period the working class, however discontented, however repressed by the Communists, nevertheless preferred them to the non-Party specialists, in whom it saw the defenders of the old regime, the partisans of private capitalism. As a result of the Five Year Plan the situation has radically changed. Not only has the economic and technical aspect of Russia undergone a transformation, but so has the consciousness of all classes and groups. Industrialization and collectivization have destroyed any tendencies towards the more or less complete restoration of private capitalism, and the rivalry at the top is no longer waged for or against such a restoration, but for the distribution of power on the basis of the existing regime of state capitalism. The power enjoyed by the non-Party specialists over industrial production and the administration is far greater than it would be under a system of private capitalism. However much they may hate the Communists, the Soviet engineers, technicians, agronomists, not to speak of the doctors and scientists, are still not interested in the restoration of private enterprise. Their struggle against the Communists is therefore destined, in spite of the sharpest possible differences of an ideological nature, to take place on the basis, and within the framework of the present economic system.

As a result there has arisen a new interrelationship between the non-Party bureaucracy and the working class. Since they both not only have a common enemy, but also wage battle on the common ground of the new system, there are times when their interests coincide, which was not so before the Five Year Plan. In the Trust and elsewhere I was able to note how the engineers and other specialists made use of the workers' discontent and directed it, or more correctly speaking strengthened it by throwing the responsibility for all abuses and shortcomings on to the Communists. "The Party orders", "the Party demands and we all have to obey", declared the specialists to the workers whenever an unpopular measure had to be carried out, whenever fresh sacrifices were called for. And although the non-Party bureaucrats enjoy the same privileges as the Communists, it is against the latter that all discontent is concentrated, since it is they alone who appear to hold the reins of political power. In this manner there is gradually being created a united front between the non-Party bureaucracy and the workers against the Communists. This is a consequence, unexpected but incontestable, of the Five Year Plans. Now that the old ruling classes have been destroyed, and even their last vestiges, the kulaks, annihilated, the Communist bureaucracy stands before the whole country as the self-evident exploiter of the people. We have entered upon the period of the ever-growing isolation of the Communists. Whatever the forms, whatever the tempo of future events in Russia, they will inevitably lead to a weakening of the Communist bureaucracy and a strengthening of their rivals, the non-Party bureaucracy.

After my departure from Russia a number of events took place there that clearly confirmed this view. Let me cite only the best known: the new Soviet Constitution of 1936 and the Moscow Trials of 1936—38. Sensing the dangerous widening of the void around the Communist bureaucracy, Stalin tried to rally the non-Party men to it by a whole series of paragraphs of a propagandist character in the new Constitution; elections, for example, since the Constitution, take place under the slogan of the 'Stalin bloc of the Communists and non-Party people'. The introduction of patriotic and nationalistic terminology had the same end. But Paragraph 126 of the Constitution none the less reaffirmed the leading role of the Party in every aspect of social life. Thus the new Constitution in its entirety, far from giving a leading role to the non-Party bureaucracy, even denied it the equality of rights so solemnly proclaimed in certain Articles. The Constitution has therefore not put an end to the struggle between the two groups; it has simply created a new political basis for its future development.

The Moscow Trials were aimed not only at eliminating all competitors and enemies of Stalin within the Party, but were also designed as a warning to the non-Party bureaucracy against any attempt on the monopoly of the Communists. This applies particularly to the liquidation of Tukhachevsky and the other Red Army generals. Circumstances themselves thrust the Red Army forward into the position of arbitrator between the two contending groups so long as it is only a question of a simple shifting of the balance of power and not of a direct struggle to wrest the monopoly of power from the Communists. The Red Army, born of the Revolution, can give the Communist bureaucracy sufficient guarantees against a White-Guard type restoration. On the other hand, given that they are placed in a position above the Party, the Red Army generals can also guarantee equality of rights between the non-Party bureaucracy and the Communist bureaucracy. The two bureaucracies of the new ruling class can rest assured that the Army will maintain 'order' in the event of any sharp expression of discontent on the part of the masses left out of consideration in all these manoeuvres at the top. Here lie the political and social roots of Soviet bonapartism. The danger of war, and war itself, bringing the generals to the forefront and fostering still more patriotic and nationalistic ideas, can only strengthen its chances. The young generals may prove themselves to have more initiative and more decisiveness than had those of the older generation, Tukhachevsky and his colleagues.

The workers, disillusioned with the results of the Revolution, are a passive mass that will inevitably be spectators rather than actors in future political events. This is the weakness of all Left currents in the Russia of today. In the first act of the drama, the front of the stage will be occupied by the new social layer, the reactionary Right of Soviet society. Only in the second act will the revolutionary groups of the Left come forward to play a politically important role. Russia in the immediate future moves not towards a revolution from below, not towards social liberation for the masses, but towards a completion and consolidation of reaction from above in a government of 'national conciliation' formed from among the leading strata.

Thus the Revolution declines. Russia sinks ever deeper into reaction. Stalin has greatly contributed to this and will contribute still more. Those who succeed him will continue on this path. What then is the meaning, the final historical result of the Russian Revolution? Was it not then simply a 'senseless riot'? Will it not fade from memory as if it had never been? A serious examination of what has taken place in Russia since 1917, viewed in the light of the historical experience of other great Revolutions, will show the superficiality as well as the fundamental incorrectness of such a conclusion.

However much revolution may appear at first glance to be thrown back from the territory it has conquered, History never turns back on its path. Whatever changes may occur in the political superstructure, even to the extent of a temporary restoration, the economic, social and technical foundations of society are changed for ever. The Stuarts, restored to the throne, could dig up Cromwell's bones and hang them on a gibbet, but they could not turn back the clock to pre-Cromwellian England. The Directory, Napoleon, and even Louis XVIII could succeed Robespierre, but the France of the States General had gone for good. Stalin might tomorrow be overthrown and executed by Red Army generals or others, the embalmed body of Lenin thrown into the gutter and trampled underfoot by a tormented and enraged people, but 'Holy Russia', peasants with wooden ploughs, landowners with their White Tsar, and the anaemic Russian bourgeoisie will never rise again!

The Revolution and industrialization has given Russia new foundations of steel. This is its national conquest, a national possession of which it cannot be deprived. By means of the tractor, the combine, the motor, a new agriculture has been added to it. The new face of Russia is still raw and bloody from the wounds of its people; but this new Russia no longer rides on a wooden cart, it has machines of iron and is learning how to drive them.

Neither the people, nor the worker, nor the working class has obtained social freedom. The tender shoots of liberty that sprang up in the first two or three years of the Revolution have long since been trodden down. But all the same, not only has Russia gone forward as a national State equipped with modern technique, but the working classes, too, have taken a giant stride along the road to social freedom. They have not only historically and spiritually matured as a result of their monstrous ordeal; but in the new technology they have also gained a new national base for their future operations. Henceforth the battle of the Russian working men and women for truth and social justice is waged—today, tomorrow—on this new base of steel.

This twofold result, spiritual and technical, of the people's revolution and the people's sacrifices can never be destroyed.

X

FAREWELL, RUSSIA; FAREWELL, HARD, YOUNG LAND!

In Yeniseisk I did not forget that my objective was to leave Russia. The patient wait for the suitable moment for action; the delicate weighing up of every move and the careful choice of every word; behind these lay a terrible impatience and a nerve-wracking desperation.

One solitary wretch—an ant lost amid 170 million equally impotent—had to brave the ponderous Leviathan, which had only to stir to crush him. And I had not only to keep out of this monster's way, but I had somehow to overcome, out-manoeuvre it—this mightiest governmental police-machine in the world.

To tell the truth, despairing thoughts that my physical strength might at any moment fail me, and moral indignation at this Government's posing as the champion of the oppressed, the standard bearer of socialism and liberty, while it in fact doomed 170 million subjects to servitude—these were what urged me to action more than cold reason, which, however it weighed up my chances, could not give me any great hope of success. The cynical hypocrisy of a Government that said one thing and did exactly the opposite infuriated me more than the brutalities and injustices themselves.

When I arrived in Yeniseisk I had another half a year of exile to do. My sentence terminated in the month of May. Would I be released then? Perhaps it was simply that the G.P.U. wanted at all costs to 'save face' by holding me until the time limit set by it had expired? The desire to part on 'good terms' with my erstwhile comrades held me back all the time: hence my inclination not to try and force the issue before May. But just the same it was necessary to find out the attitude of the Italian Embassy towards the retention of my passport and the violation of my rights as an Italian citizen by the G.P.U. I should have to frame a telegram to the Embassy on this matter in such a way that the Soviet authorities, through whose hands it would inevitably pass, would see that I was prepared to wait six months, but that I was not afraid, if the necessity arose, to take extreme measures once again. Events following on the

Kirov affair speeded up the despatch of this telegram. One day the Moscow papers came out with a 'sensation', alleging that Nikolayev, Kirov's assassin, had been in touch with the consul of a neighbouring State, who had offered him five thousand roubles in return for a 'letter to Trotsky'. Right from the outset it was obvious that this was a frame-up. Abroad the manoeuvre was soon exposed and the name of the consul revealed. In fact, he had been bought by the Soviet Government, and his name, as well as the country he represented, was carefully avoided by the Soviet press. Further, the Soviet statement on the matter itself admitted that Nikolayev had not given the consul any 'letter to Trotsky'. But the significance of all this was clear: to blacken Stalin's political enemies, to hint at that which in a year or eighteen months' time would be so brazenly proclaimed at the Moscow Trials—that Stalin's political enemies, the oppositionists, were agents of a foreign power. True, at that time I did not foresee the Moscow Trials, but in this frame-up employing the Latvian consul, an agent of the G.P.U., I understood very well that the aim was to terrorize the political exiles.

This, then, I said to myself, is the moment to show the G.P.U. that we are not afraid of their threats and insinuations. And on that same day I sent the telegram to the Embassy.

A day later I received from the Moscow post office notification that my telegram had been delivered. But no reply came from the Embassy. What could that mean? That my telegram had in fact not been delivered—in spite of the official notification from the post office? Or that the Embassy and the G.P.U. had reached an understanding at my expense? Whatever the truth of the matter, I decided that until I received notification from the Embassy that it no longer considered me an Italian citizen, I would fight for my right as a foreign subject to have my passport returned and to leave the country.

Finally I wrote a detailed report of the whole business to the Embassy, explaining how my passport had been taken away from me, and how I had been forcibly deported to Siberia and transferred from Krasnoyarsk to Yeniseisk. Again the Embassy gave no sign of life. After a three and a half months' exchange of correspondence between the Yeniseisk and Moscow post offices, I at last obtained, on April 8 1935, an official notification that "registered letter No. 1718, sent from Yeniseisk on December 26 1934, to the Italian Embassy in Moscow, had been lost in transit".

Very well. Apparently a brief telegram was allowed to reach

its destination. But a registered letter containing a full exposi-
ion of the whole affair, with a reasoned argument demonstrating
the illegality of the Soviet authorities' actions, was too embarrassing to be delivered. So they shamefacedly informed me
that it had been "lost in transit". Good. So everything was not
yet lost. Patience and perseverance!

By that time I was again unemployed. The Kirov affair did
not die down and among the political exiles the first to be
dismissed from work were those who had been taken on after
the assassination. The director of the capital construction
department was satisfied with my work and as he could not
find a suitable substitute, was reluctant to discharge me. But
after two or three sharp 'suggestions' from the director-general
of the Trust, who probably was better informed of what was
brewing in Moscow, he had to dismiss me.

For about a month I was unemployed, and I began to feel
the lack of means. My reserves in cash and kind were coming
to an end. And then, at the beginning of May, during a routine
control visit to the G.P.U., the chief said to me: "Have you
been to see the head of the Supply Department of the Gold
Trust? He needs a conscientious worker and is interested in
you. I have given him your address."

To work for the Gold Trust would indeed be a blessing.
There the rations really were rations. I was delighted and
went straight to this Supply Department. However, I had some
difficulty in getting to see the chief, and when I did see him
he gave me an evasive, and, it seemed to me, even an embarrassed answer. I began to have my doubts: why should I
be employed by the Gold Trust, when political exiles were in
principle not accepted? Unless they were going to make an
exception for me as a foreign communist?

However, the Gold Trust's alleged interest in me came to
nothing: the gold ration remained inaccessible. Puzzling my
head over this riddle for some days, I was at last suddenly
struck by the horrible thought: could this be the 'psychological
conditioning' preparing me for an extension of my exile? Was
this the sugar coating on the bitter pill they wanted me to
swallow without causing them any trouble? Yet another
winter in Yeniseisk! No, impossible!

Before two weeks had elapsed, a few days before my
sentence was due to expire, the riddle was solved.

"Citizen Ciliga, I have to inform you that by a resolution of
a Special Session of the Commissariat of the Interior on March
23rd, 1935, you have been sentenced to three years of political

exile in eastern Siberia, in Yeniseisk," the chief of the G.P.U. declared.

"But what is the charge? Why this new sentence?" I demanded, overwhelmed.

What had happened? What should I do? As though there had been an eclipse of the sun, the whole world went dark before my eyes. It seemed to me at that moment that a sentence of death would be easier to bear than this soulless cat-and-mouse game.

"I do not know the details of the charge. I was not present at the meeting in Moscow, and there are no regulations obliging the G.P.U. to give you any explanation of the sentence," he replied in an arrogant voice.

But I received an explanation from one of my companions in exile.

"Well, you're lucky, Ciliga, to be left in Yeniseisk. I was certain that for your obstinacy you would be sent farther away to a place much worse than this."

My situation appeared hopeless. The G.P.U. was doing what it liked with me. Many of my friends advised me to resign myself and wait for better times, and I almost came round to this view myself. But what better times could one hope for? I simply could not survive three more winters in Siberia. And in addition to the new sentence, the G.P.U. kept me from getting employment. Correspondence with my relatives and friends abroad, which had been permitted the year before in Krasnoyarsk, had now been stopped. During the whole of my sojourn in Yeniseisk I was not able to send a single letter abroad. Finally, even if I managed to survive three more years there, where was the guarantee that I should not be given more years of exile, even of prison? Was not the prolongation of sentences in Russia an automatic matter! The Chinese wall built by the Soviet Government almost hermetically seals Russia off from the outside world. This is the only way in which the world can be deceived about what goes on in Russia. And just because of this I could not resign myself, could not submit. I determined to act: I would have my visa or die in the attempt. In the course of the following two months I thought carefully over my plan of campaign. First, I decided that it was necessary to protest, with a certain caution but not the less firmly, against the sentence of the G.P.U. I would send this protest to the State Prosecutor of the U.S.S.R., Vyshinsky (the future chief wire-puller in the bloody Moscow Trials). I had already prepared the text of this protest and was deliberating over its final polishing when the G.P.U. presented me with a fresh surprise.

At two o'clock one morning I heard a loud banging at my door. My landlord was away and I got up, thinking in my only half-awakened state that he had returned. I called out "Who's there?" and someone answered "Militia!" Hastily throwing a coat over me, I went to the door. Two G.P.U. men stood before it. "What do you want at this hour?" I demanded.

"It's you we want," they said.

We went into my room. They showed me a search and arrest warrant. Arrest!—that means prison again, a concentration camp and the devil knew what else! There's your visa for you! . . . But I should not give up. I steeled myself for a fight. Hunger-strike, if need be even to death. Somehow an end had to be made to this pitiless cat-and-mouse torture.

"What is the matter? Why this arrest and search warrant?" I demanded.

"This is not an arrest. It's only a search," they replied.

"How is that—not an arrest? You showed me a warrant of arrest."

"Oh, that's the only form we could lay our hands on. You can see for yourself there's only search written here."

The search lasted four hours, and all the time I was not sure whether I was under arrest or not. I had nothing to fear from the search; they would not find anything incriminating among my things. Page by page the G.P.U. men went through every book and letter. I could hardly help smiling at their fruitless labour. But then they came across my correspondence with the Embassy.

"Ah, the correspondence with the Embassy . . ." They put it aside, not even reading it. The Soviet Government has more respect for the bourgeois Embassies than for proletarian solidarity. It has more regard for capitalist and fascist governments than for public opinion.

I was very concerned that the G.P.U. men should not find the draft of my statement to the Prosecutor. I managed with some difficulty, when they were already becoming tired, to profit from a momentary distraction and hide it on my person. That was the only small pleasure I got during the whole four hours. At six o'clock in the morning the search was ended. The word 'arrest' on the warrant was crossed out and they left. As soon as the door had closed behind them it occurred to me that this was certainly not the only search that had been made. I had to find out how the night had passed for my friends.

One of them lived just across the road: Comrade Boiko, a 'decist' (i.e. member of a left-Trotskyist tendency).

"He has been taken away," his old landlady told me sadly.

I made my way to an Austrian Trotskyist named Langer. He had also had a search, but had not been arrested. Together we went to a third comrade. He was not at home. They had also searched his place during the night and he had gone, like ourselves, to find out what had happened to the others. We then went to Davidov. He was not there. His wife told us that he had been arrested. Maximov likewise. In the course of the day we learned of the arrest of about a dozen of the Zinovievists. Maximov's neighbour told us that she had heard a knocking at his door and had stood at her window all the time to see if he would be taken away or not. Boiko's sad old landlady and Maximov's neighbour who had kept watch all night at her window—these were isolated instances of the sympathy felt for the exiles, but they were nonetheless expressive of the general compassion felt by the whole population. It was this bond of sympathy that made it easier for the exile to bear his burden.

The Trotskyists and Zinovievists arrested that night were accused of organizing a 'bloc'. It was evident that the G.P.U. was already preparing the amalgams that were to characterize the Moscow Trials. As a clear exposure of the opening moves in the frame-up technique, it is worth noting that some of the arrested Zinovievists (Lifschitz and others) immediately addressed a complaint to Vyshinsky, declaring that the G.P.U. was trying to force them to give false evidence to the effect that the Trotskyists had induced them to engage in illegal activity, to organize groups, etc. But the arrested men were not released. The exiled women, Davidov's wife, the left socialist-revolutionary, Galya Luzina, the socialist Eva Lozman, etc., prepared parcels for the arrested men, and we took them to the prison. As usual, all the colony lent a hand in the work of caring for the prisoners' welfare. Later the arrested men were transferred to the prison in Krasnoyarsk. They were still there when I left the country.

The machinations of the Yeniseisk and Krasnoyarsk G.P.U., who were preparing the future 'bloc of Trotskyists and Zinovievists' for the Trials, were not the only ones of which I was at once witness and victim. I would see worse at the moment of my departure. But for the moment let us keep to Yeniseisk.

During that summer the majority of the exiled Zinovievists

were sent by ship further north. As a mark of general solidarity among the exiles those who were not Zinovievists, myself among them, went to see them off. At the harbour we met others who had also come to see them off—the commissars and inspectors of the G.P.U. Seeing them, Shatsky's widow said to me with a wry smile:

"You shouldn't have come. You will only compromise yourself by this association with 'terrorists'."

"Yelena Ignatyevna, do you think there is anything that can compromise me in the eyes of the G.P.U.? It is rather I who compromise the others . . ."

Thus we joked about our miserable situation. It was, of course, a gloomy, hopeless position we were in. Sometimes of an evening I would stand on the banks of the Yenisei and, leaning against the enormous logs of timber, would contemplate the calm, vast, powerful river, following with my eyes the current flowing north, and thinking of those who had gone there. How would it go with them in the coming winter? Should I ever set eyes on them again?

I watch the long, slow sunset of the north, lasting till eleven o'clock at night. The sun goes down beyond the waters and the whole horizon, the whole sky is a multitude of tiny blue clouds, flooded with flaming light—a vast garden blazing with colour. It is beautiful and melancholy. O mighty, gracious sun! Send my greetings to friends far away in the north!

I look on the river, tranquil, powerful, wide as a sea . . . and I remember another sea, my own, the Adriatic. How is it with my relatives and friends there? Will they be able to come to my aid? They do not know my situation, nor what it is like in Russia. Last year they advised me, "in view of the reaction and of unemployment in Europe", to "somehow come to terms with my Russian comrades". Some have even sent letters to Stalin appealing to him to let me go. Europe is remote from Russia; they may grieve for me there, but it is not to be expected that they can do anything. And now matters are still worse. The G.P.U. does not allow me to correspond with the outside world; I am completely cut off from it.

Still, I took advantage of an opportunity, the departure of a friend to European Russia, to send two postcards abroad. In them I gave vent to all my despair, yet in spite of that they reached their destinations safely. "It is easier for Dante to leave his inferno than it is for me to leave mine," I wrote, careless of the censorship, feeling I had nothing more to lose. "Here it is magnificent—and terrible. No, I was not made for the Arctic."

The summer was hot, as hot as forty degrees centigrade during the day. In winter 56 degrees of frost, in summer 40 degrees of heat—that was the range of our temperature. But even in summer, as is usual with continental climates, the nights were fresh. Moreover, Yeniseisk was the northernmost town of that region to enjoy a real summer. The next locality, Vorogovo, a hundred kilometres farther north, never knew a real summer; and whatever lay still farther north—Imbarskoye, Turukhansk, Igarka, Dudinka, Dixon Island—had even less. There is a difference of temperature in those parts but no such summer as temperate regions know.

However, not even the hot Yeniseisk summer could dispel the nightmare of the freezing winter. I was able to forget it for an hour and two, and then it returned. My teeth in particular remembered it. They had become like strange bits of foreign matter in my mouth. My gums had somehow been affected and the teeth were loose. The first symptoms of scurvy . . . In the midst of summer! Then what would it be like in winter!

The search took place on the night of July 21st and 22nd. On the 24th I had already sent by registered letter to Vyshinksy, with a prepaid delivery confirmation, the "statement by Dr. Anton Ciliga, Italian citizen, former member of the Politbureau of the Central Committee of the Communist Party of Yugoslavia", containing the demand (a) for the annulment of the sentence of three years of exile in Siberia given by the Special Session of the N.K.V.D. on 23 March, 1935, as illegal and contrary to the provisions of the decree of the Central Executive Committee of the Soviets of the U.S.S.R. and the Council of People's Commissars, 5 November 1934, Paragraph 1 (g); and (b) for the right "immediately to leave the U.S.S.R.".

My statement began by referring to the fact that "the local organ of the Commissariat of the Interior in Yeniseisk has communicated to me the order of the Special Session of the N.K.V.D. on 23 March, 1935, sentencing me to a further three years of political exile in the town of Yeniseisk in eastern Siberia. This sentence is not only a monstrous exhibition of arbitrariness and cynical mockery but it is also a direct breach of the existing laws of the U.S.S.R."

There followed a concise exposition of all the "arbitrary acts" and the humiliation to which I had been subjected over the previous five years by the G.P.U., and which are already known to the reader. After this resumé I reverted to the latest affair.

"But the climax of contempt for justice is the above-mentioned order, which violates the existing laws of the U.S.S.R., which is in direct and unequivocal contradiction to the decree of the Central Executive Committee ... defining the functions and powers of the Special Sessions of the N.K.V.D. as follows: 'To give the N.K.V.D. of the U.S.S.R. the right to apply: 1) ... (g) with regard to foreign citizens who are a public danger, expulsion beyond the frontiers of the U.S.S.R.'

"No other punishment on the part of the G.P.U./N.K.V.D. for imaginary or real political crimes of foreign citizens is laid down by the law."

This limitation of the right of the G.P.U. in regard to foreign citizens was made, it was said in Russia, at the request of Roosevelt on the occasion of his country's recognition of the U.S.S.R. a year before, and had reference primarily to foreign technicians; but it now came in useful for me too. It even became the main juridical basis of my case, since the Italian Embassy remained silent about the retention of my passport and the extension of my sentence.

"I do not intend to discuss", I wrote further, "whether I am a 'public danger' or not to the established regime, nor my personal opinions on the lack of humanity in a regime that I no longer support. I attach no importance to the G.P.U.'s concern about me in this respect. But I insist that as a foreign citizen I be allowed to leave your country."

Then I gave the history of my efforts to leave the U.S.S.R. over the course of the last seven years and in particular during the last year when, having served my three years' sentence of imprisonment, I renewed my passport. "But in order to prevent my departure the Soviet Government and its organs have not scrupled to disregard not only the general laws of humanity, but even their own State laws."

"Why this strange, incomprehensible fear about my departure?" I asked. "A Great Power, a country occupying one-sixth of the surface of the globe, a country recognized by all other States and having normal diplomatic relations with them; for whose protection there exists dozens of parties and organizations in all countries; which has its own political and trade union internationals—such a State only makes itself ridiculous in fearing the departure abroad of one solitary, not very well-known person, a former participant in the Communist leadership of the small country of Yugoslavia, who came to the U.S.S.R. as a supporter of the Government and is now divorced from it by thousands of kilometres, as a result of his having seen the true situation of the people under this Government."

Then came my conclusions:

"This peculiar fear of the Soviet governing bodies of my return abroad has reached a stage when there is no act of violence, of illegality, ignominy and cowardice, to which they will not stoop if only my departure can thereby be prevented. They did not hesitate last year, when I renewed my passport, to make an attempt to buy me from the Italian authorities, negotiating in an underhand manner the annulment of my Italian citizenship. The Soviet Government, which calls itself the hope of the world, attempts to revive the trade in men, tries to buy foreign citizens in order to enslave them, to hold them as life-long prisoners in jails and in exile, by continually and arbitrarily prolonging their sentences."

I considered and re-considered this paragraph about the ambiguous behaviour of the Italian Embassy before I put it in the text. But I finally decided that it was necessary to tell both the Soviet authorities and the Embassy (to which a copy of the statement was sent) that I was aware of how things stood, and that whatever happened, whatever the risks, this time I was waging the final battle for liberty or death.

So I shot my last bolt, pointing out coldly and desparately what there remained for the G.P.U. to do if it would not let me go.

"In order that the shameful crimes of the Soviet authorities against me should reach their climax, there is only one thing lacking: that I should be quietly done away with. If this has not so far been done, it is, presumably, only because such a crime could not be kept secret either from my friends who share prison and exile with me, or from my relatives abroad.

"Bringing all these facts to your notice, I demand from you, Mr. Prosecutor of the U.S.S.R., the rescinding of the illegal order of the Commissariat of the Interior and the guarantee of permission for my immediate and unhindered departure from the U.S.S.R.

"I await an immediate and definite reply from you. Yours, etc."

I had never made a secret of what I thought of the bureaucratic regime of the U.S.S.R. But in this statement I dotted all the i's and crossed all the t's. After this it seemed to me that Moscow had only the choice between finally settling with me or expelling me from the country.

"Ah, Anton Antonovich," a local friend said to me when I

read this statement to him, "you are certain to be shot now. You should not have written so sharply. They can't stand the naked truth."

"No, on the contrary," I replied, "if there's anything at all that can save me, it is precisely this frankness."

My calculation was simple: if I kept quiet I had a hundred per cent guarantee of a quick end, since I simply would not survive the climate. So whether I were shot for my action, or perished in a concentration camp of hunger-striking, the result would be the same. On the other hand, bold action, an all or nothing gamble, gave me the chance of success, a faint hope of saving myself. Not only because I was a foreign citizen and had a legal basis for the demand to leave the country, but in the first place because the degeneration of the Russian Revolution had not then reached the stage when oppositionist Communists were shot out of hand. They were exiled, imprisoned, put into concentration camps—but not yet shot. It was not likely that such a major change of policy would take place behind the scenes and with such an unknown person as myself. It was on this calculation—in so far as it was a question of reasoning—that I based my whole tactic, my reckless *va banque* gamble . . . There were as yet no Moscow Trials and I had just the chance of coming out of the gamble successfully.

Besides sending the Italian Embassy a copy of the statement I also sent them a telegram informing them of the despatch of this letter. If the copy itself should go astray, as the letter of December 26th had done, perhaps this telegram at least would reach them.

However, I did not content myself with that. Necessity is the mother of invention. Prosecutor Vyshinsky could do as the rest of the Soviet authorities had done, and make no reply to my demands. The Embassy had been silent for half a year, why should it not remain silent for another three years, till the completion of my new sentence? If the G.P.U. was able to buy the Latvian consul, why not also some official at the Italian Embassy?—who, under cloak of ultra-fascist arguments (why should we concern ourselves with this non-fascist, let him settle his own affairs with his former comrades!), would in reality be carrying out the orders of the G.P.U. .. If the quiescence of the Embassy suggested to me its tacit consent with the methods used by the G.P.U. against me, then on the other hand the fact that my telegrams had been delivered to the Embassy and also the respect shown by the G.P.U. to my correspondence with the Embassy during the search of my room, indicated that the Embassy had not complied with the main demand of the G.P.U. to deny my Italian citizenship and thus place me entirely in its hands. These circumstances strengthened my position. There had been a note in my passport to the effect that it was issued by the Embassy on 8 November, 1934, "on the basis of a decision dated 8 August, 1934, of the Ministry of Foreign and Internal Affairs of the Kingdom of Italy". This, I thought to myself, gives me legal justification for approaching the Ministry direct. I therefore did so.

In this telegram to Rome, referring to the decision to renew my passport, I outlined the history of the illegal refusal of an exit visa and the retention of my passport by the Soviet authorities. I then pointed out that I had "received no replies to my telegrams to the Embassy for half a year, for reasons unknown to me". I ended with the words: "In any case I would ask you to inform me of the attitude of the Italian Government to the Soviet Government's contempt for my rights as an Italian citizen." In other words: If you agree with their actions, then say so openly. I also sent one copy of this telegram to the Chairman of the Central Executive Committee, Kalinin, and another to the Embassy in Moscow.

"Why do you waste so much money? They certainly won't let you go," the young girl at the Yeniseisk post office said as she reckoned up the small fortune it cost me to send these telegrams. She was eighteen years of age and quite a beauty, the black-eyed, milk-and-roses complexioned Zhenya; but, Lord, what a pessimist! In Russia there is a whole category of the unsuccessful among the youth, and Zhenya is one of them. She wanted to study in a University, to go to a large town and be in the centre of events. But somehow she failed to achieve her desire. "Why not? There are so many of the youth, even the poorest, who now study in Russia?" I once enquired of her.

"I am not a Komsomol. My father is a small employee and we are such a large family that he can't afford to give me any money to go anywhere."

In Siberia one encounters the new life, successful or unsuccessful, but there are also traces of the old, including traces of the exiles who preceded us in the times of the Tsars. There is in Yeniseisk an ancient little house. This was the headquarters of the Bolsheviks deported under the Tsar. The occupants are no longer the same but I came across the old woman who had been the landlady in those days, and she talked readily. The future President of the Ukrainian Soviet Republic, Petrovsky, and the future Secretary of the Central Executive Committee, Yenukidze, had both stayed with her.

"Petrovsky thought they would leave him in Yeniseisk and made plans to send for his wife," the old woman told me, "but I learned from my nephew who served with the gendarmes that Petrovsky and all the others would shortly be sent to Turukhansk. And that was what happened."

At that time all the Bolshevik leaders who were in Russia came together in Turukhansk. Petrovsky and three other Bolshevik deputies to the Duma; the future first President of the Soviet Republic, Sverdlov; Kamenev, who was shot as a result of the Moscow Trials; and the present dictator, Stalin. There they all spent the period of the first world war, 1914—1917. Yenukidze at that time lived in Vorogovo, between Yeniseisk and Turukhansk.

Siberia is the land of eternal exiles and has seen many things. To a Siberian an exile seems just as natural a phenomenon as an apple or a pear does to a European. During the 19th century over one million exiles were sent to Siberia; and it must be bourne in mind that the total Siberian population at the beginning of the 20th century was only eight million.

Learning that the old Bolsheviks had lived in Krasnoyarsk and Yeniseisk I did my best to find out more about their lives there. In Yeniseisk they had continued their activity, agitated among the population, issued illegal leaflets, possessed their own office for false passports and the preservations of their illegal archives. There were two factions among the Turukhansk Bolsheviks. One set around Sverdlov and Kamenev, which studied a good deal, read and discussed, actively prepared for the future; the other around Stalin, which chose the simpler, more pleasant life, and drank a great deal, waiting for better times. The whole Yeniseisk region remembers Stalin's drinking bouts. That is no hindrance to a man's career, least of all in Russia. Stalin left another souvenir of his stay in Turukhansk, a son by the wife of a peasant whose husband was at the front. In 1935 this young man was twenty years of age and still lived in the Yeniseisk region. He had not desired to join his father in Moscow, preferring to work as a fisherman. And—a curious thing—the woman with whom Stalin had lived had nothing good to say of him. She had brought up her son to dislike his father intensely. But that did not prevent him from occasionally taking advantage of his origin. Thus, after a drunken scene in the Krasnoyarsk Circus, when the militia came to arrest him he resisted strenuously, crying: "Don't you touch me, I'm Stalin's son."

Not all the exiled Bolsheviks came to power after the Revolution. Some left their bones in Siberia during the partisan struggle against Kolchak, and on the central square of Krasnoyarsk there are several graves of those who were executed.

A week later I received notification from the post office that my registered letter containing the statement had been delivered to Prosecutor Vyshinksy. Hurrah! But I received no notification that the copy of the statement and the telegram had been received by the Embassy, nor any news of the telegram to the Italian Ministry of Foreign Affairs. After three weeks of waiting in vain, I sent a telegram to Kalinin, protesting against the long delay by the post office in notifying me of the delivery of my registered letters and telegrams to the Embassy and the Ministry.

"The non-delivery of these letters and telegrams to the addressees would constitute not only a violation of my rights but also a breach of the Soviet Union's international diplomatic obligations, and in such a case the responsibility falls entirely upon the Soviet Government." Once battle is joined it is no use stopping half-way.

Another week went by, and still no reply came.

I told myself that nothing would come of it all. Who was worried about my letters and protests! The only thing left to do was to make preparations for an escape. And I feverishly began to make plans. Control on the roads and in the trains was very strict. It would therefore be necessary to talk the matter over with others, to find accomplices. Having thought about it long and carefully, I decided to approach a young worker I knew.

"Well, why not, Ciliga? That's not a difficult business. One of our comrades has just died and we have hidden his passport. Thought it might come in useful sometime. He was an engineer. Intelligent looking sort of chap. His passport should just suit you."

While awaiting the results of my efforts, and making preparations for flight if the worst came to the worst, I had to save myself from possible punitive action on the part of the G.P.U.

Would my aims not be furthered if I went to see the chief of the G.P.U. and re-opened the question of employment with the Gold Trust? Or elsewhere? By showing such an interest in work the G.P.U. would be thrown off the track and think that I was tired of all this manoeuvring, that I had resigned myself and given up the idea of getting out of the country.

In a state of high tension—impatient and nervous as I had by then become—I went to the G.P.U.

"I want to see the chief."

"The chief is busy and can see nobody."

"Tell him I am here. Let him make an appointment with me."

Whilst I was arguing the chief appeared at the door of his room, evidently having heard us talking.

"Have you come in response to the message I have just sent you, Ciliga?"

A message? An order to report? Something big, something new has occurred about which I am in the dark as yet. Everything whirls within me. One step more—and in my cursed haste and excitement I may perhaps ruin all my chances at the very last moment! My voice, which a moment ago in the argument with the secretary had been strained and jerky, becomes instantly calm, restrained.

"No, Citizen Strelnikov, there has been no message from you. I am here about the question of getting work ..."

"Then you must have missed the messenger on the way," he interrupts me. "He has just left with a request for you to attend tomorrow. I have an important announcement to make to you."

"What is it about? Tell me now, since I am here."

He refused to do so, telling me I had to come tomorrow. My friends and I were breaking our heads over this, trying to puzzle out what the announcement could possibly be.

"The day after tomorrow there is a shipment to Krasnoyarsk. That's where you will be going, for certain," one of the comrades said.

"Hurrah! Then they're letting you go!"

"Yes, but where to? Abroad or to Krasnoyarsk prison?"

At nine o'clock the next morning I reported to the chief of the G.P.U.

"You will leave tomorrow by ship for Krasnoyarsk. Get your things ready."

"Why? Have I received permission to depart?"

"I do not know. You will learn about that in Krasnoyarsk. There has apparently been an alteration in your sentence."

An alteration? Yes, but in what sense? For better or for worse? I tried to find this out in an indirect way.

"How am I going? Alone or with an escort?" This detail

would indicate the possible course of my fate—for better or for worse.

"You will go alone. A travel warrant will be given you and you will report to the Krasnoyarsk G.P.U."

The remainder of the day passed as in a dream. I regretted that the day of departure was not in a week's time. Now more than ever I wanted to talk about many things with my comrades and friends. We had lived three years of exile and prison together, lived a common life with others of the comrades scattered all over Russia, from whom we heard irregularly but still systematically. Now I should cross the frontiers of Russia and she would close the enormous iron gates of her world behind me. When should we ever again hear from each other? Through years of common struggle, common suffering, and striving for common social ideals we had drawn close to one another, as close as members of one big family—and in an instant all these ties would be broken. Should we ever meet again? In a year ... many years ... maybe never again. I was happy because I was breaking free, going home again, going to see Europe once more; but there was at the same time a sadness in so abruptly and so completely severing ties with old comrades, and with Russia. It was saddening to think of them remaining here in the same situation—prisoners. On this last day I wanted with all my heart to engrave their faces and their personalities on my memory. I said goodbye to the local people, the Siberians. They were delighted, all expressed their lively sympathy and pleasure that I had managed to regain my liberty.

The following morning, September the first, I reported to the G.P.U. for the travel warrant. In a quarter of an hour I had the warrant in my hand and was equipped to leave.

"Well, for once I've received something good from you," I told the commissar. "It would have been a pity to part without my having a single good thing to say of you."

I was called into the next room to see the chief.

"Of course, you won't be wanting to discuss the question of work any more. But yesterday, Ciliga, you wanted to say something."

Without a doubt he had noticed the change in my voice that had occurred the day before, when he had told me about the message he had sent. He must on reflection have decided that I had been agitated by something more than the question of employment. But his reaction had been a little too late ... In this perpetual duel between the G.P.U. and its victims, where it is not always a question of mere trifles, since life and death may be at stake, he had missed a good opportunity. I had gained the move.

"No, it was only about work . . .", I said to him tranquilly. He understood that he had lost the move. Thus I parted from the Yeniseisk G.P.U.

Most of the political exiles came down to the ship to see me off. There were a good hundred comrades of all parties and tendencies. It was as if in my person they wanted to send greetings not only to the freedom glimmering before me, but also to greet the far-away West, Europe and America, which through me, a witness of their lives, their struggles and sufferings, might hear the true story of their fate, and perhaps in some way help them. Some local Siberian friends were also there to say farewell.

The ship left at midday. The last goodbyes; handkerchiefs fluttering in the air; and Yeniseisk fades into the mist. I wanted to take with me a picture of that place—the mighty Yenisei, the endless taiga, the unearthly beauty of the northern sunset, the long horror of winter—and for a long time I kept my eyes fixed on that slowly receding world.

Our ship was old, worn-out; it did not make much speed. For the four hundred kilometres from Yeniseisk to Krasnoyarsk we should need about five days. American hustle and tortoise tempos so often alternate in Russia! The rhythm of speed has touched this enormous continent of Siberia only at its fringes. I stood on the deck of the ship breathing in the pure air and gazing at the landscape. Here and there are small wooden huts between the river's edge and the grandiose forests. Forest after forest moves towards us; the outlines of the shore change continually, broken by rocks and dotted with little islands. The works carried out along the banks of the river, and into which has gone so much enthusiasm, so much sacrifice and so much cruelty, are tiny forsaken dots in the vast landscape. The river banks and the forests radiate a calm power, the freshness of awakening life. Poverty is there, side by side with sprawling strength. A spirit of pioneering electrifies the atmosphere. Through the rhythm of nature one feels the movement of a people; a giant is stirring his limbs here; a new continent is awakening to the world.

Above us the vast blue sky was calm, flecked with clouds slowly moving before a gentle breeze and sparkling with light. In my imagination the clouds became an army of labour wandering from Europe and America in search of a better world . . . But shall we ever meet? Shall I see Europe once more? Will they really be concerned with the fate of their brothers in Russia? Will they understand the tragic situation of the Russian proletariat, the political exiles, those condemned to forced labour?

Towards the end of the fifth day we approached Krasnoyarsk. According to the time-table we should have docked during the day, but the ship had been unable to make headway against the powerful current a few kilometres before the town. For seven hours we had stuck on one spot. So we did not arrive before midnight.

The following morning I reported to the G.P.U. Let be what had to be—only let me get it over quickly.

I was received by one of the leading officials.

"Citizen Ciliga, I am Levshin, Deputy Chief of the Political Section for the regional department of the Commissariat of the Interior. I am instructed to inform you that, in conformity with an order of the chief administration of the Commissariat of the Interior . . . (my heart almost stopped beating as I held my breath in tense preparation for the news of rescue or ruin that must now follow) . . . you are expelled from the U.S.S.R. . . ."

I was being born a second time . . . I heard what followed in a dream.

". . . date of expulsion will be made known to you later . . . informing Moscow today that you have arrived . . . in a few days . . . an answer regarding your further journey . . ."

The edges of reality blurred, I went away like a drunken man.

A year had passed, but the general tenor of Krasnoyarsk life reamained unchanged: seize the passing moment, work intensively—hope. Some had begun their careers, some had married, others divorced; but still everything they did was done with such passionate intensity, a kind of frenzy of haste, as though the world might at any moment break to pieces under their feet—or as though it had only just been created. As a result of this passion the face of the town is changed. In the course of one year the houses and the people have somehow managed to smarten themselves up. The houses have been freshened up; there are more well-dressed people. The second house from where I am staying has recently been painted an olive green, a rare thing for these times, and day and night in front of it stands an armed militia-man. The chairman of the regional Executive Committee lives here, and he has thought up this idea in order to give himself more importance after the assassination of Kirov.

The shops have become cleaner, smarter. The formerly half-built factories are now in operation. New plants are being planned; construction on some has already begun. The metallurgical, chemical and war industries are booming. The bakery is being extended to supply the Army. Thus the town changes, as the entire country is changing. This is the dynamism of the U.S.S.R. so greatly envied by Europe. Three times in the course of the ten years I have spent here has the face of this vast land changed. It seems to remain unaltered, yet it is not. The Russia of the NEP received me in 1926; the Russia of the Five Year Plan from 1928 to 1932 saw my arrest and imprisonment; and assisting at my departure was the post-Plan Russia, that of State capitalist NEP, or—as one said then—of the "gay and well-to-do" life. Such a land, whatever may happen, will not perish.

From day to day I awaited the G.P.U.'s information on the continuation of my journey, saying goodbye to this many-peopled land that has given to the world, and to me, so many agonizing problems. How clumsily powerful it is, and yet how attractive! Youth and strength bubble up as from an inexhaustible well, yet at every step one stumbles upon injustice and cruelty. The cruelty of the rulers is compensated for by the warmth and sympathy of the people, making the most severe trials less difficult to bear. So it was then. Bidding me goodbye, these people showed me a spontaneous sympathy.

"Anton Antonovich, take care that 'they' don't kill you on the way. One cannot trust the G.P.U. ... they may say go home and then bump you off on the way ... Be particularly careful after you cross the frontier, in case their secret agents try to throw you off the train somewhere. Once past the frontier they can wash their hands of all responsibility for your death."

After the advice, a request.

"Anton Antonovich, when you get to Europe, tell the truth about the life of the people here. Don't lie like those writers who come here for a visit and go away to praise everything."

No, you may think what you like, but I myself am absolutely convinced that these men, this people, will tackle even the Stalin Government. Yes, the G.P.U. is omnipotent, but Russia, the Russian people are in the final analysis stronger than the G.P.U. This people will make its way in spite of the G.P.U., for it has still many things, many truths to tell the world.

A week had passed and Moscow still gave no signal. I again began to have doubts. Was this not after all another cat-and-mouse trick? Now I recalled the last words of Levshin's pronouncement: ". . . the date of expulsion will be made known to you later".

"Later!" This in G.P.U. jargon meant the possibility of indefinite delay! I went to see the G.P.U.

"Citizen Levshin, I protest against this fresh procrastination. When will the date of my departure be settled? In ten years or perhaps after I am dead? You have not given yourself any time limit."

Levshin assured me that it was a purely technical hitch, which would take a few days or at the most a week to straighten out.

What caused this delay I never exactly knew. Neither did I find out precisely why the decision to let me go was made. To my protest to Vyshinsky? To my telegram to the President of the Republic? To my telegrams to the Embassy and the Italian Ministry of Foreign Affairs, which never reached their destinations? To the fact that the Government preferred even my departure to the delivery of the telegrams? Since I had been sent away from Yeniseisk after I had sent the telegram to Kalinin I was inclined to believe that that had been the decisive move in the matter: *Post hoc, ergo propter hoc.* But after the Moscow Trials I recalled something that threw a singular light on the circumstances of my departure.

At that time Krasnoyarsk and Yeniseisk swarmed with men exiled as a consequence of the Kirov affair. Among the hundreds of others was Zinoviev's nephew, Zaks, and Trotsky's son, Sergei Sedov, a qualified engineer who took no interest whatever in politics, but was solely concerned with his scientific researches. Sergei had never been a member of the Party and when Trotsky was expelled from the country in 1929 he chose to remain in Moscow and carry on with his work under the Stalin regime, in contrast with his younger brother, Leon, who was passionately engaged in the political struggle and who died in Paris in 1938, after the Moscow Trials, in circumstances that have never been fully cleared up. To my question, why had the G.P.U. exiled him, Sergei Sedov replied with a bitter smile: "Because of my tainted origin." On my saying that I should soon be going abroad and that I could pass on a message to his parents, he only asked me to give them his greetings, to tell them that he was in good health and that he continued to work in his profession.

Among other exiles I met the old Bolshevik, Artun Solovyan, recently condemned in Moscow for Trotskyism. He had been sent first to Minusinsk, where the well-known Trotskyist Kossior and others were then living, and from Minusinsk he had been transferred to Krasnoyarsk shortly before my arrival. In spite of differences of opinion, I treated him with respect, for he was an Old Bolshevik, a revolutionary from Tsarist times. My confidence in him was strengthened by the fact that he had a brother well known in oppositionist circles. Solovyan expressed the desire to send to Trotsky, through me, a brief report of the situation of the exiled Trotskyists and their organization. Although I had left the Trotskyist organization in 1932, because of political differences with Trotsky, I agreed to do this as a matter of comradely solidarity and in the interests of the common struggle against Stalin. He then informed me that the text of the report would have to be drawn up in consultation with his comrades in Minusinsk.

After some time, however, Solovyan changed his plan, saying that it would be too dangerous for me to take a report, and asked me to do something else instead: to transmit to Trotsky personally or to his son Leon Sedov, a certain address and a method of communication.

"What we need here more than anything else are personal directives from Trotsky," he said.

I agreed to do this, but I also tried to convince him that a report to Trotsky would not be a danger to me if well coded.

"After all, an attempt to pass on such a letter would only be one more argument in favour of expelling me."

"No, no, you had better not give the G.P.U. any more arguments."

What did surprise me, however, was that, according to Solovyan, the Trotskyists in Minusinsk were in favour of a bloc with the Zinovievists, and an attempt to win 'the best among them' for the Trotskyist organization. From my observations in Yeniseisk it was clear that the Trotskyists shunned the Zinovievists like the plague and avoided all political discussions with them, on the grounds that it was impossible to tell who among them was a provocateur and who was not. During the last hours of my stay in Krasnoyarsk the vague suspicion lurking in the back of my mind was suddenly transformed into an absolute conviction. Solovyan had been sent to me by the G.P.U.; he was an agent-provocateur. I obtained irrefutable proof of this in the behaviour of the G.P.U. at Negoreloye Station, on the Soviet-Polish frontier.

On my arrival in Paris I did not, of course, carry out Solovyan's 'comradely mission'. On the contrary, I informed Trotsky's son, Leon Sedov, who was then in Paris, that the G.P.U. had attempted to take advantage of my expulsion to engineer a new frame-up.

At the time I did not attach great importance to this episode, regarding it as a routine manoeuvre of the G.P.U. It was not until after the Moscow Trials that it became clear to me that this manoeuvre had in fact a quite exceptional importance.

At the Moscow Trials one fact in particular struck me: the prosecution could not produce as evidence a single letter, a single document written by Trotsky. Both witnesses and accused who 'confessed': Old Bolsheviks covering themselves with filth; Zinovievists and Trotskyists who had capitulated to Stalin years previously—all of them could only 'quote from memory' Trotsky's alleged political directives on 'terrorism'. Radek, the Mephistopheles of these Trials, who after the event decided to play the role of a pseudo-Azev, also quoted 'from memory' whole passages of Trotsky's so-called terrorist instructions. "All the documents have, unfortunately, been destroyed," Azev-Radek apologized.

So Stalin and his G.P.U. were not only unable to produce any of those 'spy-terrorist' letters at the Trials, they could not even lay before the Court the most ordinary political letter from Trotsky or his son, Leon Sedov.

And that explains why Solovyan was so anxious to obtain 'letters with directives' from Trotsky or his son.

Afterwards it occurred to me—did the G.P.U., as I at first thought, only want to take advantage of my departure, to use me for the frame-up without my knowing it; or had the departure itself depended (hence the 'technical hitch') on their being able to get me to accept Solovyan's proposal? Cold shivers still run down my spine at the thought that perhaps it was only a lucky coincidence that saved me . . . But Solovyan and the G.P.U. must have been deeply disappointed. Instead of the 'letters with directives' from Trotsky for use at the Moscow Trials, they had to content themselves with reading the warning that appeared in the Russian 'Bulletin of the Opposition': "According to information received from Siberia, the political exile Artun Solovyan is an agent of the G.P.U."

I will relate in a few words why the G.P.U. was duped. There is a saying that some things are too good to be true. That is how the G.P.U. slipped up; just a minor failure to take routine bureaucratic precautions put paid to their manoeuvre.

During the final days prior to my departure I naturally expected to be subjected to the same close personal attention by the G.P.U. as I had enjoyed from the moment of my arrival in Krasnoyarsk from Yeniseisk when two agents had tailed me night and day, not leaving me out of their sight for a single instant and keeping guard outside the house when I slept. Yet during the last few days there was no one shadowing me at all. At first I refused to believe this, but was finally compelled to recognize that it was so.

This could only mean that they had me under observation in another way—through someone 'on the inside', an agent-provocateur. Someone among my acquaintances was one of their men. The question needed only to be posed for suspicion to fall upon Solovyan. A number of small details, each one unimportant in itself, taken together constituted a logical chain of presumptive evidence. What followed changed my suspicions into certainty.

I was called to the G.P.U. A few days before I had been instructed to make ready for the journey. I therefore hoped that this summons meant that the exact date and time of departure would be given me. I encountered Solovyan in front of the building. He told me that he had just come from a routine visit to Levshin. Their last talk about me before my departure, I thought to myself. Solovyan once more reminded me of my commission.

"You will now be detained," he said nervously. "We are speaking to one another for the last time and it is essential that you should remember everything clearly . . ."

How do you know, I thought, that I am going to be "detained"—that is, arrested—and that it is not simply a question of giving me the precise date of departure. Such matters are revealed only to G.P.U. agents.

Levshin informed me that I should leave the following morning by the Trans-Siberian express, with an escort up to the Soviet-Polish frontier. I was immediately placed in a state of arrest, and Levshin himself returned with me to my lodgings, helped me to get my things together and conducted me back to the G.P.U. prison, where I spent my last night in Krasnoyarsk.

In the evening Levshin came into my cell with another agent and made a thorough search of all my belongings. They took away all my correspondence, even including that with the Italian Embassy. "We are taking this with the consent of the Embassy, to whom we are handing it over," Levshin replied to my protests. They also confiscated a number of Soviet books, old editions that had become 'unreliable'; books not only by Trotsky, but also those of Kroptkin and Shliapnikov . . . Going through the books, Levshin showed particular interest in three absolutely innocuous books of fiction given me by Solovyan.

He had given me them so that the comments he had written on the margins could serve as samples of his handwriting for Trotsky and his son. Future letters could then be compared to make sure that they really came from Solovyan. The marginal notes were completely harmless and related simply to the matter of the text against which they were written. I never really appreciated the need for these 'samples of handwriting', but I thought that the Trotskyist method of communication was after all no concern of mine. Yet it was precisely these little books with their marginal notes that interested Levshin.

"What do these notes mean? Did you make them?"

"You can see for yourself that they are remarks I made when reading the books."

At the frontier post of Negoroloye itself all my belongings and all my books were examined by the G.P.U. frontier guards. I had more than a hundred books, but they put aside only two of them, and these were two of the three books given me by Solovyan. After a moment's reflection the frontier guard asked me if I had not got any books in German. I grasped what he meant. The two books from Solovyan that he had put aside were in Russian, and the third was in German— Goethe's conversations with Eckermann in the small *reclame* edition, and because of that apparently overlooked by him. In it were some marginal comments against Goethe's remarks about Byron. I had only two books in German: this one of Goethe's and a grammar. I calmly replied that I had only one and gave him the grammar. He snatched it eagerly, quickly glanced at the title and returned it immediately, saying in an irritaged tone: "And have you no other?" "No," I replied. Any further doubt about Solovyan was unnecessary.

The two books with the marginal notes in them, the ones which the G.P.U. had put aside, were taken into the office and returned to me half an hour later. The G.P.U. was clearly as concerned with checking up on Solovyan's contact with Trotsky as it was with not hampering it. Once photographed, the 'harmless' remarks of Solovyan, appropriately arranged, would constitute just the kind of 'evidence' needed for the Mocow Trials.

It was already the depths of winter in Siberia when I left Krasnoyarsk by train on 27 November. It was warm and comfortable in the Harbin-Moscow International Express. From the windows of the train the snow and ice-covered world no longer seemed terrible to me. My three guards and I had an entire compartment to ourselves. In the neighbouring compartments were only members of the Soviet nobility: officers, bureaucrats, their wives, daughters, mistresses. There was not a single compartment for the proletariat in the whole of the train. Everywhere there was comfort, cleanliness, 'culture'. The icy cold of the passing countryside and the poverty and misery of its people belonged to another world. Hundreds, thousands of kilometres rolled away behind us . . . we travelled . . . night and day . . . travelled . . .

The fields and towns of Siberia, which had so moved me two and a half years before when I saw them in full summer, splendid with the sun shining on the waving corn, now left me calm. Now it was a spell-bound, slumbering kingdom, and only the vast sweep of the horizon and the mighty forests evoked in me a feeling of unutterable awe.

From Kurgan in the centre of Western Siberia, we turned northwards towards Sverdlovsk, formerly Yekaterinburg. I had entered Siberia by the southern road from European Russia, via Samara and Chelyabinsk, but I was returning by the northern route through Sverdlovsk and Viatka. The guards were my only company. All three were young men from the people. The chief was a young commissar who had recently passed out of the G.P.U. 'Academy' in Moscow; the second, a former worker, was an N.C.O. in the special G.P.U. troops; and the third was a ranker, the son of peasants. They spoke little and during the first two days of the journey the conversation was not very animated. As a protest against the confiscation of my correspondence, my books and my study notes, I went on hunger-strike for the six days of the journey from Krasnoyarsk to the frontier. It was my farewell to the Russia of the G.P.U. and my action created a certain reserve between my guardians and myself. We talked a little about new customs and politics. The N.C.O. did his best to convince me that dancing fox-trots, charlestons, rumbas, etc., then officially authorized but formerly characterized as 'expressions of bourgeois decadence', was not a social phenomenon, but a purely technical question, arising from considerations of health, the need for physical exercise, which had not previously been 'taken into consideration'. During an argument about kolkhozes, the leader of the escort appealed for support to the train guard who happened at that moment to be passing our compartment. The latter did his best to show himself in support of the G.P.U. man's viewpoint.

"There you are! See what the workers, the people, think about it!" he said, turning to me in triumph.

Yet I detected a note of reserve in the acquiescence of the train guard. And, indeed, when later we were at Sverdlovsk and I was left alone in the compartment for a while, the guard spoke of the kolkhozes and the Stalin regime in quite a different manner. He had, of course, not the slightest reason for trying to please me, but he had every reason for not contradicting the leader of the G.P.U. escort. He even agreed to post several post cards that I had written to friends in Russia informing them that I was on my way abroad, or, at any rate, for the time being travelling in the direction of Moscow.

On the journey it took me a long time to get used to the idea that I was at last really going home. At the last minute something might crop up . . . I was also oppressed by thoughts of the fate of my Yugoslav comrades who remained behind in Russia. Perhaps I should succeed in getting away, but should I be able to do anything in Europe to secure their release? Dragich, who had made an attempt to escape from exile in Saratov and been caught in the Caucasus, had been sent as punishment to spend his last days in the infamous concentration camp on the Solovetsky Islands in the Arctic Ocean. Dedich was going from one place of exile to another. After Archangel and Narymsk, he was at that moment in Minusinsk, or en route there, since he had been awaiting transfer in Krasnoyarsk prison when I left. I had not succeeded in seeing him, but had managed to send him greetings. Kheberling and others were scattered in remote places of the Soviet concentration camp world. What did the future hold for them?

I had to traverse half of Siberia—from Krasnoyarsk to the Urals—before I began to forget for a while, ceased to brood over the fate of my best friends, and turned my thoughts to the more general question of the destiny of the country I was about to leave.

That long high chain of the Ural mountains stretches from the Arctic to the Caspian, separating European Russia from Asia. Rich in oil, iron, coal, salt, gold, platinum, and precious stones, the Five Year Plans have made it the iron axis of contemporary Russia, the central core of its empire. This 'belt of the world' was for Ptolemy and the ancient world the boundary of the earth on the north-east, as was Atlas with his Herculean

Pillars on the south-west. Today it is the armed fortress defending Russia; should the occasion arise, the granite and steel stronghold from which her invading hordes will swarm east or west, south or north.*

Without the destruction·of medieval Kiev by the Tartars, without that fundamental thrust of the Russians towards Moscow, towards the Volga, towards colonization of the immense Eurasian north, Russia's historical road would have remained closer to that of central and western Europe, but the world importance of the Russian nation would probably have been much smaller. Russia has grown mighty in moving away from the Dnieper, the Black Sea, and Europe, to become the most northerly of the great nations.

The Russian Revolution should have brought the country closer to Europe, because its basic ideas had come from the West and its inspirers and leaders had lived there. But the Russian Revolution remained isolated. Europe proved to be too senile, shattered and exhausted for any fresh revolutionary efforts. In Europe, as in ancient Rome, it is not Gracchus and Spartakus who conquer, but the Caesars: Mussolini, Hitler . . . The result is that the gulf between Russia and Europe has widened. Their failure to unite in a revolutionary synthesis has led them to be ranged against each other. Russia was thrown back towards the East and, in the person of Stalin and in his regime, the Russo-Asiatic nationalists overwhelmed the Russo-European internationalists. Basing themselves on the might of this dynamic land, the Russo-Asiatic elements are preparing not a few surprises for Europe.

Descending the mountain ridge of the Urals I seemed to hear in the voice of the wind surging from the surrounding forests an echo of Blok's prophetic poem, 'The Scythians', composed in January, 1918, and opportunely complementing the powerful revolutionary pathos of his 'The Twelve'.

It was a desperate appeal to Europe to rally to the Russian Revolution; an appeal containing a threat:

> *"Come to us! Come from the horrors of war*
> *To our peaceful embrace!*
> *Comrades! Before it is too late—*
> *Sheathe the ancient sword*
> *And let us be as brothers!*

*Today—February 1950—one may add: her planes and atom bombs—*A.C.

For the last time—come to your senses, old world!
Come to the brotherly feast of labour and love!
For the last time—to the fair brotherly feast
Calls the barbarian lyre!

The Russia of the poet Blok and the statesman Lenin, 'drenched in black blood', already looked upon Europe and the West with mixed feelings, 'both with hate and with love'. On 31 January, 1918, the treacherous epoch of Stalin was foretold; the vengeful spirit of old Europe against the young Russian Revolution and the growth of egoistic Russian and Asian nationalisms were foreseen.

'But if you come not—we have no more to lose.
We too can break faith.

. . . .
. . . .
We shall fall back far and wide
Into the cover of our thickets and our forests,
And turn to the fair face of Europe
Our ugly Asiatic snout!

Come, come to the Urals!
We'll clear the ground for battle;
We'll call upon the steel machines,
Bring mathematics to the wild Mongolian hordes!

But never shield of yours again!
Henceforth we'll wage no war of yours,
But watch with our slanting eyes
How your death-struggle swirls.'

And Blok foretold not only this ferocious, revengeful 'neutrality' but also the aggressive alliance.

'You are millions, but we swarm
A multitude upon a multitude.
Come, try the metal of your sword with ours!
Yes, Scythians we! Yes, Asiatics we!
With slanting, avaricious eyes . . .
Like those of the Vandals and the Goths
The day they came upon Rome.

I wanted to cry out to Europe from afar, from those ridges of the Urals quite close to Chelyabinsk where already a giant plant was turning out the most modern and the largest tanks in the world:

'O tired, grey-haired old Europe, what surprises are in store for you from these northern barbarians, these new Scythians, worshippers of the machine.'

The wind of the Ural mountains brought me a message for Europe, came to me like the voice of Yessinin's peasants done to death by Peter the Great: 'We shall return, we shall yet return!' . . .

How weird a feeling it gave me, this menacing whisper over my shoulder of the wind from the Ural mountains, as I sat there with my face toward Europe! Yet I did not think that Russia presented any *immediate* threat to Europe: for she had herself too many weak spots. I knew that better than anyone else. I knew from many experiences—in prison and in exile, at liberty and at work in the Soviet Trusts—the discontent of her people and the weaknesses of her technology. I remain convinced that Stalinist Russia is incapable of launching a sweeping offensive. Yet more, I was convinced (end of 1935) that the Stalinist regime could not survive a serious enemy offensive, and I remained of the opinion, in 1941, that it was not capable of successfully conducting a long defensive war.

But it is necessary to be clear about this: the weakness of the Stalin regime is in reality only a weakness of the leading group; the main strength of the Russian reaction is not exhausted. Other strata of the reaction—the military, non-Party specialists, the Church—are very strong and may at any moment replace the Stalin regime. In opposition to this reaction that appears on the surface of political life, or matures not far below it, there is another force, that of the revolutionary people hidden in the depths of Russian society. That force will rise to the surface much later. It awaits its hour and its poets . . .

This was the music of history, this murmur of long years telling Russia's strength and Russia's weakness, brought to my ears by the wind from the Urals.*

We arrived in Moscow at five in the morning. After five years of absence, and the execution of the Five Year Plan, I longed passionately to see it once again at close quarters. But I had to remain in the compartment, shunted on to a siding, under the surveillance of my escort. And that for a whole day! Our train, which had been five hours late in reaching Sverdlovsk, had 'collected' another eleven hours by the time it reached Moscow (here again one of Russia's weak points).

*Regarding the critical value of this judgement, see the preface. *A.C.*

Since the train from Moscow to the frontier did not leave until the evening, we had to wait.

The waiting was even more boring for my guardians than for me. They decided to go and have a look at Moscow. The first to depart was the leader. He did not return until the evening. Then the N.C.O. left and I remained for a long time with the ranker only. But at last he could stand it no longer, and he too departed.

"You stay here. I shall be back soon."

So I was alone. Well, should I also go and have a look at Moscow, leaving a note telling them that I should return in three hours? No, it wouldn't work out as simply as that; they would certainly get panicky and begin accusing and denouncing one another, and as a result all three would suffer. For my own sake also it would be better to avoid any complications. I had no right to compromise them; they still belonged, in spite of everything, to the ordinary people. So I waited patiently till they returned. The ranker came back two hours later and in due course the other two also arrived. I said I wanted a shave and the ranker was detailed to accompany me to the station barber. On my way I managed to catch just a glimpse of the Square before the station. Passing a letter-box, I calmly took from my pocket some letters that I had written during the absence of my guards, and without saying anything to the G.P.U. soldier, posted them. He accepted this action of mine as perfectly natural and did not say a word in protest. Thus we exchanged favours.

We left Moscow late at night and towards noon of the following day were at the frontier post of Niegoroloye. The train was leaving for Poland in two hours. The travellers alighted to take their luggage to the customs office for examination. Only I and my escort remain on the train. My luggage had already been examined in Krasnoyarsk. But ten minutes before the train was due to leave I was ordered off the train with all my belongings. I was afraid that I was going to be sent back to Moscow. Or were they going to execute me at the last moment?

The chief of the G.P.U. frontier guards was on the platform.

"Citizen Ciliga, you will take the next train. Your passport is not quite in order, there is a slight omission. The Poles might not let you in, or might perhaps turn you back."

"You don't have to worry yourselves about me and the Poles. Let me go on. I will explain the matter to them, they won't send me back."

At his evasive reply I became heated.

"Why the devil do you everlastingly play with me like this! You make out thousands of passports—and now suddenly there's something wrong with just mine—after you've been trying for years to stop me going."

"You appear to have a poor opinion of us."

"It could never be bad enough. The more I have to do with you, the more I realize you are worse than I ever thought possible."

They took me somewhere off behind the station buildings.

"Where are you taking me?" I demanded violently.

"There is no need to be afraid," the G.P.U. man replied.

"I am not afraid of anything. Nothing you could do would surprise me, not even if you put me up against the wall this very minute. But I want to know where you are taking me and why. What is this so-called 'irregularity' in my passport?"

"I am simply taking you to the waiting room. Your passport will be sent straight away to Minsk for the necessary adjustment. We shall be ready tonight and you will be able to go on. Your expulsion has been ordered by the chief administration of the State Security and it will be carried out. As for the irregularity in your passport, I see no necessity for giving you any information," the chief of the G.P.U. answered coldly.

They did take me to the waiting room. The three G.P.U. guards remained with me. The passport, however, did not come back that night from Minsk. Neither did it come back the following day; but it finally arrived on the third day, December 3rd.

Accompanied by the chief of the Niegoroloye G.P.U. and my three Krasnoyarsk guards, I went on towards Poland. Everyone was silent. What had we to say to one another? There was no place for small talk and even less for serious discussion. The train halted a short while at the frontier. I was handed my passport and a railway ticket. It was the same old passport that had been taken from me in Krasnoyarsk a year before . . .

The G.P.U. men left the train, which was taken over by Polish railwaymen and guards. The train started to move. A few minutes later we crossed the Polish frontier. I was free.

Behind me lay sprawling, mighty Russia. Behind me were years of hardship, of seeking for the truth, of fighting for the truth. In experience and emotion the richest years of all my life. Happy years.